JUVENILE DELINQUENCY

JUVENILE DELINQUENCY

DEVELOPMENT   TREATMENT   CONTROL

Ruth Shonle Cavan

Professor of Sociology on the Mary Ashby Cheek Foundation
Rockford College

J. B. Lippincott Company
Philadelphia and New York

Preface

This book is planned primarily as a textbook for college students, both undergraduate and graduate. It should be useful also to various professional groups working with delinquent children, to teachers disturbed by misbehavior of their pupils, and to the general public.

Part 1, after clearing the air of various misconceptions, defines delinquency: theoretically as stated by law, realistically in terms of what the public will stand in the way of misconduct, and factually according to actual occurrence.

Part 2 applies the concepts of individual growth and developmental social processes to the emergence and development of delinquent behavior in the individual child. The effect of numerous factors on delinquent behavior and on the production of a delinquent personality is studied: individual differences, social disorganization, social-class subcultures, peer groups, and family life. The final chapter in this part analyzes three cases in terms of different combinations of the above factors.

Part 3 concentrates on different patterns of delinquent behavior, each of which tends to develop under specific social conditions.

Part 4 treats institutional efforts at control and treatment, as carried out by public schools, community organizations, and agencies working specifically with delinquent children.

Part 5 shifts attention to legal methods of dealing with delinquents, organized in the order in which a delinquent child passes from one to another stage of the process: police, detention, juvenile court, training school, and release and aftercare.

As the above outline implies, the aim of this textbook is to integrate the broad social and cultural aspects of delinquency with the developmental processes of delinquent behavior in a person.

Study of the problems of delinquency and assembling of material in the field have extended over a number of years. It would be impossible to list all those who have contributed in some way to my preparation for writing this book—the speakers at conferences who later were buttonholed in the corridor, the administrative heads who arranged tours of their institutions, those who answered letters of inquiry or supplied published and unpublished reports. Two people should be mentioned specifically—Sherwood Norman, who read and offered invaluable comments on the chapter on detention facilities, and my husband, Jordan T. Cavan, an educational psychologist specializing in secondary education, who became the sounding board for many of my formulations and who provided critical comments on the entire manuscript.

RUTH SHONLE CAVAN

Rockford, Illinois
December, 1961

Contents

Contents, continued

Part five **Legal methods of dealing with delinquency**

Charts

Tables

Delinquency and the delinquent defined

Juvenile delinquency occurs in every community affecting some children of all religious beliefs, every socio-economic class, and each ethnic group. No area, no group is immune.

Well-adjusted children are everyone's concern. Especially in a democracy, the public as well as the government is obligated to provide facilities for rearing children—all children—to lead happy and useful lives. In the United States, great sums are spent to provide for the education, health, recreation, and personal guidance of all children. For children whose parents cannot meet basic needs of food, clothing, and shelter, special provisions are made in governmental and private welfare programs. Professions have developed that specialize in keeping children mentally and physically well and that train them for responsible adult life: obstetricians, pediatricians, child psychologists, teachers, religious educators, specialized nurses, and recreation and youth leaders of various kinds.

Parents themselves are deeply concerned. They regard rearing well-adjusted children as one of their major life projects. Middle-class parents read books on child care, conscientiously join parent study groups, and anxiously consult specialists. Lower-class parents are also concerned but rely more on traditional methods and common sense for guidance.

Nevertheless, many children are unhealthy, poorly educated, maladjusted emotionally, or habituated to misbehavior. Common sense tells us not to expect perfection of children or adults, but neither does it assent to routine acceptance of human imperfection.

This book is concerned with only one of the types of poor adjustment—delinquency.

What is juvenile delinquency?

Delinquency is misbehavior. Officially, juvenile delinquency consists of misbehavior by children and adolescents which leads to referral to the juvenile court. In some states the specifics of such misbehavior are rather explicitly stated in the law; in other states the definition of delinquency is so vague and general that the dividing line between delinquency and normal misbehavior is the verdict of public opinion, the opinion of the policeman who arrests the child, or the judgment of the juvenile court. This lack of exactness and uniformity has led some cynics to say that juvenile delinquency is whatever the law

Chapter 1

Facts and fallacies about juvenile delinquency

says it is. It would be more exact to say that it is behavior which the people of a state and their leaders believe to be a threat to public safety or a hindrance to the best development of the child, and whose prohibition they have incorporated into law.

Specifically, juvenile delinquency in different states ranges from the most serious crimes such as murder, burglary, or robbery, to irritating but trivial acts such as playing ball in the street, building a tree house in a public park, or obstructing traffic on a sidewalk. Fortunately, most delinquent acts are of the less serious variety. But there is always the fear on the part of adults that the trivial acts, if continued, may somehow lead to long-lasting or serious misconduct.

Delinquency of juveniles is centuries old

The legal concept of juvenile delinquency is new. The first legal definition was formulated and the first juvenile court was established in Illinois as recently as 1899. But the failure or inability of children and youth to live up to standards set by adults is ageold. The forbidden behavior of children and youth, along with the severe punishments dealt out, is included in the general criminal laws of different countries in different periods.

Four thousand years ago. The oldest known code of laws, the Code of Hammurabi, dating from 2270 B.C., takes account of many types of misconduct, some specifically of youth. This Code records the laws of Babylon, which must have been developing into a consistent system over many preceding centuries. The laws regulate business transactions, property rights, personal relationships, rights of master and slave, and family relationships and responsibilities.

In the period of the Code, the husband was the patriarchal head of the family, charged with many responsibilities to his wife and children. In patriarchal societies rebellion against the father, even by adult sons, was not tolerated. Punishments were severe.

Item 195 in the Code of Hammurabi states: "If a son strike his father, one shall cut off his hands." [1] Since the age of the son who would be so severely punished is not specified, the law might have applied chiefly to adult sons. It should be noted that severe punishments run all through the Code of Hammurabi, including not only physical mutilations, but death for many offenses, sometimes specified as death by drowning or burning.

Parents may now refer their children to the juvenile court for rebellion or mistreatment, but the penalty would be mild compared to early punishments.

The Code of Hammurabi also provided for the adoption of certain children, who were then expected to be loyal to the foster father. The code provides: "If the son of a Ner-se-ga (palace official), or a sacred prostitute, say to a foster father or mother, 'Thou art not my father,' 'Thou art not my mother,' one shall cut out his tongue." Another provision states: "If the son of a Ner-se-ga, or a sacred prostitute, long for his father's house, and run away from his foster-father and foster-mother and go back to his father's house, one shall pluck out his eye." [2]

Running away from home and ungovernability are still considered acts of delinquency, but the severe punishments of four thousand years ago are now abhorred.

Although in the Code there are many items concerning the care of children, inheritance of property, arrangements for the marriage of children, and proper conduct of children toward parents, public offenses such as burglary or assault are not mentioned. It may be that children were closely supervised or punished by the family, or it may be that children suffered the same punishments as adults.

Another early indication of father-son difficulties that sounds surprisingly modern comes from the translation of clay tablets dated about 1750 B.C. which were excavated in Nippur, about a hundred miles south of present-day Bagdad, Iraq. The translation is of an essay written by a professor in one of the more noted Sumerian academies, exalting the values of formal education. Boys attended school from sunrise to sunset the year round, from early youth to young manhood. Industriousness was encouraged by generous use of corporal punishment. The essay is in the form of a father's admonitions to his indifferent son. The father instructs the son to attend school, stand with respect and fear before his professor, complete his assignments, and avoid wandering about the public square or standing idly in the streets. In short, the son is to be about the business of getting an education. The father upbraids his son for lack of industriousness, failure to support him, too great an interest in material wealth, and refusal to follow his father's vocation. Many of the adjurations sound very familiar at the present time. [3]

Gradually, the severe punishments of the early laws were ameliorated, first in practice and later in amended and/or new laws. Among the Hebrews, for example, punishment by death was replaced by warnings and flogging. Finally, youth were divided into three groups, infant, prepubescent, and adolescent, with penalties increasing in severity as degree of maturity increased. [4]

Delinquency in early European experience. Old English laws provided penalties for offenses committed by children. For example, under the laws of King Aethelstan, about 924–939 A.D., any thief over twelve years old received the punishment of death if he stole

1 Albert Kocourek and John H. Wigmore, *Source of Ancient and Primitive Law, Evolution of Law, Select Readings on the Origin and Development of Legal Institutions,* Little, Brown and Company, Boston, 1951, vol. 1, p. 427. Even more severe punishments were sometimes used in other groups. Striking of either parent, cursing or disobeying, and rebelling against a parent was punishable by death, according to certain entries in the Bible.
2 *Ibid.,* numbers 192, 193 of the Code.

3 Samuel Noah Kramer, "A Father and His Perverse Son," *National Probation and Parole Association Journal,* 3 (April, 1957), 169–173. The tablet from which the above translation is taken is in the University Museum in Philadelphia.
4 Frederick J. Ludwig, *Youth and the Law, Handbook on Laws Affecting Youth,* The Foundation Press, Inc., Youth Council Bureau Project, 1955, pp. 124 ff.

more than twelve pence. (This amount was later reduced to eight pence.) However, with the passage of time, the law was eased for children, and no one under sixteen years could be put to death unless he resisted or ran away.[1]

After the Norman Conquest, a difference in responsibility was recognized for children. Eventually children under seven years old were pardoned. But severe penalties were still imposed on older children and adolescents of the same age as present-day juvenile delinquents. For example, in reviewing early crimes committed by English children, for which they received the same punishments adults would have received, Blackstone, writing in the eighteenth century, refers to the following:

girl of thirteen, burned to death for killing her mistress;

boy of ten, hanged for killing his companion;

boy of eight, hanged for burning two barns;

boy of ten, executed for killing his bedfellow.[2]

Blackstone uses these cases simply as illustrations of the youthful age at which children were considered responsible for their actions. He does not indicate how frequently children committed murder or were executed, nor does he make a statement about less serious types of juvenile misbehavior.

That there were juvenile delinquents in the seventeenth and eighteenth centuries is evident from the founding of the Hospital of Saint Michael in Rome, by Pope Clement XI, "for the correction and instruction of profligate youth, that they who when idle were injurious, may when taught become useful to the state." [3]

Other European countries followed this lead, the chief growth of reform schools coming in the early part of the nineteenth century, replacing to some extent physical punishments and imprisonment of juveniles in jail with adult criminals. At this time England had an increased problem of delinquency among city children, for whom it established Kingswood Reformatory for the confinement of the "hordes of unruly children who infested the streets of the new industrial towns" of England.[4] An English report in 1818 states that all information gathered "unites in demonstrating the lamentable fact, that juvenile delinquency has of late years increased to an unprecedented extent, and is still rapidly and progressively increasing; that the crimes committed by the youthful offenders are often of the worst description; and that an organized system for instruction in vice, and the encouragement of depravity is regularly maintained." [5]

Present concern about juvenile delinquency is but a continuation of parental and public anxiety beginning before written records. Many of the actual kinds of delinquency are the same now as thousands of years ago.

Centuries of failure. Undoubtedly the most disturbing fact about this recital of delinquency and crime on the part of children is that no society has mastered the technique of successfully initiating children into the expectations and demands of their society and thus avoiding the problem of delinquency. Today each society still struggles with the twin problems of the socialization of its children and the rehabilitation of the deviants.

Juvenile delinquency in the United States

Magnitude of the situation. Each year more than 400,000 boys and girls appear before juvenile courts; they equal 1.7 per cent of all children between the ages of ten and seventeen—the "juvenile delinquency" years.[6] When traffic violations are included, the percentage rises to 2.3. This percentage is for one year. During the entire eight years in which the juvenile court holds power over the conduct of children, the probability that a boy or girl will appear in court is considerably increased over the number who appear in any one year. It is estimated that approximately

1 *Ibid.,* p. 15.
2 Sir William Blackstone, *Commentaries on the Laws of England,* edited by Thomas M. Cooley, fourth edition edited by James DeWitt Andrews, vol. 1, Callaghan and Company, Chicago, 1899, p. 1230.
3 Cited in *Comparative Survey on Juvenile Delinquency,* Part I, *North America,* Division of Social Welfare, Department of Social Affairs, United Nations, Columbia University Press, New York (Sales Number 1952. IV. 13), p. 9.

4 *Ibid.,* p. 10.
5 Society for the Diffusion of Knowledge upon the Punishment of Death and the Improvement of Prison Discipline, London, *Report of the Committee of the Society for the Improvement of Prison Discipline, and for the Reformation of Juvenile Offenders,* Bensley and Sons, London, 1818, p. 11.
6 Since a detailed statistical analysis is given in Chapter 3, only the bare outlines of the statistical picture are given here.

20 per cent of the boys and 8 per cent of the girls appear in juvenile court during the eight-year period.

As the children born after World War II grow into childhood and adolescence, the number of delinquent children may be expected to increase. By 1970, it is estimated that youth aged ten to nineteen years will number 40 million, and by 1980 about 47 million. In 1960, there were about 30 million youth in this age bracket. Even though the rate of delinquency may remain at 1.7 per cent per year, the actual number of delinquents for whom police, juvenile court judges, child guidance specialists, probation and parole officers will have to be provided, will be tremendously increased.[1] Corresponding increases will be necessary in detention homes and correctional institutions.

The serious implication of the problem is further indicated in that the percentage of children appearing before juvenile courts has been increasing. In ten or fifteen years the percentage of adolescents who appear in court may be somewhat higher than at present, thus further complicating the practical aspects of providing services for them and of providing better preventive measures than are available at present.

In addition to the children who actually appear before the court, approximately three times as many minor offenders are handled directly by the police or through a police juvenile bureau without referral to the court. If these children are counted along with the court cases, the total is again increased.

More boys than girls. It is generally true that for every one girl brought to the attention of the juvenile courts, there are four or five times as many boys. The offenses of boys and girls are distinctly different: boys' misdeeds are centered in stealing, including temporary theft of automobiles for immediate use, and in malicious mischief; girls are apt to be referred to the court for ungovernability, running away, and sexual promiscuity. Preventive measures and rehabilitation programs must be geared to the offense. Thefts involving material goods of considerable monetary value, murders, and serious vices occur occasionally, but they are rare.

Costs of delinquency. The most serious cost is the human one—the scarring effect on children apprehended by the police, brought before the courts, and possibly sent to correctional institutions even though their offenses were not serious. To a child wavering on the crest between mild or occasional misbehavior and the more serious misconduct leading to adult criminality, the experience of arrest, trial, and correctional institution may catapult him into more serious delinquency. The child or adolescent who commits a major crime has often developed a serious character defect or emotional maladjustment which only the most skillful and lengthy treatment can change.

The financial cost is also high, with most of the payment for services coming directly from the taxpayer's pocket. The direct financial cost of public services required by delinquents—police, detention facilities, courts, and institutional care—is estimated conservatively at over 200 million dollars.[2] Property stolen by juveniles is estimated at 115 million dollars, not including property lost through acts of vandalism.

Misconceptions about causes of delinquency

What causes any child to disobey, or any adult to cut a legal corner? The causes of non-conformity to rules and laws are many. Delinquency is simply a certain type of misbehavior which has been singled out for special attention. However, many people assume that all juvenile delinquency constitutes one kind of misconduct, due to one biological cause or growing out of one kind of life experience. Actually, the contributing factors to delinquency are as varied as the types of misbehavior grouped under this general term. Let us look at some of the supposed causes, each of which is in some way related indirectly to some type of delinquency, but no one of which is a direct cause.

Are delinquents feeble-minded—or superior? The answer is neither—they represent a cross section of the juvenile population. Feeble-minded children sometimes get into difficulties: they may wander from home, expose themselves in public without intent to offend anyone, or yield to violent emotions. Many such children are committed to schools for

1 *Statistical Abstract of the United States,* 1959, U. S. Government Printing Office, Washington, D. C., 1959, p. 6. The estimates assume that the fertility level of 1955–1957 will continue to 1975–1980.

2 Subcommittee on Juvenile Delinquency, U. S. Senate, *Juvenile Delinquency Report,* Report No. 130, Washington, D. C., 1957, p. 5.

the feeble-minded where they can be given closer custody than at home. Seriously feeble-minded children would not be capable of the planning and cooperation needed to commit delinquencies. At the other extreme, brilliant children sometimes become delinquent. The commission of a delinquent act or a crime usually is not a matter of rational decision so much as a social activity carried out with others or an attempt to fulfill personal needs. Intelligence may come into the planning and execution of a crime; in fact, some of the crimes that shock the nation have been committed by young people of superior intelligence. But there is no undue tendency for brilliant children to commit crimes or to become delinquent. The motivation for delinquency and crime lies elsewhere than in high intelligence or lack of it. The manner in which a crime is committed may be related to intellectual ability. The long-established idea that most if not all delinquents and criminals are feeble-minded has been discarded. Now, one must consider whether the child has been discriminated against because of dullness or brilliance. One must look for the way in which his intelligence or lack of it have contributed to the manner in which the delinquency was committed. But a direct controlling connection between intelligence or lack of it and delinquency does not exist.

Are most delinquents seriously maladjusted emotionally? Authorities who are psychologically oriented tend to answer this question in the affirmative. The affirmative answer usually comes from clinicians, who have children referred to them showing evidence of emotional maladjustment, one evidence of which may be delinquent behavior. They rarely have association with the much larger number of delinquents who seem no more neurotic or psychotic than the average person. Here we must recognize that few people are so perfectly adjusted that they do not show some signs of tension, some rebellion to frustration, some anxieties. The important point is not whether a delinquent has some symptoms of neurosis or psychosis, but whether the conditions that underlie these symptoms are also the causes of delinquent behavior.

Criminologists who study delinquents in the community instead of the clinic are convinced that most delinquents are not seriously maladjusted emotionally. One estimate is that 25 per cent are somewhat disturbed emo-

tionally.[1] The origin of delinquency in the other 75 per cent is assumed to lie in the social and cultural features of their communities.

Are the children of some races and nationality groups "naturally" delinquent? Superficially, some racial and ethnic groups seem to have a monopoly on delinquency and crime, because their rates of arrest and court appearances are higher than the average. However, careful study of the problem points to a negative reply. High rates of arrest, court appearances, and commitments seem to be closely related to residence in disorganized (slum) areas. Whatever race or ethnic group lives there tends to have higher-than-average rates of delinquency. As each group establishes itself or its children on a firm educational and economic basis and moves from lower class to middle class status, rates of delinquency decline. Delinquency thus is a symptom of a particular phase of adjustment among racial and ethnic groups. For example, a little over a hundred years ago in New York City, the Irish, newly arrived, engaged in many fights and riots. The Irish have long since become integrated into the American pattern of conformity. Many nationality groups have experienced a similar pattern of delinquency and crime, but later become assimilated into American life. The most recent example is that of the Puerto Rican migration, chiefly after World War II, into New York City. Not yet fully adjusted, the children of this group are accused of rampant delinquency. In time, they too will take their place in American social and cultural life.

Is the family responsible for delinquency? Basically, the family carries a heavy responsibility for the character and personality formation of every child. In general, each set of parents does the best it can. Few parents wish evil for their children. But many parents are unable to give their children the love and guidance they need; many are unable to introduce their children into the cultural mores or help them meet the social expectations of the larger community. When laymen or social agencies say "the family is responsible for delinquency," they are really begging the

1 William C. Kvaraceus, *et al., Delinquent Behavior: Culture and the Individual*, National Education Association of the United States, Washington, D. C., 1959, p. 54. The estimate was made by Walter B. Miller, Graduate School of Education, Harvard University, who was Director of the Roxbury Youth Project Research, Roxbury, Massachusetts. See also Table 15, this book.

question. Parents whose children are drifting into delinquency or are actually delinquent, are themselves in need of help.

The broken home with one or both parents absent has been scored as a cause of delinquency. It is true that delinquents come from broken homes in somewhat higher proportions than nondelinquents; but there is no sharp division. Many children from broken homes are nondelinquent, and many from unbroken homes are delinquent. At most, some types of broken homes indicate an unfavorable family life; but the important factor seems to be the quality of family life rather than the physical presence of both parents.

The employed mother has also been criticized as a factor in delinquency. A somewhat higher proportion of delinquent than nondelinquent children do have employed mothers. But to hold the employed mother responsible for delinquency is another blanket assumption which needs closer study. At an earlier period when most mothers worked from dire necessity, the home with an employed mother also was often the broken home and the poverty-stricken home. The employment of the mother often left the children without adequate supervision, but its greater significance for understanding delinquency was as a symptom of unfavorable family conditions, none of which alone created delinquency, but all of which precipitated an unfavorable family situation.

Today when the trend is toward widespread employment of mothers for many reasons other than necessity, the employment of the mother may connote a desire for greater family security, continued education of children, a better home, a summer vacation, or any one of a number of things thought to be of benefit to all members of the family.

Are crime comics to blame? The debate about the relation of crime comics and television murder scripts to delinquency has strong advocates on both sides. The situation repeats the debate of the twenties about the effect of crime movies on children. One group asserts that crime pictures of any type serve as a vicarious release for hostile impulses and emotions usually repressed under social disapproval. Released, they become harmless. Their opponents believe that crime pictures derogating police and emphasizing successful criminals build hatred into children, distrust of police, and admiration of criminals. Children may regard criminals as heroes and seek to emulate their careers. Research on this lags far behind emotional expressions of opinion. Some insight comes from a study of motion pictures made in the twenties.[1] It was decided that crime pictures did not stimulate youth to attempt a life of crime. They were, however, preferred by a larger percentage of already delinquent children than of nondelinquent children. Some delinquent children stated that they had learned specific techniques for the commission of crimes from the crime motion pictures. Pictures of luxury and easily acquired wealth sometimes gave a rationalization for thievery, and both boys and girls were at times sexually aroused by certain torrid love scenes. But choice of pictures and the effect of the pictures were related to already developed interests and values. It seems probable that crime comics and television programs also are not leading causes in the commission of delinquent acts, but they may further an already existing interest in delinquency.

Is the gang responsible for delinquency? Gangs of adolescent boys (occasionally of girls) are often accused of drawing boys into delinquency and of perpetuating delinquency and passing it on to younger boys. It is true that the lone delinquent is the exception. A number of studies indicate that most acts of delinquency are carried out by two or three boys. A Chicago study found that 19 per cent of all offenders were isolates; 58 per cent of the offenses were carried out by two or three boys, 18 per cent by four or five boys, and only 6 per cent by six or more boys.[2] Among boys referred to the Passaic Children's Bureau, 23.2 per cent of first offenses had been carried out by one boy, 36.6 per cent by two or three boys, 26.9 by four or five boys, and 13.3 per cent by six or more.[3]

Although the group committing an offense is small, many boys belong to larger groups or sometimes to organized gangs. Few crimes necessitate more than a few participants, and

1 Herbert Blumer and Philip M. Hauser, *Movies, Delinquency, and Crime,* Macmillan Company, New York, 1933.
2 Clifford R. Shaw and Henry D. McKay, *Social Factors in Juvenile Delinquency,* National Commission on Law Observance and Enforcement, No. 13, vol. 2, U. S. Government Printing Office, Washington, D. C., 1931, pp. 194–195.
3 William C. Kvaraceus, *Juvenile Delinquency and the School,* World Book Company, Yonkers-on-Hudson, New York, 1945, p. 116.

a large number of boys intent on burglary, stealing a car, or destruction of property would soon become conspicuous and stand in danger of an arrest. The function of the larger group is to give approval for the delinquencies of small cliques or groups within the larger group. The clique may gain status within the larger group by daring delinquencies. The gang as such functions directly in delinquency primarily through fights between rival gangs, when the number of combatants increases the chance of success even though at the same time it may attract police attention. Its relationship to the most common kinds of delinquencies of youth is indirect.

The delinquencies of individual boys or girls have received less attention than group delinquencies and gang fights. It is suggested that the individual delinquent is quite likely to be the seriously maladjusted delinquent, whose misconduct has more relationship to his own emotional needs than to clique or gang approval.

Each of the above factors—mental capacity, emotional maladjustment, racial and ethnic affiliation, family conditions, the juvenile gang—may have some relationship to delinquency. But none of these factors has a direct one-to-one relationship with any type of delinquency. The way in which these and other influences may be interwoven in the development of delinquent behavior is elaborated in later chapters.

Misconceptions about prevention and cure

The erroneous belief that factors such as those just discussed are primary, unitary causes of delinquency impedes progress toward the prevention of delinquency and the rehabilitation of the delinquent. Science has made progress since the time of the Code of Hammurabi in understanding motivations of behavior, but it has not yet accurately pinpointed the various processes by which the crazy-quilt of delinquent acts develops. Even with the best of present knowledge, prevention and rehabilitation are difficult, and progress toward more adequate methods is slow. Many people advocate sure-shot methods of prevention and cure, some of which have little validity, while others may have an indirect or partial usefulness.

Severity versus coddling. The trend in treatment of juvenile delinquents and adult criminals has been away from severe punishments.

Nevertheless, one segment of public opinion urges severe physical punishments, imprisonment, and even capital punishment for homicide by juveniles. It is not clear whether the demand for severity emanates from honest convictions, fear because of the increase in juvenile court cases, desire in some cases for a cheap solution making little demand on the taxpayer, or an unconscious projection of all kinds of hatred and resentment against the helpless delinquent. Parallel with the demand for severity is the stigmatization of therapy and re-education as coddling. Therapy and re-education are slow processes and perform no miracles. They are, however, in line with the best that we know of how children learn and are motivated to follow the social codes.

The severe physical punishments of the past put a stop neither to juvenile delinquency nor to adult crime. Several thousand years ago capital punishment by cruel methods, cutting off of fingers or hands, branding, or flogging were common penalties. Some of these punishments continued into the nineteenth century. Imprisonment became the accepted method of punishment during the early 1800's. Isolation from society, few contacts and no communication between prisoners, and sometimes solitary confinement for years within the prison, became standard treatment. Sometimes infractions of prison regulations were punished by whipping and other forms of physical abuse. As reform schools for children and youth were built, many of the same practices were followed. But still delinquency and crime did not stop.

Gradually, various forms of education and retraining for juveniles superseded the more severe methods. At first military drill and vocational training were the standbys. Since the 1920's emphasis has shifted to psychological and social rehabilitation, with the objectives of clearing up emotional twists and of teaching socially acceptable attitudes and habits. It cannot be said, however, that any of these methods has either rehabilitated all delinquents or prevented future delinquency. The methods now are more humane than in the past, and they take account of each delinquent as an individual, seeking to reach the cause of his misbehavior. Therapy and re-education are not coddling. They demand effort on the part of the delinquent, the willingness to try to understand himself, and the readiness to live by the rules of society.

These processes may be very difficult for the free-roving youth who has rejected the more stable social institutions to live by his individual impulses or by the rules of a small group of other boys. Intelligent discipline by the family, supported by other adults in charge of juveniles, and eventually self-discipline by the juveniles themselves are among the objectives of rehabilitation. These objectives are not accomplished by severe punishments, in fact, quite the opposite.

Should parents of delinquents be punished? The erroneous belief that the family alone is responsible for delinquency has led some to demand that parents of delinquents should be punished for not preventing the delinquent behavior.

Systematic punishment of parents has been tried in a few places. For ten years (1937–1946), Judge Paul W. Alexander of Toledo punished parents. Over a thousand cases of adults, half of them parents (mostly mothers), were heard by the court on the charge of contributing to delinquency. Three-fourths of the parents pleaded guilty or were found guilty. One out of four of those convicted served an average of almost a year in prison; the remainder received suspended sentences. A review of the practice, instigated by Judge Alexander himself, revealed that there was no evidence that delinquency had been curbed by punishment of the parents. Judge Alexander concluded that in the main, punishment of parents was a form of revenge.[1]

Usually parents who are sentenced for contributing to the delinquency of their children have not done any specific thing to lead the children to delinquency. They have more often failed to rear their children to conform to laws and social rules. Their own inabilities or emotional problems are usually at the root of the failure. Nothing specific that they have done or not done to contribute to an act of delinquency can normally be pointed out to these helpless or hopeless parents.

The disastrous effects of punishing parents have often been pointed out. When the mother is imprisoned, the home is broken up and her children must be placed in institutions or foster homes or left to care for themselves. Typically, when she is released, she receives no help in reassembling her children and re-establishing her home. Meanwhile, the respect of neighbors and children for her declines. Older children are given a crutch on which to lean in shifting responsibility for their conduct to their mother. If the father is the one imprisoned, the mother must go to work or the entire family must be supported by relief agencies.

It has been found also that once judges accept the idea that punishment of parents is valid, they tend to use it in many cases and relax their efforts to arrange for the rehabilitation of children or of the family as a whole.

Many who oppose punishment of parents do not deny the powerful influence of parents on the development of children's personalities and behavior, but do absolve them from blame for the delinquency. As an alternative to punishing parents, they propose aid to parents through education and counseling.[2]

Curfews are no answer. A curfew effective at an early evening hour is an attempt at an easy way to curb outward misbehavior without digging up the roots of the problem. Curfew ordinances, often setting nine o'clock as the deadline, are popular in many cities. Parents use the curfew as a threat to get their children home, and police feel that almost any youth on the streets after the designated hour should be questioned for loitering. The public in general assumes that parents should enforce the curfew on their children and be held responsible for misbehavior after that hour.

Curfews raise numerous problems. Police are unable to determine whether young people are below or above the age set in the law. Parents dislike having their nondelinquent children questioned by the police. Many programs at churches, schools, and community centers run past the usual curfew hour and crowds of youth are legitimately on the street late at night, but may be subjected to grilling by the police.

Probably more important is the fact that a

1 Cited by Sol Rubin, *Crime and Juvenile Delinquency,* published for the National Probation and Parole Association by Oceana Publications, Inc., New York, 1958, pp. 34–35.

2 Irving Arthur Gladstone, "Spare the Rod and Spoil the Parent," *Federal Probation,* 19 (June, 1955), 37–41; Justine Wise Polier, "The Woodshed is No Answer," *Federal Probation,* 20 (September, 1956), 3–6; Polier, "Back to What Woodshed," Pamphlet No. 232, Public Affairs Committee, New York, 1956. Mr. Gladstone is a school principal, and Judge Polier is a justice in the Domestic Relations Court of New York City. Both oppose punishment of parents.

curfew does not attack the causes of delinquency or provide anything constructive. A report made in 1953 by the Conneticut State Juvenile Court, which was opposed to curfew laws, compares the enforcement of the laws to a state of siege signifying that a city's youth programs are ineffective. The report points out that only about 2 per cent of children are in trouble and that 86 per cent of all delinquencies occur before nine o'clock, but the law is imposed on all youth, innocent and delinquent alike.[1]

Various writers point out that curfew laws do not stop delinquency. The normally nondelinquent youth does not wander aimlessly about the street, and the delinquency-bent youth finds ways to evade the law or openly disregard it. The negative approach of the curfew does not bring about needed changes in personality and behavior patterns.

Recreation needed by all children. Another easy answer to the problem of delinquency is to provide enough recreation for all children. The need of all children for recreation is now generally recognized, as is the fact that in cities the back yard, the vacant lot, the attic, and the open country are not available. Community centers, churches, schools, and public recreation departments have therefore accepted the responsibility of providing space, equipment, and leadership. Recreation may be used as a means of personality development and character training, but chiefly when children are organized into small groups which meet frequently with good leaders. Even then there is no absolute assurance that delinquency will be prevented or delinquents rehabilitated. The carry-over of the effect of the limited hours of recreation into the many hours of daily life spent in other situations is not complete.

Mass recreation chiefly keeps youth out of trouble while they are on the playground or participating in the programs. But even here there is no sure relationship. Delinquency may be plotted by groups of boys presumably active in recreation; thefts have been handily made from outer clothing left on racks or from the clothing of boys in swimming in public pools. Fights are common on some playgrounds, often leading to the expulsion of the unruly children, presumably the ones

most in need of recreation. It has been noted also that once a delinquent behavior pattern has been established, youth find recreational programs under adult leadership too restrictive and tame for their tastes. A more direct approach, focused on youth likely to become, or already, delinquent, is needed in addition to the usual recreation for all youth.

What about slum clearance? The early hope that slum clearance and decent housing would prevent or cure delinquency has faded. As with recreation, everyone is entitled to clean, well-equipped housing and neighborhood services, but they do not necessarily prevent or reduce delinquency. Some early assertions that there was a direct relationship between decline in delinquency and public housing overlooked the fact that often the people displaced from old slums when land was cleared did not return to the new housing. Higher rents and a different standard of living often brought in families whose children were not delinquency-oriented. In some projects, as soon as a child is detected in delinquency, the family is evicted.[2] In these projects the delinquency rate is low, but the family has simply moved outside the project, and the delinquent child continues his activities. Nothing is solved.

On the other hand, housing projects in deteriorated areas have an opportunity to help prevent delinquency if they are designed and staffed in such a way that a community spirit can develop and groups can meet on the project. These efforts are no different from those that may be made in any community. A newly built housing project may be designed to include meeting rooms. What goes on in these rooms or in the project, however, is not a matter of material equipment but of leadership and the development of community identification and pride. These often develop only with difficulty in low-rent projects where hundreds of families, previously unknown to each other and often inexperienced in urban living, suddenly come together in a compact housing project.

Many people, when confronted by a perplexing problem, try to find a short cut to the

---

1 Frank L. Manella, "Curfew Laws," *National Probation and Parole Association Journal*, 4 (April, 1958), 165–166.

2 This policy is bitterly castigated by Harrison E. Salisbury in *The Shook-Up Generation*, Harper and Brothers, New York, 1958, also published as a Crest Book, Fawcett Publications, Inc., Greenwich, Connecticut. The author is a journalist who spent many days in first-hand contact with certain delinquent gangs and community agencies in New York City.

goal of prevention or amelioration. Many of the misconceptions already discussed stem from efforts to find easy short cuts. Some are based on wishful thinking (curfew for instance)—if only this easy solution would work. Some seem to be the result of hostility on the part of the public and an attempt to assign blame on someone (punishment of parents or severe treatment of delinquents). A few are catch-all solutions—some program is recognized as valuable in its own right and must therefore surely be a cure for delinquency (recreation, slum clearance, and adequate housing). When applicable at all, any of these programs touches only part of the problem. Delinquency is behavior, and like all behavior it is related on the one hand to inner needs and on the other to social groups and cultural ways of the groups of which the person is a member.

Delinquency is world-wide

This chapter began with the statement that juvenile delinquency is age-old. It concludes with data to point out that juvenile delinquency is also world-wide. The United States is not alone in its struggle to control delinquent behavior. Every civilized country has its own problems. It is not possible to compare rates because of different concepts of delinquency, different age limits, and differences in agencies handling delinquency. In a study of nineteen European countries, made under the United Nations, it was noted that all the countries had special institutions for long-term care of juvenile delinquents.[1] Even Iceland had one institution to accommodate fifteen boys between the ages of fourteen and eighteen. The United Nations also conducted a study in nine countries in the Middle East and Near East and in each found special recognition of youthful offenders in the general criminal code, although at the time of the study only one country, Jordan, had passed special legislation regarding juvenile delinquents.[2] In Asia and the Far East, also, laws

make special provisions for young offenders, again a recognition of delinquency and crime among youth.[3] Forms of punishment and institutions vary from country to country but are vivid evidence of the existence of delinquency.

In many foreign countries, as in the United States, juvenile delinquency seems to be on the increase. England and Wales, the Union of South Africa, Australia, New Zealand, the Federal Republic of Germany, Eastern Germany, Austria, Greece, Yugoslavia, France, Sweden, Finland, and the Philippines have all reported increases in rates or in numbers sufficiently in excess of earlier numbers to indicate an increase in rate.[4] Only a few countries reported decreases in delinquency: Switzerland, Italy, Belgium, and Canada.

Among countries reporting to the United Nations in 1960, theft of automobiles for temporary use was generally noted. A common offense in the United States, car thefts have increased in other countries with the increase in usage of automobiles since World War II. Street-corner groups and gangs have also become conspicuous abroad, as they are in certain neighborhoods in the United States. Germany, France, England, Poland, Russia, Yugoslavia, Australia, South Africa, Sweden, India, China (Taiwan), Japan, the Philippines, Argentina, and Uruguay all reported gang activity and mass rioting.[5] In addition, the usual forms of stealing, vandalism, and, among girls, sex delinquency are found. In other words, delinquency in other countries closely resembles delinquency in the United States. A few examples will point up the similarities.

English cities are plagued with "teddy boys" (and girls), so called because they wear long jackets and tight trousers reminiscent of the styles of the Edwardian era. These teenagers prowl the streets in groups, singing and milling. They break windows, scratch

1 *The Prevention of Juvenile Delinquency in Selected European Countries,* Bureau of Social Affairs, Department of Economic and Social Affairs, United Nations, Columbia University Press, New York, (Sales Number 1955.IV.12), p. 35.

2 *Comparative Study on Juvenile Delinquency,* Part V, *Middle East,* Division of Social Welfare, Department of Social Affairs, United Nations, Columbia University Press, New York, (Sales Number 1953.IV.17), p. 1. The countries covered were Egypt, Iran, Jordan, Lebanon, Saudi Arabia, Syria, Turkey, and Yemen.

3 *Comparative Survey on Juvenile Delinquency,* Part IV, *Asia and the Far East,* Division of Social Welfare, Department of Social Affairs, United Nations, Columbia University Press, New York, (Sales No. 1953.IV.27), Chapter 1. The countries surveyed were Burma, Ceylon, India, Japan, Pakistan, the Philippines, and Thailand.

4 Wolf Middendorff, *New Forms of Juvenile Delinquency: Their Origin, Prevention and Treatment,* Second United Nations Congress on the Prevention of Crime and the Treatment of Offenders, A/CONF. 17/6, United Nations, Department of Economic and Social Affairs, New York, 1960, pp. 10–17.

5 *Ibid.,* pp. 23–30, 35–59.

the paint on cars, and annoy passers-by. They annoy people on the street by walking along with them, interrupting their conversation, and then laughing at their embarrassment.[1]

A July, 1959, report from Kristianstad, Sweden, a quiet town of 27,000, reveals that Swedish youth are capable of unrestrained violence. Some two hundred youths and girls roared into the city on a Saturday in "souped-up" American cars or on motor-cycles, presumably to watch motorcycle races scheduled for the following day. Dressed in black costumes of caps, leather jackets, and jeans, they soon filled the streets, staggering from too much alcohol, and arrogantly push-ing residents off the sidewalks. When op-posed, they began fighting and destroying property. Police were supplemented by troops from a nearby army base. By morning, twenty persons were in hospitals. The mob broke windows and burned public toilets and tents in the public camp ground set up for the use of motorcyclists taking part in the races. Another Swedish city had the same experi-ence earlier, and both cities have now banned future motorcycle races. Some members of the gang said their idol was Marlon Brando, American movie hero in "The Wild Ones," a story of young motorcycle toughs who ter-rorized a small town in California.[2]

A newspaper report from Belgrade, Yugo-slavia, describes the concern of officials with a renewal of teen and youth gang disturb-ances, which had been common earlier but infrequent for the past several years. Street-corner fighting and unprovoked attacks on citizens by small groups of youth are typical of the disturbances. An unusually violent disturbance occurred in Belgrade in February, 1959, when a group of "siledzije" (wild ones) boarded a street car, blocked the doors, and attacked passengers. The driver was beaten up. The fight was continued in the streets of Belgrade until some 300 people were in-volved. Six of the "wild ones" were arrested, two being given the maximum sentence of fifty days and the others sentenced to fifteen to thirty days. The "wild ones" wear jet black trousers and blue, fleece-lined windbreakers, but otherwise scorn as effeminate the distinc-tive costumes and peculiar hair cuts worn by

teen gang members in some other countries.[3]

France presumably had its first experience with juvenile delinquent gangs in 1959. Calling themselves *Les Gadjos* (the meaning of which is not clear), they have attacked citizens on the streets with bicycle chains, in one instance threatened to fire a wheat field if the owner did not pay them a large sum, and in another instance sacked their school. Intergang fights have been observed, and some battles with police have occurred. Since these gangs of youths wear black imitation leather jackets, they are nicknamed *Les Blousons Noirs* (the black jackets). They are devotees of the late James Dean.[4]

Italy, with a low rate of juvenile delin-quency, nevertheless is disturbed by the un-restrained activities of teenage boys. In the prosperous northern cities especially, gangs of boys, often from respectable, well-to-do families, molest and attack citizens and are charged with committing many robberies. Among their activities are harrassing drivers of new expensive cars and damaging the cars, molesting unescorted women, and raiding couples in parked cars. The boys do not wear any unusual type of dress but prefer brightly colored shirts and blue jeans, or, on occasion, white jeans. Police in the cities with most an-noyance are attempting to bring them under control; they are arrested in large numbers in "drives," lectured, and released. When not actually injuring anyone, they add to the irritation of people by roaring past on motor-cycles with mufflers tampered to give the maximum of noise.[5]

From Argentina comes a report of "bar gangs," so called because they usually hang around a bar, cafe, or store. Their activities begin with disrespect for others, insults to passers-by, and indecent remarks. They progress to damaging property and parked automobiles. Minor thefts and then robberies follow. These activities are not new but have increased. The gangs are made up for the most part of minors.[6]

Not all delinquency in other countries comes from undisciplined gangs. Delinquen-cies grow out of individual unfavorable family

1 From the Daily News Foreign Service, *Chicago Daily News*, (July 23, 1958), p. 6.
2 *Salt Lake Tribune*, July 27, 1959 and *Deseret News*, July 28, 1959.

3 Reuters News Service in *The New York Times*, April 19, 1959.
4 "Letter from Paris," *The New Yorker*, 35 (Septem-ber 5, 1959), 95–96.
5 Story by Paul Hoffman, *The New York Times*, July 12, 1959.
6 Middendorf, *op. cit.*, p. 58.

backgrounds in other countries as well as in the United States. In Japan, for example, the retention of feudal customs may be a factor in the deliquencies and crimes of youth. Jiro Mashike, at the age of eighteen, was selected at a family conference to marry the young widow of a member of a wealthy branch of the family and to adopt her daughter. By this maneuver, the wealth was to be retained within the family connection. Jiro, however, was an unwilling groom and not ready for the responsibilities thrust on him. Soon after the marriage, he ran away, tried without success to fulfill a childhood dream of becoming a professional wrestler, and ended with a band of hobos. He was caught on a marauding expedition for food and clothing and placed in the custody of a national juvenile reform institution.[1]

England's problems are not limited to teddy boys. Boys steal and girls run away from home. A girl of sixteen with an I. Q. of 100 had been placed in a hostel (residential home) for delinquents on probation and referred to a clinic for guidance. She was from a home with a neurotic father and a dull and inefficient mother. The moral standards were low. The girl had been running away from home and spending much time in dance halls and night clubs in undesirable company. She had a good school and work record, affected to some extent by the home conditions. She was deeply resentful toward her parents. Classified as in need of care and protection, she remained at the hostel receiving treatment at the clinic for six months. Her general behavior improved and she became more stable and less tense and anxious.

After her return home, she slipped back into undesirable behavior and ran away. A year later she was living and working in a different part of the country. She had not become actually delinquent but was known to the police because of her associations with persons guilty of wrongdoing.[2]

No easy way out

Through thousands of years of history, in countries around the world, parents and public leaders have struggled with the problem of misbehavior of children and youth. In other areas of well-being advances made in some countries are filtering through distance and language barriers into other countries. These advances include improvement and extension of education, increased health and longevity, control of poverty and unemployment, and easing the arduous task of physical labor needed to sustain life. But in the prevention and cure of juvenile delinquency and adult crime, the record of civilization makes a poor showing.

Most children grow up to become responsible adults; most individual acts of delinquency do not lead to a delinquent personality or to professional adult criminality. The usual methods of child rearing and discipline are probably adequate for the great mass of children. But the hard core of delinquents who set themselves apart from society and contribute heavily to adult criminality slip through the meshes of ordinary child-rearing methods. For this group, no country has any sure way of preventing the development of the confirmed delinquent or of accomplishing rehabilitation.

1 Soichi Morita, "Family Tension in Juvenile Cases in Japan," *Focus* 33, (1954), 18–21.

2 Tadeusz Grygier, "The Probation Hostel in England, Part II, Psychiatric Considerations," *Focus,* 31 (1952), 168–172.

Bibliography

Gladstone, Irving Arthur, "Spare the Rod and Spoil the Parent," *Federal Probation,* 19 (June, 1955), 37–41.

Kramer, Samuel Noah, "A Father and His Perverse Son," *National Probation and Parole Association Journal,* 3 (1957), 169–173.

Ludwig, Frederick J., *Youth and the Law, Handbook of Laws Affecting Youth,* The Foundation Press, Inc., Brooklyn, New York, 1955.

Manella, Frank L., "Curfew Laws," *National Probation and Parole Association Journal,* 4 (1958), 161–168.

Polier, Justine Wise, *Back to What Woodshed?* Public Affairs Pamphlet No. 232, Public Affairs Committee, New York, 1956.

———, "The Woodshed is No Answer," *Federal Probation,* 20 (September, 1956), 3–6.

Rubin, Sol, *Crime and Juvenile Delinquency,* Oceana Publications, Inc., New York, 1958, Chapter 2.

Solomon, Ben, "Why We Have not Solved the Delinquency Problem," *Federal Probation,* 17 (December, 1953), 11–19.

Stullken, Edward H., "Misconceptions about Juvenile Delinquency," *Journal of Criminal Law, Criminology and Police Science,* 46 (1956), 833–842.

Juvenile delinquency refers to the failure of children and youth to meet certain obligations expected of them by the society in which they live.

Legal definitions

The Children's Bureau, a federal agency, uses a legal definition of delinquency in its reports:

Juvenile delinquency cases are those referred to courts for acts defined in the statutes of the State as the violation of law or municipal ordinance by children or youth of juvenile court age, or for conduct so seriously antisocial as to interfere with the rights of others or to menace the welfare of the delinquent himself or of the community.[1]

Variety of laws. Each state, the District of Columbia, Puerto Rico, and the federal government have all passed laws defining the types of behavior that justify bringing a child or youth before a special juvenile court. Fifty-three varying legal definitions are based on the underlying principle of protection for the child and community. However, they vary in many details.[2]

The first juvenile delinquency law, passed by the State of Illinois in 1899, specifies many exact kinds of delinquency in addition to the offenses covered by the criminal laws. Many other states have also passed an omnibus type of law.

"Delinquent Child" defined. Sec. 1. Be it enacted by the People of the State of Illinois, represented in the General Assembly: That for the purposes of this Act a delinquent child is any male who while under the age of 17 years, or any female who while under the age of 18 years, violates any law of this State; or is incorrigible, or knowingly associates with thieves, vicious or immoral persons; or without just cause and without the consent of its parents, guardian or custodian absents itself from its home or place of abode, or is growing up in idleness or crime; or knowingly frequents a house of ill repute; or knowingly frequents any

---

1 *Juvenile Court Statistics, 1957,* Children's Bureau, Statistical Series No. 52, Children's Bureau, Washington, D. C., 1959, p. 4.
2 Students who wish to learn about the specifics of a given state should consult the statutes for that state or a collection of laws, such as Wendell Huston, compiler, *Social Welfare Laws of the Forty-Eight States,* Wendell Huston Company, Seattle 4, Washington. This publication is kept up to date through supplements.

Chapter **2**

Juvenile delinquency defined

policy shop or place where any gambling device is operated; or frequents any saloon or dramshop where intoxicating liquors are sold; or patronizes or visits any public pool room or bucket shop; or wanders about the streets in the night time without being on any lawful business or lawful occupation; or habitually wanders about any railroad yards or tracks or jumps or attempts to jump onto any moving train; or enters any car or engine without lawful authority; or uses vile, obscene, vulgar, or indecent language in any public place or about any school house; or is guilty of indecent or lascivious conduct.

Another, more flexible type of law is represented by that of New Mexico. After specifying that a juvenile delinquent is a person under eighteen who has violated laws, ordinances, or regulations of the state or its political subdivisions the law continues that the delinquent is one:

who by reason of habitually refusing to obey the reasonable and lawful commands or directions of his or her parents, parent guardian, custodian, teacher, or any person of lawful authority, is deemed to be habitually uncontrolled, habitually disobedient, or habitually wayward; . . . or who habitually is truant from school or home; . . . or who habitually deports himself as to injure or endanger the morals, health, or welfare of himself or others.

According to juvenile delinquency laws, children are held accountable not only for many laws applying to adults but for a variety of additional restrictions on behavior not imposed on adults. State laws average eight or ten specific acts of delinquency, whose variety is shown in the following list.

Violates any law or ordinance

Habitually truants

(Knowingly) associates with thieves, vicious or immoral persons

Is incorrigible

Is beyond control of parent or guardian

Is growing up in idleness or crime

So disports self as to injure or endanger self or others

Absents self from home (without just cause) without consent

Conducts self immorally or indecently

(Habitually) uses vile, obscene or vulgar language in public place

(Knowingly) enters, visits house of ill repute

Patronizes, visits policy shop or gaming place

(Habitually) wanders about railroad yards or tracks

Jumps train or enters car or engine without authority

Patronizes saloon or dram house where intoxicating liquor is sold

Wanders streets at night, not on lawful business

Patronizes public poolroom or bucket shop

Conducts self immorally around school (or in public place)

Engages in illegal occupation

Is in occupation or situation dangerous or injurious to self or others

Smokes cigarette (or uses tobacco in any form)

Frequents place whose existence violates law

Is found in place for permitting which adult may be punished

Is addicted to drugs

Is disorderly

Begs

Uses intoxicating liquor

Makes indecent proposals

Loiters, sleeps in alleys, is a vagrant

Runs away from state or charity institution

Is found on premises occupied or used for illegal purposes

Operates motor vehicle dangerously while under influence of liquor

Attempts to marry without consent, in violation of law

Is given to sexual irregularities [1]

Flexible laws are more adjustable to the passage of time and to local areas and groups than are the rigid laws. The more specific the law is, the more quickly it becomes dated. Opinions change as to what is undesirable behavior. Such behavior itself may change; for instance, the Illinois law forbids certain behavior on or around railroad trains, but nothing is said about automobiles, which were few at the time the law was passed. Smoking, forbidden in some states, was formerly thought undesirable—even immoral—but is now a common practice among adults and older adolescents. Finally, what is regarded as undesirable in one region, one social class, or one ethnic group may be regarded as normal or even desirable in some other group.

Legal age of delinquent children. Many states do not specify an age below which a child would not be considered capable of judging right and wrong conduct. When a lower age limit is specified, it is usually seven years; that is, below the age of seven a child would not be held responsible for his conduct, no matter what he did. His parents, however, might be held responsible for failure to supervise him.

The upper age limit for juvenile delinquency varies in different states from sixteen to twenty-one years. The most commonly used upper limit is the eighteenth birthday: on one day the boy is still seventeen years old, and misconduct would bring him to the juvenile court as a juvenile delinquent; the next day he celebrates his eighteenth birthday, and misconduct would bring him to a court that handles adult criminal cases. However, after his eighteenth birthday, he would not be held in any court for misconduct of the type specified only in juvenile delinquency laws.

Table 1 gives a summary of the ages below which a child would be classified as a juvenile delinquent. In some states—Illinois, for instance, the upper age limit is a year or two higher for girls than for boys. In general, however, the eighteenth birthday is the dividing line between juvenile and adult in the world of misconduct.

1 Rephrased from Frederick B. Sussmann, *Juvenile Delinquency,* Oceana Publications, 80 Fourth Avenue, New York, 1950, revised and updated by publisher's editorial staff, 1959, p. 21.

In a large number of states, children (usually of adolescent age) who have committed a very serious crime (for example, murder) must or may be tried in the criminal courts as would adults and are subject to adult penalties. New Mexico, whose juvenile delinquency law was cited above, has a provision that if a boy or girl aged fourteen or over is charged with a felony and this adolescent is not a "fit subject for reform or rehabilitation," the juvenile court may transfer the case to the criminal court. Under the age of fourteen, however, the child, no matter how unpromising he might seem or how serious the crime he had committed, would still be considered a juvenile delinquent, subject to the juvenile court. In some other states, children of still younger ages may be tried in the adult criminal courts for serious crimes. In the late forties, a boy of twelve was tried in the Criminal Court of Cook County (Chicago), Illinois, for murdering a playmate, and about the same time in a western state another boy of twelve was sentenced to a long term in prison (for adults) for killing his sister.

Some states have passed laws for older adolescents, setting up special categories of misconduct and specialized courts. These provisions are intermediate between juvenile delinquencies and courts on the one hand and adult crimes and criminal courts on the other.

Other official definitions. Three official definitions other than the one cited from the Children's Bureau are also in common use. The most sweeping defines delinquent children as children of juvenile delinquency age who have been arrested or picked up informally by the police. Most of these children are released or in some cities handled by special youth bureaus attached to the police department. A minority are referred to the juvenile court; these are the children classified by the Children's Bureau as delinquents. Many of them are handled informally, without a written record of being adjudged a juvenile delinquent. Some people argue that only those adjudged delinquent should be classified as juvenile delinquents. Another and still more restricted group consists of children committed to correctional institutions. Research on delinquency may be based on any one or more of these definitions. In order of size they are arrests (largest number), referrals to

Table 1

Age Below Which Boys and Girls Are Under the Jurisdiction of Juvenile Courts for Delinquency, in Fifty States and the District of Columbia

Age	Number of States		
	Same age for boys and girls	Different age Boys	Girls
Below age 16............	4	3	
" " 17............	7	1	
" " 18............	33		4
" " 19............		1	
" " 20............			
" " 21............	2		1

Data: *Juvenile Court Statistics, 1957*, Children's Bureau Statistical Series No. 52, Children's Bureau, Washington, D. C., 1959, pp. 13–17; supplemented by Paul W. Tappan, *Juvenile Delinquency*, McGraw-Hill Book Company, New York, 1949, p. 14.

court, informal or adjudicated cases (about equal in number), and institutionalized cases.

Whatever the classification, all have as their base the offenses specified in the juvenile delinquency law of the state. Deviation from this law, when it is detected and the child is either brought in by police or otherwise referred to the juvenile court, constitutes delinquency of an official type.

Nonlegal definition of delinquent behavior

When attention is centered on legal processes, the legal definitions are applicable. But when one is concerned with tracing the development of delinquency or with its prevention and the rehabilitation of children with behavior problems, perhaps outside the legal procedures, a looser definition is advantageous. According to one such definition, a juvenile delinquent: ". . . is any child or youth whose conduct deviates sufficiently from normal social usage to warrant his being considered a menace to himself, to his future interests, or to society itself." [1]

Such a definition (as is true also of some of the more flexible legal definitions) immediately raises all kinds of questions. What is normal social usage? Who decides whether the child is a menace to himself or his future interests? Who decides what constitutes a menace to the community? Many people make these decisions—parents themselves, teachers, ministers, youth leaders, and many others. In extreme instances, these people

1 C. V. Good, *editor, Dictionary of Education,* McGraw-Hill Book Company, New York, 1945, p. 23.

may notify the police or refer a child to the juvenile court. But they may also refer the child to a social agency which is less concerned about legal definitions than with the personal and social adjustment of the child in his particular social groups.

Interest in development and adjustment rather than legality also eliminates the age limitations. Misbehavior similar to legal delinquency may begin in the preschool period and may continue into later adolescence or early adulthood, when it may be abandoned or may lead into professional adult criminal behavior.

Public intolerance as a measure of delinquency

The preceding section suggests the need for a formulation of delinquent behavior in terms of public tolerance, intolerance, or outright condemnation. The basis of this formulation is the recognition of a continuum of behavior to replace the usual tendency to think of behavior as a dichotomy of good and bad, delinquent and nondelinquent. Figure 1 schematizes the concept. For purposes of convenience in discussion, seven stages are recognized. The central stage, called D in the figure, represents the expected, "average" behavior of children. Average behavior basically conforms to the values of society, but there is considerable flexibility in behavior in ways which do not threaten or attack the values or the structure of society by which values are maintained. The expectation is not for perfection but for essential conformity softened by minor deviations. This area is one of tolerance; public opinion not only does not condemn the foibles and vagaries of youth but views them with amusement or approval as indicative of ingenuity, cleverness, or a desirable amount of competitiveness and aggressiveness.

Examples of class D behavior among children would be an occasional truancy, helping oneself to the fruit in someone's backyard, rowdyism after a hotly contested basketball game, nuisance activity on Halloween but without deliberate destruction of property, coming home later than the hour set by parents but not staying away all night, and fighting under provocation but without deliberate injury to the opponent. The public "puts up" with much behavior of this type. When penalties are applied they are slight and short-run. The child is not handicapped by being officially labeled a delinquent through a court hearing or removed from the community by commitment to a correctional school.

Two variations from class D occur: one represents underconformity to the norms of class D, the other overconformity. In Figure 1, underconformity is shown to the left and overconformity to the right of the D or tolerance area. Children and youth who strain the limits of tolerance too far (areas C and E) are merely tolerated. Penalties are not heavy, but disapproval is evident. On the underconforming side, the youth is criticized for "going too far," "straining everyone's patience," or "beginning to get into trouble." On the overconforming side, the child or youth is overly careful of his behavior, beyond the expectations of the public for his age. He is too conscientious, too anxious to please by conforming to perfect standards. Adults tolerate him but feel that he is "afraid to do anything," or is not "red-blooded" or courageous. Children in both areas, C and E, are regarded as members of the in-group, the central group D, but as having begun to stray beyond approved boundaries. In both cases efforts are made to bring them back within the area of tolerance. Those with type C behavior are restrained; those with type E behavior are stimulated and encouraged to show more spirit and less docility in their behavior. Usually children with type C behavior arouse more concern than those with type E behavior. They are edging toward delinquency, a shift which is regarded as a threat and a potential danger to the area of tolerance. Nevertheless, they are thought of as misbehaving rather than as delinquent. Their difficulties are usually handled by parents and the school, occasionally by police when misconduct occurs in public places, only rarely by juvenile courts.

Areas C and E are flanked by distinctly disapproved areas of behavior. Children in area B feel the full weight of public disapproval. They are frequently dishonest, untruthful, deceitful, and destructive. Parents and school are no longer able to restrain or discipline them. The police take over. Nevertheless, these children and youth are not regarded as confirmed delinquents. Police release many to their parents or refer them to some social agency, but always with the

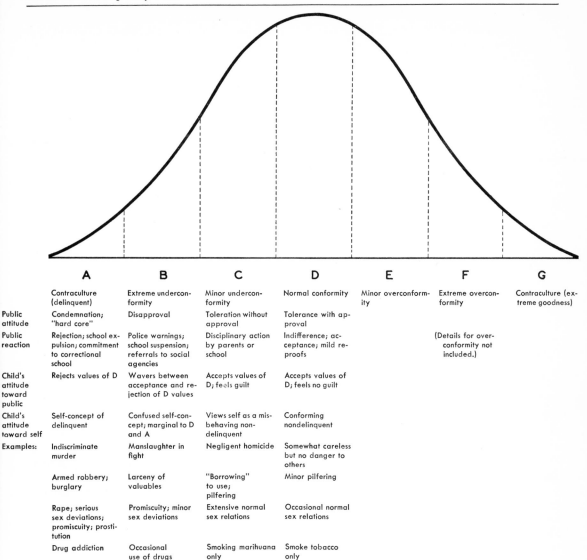

	A	B	C	D	E	F	G
	Contraculture (delinquent)	Extreme underconformity	Minor underconformity	Normal conformity	Minor overconformity	Extreme overconformity	Contraculture (extreme goodness)
Public attitude	Condemnation; "hard core"	Disapproval	Toleration without approval	Tolerance with approval			
Public reaction	Rejection; school expulsion; commitment to correctional school	Police warnings; school suspension; referrals to social agencies	Disciplinary action by parents or school	Indifference; acceptance; mild reproofs		(Details for over-conformity not included.)	
Child's attitude toward public	Rejects values of D	Wavers between acceptance and rejection of D values	Accepts values of D; feels guilt	Accepts values of D; feels no guilt			
Child's attitude toward self	Self-concept of delinquent	Confused self-concept; marginal to D and A	Views self as a misbehaving non-delinquent	Conforming nondelinquent			
Examples:	Indiscriminate murder	Manslaughter in fight	Negligent homicide	Somewhat careless but no danger to others			
	Armed robbery; burglary	Larceny of valuables	"Borrowing" to use; pilfering	Minor pilfering			
	Rape; serious sex deviations; promiscuity; prostitution	Promiscuity; minor sex deviations	Extensive normal sex relations	Occasional normal sex relations			
	Drug addiction	Occasional use of drugs	Smoking marihuana only	Smoke tobacco only			

implied threat that another instance of misbehavior will mean the juvenile court and possible commitment. Young people in this area of behavior are therefore in an anomalous position. Disapproval pushes them toward affiliation with other delinquents; they are often socially ostracized and informally penalized. At the same time, the position of the confirmed delinquent may still repel them. On the side of the overly conforming youth, area F, disapproval also is expressed. Such epithets as "goody-good," "teacher's pet," "drip," "scaredy-cat," and "sissy" are freely used. These young people are not publicly or officially penalized as are the underconforming youth, but they may be socially avoided and driven into association

Figure 1. Hypothetical Formulation of a Behavior Continuum.

with other overconforming youth. Areas B and F are the ones where children tend to stabilize their self-conceptions as "average," delinquent, or "better than other people."

If children and youth whose behavior falls into areas B or F are not drawn back into the centrally located areas of behavior, as many of them are, they tend to develop behavior of types A or G. Behavior becomes consistently under- or overconforming, as the case may be. The delinquent child has become the "hard-core" or "real" delinquent, who tends to make delinquency a central and important part of his life. The overconforming child has become "saintly," or "too good to be true." The attitude of the public toward these extreme groups is to reject them, in attitude and perhaps physically. The delinquent child comes within the legal definition of delinquent and usually has a juvenile court hearing, followed by probation or commitment to a correctional school. The over-conforming child is socially ostracized and at adolescence may voluntarily withdraw into some isolating religious group.

The discussion will now be concerned only with the delinquent child, although the same processes leading to delinquency seem applicable to the overconformer as well. The confirmed delinquent is not only rejected by the community at large, but in turn rejects the community. He tends to drop out of groups and institutions that expect his behavior to go no further than that permitted in the area of tolerance. He truants from school and quits school as early as possible. He refuses to enter community centers, churches, or public recreational areas or is ejected from them because of misbehavior. Sometimes he declares war on such institutions and enters them to riot or forces an entrance at night to wreck the inside of the buildings. With others of his kind he builds up a secluded social world, with its own peculiar scale of values, roles of activity, and levels of status. What the public thinks, what the area of tolerance in behavior permits, no longer matter greatly to him.

This peculiar world of the confirmed delinquent or the older skilled criminal is popularly referred to as the underworld. Sociologists sometimes call it the delinquent subculture. It is, however, more than a subculture, a term that implies simply some marked differences from the general culture. The extreme of delinquency (or of overconformity) is not only different from but is opposed to the dominant culture as typified by area D. The term contraculture is more significant than subculture in pointing up the characteristics of the extremes of the continuum between excessive underconformity and excessive overconformity.[1]

Any contraculture has developed values and modes of behavior that are in conflict

1 J. Milton Yinger, "Contraculture and Subculture," *American Sociological Review*, 25 (1960), 625–635.

with the prevailing culture (see Figure 1, areas A and G as opposed to area D). These values and modes of behavior tend to be the opposite of those of the prevailing culture. They have, however, grown out of the tensions and conflicts which characterized the failure of some youth in areas B and F to come to adjustment with the expected or demanded behavior of area D.

Figure 1 shows a bell-shaped curve superimposed on the behavior continuum that runs from the confirmed delinquent to the confirmed overconformer. It is difficult to find statistical proof to support the curve. We know that less than 1 per cent of all boys and girls between the ages of ten and seventeen are committed to a correctional school in any one year, and that only about 2 per cent face a hearing in juvenile court (area A). Police take another 7 per cent into custody but do not refer them to the court (area B). A rough guess based on statistical material presented in Chapter 3 would place about 20 per cent in area C. If we assume the same proportions in areas G, F, and E respectively, about 42 per cent would be in area D.

Several conclusions and observations can be made. The more serious a misbehavior is regarded by the public, the fewer are the children who indulge in that behavior. The younger the child, the more likely it is that his behavior will fall into areas D or C rather than A. Adolescents may spread out over the entire continuum in decreasing numbers from D to A, but they make up most of the delinquents in area A.

This formulation of delinquency as part of a continuum, with public opinion defining the stages at any given place and time, is adaptable to considerable manipulation. As will appear later in the text, it helps to clarify differences in delinquency among social classes, the difference in levels of seriousness of delinquency found in the same geographic area, and the difficulty of drawing hard-core delinquent gangs back into conformity.

Who is the delinquent?

At what point along this continuum of behavior is anyone justified in labeling a boy or girl as a delinquent? The law labels any child as such who presumably has committed even one act of delinquency, however mild. The legal definition is inadequate, however, for the understanding of the child's position in his society, the tolerance or disapproval of the public, or the building up of a concept of delinquent personality. An essentially conforming child may commit a few acts of delinquency but still feel himself to be part of the central or D group, holding D values and feeling guilty when he deviates beyond the area of tolerance. The self-concept of delinquency or the delinquent personality is a product of extreme deviation and especially of acceptance of a delinquent contraculture.

The misbehaving nondelinquent and the confirmed delinquent can be distinguished in several ways. Culturally, the misbehaving nondelinquent is socialized in the prevailing values of his large cultural group, that is, social class or ethnic group. He accepts the values of his culture but occasionally performs acts that are contrary to them. These acts are likely to be within the area of tolerance on the bell-shaped curve. The delinquent has for various reasons escaped such socialization. In time he tends to become socialized in a delinquent set of values and customs, referred to variously as the underworld, delinquent subculture, or delinquent contraculture. The delinquent contraculture not only differs from the general culture, but has values that are opposed to or destructive of those in the general culture.

Socially, the misbehaving nondelinquent retains his association with conforming groups such as family, school, church, and community center. He accepts the fact that authority is necessary, even though he may defy it at times. His intimate groups are conforming though at times misbehaving. In contrast, the delinquent person associates with other delinquent persons, who form his intimate or reference group. He seeks their good opinion, and he values status in the delinquent group more than in conforming groups. He often cuts himself off physically from conforming groups through truancy from school and home and avoidance of church and community center. He comes to regard as enemies the representatives of conforming institutions, such as, for example, teachers and police.

Psychologically, the misbehaving nondelinquent conceives of himself as conforming, honest, fair, and a member of the conforming community. He feels guilty when he misbehaves, even when he is not caught. In contrast, the delinquent person regards his acts as "right" and justifiable under the circumstances of his life. Although he would not label himself as a delinquent, he conceives of himself as tough, able to "outsmart" others, and justified in taking what he needs or wants with little regard for the rights of other people.

A relatively minor proportion of delinquents fall outside this formulation—the emotionally disturbed whose delinquency is a response to uncontrollable inner pressures. Disturbed delinquent children may be found within either the normal culture or the delinquent contraculture. If such a child is a member of a delinquent group he often fails to achieve high status because of his erratic and unreliable behavior. Some disturbed children are completely ungrouped, sometimes divorced from the values of both the dominant culture and the delinquent contraculture. Inner pressures may lead to a chain of compulsive acts or to violent outbursts. Other children tend to retreat into an unrealistic world of their own which they may share with others, as among some juvenile drug addicts.

It is evident that not all children who commit delinquent acts conceive of themselves as delinquent or have delinquent personalities in the sense that delinquency is a central part of their values or behavior. There are stages of delinquency. Also, it is evident that many cultural, social, and psychological factors contribute to the formation of a delinquent personality—so many and in such varying degrees and combinations that it is not possible to diagram the process of development with much precision. However, the factors can be discussed separately, and certain interrelationships can be found.

Use of different definitions

Whether one uses the strictly legal definition of delinquency or a looser definition of damaging misbehavior depends upon the purpose of the research or the practical programs. When police, court, and correctional procedures are the focus of attention, the legal definitions are pertinent. When emphasis is upon development of misbehavior, prevention, or readjustment, the wider definition in terms of deviation from expected social norms is more appropriate. In this text, Parts 2, 3, and 4 supplement legal concepts with behavioral concepts in attempting to trace the development of misbehavior and methods of prevention. Part 5 clings more closely to legal concepts since it is a discussion of legal procedures.

Bibliography

Bloch, Herbert A., "Juvenile Delinquency, Myth or Threat," *Journal of Criminal Law, Criminology and Police Science,* 49 (1958), 303–309.

Cavan, Ruth Shonle, "The Concepts of Tolerance and Contraculture as Applied to Delinquency," *Sociological Quarterly,* 2 (1961), 243–258.

Clinard, Marshall B., *Sociology of Deviant Behavior,* Rinehart and Company, New York, 1957, Chapter 1.

Huston, Wendell, compiler, *Social Welfare Laws of the Forty-eight States,* and supplements, Wendell Huston Company, Seattle, Washington, 1937.

Lundberg, George A., Clarence C. Schrag, and Otto N. Larsen, *Sociology,* Harper and Brothers, New York, 1954, Chapter 10.

Sussman, Frederick B., *Law of Juvenile Delinquency,* Oceana Publications, New York, 1959.

Yinger, J. Milton, "Contraculture and Subculture," *American Sociological Review,* 25 (1960), 625–635.

Many of our ideas about delinquency and the delinquent child are gained from statistical reports. The explicit figures of a statistical statement inspire confidence in the layman, who often accepts them uncritically. Nothing, however, is more misleading than statistics which are not understood and evaluated. This chapter presents the chief sources of statistics, what they include, and what they tell about delinquency.

No nationwide statistics comparable to census reports on the population exist. The best estimates on a national basis come from the Federal Bureau of Investigation and the Children's Bureau. Studies in individual localities help to round out the picture.

Arrests of juveniles

The most inclusive statement of children and adolescents who get into trouble comes from the Federal Bureau of Investigation in reports of the number of arrests made during a given year.

Limitations of arrest data. Police departments decide individually whether or not to co-operate with the Federal Bureau of Investigation in filling out the report blanks sent to them by the Bureau. No representative of the FBI makes visits to each police department to secure data corresponding to the door-to-door calls by representatives of the Census Bureau. Also, since the reporting is on a voluntary basis, the departments that co-operate do not constitute a carefully chosen representative sample of the population such as one would find in a carefully planned research project.

In its reports, the FBI carefully states the basis for each statistical table; the reader must take into account this basis in interpreting the tables. For example, the report on age of people arrested given in the *Uniform Crime Reports* for 1959 is based on 1,789 cities over 2,500 in population, with a total population of 56,187,181.[1] This figure is 30.6 per cent of the 177,709,512 estimated total population of the United States for 1960. The arrest figures by age do not equally represent all portions of the United States. For instance, small villages under 2,500 population and rural areas are not included. It is also known

that some regions of the country do not respond as fully as others.

The classification of offenses is controlled up to a certain point. The FBI sends to each co-operating office a list with definitions of the offenses into which the data are to be classified by the local office. This crime classification does not include all the many types of minor offenses for which juveniles may be arrested but only those for which adults would also be arrested. For example, in the table of offenses for which persons under eighteen years of age were arrested in 1958, fully 29.8 per cent of the offenses are grouped together under the heading "all other offenses." Also, traffic violations are not included in the *Uniform Crime Reports* for 1959, although it is estimated that 30 per cent of all juvenile court cases are for traffic violations.[2] The omission of traffic violations among arrests gives an incomplete picture of the legal problems of juveniles.

Another point to be noted is that the data are for arrests. Children who might be reprimanded by the police without formal arrest are not included. No report is made on the dispositions of arrests for the youthful ages. Other sources show that about one-fourth are referred to the juvenile court. A very few with serious offenses are handled by criminal courts. By far the greater proportion, virtually

---

1 Federal Bureau of Investigation, U. S. Department of Justice, *Uniform Crime Reports for the United States, 1959,* U. S. Government Printing Office, Washington, D. C., 1960, p. 93.

2 I. Richard Perlman, "Delinquency Prevention: The Size of the Problem," *Annals of the American Academy of Political and Social Science,* 322 (1959), p. 3. Mr. Perlman is Chief of Juvenile Delinquency Statistics of the Children's Bureau.

Crime Classification

Description	Remarks
1. Criminal homicide.	(1) Murder and nonnegligent manslaughter: All willful felonious homicides as distinguished from deaths caused by negligence. Excludes attempts to kill, assaults to kill, suicides, accidental deaths or justifiable homicides. Justifiable homicides are limited to: (a) killing of a felon by a peace officer in line of duty; (b) killing of a holdup man by a private citizen. (2) Manslaughter by negligence: any death which the police investigation establishes was primarily attributable to gross negligence of some individual other than the victim.
2. Forcible rape.	Forcible rape, assault to rape, and attempted rape. Excludes statutory offenses (no force used—victim under age of consent).
3. Robbery.	Stealing or taking anything of value from the person by force or violence or by putting in fear, such as strong-arm robbery, stick-ups, robbery armed; assault to rob and attempt to rob.
4. Aggravated assault.	Assault with intent to kill or for the purpose of inflicting severe bodily injury by shooting, cutting, stabbing, maiming, poisoning, scalding, or by the use of acids, explosives, or other means. Excludes simple assault, assault and battery, fighting, etc.
5. Burglary—breaking or entering.	Burglary, house-breaking, safecracking, or any unlawful entry to commit a felony or a theft, even though no force was used to gain entrance and attempts. Burglary followed by larceny is not counted again as larceny.
6. Larceny—theft (except auto theft).	(1) Fifty dollars and over in value; (2) under $50 in value. Thefts of bicycles, automobile accessories, shoplifting, pocket-picking, or any stealing of property or article of value which is not taken by force and violence or by fraud. Excludes embezzlement, "con" games, forgery, worthless checks, etc.
7. Auto theft.	Stealing or driving away and abandoning a motor vehicle, including the so-called joy-riding thefts. Excludes taking for temporary use when actually returned by the taker, or unauthorized use by those having lawful access to the vehicle.
8. Other assaults.	Assaults and attempted assaults which are not of an aggravated nature.
9. Forgery and counterfeiting.	Making, altering, uttering, or possessing, with intent to defraud, anything false which is made to appear true. Includes attempts.
10. Embezzlement and fraud.	Fraudulent conversion, embezzlement, and obtaining money or property by false pretenses.
11. Stolen property; buying, receiving, possessing.	Buying, receiving, and possessing stolen property and attempts.
12. Weapons; carrying, possessing, etc.	All violations of regulations or statutes controlling the carrying, using, possessing, furnishing, and manufacturing of deadly weapons or silencers and attempts.
13. Prostitution and commercialized vice.	Sex offenses of a commercialized nature and attempts, such as prostitution, keeping bawdy houses, procuring, transporting, or detaining women for immoral purposes.
14. Sex offenses (except forcible rape, prostitution and commercialized vice.)	Statutory rape, offenses against chastity, common decency, morals, and other offenses. Includes attempts.
15. Offenses against the family and children.	Nonsupport, neglect, desertion, or abuse of family and children.
16. Narcotic drug laws.	Offenses relating to narcotic drugs, such as unlawful possession, sale, or use. Excludes federal offenses.
17. Liquor laws.	State or local liquor law violations except "drunkenness" (class 18) and "driving while intoxicated" (class 22). Excludes federal violations.

Crime Classification (*Continued*)

Description	Remarks
18. Drunkenness.	Drunkenness or intoxication.
19. Disorderly conduct.	Breach of the peace.
20. Vagrancy.	Vagabondage, begging, loitering, etc.
21. Gambling.	Promoting, permitting, or engaging in gambling.
22. Driving while intoxicated.	Driving or operating any motor vehicle while drunk or under the influence of liquor or narcotics.
23. Violation of road and driving laws.	Improper handling of a moving motor vehicle.
24. Parking violations.	Improper or overtime parking.
25. Other violations of traffic and motor vehicle laws.	Traffic and motor vehicle violations other than classes 22–24.
26. All other offenses.	All violations of State or local laws except classes 1–25.
27. Suspicion.	Arrests for no specific offense and released without formal charges being placed.

Data: Federal Bureau of Investigation, U. S. Department of Justice, *Uniform Crime Reports for the United States, 1959,* U. S. Government Printing Office, Washington, D. C., 1960, pp. 26–27.

three-fourths, the police handle themselves, sometimes with a reprimand, sometimes through special police youth bureaus.[1]

Offenses for which juveniles are arrested. The FBI reports do not classify offenses of juveniles by sex, race, or size of city. They do show distribution of types of offenses. According to Table 2, columns 3 and 5, juveniles are very busy with larceny, burglary, disorderly conduct, auto theft, and the minor offenses grouped under "all other offenses." Many are picked up by the police "on suspicion" or as suspicious characters and later released without formal charges being placed against them. Contrary to public opinion, they rarely are arrested for crimes implying or involving physical force (carrying weapons, forcible rape, aggravated assault, or homicide) or for personal vices (vagrancy, narcotic law violations, violation of liquor laws, prostitution, or gambling). They also are rarely involved in financial crimes based on clever manipulation of the victim or on highly developed skills, such as forgery and counterfeiting, or embezzlement and fraud. They seem to be involved in getting money or automobiles and other property by the very direct method of taking it without contact with the owner; note that the proportion of robberies, where money is taken from the person of the victim, is low. Otherwise, they are involved in minor offenses and disorderly behavior, much of which might be thought of by the delinquents

[1] *Ibid.,* p. 4.

as adventurous, recreational, or releasing of tensions.

Juvenile delinquents play only a small part in the total array of offenses in the United States. Only 12.3 per cent of all arrests are of persons under the age of eighteen. However, they have certain distinctive crimes. Approximately one-half to two-thirds of all arrests made for automobile thefts, burglaries, and larcenies are of persons under eighteen (Table 2, column 4). They also have approximately double their proportionate number in arrests for robbery. But they contribute less than their proportionate number to arrests for other types of physical aggressions and for personal vices.

As compared with standards set by law, the statistical reports of arrests narrow our conception of delinquency to certain kinds of legal violations.

Juvenile court cases

The statistical data on court cases come from an entirely different federal agency than the FBI—from the Children's Bureau in the U. S. Department of Health, Education, and Welfare. The two agencies do not attempt to co-ordinate their statistical reports.

Limitations of juvenile court reports. The Children's Bureau began collecting information on a uniform basis from juvenile courts in 1926. As with the FBI reports, the information was secured on a voluntary basis. Naturally, reports came from only a fraction of the courts, and did not fairly represent the entire

Table 2

Number of Arrests of Persons Under Eighteen in Relation to Total Arrests and to Type of Offense, 1959 for 1,789 Cities Over 2,500 in Population

Offense charged	Number of persons arrested Total all ages	Number of persons arrested Under age 18	Percentage for each offense under age 18	Percentage of all under age 18 arrested for each offense
Total......................................	2,612,704	320,669	12.3	100.0
Criminal homicide:				
(a) Murder and nonnegligent manslaughter.....	2,610	173	6.6	.1
(b) Manslaughter by negligence.............	1,319	75	5.7	.0
Robbery....................................	15,379	4,032	26.2	1.2
Aggravated assault........................	29,860	2,734	9.2	.8
Other assaults.............................	97,118	8,025	8.3	2.5
Burglary—breaking or entering..............	65,044	34,057	52.4	10.6
Larceny—theft.............................	132,441	64,717	48.9	20.2
Auto theft.................................	33,409	21,234	63.6	6.6
Embezzlement and fraud....................	21,009	509	2.4	.1
Stolen property; buying, receiving, etc..........	6,115	1,848	30.2	.6
Forgery and counterfeiting..................	12,007	918	7.6	.3
Forcible rape..............................	4,002	751	18.8	.2
Prostitution and commercialized vice...........	18,514	207	1.1	.1
Other sex offenses (includes statutory rape)......	29,269	5,516	18.8	1.7
Narcotic drug laws........................	10,562	457	4.3	.1
Weapons: carrying, possessing, etc.............	22,231	3,551	16.0	1.1
Offenses against family and children...........	26,042	319	1.2	.1
Liquor laws...............................	61,718	11,347	18.4	3.5
Driving while intoxicated.....................	109,678	777	.7	.2
Disorderly conduct.........................	323,353	33,581	10.4	10.4
Drunkenness...............................	1,011,427	8,826	.9	2.7
Vagrancy..................................	109,116	6,663	6.1	2.0
Gambling..................................	68,082	908	1.3	.3
Suspicion..................................	99,663	17,912	18.0	5.6
All other offenses..........................	302,736	91,532	30.2	28.5

Data: Federal Bureau of Investigation, U. S. Department of Justice, *Uniform Crime Reports for the United States, 1959,* U. S. Government Printing Office, Washington, D. C., 1960, p. 100.

United States. Also, they came from different courts in different years. For example, in 1949, 413 courts in twenty-two states reported, but only 218 of these courts reported each year from 1946 to 1949. In 1955, 1,549 courts in forty-one states, representing 66 per cent of the child population, reported completely, and an additional 127 courts made partial reports. The courts reporting continued to change from year to year, with only 383 reporting over a period of years.[1]

These early reports included not only the number of cases but the age of children, reason for referral to the court, place of detention pending disposition of the cases, and final disposition. Later, the Bureau revised its methods of collection and coverage.

Beginning with the 1956 report, data were based on a carefully selected sample of 502 juvenile courts, chosen with the technical assistance of the Bureau of the Census to give a fair sample of the entire population with reference to region, population density, rate of growth, per cent of nonwhite population, principal industry, type of agriculture, and similar items.[2] The selected courts have responded well to the request for information, and it is anticipated that all of them eventually will be included. From such a sample, uniform from year to year, it becomes possible to make estimates of delinquency for the nation as a whole, rather than to give the actual figures for a limited and shifting group

1 *Juvenile Court Statistics, 1946–1949,* Children's Bureau Statistical Series, No. 8, Children's Bureau, Washington, D. C., 1951, p. 1; *Juvenile Court Statistics, 1955,* Children's Bureau Statistical Series No. 37, Children's Bureau, Washington, D. C., 1956, p. 2.

2 I. Richard Perlman, "Reporting Juvenile Delinquency," *National Probation and Parole Association Journal,* 3 (1957), 245.

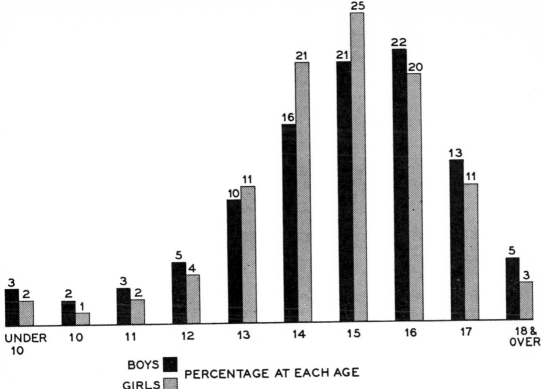

Figure 2. Distribution of Delinquency by Age.
(Data from *Juvenile Court Statistics*, 1957)

of courts. Items of information are limited to number of cases, sex, urban or rural location, and method of handling used by the court. Nothing is included on age, nature of the offense, or disposition of the case.

Estimated number of court cases. For 1959, it was estimated that 416,000 different children, or 1.7 per cent of all children aged ten through seventeen, were referred to juvenile courts.[1] This figure excludes child traffic violators, whose cases are not uniformly heard in juvenile court. Most of these children have been arrested and are referred to the court by the police. However, about 29 per cent of the children in court are referred by parents, teachers, social workers, and other adults in the community who have become aware of delinquent activity. These children do not pass through the hands of the police.[2]

Some children appear before the court more than once in a year. Approximately 67,-000 children, or 16 per cent of delinquent children, are recidivists or repeaters within a twelve-month period.[3] When the entire juvenile delinquency period, ten to seventeen years, is considered, the chance of recidivism is greatly increased.

Characteristics of court cases. A distinction must be made between delinquent children, or the actual number of different boys and girls appearing in court in the course of a year, and number of court cases, or the appearances in court including the recidivists. The characteristics presented below are based on court appearances or cases rather than on individual boys and girls.

Cities report a much higher proportion of delinquents relative to child population than do rural areas. In 1959 the rate of juvenile delinquency cases disposed of by juvenile courts, per 1,000 population aged ten through seventeen, was 13.5 for rural areas, 27.1 for semirural areas, and 40.3 for cities.[4] Discussion in Chapter 6 further reveals that within a given city, rates for boys of delinquency

1 *Juvenile Court Statistics, 1958*, Children's Bureau Statistical Series, No. 61, Children's Bureau, Washington, D. C., 1960, pp. 1.
2 Perlman, "Delinquency Prevention: The Size of the Problem," p. 6.

3 *Juvenile Court Statistics*, 1959, p. 1.
4 *Ibid.*, p. 9.

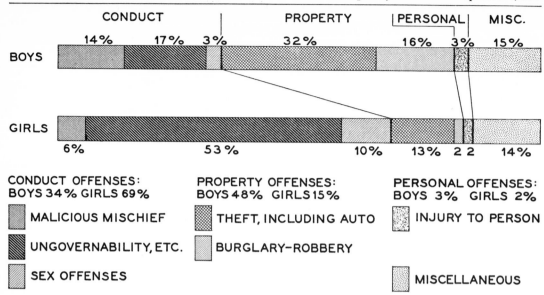

Figure 3. Types of Offenses of Boys and Girls, Percentage Distribution. (Data from *Juvenile Court Statistics,* 1957)

age, by small areas or neighborhoods, may vary from 0 to 250 cases per 1,000 during a three-year period.

Boys far outnumber girls in court appearances (and in actual engagement in delinquency). The ratio is consistently about four boys to one girl, year after year.[1]

In 1957, 3 per cent of the boys' cases and 2 per cent of the girls' cases involved children under the age of ten (Figure 2). Ten per cent of the boys and 7 per cent of the girls were between ages ten and twelve. Delinquency increased rapidly in the age thirteen group and continued at a high rate throughout adolescence or until the upper age limit set by law was reached. Over half of all boys (59 per cent) were between the ages of fourteen and sixteen, with the median age at 15.5 years. Of the girls, 66 per cent were between the ages of fourteen and sixteen, with the median at 15.4 years. These figures are based on the state reports of fifteen states, widely scattered over the United States, and accounting for almost half of all delinquency cases.[2]

1 *Ibid.,* p. 8.

2 *Juvenile Court Statistics, 1957,* Children's Bureau Statistical Series, No. 52, Children's Bureau, Washington, D. C., 1959, p. 6. The fifteen states are California, Connecticut, Florida, Iowa, Michigan, Mississippi, Missouri, New Mexico, North Carolina, Ohio, Oregon, Utah, Vermont, Washington, and Wisconsin.

Boys and girls appearing in juvenile court differ greatly in the offenses that brought them there, as Figure 3 shows. Some form of stealing brought 48 per cent of the boys but only 15 per cent of the girls to the attention of the court. Carelessness or mischief was the second most common offense of boys but was rather low for the girls, whose second most frequent offense was running away, followed by ungovernability, truancy, and sex offenses. The girls show a wide variety of offenses, whereas the boys' offenses tend to be concentrated in some form of stealing. It should be noted that due to the greater number of delinquent boys than girls, more individual boys than girls are involved in each type of offense, even when the percentage of girls in a given offense exceeds the percentage of boys involved in the same offense.

The concentration of boys' offenses in stealing is shown more sharply when all of each boys' delinquent acts are known. Such a cumulative amassing of delinquencies has been made for 500 delinquent boys in two Massachusetts correctional schools. Table 3 shows these cumulative figures. According to the cumulative figures, the boys had an average of 2.3 delinquencies up to the time they reached the average age of fourteen years, eight months.

Traffic violations. In figures both for arrests and court cases, traffic violations have been omitted. It is estimated that in addition to the 483,000 delinquency cases heard in juvenile courts each year, another 290,000 cases of traffic violations are heard in juvenile courts. In some states, cases of traffic violations by juveniles are heard in the same courts that handle adult cases. Hence the total number of cases of juvenile traffic violation would exceed the figure of 290,000 per year.[1]

In years past, traffic violation was not a frequent offense of youth, but with the tremendous increase in the number of teenage drivers, traffic violations have also increased. Table 4 shows the number of juvenile court cases involving nontraffic and traffic violations of laws in ten counties containing large cities, and the percentage of the total cases that fall into the category of traffic violation. These cities are all ones in which the juvenile court has jurisdiction over at least some types of traffic violations by juveniles.

Opinions differ as to whether traffic violations should be handled by the juvenile court or by whatever special traffic or other court handles adult traffic violations. Many traffic violations among both juveniles and adults are not criminal in the sense that they harm some other person or destroy property; they may be minor violations of parking ordinances, failure to reduce speed sufficiently in a slow zone, and so on, due to carelessness or for the convenience of the driver, who "takes a chance" with full knowledge that he may have to pay a fine. Other violations, however, are serious in nature: speeding, disregard for

1 *Juvenile Court Statistics, 1959,* p. 2.

pedestrians, leaving the scene of an accident, driving without a license, driving while intoxicated, and so forth. While the former type may be handled in routine fashion, the latter stems from a disregard for the safety of self or of other people. Juveniles involved in serious

Table 3

All Known Delinquencies of Five Hundred Correctional School Boys

Delinquency	Percentage of boys
Burglary, attempted burglary, and intent to commit burglary	59.0
Larceny, excluding automobiles	58.4
Larceny of automobiles	19.8
Crimes against the public order, (e.g., breaking windows, destroying property, stealing rides, ringing false alarms, etc.)	32.4
Stubbornness	16.0
Running away	17.0
Truancy	12.8
Assault and battery	5.4
Sex offenses	3.6
Robbery	2.4
Arson	2.2
Drunkenness	2.0
Average number of delinquencies per boy	2.3
Average age of boys	14 years 8 months

Reprinted by permission of the publishers from Sheldon and Eleanor Glueck, *Unraveling Juvenile Delinquency,* Harvard University Press, Cambridge, Mass., Copyright 1950 by the Commonwealth Fund, pp. 28, 37.

Table 4

Nontraffic and Traffic Cases Disposed of by Juvenile Courts in Certain Counties Containing Large Cities, 1957

County containing city of:	Total juvenile court cases:	Nontraffic delinquency cases:		Traffic cases of juveniles:	
		Number	Percentage	Number	Percentage of total
Albuquerque.......... 3,704		1,476	39.8	2,228	60.2
Cincinnati............ 6,703		4,791	71.5	1,912	28.5
Cleveland............ 7,976		4,029	50.5	3,947	49.5
Los Angeles.......... 10,508		8,761	83.4	1,747	16.6
Memphis (city)........ 5,102		3,117	61.1	1,985	38.9
Milwaukee........... 8,029		6,211	77.3	1,818	22.6
Minneapolis.......... 3,821		2,171	56.8	1,650	43.2
San Francisco......... 6,845		3,583	52.4	3,262	47.6
Seattle.............. 7,342		3,279	44.7	4,063	55.3
St. Paul............. 3,967		1,543	39.0	2,424	61.0

Data: *Juvenile Court Statistics, 1957,* Children's Bureau Statistical Series, No. 52, Children's Bureau, Washington, D. C., 1959, pp. 13–17. Cases handled officially and unofficially are combined for both types of delinquencies. Courts varied greatly as to whether cases of both types were handled officially or unofficially.

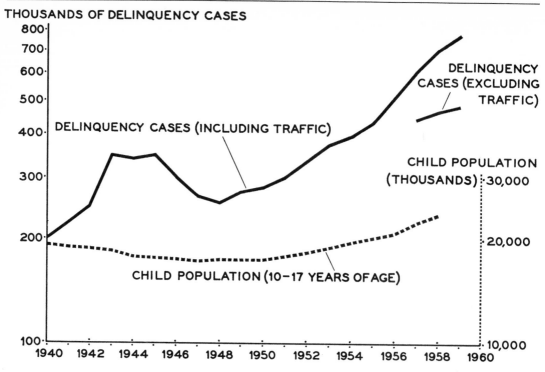

Figure 4. Trend in Delinquency Rates, semilogarithmic scale. (Data from *Juvenile Court Statistics,* 1957)

traffic violations are perhaps as much in need of the supervision of court and probation officers as are juveniles who commit the more generally recognized forms of delinquency.

Is delinquency increasing? This is a controversial question because of the many factors that must be taken into account in determining whether increasing statistical trends indicate genuine increases in misbehavior. The trend since about 1938 seems to have gone as follows:

No marked change in delinquency occurred from 1938 until 1940, when a gradual and then a rapid increase came, reaching a high peak in 1943, dropping a little in 1944, and slightly surpassing the 1943 peak in 1945. (See Figure 4.) The frequency of court cases in 1945 was almost 70 per cent above that of 1938. Whatever the specific factors involved, the war years saw a tremendous increase in cases brought before juvenile courts. During this same period, the number of children between ten and seventeen years of age changed very little; in fact, it decreased slightly. The increase in court cases was not due merely to a larger number of children—

and therefore of potential delinquents—during this time. From 1945 to 1948, the number of court cases dropped spectacularly, although it did not decline to the 1938 level. This drop corresponded to the end of the war and the readjustment of families. The prosperity born of the war continued. The decline was of short duration, however, and by 1950 a still more spectacular upward trend had begun, at the same time that the child population between ages ten and seventeen had also begun to increase. However, the upward trend of court cases was not simply a result of more children and therefore more cases. From 1950 through 1957, the trend has been an increase in court cases outstripping the increase in child population. Between 1950 and 1957, the population aged ten through seventeen years increased 27 per cent; court cases 115 per cent.[1]

Caution should be used in interpreting these figures. They refer only to cases heard in juvenile courts. It is generally assumed that they indicate a genuine increase in acts of de-

1 *Juvenile Court Statistics, 1956,* Children's Bureau Statistical Series, No. 47, Children's Bureau, Washington, D. C., 1957, pp. 6–7; *Juvenile Court Statistics 1957,* pp. 8–9. Statistics for 1958 are on a different basis and not comparable. Edward E. Schwartz, "Statistics of Juvenile Delinquency in the United States," *Annals of the American Academy of Political and Social Science,* 261 (January, 1949), 9–20.

Table 5

Disposition of Delinquency Cases (Exclusive of Traffic Offenses) in Juvenile Courts in Fifteen States, 1957, Percentage Distribution

Type of disposition	Total	Official cases	Unofficial cases
Dismissed, adjusted, or held open without further hearing..........................	45	23	54
Probation officer to supervise.................	27	38	15
Committed or referred to:			
Public institution for delinquents..............	7	14	1
Other institution, agency, or individual........	9	14	11
Other disposition...........................	12	11	19
Total......................................	100	100	100

Data: *Juvenile Court Statistics, 1957*, Children's Bureau Statistical Series, No. 52, Children's Bureau, Washington, D. C., 1959, p. 7.

linquency. However, to some extent at least, the increase might be the result of a change in police policy, in the number of cases referred to the court rather than handled directly by the police, or even in the number of arrests made, which might tend to increase the number of cases referred to the courts. A slight increase in delinquency rates, published in newspapers across the land, tends to frighten people and to create an outcry for greater vigilance by the police and more authoritative handling of cases. Thus the number of cases may be artificially built up without an actual or a proportionate increase in the number of delinquents. Also, it is not clear what the effect is on marginally delinquent youth when they feel that the public has turned against them and that the police are overly watchful. Do they tend to conform or does the air of suspicion push them over the edge into truculence and retaliation? Although we may wish to discount the increase in misbehavior, it is true that a greater proportion of children than formerly are being arrested and brought before the court.

Disposition of cases. The statement has been made that police take independent authority over three-fourths of the children whom they arrest. The remaining fourth of arrest cases, plus children referred directly to the court, receive attention from the juvenile court. About half the cases are handled unofficially by the judge or an appropriate court officer; these cases are not placed on the official court calendar, and no public record remains. The other half of the cases—typically the more seriously delinquent ones—are handled officially: the case is placed on the official court calendar for adjudication by the judge, and court action is begun through the filing of a petition or other legal paper.

More than half of the unofficial cases result in a reprimand or in the release of the child without further hearing; a few children are placed on probation; almost none are committed to a public institution, although about a tenth are referred to other types of institutions. (See Table 5). Less than a fourth of the official cases are dismissed or adjusted without further hearing. Many are referred to a public or other institution or agency; most of the remainder are placed on probation, during which they usually continue to live in their own homes. Thus most delinquents brought to court attention remain in their own homes and neighborhoods, in association with their old friends, and are subject to the influences that led to their delinquency. The shock of court appearance and the supervision of probation officer or social agency is often insufficient to counterbalance delinquent influences, and many children appear again in court during the age period of ten through seventeen years. Even those committed to a public correctional school are away from their homes for a short time only; the median length of stay is 9.7 months.[1] Delinquency that began in the local community continues to be a community issue, and adjustment, if it occurs at all, usually must take place in the home community.

In some states, a small minority of children who have committed felonies, such as mur-

1 *Statistics on Public Institutions for Delinquent Children, 1958*, Children's Bureau Statistical Series, No. 59, Children's Bureau, Washington, D. C., 1960, p. 7.

Boys wandering the streets at night are often stopped and questioned by the police, in this case a juvenile officer in plain clothes. By such supervision, incipient delinquent behavior may be nipped in the bud, or leads may be uncovered to more serious situations. If no delinquent behavior is involved, boys may simply be directed to return to their homes. (Courtesy George Harris, photographer, and St. Louis Police Department)

der, armed robbery, or aggravated assaults may be tried in the adult criminal courts. If found guilty, these children may be placed on probation, committed to adult prisons or to juvenile institutions, or (in theory at least) executed if the state laws permit capital punishment.

Delinquent behavior not officially reported

Not all children who commit delinquent acts are included among the arrest or court cases. Some misbehavior even of a serious nature is not detected by responsible adults; some is detected, but not by the police, and is not referred to the police. Neighbors may adjust payment for property damage with the parents of the offending child; storekeepers may stop a young shoplifter as he leaves the store and relieve him of stolen articles; schools adjust many types of delinquent behavior occurring in and near school property. Many minor delinquencies are simply passed over by observers, even by the victims, as part of the process of growing up.

A complete cataloguing of delinquency calls for inclusion of the unrecorded delinquency. The conception of delinquency changes to some extent with such inclusion. Delinquency, especially of minor types, is found to be very widespread throughout the community permeating all social classes.

Unreported delinquents: New York. Attention was forcibly directed to the incomplete nature of official reports in 1936, when Sophia Moses Robison published a report called *Can Delinquency Be Measured?* [1]

Dr. Robison's interest grew from her observations that previous studies tended to show a high concentration of delinquency in slum

1 Published for the Welfare Council of New York City by Columbia University Press, New York, 1936.

areas and little delinquency in well-to-do areas. She contended that many cases of delinquency in the latter areas were not referred to the police and courts and also that certain cases were handled by nonpublic agencies, although the offenses came within the legal definition of juvenile delinquency. She began to search for a more definite concept of delinquency than that given by the official police and court statistics. Her study was limited to New York City.

She secured detailed reports on delinquent behavior of children referred to three official agencies: the Crime Prevention Bureau, the Children's (juvenile) Court, and the Bureau of Attendance of the Board of Education, as well as from forty private agencies whose clientele was not limited to delinquent children. Table 6 gives Dr. Robison's results.

Her study shows that when juvenile court statistics alone were used as the basis for frequency of delinquency, a third of the cases were overlooked, exclusive of serious truancy. Children under treatment at private agencies often came from upper-middle- or upper-class families, children erroneously believed to be immune to delinquent impulses. Many of these children were not included in court statistics.

Unreported delinquents: Washington, D. C. Dr. Robison's study was followed by similar studies confirming the conclusion that each city has children perpetrating delinquent acts who are not brought to the attention of the juvenile court nor to the police. A study for June, 1943 to May, 1944 in the District of Columbia encompassed the juvenile court,

Table 6

Total Delinquent Children Known to Three Official and Forty Unofficial Agencies, New York City, 1930

Total delinquents, exclusive of truants, known to all agencies...............	10,374
Percentage handled by each type of agency:	
Children's Court..................	68.3
Official agencies other than court....	20.4
Unofficial agencies...............	8.0
Mental hygiene clinics.............	3.3
	100.0
Total truancy hearings, school year 1929–30, 25,559	
Wilful truants...................	3,000
Truants recorded in files of unofficial agencies.....................	668
Total wilful truants...............	3,668
Of these, serious delinquents because of truancy.........................	1,579
Total delinquency including truancy.......	11,953
Handled by Children's Court.........	59.3

Data: Based on Sophia Moses Robison, *Can Delinquency Be Measured?* Published for the Welfare Council of New York City by Columbia University Press, New York, 1936, pp. 52, 130.

divisions of the police department working with juvenile delinquents, two public welfare agencies, and a department of the Board of Education. Table 7 shows that when the count of juvenile delinquency is limited to juvenile court records, it includes only 43 per cent of the actual total of known delinquent children. Almost a third of all cases, including the large number of cases of truancy, were handled by the Board of Education.

Volume of unreported delinquency. The cumulative record of 114 boy participants in a

Table 7

Number of Alleged Juvenile Delinquents Reported by Six Public Agencies, District of Columbia, June 1943—May 1944

Reporting Agency		Number of children	Percentage
Juvenile Court..		3,384	43
Woman's Bureau, Metropolitan Police Department......................	1,153		
Boys' Service Division, Metropolitan Police Department.................	40		
Receiving Home for Children, Board of Public Welfare.................	810		
Protective Service, Board of Public Welfare.........................	17		
Department of Attendance and Work Permits, Board of Education.........	2,785		
Total of children from five agencies.................................		4,444*	57
Total of children from all agencies.................................		7,828	100.0

Data: Based on Edward E. Schwartz, "A Community Experiment in the Measurement of Juvenile Delinquency," *Yearbook, 1945 National Probation Association,* New York, 1945, reproduced by Federal Security Agency, pp. 11, 21.

   * 361 children were registered at more than one agency, but not with the juvenile court. The juvenile court had 767 children who were also registered with another agency; these are not shown separately in the Table.

Table 8

Recorded and Unrecorded Delinquencies of 101 Boys Over a Period of Time

| | Delinquencies | |
Delinquency	Number	Percentage
Minor delinquencies, such as truancy, petty theft, trespassing, running away, being stubborn, etc.............................4,406		68
Violation of city ordinances, such as vending without a license, playing ball in streets, swimming or fishing in forbidden places, violating the curfew law, etc..1,394		22
Serious offenses, such as burglary, larceny, assault, drunkenness, sex offenses, etc... 616		10
Total..6,416		100

Data: Fred J. Murphy, Mary M. Shirley, and Helen L. Witmer, "The Incidence of Hidden Delinquency," *American Journal of Orthopsychiatry,* 16 (1946), 686–696.

special youth study in the Cambridge-Somerville, Massachusetts, area was that sixty-four acts of delinquency per boy over a five-year period (or one delinquency per month) occurred. These boys were from the lower and lower-middle class, and many had been referred to the study because they had shown signs of delinquent behavior. All had had some counseling over a five-year period from age eleven to age sixteen.[1]

Of the 114 boys, only thirteen had not committed an act that could be classified as legal delinquency. Of the remaining 101 boys, sixty-one were unofficially delinquent with no court record, and forty had court records. Table 8 shows a grouping of the 6,416 acts of delinquency attributed to the boys during the five-year period. The majority of the delinquencies are minor in nature. So trivial are many of them that they fall into segments C and D of the bell-shaped continuum of behavior presented in Chapter 2—in other words, they represent the normal deviations anticipated and tolerated by society.

Comparison of high school and correctional school students. Several studies have probed the backgrounds of high school or college students, socially accepted and playing the role of nondelinquents. In one study high school and correctional school students are compared as to frequency and seriousness of delinquent acts.[2]

Twenty-one items of legal delinquency were used as the basis for the study. The formal terms of the law were translated into language more understandable to adolescents. Thus robbery became "used force (strong-arm methods) to get money from another person," and "incorrigibility" or "ungovernability" became "defied parents' authority." Questionnaires were anonymously filled out by high school students in three small western communities and by inmates in a western state training school for delinquents. It was not possible to secure arrest records for the high school students; therefore this group may have a few students who have been arrested or who are on probation; in fact, a few might have spent some time in a correctional school.

Every offense on the list presented to high school students, shown in Tables 9 and 10, was checked by some high school boys and girls, although often by only a few. A much higher percentage of the training school boys and girls checked offenses. The greater number of offenses by training school boys was particularly noticeable in stealing and fighting. Training school girls exceeded high school girls in fighting and sex relations. The com-

1 F. J. Murphy, M. M. Shirley, and H. L. Witmer, "The Incidence of Hidden Delinquency," *American Journal of Orthopsychiatry,* 16 (1946), 686–696.

2 The present discussion is based on James F. Short, Jr. and F. Ivan Nye, "Extent of Unrecorded Juvenile Delinquency, Tentative Conclusions," *Journal of Criminal Law, Criminology and Police Science,* 49 (1958), 296–302. Other aspects of the complete study are found in Short, "A Report on the Incidence of

Criminal Behavior, Arrests, and Convictions in Selected Groups," *Research Studies of the State College of Washington,* 22 (June, 1954), 110–118; Short and Nye, "Reported Behavior as a Criterion of Deviant Behavior," *Social Problems,* 5 (1957–58), 207–213; Short and Nye, "Scaling Delinquent Behavior," *American Sociological Review,* 22 (1957), 326–331. An earlier study by Porterfield compared admitted delinquencies of college students with offenses of juvenile court cases; every college student had committed one or more offenses, the average being 17.6 for men and 4.7 for women. See Austin L. Porterfield, *Youth in Trouble,* The Leo Potishman Foundation, Fort Worth, Texas, 1946, pp. 37–51.

Table 9

Reported Delinquent Behavior Among Boys in High School and Correctional School

Type of offense	Per cent admitting commission of offense		Per cent admitting commission of offense more than once or twice	
	High school	Correctional school	High school	Correctional school
Driven a car without a driver's license or permit..........75.3	91.1		49.0	73.4
Skipped school....................................53.0	95.3		23.8	85.9
Had fist fight with one person.........................80.7	95.3		31.9	75.0
"Run away" from home..............................13.0	68.1		2.4	37.7
School probation or expulsion........................11.3	67.8		2.9	31.3
Defied parents' authority............................33.1	52.4		6.3	23.6
Driven too fast or recklessly.........................46.0	76.3		19.1	51.6
Taken little things (worth less than $2) that did not belong to you..60.6	91.8		12.9	65.1
Taken things of medium value ($2–$50)................15.8	91.0		3.8	61.4
Taken things of large value ($50)..................... 5.0	90.8		2.1	47.7
Used force (strong-arm methods) to get money from another person................................. (6.3) *	67.7		(2.4) *	35.5
Taken part in "gang fights"..........................22.5	67.4		5.2	47.4
Taken a car for a ride without the owner's knowledge.....14.8	75.2		4.0	53.4
Bought or drank beer, wine, or liquor (including drinking at home)......................................57.2	89.7		29.5	79.4
Bought or drank beer, wine, or liquor (outside your home)...(43.0) *	87.0		(21.1) *	75.0
Drank beer, wine, or liquor in your own home...........(57.0) *	62.8		(24.1) *	31.9
Deliberate property damage.........................44.8	84.3		8.2	49.7
Used or sold narcotic drugs......................... 2.2	23.1		1.6	12.6
Had sex relations with another person of the same sex (not masturbation)................................ 8.8	10.9		2.9	3.1
Had sex relations with a person of the opposite sex......40.4	87.5		19.9	73.4
Gone hunting or fishing without a license (or violated other game laws)......................................62.7	66.7		23.5	44.8
Taken things you didn't want........................22.5	56.8		3.1	26.8
"Beat up" on kids who hadn't done anything to you.......13.9	48.7		2.8	26.2
Hurt someone to see them squirm.....................15.8	33.4		3.2	17.5

Data: James F. Short, Jr., and F. Ivan Nye, "Extent of Unrecorded Juvenile Delinquency," *Journal of Criminal Law, Criminology and Police Science,* Northwestern University School of Law, 49 (1958), 297.

* These questions were omitted from the schedule given to high school students in the western state. The percentage in parentheses are from a sample of midwest high school students.

parison of high school and training school youth is significant for repeated offenses. Relatively few high school youth repeated, compared to the number of repeaters among training school youth. In a more detailed analysis, the authors indicated that in their sample of students, a small percentage of both boys and girls exceeded the training school groups in delinquency, but that in general the boys and girls sent to the training school were more persistently and seriously delinquent than the high school students.

Many of the delinquencies seem to represent the minor acts of deviation tolerated by society. These would be represented by acts very common to both high school and correctional school students. These acts not being highly disapproved, high school students probably engaged in them with little feeling of guilt. Among correctional school students, they were probably incidental to other, more serious types of delinquency which brought them to court conviction. Among boys, deviations tolerated are driving a car without a license or permit, skipping school, having fist fights with one other person, taking things worth less than $2, buying or drinking beer, wine, or liquor, including drinking at home, and going fishing or hunting without a license. All these were checked by more than half of

Table 10

Reported Delinquent Behavior Among Girls in High School and Correctional School

Type of offense	Per cent admitting commission of offense		Per cent admitting commission of offense more than once or twice	
	High school	Correctional school	High school	Correctional school
Driven a car without a driver's license or permit	58.2	68.3	29.9	54.4
Skipped school	41.0	94.0	12.2	66.3
Had fist fight with one person	28.2	72.3	5.7	44.6
"Run away" from home	11.3	85.5	1.0	51.8
School probation or expulsion	3.7	63.4	0.2	29.3
Defied parents' authority	30.6	68.3	5.0	39.0
Driven too fast or recklessly	16.3	47.5	5.4	35.0
Taken little things (worth less than $2) that did not belong to you	30.0	77.8	3.5	48.1
Taken things of medium value ($2–$50)	3.9	58.0	0.6	29.6
Taken things of large value ($50)	1.3	30.4	0.9	10.1
Used force (strong-arm methods) to get money from another person	(1.3) *	36.7	(0.3) *	21.5
Taken part in "gang fights"	6.5	59.0	1.1	27.7
Taken a car for a ride without the owner's knowledge	4.5	36.6	0.6	20.7
Bought or drank beer, wine, or liquor (include drinking at home)	44.5	90.2	17.6	80.5
Bought or drank beer, wine or liquor (outside your home)	(28.7) *	83.9	(10.8) *	75.3
Drank beer, wine, or liquor in your own home	(54.2) *	71.1	(16.4) *	42.2
Deliberate property damage	13.6	65.4	1.6	32.1
Used or sold narcotic drugs	0.5	36.9	0.3	23.8
Had sex relations with another person of the same sex (not masturbation)	3.6	25.0	0.5	12.5
Had sex relations with a person of the opposite sex	14.1	95.1	4.8	81.5
Gone hunting or fishing without a license (or violated other game laws)	20.3	27.5	3.9	21.3
Taken things you didn't want	3.6	43.0	0.6	13.9
"Beat up" on kids who hadn't done anything to you	3.1	37.8	0.9	18.3
Hurt someone to see them squirm	9.3	35.4	1.1	20.7

Data: James F. Short, Jr., and F. Ivan Nye, "Extent of Unrecorded Juvenile Delinquency," *Journal of Criminal Law, Criminology and Police Science,* Northwestern University School of Law, 49 (1958), 297.

* These questions were omitted from the schedule given to high school students in the western state. The percentage in parentheses are from a sample of midwest high school students.

the high school boys and by still more correctional school boys. Correctional school boys had many more repetitions of these offenses than high school boys, and in addition had more often committed more serious offenses found among only a few high school boys. Girls typically act delinquently less often than boys. Nevertheless 30 per cent or more of the high school girls had driven a car without a driver's license, skipped school, defied parents' authority, taken little things worth less than $2, and bought or drunk beer, or wine, including drinking at home. Higher percentages of correctional school girls had commit-

ted these offenses; in addition they often had more serious offenses on their records and a higher rate of recidivism.

One could surmise that driving without a driver's license, skipping school, taking little things, drinking light alcoholic beverages, done in moderation and not very often repeated, are within the tolerated deviations for normal youth. In addition, boys may escape serious penalties for a moderate amount of fighting and evading hunting and fishing laws; girls may show some defiance of parents' authority. But when these tolerated deviations are often repeated or are combined

with other, more serious offenses, which threaten or injure other people or their property, youth may find themselves under arrest, in juvenile court, and committed to a correctional school.

In other words, the delinquency that comes to the courts' attention is a combination of an immoderate amount of "normal" deviation and serious offenses which threaten or injure.

These studies throw new light on the ear-

Stealing is a frequent offense of teen-age girls, as shown in Table 10. Juvenile shoplifters usually work in small groups. The picture at right shows three girls stealing a blouse and concealing it in a large purse. One of the girls is acting as the "lookout." Juveniles are usually amateurs; they conceal merchandise in their jackets, books, briefcases, and large pocketbooks. This picture is posed to show a typical procedure. (Courtesy Director of Security, Carson, Pirie, Scott and Co., Chicago)

lier studies which seemed to show that many delinquent children were in some way escaping detection. Some serious offenders of course do escape detection, but, in general, it seems that many of the undetected offenders are actually acting within the area of tolerance for deviating behavior.

An interpretation of the statistical studies

The percentages given in this chapter support the hypothesis of the bell-shaped continuum presented in Chapter 2. Although the studies of high school and college students seem to indicate that all students have at some time committed at least a minor act of delinquency, it seems safe to assume that small percentages of youth could be found who were free or virtually free from delinquency—Sections E, F, and G of the curve. The high school students, with their small proportion of serious delinquencies and large proportions of tolerated misbehavior, represent Sections C and D. The arrested youth fit into Section B, and the court and correctional school cases into Section A.

Bibliography

Murphy, Fred J., Mary M. Shirley, and Helen L. Witmer, "The Incidence of Hidden Delinquency," *American Journal of Orthopsychiatry,* 16 (1946), 686–696.

Perlman, I. Richard, "Delinquency Prevention: The Size of the Problem," *Annals of the American Academy of Political and Social Science,* 322 (1959), 1–9.

————, "Reporting Juvenile Delinquency, *National Probation and Parole Association Journal,* 3 (1957), 242–299.

Porterfield, Austin L., *Youth in Trouble,* Leo Potishman Foundation, Fort Worth, Texas, 1946.

Robison, Sophia Moses, *Can Delinquency be Measured?* Columbia University Press, New York, 1936.

Schwartz, Edward E., "A Community Experiment in the Measurement of Delinquency," *Yearbook 1945, National Probation Association,* New York, 1945, 157–182.

Short, James F., Jr., "A Report on the Incidence of Criminal Behavior, Arrests, and Convictions in Selected Groups," *Research Studies of the State College of Washington,* 22 (June, 1954), 110–118.

————, and F. Ivan Nye, "Extent of Unrecorded Juvenile Delinquency, Tentative Conclusions," *Journal of Criminal Law, Criminology and Police Science,* 49 (1958), 296–302.

————, "Reported Behavior as a Criterion of Deviant Behavior," *Social Problems,* 5 (Winter, 1957–1958), 207–213.

————, "Scaling Delinquent Behavior," *American Sociological Review,* 22 (1957), 326–331.

The development of delinquent behavior

Both conforming and delinquent children are in the process of development from infancy to adulthood. Early adulthood is a relatively stable stage of life, physically, mentally, in personality, and in behavior. Growth has been attained, the pattern of life has been set. Prior to this stabilization, children and youth pass progressively through a series of growing and learning stages.

Development toward maturity is based on the physical and mental capacities apparent at birth or contained in the genes for later development. Physical and mental growth follows a generally uniform line for all human beings, predictable in advance. Normal deviations are contained within a relatively narrow range; only a very small percentage of human beings deviate so much that special provisions must be made for them.

Human beings also have a variety of needs, the simplest of which are the need for food and physical comfort. Other strongly felt needs are for love and approval. These needs appear early in life and are refined and augmented as time goes on. Satisfaction of the needs brings contentment; denial of the needs leads to discontent and unhappiness, which may be expressed in a number of ways. The expression may be overt through temper tantrums, fighting, or screaming (later profanity); or it may be contained internally through repression, resignation, or withdrawal.

Maturation and need satisfaction are molded by the culture within which a child lives. By the process of socialization, the child learns slowly and sometimes painfully what is expected of him by the adults close to him, by his peers, and by the institutions of his society. His parents, his friends, his school, and his church are probably the dominant socializing agencies. He learns to use his growing physical strength and mental abilities according to the expectations and behavior systems presented by these agencies. He gradually accepts their standards of behavior and their ways of meeting needs and of controlling dissatisfactions.

The people who shape a child's growth serve another function in addition to that of impressing cultural patterns on the child. By their personal attitudes and behavior toward him they instill in him his personal concept of himself—the heart of his personality.

Chapter **4**

The developmental process, normal and delinquent

The child moving toward adjusted maturity not only is molded by his social world but learns to fit into it. He is offered and accepts compatible roles to play in his world; he forms a self-concept that both harmonizes with his roles and satisfies his inner needs. These roles and self-concepts are an outgrowth of the culture in general, and hence vary according to the society and to some extent, in subcultures within one society. When subcultures conflict or compete, the child has difficulty in finding roles and self-concepts that are compatible and satisfying.

He will find himself more at home and more readily accepted in some groups than in others. These groups are more influential in shaping his personality than those groups which are indifferent to or reject him. Invariably these groups maintain cohesion through love, friendship, and loyalty. They are called reference groups. Their influence, good or bad, outweighs the influence of formal institutions.

Organization of behavior in developmental stages

Developmental stages can be recognized in many ways. The organization of schools into preschool, kindergarten, elementary school, junior and senior high school, and college rests on the changes in the growth and capacity of children. Playthings and books are also adapted to stages of growth; many toys and books are marked by the manufacturer for particular age groups. Parents implicitly recognize stages of growth in the tasks they assign to children of different ages, the amount of freedom allowed, bedtime enforced, and foods provided.

Laws affecting children are patterned to progressive stages of development. In general, the child under seven years is conceded not to be legally responsible for his behavior. From seven to approximately eighteen, he is held responsible to some extent, but emphasis is also placed on the failure of adults to guide him. Above the age of seventeen (and in some states at earlier ages), he is held fully responsible for certain crimes. Court procedures are adapted to these stages; special institutions receive delinquent children, older adolescents, and adults.

Developmental tasks and roles. Educationists tend to think of developmental stages in terms of developmental tasks—the growth increment that the child is expected to attain during a certain age period. Robert J. Havighurst has defined a developmental task as a "task which arises at or about a certain period in the life of the individual, successful achievement of which leads to his happiness and to success with later tasks, while failure leads to unhappiness in the individual, disapproval by the society and difficulty with later tasks." [1] This point of view emphasizes developmental stages from the point of view of the progression that society expects the child to make. The child who does not meet these expectations, whether because of inability, lack of interest, or some emotional blocking, is soon out of step with his age mates. He is susceptible to feelings of inferiority and prone to seek satisfactions outside the normal group associations, although not necessarily through delinquency.

Another approach to developmental stages is from the point of view of society itself, which out of past experience has developed a set of interrelated roles for each age and sex group. These are called age-sex roles. [2]

Age-sex roles are closely related to the developmental process. First, each age level has its own roles. Ideally, these roles grow out of and are based upon the roles of the preceding period; they also are practically possible within the range of maturation of the age level. They reflect the developmental tasks. Second, almost immediately upon birth boys and girls are inducted into a different succession of roles, which parallel but do not completely duplicate each other. Even in school, where boys and girls share the same curriculum, many distinctions are made in physical education and sports, clubs that appeal to only one sex, and sex-linked differences in classes (woodwork versus home economics). Outside the school, boys and girls are separated in most organized clubs until adolescence, when the culture expects a coordination of masculine and feminine roles.

Note has already been taken of the differences in delinquencies of boys and girls. These differences are closely related to the general pattern of role differences for boys and girls, or in some cases to the inability of the boy or girl to accept the appropriate age or sex role.

Boys and girls who accept the masculine-feminine division and are able to keep pace with the developmental aspect of changing roles are guided stage by stage into the culturally devised roles of adulthood. But all children do not fit into these prescribed roles with equal ease.

Infancy

Influence of mother. Infancy, as used here, covers the period from birth to thirty months. Physical needs predominate in the young baby. His helplessness makes him completely dependent on others, usually on his mother. He is not, however, passive, but makes his wants known by crying and random kicking and flailing of arms. When he is fed and warm he responds by sleeping. After a time, he associates his mother with the satisfaction of his needs and is comforted by her presence.

Tremendous emphasis has been placed by some child psychologists on techniques of infant care, stressing, for example, the values to be gained by the child from breast feeding, certain techniques of toilet training, and so forth. Ralph Linton, however, from his vantage point as an anthropologist familiar with many cultural patterns of child training, asserts that the precise techniques customary in the culture are of minor importance compared to the influence of parental attitudes

1 Robert J. Havighurst, *Human Development and Education*, Longman's Green and Company, New York, 1953, p. 2.
2 Leonard S. Cottrell, "The Adjustment of the Individual to His Age and Sex Roles," *American Sociological Review*, 7 (1942), 617–620.

toward the infant.[1] During the early stages of infancy, the desirable attitude is visualized in American culture as loving, tolerant, and permissive. The baby's needs are to be met promptly and as completely as possible.

Developing a feeling of trust. From such treatment, the baby accomplishes his first developmental "task," a feeling of trust in others and in his environment. This trust lays the foundation for later self-confidence and friendliness toward others. Having been treated considerately, he anticipates consideration; he is also ready to give consideration to others. Without the development of trust, he enters the later stages of babyhood with some feeling of fear, uncertainty, and suspicion, which then must be dissipated before good adjustment can be accomplished.[2]

If, however, the baby is not loved and given a sense of trust, if he feels unwanted, rejected, and insecure, he may develop serious maladjustments, ranging in individual children from frightened withdrawal from social contacts to aggressive and hostile attacks on physical environment and people. At this point there is a connection with delinquency, not in babyhood, but sometimes beginning by the age of four with types of misconduct that would be considered delinquency in an older child. Not to create a long diversion at this point, the ramifications of deprivation of love for later delinquent behavior are discussed in Chapter 10.

Achieving limited autonomy. As the child grows, he gains a considerable degree of autonomy, which he usually grasps eagerly. He learns to walk, feed himself, talk, control elimination, pull on his clothing, carry out simple requests, and obey simple commands. His autonomy is never complete, however. As he becomes mobile, strong, and investiga-

tive, he finds he must conform to restraints. Learning to yield to authority is one phase of the developmental task of becoming autonomous. He may safely exercise autonomy only within the cultural limitations, only within the role of the obedient child. His mother is still his chief teacher, and her most effective method is through the child's desire to please her because he is still dependent upon her and still needs her love and protection.

Some children do not easily accept the imposition of authority, and a few violently resist curbing of their desires. Early resistance to control includes screaming, kicking, hitting, or conversely, complete passivity and refusal to conform or even to stand upright. Angry children, frustrated in their desires, may throw toys, pillows, or other small objects; tear up plants or books; or throw food on the floor. Sometimes these are spontaneous expressions of anger, but sometimes they are the things that the child knows will irritate the mother.

In addition to curbing the child's range of mobility and physical activities, the mother imposes whatever her culture prescribes as the routine of daily life during later babyhood: when, where, and how to wash hands, take baths, eat, dress, eliminate, sleep, play, and all the actions which will eventually become habitual.

Gradually, the mother imposes her standards of behavior on the child through expressions of approval and rewards when he conforms and disapproval and punishment when he refuses.

His autonomy thus is circumscribed by the cultural limitations for a child of his age and sex.

During this process the mother's role is to love, understand, and guide the child into his role. If the mother is not able to do this, the child has difficulty controlling his behavior. The mother may already have rejected the child and hence destroyed some of his desire to please her, or she may use methods of training that are so harsh they arouse the child's hostility and resentment.

The child then may continue his violent reactions toward his parents or later his teachers. As he grows older and stronger, he may become a threat to the safety of younger children, or even of his mother.

---

1 Ralph Linton, *Culture and Mental Disorders,* Charles C Thomas, Springfield, Illinois, 1956, pp. 11, 36–37.

2 The importance of the development of an attitude of trust during the first year of life and of freedom to develop autonomy during the second year is especially emphasized by Eric Homburger Erikson, "Growth and Crisis of the Healthy Personality," Chapter 12 in Clyde Kluckhohn, Henry A. Murray, and David M. Schneider, editors, *Personality in Nature, Society and Culture,* Alfred A. Knopf, New York, 1955. See also Erikson, *Childhood and Society,* W. W. Norton and Company, New York, 1950. Dr. Erikson is a member of the Senior Staff, Austin Riggs Foundation, and Professor of Psychology in the Department of Psychiatry, University of Pittsburg.

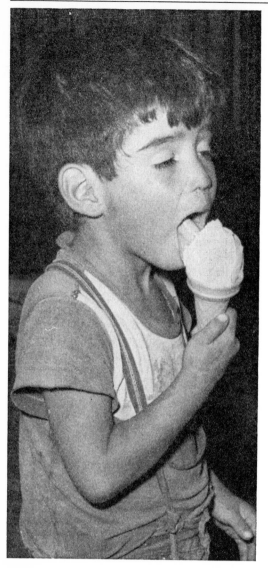

Young children receive much satisfaction through individual physical pleasures, such as a large ice cream cone. Sharing pleasures with associates is less important than it will become later. (Courtesy Our Lady's Youth Center, El Paso)

Early childhood—thirty months through five years

The child is expected to come into early childhood with a basic feeling of trust, a modified autonomy in handling daily affairs, and a fair acceptance of daily routines. He should have begun to curb the most violent of his emotional reactions. He has probably begun to learn that objects (toys, clothes) belong to certain people.

Developmental tasks. During early childhood he continues his mastery of routines and learns more about how and where he may exercise initiative and independence. At times, especially when ill or under emotional stress (as at the birth of a younger child), or at a time of marked change (as moving to a new city), he may tend to revert to baby ways—to wet the bed, use baby talk, or want to be carried. But he also pushes ahead. This vacillation is normal for his age, since his roles and self-concept are not yet well rooted.

The young child is also beginning to have a private life, a family life, and a public life. He begins to inhibit or to conceal curiosity about or experimentation with his sex organs and those of the opposite sex. Direct sexual curiosity often is replaced by an interest in naughty words, usually pertaining to toilet processes. He learns to be modest—to show a certain reticence in talking about elimination and to avoid nudity before strangers or in public.

The cultural pattern of sex roles is delineated during early childhood. The child normally begins to identify with the parent of his own sex, although the mother still remains in a strong affectional position with both boys and girls. Not only does the father replace the mother as the ideal self-concept for the boy, but the mother impresses on her son the desirability of being "daddy's boy," "a little man," brave in the face of childish fears, tearless under mild pain. The little girl is encouraged to pattern her activities after the mother. As children accept the sex roles, they begin to play more and more with children of their own sex—a separation of playmates that continues until adolescence.

The child now not only obeys his mother to please her but has learned the rudiments of right and wrong as taught by his parents. Even when they are not present, he is beginning to conform to their standards of right and wrong. He has the beginnings of a conscience although it is still primarily a reflection of what his parents stand for. He has gone so far as to adopt their standards, to begin to internalize their beliefs and values.

Misbehavior in early childhood. Nevertheless, the child's facade of personal control and social adjustment has weaknesses. When he is thwarted, emotions run high, but subside quickly. Of the young child it has been said that "in a flash of anger, if his strength were equal to the job, there is little doubt that he would kill without compunction." [1]

Quarrels and conflicts with other children are common. Girls tend to quarrel, and boys tend to fight. Much of the conflict is over possessions or is retaliation for being hurt. Thwarting and frustration may elicit bitter words or hard blows. Difficulties in social adjustments are the chief cause of conflicts as children compete to play with other children or to play games. This source of conflict continues into middle childhood. The expression of conflict changes, however, probably under adult authority, from violence to the person of the opponent, to violence displaced to the property of the opponent, to neutral objects, or to weaker scapegoats, such as younger children. Finally, physical violence is replaced by verbal tirades, name-calling, and the like.

Although culture pressures are felt by children and they make an effort to conform to please their parents, tolerance for failure to come up to conventional standards of conduct is still great. Allowances are made for the child's inability to exercise complete self-control or to handle social relationships smoothly. However, toleration by neighbors begins to wear thin if the child does not respond to suggestions not to tear up flower beds, not to take home toys, or not to hurt smaller children.

Parents, more than children, are likely to be held responsible and criticized, or they may be brought into court on a charge of neglect. The child is presumed to belong to its parents and it is their responsibility to care for, teach, and control him. In extreme cases the child may be removed from his parents by court order and placed in a foster home or child-care institution. The child may act in a way that would bring extreme penalties at a later age, but he is not considered to be delinquent because of the presumption that he does not understand the harmfulness of his acts or is unable to use the judgment necessary to control his behavior.

Middle childhood—six to thirteen years

Until the child enters school, he has been in the protective atmosphere of his family or the semiprotective care of preschool or

1 L. Joseph Stone and Joseph Church, *Childhood and Adolescence, A Psychology of the Growing Person,* Random House, New York, 1957, p. 148. The authors are child psychologists.

kindergarten for a few hours a day. Upon entrance into the school system, he makes a transition to a formal institution, usually with definite routines and rules. A few schools may follow a permissive program, but in most overcrowded public schools conformity is thought necessary to prevent bedlam. There is less tendency to treat the child in terms of his individual idiosyncrasies (as parents may do) and a greater tendency to expect conformity to the school-child role. He is expected to adapt himself to the school and to community expectations of good behavior on the street, in a bus, and in stores.

Tasks of middle childhood. One of the tasks of middle childhood is to learn rather quickly what is expected in public. Failure to conform brings marked disapproval. School and public tolerance of misbehavior rapidly declines as the boy or girl becomes older, larger, and louder. They are no longer referred to tolerantly as naughty little children but are considered rude, presumptious, or predelinquent. They are now "old enough to know better," that is, their mental development is sufficient to give some judgment of behavior and responsiveness to community expectations.

Differentiated roles for boys and girls continue. Boys develop aptitudes for physical activities and seek mastery and control of their environment. They are eager for sports; they want to explore; they want to manipulate and make things. Girls are more passive and accepting. Whether these differences are innate or are the result of training is a moot question.

Separate peer groups of boys and girls form, dissolve, and re-form. They begin to absorb more and more of the time and allegiance of their members, thus drawing them away from earlier complete identification with parents. The peer group becomes a place for exchange of knowledge, experimentation in new activities, and development of loyalties for one's own age and sex. Peer groups increase in importance in the child's development until adulthood, when marriage detaches the boy or girl from the peer group as the most significant reference group and attaches him or her again to a family group.

During middle childhood, children become increasingly independent of their parents, not only in supplying physical needs but in making decisions and moral judgments. A conscience

This small, informal play group is typical of early and middle childhood. When ages differ, the younger children learn the games and folkways of childhood from the older. If, as sometimes happens, the older children are delinquent, the younger ones learn delinquency as a matter of course. (Courtesy Our Lady's Youth Center, El Paso)

normally develops, based less on parents' specific approval and more on abstract values of what is right and what is wrong.

By the end of the period, the child normally has acquired the basic skills of reading, handwriting, spelling, and arithmetic. By the age of twelve or thirteen he has learned these basic skills well enough to get through life at a working-class or perhaps a lower-middle-class level.[1] In high school and college he builds on these skills and applies them to more difficult problems. If he does not accomplish this important developmental task of mastering basic skills at the expected rate during elementary school, he is increasingly handicapped with each added year.

Delinquency in middle childhood. Much delinquent behavior is still handled by parents

1 Havighurst, *op. cit.*, p. 33.

or schools; older children may be referred to the police. Schools have their own system of rules, "policing" of corridors and playgrounds, and stated punishments. Truancy, vandalism within the school building, and fighting are handled by school authorities; only the most flagrant incidents by older children are referred to the police.

Middle childhood delinquency takes several forms. The child may have failed to accomplish successfully some of the earlier developmental tasks. He may have explosive temper tantrums in school, be noisy during class periods, or be unwilling to conform to school regulations. Boys experience greater difficulty in conforming than girls. The school expects the child to have learned these self-controls at home in the preschool period. Without them, he is unable to fit into the expected school-child role.

The child may have failed to form a clear concept of property as a private possession—again a developmental task of preschool years. He may pilfer from other children's desks or lockers or from the teacher's purse or destroy property. In the early part of the period, these children are not stealing in the usual sense of the term; they are attracted by some object that they cannot resist, or they act on impulse. They have not yet firmly established values of right and wrong or strong controls over their behavior. Toward the end of the period, taking things often comes into the usual category of stealing with some preliminary planning.

The child may not have learned to accept the degree of authority necessary in any large group of children. He may defy, evade, or vent hostility directly or indirectly at the teacher. Older boys sometimes court physical combat with teachers, not so much to overcome the teacher as to show disdain and defiance.

Other misbehavior takes place outside the school. Some of it is experimental. The peer group has heard or read of some daring exploit. Can they carry out the project? Dare they try? Are they brave enough, strong enough? If the exploit has been forbidden by adults or is known to be unlawful, it may achieve added fascination.

Other middle childhood delinquencies are recreational in nature and may not be thought of by the child as misbehavior. Several city boys who were brought into juvenile court for damaging public property explained that they were building a hut in one corner of a park shelter; their apartment house did not have a place for a hut. Two boys of ten amused themselves for two afternoons before being intercepted by the owner in stripping asbestos shingles from the roof of a garage and sailing them through the air like gliders. The damage approached $75. Three boys nearing adolescence filled an idle evening by wandering through a crowded parking lot puncturing tires and snapping off radio antennae. Since they made no effort at secrecy, they were quickly apprehended by the police. Their explanation was simply that "it was something to do."

Some of these destructive recreational activities may be concealed expressions of hostility. At times the hostility is open. Three boys who were constantly in trouble at school broke into their school at night and wrecked the principal's office. They also stole as much canned fruit from the cafeteria as they could carry to their "clubhouse," an empty garage. Their pleasure was increased the next day in school when the angry principal appeared before each class to demand a confession from the culprits, which of course he did not receive.

Middle childhood and some adolescent delinquency is the result of excess exuberance on some occasion when moderate exhilaration is expected. Halloween, New Year's Eve, or the evening of a certain ball game may be accepted by the public as times for high spirits. Carried away, children and teenagers may go to excesses with property damage and injuries to each other or to anyone who gets in their way.

Some children in middle childhood are referred to the juvenile court with or without arrest. Of all juvenile court cases in fifteen states, a fifth are of children in middle childhood, the percentage increasing from about 3 per cent for children under ten years of age to 10 per cent for those aged thirteen.[1] Among the younger children, few are destined to become habitual delinquents. A study of children in contact with the Youth Bureau of the Detroit Police Department indicated that approximately 80 per cent of the ten- to twelve-year-old boys had only one encounter with the police. Their episodic offenses were not indicative of continued delinquency. They tended to be contrite and worried when in the hands of the Youth Bureau, or tried to bluff by pretending their behavior was just a lark.[2] Girls, also with a high percentage of one contact only (about 60 per cent), tended to indulge in many of the same kinds of delinquencies as boys, especially stealing. With adolescence their misconduct tended to shift to a greater frequency of incorrigibility and sexual misconduct.[3] The delinquency of middle childhood is in line with other phases of development of this period. Delinquency tends to be adventurous experimentation, often not clearly separated in the child's mind from other types of adventure and fun.

However, some children have continued encounters with the police and later become

1 *Juvenile Court Statistics, 1957*, Children's Bureau Statistical Series, No. 52, Children's Bureau, Washington, D. C., 1959, p. 6.
2 William W. Wattenberg, "Ten-Year Old Boys in Trouble," *Child Development*, 28 (1957), 43–46; Wattenberg and F. Quiroz, "Follow-up Study of Ten-Year Old Boys with Police Records," *Journal of Consulting Psychology*, 17 (1953), 309–313; Wattenberg, "Eleven-Year Old Boys in Trouble," *Journal of Educational Psychology*, 44 (1953), 409–417; Wattenberg, "Normal Rebellion—or Real Delinquency?" *Child Study*, 34 (fall, 1957), 15–20.
3 William W. Wattenberg and Frank Saunders, "Sex Differences among Juvenile Offenders," *Sociology and Social Research*, 39 (1954), 24–31.

Table 11

Age of First Misbehavior and of First Court Appearance, Five Hundred Massachusetts Correctional School Boys, Percentage Distribution

Age	First misbehavior	First court appearance
Under five............	4.0	—
Five to seven..........	44.4	0.8
Eight to ten...........	39.2	27.6
Eleven to thirteen......	10.6	45.8
Fourteen to sixteen.....	1.8	25.8
Total................	100.0	100.0

Based on Sheldon and Eleanor Glueck, *Unraveling Juvenile Delinquency,* Harvard University Press, Cambridge, Massachusetts, Copyright 1950 by the Commonwealth Fund, pp. 27–28.

confirmed or serious delinquents in adolescence. A study of 500 boys in a Massachusetts Correctional School shows the progression of misbehavior and delinquency in the middle-childhood period. In fact, some were notably misbehaving in early childhood. Table 11 shows the percentage distribution of ages at first serious misconduct and at first court appearance, which came several years after misbehavior had first been noted. The misconduct included stealing, truancy, destructive mischief, stubbornness, tantrums, disobedience, running away, stealing rides, junking, and sex offenses. These children who continue into serious delinquency and commitment to correctional school represent only a small proportion of misbehaving boys. An urgent problem is to find means of distinguishing the potential delinquent from the normally deviating child.

Adolescence—age thirteen to early adulthood

From middle childhood, the boy or girl steps not only into adolescence physically defined but into a period of social change and decision-making. In general, adolescence is a period of unco-ordination for many youth.

Stresses of adolescence. Physically, at some time during adolescence, the girl becomes a woman, the boy a man. The growth process does not go on at the same rate for all parts of the body. At one point the face may seem all nose, or the feet may seem too large for the rest of the body. Not all adolescents make equal progress. A boy or girl may appear to be a giant physically among age mates who are still midgets. Or a middle teen-ager may still be a child whose piping or soft

child's voice mingles strangely with the deeper voices of boys or the clear tones of girls of the same age but with greater physical maturity. Moreover, boys and girls do not develop at the same pace. Girls experience the normal preadolescent growth spurt at about age eleven, puberty (first menstruation) at age thirteen, followed by added growth to adult womanhood. The developmental pattern for boys is similar, but begins a year or two later. Girls become interested in boys about two years before boys of their own age are interested in them.

Eventually, both boys and girls achieve physical and sexual maturity during adolescence. They know what their permanent stature and formation of their facial features will be. One difficult task for less favored adolescents is to accept themselves as they are—as boy or girl and as having certain individual physical characteristics that may not coincide with their conception of the ideal adolescent.

In other than physical areas, adolescence is also a period of lack of co-ordination. A sociologist, Kingsley Davis, has pointed out that adolescence is a time soon after puberty when the youth is physically equal or superior to the adult, but is socially subordinate.[1] Wishing to achieve full independence, he nevertheless finds himself still dependent on his parents for support and guidance. He is still a schoolboy, compelled by state law to attend school until a given age, despite any inclination he may have to leave school for a job. In our complex society many years of study are needed, and family and social expectations often prolong education long past the legal age limit. Social adolescence is correspondingly prolonged. The long-continued status as a schoolchild is especially trying to the adolescent who does not aspire to a status beyond that of workingman, and who has acquired all that he is ever likely to of basic skills by the time he is thirteen.

Sexual interests and drives come to full physical development during adolescence, and the stimulations of our culture tend to bring them to a high point of personal interest. Nevertheless, the approved developmental sexual task of adolescence is not to express sexual drives but to contain and inhibit them until the late teens or early twenties (a period

1 Kingsley Davis, "Adolescence and the Social Structure," *Annals of the American Academy of Political and Social Science,* 236 (1944), 8–16.

of five or ten years), when marriage is socially approved. Most adolescents, especially boys, find it hard to accept this waiting period. Consequently, experimentation with sex is widespread. If inhibitory attitudes and compensatory or substitute interests have not been built into the child, raw sexual impulses may erupt into action.

The final development of the masculine or feminine role usually comes during adolescence. Younger children usually make their identification with the parent of the same sex, with each parent also impressing on the child of the opposite sex what his role should be. The boy thus usually receives from both father and mother pressure toward the masculine role. The girl similarly is turned toward the feminine role. However, the girl usually spends more time with the mother than the boy does with his father. She therefore has a personal model to follow; however, if she and her mother are not compatible, conflicts are likely to develop. The boy, in less constant association with his father and with greater freedom in the community, has more choice of a masculine model. If he and his father are not compatible, he may more readily find and adopt a model outside the home. This model may be more or less suitable than his father, depending upon his experiences with others.

The adolescent begins to substitute his peer group for his family as his most important reference group. The peer group sets his standards, controls his behavior, provides his companions, and shapes his attitudes for the future. If the peer group holds the same values and attitudes as the parents of its members, the influence of the parents will be reinforced. However, if the members of the peer group are on antagonistic terms with their parents, they may actually oppose the parents and form a little closed circle or society of their own. Typically, this withdrawal from adult society is temporary, and the older adolescent emerges from his seclusion to re-enter the adult world.

As an adolescent, the boy or girl acquires new tastes and new ideas of recreation, all of which require money for their fulfillment. The girl wishes a full wardrobe of clothing, with dresses and coats for many different occasions; she wants to patronize the beauty parlor. The boy has also become interested in clothing and in having his own car. Both boys

and girls want their own radios, TV sets, phonographs, and records for exclusive use in listening to and seeing the favorite teen-age programs and music of the month. Special advertising campaigns urge youth to buy these teen-age products. It is estimated that 9 billion dollars are spent annually by teen-agers, much for special but not essential teen-age goods.[1] These expenditures come from families or from the earnings of teen-agers themselves. Teen-agers unable to meet the current standards of expenditure are likely to feel resentful and deprived.

Adolescence is a period of decision about education and vocations. The teen-ager who drops out of school at the earliest possible age is likely to be retarded and to have several years less schooling than his age would imply. He usually wants to work, but, young and unskilled, often finds it difficult or impossible to find an employer who can use him. He often passes from one temporary job to another, spending much of the next few years in idleness and without adequate income. The youth who continues in school is working for a future objective—an adequate job, but may undergo frustrations because of his semidependent status at home.

Some of the uncertainty of adolescence can be seen from Table 12, which gives the legal age for securing certain privileges and assuming certain responsibilities regarded as belonging to the adult. In addition to such laws, the customs of families and communities add further uncertainty.

The anomalous position of adolescents has been compared by Kurt Lewin to that experienced by someone coming into a new town. Even when the person has objectives he is not certain which moves will lead him toward achieving his goal.[2] The adolescent sees himself as ready to leave childhood and enter adult life. As a child, he has become familiar with certain types of groups and experiences open to him. The established adult has other groups and experiences open to him, and has lost some of those of childhood. The adolescent is between these two groups. His

1 "Teen-age Consumers," *Consumer Reports*, 22 (March, 1957), 139–142; Ralph W. England, Jr., "A Theory of Middle Class Juvenile Delinquency," *Journal of Criminal Law, Criminology and Police Science*, 50 (April, 1960), 535–540.
2 Kurt Lewin, "Field Theory and Experiment in Social Psychology," *American Journal of Sociology*, 44 (1939), 868–897. Lewin, who died in 1947, was a distinguished social psychologist.

Table 12

Age for Acquiring Adult Status in Various Privileges and Responsibilities

	Illinois	Georgia
Voting	21	18
Service in the armed forces, selective service	18	18
Marriage without consent of parents	21–18 *	17–18
Marriage with consent of parents	18–16	17–14
End of compulsory education	16	16
Purchase intoxicating beverages	21–18	21
Secure driver's license	15	16
Minimum age for execution of a will	18	14
Cease to be treated as a juvenile delinquent	17–18	16

Data: Parnell Callahan, *Legal Status for Young Adults*, Oceana Publications, Inc., New York, 1958, pp. 8, 27, 28, 38, 44, 49, 58, 78, 81.
* Where two ages are given the first applies to males, the second to females.

"life space" (range of geographic mobility, breadth of social contacts, and remoteness of future goals) has increased over that of childhood, but the adult future that he sees before him is not well defined. If he moves too rapidly into certain new experiences or seeks affiliation with certain more sophisticated groups, he is rebuffed and told he is not ready; but, if he clings to his old childhood life space, he may be rudely reminded that he is no longer a child. At the same time he is coping with bodily changes in growth and sexual development which often disturb him.

Lewin compares the uncertain adolescent to the marginal man in an underprivileged minority group who is unhappy with his minority position but unable to move into the dominant group. He attributes characteristics found in many adolescents to this situation: shyness, sensitivity, and aggressiveness resulting from the unclearness of the adolescent's position; inner conflict due to differences in values, attitudes, ideologies, and styles of living of the child and the adult; emotional tensions resulting from his conflict; and readiness to take radical positions to the right or the left as part of the general uncertainty of being free from the childhood position but without firm roots in the adult position.

Adolescent delinquency. Delinquency in adolescence may grow out of delinquency in middle childhood, or may develop from the special stresses and dissatisfactions of adolescence. The man-size adolescent may roughhouse with all the abandon of the eight-year-old, but may do serious injury to his opponent or damage to property. Much delinquency hinges on the enforced attendance at school by the unwilling and sometimes retarded boy or girl. Fighting in school, chronic truancy, and spiteful vandalism account for much adolescent delinquency, especially on the part of boys. Girls, now sexually mature and resentful of home restraints, are reported for ungovernability, running away, and sexual promiscuity.

Other adolescent delinquency may turn the boy toward a criminal future. The masculine role may develop through a delinquent peer group or in the shadow of successful adult criminals. Thefts are planned and become more daring; their motivation is typically adolescent, however, to buy clothes, to pay for dates, or to participate in sports. When the time comes for settling into a job, the job chosen may be in affiliation with an adult criminal organization or an independent specialization in some type of crime.

Growth of delinquent behavior as a developmental process

Delinquency may be thought of in the same way as conforming behavior, as the persistent development of a certain kind of behavior from the impulsive activity of the baby through the partially random milling around of the middle-stage child to the planned delinquencies of the adolescent and eventually the admission of the trained delinquent into an adult occupation of crime. Delinquent behavior is similar to conforming behavior in the adjustment of kinds of misbehavior to the maturing capacities of the child. The little child's misbehavior is impulsive, unplanned, and of short duration, as is his conforming behavior. The delinquency of the child of middle years is random and thoughtless, in that he seeks immediate gratification, as he does in much of his conforming behavior. He makes many choices between conforming and deviant behavior, not so much in terms of values of right and wrong, as in terms of the amount of pleasure received relative to disapproval and punishment. In some instances the pleasure derived from misbehavior may exceed the pain of disapproval and punishment.

The adolescent's delinquency parallels his conformity behavior. Although some delinquency may still be impulsive, he is able to plan his delinquencies in advance, to cooperate with his companions in organized delinquent ventures, and to postpone a planned delinquency until the situation is propitious for success. He feels pride in a successful delinquency and secures status among his peers. His actions regarding conformity and delinquency are becoming deliberate and selective. Since adolescent delinquency at least in part grows out of the unco-ordination and dissatisfactions of adolescence, many adolescents find as they near adulthood that the satisfactions they may secure as conventional adults outreach the satisfactions of delinquency, and they enter the conventional stream of life. But a few have so thoroughly organized their lives and found their satisfactions in delinquency and crime that they continue into a criminal vocation.

Since the child enters life with no conception of conformity, it is not surprising that misbehavior follows a general pattern of decreasing frequency. Babies are most nonconforming, older adolescents most conforming. This statement is contradictory to public opinion, which assumes that misbehavior in the form of delinquency has a great upsurge during adolescence. Actually, the process of socialization continues during all of childhood and adolescence and is increasingly effective. The opinion that delinquency has an adolescent upsurge seems to spring from two sources. First, as young people approach adulthood they are able to plan and execute more startling and serious delinquencies, just as they are able to master more difficult school subjects or hold a more demanding job than at a younger age. Second, the manner of handling misbehavior changes.

The daily misbehavior of preschool children is known only to the family. The child of middle years is under close control by the school and organized children's groups during much of the time. In adolescence, the police and juvenile court step into the picture. Escapades and delinquencies become matters of public knowledge and often of official record; they are played up in newspapers. The impression is given that a totally new type of behavior has emerged with adolescence.

Public tolerance also follows the developmental growth of the child. The young child is regarded as a precious heritage of his family and to some extent of the community. He is protected from public censure. His misbehavior is regarded as a temporary lapse; he is not ejected from family or neighborhood. He remains a member of these primary groups, even though intermittently deviant. The adolescent receives less tolerance from the community and often less from his family. He is regarded as dangerous to society, to be ejected (committed to correctional school or prison), or placed under surveillance (probation), or required to make restitution for property stolen or destroyed. Statistical trends showing an increase of arrests and court appearances culminating in adolescence are primarily a reflection of the way in which delinquency is defined and treated. The spurt in delinquency during adolescence is also partly due to the restrictions legally placed on development toward adulthood. School does not seem to lead anywhere for some children, yet they must remain in attendance; therefore they truant. Many wish to work but are not allowed to until a certain age; therefore they have idle time for minor delinquencies and may commit crimes to obtain money. Some girls wish to marry, but the law forbids them; they may therefore enter temporary and unstable sexual relationships. Eventually, adolescents reach the age where these and other laws do not apply.

This discussion of developmental patterns of delinquency has not taken account of special influencing factors which help to determine whether a child develops along conforming or delinquent lines. Chief among these factors are the individual differences among children, the cultural patterns of their communities, and the early influence of their families. These are discussed in that order.

Bibliography

Cottrell, Leonard S., "The Adjustment of the Individual to His Age and Sex Roles," *American Sociological Review,* 7 (1942), 617–620.

Davis, Kingsley, "Adolescence and the Social Structure," *Annals of the American Academy of Political and Social Science,* 236 (1944), 8–16.

Duvall, Evelyn Millis, *Family Development,* J. B. Lippincott Company, Philadelphia, 1957.

Erikson, Erik H., *Childhood and Society,* W. W. Norton Company, New York, 1950.

———, "Growth and Crisis of the Healthy Personality," Chapter 12 in Clyde Kluckhohn, Henry A. Murray, and David M. Schneider, editors, *Personality in Nature, Society, and Culture,* Alfred A. Knopf, New York, 1955.

Gesell, Arnold, and Francis L. Ilg, *The Child from Five to Ten,* Harper and Brothers, New York, 1946.

———, *Infant and Child in the Culture of Today,* Harper and Brothers, New York, 1943.

———, and Louise Bates Ames, *Youth, the Years from Ten to Sixteen,* Harper and Brothers, New York, 1956.

Harris, Dale B., and Sing Chu Tseng, "Children's Attitudes toward Peers and Parents as Revealed by Sentence Completion," *Child Development,* 28 (1957), 401–411.

Havighurst, Robert J., *Human Development and Education,* Longman's Green and Company, New York, 1953.

Liccione, John V., "The Changing Family Relationships of Adolescent Girls," *Journal of Abnormal and Social Psychology,* 51 (1955), 421–426.

Lynn, D. B., "A Note on Sex Differences in the Development of Masculine and Feminine Identification," *Psychological Review,* 66 (1959), 126–135.

Murray, Henry A., and Clyde Kluckhohn, "Outline of a Conception of Personality," Chapter 1 in Clyde Kluckhohn, Henry A. Murray, and David M. Schneider, editors, *Personality in Nature, Society and Culture,* Alfred A. Knopf, New York, 1955.

Schoeppe, Aileen, "Sex Differences in Adolescent Socialization," *Journal of Social Psychology,* 38 (1953), 175–185.

Stone, L. Joseph, and Joseph Church, *Childhood and Adolescence, A Psychology of the Growing Person,* Random House, New York, 1957.

Symonds, Percival M., *The Ego and the Self,* Appleton-Century-Crofts, Inc., New York, 1951.

Although all children tend to follow a uniform trend in maturation and, in a given culture, in behavioral development, the factor of individual differences cannot be overlooked. Children are known to differ in physique, rate of growth, mental ability, and temperament. They are also affected by the way in which they are treated by their mothers and those in close relationships with them during their early childhood. Often it is difficult to distinguish inborn traits and capacities from the social influences of early childhood. These individual differences and the organization of such qualities into personality types are important to understanding delinquency.

Chapter **5**

Individual differences among delinquents

The search for a cause

For many years, criminologists have sought for one factor in the individual's body or mind which would automatically account for delinquency and crime. Scientists and laymen alike have found it difficult to accept the fact that, basically, delinquents and nondelinquents, criminals and noncriminals are much alike in biological make-up and in their responses to social and cultural influences. As Lawson G. Lowrey, a psychiatrist, has written,

. . . despite extensive research and many ingenious efforts to delimit them, there are no such entities as "delinquent" or "criminal" personalities. To be sure, there are delinquents and criminals and, naturally, each has a personality, normal or abnormal, but all attempts to establish a distinctive delinquent or criminal *type* have eventually come to naught.[1]

In spite of this and similar blunt statements denying criminal personality types, one attempt after another is made to isolate particular traits or personality types that can definitely be labeled as criminal and, among children, as forecasting the potential criminal. Reputable researchers continue to make studies to find characteristics that predispose certain people to crime. These studies must be evaluated. The studies of individual charac-

teristics of delinquents and conformers cannot be dismissed as belonging to the past.

Another reason for considering individual characteristics is that differences in physique, mental traits, temperament, or personality formation may have an indirect effect on behavior and therefore under certain circumstances influence the child to become delinquent. For example, the undersized boy who cannot star in athletics may find his small size of use to a delinquent group which needs someone small to squeeze through a transom into a store, or a childish-appearing boy to stand as lookout for the police. But there is certainly no inevitability about this. More often, the undersized boy finds a useful, legitimate role to play in some area other than athletics, as in an academic or artistic field.

Caution is needed in evaluating the attempts to link delinquency and crime irrevocably with some specific personality trait or type. Each theory that has developed has stemmed from general trends of scientific thought and research. Often the theories are valid in the field in which they originated; sometimes, however, they must be validated by further research. The desire to solve the problem of delinquency has led some persons to apply a theory, which holds validity in one field, indiscriminately to the explanation of delinquency and crime. Thus biological explanations of criminal behavior followed soon after Darwin's theory on the evolution of man from lower forms of animal life. Psychological theories were formulated soon after men-

1 Lawson G. Lowrey, "Delinquent and Criminal Personalities," Chapter 26 in J. McV. Hunt, editor, *Personality and the Behavior Disorders*, vol. 2, Ronald Press Company, New York, 1944, p. 794. This chapter gives an excellent survey of the many attempts to find a unitary cause of all crime, dating back to 1812.

tal testing demonstrated differences in mental ability. With the development of Freudian theories, there have been attempts to find delinquent personality types rooted in the id.

Theories of a biological criminal type

Criminal as a primitive savage. The discoveries and interpretations of Charles Darwin, who published *The Descent of Man* in 1871, had a powerful influence on thinking about the causes of criminal behavior, first in Europe, and after 1890, in the United States. Darwin himself did not develop a theory of criminology, but his theory of the evolution of man from lower animal forms opened the way for several interesting criminological theories, since discarded scientifically, but traces of which remain in current theories. Darwin's theory led to the supposition that men could be aligned on a graduated scale, some being more animal-like in characteristics than others. Criminologists readily assumed that criminals were animal-like.

The leader in developing biological theories of criminal behavior was Cesare Lombroso, an Italian physician and psychiatrist (1835–1909).[1] Lombroso made the concept of incomplete evolutionary development the basis of an elaborate theory. This theory of atavism, or reversion to an early type of man, was widely accepted in the United states from about 1890 to 1910. American writers described the criminal as a savage in the midst of civilization, who had been hurled back thousands and thousands of years; the juvenile delinquent was often stigmatized as "the child born centuries too late," who presumably would have been at home in an early type of savage society but did not fit into twentieth century society.[2]

Lombroso and his followers believed that the brain of the criminal differed structurally —and therefore in the way it functioned— from the brains of noncriminals. Other scientists disagreed. Different scientists dissected and studied the brains of criminals who had died or been executed. The end of the controversy in the United States came about 1910 with the abandonment of the idea that a criminal brain existed as a structural anomaly.

1 Arthur E. Fink, *Causes of Crime, Biological Theories in the United States, 1800–1915,* University of Pennsylvania Press, Philadelphia, 1938, p. 100.
2 Cited from various writers by Fink, *op. cit.,* pp. 100–101.

Lombroso thought that the criminal revealed his criminality in observable physical peculiarities and therefore could be spotted while still alive.[3] These peculiarities, the stigmata of criminal behavior, included the following characteristics: low, narrow forehead, large jaws and cheekbones, outstanding ears, hairiness, precocious wrinkles, predominance of left-handedness, prehensile foot, and an arm span greater than the individual's height. When it was pointed out to him that some of the anomalies could be developed in the lifetime of the individual, Lombroso added a new criminal type, the degenerate, who represented a degradation from the normal process of development, a condition considered to be hereditary. He still clung to the idea that the degenerate could be identified by physical traits, e.g., thin upper lip; large ears, jaw, and cheekbones; and a ferocious squint. Further objections led Lombroso to modify his theories to include in his classification occasional criminals, criminals by contracted habit, criminal madmen, and criminals of passion. But he continued to believe that the true or born criminal was central in the classification of criminals.

Another related theory held that the criminal was a person arrested in individual development. The discovery that the human fetus seemed in its development to pass through stages traversed in the biological evolution of man led to the unjustified expansion of this theory to include the psychological and social development of children after birth. G. Stanley Hall, outstanding psychologist at Clark University, was especially fluent in expounding this theory. It required only a simple extension of this theory to explain delinquency and crime as a case of arrested development of the child, corresponding to some early, untamed stage of development of the human race.[4] Studies were made of living delinquents and criminals to try to find some

3 Cesare Lombroso, *Crime, Its Causes and Remedies,* Little, Brown and Company, Boston, 1912. This translation gives Lombroso's modifications of his early theories, which are outlined in the introduction. For summaries of Lombroso's theories see Ruth Shonle Cavan, *Criminology,* Thomas Y. Crowell Company, New York, 1955, pp. 681–685, or George B. Vold, *Theoretical Criminology,* Oxford University Press, New York, 1958, chapter 4.
4 There is of course no proof that in its early stages of development the human race was savage and brutal. No record remains of those early prehistoric days beyond a few types of stone implements.

physical or mental evidence of arrested development.[1]

In time, more extensive and careful research undermined the theories of delinquent and criminal biological types. Some criminals did have biological or physical peculiarities, but the relation of these to crime could not be established. Perhaps the most effective dismissal of the biological theories was a study by Charles Goring comparing English criminals with noncriminals, which revealed that there was no special physical type of criminal.[2]

Juvenile delinquents. The theories of Lombroso and his associates as they pertained to juvenile delinquents rather than adult criminals received a setback from a careful study made in the late thirties at the Institute for Juvenile Research, Chicago. The subjects were 4,000 grade school boys in two socioeconomic areas with high rates of delinquency. The data assembled for each boy were based on a medical examination, a neurologic review, a series of sixty-three anthropometrical measurements and indices, and extensive social and morphological information. The boys were aged six to seventeen; they were studied in three racial-social groups, Caucasoid, Negroid, and Mexican. The boys classified as delinquent either had an official record of delinquency or were known by persons and agencies in the areas to engage in delinquent practices. Those who made the examinations had no knowledge as to which of the boys had a record of delinquency and which had not. In fact, the classification into delinquent and nondelinquent was not made until the testing and collection of information had been completed.[3]

No relation was found between Lombrosian-type stigmata and criminal and delinquent behavior. Among white boys, no significant physical differences were found between delinquents and nondelinquents. Among Negro boys, some differences existed in gross physical appearance. In general, the researchers concluded that, in the areas studied, delinquents had fewer of the so-called stigmata of crime than had the nondelinquents. The delinquents tended to be superior from a medical and neurological standpoint; intelligence did not differ between the two groups.

Later physical studies of criminals and delinquents. The various refutations of Lombroso's theories did not refute the basic idea that criminals and delinquents are in some way organically deficient or at any rate different from the average run of people. If they can be proved different structurally, the theory contends, then they must be different in ways of thinking, feeling, and acting. Such relationships are difficult if not impossible to establish, especially when gross physical features are equated with the complexities of delinquent or criminal behavior. But attempts are still made to establish such relationships.

One of the most elaborate studies was made in the thirties by Ernest A. Hooton, in which elaborate physical measurements were made on 17,076 male prisoners and various groups of noncriminals.[4] Over a hundred measurements were used, including exact measurements of the head, forehead, nose, chin, shape of features, and classification of the abundance and color of hair. The men were also classified by stature and body build. No measurements of intellectual capacity or personality were made, and social or cultural factors were not considered. Hooton failed to find any stigmata of crime, but came to the conclusion that criminals were by heredity organically inferior and that crime resulted from the impact of environment on low-grade human organisms. Without further ado, he concluded that the only way to eliminate crime would be to "extirpate" all physically, mentally, and morally unfit persons, or to place them in complete segregation.

Upon publication of Hooton's study, controversy raged in book reviews and articles. A few writers supported Hooton's conclusions, but more sought to refute them, pointing out deficiencies in his selection of criminals and noncriminals for comparison and condemning his bland assumption that physical structure is an indication of psychological

1 Fink summarizes various of these studies, *op. cit.,* chapter 5.

2 *Abridged Edition of the English Convict,* His Majesty's Stationery Office, London, England, 1919. Discussion may be found in Cavan, *op. cit.,* pp. 684–685, and Vold, *op. cit.,* pp. 52–55.

3 This unpublished study was made by representatives of four professions: B. Boshes, physician; Solomon Kobrin, sociologist; E. Reynolds, physical anthropologist; and S. Rosenbaum, statistician.

4 Ernest A. Hooton, *The American Criminal: An Anthropological Study,* Harvard University Press, Cambridge, Massachusetts, 1939, three volumes. In more popular form the study was published as *Crime and the Man,* Harvard University Press, Cambridge, Massachusetts, 1939.

Table 13

Body Types, Temperamental Types, and Psychiatric Types Postulated by William H. Sheldon

Body type	Temperamental type	Psychiatric type
Endomorphic: predominance of digestive, assimilative function; person is fat	Viscerotonia, relaxed, gluttonous, loves comfort, sociability, craves affection	
Intermediate types between endomorphic and mesomorphic		Manic
Mesomorphic: predominance of bone and muscle; person is muscular, active	Somatotonia, vigorous, active	
Intermediate types between mesomorphic and ectomorphic		Paranoid
Ectomorphic: predominance of mental functions; person is thin	Cerebrotonia, inhibited, shrinks from contacts, self conscious, feelings of inadequacy	
Intermediate types between ectomorphic and endomorphic		Heboid

motivations and social adjustment. Hooton also overlooked the fact that his statistics showed that a much higher percentage of criminals and noncriminals had the same characteristics than had different ones. They did not fall into two distinct groups.

At present one reads little about Hooton's studies, which seem to have had little effect on most researchers or on preventive or treatment methods. He serves, however, as a link to another body of research, dealing with the physical characteristics of juvenile delinquents.

Body types of juvenile delinquents. Another approach to physical marks distinguishing delinquents has been made by William H. Sheldon through a theory of somatotypes or body types.[1] Sheldon's theory postulates three body types, each of which is represented by a clearly defined type which shades off in either direction into the two other types. Each body type has a related type of temperament. Each merging body type that is a combination of two clear-cut body types has a corresponding psychiatric type.[2] The various relationships are shown in Table 13.

Sheldon later applied his theory to delinquency, using as subjects 200 young men referred to Hayden Goodwill Inn, a Boston social agency, by courts, parole officers, and others.[3] With a capacity of eighty boys, the agency had contacts with about 500 youths a year, varying from fifteen to twenty-one years of age. The boys were scored subjectively on a scale running from 0 to 10 in terms of the interference of various factors with adjustment. The factors were mental insufficiency, medical insufficiency, first-order and second-order psychopathy, alcoholism, homosexuality, and primary criminality. Only the last three would be treated legally as crime. Sheldon, however, uses his score to indicate degree of criminality. He then classified the boys by somatotypes and related these to the assumed degree of criminality. His conclusion was that delinquency is mainly lodged in the germ plasm and should be weeded out by selective breeding.

Sheldon's conclusions were challenged by the criminologist, Edwin H. Sutherland, who reclassified Sheldon's 200 subjects on a more meaningful scale of delinquency and crime (running from those with no delinquency to gangsters engaged in major crimes). He found a slight tendency for mesomorphic and

1 A predecessor with a similar theory was E. Kretschmer, whose book *Physique and Character* (Harcourt, Brace and Company, New York, 1925) set forth a theory of three body types: pyknic, with a heavy thickset body; asthenic, with a thin, underdeveloped body; and athletic, with a well-developed, muscular body. Kretschmer was interested in trying to relate types of mental illness to body type.

2 William H. Sheldon *et al.*, *The Varieties of Human Physique*, Harper & Brothers, New York, 1942; William H. Sheldon, *The Varieties of Temperament*, Harper and Brothers, New York, 1949.

3 William H. Sheldon, in collaboration with Emil M. Hartl and Eugene McDermott, *Varieties of Delinquent Youth*, Harper & Brothers, New York, 1949. For a sociological evaluation by a criminologist, see Edwin H. Sutherland, "Critique of Sheldon's *Varieties of Delinquent Youth*," *American Sociological Review*, 16 (1951), 10–13.

Table 14

Sheldon Body Types Applied to Delinquents and Nondelinquents, Percentage Distribution

Body types	496 delinquent boys		482 nondelinquent boys	
Endomorphic component dominance				
Extreme endomorphs......................	1.2		5.0	
Endomorphs............................	2.8		4.8	
Mesomorphic endomorphs...................	3.2		1.5	
Ectomorphic endomorphs....................	4.6		3.7	
Total endomorphs......................		11.8		15.0
Mesomorphic component dominance				
Extreme mesomorphs.......................	23.2		7.1	
Mesomorphs............................	16.9		12.2	
Endomorphic mesomorphs..................	13.3		3.1	
Ectomorphic mesomorphs...................	6.7		8.3	
Total mesomorphs.....................		60.1		30.7
Ectomorphic component dominance				
Extreme ectomorphs.......................	1.8		14.5	
Ectomorphs............................	5.0		14.7	
Endomorphic ectomorphs...................	4.2		3.1	
Mesomorphic ectomorphs..................	3.4		7.3	
Total ectomorphs......................		14.4		39.6
No component dominance				
Balanced types........................	13.5		14.7	

Reprinted by permission of the publishers from Sheldon and Eleanor Glueck, *Unraveling Juvenile Delinquency,* Harvard University Press, Cambridge, Massachusetts, Copyright 1950 by the Commonwealth Fund, p. 193.

manic components to increase and ectomorphic and heboid components to decrease with increasing criminality. The differences between the seriously delinquent and the nondelinquent boys were not statistically significant.

Another attempt to fit Sheldon's somatotypes to delinquency was made by Sheldon and Eleanor Glueck in their massive comparison of 500 correctional school youths and 500 nondelinquents in the Boston area.[1] Considerable effort was made to select nondelinquent boys who not only matched the delinquents in residence in underprivileged area, age, ethnic origin, and intelligence rating, but who were virtually free of any delinquency, even of the most trivial kind. They succeeded to the extent that only 26 per cent of nondelinquents had records of such casual offenses as smoking, hopping trucks, once or twice taking small articles from stores, crap-shooting, sneaking into movies, and occasionally truanting from school. The other 74 per cent had not done even these things.

1 Sheldon and Eleanor Glueck, *Physique and Delinquency,* Harper & Brothers, New York, 1956. A brief statement is contained in the Glueck's *Unraveling Juvenile Delinquency,* Harvard University Press, Cambridge, Massachusetts, 1950, Chapter 15.

The study therefore compares extremes—the most seriously delinquent with the most devout conformers. On the bell-shaped curve of continuity given in Chapter 2, class A was compared with classes F and G and a few of class E. The middle group of "normal" boys was omitted.

According to the Glueck study, as shown in Table 14, about 14 per cent of both the delinquent and the nondelinquent boys had balanced types of personality: that is, none of the three body types dominated. The difference in the percentages of delinquent and nondelinquent endomorphs was very slight. However, the difference among mesomorphs was very large, with a ratio of two delinquents to one nondelinquent. Among ectomorphs the difference was still greater, but tended to the opposite direction, with one delinquent to almost 2.7 nondelinquents. In general, it might be said that mesomorphs (active, muscular types) might be expected to be numerous among delinquent boys, since much adolescent delinquency takes the form of stealing, destruction of property, truanting from school or home, conflicts with parents, and fighting. It should be noted from the table that the highest proportion of delinquent mesomorphs were extreme mesomorphs. In correlating other traits with body type, the Gluecks found that the mesomorphs who became delinquent often had traits not usually found with this body type—destructiveness, feelings of inadequacy, or emotional conflict. Ordinarily, the mesomorphs are somewhat emotionally stable and not given to emotional conflicts. The conclusion is therefore drawn that when the mesomorph has traits disharmonious with his body type, the outcome is likely to be delinquency. It is worth noting also that in general the vigorous, muscular mesomorph is quite likely to express his problems in overt action rather than to inhibit his emotions.

A different set of relationships was found for the ectomorphs, who were the most dominant type among the nondelinquents but constituted only a small percentage of the delinquents. Although ectomorphs are sensitive, their inhibitions and feelings of inadequacy would generally prohibit the customary type of active adolescent delinquency. However, under the stress of environmental pressures, ectomorphs tend to become delinquent. This reaction is in line with their general sensitivity.

Thus the findings tend to indicate that mesomorphs are motivated toward delinquency by traits incompatible with their body type, that ectomorphs are more responsive to environmental situations, and that endomorphs and balanced types seem to have no special internal or external factors that distinguish them in tendency toward delinquency.

The Gluecks conclude that there is no delinquent personality or stable combination of traits that determines that a given individual will become delinquent.

In all studies of physical or biological types, the overlap between the physical characteristics of delinquents and nondelinquents or criminals and noncriminals is very great. The analysis by the Gluecks, trying to determine why some boys of a given body type are delinquent and some not, shows that other factors, often social and cultural in nature, in addition to traits that are assumed to be innate are markedly influential.

Theories of mental capacity and delinquency

When psychological testing first developed, in the period preceding World War I, the differences in mental ability as shown by tests were seized upon by many scientists and laymen alike as the explanation for many types of behavior—delinquency and crime among them.[1] The neatly ranked scores of the tests were taken at face value as indicators of the degree of innate ability. The effect on scores of schooling, family educational background, and degree of familiarity with the English language and American customs was not yet known, as it is today. Therefore any group—racial, foreign-born, economic—with low scores was branded as innately inferior to the group upon which the tests had been standardized, usually a middle-class white urban group. If low test scores and delinquency were associated together in any group, it was assumed that inferior mental ability was the cause of the delinquency. The situation was further clouded by the fact that standards for giving, scoring, and interpreting the earlier tests were not yet well established, and many untrained people gave tests and drew individual conclusions.

Early studies. Perhaps the most outspoken of those who believed that dullness and feeble-mindedness were the chief causes of delinquency and crime was Henry H. Goddard, Director of the Research Laboratory of the Training School for Feeble-Minded Girls and Boys at Vineland, New Jersey.[2] Goddard thought that criminals fell into two classes: those who committed crimes wilfully or through neglect and carelessness and therefore were responsible for their acts; and those whose offenses were the result of some defect which removed full responsibility. He did not believe that criminality itself was inherited but that inherited low mental ability impaired judgment, self-control, and the ability to distinguish right from wrong. If the feeble-minded person was also nervous or impulsive he was almost sure to become a criminal. In one statement, Goddard asserted that low-grade mentality, much of it feeble-mindedness, is the greatest single cause of crime and also that "every feeble-minded person is a potential criminal."

1 George B. Vold, *Theoretical Criminology*, Oxford University Press, New York, 1958, Chapter 5, gives a brief summary of the changing findings and attitudes regarding intelligence test scores of criminals.
2 Henry V. Goddard, *Human Efficiency and Levels of Intelligence*, Princeton University Press, Princeton, New Jersey, 1920; *Feeble-Mindedness, Its Causes and Consequences*, Macmillan Company, New York, 1914.

Goddard was familiar with the various studies made of offenders in institutions, which showed from 10 to 80 per cent of the inmates to be of low mentality. He also traced the family histories of 327 families with children at the Vineland School.[1] Although his imprecise methods tended to load his findings in favor of crime in these families, he found that only 10 per cent of the families and 1 per cent of the individuals involved were criminal. He went to great efforts to counter the low percentage, since it refuted his earlier convictions.

Refutation of the theory of feeble-mindedness as a cause of crime. The great divergence in the proportions of low mentality found in different but similar institutions and the increasing precision of tests threw doubt on some of the earlier statements of the close relationship of feeble-mindedness and crime. The issue was conclusively settled insofar as adult crime was concerned by a precisely scientific study made by Carl Murchison just after World War I.[2] Murchison was Chief Psychological Examiner at Camp Sherman, Ohio, and therefore had access to the tests given to all draftees during World War I. He tested the prisoners at Ohio Penitentiary, at the invitation of the warden, and later was able to secure tests from men in nine or ten other prisons. He compared the scores of the prisoners with those of the soldiers, taking into account race, native or foreign birth, and region. The results unequivocally proved that prisoners and soldiers, men of much the same age, had essentially the same range of mental test scores, that the great majority of both classes fell into the average range, and that both groups had men of low and high mentality in about the same proportions. Murchison discusses many of the factors that might affect the scores of both soldiers and prisoners, many of which offset each other. Regardless of these factors, the evidence was overwhelming that adult male prisoners were a representative cross section of the population of the United States insofar as mental ability was concerned.

Mental ability and juvenile delinquency. The studies cited were made on adult criminals. While their findings undoubtedly apply also

to juvenile delinquency insofar as any automatic relationship between feeble-mindedness and delinquency is concerned, the question of mental ability and delinquency needs further exploration.

There is little evidence among cases brought to juvenile court that low-grade, feeble-minded boys and girls are numerous. Many such children are protected and cared for at home, where, with kind treatment, they create no disturbance. Others, who cannot be cared for at home, are placed early in special institutions for the feeble-minded, either private or state, but usually the latter. In many states the juvenile court judge has jurisdiction over the commitment of feeble-minded children to special institutions as well as over delinquent children. The obviously feeble-minded child who is brought in on a delinquency charge can be committed to a special institution or school for training or custodial care rather than to a correctional school. Thus a cordon of protective care is thrown around the child of obviously low mentality, whether his difficulty is simply inability to adjust to the normal demands of society or consists of delinquent acts.

The crux of the problem of mental ability and delinquency, then, lies in the range from dull-normal to brilliant—the average run of children found in any community, who are attending school if still of school age, who find jobs of one sort or another, and who in time will marry. Several problems need to be examined, among them to determine whether comparable groups of delinquent and nondelinquent children have a distribution of mental test scores approximately the same or differing significantly. Since it is known that scores vary according to the amount of education and cultural background, a fair comparison can be made only when delinquents and nondelinquents are matched on such factors.

Identity of background is provided in the comparison of delinquent children made by Healy and Bronner with the brother or sister closest in age. Race, ethnic, and general family background were identical. The intelligence quotients of the two groups showed very little difference. The delinquents had 14 children with I.Q. above 110 (superior), the nondelinquents 18; in the middle or average range of 90–110, the delinquents had 84 children, the nondelinquents 76; below 90, in the dull and feeble-minded ranges, the de-

1 Goddard, *The Criminal Imbecile*, Macmillan Company, New York, 1915.
2 Carl Murchison, *Criminal Intelligence*, Clark University, Worcester, Massachusetts, 1926.

linquents had 7 and the nondelinquents 11. Seriously feeble-minded were not included in the study.[1] The authors further state that I.Q. was not related to the length of time for treatment required to help the delinquents.

A California study compared 300 children referred to a child-guidance clinic in X County (a rural county), with 300 school children matched for community of residence, sex, and age.[2] The mean I.Q. of the delinquents was 86.7, and of the control group of nondelinquents, 89.3. In another study of 500 consecutive cases of delinquents in X county, the average I.Q. of the delinquents was 92.5. This I.Q. was compared with that of the 3,000 school children upon whom the Stanford-Binet test had been standardized. The school children had an average I.Q. of 101.8; they came from a better educational and social background than the delinquent children. The first comparison given between 300 delinquent and 300 nondelinquent children was based on children from similar backgrounds.

Another problem is the relation of mental ability to the type of delinquency. Merrill found that, regardless of I.Q., the most frequent delinquency was stealing.[3] Children brought to the clinic because of forgery, defiance of parents, and malicious mischief tended to have better-than-average I.Q.'s. Those referred for sexual misconduct, truancy, vagrancy, and assault tended to have I.Q.'s below average. However, the differences were slight.

Still another problem related to intelligence is the amount of recidivism. Does the intelligent child learn more readily than the dull child that delinquency may bring unpleasant results and that he must control his behavior? Or does he devise more clever ways to avoid detection? Merril found no significant difference in the distribution of I.Q. scores between single offenders and recidivists.[4] Others who have studied the same problem differ in their findings; some studies indicate a lower I.Q. among recidivists, while others show no difference.

1 William Healy and Augusta F. Bronner, *New Light on Delinquency and its Treatment,* Yale University Press, New Haven, Connecticutt, 1936, pp. 75–76, 162, 190, 198.
2 Maud A. Merrill, *Problems of Child Delinquency,* Houghton Mifflin Company, Boston, 1947, p. 338.
3 Ibid., pp. 173–174.
4 Ibid., p. 117. Other studies are cited.

Merrill concludes that intelligence level as measured by tests has little relation to the choice of a criminal career or its persistence. Intelligence may play a significant role in some delinquency, but it is not an isolated factor; the total personality is involved.

Classes of children who typically test low. It is now known that almost all intelligence tests do not test "pure" native ability, but test ability as it is strained through informal and formal education, ability to understand and communicate in English, and motivations. In general, children whose parents have a low level of education and who have been unable to give their children an extensive vocabulary, a background of culture, and an interest in reading tend to test lower than children whose parents have given their children such benefits. Children who test low are found among lower-class families and among certain foreign-born groups. If these children are compared with children of American middle-class background, the scores of the two groups will overlap, for there are dull and bright children in both, but the average scores for the deprived group will be lower than those for the American middle-class group.

Certain lower-class and foreign-culture groups contain within their ways of life attitudes and customs that accustom their children to certain types of behavior which are accepted as normal in the group, but are considered delinquent legally or by other groups in the larger community. Since intelligence test scores for the entire group may tend to run low, it is easy to make the mistake of attributing the delinquency to low mentality rather than to the cultural way of life of the group.

Indirect effect of physical and mental deviations on delinquency

Inherited physical and mental differences exist, but they do not set one segment of the population aside as potential delinquents and criminals. They cannot, however, be dismissed without consideration of the part they play in the development of children. The roles offered to children are adapted to the normal, average child. Even slight deviations (such as left-handedness) call for special adjustments on the part of the child. The child who is either very dull or very brilliant, feeble, crippled, muscular if a girl, or pretty

if a boy, does not fit into the pattern of expected physical development or customary
social roles. Moreover, the lack of adjustment
usually increases as the child grows older.
When he fails to make the normal progress
in development or is unable to accept the role
offered, he is hindered by that failure as well
as by the original handicap. He tends to
move further and further out of step with the
normal group.

It does not follow that he becomes delinquent, but he is very likely to feel left out,
inferior, and inadequate. On the other hand,
sometimes the handicap presents a problem
which he is determined to solve, especially if
he receives some interested help from adults
in forming a constructive attitude toward the
handicap. Many fall into a middle group,
accepting their handicap realistically and
feeling neither inferior nor determined to
excel at any cost.

The dull-normal child may react in similar
ways: he may feel inferior or accept his
status realistically or make an effort to excel
in some line. The brilliant child often feels
different and may regret or try to hide his
brilliance when it seems to set him apart
from other children. Occasionally he may
use his brilliance in some clever delinquency
or in trying to devise "the perfect crime."

Which of these directions adjustment will
take seems to depend upon the way in which
the child is treated by children and adults
about him and the help that he is given in
finding a satisfactory role. The physical or
mental deviation itself does not cause delinquency, but if he is rejected from normal
groups and excluded from normal roles, delinquency may be one of the alternative
choices open to him.

Theories of delinquent personalities

As theories linking delinquency and crime
with mental defectiveness faded out and
clinical psychology and psychiatry came to
prominence, the never-ending search for a
single cause of delinquency shifted to personality disorders. Some psychiatrists have
asserted that all delinquents are neurotics.
Others have classified delinquents into several different types. When great care is taken
in interviewing or when standardized tests are
used, the results usually show that half or
more of the delinquents do not have pathological or maladjusted personalities.

Syndromes of delinquent behavior. One type
of classification has been devised by Lester E.
Hewitt and Richard L. Jenkins, a psychiatrist
with experience in child guidance programs.
The classification is based upon the records of
500 children referred to the Michigan Child
Guidance Institute, 78 per cent of whom
were boys. By statistical methods, syndromes
or clusters of related traits were discovered;
each syndrome was considered to be symptomatic of a fundamental pattern of maladjustment. With the cases classified into types
by syndromes, environmental factors associated with each type were sought. The type of
maladjustment and the environmental situation were regarded as closely related and
exerting reciprocal influence.

Hewitt and Jenkins discovered three syndromes, described below. Taken together,
they comprised only 195 (39 per cent) of
the 500 cases. The remaining 305 cases (61
per cent) did not fit into the syndromes.
These cases, even though they account for
almost two-thirds of the total were not discussed; presumably they did not have maladjusted personalities, although they had been
referred to the Michigan Child Guidance
Institute.[1]

**Type 1. Unsocialized aggressive behavior
syndrome.** The child is defiantly aggressive
toward others, disregards their rights as fel-
low-persons, and lacks a feeling of responsibility in interpersonal relations. The six items
found associated in this syndrome were assaultive tendencies, initiatory fighting, cruelty,
open defiance of authority, malicious mischief, and inadequate guilt feelings.

These children usually came from deteriorated homes, often in the country or on
the edge of some town. Their parents had
little education. The children often were unwanted, probably illegitimate. They felt rejected. The relationship between the parents
usually was poor.

The children tended to steal, to lie, and to
treat others badly. They could not get along
with other children. Many were the "lone
wolf" type.

1 Lester E. Hewitt and Richard L. Jenkins, *Funda-
mental Patterns of Maladjustment: The Dynamics of
Their Origin,* State Printer, Springfield, Illinois, 1946.
See also Jenkins, "A Psychiatric View of Personality
Structure in Children, Yearbook 1943," *National
Probation Association,* New York, 1943; Jenkins and
Hewitt, "Types of Personality Structure Encountered
in Child Guidance Clinics," *American Journal of
Orthopsychiatry,* 14 (1944` 84–94.

Fifty-two cases (10.4 per cent) fell into this syndrome.

Type 2. Socialized delinquency behavior syndrome. Seven traits were used to form this syndrome, three of which (including one of the first three) had to be present for a child to be placed in this classification: association with undesirable companions, gang activities, co-operative stealing, furtive stealing, habitual truancy, running away from home overnight, and staying out late at night.

Children with this syndrome usually lived in deteriorated inner city areas with a tradition of delinquent behavior among children. They usually were typical gang members, loyal to the standards of the gang but not socialized into the standards of the larger community. The child was aggressive, a bully, and hostile to groups other than his gang. This type of delinquent has been called the pseudo-social type, adjusted to his own gang and its culture but unadjusted to conventional social life.

Seventy cases (14 per cent) fell into this syndrome.

Type 3. Overinhibited behavior syndrome pattern. The associated traits are seclusiveness, shyness, apathy, worrying, sensitiveness, and submissiveness.

The home background of the children in this classification was better than that of those in the other two syndromes, but the atmosphere was repressive. The mother might be ill. The child might have some physical defect. The child felt insecure at home. He tended to hide behind a shell of inhibition, but suffered from inner conflicts.

This child was more neurotic than delinquent. Overt symptoms were tics, nail-biting, and disturbances of sleep.

Seventy-three cases (14.6 per cent) fell into this syndrome.

The Hewitt-Jenkins classification differs from many of the others in that it does not imply that traits associated with delinquency are hereditary. The social environment in which the child has been reared is a dominant factor in personality formation, although this does not rule out the possibility of individual differences that might affect the interaction between child and environment.

Delinquency and ego control. A somewhat different classification was made by Albert J. Reiss, Jr., a sociologist, of 1,110 white male juvenile delinquents who were probationers of the Cook County Juvenile Court (Chicago).[1] The classification was made by psychiatric social workers and, in extreme or doubtful cases, by psychiatrists.

The percentage found to have integrated personalities is significant—65.7 per cent. The delinquent person in this group, according to Reiss, in all probability will become a mature independent adult. Whether the adult will be delinquent or nondelinquent is not stated.

A second type identified by the psychiatrists, amounting to 22.1 per cent, consisted of delinquents with relatively weak ego controls[2] who are described as very insecure persons with low self-esteem or as highly aggressive and hostile persons. Usually, they suffer from internal conflicts and show symptoms of marked anxiety.

The third type in Reiss's series consisted of the group (12.2 per cent) with defective superegos. These delinquents have no internalized or personally accepted social values; they do not submit to the controls of middle-class society. They do not have a well-developed conscience and, when they misbehave, have little sense of guilt. Boys of this type usually identify with an adolescent delinquent gang which rejects middle-class norms.

Although this classifications bears some resemblance to that of Hewitt and Jenkins, the two series of types are not comparable. What seems important is that both studies, using somewhat different methods of isolating maladjusted personalities, report that the majority (65.7 and 61.0 per cent) of the cases exhibited no unusual personality defects.

1 Albert J. Reiss, Jr., "Social Correlates of Psychological Types of Delinquency," *American Sociological Review,* 17 (1952), 710–718.
2 Ego is the term used by Freud and adopted by psychologists and psychiatrists to refer to the active, practical part of the personality which guides the person in his day-by-day adjustment to the realities of his life. It provides the balance between the id (the basic urges, primitive impulses, often described as selfish, destructive, evil) and the superego (conscience), which sets forth the values and ideals for behavior. A weak ego is one that cannot maintain the balance between self-centered unsocial impulses and ideal standards. The unsocial impulses tend to predominate, and the person seeks immediate gratification for them regardless of social disapproval. If the behavior is inhibited, the person suffers from internal conflicts and exhibits neurotic symptoms. —Joseph Jastrow, *Freud, His Dream and Sex Theories,* Pocket Books, Inc., Rockefeller Center, New York, 1932, pp. 86–92.

Table 15

Percentage of Delinquents and Nondelinquents With Different Types of Pathology

Description	Delinquents	Nondelinquents
No conspicuous pathology..........................	48.6	55.7
Asocial, "primitive," poorly adjusted, unstable........	16.9	5.9
Organic disturbances of the central nervous system.....	0.8	0.2
Psychotic trends, or divorce from reality..............	0.4	1.6
Neuroticism, causing the person to suffer more than average insecurity and anxiety and to develop protective devices that are not culturally approved and that lead to conflicts difficult to solve.........	24.6	35.8
Marked neuroticism, interferes with efficient adaptation..................................... 3.2		5.1
Mild, does not prevent efficient adaptation.........16.3		23.2
Trends not classifiable as above................... 5.1		7.5
Psychopathy, superficial personal relations, less severe than psychosis but more severe than neuroticism....	7.3	0.4
Undifferentiated pathology.......................	1.4	0.4
Total..	100.0	100.0
Number of cases................................	496	495

$$X^2 = 77.85; \ P < .01$$

Reprinted by permission of the publisher from Sheldon and Eleanor Glueck, *Unraveling Juvenile Delinquency*, Harvard University Press, Cambridge, Massachusetts, Copyright 1950 by the Commonwealth Fund, Table on p. 239 and accompanying explanations. In Chapter 18 the Gluecks also give individual tables for forty-two Rorschach tests, comparing the individual characteristics of delinquents and nondelinquents. To the extent that they are applicable, they support Table 15, which is in part based upon them.

A weakness of both studies is that no comparable study of nondelinquent children was made. Might not nondelinquents also show somewhat the same percentage of maladjusted personalities? If so, delinquency could not be attributed directly to the maladjustment, but to other factors in the environment. This suggestion seems reasonable in view of the high percentage of delinquency among children whose personalities were not maladjusted. For two-thirds of the children some explanation other than maladjusted personality has to be assumed.

Pathological characteristics of delinquent and nondelinquent children. A comparison of pathological characteristics of delinquent and nondelinquent children is provided in the Glueck study of 500 correctional school and 500 nondelinquent boys matched for residential area, age, ethnic origin, and intelligence rating.[1] The results are shown in Table 15.

An important factor is that almost half of the delinquents and only slightly more than half of the nondelinquents had no conspicuous mental pathology. Stated in reverse, 51.4 per cent of delinquents and 44.3 per cent of nondelinquents were found to have some type of pathology; the excess of delinquents over

1 Glueck and Glueck, *Unraveling Juvenile Delinquency, op. cit.*, p. 239.

nondelinquents with pathological traits is only 7.1 per cent. According to this table, then, delinquent behavior cannot be attributed directly to maladjustment or to mental or emotional disturbances except, possibly, in 7.1 per cent of the cases.

Some comparisons of the specific pathologies help to throw light on delinquency. In both groups, the more serious pathologies (organic disturbances, psychotic trends) occur only rarely, and in both neuroticism is common, with mild kinds of neurotic reactions predominating.

Some interesting differences appear. Almost three times as many delinquents as nondelinquents were found to be asocial, "primitive," poorly adjusted, and unstable. Also, psychopathology, often associated with aggression, was more common among delinquents, although infrequent in both groups. Combining the two types, some 24 per cent of the delinquents, compared with 6 per cent of the nondelinquents, had tendencies toward aggressive behavior. This figure cannot be compared with the Hewitt-Jenkins and Reiss Studies directly; however, Hewitt-Jenkins found 10 per cent who were of the unsocialized-aggressive type and another 14 per cent who were socialized into delinquent gangs, usually aggressive in some of their activities.

Reiss found 12.2 per cent with defective superegos and also refers to some of those with weak ego controls as aggressive. These loosely comparable findings give support to the supposition that male delinquents include more than their share of aggressive boys. Whether this aggression comes from internal frustrations or from the traditional culture pattern of gangs, or both, is not clear.

Neuroticism, accounting for a high percentage of both groups, nevertheless is more characteristic of nondelinquents than of delinquents. This finding may be due in part to the fact that the nondelinquent boys selected by the Gluecks were overly conforming and were probably inhibiting normally acceptable expressions of emotions and desires. In both groups most of the neuroticism is so mild that it does not prevent efficient adaptation; therefore it is probably not a serious factor in delinquency.

Individual differences in the socio-cultural setting

One by one the attempts to find a unitary explanation of all delinquency have failed. Hereditary factors do not account for delinquency, nor has any one type of personality or of pathology been found that is so closely associated with delinquency that it can be thought of as determining the delinquent behavior. When delinquents and nondelinquents are compared, with background factors held constant, differences are very slight. The conclusion may be drawn that in general delinquents and nondelinquents share very much the same distributions of physique, intelligence, and personality characteristics and types.

The slight differences that appear are not ones that set the delinquent apart as a differ-

ent type, but seem merely slight variations in the frequency with which some characteristic appears in delinquents and nondelinquents. One might assume that there is a slightly greater tendency for children with certain characteristics to become involved in delinquent rather than nondelinquent behavior. But certainly there is no direct causative relationship, or all children with the characteristic would become delinquent.

Two important factors influence the development of the child: one is the culture of the person's group, which determines what behavior is permitted, disapproved, or condemned; the other is the social interrelationship that the person has with other people. The two influences are closely related, since the culture determines the range of social relationships and these in turn are the means of passing the culture on to children. How individual characteristics are defined and what means are provided to control or give expression to idiosyncrasies are part of the socio-cultural situation. Thus each child works out his adjustment to himself as a unique being through the guiding complex of socio-cultural relationships which he experiences. Human beings are remarkably pliable and flexible. If delinquency seems to be predominant in certain groups or areas, it is most likely that it is because the socio-cultural pressures are uniform in these groups or areas.

Although unfavorable individual characteristics do not seem to be the taproot of delinquency, general interest in the development of well-adjusted children indicates a need to recognize that some children have physical, mental, or socio-cultural obstacles to their fullest development and that these children, delinquent or nondelinquent, need help in making adjustments.

Bibliography

Fink, Arthur E., *Causes of Crime, Biological Theories in the United States, 1800–1915,* University of Pennsylvania Press, Philadelphia, 1938.

Glueck, Sheldon and Eleanor, *Physique and Delinquency,* Harper & Bros., N. Y., 1956.

———, *Unraveling Juvenile Delinquency,* Harvard University Press, Cambridge, Massachusetts, 1950.

Goddard, Henry V., *Criminal Imbeciles,* Macmillan Company, New York, 1915.

———, *Feeble-mindedness, Its Causes and Consequences,* Macmillan Company, New York, 1914.

———, *Human Efficiency and Levels of Intelligence,* Princeton University Press, Princeton, New Jersey, 1920.

Goring, Charles, *Abridged Edition of the English Convict,* His Majesty's Stationery Office, London, England, 1919.

Hewitt, Lester E., and Richard L. Jenkins, *Fundamental Patterns of Maladjustment: The Dynamics of Their Origin,* State Printer, Springfield, Illinois, 1946.

Hooton, Ernest A., *Crime and the Man*, Harvard University Press, Cambridge, Massachusetts, 1939.

Jenkins, Richard L., "A Psychiatric View of Personality Structure in Children," Yearbook 1943, *National Probation Association*, New York, 1943.

————, and Lester E. Hewitt, "Types of Personality Structure Encountered in Child Guidance Clinics," *American Journal of Orthopsychiatry*, 14 (1944), 84–94.

Lowrey, Lawson G., "Delinquent and Criminal Personalities," Chapter 26 in J. McV. Hunt, editor, *Personality and the Behavior Disorders*, vol. 2, Ronald Press Company, New York, 1944.

Murchison, Carl, *Criminal Intelligence*, Clark University, Worcester, Massachusetts, 1926.

Reiss, Albert J., Jr., "Social Correlates of Psychological Types of Delinquency," *American Sociological Review*, 17 (1952), 710–718.

Sheldon, William H., *The Varieties of Temperament*, Harper and Brothers, New York, 1949.

————, et al., *The Varieties of Human Physique*, Harper and Brothers, New York, 1942.

————, with collaboration of Emil M. Hartl and Eugene McDermott, *Varieties of Delinquent Youth*, Harper and Brothers, New York, 1949.

Vold, George B., *Theoretical Criminology*, Oxford University Press, New York, 1958.

Chapter **6**

Social disorganization and delinquency

Children work out their physical, mental, and behavioral development within the cultural standards, demands, and provisions of their society. In the United States, not all children are reared in precisely the same cultural milieu. Many subcultures give their own characteristic interpretations of the basic culture. Chief of these subcultures are the social classes, foreign and ethnic culture groups, and certain racial groups.

Several characteristics of subcultures are related to the study of juvenile delinquency. Subcultural groups tend to isolate themselves voluntarily from other groups, thus having a geographic base; in large cities the geographic base is a neighborhood or small local community, often bounded by a heavy-traffic street, factories, or railroads. Unless there is some major change in land usage or redevelopment, these local areas may remain in the same condition—or gradually deteriorate—from one decade to another. A neighborhood known as a high-rate delinquency area in 1910 is very likely to top other areas in delinquency in the 1960's. This characteristic and others remain virtually the same, even though different groups of people flow through the area. The neighborhood acquires a reputation that draws certain people into it and at the same time impresses itself upon the lives of its residents. Thus in any large city there are areas populated by homeless vagrants, by newly arrived immigrants or migrants, or by a distinctive social class. Each of these groups brings in its own subculture, but each is also colored by the cultural traditions and customs of the area. Some of the earlier studies of cultural influences on delinquency were made through plotting the rates of delinquency for small geographic areas of cities and then contrasting areas with high and low incidences of delinquency.

Variations of delinquency rates in urban neighborhoods

The rate of delinquency in many cities is not conspicuously high when the entire city is treated as a unit. Observation has led to the conclusion that some areas contribute more heavily than others to the total delinquency rate. In the twenties, detailed studies of small areas within cities highlighted the fact that 20 to 30 per cent of all boys in some neighborhoods were brought before the juvenile court during a period of three to five years, contrasting with other neighborhoods in which less than 1 per cent appeared in court. Later studies have confirmed these earlier findings. Table 16 gives the contrasting rates.

Chicago (Figure 5) illustrates the city pattern of delinquency.[1] In general, the high rates are in and on the edge of the central business district and in extensions to the west and south, occupied by newcomers. The high rates in certain outlying areas are due to the social deterioration of the area, with many taverns, opportunities for gambling, and streetwalkers. In Chicago and elsewhere, research showed that high-rate areas often were in the oldest parts of the city, near the central business district or industrial areas.[2] Other high-rate areas were near noisy, odorous, or dirt-producing factories, or near railroads or swamps. Characteristics of the areas were poverty, poor health, and high incidence of mental disease, suicide, adult arrests, and chronic alcoholism. These were the typical lower-class areas of a large city.

1 The data for the map is from Institute for Juvenile Research, Chicago, based on the number of boys appearing in the Family Court of Cook County during 1953–1957 on official petitions of delinquency. The rate consists of the number of boys for the five years computed as a percentage of the total boy population per area aged twelve through sixteen.
2 Clifford R. Shaw, Henry McKay, and associates, *Juvenile Delinquency and Urban Areas,* University of Chicago Press, Chicago, 1942.

Table 16

Variation of Male Juvenile Delinquency for Local Urban Areas Shown as Rates Per Hundred Boys of Specified Age

City	Period [§]	Number of areas	Age for computing rates	Juvenile court cases as rate per hundred boys			
				Lowest	Highest	Median	City rate
*Cleveland and suburbs	1928–1931	40	10–17	0.6	37.7	7.1	8.9
*Denver	July 1924 to July 1929	33	9–18	0.9	14.3	—	—
*Philadelphia	1926–1928	134	10–15	0.0	22.6	4.7	5.6
*Seattle	July 1926 to June 1929	38	10–17	2.0	24.0	7.4	9.0
*Richmond	May 1927 to April 1930	19	10–17	1.6	25.1	10.7	12.3
*Birmingham	May 1927 to April 1930	23	10–15	1.2	20.8	7.1	7.5
*Boston	1931–1934	14	7–16‖	2.8	21.4	6.5	7.7
†Baltimore	1939–1942	155	6–17	0.0	20.8	Mean 4.2	—
‡Chicago	1953–1957	75	12–16	2.1	21.0	—	8.3

* Clifford R. Shaw, Henry D. McKay, and Associates, *Juvenile Delinquency and Urban Areas*, University of Chicago Press, Chicago, 1942. Rates for a number of other cities are given, all showing essentially the same pattern of distribution.
† Bernard Lander, *Towards an Understanding of Juvenile Delinquency*, Columbia University Press, New York, 1954, p. 22.
‡ Henry D. McKay, "Rates of Delinquents by Communities in Chicago, 1953–1957," Institute for Juvenile Research, Chicago, June, 1959, mimeographed.
§ Notice that number of years in the period studied and age of the base population differ from city to city. Comparisons between cities cannot be made. The table shows, however, that in each city one or more areas had no or almost no boys appearing in court during the period studied, whereas other areas had from 14.3 to 29.6 boys per 100 boys of specified age.
‖ Male and female combined.

Some areas were inhabited by groups newly arrived to the city and often in conflict with each other. Other areas, although occupied by only one cultural group or race, nevertheless had high rates of delinquency, crime, and vice. In these areas social disorganization—lack of social control—overrode an orderly way of living. In other lower-class areas the population seemed to be more stable and uniform in background; crime might exist but it was organized and orderly.

In contrast to the high-rate areas, moderate or low rate areas of delinquency and crime tended to be physically attractive and inhabited by families with adequate income and a minimum of personal and family disorganization—in short, by middle-class and upper-class people.

For the purposes of discussion, three types of areas—three cultural types—are used: disorganized communities, stable lower-class communities, and middle- and upper-class communities. The tendency of people to live with others of their kind makes it possible to think in terms of geographic communities. The significance, of course, is not in the physical features of the community except as these are symbols of the cultural life and the type of social organization. The significance is in the pattern of daily life that encompasses the people who live in the community.[1]

From disorganization to organization

Social disorganization refers to situations in which interpersonal bonds and institutional control are weak and hence ineffective in controlling behavior. The concept of social disorganization as a factor in delinquency and crime was developed during the twenties and thirties, more or less abandoned as immigrant groups (the prime examples of social disorganization) became adjusted, and now

1 The social classes differ both in numbers of people and in degree of influence. A general estimate for the United States places 3 per cent of the population in the upper class, 9 per cent in the upper-middle, 36 per cent in the lower-middle, 35 per cent in the upper-lower, and 17 per cent in the lower-lower. The percentages would vary from one city to another, depending upon the economic opportunities for one class or another. The middle class is usually regarded as most influential in governing the total social organization. Carson McGuire, "Social Stratification and Mobility Patterns," *American Sociological Review*, 15 (1950), 200.

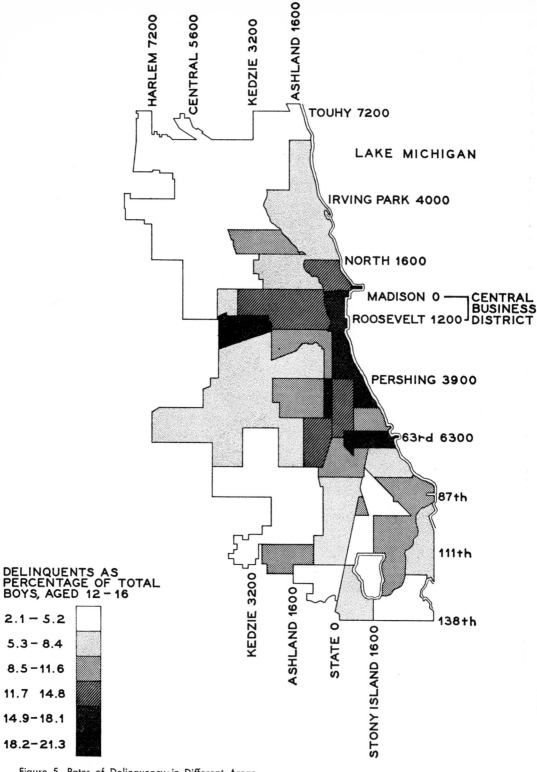

HARLEM 7200
CENTRAL 5600
KEDZIE 3200
ASHLAND 1600

TOUHY 7200

LAKE MICHIGAN

IRVING PARK 4000

NORTH 1600

MADISON 0 ———
CENTRAL
BUSINESS
DISTRICT
ROOSEVELT 1200 —

PERSHING 3900

63rd 6300

87th

111th

138th

DELINQUENTS AS
PERCENTAGE OF TOTAL
BOYS, AGED 12 - 16

2.1 - 5.2
5.3 - 8.4
8.5 - 11.6
11.7 14.8
14.9 - 18.1
18.2 - 21.3

KEDZIE 3200
ASHLAND 1600
STATE 0
STONY ISLAND 1600

Figure 5. Rates of Delinquency in Different Areas
of Chicago.

again found useful for an understanding of certain high-delinquency-rate areas peopled by groups that find adjustment difficult.

In the twenties and thirties, when the children of the immigrants who poured into the United States prior to World War I were growing into maturity, a stock explanation for much of the delinquency in lower-class, high-delinquency areas, was the difficulty of adjustment for the American-born children of foreign-born parents. Neither completely foreign nor American in associations and culture, many of them escaped effective social controls over their behavior. Immigration was virtually brought to an end by the combined effects of World War I, restrictive immigration legislation in the twenties, the depression of the thirties, and World War II. During this long period, the descendants of the immigrants came to maturity, and many of them left the foreign colonies in which their parents or grandparents had sought security among others of their own nationality. They became Americans, fitting themselves into the social class system. Others, however, remained in the old areas or moved almost *en masse* to other areas, retaining some of the old ways but partially adapting themselves to American life.

Meanwhile, urban demands for additional factory workers brought influxes of people from the rural South (both white and Negro), Mexico, and Puerto Rico. In the fifties and sixties, many members of these groups have been repeating the processes by which European immigrants and their children became assimilated into urban American culture and/or adjusted to urban institutions. The remnants of European immigrant groups, rural southerners, Mexicans, Puerto Ricans, and Negroes usually are found in different cities; sometimes one group constitutes almost the entire lower class of a given city. In other cities, especially in large industrial cities, a variety of people elbow each other for living space.

When any one of these groups remains settled in one locality, it tends to have the usual problems of the lower class. When a group moves into new social situations, its members face varied additional problems, the chief of which are adjusting to large-city living from a previous rural background where the family group could exert adequate control over the children, securing a level of education adequate for upward mobility in the city, learning the English language, breaking barriers against the advancement and acceptance of people of dark skin—found among some members of several groups—and accepting new cultural values and customs. These personal problems are closely related to social disorganization.

Disruption of family control. The chief agency of control among Mexicans, Puerto Ricans, and southern Negroes before migration was the family.[1] Mexicans and Puerto Ricans had strongly organized patriarchal families. Rural Negro families were often organized around the mother or grandmother and were frequently given additional stability by the white employer, who assumed a paternal interest in his Negro employees.[2] The family control was based on the recognition of a head of the family, who exerted authority over other members and especially children, and a high degree of loyalty within the family. Implementation of authority came through the ability of the head to control the money-earning enterprises of all members and to hold the family purse, as well as through almost hourly association among the members. The family organization was recognized in the local community as extremely important for social control; any recalcitrant youth was pressured back into conformity by the entire community. Both personal and institutional control reached a highly coordinated level.

With migration to industrial cities, the family controls tend to disintegrate. Each member of the family may work in a different factory and receive, and hence be in a position to control, his own earnings. A frequent cause for dispute in these families comes when adolescents begin to earn and refuse to turn over their earnings to the head of the family to be used at his discretion for the entire family. Recreation is largely outside the family and takes children and adolescents away from family supervision. The American tendency to organize recreation on an age and sex rather than on a family basis may split the former family group into a half-dozen

1 The discussion of southern migrants into cities is limited to Negroes, since their problem is much more acute than the problem of migrant southern whites.
2 Certain distinctive aspects of the Negro family are discussed in Chapter 10.

individuals, each engrossed in his own leisure activities. Sometimes the family as a social group disintegrates. The discouraged father may desert. Adolescent children may leave home to support themselves in a hit-or-miss fashion.

Ineffective institutional controls. Conventional institutional controls are also weak in these communities. Some groups, such as newly arrived Negroes, who try to support "store-front" churches, organize small, ineffectual churches. Migrants of the Catholic faith often find a Catholic church operating in the area, but not always one that uses their native language.

American institutions try to be helpful but often fail because of language differences or because of unfamiliarity with the background and culture of the incoming group. Public schools are often crowded in the teeming migrant areas, and they are taught by middle-class American teachers who try to make southern Negroes, Mexicans, and Puerto Ricans conform to the behavior patterns of the middle-class urban culture in only a few years' time. Community centers face many of the same problems as public schools.

During the period of social disorganization, when neither the native nor the American urban controls prevail, children tend to follow their own impulses, either individually or in little cliques and informal groups. They have somehow slipped into the gap between the old culture and the new.

Much urban delinquency arises because of inadequate social control. When people in a given neighborhood or larger community become stabilized in residence, they become acquainted and reassert their organizing ability. They tend to duplicate the institutions with which they were familiar—the churches, clubs, and leisure activities. In time, these institutions become sufficiently modified to adapt to urban life. Parents grow old and lose their dominance, and children then follow an urban type of family life. As this process goes on, urban American institutions slowly take over control.

Sometimes, in the period of disorganization and reorganization, not only delinquency but also adult crime becomes a prominent feature of the area. The community is defenseless against the inroads of crime, which sometimes takes the form of organized rackets or syndicates. These, too, may become a permanent part of the total social organization, effecting various compromises with the local law-abiding organizations and the police.

Cultural conflicts

When various groups holding particular cultural values are brought together, their differences, inconsistencies, and contradictions come into open conflict. Activity which one group may regard as right, as something always to be done, another group may condemn as wrong and never to be done. Several kinds of conflict are present in urban migrant colonies.

Groups with different values living in adjacent areas or intermingled in the same neighborhood, meeting on the streets, and living in the same tenements, experience many clashes of cultural values and daily customs. According to both Mexican and Puerto Rican culture, the adolescent girl must be protected so that she remains a virgin until the time of marriage. In the lower-class Negro group, freedom of sex relations on the part of the adolescent girl is typically regarded as natural, an illegitimate baby is welcomed, and the girl is not rejected by her mother's family. (The Negro girl who becomes a prostitute, however, is condemned in the lower class, and all forms of premarital sex relations for girls are outside the bounds of middle-class Negro values.) American urban culture encourages girls and boys to join mixed youth groups, but condemns premarital sex relations. Thus the Puerto Rican family may try to keep the adolescent daughter at home in the evenings, the community center beckons her to come unattended to mixed youth dances, and the Negro boy, whose color may be no darker than that of a mixed-blood Puerto Rican girl, may urge her into an illicit affair. Whatever the girl does, her behavior is approved or condoned by only one of the three groups and disapproved or condemned by the other two.

The adolescent girl who is subject to these conflicting cultural pressures may not be able to make a clear-cut choice, since any such choice cuts her off from some groups which are important to her and may, in fact, set her adrift without group affiliation. She may internalize the conflict of the cultures, trying to live according to more than one code, or vacillate between two or more codes. She then becomes personally disorganized, without loyalty to any group or adherence to any consistent set of values or codes.

The boy may be in a similar position. He may be torn between the urging of a street gang to participate in an aggressive attack on a rival gang, his parents' admonition to fight only in defense of his honor or the honor of his mother and sisters, and the middle-class expectation that he will fight only in self-defense against physical injury. His life becomes inconsistent as he shifts from one set of values to another.

Another type of conflict occurs between the values of the migrant group and the official or legal standards of the American urban community. An example that plagues many families and adolescents is the variation in attitudes toward schooling. In the areas from which many migrants came, a few years' schooling or, at most, mastery of the basic skills is regarded as adequate. It is important for the child to begin to earn money for his own support or to help the family at an early age. The school laws may require attendance until age sixteen. With his family and his own inclination on one side and the school laws, attendance officers, and juvenile court on the other, the adolescent is caught between two opposed sets of cultural values. He may not be disorganized himself on this matter: he does not want to continue in school until age sixteen. But he is subject to the penalties growing out of a set of values which believes in and demands many years of education. This situation is the same one found generally in lower-class communities when middle-class values are imposed through schools, churches, community centers, and police. With the migrant groups, however, the contrast may be more extreme, the group may be less ready to accept the middle-class concepts, and it may resist them more strongly.

Crime and delinquency in disorganized areas

Adult crime as well as delinquency abounds in the disorganized area.

Adult crime. Some adult crime is "small-time" thieving and purse-snatching. Violent adult crime, such as armed robbery or rape, may also exist. The adult criminals may operate individually, in small organized groups called mobs, or in large groups. Adult crime is likely to be based on force—breaking into buildings or injuring people—and unlikely to be organized into a business, such as operation of a house of prostitution or gambling. Adult crime familiarizes children and youth with crime and may open opportunities for youth to become affiliated with older criminals.

Juvenile delinquency and unsupervised peer groups. The importance of the peer group in middle childhood and adolescence has already been discussed in Chapter 4. In the disorganized lower-class community, where family control is weak, peer groups assume unusual importance in giving the boy a way in which to organize his activities and to find status and security. The peer groups tend to be unsupervised by adults and detached from institutional or family control.

Supervised groups are not dominant in the lower class as they are in the middle class. They must compete with numerous spontaneous peer groups, especially in the disorganized slum areas, where both family and social organization are weak. For only a limited portion of the lower class are the school and the community center of marked importance. Embodying middle-class values and staffed primarily by middle-class leaders, the typical supervised program offered to lower-class youth appeals chiefly to young children or to upwardly mobile adolescents. In fact, organized programs often pull away from the chief values and considerations of the lower class, attempting to convert lower-class youth to middle-class values and ways of life. They succeed with some, but for many the school is simply something to be endured and the community center an alien cultural island to be ignored. For many boys the street-corner crowd or the semi-self-organized club (gang) becomes the chief agency to help them implement lower-class values and objectives into roles that they can fill.

Lower-class peer groups do not as a rule function in harmony with the adult supervised groups, but oppose them. The adolescent, especially the boy, who attempts to keep a foothold in both organized group and peer group, fails to get the full approval of either. He must make a choice or live on the fringe of both groups. Each type of group represents a different set of values. The supervised group is oriented toward conformity, often to middle-class values. The peer group is autonomous and seeks its own way of life. Each group regards the other as a threat to its values and functions.[1]

Detached peer groups and the delinquent contraculture.

In the autonomous peer groups detached from adult control, codes of conduct and activities are likely to develop independently of any adult group. Activities tend to be erratic and violent, without consideration of consequences. The boys refer to their group as their "crowd," "gang" (without the implication of crime), or "club." The more violent groups, however, are the ones referred to in newspapers and popular speech as gangs with an implication of criminal activity.

In extreme cases, the delinquent gangs are pitted against virtually all agencies of law and order. They are beyond the limits of toleration of their own parents and community groups as well as middle-class institutions. They tend to invert the social values of the dominant middle-class and the more stable lower-class community. They have developed a delinquent contraculture.

Not all delinquency that occurs in lower-class communities is of a group type. A minority of boys carry out their delinquencies alone. However, the more common type of delinquency has some relation to peer-group membership. Peer-group delinquency, especially when it takes the extreme form of a contraculture, gains prestige and permanency. Skills and rationalizations are readily passed from group to group and from older to younger boys.

Delinquent groups in a newly disorganized community

To sharpen the perception of delinquent groups, three illustrations are presented from a study of a newly disorganized Chicago community.

The Chicago community known as Hyde Park was first settled in 1856, but was not well integrated into the city until the 1890's, when the World's Fair was held in the area and the University of Chicago was built

there. The World's Fair bequeathed to the city parks, poorly constructed buildings, and hotels which later became deteriorated slums. The university set the tone of the community as an upper middle-class cultural area. The community was not immune to population changes characteristic of Chicago, and in the 1940's its poorer buildings were filled by the tide of Negro imigrants from the South sweeping across the city and into Hyde Park. In 1950 there were 2,700 nonwhites (primarily Negroes) in Hyde Park; six years later there were approximately 14,500, an increase of 400 per cent. Whites moved out in about the same numbers. Tension grew between lower-class Negroes and lower-class whites, but the middle-class residents often were the objects of aggression; there were many cases of robbery and some cases of rape.

Strong community groups formed and projects were set in motion to demolish the most deteriorated buildings and to rebuild. This movement caused many people to move away from the area. Semitransient families filled the vacancies until such time as the buildings were demolished. Many of these families were Puerto Ricans.

The community agencies in the area were unable to cope with disorderly delinquent groups springing up. The Welfare Council of Metropolitan Chicago initiated a pilot project in co-ordinated and enlarged community services, which operated from 1955 to 1958. As part of the plan, group workers called street-club workers were employed to work with unsupervised and often unorganized groups of boys.[2]

When the street-club workers went into the area they did not find well-structured groups. One large conglomeration of about 100 white boys was referred to as a "crowd-form." The boys had some feeling of belonging in this grouping, but actually it did not meet as a total group. Fifteen or twenty of the boys might be found together. They seemed to have no objectives but felt the need for some "protective alliance" against the large numbers of Negroes moving into the area. They felt alienated from community life, unwanted by respectable Hyde Park, which was backing the demolition of buildings, selected as

---

1 Fritz Redl, "The Psychology of Gang Formation and the Treatment of Juvenile Delinquents," *Psychoanalytic Study of the Child,* Volume 1, International Universities Press, New York, 1945, pp. 367–377. Redl makes the point that a member of a lower-class peer group may associate with—even love—someone from an opposing group, but must never identify with him or permit him to influence peer group policy.

2 The discussion of clubs and gangs is from Charles H. Shireman, *The Hyde Park Youth Project, May 1955 —May 1958,* Welfare Council of Metropolitan Chicago, Chicago, undated.

the target of stricter law enforcement. Under the guidance of the street workers, smaller, more cohesive clubs, whose activities could be directed to definite purposes, began to form.

Another loosely formed group was composed of fifteen Negro boys ranging in age from fourteen to seventeen, who called themselves the Clovers. They are described as follows:

They were being accused by members of the immediate adult community of theft, intimidation, assaults and disturbingly aggressive boisterous behavior. Their relationship to social institutions and to the adult community was, for the most part, negative. They felt that the community's adults were "against them" and did not want them in the neighborhood. The adults were frustrated and alarmed because they were confronted with a teenage problem which had never before existed to serious degree in the neighborhood. The youths' southern background and their lower economic status added to the gulf between them and the community. Very few of the group members were employed; almost all were attending school.

The worker's initial contacts found the youths without any group structure. They were just a collection of individuals and subgroups who "hung around" together for companionship. Group decisions to engage in antisocial activities were few. However, they would band together to combat any group from outside the community or whose racial origins were different from theirs. There were several active subgroups and individuals who engaged in vandalism, assaults, thefts, and shoplifting. At no time were any members of the group reprimanded for a delinquent act by the group as a whole, nor was there any strict code of behavior among group members, between whom there was occasional fighting.[1]

Older boys may achieve a degree of organization not usually found among young adolescents. The Trojans are an illustration of an organized group.

The Trojans were an all-white male group of seventeen boys. One member was fifteen, nine were sixteen and the rest ranged in age from seventeen to nineteen. Six members were in school, four attending a vocational high school . . . and two a general high school. Those attending school were frequent truants. Only three of the boys out of school were regularly

employed, the rest working occasionally at odd jobs—minor janitorial duties, gardening and the like. They tended to come from lower to upper-lower class families.

[The street worker] describes the group life of the Trojans as follows:

The Trojans can be classified as a Social and Athletic Club. They wore identifying jackets in the club colors of blue and gold and displayed the club insignia, a Greek helmet. They had a constitution, elected officers and at least attempted to conduct meetings according to parliamentary procedure. Formal meetings were held, usually once a week, in a basement located in an apartment where one of the members lived. The furnishings included chairs, tables, radio and phonograph, a separate bedroom with three beds, an announcement board and a bookcase. The members spent a great deal of time in the club house playing cards (usually not for money) and just sitting around. They held their meetings and some of their parties here. Their relationship with the rest of the people in the building was bad and often they could not use the place at all for short periods of time. The beds were frequently used by members who couldn't go home for one reason or another. Girls were encouraged to visit the club room and often did. The bedroom was occasionally used for assignations but the members preferred not to use it for this purpose because of the danger of discovery.

The Trojans had poor relations with the social institutions with which they were in contact, although they were perfectly willing to use and exploit them. For example, they would express anti-Semitic comments while they attended dances at Sinai Temple. They used the gyms of both the Hyde Park Neighborhood Club and Church of the Redeemer but displayed little regard for the property of these institutions and deliberately defied the regulations set up by them. They were expelled from the YMCA. They delighted in tormenting "Y" personnel and sometimes entered the building expressly for the purpose of doing so. The Trojans' out-door "hang-out" was a long metal bar in front of the "Y" lawn. They frequently blocked the sidewalk, making it difficult for people to pass and talked loudly with much profanity. Frequently women and passers-by whom they considered odd would be singled out for insulting and derogatory remarks. In the Neighborhood Club it was a full-time job to keep them under control. They were extraordinarily demanding and did not readily accept explanations. They often went where they had been expressly told not to go and used equipment which they had been expressly told not to use. They very deliberately dawdled when informed that their

1 Shireman, *op. cit.,* pp. 115–116.

time was up and when warned about it continued the use of the loud, profane speech that was their natural vernacular.

The police were also seen by the Trojans as a nuisance. Most of them knew of examples of police bribery and had engaged in it or witnessed it in the case of traffic violations. Some members even expressed a desire to be a policeman "in order to make some money."

The Trojans' relationship with all the other white groups in the community was fair except in instances in which there were class differences. Young Southern whites were treated with contempt, while young upper-middle class whites were viewed with envy. Negro groups were feared. The Trojans committed few antisocial acts collectively. They may all have engaged at once in a drinking bout, drag race, bumper tag on the city's streets, but most antisocial acts were committed by individuals and cliques. No member of the group was arrested during the period of the worker's association with them [seven months]. Individual members had in the past been arrested and placed on probation for car theft, larceny and rolling drunks. During the period of the worker's contact with them they had no conflicts with other groups although individual members attempted to promote such conflicts with several groups. To the worker's knowledge, about six members engaged regularly in petty thievery such as robbing candy and pop in stores. Most of the boys engaged in heterosexual activity and a few visited prostitutes. They did not engage in sexual behavior with the girls who associated regularly with them. They looked for sex in the "pick-up," out of the neighborhood.

The group had no trouble in securing alcoholic drinks. Some members passed for twenty-one and had false I.D. cards. All the members drank regularly, often to intoxication. Malicious mischief and vandalism were directed against the schools they attended. It was never planned but was, rather, the result of sudden violent impulse.[1]

The above illustrations bring out the interrelatedness of radical change in cultural and racial groups, failure of social control by local institutions, and the development both of milling, unrooted peer groups and of organized peer groups.

The dilemma of the Negro delinquent

Negroes are found at all points on the social scale and in communities of many degrees of social organization. The lower class

1 Shireman, *op. cit.*, pp. 113–114.

has one problem not common to the earlier lower-class white immigrant groups. The progress of lower-class Negroes upward into middle-class status is hampered at many points—educationally, in employment and choice of occupation, in residential choice, and in cultural participation. The lower-class Negro youth sees fewer possibilities than the white youth for improving his status. He is more likely to feel hopeless or frustrated. In some communities, Negroes become resigned to their position and do not struggle aggressively and overtly against it. In others, however, a degree of aggression is a permanent feature. When Negroes move in large numbers into a northern city, they suffer marked social disorganization. In time, they reorganize into some kind of stable community, and a certain proportion move upward into middle-class status.

Lower-class Negro aggressiveness. In the South, Negroes tend to confine their aggressive actions to other Negroes. The dominant whites tend to be tolerant of Negro toughness and aggressiveness so long as these are confined to the Negro community. Aggressiveness toward whites is not tolerated and is likely to bring swift and brutal retaliation in direct action, often outside the law. Aggressiveness is also often reduced by the training that Negro children receive in assuming a humble manner toward whites; this is a survival technique with its roots in the days of slavery, when any show of hostility was severely punished.[2] Unable to express hostility toward whites, Negroes tend to turn it back upon their own race, in quarrelling, fighting, and numerous homicides. The meek Negro received approval and aid from whites; aggression within the race is regarded tolerantly as a display of the "natural temperament" of the Negro.[3]

2 Allison Davis, Burleigh B. and Mary R. Gardner, *Deep South,* University of Chicago Press, Chicago, 1941, pp. 498–538; E. Franklin Frazier, *Negro Youth at the Crossways,* American Council on Education, Washington, D. C., 1940, pp. 41–51. The recent pressures in the South of Negroes on whites to obtain certain civil rights have been carried on through courts and by passive resistance, not by overtly aggressive behavior; moreover, these efforts are typical of middle-class, not lower-class Negroes.
3 Hortense Powdermaker, "The Channeling of Negro Aggression by the Cultural Process," Chapter 38 in Clyde Kluckhohn, Henry A. Murray, and David M. Schneider, editors, *Personality in Nature, Society, and Culture,* Alfred A. Knopf, New York, 1955.

In the border cities, lower-class girls as well as boys accept indignities from whites with bitterness and a show of retaliation. A fourteen-year-old girl related the following incident about another girl.

This girl and several of her friends were on the sidewalk when a white woman, pushing a baby carriage, wheeled the carriage over the feet of one of the Negro girls. When the girl protested, the white woman said, "Put your feet in your pocket. Why don't you keep your feet out of the way?" The Negro girl began to strike the white woman, who snatched her baby and began running, the Negro girl following and beating her, and the girl's friends running behind, laughing, and yelling. The girls chased the woman several blocks to the police station, then ran away before the police could catch them.[1]

In the North, resentment of whites may be shown in many ways by lower-class Negro youths. If they have recently come from the South, they find themselves with many new areas of freedom, and sometimes they make this freedom a license for insolent aggressive behavior, pushing and shoving white people on the sidewalks and instigating fights. Continued exclusion of Negroes from certain institutions such as restaurants, parks, swimming pools, and certain residential neighborhoods, either as a matter of policy or by overt repulsion from whites, keeps alive the smoldering embers of resentment.

In some northern cities, boys in lower-class areas of compact Negro population follow the pattern found in white lower-class areas and organize into gangs having all the general characteristics of the white gangs. In these large, solidly Negro areas, Negro gangs meet primarily other Negro gangs. They fight with each other to maintain control over the territory that each gang regards as its own, in which the gang members may freely move without fear of molestation by a rival gang. On the periphery of the Negro area, Negro gangs fight white gangs in adjacent neighborhoods, not necessarily because they are white but because they are a threat to the security of the home territory. However, fights on the basis of color also sometimes materialize.

The lower-class boy's dilemma. The pre-

carious balance that the lower-class Negro boy maintains between crime and legality is well illustrated by the case of Smokey.[2]

Smokey, a Negro boy of seventeen, had been born in Florida but brought to New York City by his parents when he was a small child. Father, mother, and five children, of whom Smokey was the eldest, lived in a housing project in a gang-ridden area of Brooklyn. Smokey had a number of stabilizing elements: his parents were both present in the home; they were interested in and concerned for their children, holding them to strict discipline. The father, a machinist, supported the family and the children were adequately clothed. Smokey loved his mother and was respectful and affectionate toward his father. He did not want to do things to hurt them. In addition to attending school, Smokey held a part-time job as a messenger boy. He looked forward to the day when he might become a policeman. He had a girl with whom he went steadily, and he looked forward to marriage in the future. All these things point toward a well-organized adolescence and a stable and conventional future.

However, Smokey also had experiences and relationships that pulled him in the opposite direction. At the age of thirteen he found that he could not remain outside a street gang without repeatedly being beaten up. He therefore joined one of the stronger gangs and became a leader. He felt responsible for his gang and its reputation and he came to depend on it for affection, approval, and status. He had not been able to avoid all delinquency and was on probation. His parents knew he belonged to a gang but did not know it was a "bopping" gang, that is, one that included gang fights in its regular activities.

Soon after he had related these facts to a reporter who had befriended him, a critical event happened which broke the slender threads that held him to a conventional life and future. He had beaten up a boy and taken money from him, both serious offenses. He was arrested, and his parents learned of his life with the gang. His father had to borrow $300 for bail. Since the housing project had a policy of ordering out any family who had a child in trouble, the family was given an eviction notice to move within two months. His parents therefore were

---

1 Abstracted from Frazier, *Negro Youth at the Crossways, op. cit.,* p. 78.

2 Abstracted from Harrison E. Salisbury, *The Shook-up Generation,* Fawcett Publication, Inc., Greenwich, Connecticut, 1958, Chapter 4. This book, written by a journalist, is based on first-hand observations, conversations with gang boys, and interviews with ministers and social workers in the gang areas of New York City.

angry with him. The move would entail more debt, since some private apartment owners require a preliminary payment of several hundred dollars as "key money." He was in jail a week and therefore lost his job. With his world tumbling around him, Smokey saw no reason to continue school. And in addition to these disturbing events, Smokey's girl, aged fifteen, told him she was pregnant. He therefore stopped going with her.

The sudden change precipitated by his assault on the other boy was more than Smokey could handle. He "gave up" and turned in the direction of personal disorganization and seemingly toward more crime. He increased his drinking, which had been moderate before, and lost status with his gang which became involved in more fighting. He became belligerent and ready to fight anyone. The reporter noted that in all probability when his case comes to trial he will be sentenced to prison unless he is again placed on probation; he is now past the age for the juvenile court.

Continuity of the criminal contraculture

Certain areas in many large industrial cities of the United States have a continuous history of population change, social disorganization, delinquency, crime, and conflict. Once established, the criminal contraculture tends to continue, unless some radical change occurs in the social and economic status of the area. A brief sketch of one Chicago area will illustrate a number of points already made regarding population change, disorganization, delinquency, crime, and integration of crime into the community.

Over the years one of the most notoriously criminal and demoralized areas in Chicago has been the old Maxwell police district, often referred to as "Bloody Maxwell." It is a strip one by two miles in size, southwest of the central business district, enclosed on two sides by the river and a heavy band of railroad property. Chicago was founded in the 1830's; from 1850 on Bloody Maxwell was the stronghold of hoodlums, robbers, and burglars.[1] As one decade followed another, new immigrant groups crowded out many of the preceding residents and were in turn crowded out by others. In the seventies, the Irish predominated. They fought alone unless they were outnumbered. As Germans and Jews began to come in, the Irish began to

form gangs to combat the invaders of their territory. German and Jewish hoodlums organized in turn. Often in mixed areas one gang would have members of several nationalities, usually with an Irish leader. The gangs both fought and stole, sometimes specializing in one type of stealing such as shoplifting or burglary. Italians, Bohemians, Greeks, and Poles came later, remaining until the 1930's; the fighting continued. The gang members were in their teens and early twenties. Arrests of boys under age sixteen were common; the average age was about twenty.

School children of the area had their gangs. One feud between rival gangs in the same school began in 1881 and continued, with different participants, for almost thirty years. Although the boys called themselves the Irishers and the Bohemians, gang membership was based not on nationality but on place of residence. The boys carried knives and revolvers to school. Most of their battles were in the streets or schoolyard, but occasionally one erupted inside the school building. Over the years, a number of boys were injured, sometimes seriously, and several were killed. The last great clash came in 1905, when the two groups, armed with guns, lined up twenty-five strong on each side. The arrival of the police prevented the battle. For several years afterward, every boy who attended the school in question was searched for weapons before entering the building. The ages of the boys ranged from ten to fifteen.

Adult gangs of the area also were long-lived. The Valley gang in Bloody Maxwell was in existence forty years, surviving the imprisonment of at least one leader and the murder of another. In its early history the gang controlled the social and political life of the area, various members having relatives on the police force. Later they came into conflict with the police, killing two. The leader was imprisoned and the gang almost disintegrated. However, it revived. In the twenties, during the prohibition period, the gang worked itself into a strong position, and various leaders accumulated wealth and moved their residences away from the district and into suburban areas. They employed skilled lawyers and as a rule were able to avoid conviction or imprisonment. The occasional one who was imprisoned was sometimes able to make private political arrange-

---

1 Herbert Asbury, *Gem of the Prairie, An Informal History of the Chicago Underworld,* Alfred A. Knopf, New York, 1940, pp. 211 ff.

ments to come and go as he pleased from jail or prison.[1]

In the twenties, Bloody Maxwell was one of the slum areas peppered with boys' gangs according to Thrasher's study of that decade. They represented four or five nationalities; sometimes one predominated, sometimes the gang was mixed. Fighting continued. Some of the gangs, as they came to adulthood, organized as semicriminal athletic clubs, sponsored perhaps by a local political club. Some gangs, initiated as play groups, developed vicious criminal activities. In the twenties, the percentage of youth arrested and brought to the juvenile court, while not the highest in Chicago, was well above average and placed the area in the high-delinquency category.[2]

In 1950 the old Bloody Maxwell area was heterogeneous both in nationality and along racial lines. In the white areas of the district, the percentages of foreign-born ran from 18.5 to 55.8 for small areas, compared with an over-all city percentage of 14.5 per cent. In a broad band across the area the population was 66.0 to 99.9 per cent Negro, representing the heavy influx of poor southern Negroes following the same route into Chicago via the slums that many immigrant groups previously had followed.[3] Population density was high and home-ownership rates were low. In 1953–57, in the southern part of Bloody Maxwell, 9.8 per cent of the estimated male population aged twelve to sixteen years were brought before the Family Court (includes juvenile court); in the northern (Negro) section, the percentage of boys appearing in court was 14.5. Eight other city areas had higher rates of delinquency, the highest being 21.0. The city-wide rate was 8.3.[4]

This brief historical statement of gang succession and the persistence of delinquency in one continually disorganized and crime-ridden area brings out several points. The area was established as tolerant to hoodlums and crime soon after the founding of Chicago; the tradition continued in spite of changes in the nationality and the race of the residents. The constant change maintained a state of partial disorganization. At the same time in the white areas, where stability of residence is greater than in the Negro areas, businesses have grown and economic status improved. The rapid turnover of population indicated that at all times there were avenues of escape for many of each new group, either in legitimate business or through crime. Nevertheless, the fighting among gangs continued, based on antagonisms among the different cultural groups, combined with resistance to the invasion by a group of different culture.

A distinction must be made between the criminal history of an area and of a specific nationality or racial group. The area, by reason of the turnover of population and the constant influx of newcomers unfamiliar with city life, may remain the site of gangs and crime from one decade to another. If population stabilizes in some neighborhood, a conventional lower-class or an integrated type of conventional-criminal community may develop, only to be torn apart if a new unadjusted group pushes into the area when the process begins again. As far as any one cultural group is concerned, it may begin its life in the city in a state of loose cohesion leading to disorganization. A crucial period seems to occur when the first American-born or urban-reared generation is growing up, unassimilated into either the parental or the American urban culture. This is often the stage of juvenile delinquency. Most of these young people emerge into adulthood as conventional Americans. A few shift over into illegal syndicates and rackets; a few go down the scale to vagrancy and petty crime. By the third generation, the children of at least the majority of the group are completely assimilated into American life.[5]

---

1 Asbury, *op. cit.*, pp. 219, 221; Frederic M. Thrasher, *The Gang*, University of Chicago Press, Chicago, 1927, pp 11–15, 199–200, 433–434.

2 Clifford R. Shaw and Henry D. McKay, *Social Factors in Juvenile Delinquency*, A Study . . . for the National Commission on Law Observance and Enforcement, Vol. 2, No. 13, U. S. Government Printing Office, Washington, D. C. 1931, pp. 30, 42.

3 Charts from the Chicago Plan Commission and Chicago Community Inventory, University of Chicago, Chicago.

4 Department of Sociology, Institute for Juvenile Research, Chicago, Illinois.

5 Richard A. Cloward and Lloyd E. Ohlin, *Delinquency and Opportunity*, Free Press, Glencoe, Illinois, 1960, 191–202 has a somewhat similar analysis.

Bibliography

Asbury, Herbert, *Gem of the Prairie, an Informal History of the Chicago Underworld,* Alfred A. Knopf, New York, 1940, pp. 211 ff.

Asbury, Herbert, *The Gangs of New York, an Informal History of the Underworld,* Alfred A. Knopf, New York, 1937.

Cloward, Richard A., and Lloyd E. Ohlin, *Delinquency and Opportunity, a Theory of Delinquent Gangs,* Free Press, Glencoe, Illinois, 1960.

Cohen, Albert K., *Delinquent Boys, The Culture of the Gang,* Free Press, Glencoe, Illinois, 1955.

———, and James F. Short, Jr., "Research in Delinquent Subcultures," *Journal of Social Issues,* 14, No. 3 (1958), 20–37.

Handlin, Oscar, *The Newcomers, Negroes and Puerto Ricans in a Changing Metropolis,* Harvard University Press, Cambridge, Massachusetts, 1959.

Reaching the Fighting Gang, New York City Youth Board, New York, 1960, Chapters 2 and 3.

Redl, Fritz, "The Psychology of Gang Formation and the Treatment of Juvenile Delinquents," *Psychoanalytic Study of the Child,* Volume 1, International Universities Press, New York, 1945, pp. 367–377.

Salisbury, Harrison E., *The Shook-up Generation,* Fawcett Publications, Inc., Greenwich, Connecticut, 1958.

Sellin, Thorsten, *Culture Conflict and Crime,* Social Science Research Council, New York, 1938.

Shireman, Charles H., *The Hyde Park Youth Project, May 1955—May 1958,* Welfare Council of Metropolitan Chicago, Chicago, undated.

Thrasher, Frederic M., *The Gang,* University of Chicago Press, Chicago, 1927.

Negro delinquency

Dai, Bingham, "Some Problems of Personality Development among Negro Children," Chapter 35 in Clyde Kluckhohn, Henry A. Murray, and David M. Schneider, editors, *Personality in Nature, Society, and Culture,* Alfred A. Knopf, New York, 1955.

Frazier, E. Franklin, *Negro Youth at the Crossways,* American Council on Education, Washington, D. C., 1940, pp. 19–28.

"Juvenile Delinquency among Negroes," Yearbook 28, *Journal of Negro Education* (Summer, 1959), entire issue.

Lander, Bernard, *Towards an Understanding of Juvenile Delinquency,* Columbia University Press, New York, 1954.

Powdermaker, Hortense, "The Channeling of Negro Aggression by the Cultural Process," Chapter 38 in Clyde Kluckhohn, Henry A. Murray, and David M. Schneider, editors, *Personality in Nature, Society, and Culture,* Alfred A. Knopf, New York, 1955.

The lower class is the world of the unskilled and semiskilled laborer. At the lowest level, it is the world of the unemployable, the handicapped, and the economically distressed whose level of living is very low and one of whose chief sources of income is some form of relief payments. At its upper level, some aspire to move upward into the lower levels of the middle class.

The subculture of the lower class is often misjudged as being a deviation or a decline of middle-class values, goals, and customs. On the contrary, lower-class subculture has positive values and meanings for the people living in it and provides numerous ways in which to meet needs and gain satisfactions. It must be judged in terms of these meanings and not as a degenerate type of middle-class subculture.

The lower class of many cities has grown out of the multicultural disorganized groups of a generation ago. It is often composed of distinct groups, separated from each other by remaining differences of ethnic culture. A given city may have many or few of these subgroups. In New Haven, for example, the lower class is composed primarily of people of European background.[1] Only 7 per cent of the heads of families are from old Yankee stock; most are of partially assimilated European stock resident in the United States for several generations. Each group—Italians, Poles, Lithuanians, Finns, Jews, and Hungarians—lives in a distinctive area, with social activities carried on within the area. In other cities, the lower class includes large contingents of settled Mexicans, Puerto Ricans, or Negro Americans. In still others, white Americans of long standing are prominent. In Elmtown, a city of 7,000, three out of five lower lower-class families had ancestors in Elmtown prior to the Civil War.[2]

Lower-class values

Lower-class values often seem to be a contradiction of middle-class values. Although lower-class people express scorn for the niceties of the middle class, their subculture is not a contradiction of the middle-class subculture; it has developed out of the ne-

Chapter **7**

The lower class and the integrated criminal community

cessities of their living conditions.[3] Well-developed and co-ordinated values such as those listed below indicate a stabilized lower-class community that has maintained its residence for some time in one area.

1. Supplying immediate physical needs is a positive value. Lower-class individuals are frequently haunted by fears of hunger and cold; money is spent as it is acquired. When there is extra money, there is a tendency to overeat or to buy unnecessary clothing or even luxuries. Lower-class groups have their own ideas of what constitutes a decent standard of living and they try to meet this standard. Extra money may be spent on showy articles, a fine automobile, or an expensive TV set. Permanent economic security through savings and investments is not a lower-class value.

2. The lower-class subculture has its own concept of family-centeredness. The stable family unit often is the mother and children (and, in time, grandchildren). Men assume only limited responsibility for the support of the family and for remaining steadily with the family. Serial marriage is accepted. Miller, referring primarily to the lower-class Negro family, speaks of the female-based household.[4] Women accept the task of holding the family together and caring for the children.

1 August Hollingshead and Frederick C. Redlich, *Social Class and Mental Illness,* John Wiley and Sons, New York, 1958, pp. 95–135.
2 August B. Hollingshead, *Elmtown's Youth,* John Wiley and Sons, New York, 1949.
3 Allison Davis, *Social Class Influences upon Learning,* Harvard University Press, Cambridge, Massachusetts, 1948; Hollingshead and Redlich, *op. cit.;* Walter B. Miller, "Lower Class Culture as a Generating Milieu of Gang Delinquency," *Journal of Social Issues,* 14 (April, 1958), pp. 5–19.
4 Miller, *op. cit.*

3. Toughness and the ability to look after oneself early in life are positive values. Child care does not throw a protective shield of supervision around the child, who early begins to share in the life of the street and to remain away from home late into the evening. The girl must be strong and agile to be able to protect herself against unwelcome aggressions from boys and men. The following statement is illustrative:

Maureen was a strong, tough girl. If a boy used filthy language, and the boys liked to use obscenity before the girls, Maureen told him off in the same words. She knew them all. If a boy got rough with her she knew where to hit him so it would hurt most.[1]

The lower-class boy or girl does not necessarily wait until someone else strikes the first blow before fighting (a part of the middle-class credo). He anticipates trouble, or he starts trouble. The boy, as a man, will do hard physical labor and must be able to compete on a physical level.

4. Lower-class boys and girls leave school early, find whatever jobs they can, and marry early. They assert their masculinity and femininity early in life. For the boy, this often means early sex relations carried out as a group enterprise. For the girl the pattern varies. In some lower-class groups the respectable girl is expected to remain a virgin; in others she may flirt and enter rather casually into sex relations, but not as a prostitute. She flaunts her femininity through tight clothing and an exhibitionist manner of walking. The casual nature of sex relations among many lower-class boys and girls shocks middle-class adults. But lower-class people in turn are rather scornful of the subterfuges of middle-class youth—heavy petting or clandestine sex relations contrary to the middle-class code.

5. Autonomy is highly valued and is supported by an aggressive attitude against authority. Among children and youth, the chief targets of authority are fathers, teachers and school administrators, social workers, and the police. Boys especially fight back at these adults. On the other hand, when life becomes too precarious for youth, they sometimes seek refuge under authority: they ask to re-

main in the detention home or in jail, or they recidivate soon after a period of confinement in a way that suggests they are courting discovery and arrest.

6. In methods of attaining objectives, high value is placed on the ability to "outsmart" others. Hard work or academic success are less valued than cleverness and dupery as roads to success. The "smart," shrewd person is admired; the gullible person or one who works for his money has lower status.

7. Leisure time, presumably filled with constructive activities in the middle class, is the time for excitement, dangerous pursuits, and invited trouble in the lower class. A study of New Haven showed that lower-class youth move in crowds to the downtown area, amusement parks, roller skating rinks, or beaches, or go on exploring expeditions to communities other than their own. They may be questioned by the police, arrested, or sent home. Older boys haunt the public amusement parks, looking for pickups or dates and an opportunity to pet.[2]

Except for such gang excursions, much of the lower-class adolescent's life is contained within the lower-class community. In cities where the lower class is made up of a number of different ethnic or racial groups, much of the everyday life is encompassed by the ethnic or racial geographic neighborhood, forays outside being made chiefly by men going to work and gangs of youth searching for excitement.

8. Lower-class communities formed of newcomers to a city often are without social structure, even when the people are of the same background. In time, civic organizations, clubs, and business houses are established and give some institutional control to the community. In some communities, certain of these indigenous institutions may be illegal; nevertheless, they tend to control behavior.

The stable lower class

The lower class falls into several different types. Long residence and little intrusion of different cultural groups tends to create a stable lower-class culture, characterized by the first seven values described. The delinquencies that develop embody many of these characteristics. Since they reflect the subculture, they are tolerated by the adults.

1 Harrison E. Salisbury, *The Shook-up Generation,* Fawcett Publications, Inc., Greenwich, Connecticut, 1959, p. 57.

2 Hollingshead and Redlich, *op. cit.,* pp. 114–135.

Delinquency in a small city. The study of Elmtown, population 7,000, draws a clear picture of delinquency as the activity of loosely bound cliques which dissolve when the adolescents become adults. The characteristics are more clearly observed when contrasted with middle-class behavior in the same city.[1] Another factor influencing delinquency is the status accorded to adolescents who drop out of school. Many lower-class adolescents of school age become chronic truants and, if possible, permanent dropouts. Boys, trying to be adult, live up to the lower-class supposition that they are adult since they no longer attend school. A boy is accorded a man's status when he can walk up to the bar, nonchalantly order a "shot" of whisky, drink it, and order another. Smoking at an age as young as fourteen is common for both boys and girls. Other traits of identification with manhood are ownership of an automobile, or at least having access to one, the ability to pick up girls, gambling, the use of firearms for excitement, admission to commercial dance halls and houses of prostitution, and a smart style of dress affected by other youths. These activities are patterned after those of men in the lower class. They often call for the spending of more money than the adolescent has from his scant and irregular earnings. Consequently, some boys become involved from time to time in stealing money, gas, an automobile, or a gun. The gun is not used to threaten anyone but is shot off as a group speeds along the highway.

Fighting is another lower-class male youth activity in Elmtown. This is not gang fighting, although it may be symbolic of tension between small cliques. The fights start in a commercial dance hall between two boys from different cliques, often half drunk, for the favor of one girl. When quarreling starts, the manager of the hall tries to part the boys or pushes them outside. Each boy's fellow clique-members stand by, and if one boy draws a knife or unfairly attacks his opponent, the two cliques enter into a free-for-all. The girls enjoy these fights, but often have left the scene by the time the fight has ended. Sometimes the competition over a girl or an altercation that arises in the parking lot is the result of feuds between cliques or grows out

of concealed antagonism between upper-lower- and lower-lower-class boys.

Delinquency in a large city. In stabilized lower-class urban communities, much the same situation exists as in Elmtown. Adults do not expect complete conformity from youth, but neither do they expect outright crime. Working-class men look back nostalgically to their own adolescent exploits, recalling how they "got away" with some minor delinquency, and are not inclined to censure their sons for similar behavior. At the same time, they expect these sons to move on into conventional lower-class adulthood, with marriage, fatherhood, and a steady job.[2]

The delinquencies so far discussed are not serious crimes. The lower class is lenient about many of these activities, such as fighting, drinking, and illicit sex relations. It may even condone activities over the border line of criminality. For example, a father defended his son, who had been committed to a state correctional school. He was quoted in a newspaper story as saying, "Sure he stole a couple of cars. But he never stripped them. He's not a bad boy." But the lower class heartily condemns other kinds of crime. Forcible rape, wanton murder, injury to women and children, and theft from people in need are some of the crimes that are condemned in the stable lower class.

The integrated conventional-criminal community

Very different from both the disorganized and the stable lower-class community is the one that tolerates adult criminality organized on a businesslike basis—prostitution, gambling, illegal sale of alcoholic beverages or narcotic drugs, purchase and resale of stolen articles, extortion, and the many other illegal ways that men devise to get money. These types of crime are carried on by a permanent organization, often as well organized as a successful legitimate business. The criminals are settled residents of a community, and while they do not seek publicity, neither do they hide furtively in fear of arrest. They carry on their businesses with the protection of police and corrupt politicians who are paid to leave them alone.[3]

Integration of conventionality and crime. In

---

1 Hollingshead, *Elmtown's Youth, op. cit.,* pp. 102–120, 302–307, 403–424. The description refers to the lower-lower class; the upper-lower class emulates the lower-middle class.

2 Based on an unpublished study by Sidney Peck.

3 For a discussion of organized crime see Ruth Shonle Cavan, *Criminology,* Thomas Y. Crowell Company, New York, 1962, Chapter 6.

integrated communities the adult criminal contraculture has reached a high point of efficiency, and to maintain itself has turned to compromises with the noncriminal groups in the same area, whose toleration of orderly crime is high. For example, the criminal may not only affiliate with a church but make generous contributions to it as a way to dignify his status. His contribution is gratefully received, and no questions are asked as to its origin. As a reward, he may be made an officer of the church or be asked to serve on a building committee, but not on a committee to eradicate crime from the community. The criminal group may tacitly agree to carry on its activities quietly and not to bring disgrace on the area. It may therefore make arrangements to pay police or local politicians not to make raids or arrests. The conventional group is proud of its orderly community and the low number of arrests, and eyes are shut to police and political corruption. This coexistence gives orderliness to the community, but it also protects the existence of criminal activity.

When conventional and criminal groups accept each other and benefit from each other without merging their different sets of values, the community is referred to as integrated.[1] Many degrees of integration exist, of course, and, like any compromise, the relationship may break down. A vigorous drive against crime would disturb it, as would the introduction of some new type of crime that disregarded the sensibilities of the community.

The integrated community is to be distinguished from the disorganized community. Adult crime and juvenile delinquency tend to be less violent physically and less aimless, less an emotional explosion and more a planned and controlled procedure. In the disorganized community, delinquency and crime seem to be more in the nature of a protest or a gesture of hopelessness, while in the integrated community, there is a striving for specific goals.

In general, the goals of organized crime are similar to certain materialistic goals of the conventional community—money, success, power, and status in one's chosen group

of associates. The illegal aspect centers in the means used to attain the goals. One may surmise that through the earlier conflict of cultures, accompanied by disorganization and personal frustration, reaching goals became more important than the means used.[2]

Multiple choices for youth. The integrated conventional-criminal community provides youth with a choice of means to obtain the coveted goals of money and success—a legal way and a criminal way. Each means is supported by people of substance and standing; each is organized; each is known in the community; and each is in need of young recruits. The choice is not always deliberate on the part of youth. It often comes gradually from participation with both groups and an eventual closer relationship with one. Many factors enter into the choice. The adult criminal leaders may hold a higher degree of financial success than any conventional person in the area. If the boy is not well adjusted at school and does not regard higher education as a road to success, crime may be an alternative. The pressures of the family are undoubtedly also important. The integrated community may be said to encourage delinquency and the entrance of the delinquent into adult crime.

At the same time, however, integrated criminal activities tend to regulate and control delinquency. A selective process determines which promising adolescent delinquents will be permitted to join a criminal

1 Richard A. Cloward and Lloyd E. Ohlin, *Delinquencies and Opportunity, a Theory of Delinquent Gangs,* Free Press, Glencoe, Illinois, 1960, pp. 150–170; Solomon Kobrin, "The Conflict of Values in Delinquency Areas," *American Sociological Review,* 16 (1951), pp. 653–661.

2 The theoretical background for the pursuit of approved goals (in this case money and status) by illegal means comes from Robert K. Merton, *Social Theory and Social Structure,* Free Press, Glencoe, Illinois, revised 1957. In this and in earlier writings, Merton sets forth the following possibilities for reaching approved goals: 1. Conformity—the goals and the means to achieve them (norms) are both approved by the larger society; 2. Innovation—the person cannot achieve the goals by approved means and innovates or invents unapproved or illicit means, for example, delinquent or criminal means; 3. Ritualism—emphasis on approved means as all-important, with little regard to the goals (for example, one must be honest even if it means starvation); 4. Retreatism—abandonment both of goals and of means and retreat from reality and effort, for example, chronic drunkenness, vagrancy, or drug addiction; 5. Rebellion—rejection of both goals and means and the attempt to institute new ones. The process called innovation is applicable to some kinds of delinquency and crime, and retreatism to other types.

Innovation indicates a lack of co-ordination or a disruption between goals and norms when cultural controls over individuals break down. It is referred to as *anomie.* The same term is applied to individuals who have lost their sense of social cohesion.

organization. As an adolescent, the youth may belong to a delinquent group, which becomes a training ground for him. But the entire group is not admitted to the adult criminal group; an individual selection is made. Since criminal as well as legitimate businesses call for clear thinking and steady nerves, the existence of criminal organizations in a lower-class community may have a stabilizing effect on the delinquent activities of youth without stamping them out. The irresponsible, impulsive delinquent or the one who becomes personally demoralized through chronic drinking or drug addiction is passed by. The sought-after youth is the one who is clever, astute, bold, co-operative, and who accepts the contraculture. The uncontrolled delinquent therefore tends to lose status in his own group, while the delinquent headed for adult criminality rises to the top.

These integrated communities function most smoothly when they represent an integration of culture and race as well as an occupational integration. The ethnic community, which may afford legitimate and illegal occupational openings to boys of its own ethnic group, may have little to offer a minority or newly arrived group of different cultural or racial background. As far as the stable ethnic element is concerned, job opportunities and status may be controlled by the ethnic leaders, who perhaps represent large interlocking kinship groups. These job opportunities are open to members of the ethnic group, but completely closed to others. A white European ethnic community may have no place for the incoming Negro, Mexican, or Puerto Rican youth. Likewise, the well-established Negro community may have nothing to offer to members of the white race. Under such conditions, tensions and conflict may arise between competing groups of adolescents.

An illustration of an integrated conventional-criminal community

An illustration of an integrated community is afforded by the lower-class Negro community in Chicago in the early forties. At this time, Negroes in Chicago fell into rather well-defined social classes. The Negroes, who came in a tremendous influx during World War I, had had time to become assimilated into the various social classes; residential areas had been stabilized; Negro institutions

and businesses were well established; and public institutions had adapted to the presence of Negroes. Few Negroes migrated to Chicago during the thirties, and the second great influx of the forties and fifties had not begun. The discussion in this section is based on a study of the Chicago Negro community of about 1940.[1]

Adult crime. At the bottom of the social class hierarchy in Chicago was the thin but solid layer of the Negro criminal underworld. This underworld encompassed "the tougher taverns, the reefer pads, the gambling dens, the liquor joints, and the call-houses and buffet-flats where professional prostitutes cater to the trade in an organized fashion."[2] Although payments were made to policemen on the beat and to minor ward politicians, these activities were not openly protected by a political "fix." The only well-organized illegal activity, well protected from police interference, was the policy game, sometimes called the poor man's game. The operation of the policy game was not limited to the underworld. In fact, it was regarded as a legitimate business and gave employment to many Negroes and wealth to a few at the head of the organization.

In the lower class about half the people, the "shadies," were connected in some way with illegal activities. Most of the other half had organized their lives around respectability and religion. In the middle class, the proportion of shadies was greatly reduced. In the upper class, respectability predominated, but a few very successful shadies claimed membership in this class, offsetting the illegal source of their income by contributions to civic causes and investments in legitimate businesses.

Since all the illegal activities were carried on with little or no concealment, they were part of the daily life of the lower class, where most of them existed. Although the policy game has been illegal in Illinois since 1905, the local syndicate that operated the game in

1 St. Clair Drake and Horace R. Cayton, *Black Metropolis: A Study of Negro Life in a Northern City,* Harcourt, Brace, and Company, New York, 1945. Since this study was made, many more southern Negroes have poured into Chicago, primarily working class. Various central areas of the city now display all the characteristics of disorganized communities. At the same time, other areas still represent the integrated conventional-criminal community.

2 Drake and Clayton, *op. cit.,* pp. 610–611. Reefer pads are hangouts for smokers of marijuana cigarettes.

Chicago employed a total of 5,000 persons with a weekly payroll of $25,000 and had an annual gross turnover of at least $18,000,-000. Ticket sellers were permitted to retain 25 per cent of the money taken in for tickets. Of the fifteen controlling members of the syndicate, twelve were Negroes.[1]

Lower-class youth are familiar with the policy game as well as with other types of illegal activities. They receive informal training on how to get something for almost no expenditure of effort or money. Successful policy men are living examples of how a Negro may become wealthy and respected in his own group, although he is shut out of conventional legal business avenues to success because of race.

Peer groups in the integrated community

The street-corner crowd or club is perhaps the most characteristic form of adolescent peer group in the integrated community. The term came into use with a study of an integrated Italian ethnic neighborhood in an eastern city.[2] That the neighborhood was Italian is much less important than that it had already passed through the first stages of adaptation to American culture, and was ethnic rather than alien in culture.

The ethnic community that had bred this corner group was stabilized and essentially law-abiding. However, certain types of organized crime (gambling, for example) operated from the community but were accepted in the local mores as justifiable ways

to make a living. There was no public movement or police action against them. Legitimate business, organized criminal groups, and politicians worked amicably together.

The term, *corner boys,* was coined by Whyte to describe adolescent boys and young male adults hanging around a particular corner taken over as one group's meeting place. The group had its origin in early childhood among boys who lived near each other. The nucleus of what became a permanently established group that lasted into adulthood was a spontaneous play group formed in middle childhood. In school the boys met other boys; however, the groups did not originate in the school.

The corner group was organized around a system of mutual obligations giving it cohesion. The experience of the group outside its own neighborhood was limited, and members lacked social assurance. They drew together, and felt obligated to help each other financially and otherwise. The leader, especially, was obligated to help the followers or he would lose status and prestige. He often had little money for his own use because of the financial needs of other boys. As young adults the boys married and held jobs, but still returned to the corner night after night, except for one night a week when they took out their wives.

The corner boys were not committed to delinquency as a way of life, nor were they outlaws against either their own or the middle-class mores. As adolescents they sometimes had skirmishes with similar groups over invasions of territory or over girls; but there was no intent to injure anyone. They were not considered seriously delinquent by the community nor were they hunted by the police. Most of their time was spent "hanging" on the corner, milling about, sitting and talking, or engaging in social affairs. They operated well within the tolerance limits of their own community, although some of their activities were border-line delinquencies.

During adolescence the corner boys came to the time of decision about their future lives. Criminal as well as legitimate businesses in the local area had openings for them. Some entered local legitimate businesses, but others became affiliated with organized criminal groups operating illegal businesses. This choice involved a certain withdrawal from legitimate groups but did not make outlaws of

1 In policy games (the origin of the name is obscure), for a small sum of money, a person buys a ticket with the number of his choice on it. He keeps one copy of the ticket and the other is forwarded to the headquarters for the game. Each day a number of lucky or winning numbers are drawn from among these tickets. The holders of the tickets with these numbers receive a sum of money far in excess of the small amount paid for the ticket. The operators of the game keep the remainder of all money received. In some cities the drawing of winning numbers (open to trickery) has been replaced by using the last three numbers of some list of figures regularly published in the daily newspaper; at one time the Federal Reserve Clearing House Report was used. The policy game is only one of numerous types of gambling illegally flourishing in the United States, but it is virtually the only one that operates in Negro communities. See "Gambling," the entire issue of the *Annals of the American Academy of Political and Social Science,* 269 (May, 1950); Estes Kefauver, *Crime in America,* Doubleday and Company, Inc., Garden City, New York, 1951.
2 William F. Whyte, *Street Corner Society, the Social Structure of an Italian Slum,* University of Chicago Press, Chicago, second edition, 1955.

the boys. They readily adopted the codes and philosophy of organized crime and fitted themselves into the adult criminal world. They also remained the nucleus of the young adult corner-boy group.

A few of the corner boys became "college boys," encouraged by their teachers and the local community center. They were upwardly mobile and gradually withdrew from close participation in the corner crowd to find a place in legitimate occupations.

Reports of similar communities where legitimate and illegitimate businesses exist without conflict indicate a wider range of delinquency on the part of street-corner groups, especially during the preadolescent and early adolescent years. Rowdiness, defying adult authority (to the point of forcing adults to call the police), horseplay, minor shoplifting, an occasional larceny, burglary, vandalism (often at the school or community center), and sexual exploits appear infrequently but regularly. These activities may not be regarded as abnormal by the community. With suffi-

Loafing on the loading platform of a business house near the area in which they live is part of this group's daily routine. The boys are interested in girls in the neighborhood, who sometimes are regarded as auxiliaries to the boys' gang. (Courtesy New York City Youth Board)

cient provocation, police may be called; but they will usually handle the matter without referral to the juvenile court. With later adolescence, most of the boys move into some type of regular occupation, legal or illegal, while the few who do not, drift into petty thievery and vagrancy.

Hypotheses of lower-class delinquency

Heightened interest in lower-class delinquency during the fifties and early sixties led to the publication of several hypotheses concerning the origin and continuance of certain types of lower-class delinquency. The hypotheses grew out of earlier objective research but were not validated by new research.[1] Little attempt has been made to co-ordinate the hypotheses.

The spectacular exploits of gangs of boys have provided the framework for most of the hypotheses. Delinquency of individuals has been almost entirely disregarded in recent hypotheses. Girl delinquency has been likewise by-passed.

The theories are briefly stated here and related to the preceding discussion of disorganized and lower-class communities.

Delinquency as a normal part of lower-class culture. According to one school of thought, for which Kvaraceus and Miller are the chief spokesmen, the delinquent gang that gradually moves into conformity with adult lower-class norms is oriented to lower-class culture.[2] The normal lower-class concerns of accepting or fomenting trouble, of toughness, smartness, excitement, fate, and autonomy are expressed by the street-corner groups not only in their normal activities but in their delinquencies. In less flamboyant fashion, lower-class adults achieve the same results that adolescent boys achieve through delinquency. The boys are in preparation for normal adult lower-class life. The delinquent acts are functional for the boys in terms of the demands that will be made on them as adults. For example, episodes of wildness to break the monotony of street-corner existence is similar to the alternation of dull routine work broken periodically by the excitement of gambling, getting drunk, or engaging in sharply competitive sports as participant or spectator.

The authors point out that some lower-class gang activity, while illegal, is not an intentional rebellion against middle-class standards nor a protest against barriers to upward mobility. Illegality is incidental to the urge to achieve lower-class normal adjustment.

The type of delinquency that reflects lower-class concerns is most likely to be found in the stable lower-class community. The authors do not deny the problems of lower-class

boys who want to achieve upward mobility, but are unable to break away from lower-class cultural habits. They also recognize that spectacular upward mobility into wealth occasionally occurs, although less often than in the past, when a constant influx of immigrants brought great numbers of temporarily unadjusted people into the slums, some of whom later would make phenomenal strides upward. The authors state that nonaspiring lower-class boys, who are content to remain where they are, are more numerous than is often supposed and that, in fact, this group may be increasing in numbers.

The discussion in this text of the stable lower-class delinquent is essentially an exemplification of the point of view stated above.

Delinquency as the response to frustration. Another school of thought, led by Albert K. Cohen, emphasizes the point of view that basic lower-class gang delinquency is a protest against the middle-class culture, a theory based on the fact that many lower-class youth are unable to enter the middle class and to share in its rewards. In contrast to Miller's emphasis on the stable lower-class group with few aspirations to move upward, Cohen emphasizes the upwardly aspiring but frustrated group that has developed a delinquent subculture of protest and vengeance.[3] The two theories, apparently in conflict, are not if one accepts each as applying to a certain segment of the lower class.

The characteristics of this type of delinquent subculture are described as follows:

1. Awareness by youth of a better way of living in other, middle-class communities, and dissatisfaction with their own lives.

2. Partial acceptance of middle-class values but denial of them since they cannot be attained, and inversion of values.

3. Grouping of boys who face the same problems and who are groping toward the same solutions.

4. Development of activities which are nonutilitarian and serve no practical purpose. Stealing because of the daring involved, with later destruction of what is stolen.

5. Activities which are malicious, hostile, aggressive. Tricks are played on storekeepers, old people, and younger children who cannot retaliate.

1 Research specifically aimed at testing the hypotheses began in the early 1960's and may be expected to continue, probably with modification of the original hypotheses.

2 William C. Kvaraceus and Walter B. Miller, *Delinquent Behavior, Culture and the Individual,* National Education Association of the United States, Washington, D. C., 1959, especially Chapter 9; Walter B. Miller, "Lower Class Culture as a Generating Milieu of Gang Delinquency," *Journal of Social Issues,* 14 No. 3 (1958), 5–19.

3 Albert K. Cohen, *Delinquent Boys, The Culture of the Gang,* Free Press, Glencoe, Illinois, 1955.

6. Negativistic activities, that is, values of the larger society are inverted. Values which the dominant society regards as good, the delinquent group scorns. School attendance is a positive value of the middle class; truancy is a positive value of the delinquent subculture.

7. Although stealing is the most common delinquent activity, the delinquent gang is versatile in its activities. Few adolescent gangs settle into one kind of delinquency. They steal, maliciously annoy other people, become drunk, are rowdy on the streets, and fight. They do not specialize in a delinquent activity.

8. The delinquent gang does not look very far ahead in its activities. This characteristic is not limited to delinquent gangs but is a general lower-class trait. However, the consequences for the gang member may be very serious if he does not consider the outcome to which stealing or violent fighting will lead him.

9. Finally, the delinquent gang emphasizes group autonomy or resistance to conformity and authority. The gang tends to be hostile to other groups. It tends to set up its own codes and methods of control over its own members. Groups differ greatly, however, in the degree of organization which they attain.

Cohen does not assume that all lower-class boys are upwardly aspiring or that gang delinquency is the answer for all who are. The delinquent subculture is one solution. It arose at some point in the past when boys with similar frustrations found themselves in interaction and devised ways to meet their feelings of frustration. The ways are through protest types of delinquency and the building up of an independent prestige and security system within the gang itself. This system of offsetting frustration becomes institutionalized in the values and customs of the gang and is passed on to others. Once formed, the delinquent subculture, as exemplified in the gang, may attract almost any youth who has not found status and satisfactions in the normal culture.

The attributes of the middle-class culture become known to lower-class children through schools with mixed middle- and lower-class children and by way of middle-class teachers and settlement house staffs. Lower-class children also see and read about middle-class success. However, lower-class children are at a disadvantage in competing with middle-class children, since their lower-class parents have not been able to give them the values and habits needed for middle-class participation. This orientation to society frustrates lower-class children who aspire to become successful middle-class people, but do not have the preparation for participation in and acceptance by the middle class. Therefore they are denied middle-class status.

Lower-class children also absorb some of the cultural elements of their own class— corner-boy elements of loyalty to friends, sharing, having fun—and also middle-class or college-boy culture or ambition, striving, and planning for the future. The boy, therefore, has ambivalent values, which may be resolved in one of three ways. The boy may accept the corner-boy status and in time become absorbed into lower-class culture; he may by extra effort detach himself from his corner-boy, lower-class culture and position and affiliate himself with the middle class; or he may affiliate himself with the delinquent subculture and become a member of a delinquent gang. This gang offers him status on a level completely different from middle-class standards. In fact, the delinquent subculture is a repudiation of middle-class standards. By this repudiation, the delinquent boy no longer feels constrained to curb hostility or aggression; he no longer consciously feels guilty when he breaks middle-class standards or inferior when he fails to reach middle-class aspirations. However, if the boy has previously internalized some middle-class values, they may still plague him, perhaps unconsciously. In the effort to still their nagging, the boy may over-react; he may become excessively hostile or aggressive against the middle-class values. Hence the destruction of property by the delinquent boy has value to him as a defiance of the property values of the middle class.

Delinquency as an answer to frustrated middle-class aspirations becomes a more effective answer when it is part of the culture of a group. The lone delinquent may still be subject to ambivalent values, but the gang gives its members support and status within its own circle. It becomes the reference group for the delinquent boy, who then may more easily disregard earlier reference groups (family) or the pressures of alternative reference groups (school, club). The status or prestige that the boy secures in the delinquent

gang is not acceptable to nondelinquent society, either lower-class or middle-class. The
delinquent boy therefore constantly loses
status in the outer society at the same time
that he gains status in the gang. In time he
moves over almost completely into the delinquent subculture (as an adult into crime)
where he seeks most of his satisfactions,
makes his friends, and centers his activities.

Cohen emphasizes that the delinquent subculture applies only to certain types of delinquency; many other types also exist, even in
the lower class.

Aspirations for upward mobility. Since both
Miller and Cohen base their hypotheses of
lower-class delinquency either on contentment with the lower class or thwarted aspiration to move upward, it is important to determine how much upward mobility there is and
how many boys aspire to move upward. In
Elmtown, a city of 7,000, 60 per cent of the
lower-lower-class families had held this position since before the Civil War; it may be assumed that many of the remaining 40 per
cent had also been lower-class through several generations.[1] Upward mobility is not
given; the discussion, however, makes clear
that few lower-lower-class children move upward, although upper-lower-class children
are sometimes successful in moving into the
lower-middle class. In New Haven, 70 per
cent of the upper-lower-class families were
satisfied with their way of life, and their children were not striving upward.[2] About 30 per
cent of all upper-lower-class families had
moved upward from the lower-lower class.
Upward mobility seems to be limited to a minority of the lower class and to one step upward. Few aspired to make the leap from
lower-lower class into a status of middle-class
wealth.

Various studies have attempted to probe
the aspirations of individual boys. Aspirations are limited to a minority of boys who
do not think in terms of great leaps upward.
Lower-class boys who aspire to be upwardly
mobile tend to be realistic in their yearnings.
The son of the unskilled laborer wishes to
become a skilled mechanic; the boy whose
father completed sixth grade wishes to attend
a vocational school.[3] Moreover, in all social

class levels, the brighter boys are more likely
to aspire to an occupational position above
that of their fathers than are the boys of average or low ability. However, regardless of
mental ability, only 12 per cent of the lower-
class boys aspired to a college education, according to one study, compared with 80 per
cent of the highest class (majority white color)
included in the study, a finding that confirms
the limited upward vision of even the bright
lower-class boys.[4] A selective process goes on
also with reference to personality and family
background. The upwardly aspiring boys
tended to be energetic, enthusiastic, and
ready for adult roles. Family relationships
were friendly; the boys did not, however, accept their fathers as exact role models, a cir-
cumstance that opened the way for seeking a
role of higher status. Boys content to remain
in their original status or desiring to move
downward were less secure and venturesome
and more likely to be entangled in family
conflicts.[5]

A clue to the frustration of lower-class boys
comes from the preceding paragraph. The
boys who are likely to stop trying to move upward and who move into delinquency may
be those poorly adjusted and from families in
conflict. Perhaps the boy's frustration does
not come completely from middle-class barriers but, at least in part, from his own unsolved problems.

Another suggestion is that some groups are
more readily welcomed into the middle class
than others. European immigrants of the
same race and cultural heritage as old-line
Americans could overcome the barriers.
Dark-skinned peoples, who now make up a
large proportion of the lower class, find the
upward climb more difficult. However, the
sizable middle-class groups among these peoples attest to the feasibility of upward mobility.

1 August B. Hollingshead, *Elmtown's Youth,* John
   Wiley and Sons, New York, 1949.
2 August B. Hollingshead and Frederick C. Redlich,
   Social Class and Mental Illness, John Wiley and
   Sons, New York, 1958, p. 104.
3 Hollingshead and Redlich, *op. cit.,* pp. 114–135;
   William H. Sewell, Archie O. Haller, and Murray A.
   Straus, "Social Status and Educational and Occupational Aspirations," *American Sociological Review,*
   22 (1957), 67–73; LeMar T. Empey, "Social Class
   and Occupational Aspiration: A Comparison of
   Absolute and Relative Measurement," *American Sociological Review,* 21 (December, 1956), 703–709.
4 Joseph A. Kahl, "Educational and Occupational
   Aspirations of 'Common Man' Boys," *Harvard Educational Review,* 23 (Summer, 1953), 186–203.
5 Elizabeth Douvan and Joseph Adelson, "The Psy-
   chodynamics of Social Mobility in Adolescent Boys,"
   Journal of Abnormal and Social Psychology, 56
   (January–May, 1958), 31–44.

In view of the above studies and suggestions, Cohen's hypothesis of gang delinquency as the result of mobility frustration seems limited to a minority of the lower class.

Variants of the delinquent subculture. Cohen and Short have provided a tentative statement of the differentiation of delinquency into specialized types, namely, among boys, delinquency oriented around conflict, around serious criminality, and around drug addiction.[1] These specialized types are regarded as developing during adolescence, as variants of the basic or "parent" type of delinquency, in which delinquencies are varied and diffuse. Their implication is that the basic type of delinquency develops first among young boys and later may become specialized into one of three types. This approach fits into the known pattern of delinquency of preadolescent boys, which is varied and inconsistent without planning for specific utilitarian goals. Specialization during adolescence is consistent with the general tendency of adolescents to focus their main activities on discernible goals, although not with the specific intent and determination of adults. The social conditions under which the different types of delinquency arise and the personal factors that would lead a boy to affiliate himself with one or another type of delinquent subculture are not made clear by Cohen and Short's discussion.

Delinquency in relation to opportunities for success. The research team of Cloward and Ohlin, after critical analysis of a number of hypotheses of the origin of delinquency, including those of Miller, Cohen, and Short, proposes the hypothesis that delinquent subcultures develop when both legitimate and illegal opportunities for success are lacking.[2] Disregarding the minor types of delinquency that grow out of lower-class cultural concerns (as discussed by Miller) and the concept of a diffuse, basic delinquency subculture as developed by Cohen, they turn their attention to the three more serious specialized types called the criminal, the conflict, and the retreatist (drug addiction).

At the basis of a delinquent subculture lies the inability of lower-class youth to achieve the symbols of success—primarily financial

success—that Cloward and Ohlin conceive of as running throughout all social classes. Unlike Cohen, they do not consider that actual participation in the middle class is what lower-class youth desire; they want wealth, but often are content with the lower-class culture and their close associates in their peer groups. Combining class membership with improved economic position, they find four possible combinations. These are listed below, with the type of peer group involved and the name of the researcher interested in each type.

Type 1: Wants membership in the middle class and better economic position. Typical is the "college boy" who wishes to separate himself from the lower class and through education to enter the middle class and also improve his economic position. Whyte discussed this type as an offshoot of corner-boy groups.[3] The boy of this type avoids delinquency and eventually leaves the corner group and the lower-class community.

Type 2: Wants membership in the middle class even though he cannot improve his economic status. He values middle-class status and the middle-class way of life more than increased income, which he might secure through delinquent and criminal activities if he remained in the lower class. He avoids delinquency and seeks education and association with middle-class people. Cohen's hypothesis of the origin and in part of the continuity of the basic delinquent subculture is concerned with boys of Types 1 and 2, who are thwarted in their desire for upward social mobility.

Type 3: Is not concerned about middle-class status but wishes to improve his economic position. This boy prefers his lower-class way of life to that of the middle class. He is not concerned about rebuffs from the middle class. He is, however, a candidate for a position in the adult criminal world, since in all probability he will not be able to secure the wealth he wishes through legitimate means. Cloward and Ohlin are concerned primarily with boys in this classification and the variations in their opportunities for financial success, whether legitimate or criminal.

Type 4: Is not concerned with either middle-class membership or improved economic position. He is content to remain in the lower class. This type, discussed by Miller, fits into

---

1 Albert K. Cohen and James F. Short, Jr., "Research in Delinquent Subcultures," *Journal of Social Issues,* 14, No. 3 (1958), 20–37.
2 Cloward and Ohlin, *op. cit.*
3 Whyte, *op. cit.*

the adjusted and stable lower-class culture.

All three kinds of delinquent subculture with which Cloward and Ohlin are concerned are of Type 3. According to their hypothesis, whether a boy becomes an adult criminal, a member of a fighting gang, or a drug addict depends upon the opportunities that he finds in his community for financial success. The goal for all is the same—financial success. This is an approved goal, with approved legal ways of attaining it. However, especially in the lower class, many legitimate avenues for success are closed to the boys. They may not have enough education, sufficient savoir-faire, the right color of skin, or the desire to strive for success according to approved methods. However, in some lower-class communities organized criminal methods exist for gaining wealth and prestige through such illegal businesses as gambling, prostitution, illegal sale of liquor or drugs, extortion, graft, and the like. These communities usually are ones, as described earlier in this chapter, in which conventional and organized criminal groups have compromised to the point of maintaining an orderly community. In these neighborhoods, although boys may be denied legitimate means to success, they are saved from frustration through their incorporation into groups providing for criminal means to success.

However, not all boys are accepted into adult criminal organizations, and in some communities the degree of disorganization is so great that organized crime has not developed. At the same time legitimate means to financial success are also lacking. The combination of the absence of any avenue to success and the weak social controls of the disorganized area leads to the development of conflict and its embodiment in fighting gangs. Within their gang and in combat with other gangs, boys achieve status and prove their worth even though they are shut out of avenues to financial success.

Carrying their analysis still further, Cloward and Ohlin turn their attention to boys who are shut out of both legitimate and illegitimate means to success but who, unlike the conflict group, do not rebel against the existing social structure, but retreat from the struggle through the use of narcotic drugs. These boys have failed in gaining success through legitimate means and have internal prohibitions against illegal means, or they may have failed in the use of both legitimate and illegitimate means. In still other cases they may have tried to affiliate with a conflict group but have been rejected by the members of the group. The retreat into drugs further hinders the boy's chances of success along any line. Although not all drug users become members of groups organized around drug addiction, enough do to make the concept of a retreatist subculture with its own set of values and roles feasible.

In the main body of this chapter and the preceding one, concrete, factual material was presented on different types of communities and the types of delinquent peer groups and gangs typical of each. The discussion of hypotheses just completed shows the attempts that have been made to find some general principles to account for the different kinds of delinquency. Both the factual descriptions and the hypotheses present communities and types of delinquency as though they fell into distinct types. Actually, much overlapping occurs in types of communities and in the kinds of delinquent subcultures that develop in them. Differences often are matters of degree of variation rather than of separation into discrete types. It is probable that further research will refine and modify the hypotheses just discussed.

It is necessary to point out again that the hypotheses are concerned only with delinquent subcultures as embodied in peer groups, not with individual acts of delinquency.

Bibliography

Cloward, Richard A., and Lloyd E. Ohlin, *Delinquency and Opportunity, A Theory of Delinquent Gangs,* Free Press, Glencoe, Illinois, 1960.

Cohen, Albert K., *Delinquent Boys, The Culture of the Gang,* Free Press, Glencoe, Illinois, 1955.

————, and James F. Short, Jr., "Research in Delinquent Subcultures," *Journal of Social Issues,* 14, No. 3 (1958), 20–37.

Davis, Allison, *Social Class Influences upon Learning,* Harvard University Press, Cambridge, Massachusetts, 1948.

Drake, St. Clair, and Horace R. Cayton, *Black*

Metropolis: A Study of Negro Life in a Northern City, Harcourt, Brace and Company, New York, 1945.

Hollingshead, August B., *Elmtown's Youth,* John Wiley and Sons, New York, 1949.

————, and Frederick C. Redlich, *Social Class and Mental Illness,* John Wiley and Sons, New York, 1958.

Kobrin, Solomon, "The Conflict of Values in Delinquency Areas," *American Sociological Review,* 16 (1951), 653–661.

Kvaraceus, William C., and Walter B. Miller, *Delinquent Behavior, Culture and the Individual,* National Education Association of the United States, Washington, D. C., 1959.

Merton, Robert K., *Social Theory and Social Structure,* Free Press, Glencoe, Illinois, 1957.

Miller, Walter B., "Implications of Urban Lower-Class Culture for Social Work," *Social Service Review,* 33 (September, 1959), 219–236.

————, "Lower Class Culture as a Generating Milieu of Gang Delinquency," *Journal of Social Issues,* 14, No. 3 (1958), 5–19.

Salisbury, Harrison E., "The Shook-up Generation," Fawcett Publications, Inc., Greenwich, Connecticut, 1958.

Thrasher, Frederic M., *The Gang,* University of Chicago Press, Chicago, 1927.

Whyte, William F., *Street Corner Society, the Social Structure of an Italian Slum,* University of Chicago Press, Chicago, second edition, 1955.

Chapter **8**

Middle-class and upper-class delinquency

In the medley of social classes and other types of subcultural groups, the middle class is presumed to be dominant. In terms of numbers it can make its force felt more than can the small upper class. In community and institutional leadership it surpasses the more numerous lower class.

Middle-class values

As is true of any subculture, the middle class has a distinctive way of life with rather definitely defined goals toward the accomplishment of which children and youth are directed. The restraints imposed upon children are partially offset by approved or condoned avenues of release as well as by rewards for conformity. However, the frustration and deprivation are rarely completely compensated by release and rewards. The failure of the subculture to encompass the whole of life —completely to socialize the child—opens the way to delinquency.

Middle-class values and goals. Middle-class values and goals tend to be well defined and consciously accepted by adults, who deliberately impose them upon children. The child is caught early in a web of planned socialization.[1]

1 Factual material comes primarily from the sources that follow: Albert K. Cohen, Jr., *Delinquent Boys, The Culture of the Gang*, Free Press, Glencoe, Illinois, 1955, pp. 88–91; Allison Davis, *Social Class Influences upon Learning*, Harvard University Press, Cambridge, Massachusetts, 1948, pp. 29 ff.; William C. Kvaraceus and Walter B. Miller, *Delinquent Behavior, Culture and the Individual*, National Educa-

1. The middle-class subculture is family- and home-centered. Preservation of marriage is important. Child-rearing becomes an end in itself and is directed toward the twin goals of a well-balanced personality and the acceptance of middle-class goals. The influence of the parents is supplemented by public schools, staffed primarily by middle-class administrators and teachers, and by such organizations as the Scouts and other middle-class youth organizations.

2. Success, especially of a material nature, is a strong motivating factor among adults, who guide children in the pathway to success. Many years of education are accepted as normal preparation for future success. The middle-class boy or girl remains a schoolchild until the late teens and sometimes extends his adolescence through four years of college. The unco-ordinated position of the adolescent has already been discussed in Chapter 4.

3. Success is more a future than a present goal. Hence children are taught to plan for the future, save money, avoid disgrace, and curb impulsive actions. Spontaneous and impulsive actions lie outside the approved pattern.

4. Competitiveness is encouraged as necessary to success. But the competitiveness must be restrained and carried out within the framework of school, sports, or organized competitions. Proving one's worth through physical aggression or fighting is taboo.

5. Material possessions are prized as symbols of class security and success. Middle-class families often own or are in the process of buying their homes; they have invested large sums of money in prized household articles and a car. The child feels pride also in what the family possesses and its care. He may extend this attitude to the possessions of others. At the same time, stealing or destruction of property may become a way of expressing resentment or defiance.

Middle-class peer groups

Supervised free time. The free-time activities of middle-class children and youth outside family and school tend to fall into two rather

tion Association of the United States, Washington, D. C., 1959, pp. 77–79; and Martin B. Loeb, "Implications of Status Differentiation for Personal and Social Development," *Harvard Educational Review*, 23 (Summer, 1953), 168–174.

distinct categories: adult-supervised and un-supervised peer-group activities.

In the middle class, supervised activities play a dominant role in organizing free time. Family and school controls are highly developed and are projected into the child's free time through organized youth groups and extra-curricular activities. Dancing lessons, music lessons and practice, dramatic lessons, choir practice, meetings of youth organizations (such as the Scouts), and active sports after school consume much of the nonschool time of middle-class children. Home amusements, including radio and television programs, fill additional time. At least until mid-adolescence, motion picture attendance is usually limited to one show a week.[1]

Although these supervised activities cannot be compared with the natural groupings of children, they are popular with middle-class children and young adolescents. None of them have quite the compulsion of school, although some children undoubtedly participate in them under parental pressure.

Organized supervised groups have certain characteristics in common that set them off from the natural peer group. Foremost among these is the predictability of their activities. Each organization or supervised activity tends to have a certain objective, sometimes formulated on a national level and available in printed form. The program is carried out under adult leadership; even when the members make their own plans they do so within limits set by the organization or the leader. The groups meet at a fixed place at stated times. They own equipment bought by or given to the group, with ownership remaining under adult control. This property is not subject to disposal or unauthorized use by members.

The actions of members are also predictable. Leaders replace parents as agents of control. The program tends to bridge the gap between the lessening control of parents and the emergence of the self-control of adulthood. Members are stabilized in their activities, fixed in the ways of conformity to some larger and more formal social group. Meetings are not occasions for letting off steam or planning deviant activities. Youth who do not want to conform may drop out or be dropped from the group, just as youth drop out of school—another conforming group.

Parents view the supervised groups as secure places for their children, who otherwise might run the streets or get into "bad company." The leaders tend to be of the same social class as the parents and hence reinforce the teachings of the parents. Programs also tend to be middle-class in objectives and practices. Therefore, supervised groups are a bulwark against deviant behavior.

Children receive many satisfactions from supervised and organized groups. Accustomed to adult supervision at home and in school, middle-class children do not resent the leader, who may in fact bring some release from strict parental supervision. The organizations gather together children of the same age and sex into a wider scope of activities than they would be permitted without supervision. The child identifies with the leader, internalizes the values and works for the goals, and proudly wears the uniform, scarf, badge, and pin that symbolize common values and unity. If the organization has prestige among other middle-class children and adults, each member feels security of social status. Thus despite their formality, organized groups serve many of the functions of natural peer groups.

Unsupervised peer groups. In addition to organized groups, many middle-class children also belong to natural peer groups. The time left over from school and organized activities, however, is often meager. Many of the peer groups are small clusters of friends meeting at the homes of different members. In childhood, they are not likely to be free-roaming groups. Not until adolescence do middle-class children achieve much autonomy in their group activities, and even then freedom of action tends to be contained within the middle-class area of tolerance.

However, no social class can provide for complete control. Tensions arise, for individuals or for groups, which may be worked off individually or through unsupervised groups. In time, patterns of behavior may arise to facilitate adjustment. These are supported by the age and sex group but may be unknown to adults. Sometimes these special patterns of behavior, originating in the youth group itself, are referred to as a youth culture, or

1 W. Ward Cramer, "Leisure Time Activities of Economically Privileged Children," *Sociology and Social Research,* 34 (1949–1950), 444–450.

adolescent subculture. They are, however, chiefly temporary deviations from the class subculture, sufficiently minor to permit the adolescent to return to full acceptance by his social class at any time.

The unsupervised peer group provides the locus for certain types of juvenile delinquency. The group builds up standards of what may and may not be done; it thus exerts controls over the actions of individual members. It also shields each member with a shroud of secrecy from outside prying. Conformity to the group norms and expectations brings status and approval. And finally, the group action gives courage to the faltering individual. Unlike the lower-class youth, the middle-class youth sees little of delinquency and crime in his home or immediate neighborhood. He is relatively unfamiliar with arrests and court hearings. Therefore a foray into delinquency is for him a more daring and fearful experience than it is for the lower-class youth.

Middle-class delinquencies

Discussion of middle-class delinquency is largely speculative and pertains primarily to males. In view of the lack of precise data, discussion is limited to two types: attempts to attain middle-class goals through violation of mores and attempts to become adult when the mores prescribe continued adolescence.

Cheating. Continued education as a secondary goal to future success and as a matter of family pride may come to have exaggerated importance to the middle-class adolescent. Remaining in school becomes more important than actual success in academic work. Failure blocks future education and is regarded as a disgrace to the entire family. Children and youth who do not have the ability or desire to make the effort to pass a course look for some "out." The lower-class child in a similar position truants or drops out of school as soon as he legally can without feelings of guilt or family disapproval. The middle-class boy often finds his solution in cheating. The lower-class boy who persistently truants is handled as a delinquent; the middle-class boy who persistently cheats is at most penalized by the school. Cheating, strictly speaking a type of dishonesty, is tolerated and condoned so long as the student remains in school.

Most of what is known about cheating comes from college students, who are prima-

rily middle-class. The prevalence of cheating and its approval by youth is shown by a study made in a small urban college. Fifty-seven per cent of the students and 75 per cent of all seniors cheated on examinations.[1] Cheating was not regarded as basically dishonest by 53 per cent of the students; only 13 per cent thought it was basically dishonest, and 33 per cent were uncertain of their attitudes. Only 12 per cent said they would report cheating, although the honor system demanded that they do so.

Teachers tend to be lenient toward cheaters. In one college where cheating could lead to expulsion this measure was rarely used. Some teachers talked to cheating students and then permitted them to complete their tests; others felt that the students' ethics were not their concern; still others expressed the opinion that students represented a lower class than the professors and that nothing better could be expected of them. Other evidence suggests that some teachers may be lenient because they themselves cheated in college. An investigation in New York in 1960 uncovered the commercialization of cheating on term papers, theses, and examinations, whereby "ghostwriting agencies" prepared papers or sent someone to take a test on almost any subject for fees ranging from $12.50 to one fee of $3,000. The clients of these agencies included public school teachers working for advanced degrees and increases in salary as well as students seeking admission to professional schools. Parents also were found among the clients, purchasing papers and book reports for their children.[2]

It seems that cheating is a type of dishonesty supported by middle-class ambition for success and is tolerated by adults. In fact it might be said that cheating permeates a number of areas of middle-class life among adults as well as children. Income tax evasion and failure to observe business ethics under the pressure of competition are examples. In these ways, children and adults alike who would regard taking money or property as criminal seek to gain an advantage for themselves in order to attain or maintain certain middle-class goals.

1 Marvin L. Hendricks, "Changing Mores Concerning Cheating on Examinations," *School and Society,* 86 (1958), 413–414.
2 "At Exam Time—Cheating in College: How Much and How Bad," *U. S. News and World Report,* 48 (May 23, 1960), 108–112.

Cheating may be an individual activity, although supported by the large peer group of youth. However, it may be supported and furthered by small peer groups or, in college, by fraternities which accumulate and retain for the use of the members past examination questions and term papers.

The automobile-alcohol-sex combination. Much of the misconduct attributed to middle-class adolescents is a perversion of normal adult activities to serve irregular adolescent functions during the period when adolescents are ready in many ways for adulthood but are held in a nebulous preadult status. A prominent type of middle-class misconduct (sometimes reaching the proportions of delinquency) is the co-ordinated behavior system built up around the automobile, alcohol, and sex behavior. Whereas in the adult middle class these three items serve some utilitarian functions and are brought under the control of a co-ordinated pattern of life, among adolescents they are detached from utilitarian functions and adult goals. One formulation points out that cars, used mainly for transportation by adults, are used mainly for pleasure by adolescents.[1] Examples are speeding, drag racing on public highways, parking with a girl for sexual purposes, and playing "chicken." The latter is a "game" whereby two cars are driven rapidly toward each other as though for a collision. The driver who first turns aside to avoid a crash is "chicken." Occasionally neither driver is "chicken," and a head-on collison results. "Borrowing" someone's car without permission is justified by the statement that the borrower only wanted the car for a little fun and did not intend to keep it. Speeding, racing, and playing "chicken" all break the speed laws; "borrowing" a car is theft.

Uninhibited and usually illegal use of alcohol is another aspect of the middle-class teen-age behavior system. The customary restrained social use of alcoholic beverages among middle-class adults tends to become unrestrained among youth. Alcoholic drinks are obtained illegally: some hanger-on at a tavern is bribed to buy bottled liquor for under-age youths, or adolescents surreptitiously and without permission take bottles from their parents' supply. Others lie about their age, falsify birth certificates to show they are of legal age to buy liquor, or borrow a birth certificate from an older companion.

The third component, sex, is usually detached from any sense of personal responsibility in its earliest manifestations. Also, it tends to cut across social-class lines. Middle-class adolescent boys tend to have their first sex experiences with prostitutes or with pick-ups, almost invariably members of the lower class. Only when they become a little more mature and have developed lasting dating relationships with girls of their own class do they begin to have intercourse with middle-class girls. Underlying motivations for teen-age boys are curiosity about an exciting experience of which they have heard from other boys and the desire to prove to themselves and their male friends that they are virile, masculine, and mature. The first sex experience, especially, is often shared by a group of boys who are friends.[2] By constant talk and daring they nerve themselves to the point of entering a house of prostitution and arranging to visit the prostitutes. Some boys find their first sex experience with pick-ups; usually a small group of boys cruise around in a car until they find a girl who rather obviously is inviting an approach. They drive to a secluded spot, and one by one the boys have intercourse with the girl.

The early shared sex experiences serve a number of functions for the boys. Whether or not the experience has been satisfying, the boys brag about it afterward in the group. They build up status within the group and pride themselves on having achieved sophistication and maturity. Also, the group nature of the experience serves to solidify the group and to increase the members' sense of identification. The sense of group unity is limited to the boys. The girl is a transient in her contact with the group. The boys often never see her again; in fact, if the girl shows any desire to establish a pair contact with one of them, she is usually dropped immediately. For the boys, the meaning of the shared experience is entirely different from other sexual relationships held exclusively with one girl on the basis of friendship with the girl. In these relationships the girl is very likely to be near or of the boy's own social-class status.

Whatever the type of partner, middle-class

1 Ralph W. England, Jr., "A Theory of Middle Class Juvenile Delinquency," *Journal of Criminal Law, Criminology and Police Science*, 50 (1960), 535–540.

2 Lester A. Kirkendall, *Premarital Intercourse and Interpersonal Relationships*, manuscript.

boys tend to regard sexual activity as a masculine prerogative. Prostitutes regard it as a way to make a living; pick-ups are looking for physical pleasure, adventure, and sometimes a temporary feeling of being wanted. Middle-class girls try to find a more idealistic justification, usually the belief that they are in love or that intercourse is the preliminary to marriage.[1]

The sexual activities of middle-class adolescents sometimes come to light not through arrests but through venereal disease infections whose symptoms have taken the adolescent to a physician. The types and degrees of involvement are shown in the following case, which emphasizes the sexual involvement.[2]

Nineteen white boys, ranging in age from fifteen to seventeen, were all in school when they first came to professional attention. They lived in a large city where their fathers were employed in an aircraft industry, owned and operated their businesses, or were professional men. They lived in a good residential area, where all but one of the families were homeowners. There were no broken homes. The boys were better than average in school work and were active in school affairs, including athletics. They carried on their recreational activities together, spending two evenings each week at a popular teen-age hangout where the curfew was not observed and where they could learn of parties that they might crash. The boys were accustomed to sexual intercourse, the average age of first experience being fourteen. They rationalized their sexual activities on the basis that they were "natural." Four of the boys had also had some homosexual experience. The parents were apparently unaware of their sons' activities until a sixteen-year-old boy, Jack, went to a clinic for aid because of painful symptoms, which turned out to be the result of a gonorrheal infection contracted from a prostitute. He passed the infection on to Phyllis, a fifteen-year-old junior high school student who had begun her sexual activities two years before. She was a mediocre stu-

dent with a history of truancy. Her father, an engineer, had a good reputation and was active in church affairs, as indeed Phyllis was also. Her mother was a patient in a mental institution. Phyllis was a complacent sexual partner and seemed to have no moral scruples regarding sexual intercourse with a variety of boys. Jack accordingly introduced his eighteen friends to her in the course of two weeks. Several became infected.

For many adolescents the automobile, alcohol, and sex are woven into a co-ordinated system of behavior that becomes habitual, well rationalized, and widely diffused. The automobile not only provides a means for excitement but puts miles between the occupants and the sources of adult controls; it also provides a private lounge for drinking and for petting or sex episodes. Alcohol releases inhibitions built up against sex activities and reduces the ordinary precautions against dangerous driving. It is not known how widely this behavior system has permeated the middle-class adolescent population. Certainly many adolescents do not subscribe to it or are only mildly or occasionally involved.

The peer group forms the little social world in which much of the automobile-alcohol-sex combination of behavior takes place. It is rationalized by the peer group and passed on from one member of a group to another.

Although the automobile-drinking-sex system of behavior contains many legal violations, the behavior is not regarded as illegal or reprehensible by adolescents. They do not place it in the same category as stealing or assaults, but rather as private personal behavior. Many adults take the same view. If the adolescent is otherwise meeting his middle-class obligations and making progress toward future goals, his week-end indiscretions are overlooked. Thus middle-class adolescent misconduct, whether outrightly illegal or simply unrestrained, comes within the area of tolerance of the middle class.

Hypotheses of the automobile-alcohol-sex type of misconduct. Little organized objective research has touched on middle-class delinquency. Various hypotheses have been advanced, pertaining especially to the automobile-alcohol-sex behavior pattern.

1. The age-sex identification hypothesis. According to this hypothesis, the middle-class boy has difficulty in changing from his

---

1 Albert J. Reiss, "Sex Offenses: The Marginal Status of the Adolescent," *Law and Contemporary Problems,* (Spring, 1960), 310–333.

2 *Venereal Disease in Children and Youth,* U. S. Department of Health, Education, and Welfare, Public Health Service, Bureau of State Services Communicable Disease Center, Atlanta, Georgia (undated, statistics include 1959), pp. 18–19.

childhood identification with his mother, female teachers, and other women who supervise him to an adult masculine identification. The situation grows out of present urban conditions, in which men have little time to spend with their sons. In addition, the long continued education of middle-class boys keeps them under female supervision almost to manhood and prevents association with men in work. The adolescent boy rebels against his feminine identification. Since he identifies the feminine role with goodness and the masculine role with toughness, he tends to repudiate goodness and to cultivate tough attitudes and behavior. However, middle-class values oppose physical toughness and violence. Therefore, runs the hypothesis, he seeks expression of masculine toughness in danger-courting activities such as playing "chicken," racing, or sexual orgies.[1]

2. Another hypothesis is opposed to the age-sex role hypothesis. England contends that middle-class boys are not so thoroughly identified with a feminine role that they must rebel against it through symbolic over identification with the masculine role. He contends that a more or less independent teen-age culture is emerging from our general culture, functional to teen-agers but often in opposition to the values of the general culture.[2]

He traces the emergence of the teen-age culture or behavior system to the fact that for a century or more American society has gradually squeezed teen-agers out of the productive economy, without providing an alternative role yielding satisfactory status and importance to society. Because they are neither children nor adults, adolescents play at being adults, but their play has no significance for the adult-organized society. The teen-age behavior system has gained strength, especially since World War II, through the ease with which adolescent fads and activities shuttle back and forth across the country via television, motion pictures,

magazines, and newspaper stories that either cater to adolescent tastes or discuss their problems.

Moreover, adolescents have more money to spend than ever before, and the new market is being carefully exploited by commercial and entertainment organizations which offer uniformly to teen-agers in all parts of the country the same popular music, reading material, and distinctive clothing.

Adolescents tend to develop a closed social world of their own, in which they develop not only their own types of entertainment and clothing, but their own status system, codes of behavior, and methods of control. Much of their behavior seems irresponsible to adults (not necessarily delinquent) but since it is approved by the adolescent social world it has functional value for adolescents. As adolescents mature and are admitted to the adult world they leave behind the foibles of the adolescent social world.

3. A third attempt to explain middle-class delinquency, again chiefly on the basis of the pleasure-seeking automobile-alcohol-sex combination, comes from Walter B. Miller, who regards such delinquency as an upward diffusion of lower-income attitudes and activities.[3] Much of the diffusion comes by way of songs and music, originating in the Negro lower class, passed along to the white lower class, and adopted by middle-class whites with some adaptations to middle-class standards. These songs especially emphasize Negro lower-class sexual and marriage patterns—unmarried lovers, desertion, and blighted romance. They are diffused upward primarily through such mass media as radio and records. Styles of dress, manners, and slang are also diffused upward through motion pictures and fiction. Toughness, daring, indulgence, hardness, and autonomy are listed by Miller as lower-class traits which have diffused upward.

In lower-class subculture the above characteristics are functional in meeting life situations. As middle-class youth modify them to fit the middle-class subculture they become fads, one of whose functions is to shock and distress parents and other adults. They are thus a symbol of rebellion against the domination of the adult generation.

Miller does not regard the adoption of

---

1 For a discussion of this point of view see Albert K. Cohen, *Delinquent Boys, The Culture of the Gang,* Free Press, Glencoe, Illinois, 1955, pp. 157–159; Cohen and James F. Short, Jr., "Research in Delinquent Subcultures," *Journal of Social Issues,* 14 (1958), 28. The theoretical basis for the age-sex role hypothesis comes from Talcott Parsons, "Certain Primary Sources and Patterns of Aggression in the Social Structure of the Western World," *Psychiatry,* 10 (1947), 167–181; Parsons, "Age and Sex in the Social Structure of the United States," *American Sociological Review,* 7 (1942), 604–616.

2 England, *op. cit.*

3 Kvaraceus and Miller, *op. cit.,* pp. 79–84.

these lower-class characteristics by middle-class youth as a new manifestation; youth have been restless in times past and have used many other fads to express their inner turmoil. His implication is that when lower-class diffusion passes away some other fad will replace it.

4. A fourth hypothesis to account for much adolescent delinquency is that in all cultures adolescents undergo tensions during the period in which they pass from adolescent to adult status. The intensity of the experience is related to the period of time between biological maturity and actual admission into adulthood (a long period in the United States for the middle-class youth), when insecurities and uncertainties beset the adolescent. Many societies use institutionalized ceremonies, rites, rituals, and tests in which each youth participates when he reaches a given age. Having passed through these ceremonies and tests, the youth is considered an adult, ready to share the privileges and responsibilities of the adult world. In the United States, such institutionalized ceremonies are lacking, and the adolescent is left to flounder as best he can. Adolescents seek out symbols and rituals to define their status, courage, maturity, and readiness for adult life. They accept artificial symbols of adult life, specifically, the automobile, liquor, and illicit sex activity.[1]

Limitations of the hypotheses. The four hypotheses—none as yet adequately supported by research—have several limitations.

1. All hinge on one pattern of adolescent behavior—that of automobiles, alcohol, and sex. This pattern is similar to adult vice in that it is essentially self-harmful rather than harmful to others. It tends to differ from adult vice in that it usually does not become deeply ingrained and usually is a transitory deviation from approved middle-class values and norms. Other types of delinquency (for example, cheating to attain middle-class goals) are ignored by the theorists.

2. The theories are limited to behavior of the adolescent period. Pre- and postadolescent individuals are not covered by the hypotheses.

3. The social conditions cited as account-

able for delinquency are presented as general among middle-class youth. No attempt is made to explain why some youth respond with rebellion and delinquency while others conform to approved behavior.

4. The delinquencies cited and the hypotheses are primarily applicable to boys.

5. In no case has empirical research actually been carried out to prove or disprove the validity of any of the four hypotheses. It is not even known how widely diffused the automobile-alcohol-sex behavior system is among middle-class youth. The behavior is self-contained within the middle class, tolerated by adults, and rarely leads to a court appearance. The hypotheses are discussed at some length here because they indicate an increased awareness of deviant behavior among middle-class youth.

Upper-class delinquency

Very little precise knowledge is available about juvenile delinquency among upper-class children and youth. Maps showing rates of court appearances indicate that the lowest rates tend to be in upper-class residential areas.[2] From general studies of social-class subcultures one would infer that there actually is less delinquency, that much of what occurs is contained within the institutional framework of the upper class, and that police tend to turn delinquents over to their parents.

Upper-class values. The core of the upper class has been securely anchored in its position for at least several generations. The impress of the subculture on children comes with the weight of authority and tradition.[3]

1. Highly valued is the sense of the family's continuity and of belonging to the kinship group. Authority is vested in the older members of the kinship, who often control the financial resources. Pride of family acts as a restraint on the child's behavior. Motivation is not for future individual success (as in the middle class) but for the maintenance of family prestige and honor.

2. The family takes the initiative in plan-

1 Herbert A. Bloch and Arthur Niederhoffer, *The Gang, A Study in Adolescent Behavior*, Philosophical Library, New York, 1958, pp. 17–18, 25–31. Chapter 4 gives a survey of puberty rites in primitive societies and Chapter 5 some contemporary counterparts.

2 Clifford R. Shaw, Henry McKay, and Associates, *Juvenile Delinquency and Urban Areas*, University of Chicago Press, Chicago, Illinois, 1942.
3 Based primarily on Ruth Shonle Cavan, *The American Family*, Thomas Y. Crowell Company, 1953, Chapter 5.

ning the child's life. The son attends the same university as his father and enters the family profession or business. Supervision from childhood on is close. The upper-class child usually attends a private school with other upper-class children. His social life is circumscribed by upper-class private clubs and camps. He is insulated against contacts with children of other subcultures.

3. The security of each member of the family is important—not only financial security but also protection from criticism or arrest. The kinship family tends to be a self-contained community, looking after all the needs of all members, worthy or unworthy. This family protection may become a license to disregard of the law on the part of a few members of the family, or of youth before they settle into responsible adult roles.

The constraints placed on children and youth by these kinship values and their implementation are eased by the vast possibilities for satisfactions offered by families with secure social positions and ample money. It is part of the upper-class mores that money should be conserved and increased; nevertheless, there is no need to scrimp or sacrifice present pleasures for future financial needs. Profligacy is discouraged, but expenditures on the scale normal within the upper-class subculture are expected and encouraged. Social life, camping, hobbies, and travel with the family are normal for the younger child; a sports car, a boat, and foreign travel are often given to the older youth, while they follow sports such as skiing, polo, skeet, and sailing.

Misbehavior and delinquency. The behavior of which the upper-class itself disapproves strongly is the violation of upper-class mores; it may or may not also include a violation of law. The temptation to steal is less urgent than in many other groups, and therefore experiences with the police are less likely to occur. Much of the control of delinquency is in the hands of parents, tutors, and school personnel. The child who exceeds the limits of toleration is sent to a private residential school, the adolescent to a military school. The family thus takes over some of the functions of the juvenile court with its power to commit a child to a public correctional school. Other misbehaving children are defined as maladjusted rather than delinquent and are placed under the care of a private psychiatrist. Financial restitution is made for property damage or to appease an outraged victim. In many ways the upper class does its own policing, punishing, and rehabilitating, guiding the child back into the upper-class patterns of behavior.

Social class and delinquency

The social-class subcultures do not give a complete explanation of delinquency, but they form the broad background within which delinquency operates. Each social class has within its subculture the seeds of certain types of delinquency. In each class the process of socialization bears heavily on children and creates dissatisfactions and frustrations. Each class condones certain evasions and exaggerations, which often are ways to attain certain personal satisfactions or class values without all the rigors of following prescribed procedures. These delinquencies are tolerated by the class that generates them, but not necessarily by other classes or by the common culture of the society.

Many adolescents in all classes seem to have special problems in the transition from childhood to adulthood. The standards and the approved means of reaching the standards differ from class to class. In each class some adolescents, as they fumble their way to the coveted status, violate some laws and some of the mores of their class. Often the misconduct is some form of self-indulgence viewed by adolescents as proof of manhood. Usually the social class is tolerant in its attitudes, so long as the adolescents are moving toward fulfillment of the goals of adulthood.

Although some delinquency is of an individual nature (see Chapter 13), the class-typed delinquency tends to be imbedded in youth peer groups. Generally, the deviant behavior systems of a class spread across the country, giving local groups the feeling of having the support and approval of all youth. Specifically, the deviations in a given community are carried out by peer groups operating on a friendship basis without organization or formal structure. The members know who is in their group and they respond to natural leaders, but they rarely have a name or elected officers. At most, the membership is circumscribed by the custom of meeting at some favored spot at a given time.

Bibliography

Bloch, Herbert A., and Arthur Niederhoffer, *The Gang, A Study of Adolescent Behavior,* Philosophical Library, New York, 1958.

Bohlke, Robert H., "Social Mobility, Stratification Inconsistency and Middle Class Delinquency," *Social Problems,* 8 (1961), 351–363.

Cavan, Ruth Shonle, *American Family,* Thomas Y. Crowell Company, New York, 1953, Chapter 5.

England, Ralph W., Jr., "A Theory of Middle Class Juvenile Delinquency," *Journal of Criminal Law, Criminology and Police Science,* 50 (1960), 535–540.

Kvaraceus, William C., and Walter B. Miller, *Delinquent Behavior, Culture and the Individual,* National Education Association of the United States, Washington, D. C., 1959.

Loeb, Martin B., "Implications of Status Differentiation for Personal and Social Development," *Harvard Educational Review,* 23, No. 3 (Summer, 1953), 168–174.

Parsons, Talcott, "Certain Primary Sources and Patterns of Aggression in the Social Structure of the Western World," *Psychiatry,* 10 (1947), 167–181.

———, "Age and Sex in the Social Structure of the United States," *American Sociological Review,* 7 (1942), 604–616.

Reiss, Albert J., "Sex Offenses: The Marginal Status of the Adolescent," *Law and Contemporary Problems* (Spring, 1960), 310–333.

Shaw, Clifford R., and Associates, *Delinquency Areas,* University of Chicago Press, Chicago, 1929.

———, Henry D. McKay, and Associates, *Juvenile Delinquency and Urban Areas,* University of Chicago Press, Chicago, 1942.

The delinquency of girls is of a different kind than the delinquency of boys. Delinquency of boys reflects young male aspirations on the one hand and social expectations on the other. In similar manner, the delinquency of girls is closely related to feminine aspirations and social expectations for girls. Certain connections draw the masculine and the feminine patterns of delinquency together, especially during adolescence, just as the ordinary social activities of boys and girls begin to merge during adolescence. In other words, delinquency of boys and of girls is part of the total life organization for the two sexes as decreed by the particular subculture in which the adolescent lives.

Characteristics of girl delinquency

As was pointed out in Chapter 3, about four boys appear before juvenile courts for every one girl. Although police juvenile officers are more likely to release young girls than boys without a court hearing, or to refer the girl directly to a social agency, this differential treatment accounts for only part of the differences in court cases. Even in socially disorganized areas, girls do not have the free run of the community to the same extent as boys; the family control is greater for girls; the social expectations differ.

Types of delinquency. These differences in the roles of boys and girls in the family and the community are reflected in the types of delinquency characteristic of boys and girls. The delinquencies of boys are overt and aggressive, in the form of thefts or malicious mischief carried out in public places. Girls are primarily in a struggle with adult authority, which they express in incorrigibility or by running away. Sexual promiscuity also is often entered on the girl's record of delinquency, but not on the boy's, although boys are fully as prone to this behavior as girls. Injury to another person is very rare for both boys and girls.

Early beginnings of delinquency. Little girls as well as little boys begin delinquent behavior in early childhood. Police pick up both boys and girls as young as six or seven years, although they do not usually refer them to the juvenile court at these early ages. Delinquency for both boys and girls reaches its highest point during adolescence; girls'

cases especially tend to be concentrated at ages thirteen and over.

This concentration is related to changes in the type of delinquency as girls pass from childhood into adolescence. A Detroit study shows that girls below the age of twelve were guilty primarily of stealing small objects, usually through shoplifting—the same offense for which little boys are usually picked up.[1] With early adolescence girls were referred to the police primarily for incorrigibility, truancy from home, and some sex offenses. In mid-adolescence, girls were most frequently charged with sex offenses and disorderly conduct, with some continuation of incorrigibility and truancy from home. Boys in the meantime had shifted from petty thievery to more serious kinds of stealing and some instances of assault.

The above discussion of differences between boy and girl delinquencies is based on percentages of the total number of delinquent boys or delinquent girls. However, since boys exceed girls greatly in numbers, in no type of delinquency do more girls than boys commit the offense. Figure 6 shows the percentage of offenses committed by boys and girls in Onondaga County, New York. Not even in the typically feminine offenses of ungoverna-

---

1 William W. Wattenberg and Frank Saunders, "Sex Differences among Juvenile Offenders," *Sociology and Social Research*, 39 (1954), 24–31; Wattenberg, "Differences Between Girl and Boy Repeaters," *Journal of Educational Psychology*, 47 (March, 1956), 137–146.

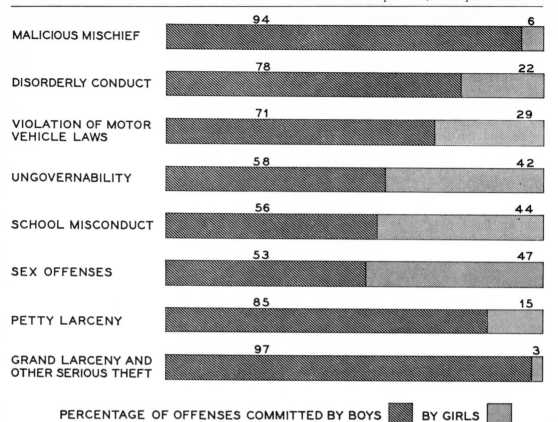

MALICIOUS MISCHIEF 94 | 6

DISORDERLY CONDUCT 78 | 22

VIOLATION OF MOTOR VEHICLE LAWS 71 | 29

UNGOVERNABILITY 58 | 42

SCHOOL MISCONDUCT 56 | 44

SEX OFFENSES 53 | 47

PETTY LARCENY 85 | 15

GRAND LARCENY AND OTHER SERIOUS THEFT 97 | 3

PERCENTAGE OF OFFENSES COMMITTED BY BOYS ▨   BY GIRLS ▨

Figure 6. Percentage of Offenses of Each Type Committed by Boys or Girls, Onondaga County, New York, 1957–1958. (Data from R. H. Hardt, *A Delinquency Profile of Syracuse and Onondaga County, New York, 1957–1958*)

bility, school misconduct, and sex offenses do girls exceed boys in number.[1]

Lack of studies of delinquent girls

Almost no studies have been made of delinquency among girls or of delinquent girls themselves. All the mammoth delinquency studies, such as those of the Gluecks, have been limited to boys.[2]

The discussion of delinquency among girls therefore must be based on fragmentary re-

1 Onondaga County, New York, was selected because it has been carefully studied, and published statistics are available.
2 In 1934, Sheldon and Eleanor Glueck published *Five Hundred Delinquent Women*, Alfred A. Knopf, New York, which dealt with women who had been in the Massachusetts Reformatory for Women. However, none of their many studies has been on delinquent girls.

ports and general, rather speculative knowledge of social and personal factors in the development of girls.

Several reasons may be suggested for the greater emphasis on studying the delinquent behavior of boys. The recurrent frequency of male delinquency generates a greater source of social disorganization. In addition, many juvenile delinquents continue their misconduct and become the adult criminals of the next decade. Since adult male criminals exceed adult female criminals eight to one (double the ratio for juvenile delinquents), the assumption is that boys are more likely to continue into adult criminality than are girls. Moreover, the offenses of boys attack some of our most cherished values, since they usually involve destruction or theft of someone else's property. Girls' offenses primarily tend to harm themselves and are often outgrown as the girls reach a level of maturity where they are no longer in school or under the authority of parents. Minor sex offenses (promiscuity) are often curbed by marriage.

Actually, a valid point could be made that girl delinquency is a more serious problem than boy delinquency. If girls carry their problems into marriage, their lack of adjustment may affect the rearing of their children, sons as well as daughters. The chapter on the family emphasizes the influence that mothers have on the conduct of their sons. One way to curb the delinquency of boys might be to give more attention to the delinquency of girls.

Social backgrounds of delinquent girls

One of the early studies of Chicago, which established the location of high-delinquency areas included an ecological map of the residences of delinquent girls who had appeared before the juvenile court during 1917–1923. The distribution of rates resembles that for boy delinquents. The highest rates were in certain areas adjacent to the central business district, populated primarily by newly arrived immigrant groups; high rates also extended into a concentrated Negro slum area. The rates declined toward the periphery of the city as local communities increased in socio-economic status. When rates for boys and girls are compared by square-mile areas, a great similarity is evident; in general, areas with high boy rates also have high girl rates, so much so, in fact, that the correlation between the two series of rates is 0.79 ± 1.024.[1] Studies made in the twenties and thirties of other cities—Cincinnati, Seattle, Minneapolis, St. Paul—show the similarity between the geographic distribution of rates for boys and girls.[2] For only one of these cities, Cincinnati, is the correlation between the boys' and the girls' series of rates given. It is $.95 \pm .01$, showing an even closer correspondence of high and low rate areas for boys and girls than was shown for Chicago.

In general, delinquency among girls flourishes in the same lower-class and especially culturally disorganized and socially deprived areas that contribute to the delinquency of boys. Certainly in these areas there are examples of adult female crime as judged by arrest rates as well as of all types of male delinquency and crime.[3]

1 Clifford R. Shaw and Associates, *Delinquency Areas,* University of Chicago Press, Chicago, 1929, pp. 137–160.
2 Clifford R. Shaw and Henry D. McKay, *Juvenile Delinquency and Urban Areas,* University of Chicago Press, Chicago, 1942, pp. 250, 363, 419, citing studies made by Norman S. Hayner and Calvin F. Schmid.
3 Ernest R. Mowrer, *Disorganization, Personal and Social,* J. B. Lippincott Company, Philadelphia, 1942, pp. 181–183.

Although the correlation between rates for different areas is very high, it is not complete. In each city a few areas noted for high rates for boys have low rates for girls, or vice versa. Cultural and social factors may account for such differences.

Types of delinquency by social class

The influence of social-class and ethnic subcultures on delinquency has been demonstrated for boys; such influence is also evident in girl delinquency. Since the subcultural values and customs for girls differ from those for boys, the direction of pressure also differs.

Middle-class girls. Although middle-class girls approach equality with boys in many respects, certain restrictions are made which affect actual misconduct and define what is allowed. In general, girls have less freedom of movement than boys, that is, they are more carefully and continuously supervised than boys. It is contrary to middle-class mores for girls, individually or in small cliques, to leave their homes, especially in the evenings, unless their mothers know with whom they will be, where they are going, and when they will probably return home. Underlying these restrictions is the primary middle-class goal for girls—a good marriage. The girl who is talked about, who is not respected, who is known or thought to be sexually promiscuous, or who becomes pregnant before marriage loses much of her value as a potential mate. The exception is perhaps the practice of sex relations between a couple in love who are soon to be married; this justification rarely applies to the middle-teen girl, however, since she is regarded as a school girl whose main objective is the completion of her education. The pressure of cultural concepts then on the girl is toward obedience to parents, restriction of activities, and conformity to the mores, especially the sexual mores.[4]

The middle-class girl does not feel pressure to assert herself competitively in preparation for future money-making. Most middle-class girls expect the husband to be the main support of the family, the dominant one in making decisions, and the protector against the harshness of the outside world. They may plan to work before they have children or

4 Ira L. Reiss, *Premarital Sexual Standards in America,* Free Press, Glencoe, Illinois, 1960. This book examines in detail the various shades of meaning given to different types of premarital sex relations, especially in the middle class.

after the children are in school, but they regard their income as secondary to that of the husband.

The girl learns these self-concepts and the corresponding roles from her mother. The approved middle-class girl is the one who accepts her mother as her model. The point is often made that the middle-class boy first models after his mother and his female teachers, and in adolescence must break this identification in order to achieve a masculine identification. The girl is not called upon to make such a transition. If she internalizes her mother's teachings and patterns her conduct accordingly, she moves smoothly from childhood through adolescence into adulthood, retaining her mother as her model.

These cultural expectations place certain strains on some middle-class girls. If her mother holds the reins of supervision too tightly or if the girl cannot accept her mother as a model, she may defy her mother and remain away from home late at night, date boys of whom her mother does not approve, or become a partner of some boy in the automobile-alcohol-sex combination already discussed in Chapter 8 as typical of delinquency among middle-class boys. If she associates her women teachers with her mother, she may defy them also. She is very likely to feel rejected and, in fact, may be rejected because of her behavior.

She may also be rejected by other middle-class girls, who adhere to the cultural code. She may find friends among other rejected girls or she may turn to boys to give meaning to her life. Her contacts with boys are unlikely to be with those selected and supervised by parents, teachers, and youth leaders. Lacking both love and confidence in herself, she grasps eagerly for the attention of boys. Heavy petting and sometimes sex relations on a casual and permissive basis follow. She may not be widely promiscuous, but her relationships with boys are not backed by mutual affection or a feeling of responsibility on the part of the boy (as is often true when a boy and girl who are in love or fond of each other engage in heavy petting or intercourse). Her actions are self-defeating, however, since the boy who may trade on her sexual permissiveness at the same time often crosses her from his list of admired girls, eligible for marriage with him at some later date.

The girl who has reached this point is violating middle-class mores and delinquency laws at several points. She is considered "ungovernable" by her parents and teachers, and legally she is a sexual offender. Her violations of the code are likely not to extend to public disorderliness and may be known only in her school, to her parents, and to a limited group of other adolescents. Middle-class adults are less likely to look upon her as a delinquent than as a misguided, troubled, maladjusted adolescent who needs help. She is quite likely to be referred to a child guidance clinic or a private psychiatrist. Even if parents in desperation refer her to the juvenile court as incorrigible or she is caught by police in some escapade, she is very likely to be handled informally or referred to a social agency rather than to receive a formal hearing in the juvenile court.

Considerable effort is expended to bring the middle-class girl delinquent back into the framework of the subculture, to restore her respectability, and to improve her potential to be marriageable.

One hypothesis advanced to explain middle-class boy delinquency is also applicable to girls, that of England, which supports the concept of a middle-class youth "culture," operating to serve functions of youth but not applicable—even repulsive—to adult middle-class people.[1] This hypothesis seems more appropriate as an explanation for the vagaries of youth than for outright delinquency.

Lower-class girls. The cultural expectation for lower-class girls, as for middle-class girls, is marriage. However, lower-class girls tend to leave school as soon as possible and to be married by the mid- or late teens. The road to marriage often includes several types of sex relations.[2] One is a casual, unromantic relationship with a boy or man higher in the social-class scale. The higher-class youth is looking for uncomplicated sexual pleasure; the girl for an evening of fun, which the youth will provide and for which he is compensated by sexual privileges. These episodes

1 See Chapter 8.
2 An excellent discussion of sexual offenses of lower-class girls is contained in Albert J. Reiss, "Sex Offenses: The Marginal Status of the Adolescent," *Law and Contemporary Problems*, 25 (1960), 309–333. See also Winston W. Ehrmann, "Influence of Comparative Social Class of Companion upon Premarital Heterosexual Behavior," *Marriage and Family Living*, 17 (1955), 48–53; August B. Hollingshead, *Elmtown's Youth*, John Wiley and Sons, New York, 1949, Chapters 9, 12, 15, 16.

are concealed from her family and friends.

Another type of sex experience of the lower-class girl is with youth of her own class and near her own age. These are casual events, without romance or obligation if the girl should become pregnant. In Elmtown, a city of 7,000, boys typically drove to nearby towns where they were accepted as partners for the evening by local girls. Meanwhile, Elmtown girls were accepting partners from other cities. Both boys and girls thus preserved their reputation among their friends in their own cities. In large cities, girls must also be circumspect, since a reputation for promiscuity or prostitution lowers the girl's prospects for marriage and increases the chance of arrest.

Finally, lower-class girls and boys eventually reach a marriageable age—the girl in the mid- or late teens, the boy in his late teens or early twenties. With a steady, affectionate relationship, sexual relations are anticipated and less concealment is necessary. If the girl becomes pregnant, marriage follows as a matter of course.

Cases of individual girls show that sexual relations, carried out with circumspection, do not usually lead to arrest. If the girl makes sexual activities a central part of her life, becomes publicly conspicuous in securing partners, and seems on the road to prostitution, she is more likely to be arrested. Sometimes, sexual relations are only one part of a wider pattern of related delinquent activities. For example, a girl is in conflict with her parents and teachers; she runs away from home to another city or to a different part of her own city if it is large. She is immediately faced with the need for money. Since she is still of school age she cannot find work. She may then solve the problem of money for a room, food, and other necessities by permitting herself to be picked up by men whom she meets around taverns. Some shoplifting or petty larceny supplies a supplement. In time she is very likely to be arrested. In many cities it is routine for such a girl to be given a physical examination which will reveal whether she has had intercourse, is pregnant, or has a venereal disease. She may then be charged with being a sexual offender, although her illegal sexual activities are simply part of a wider pattern of misbehaviors, all of which, incidentally, are an effort to solve personal problems.

The involvement of lower-class young girls in illicit sex relations is shown through investigations of venereal disease infections. In tracing networks of infectious syphilitic contacts, public health agencies sometimes uncover extensive chains of contacts, including anywhere from forty to 600 persons. Not infrequently girls of thirteen to sixteen have contacts with men who have become infected from older professional prostitutes; these young girls then pass the infection along to others in the course of promiscuous sex relations. Contacts may be made in youth clubs, taverns, or restaurants which serve as teen-age hangouts; the place of intercourse often is an automobile. Young girls often are introduced by a mutual friend to the youth with whom they later have intercourse; or they become acquainted informally in the hangouts. In a network of related contacts involving forty-seven persons of lower socioeconomic status, the following teen-age girls were involved: [1]

Betty, a girl of sixteen, unmarried, rarely frequented bars; parents separated, mother an alcoholic. Eventually became pregnant by a married man, Boris, who infected her.

Helen, aged fourteen, sister of Betty, who introduced her to Boris, with whom she had intercourse. She had had trouble with the police and was a habitual truant. She also had intercourse with a twenty-nine-year-old man met at a bar, and with a thirty-year-old man.

Ellen, aged eighteen, with an eight-month-old illegitimate daughter. Her mother was dead and her father lived in another state; she lived with a married sister. She was known as a "problem child." She contracted syphilis from Boris and passed it on to another man.

Gilda, aged nineteen, married but separated from her husband; she had sexual relations with Boris and other men.

Marian, aged thirteen, an eighth grade student who was a habitual truant. She contracted syphilis from a man who had contracted it from Ellen.

Lorraine, aged seventeen, contracted syphilis from her husband, who had contracted it

1 *Venereal Disease in Children and Youth*, U. S. Department of Health, Education, and Welfare, Public Health Service, Bureau of State Services Communicable Disease Center, Atlanta, Georgia (undated, statistics cover 1959), pp. 15–24.

from his mother-in-law, who had had contacts with Boris.

In a network of eighty-three persons in the lower socio-economic level, half of the girls involved were under nineteen years old, half of the men under twenty-four. One of the youngest, Zeena, aged twelve, came from a broken home. She was a habitual truant, and bragged about having syphilis. She hung around a drive-in where soft drinks and sandwiches were served. She had had sex relations with eight men. Three other teen-age girls named six, twelve, and twenty-two male contacts. Descriptions of other and larger infectious networks are similar, usually with approximately half the girls being in their teens.

While still of juvenile delinquency age, few girls are professional prostitutes in the sense that they demand and receive payment for intercourse. Their sex relations tend to be casual venturesome experiences for pleasure or popularity or in imitation of slightly older girls who permit sex relations. However, as they become known as easy marks among boys and men, they drift toward prostitution.

Variations in lower-class values for girls

The values and customs of some ethnic subcultures may differ from those just described. For example, among Italian ethnic groups and those with a Spanish tradition (Puerto Rican and Mexican) virginity at marriage is highly valued for girls. Among families that follow the ethnic traditions, girls are closely supervised. Compact self-contained communities may show a surprising difference in the delinquency rates of boys and girls. In a midwest city of moderate size, in lower-class Italian neighborhoods the most

disorganized of the neighborhoods had no more girl delinquents than neighborhoods with a higher degree of stability. The rate for boys in the highly disorganized area was double the rate in the more stable areas. Inquiry revealed that it was part of the value system of the Italian-born parents that the girls should be carefully protected but that the boys should gain their entrance into manhood through greater freedom, which in the American city often led into delinquency.[1]

In a study of the Italian community in an Eastern City the same emphasis on supervision and chastity of girls is brought out.[2] Young Italian men, free to follow their personal inclinations in sexual matters, tended to seek sexual partners outside the Italian community, and respected the Italian mores that frowned upon pair-dating. When the time came to marry, they turned to the protected Italian girls for wives.

Somewhat the reverse of this cultural attitude is found in the lower-class Negro community, in which sexual promiscuity of girls is accepted casually, both by the girl's family and by young men in the community.[3]

The pull of bright light areas

Many large cities have one or more "bright light" areas where commercial recreation abounds. Some such areas may be dominated by theaters and concert halls of the highest type but have questionable places of amusement on the side streets; others, removed from the center of the city, may be dominated by taverns, public dance halls, and night clubs, all permitting young girls to enter or to loiter near the entrance. These institutions draw girls who are interested in quickly attracting young men with sufficient funds to give them an evening of entertainment in return for sexual favors. In some such areas the rate of girl delinquency is abnormally high, whereas the rate of delinquency for boys of the same age is lower than would be anticipated, although well up the scale in the boys' series.

Seattle in the thirties provided an example.[4] The area with the highest rate of girl delin-

Restless, footloose teen-aged girls often loiter in bus or railroad stations. They may have some legitimate reason for being there. For some girls, however, the loitering is the prelude to chance acquaintanceships with strange men. In some cases such contacts may eventually lead the girl into the familiar combination of sex delinquencies, running away from home, and petty thievery. Places where girls tend to loiter are regularly patroled in some cities by youth police officers, as in the photograph, or by policewomen. (Courtesy George Harris, photographer, and St. Louis Police Department)

1 Unpublished study made by the author in the 1930's when the Italian colony was still intact.
2 William Foote Whyte, "A Slum Sex Code," *American Journal of Sociology*, 49 (1943), 24–31.
3 See Chapter 10.
4 Shaw and McKay, *op. cit.*, pp. 363–365, from study by Norman Hayner.

quency ranked fourth from the top in boy delinquency. The area is described as having a high concentration of the commercial recreational businesses in the city: two-thirds of all cafes with dancing, two-thirds of all massage and bath establishments, half of the theaters, a fourth of all places selling liquor, and a fifth of the public dance halls. Girls in the district crowded these establishments as well as the movies, swimming pools, and skating rinks. Only Oriental girls living in the area were absent. The area was given the striking epithet of the "hunting ground" of the city. An area like this draws many restless girls at an age when boys of the same age are less interested in dancing and sex than in roving gang activities. The companions of the girls are likely to be older youths past the age of juvenile court jurisdiction.

Group associations

A higher percentage of girl delinquents than of boy delinquents are without definite group or gang association: 86 versus 67 per cent, according to a Detroit study of police cases.[1] In general they are less well-adjusted socially than boys, both with those their own age and adults.

Peer groups and delinquency. Small cliques and groups of girls may make their forays into night life a joint project. The girls offer protection to each other and exert mutual control; they lessen the chance that some man will try to pick up a girl without her willingness. They may meet a group of boys in a tavern or dance hall and drink, talk, and dance together. Depending upon the interests of the girls, at the end of the evening they may leave as a mutually protective group, or they may pair off with boys or men to continue into petting and sexual activities. The professional streetwalker usually operates alone; her objective is to make money, and her reputation is measured against that of other prostitutes and not against the conventional standards of morality. Even the promiscuous teen-age girl is not "selling herself" for money; she wishes to avoid the designation of prostitute. She is looking for fun, excitement, entertainment, perhaps small gifts. She still hopes to preserve her reputation and eventually to marry. The clique or group of girls aids her to achieve these objectives.[2]

Aggressive groups or gangs of girls are rare. Girls, in general, whether by nature or training, usually engage in quiet activities, whereas boys are usually more active. Girls are more compliant, boys more aggressive. Girls are more closely supervised and tend to have many social activities in their homes; boys are permitted to rove the community.[3] Occasionally, however, a peer group of delinquent girls carries on unsupervised and aggressive activities. An isolated attack by such a group is occasionally reported in a city newspaper. One such incident involved an attack on two girls, aged thirteen and fifteen, by a band of eight teen-age girls, known to hang out on a corner in the area. The attacking girls were dressed in blue jeans and were smoking cigarettes. They engaged the two girls, not delinquent nor members of their group, in an argument and then followed the two as they tried to evade their attentions. They first flicked ashes in the girls' faces and threatened to poke the cigarettes in their eyes, then pushed the girls around and flung one in the gutter, injuring her. The other escaped and ran for help. The attackers were not immediately caught, nor was the reason for the attack known.

Relation of girls to boys' delinquent gangs. Among preadolescents, a girl or two may be admitted to a boys' gang on equal terms. She is usually an active tomboyish type who can equal the boys in physical strength and daring. With adolescence, when boys and girls become aware of sex differences and become interested in those of the opposite sex, the girls are likely to drop out of the gang. While in, they participate in the boys' activities.[4]

Adolescent girls may become adjuncts of boys' gangs, individually or in groups, but are not accepted on a basis of equality. Girls who are the "steady dates" of members, especially of leaders, are tolerated on the fringe of the gang. Groups of girls may become subordinate auxiliaries of gangs, supplying dating partners for dances, sexual partners in a discreet way, or a protective front for the boys during times of active intergang fighting.

teen-age girls tend to date by cliques before they have the self-assurance to pair-date, *op. cit.*, pp. 408–413.

3 Frederic M. Thrasher in his book *The Gang*, University of Chicago Press, Chicago, 1927, based on a study of Chicago gangs of the 1920's, notes the scarcity of girls' gangs.

4 Thrasher, *op. cit.*, pp. 225–227 describes such a gang; it was an oddity rather than the customary thing.

1 Wattenberg and Saunders, *op. cit.*
2 In his study of Elmtown, Hollingshead notes that

Girls may carry the boys' weapons before and after a gang fight; if police interfere, no weapons are found on the boys. Police hesitate to search the girls, since the customary policy is that only policewomen may search girls or women.

Older cliques or gangs of youth who engage in robberies of stores or taverns may depend upon a girl to enter the place several times previous to the burglary to take note of windows, doors, where cash is kept, and so on. The girl does not participate in the actual break-in and hence cannot be connected with the crime, although later she may share directly or indirectly in the proceeds.

The organization of these groups of girls is discussed in Chapter 14. They may be organized on an age basis, if the boys are so organized. They adopt a name derived from the gang's name, but indicating a lower status, perhaps by the adding of "-ette" to the gang's name, indicating smallness, that is, lower status. In other gangs, the girls' groups are called debutantes, pointing up their social function. If the boys wear a distinctive jacket or cap, the girls wear a similar one to indicate their relationship. Although the girls' groups are as a whole subordinate to the boys' gangs, each girls' group is internally organized with its own leaders. It seems, however, to have few activities independently of the boys' gang, and its chief function is to cater to some need or desire of the gang. The gangs thus accept the lower-class concept, especially dominant in some ethnic groups, that the male is dominant, the female subordinate.

Individual girls who date delinquent boys often benefit indirectly from the delinquencies. The theft of an automobile may be for the purpose of taking a girl out for an evening; the stolen jewelry may include a gift for the girl; the money stolen or secured from the sale of stolen property may provide for an evening's entertainment or for gifts. When the delinquent youth marries, he may support his wife through his thefts. The girl may or may not be aware of the delinquencies; if she is, she may find the boy attractive because of his daring; or she may simply ignore the origin of the money or gifts. She benefits from the boy's delinquencies but she is not legally responsible.

In summing up delinquencies of girls, we may conclude that the sex exploits and incorrigibility for which girls are arrested are only part of a more inclusive pattern of delinquent activities which sometimes includes relationships with delinquent boys. At the same time, a large proportion of girls who are arrested seem not to have group affiliations.

A problem of interpersonal relations

Girl delinquents resemble boy delinquents in age distribution, concentration in lower socioeconomic areas, and background of disorganized family life. Delinquent boys seem to be struggling to reach masculine values of success and status through various competitive devices such as outwitting police, showing courage superior to that of other delinquent boys, and finding a way to gain money without hard work. The delinquent girl is concerned with evading unpleasant interpersonal relationships at home and establishing successful relationships with boys, often defined in terms of sexual attraction. The confirmed delinquent boy moves into adult crime usually of a financial nature; the confirmed delinquent girl moves into prostitution and minor forms of stealing; or into a common-law or legal marriage where her support may come from the criminal activities of her husband.

Bibliography

Cohen, Albert K., *Delinquent Boys, The Culture of the Gang,* Free Press, Glencoe, Illinois, 1955, pp. 137–147.

————, and James F. Short, Jr., "Research in Delinquent Subcultures," *Journal of Social Issues,* 14, No. 3 (1958), 34–36.

Galvin, James, "Some Dynamics of Delinquent Girls," *Journal of Nervous and Mental Diseases,* 123 (1956), 292–295.

"Girl Delinquent, Age Sixteen," *Harper's Magazine,* 164 (1932), 551–559.

Glueck, Sheldon and Eleanor, *Five Hundred Delinquent Women,* Alfred A. Knopf, New York, 1934, pp. 34–42, 147–152.

Greenwald, Harold, *The Call Girl: A Social and Psychoanalytic Study,* Ballantine Books, New York, 1958.

Hardt, R. H., *A Delinquency Profile of Syracuse and Onondaga County, New York, 1957–1958,* Youth Development Center, Syracuse University, Syracuse, New York, 1960.

Lynn, D. B., "A Note on Sex Differences in the Development of Masculine and Feminine Identification," *Psychological Bulletin,* 66 (1959), 126–135.

Schoeppe, Aileen, "Sex Differences in Adolescent Socialization," *Journal of Social Psychology,* 38 (1953), 175–185.

Wattenberg, William W., "Differences between Girl and Boy 'Repeaters'," *Journal of Educational Psychology,* 47 (1956), 137–146.

———, "Girl Repeaters," *National Probation and Parole Association Journal,* 3 (1957), 48–53.

———, "Recidivism among Girls," *Journal of Abnormal and Social Psychology,* 50 (1955), 405–406.

———, and Frank Saunders, "Sex Differences among Juvenile Offenders," *Sociology and Social Research,* 39 (1954), 24–31.

The subcultures with their crosscurrents and unstable truces frame the social world within which children develop. Children first learn the demands and prohibitions of their subcultures through such intimate reference groups as the family and the peer group. The family makes the earlier and more profound impact. The early nurturing functions of parents (the child's first reference group) were discussed in Chapter 4. Under favorable conditions, a young child successively acquires a sense of trust, learns acceptance of authority, and develops personal values. With these fundamental learnings, the child is able to identify with and learn from his parents, and also to develop amicable and co-operative relationships with other people. This immediately raises the question whether delinquent children have as favorable a relationship with their parents as nondelinquent children.

Identification with parents

Children learn attitudes and secure personal emotional satisfactions primarily from people whom they admire and wish to emulate as models—in other words, from persons with whom they can identify. Whether a child can or cannot identify with a particular person depends in large measure on how he is treated by that person. Thus the young child's relationship to his parents is very largely a matter of how the parents feel and act toward the child. The externals of a family situation, such as a broken home or poverty, are important primarily as they affect the relationship between parents and children.[1]

Sources of information. The dynamics of parent-child relationships are understood mainly through the analysis of individual cases that have come to the attention of psychiatrists and clinical psychologists. A child, delinquent or otherwise, who seems to be emotionally disturbed may be brought to the private practitioner or the child guidance clinic. Especially with young children, the root of the problem usually goes back to the child's relationship with his parents. Since only obviously disturbed children are brought for diagnosis and treatment, the evidence from these cases is inadequate for understanding the relation of parent-child relation-

Chapter **10**

The family setting of delinquency

ships to delinquency. Delinquent children with or without emotional disturbances rarely come to the attention of psychiatrists.

Comparative statistical studies of delinquent and nondelinquent children with reference to family background are another source of information. These studies do not explore the dynamics of the family relationships but show the prevalence of certain family conditions among delinquents as compared with nondelinquents.[2]

The mother's attitude toward the boy. In all discussions of parent-child relationships, the attitude of the mother toward her children is regarded as most significant. The warm, loving mother is the one with whom the child can identify and from whom he receives a sense of worth and self-confidence. The rejecting mother not only does not secure the child's identification but creates in him a sense of unworthiness and of resentment toward herself.

A commonly held psychiatric view is that virtually all delinquency is an indication of early parental neglect or rejection. The statistical data to be presented throw doubt upon such sweeping assumptions. The great importance of family relationships cannot be doubted, and such parental attitudes as neglect, indifference, hostility and rejection are

1 Among adolescents, such externals may have a more direct effect since they help to determine the adolescent's relationship to persons outside the family.

2 Typical of clinical studies are the references in the Bibliography to Bettelheim, Eissler and Federn, Gardner, Healy, Jenkins, and Redl and Wineman. Typical of the comparative statistical studies are Axelrad, Glueck and Glueck, McCord and McCord, Monahan, Nye, and Reiss. The discussion draws from both of these lists as well as from a variety of other sources.

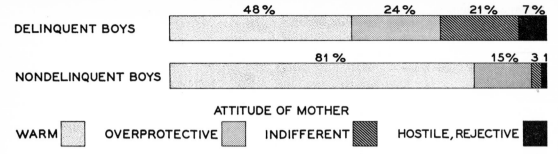

Figure 7. Affection of Mother for Boy among Five Hundred Delinquent and Five Hundred Nonde-linquent Boys. (Data from Glueck and Glueck, *Unravelling Juvenile Delinquency*, Harvard University Press)

closely associated with delinquent behavior. However, by every measure of family relationships used in comparative statistical studies, a large percentage of the delinquents —often almost half—have good parental relationships. Conversely, at least a minority of nondelinquents come from homes with unfavorable emotional relationships. A complete contrast in family relationships does not differentiate delinquents from nondelinquents.

Several explanations account for this situation. Comparative statistical studies, limited to lower or lower-middle class boys, show more unfavorable family relationships among delinquents than nondelinquents. According to one study almost twice as many nondelinquent boys as delinquent boys had warmly affectionate mothers, as Figure 7 shows. The mothers of delinquent boys tended to be overprotective, indifferent, or, in a limited number of instances, hostile or rejective. On the one hand, nondelinquents with some unfavorable family relationships may also have other favorable relationships that overcome the effect of the unfavorable ones. For example, an affectionate relationship with one parent may neutralize the effect of a hostile relationship with the other parent. On the other hand, delinquents may have some favorable relationships but a preponderance of unfavorable ones. For a complete analysis, the total family complex would have to be known. Such an analysis is often found in psychiatric or social work case studies. Since they have been made for a limited number of highly selected individuals, they do not provide any indication of the specific relationships most frequently associated with delinquency. Such information is

needed as the background for preventive measures, such as family discussion groups or community programs, which might strengthen family life.

Another explanation of the overlap of family situations between delinquents and nondelinquents is the influence of such cultural and social factors as have been discussed in the preceding chapters. These nonfamily influences may pull the child into delinquency; or they may set a barrier between him and delinquency, even when family influences are prodelinquent.

The record of adult criminality of men is also related to their boyhood family relationships, as shown by a study based on records of family relationships for 253 boys whose average age was eleven years. Sixteen years later, a restudy was made, with the original group classified into two groups on the basis of whether or not as adults they had been convicted of some crime. For each of many types of family relationships the percentage of criminal and noncriminal sons was computed. The analysis clearly answers this question: In a family of a certain type what are the chances that at least one adult criminal son will be produced? [1]

Neglecting mothers were most likely to have an adult criminal son; three-fourths of the neglecting mothers fell into this group, as Figure 8 shows. Approximately half of the passive, absent, or cruel mothers had a criminal son. Overprotective mothers were more likely to have noncriminal than criminal sons. The record for loving mothers was especially significant inasmuch as the kind of love made a vast difference. As many loving neurotic

1 William and Joan McCord, *Origins of Crime*, Columbia University Press, New York, 1959. A report on the original study of the boys is found in Edwin Powers and Helen Witmer, *An Experiment in the Prevention of Delinquency: The Cambridge-Somerville Study*, Columbia University Press, New York, 1951.

TYPE OF MOTHER

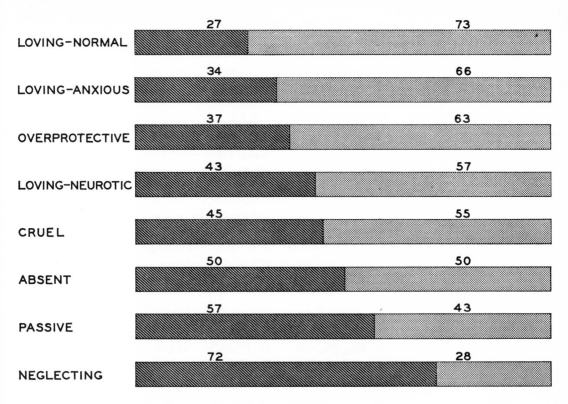

Figure 8. Types of Mother in Relation to Criminal and Noncriminal Sons. (Data from McCord and McCord, *Origins of Crime*, Columbia University Press)

mothers as cruel mothers had criminal sons. As would be expected, loving normal mothers had the best record, but even in this group a fourth had criminal sons. The sons referred to are only those who were included in the study project. Some of the mothers with a criminal son no doubt had other sons who may have been exemplary in their behavior. It would then be necessary to assume that their attitude toward sons who later became criminals differed from their attitude toward conforming sons.

Tables from the Glueck study suggest a conflict in the minds of many boys, but more especially of delinquent boys.[1] Two-thirds of the delinquents (and 90 per cent of the nondelinquents) were closely attached emotionally to their mothers. However, only 22 per cent of the delinquents (but 71 per cent of nondelinquents) felt that their mothers were deeply concerned for their welfare and went

1 Sheldon Glueck and Eleanor Glueck, *Unraveling Juvenile Delinquency*, Harvard University Press, Cambridge, Massachusetts, 1950, pp. 127–129.

to great trouble to provide training and discipline; 59 and 28 per cent respectively felt the parents were well-meaning but did not provide helpful training; 19 and 1 per cent respectively felt their mothers were little concerned for them and were selfish, prejudiced, or rejective. Thus the delinquent boys' emotional attachment to the mother seemed to exceed their feeling that she was deeply concerned for their welfare. This discrepancy between love for the mother and evaluation of her concern was much greater among delinquent than nondelinquent boys.

The data presented above and a vast amount of other data from the two studies cited seem to show an association between deviation and either actual or felt rejection by the mother. Whatever the dynamics involved, boys who felt that their mothers were rejecting, neglectful, or indifferent more fre-

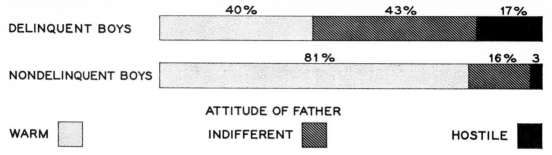

Figure 9. Affection of Father for Boy among Five Hundred Delinquent and Five Hundred Nondelinquent Boys. (Data from Glueck and Glueck, *Unravelling Juvenile Delinquency*, Harvard University Press)

quently became delinquent or criminal than did boys who felt sure of their mothers' love and concern. The difference is a matter of degree, however, as the delinquent and nondelinquent boys are far from falling into two groups, the first with rejecting mothers and the second with loving mothers.

The father's attitude toward the boy. As was true for the mother's attitudes, paternal attitudes of indifference, hostility, neglect, and rejection were more often found among parents of delinquent than nondelinquent boys (Figure 9). Warm, cordial, and friendly feelings on the part of the father were associated with nondelinquency more often than with delinquency on the part of the son. However, for every type of attitude, a large overlap existed between delinquent and nondelinquent boys.

Adverse attitudes were not all on the father's side. Among the Glueck cases, only half as many delinquent as nondelinquent boys were attached to the father (32.5 per cent versus 65.1 per cent).[1] Delinquent boys more often than nondelinquent were indifferent or hostile to their fathers or were noncommittal. The percentage of boys who were attached to the father was much lower among both delinquents and nondelinquents than the percentages attached to the mother. This finding supports the theory that the mother is the most significant figure for the child, even into the early adolescent period.

About a fifth of the delinquent boys compared with two-thirds of the nondelinquent boys in the Glueck study felt that their fathers had provided them with training and were

1 Glueck and Glueck, *op. cit.*, p. 126.

deeply concerned.[2] Fully a third of delinquents felt the father's attitude toward their welfare was poor, but only one in twenty of the nondelinquents shared this feeling.

Discipline by parents. Both the McCord and the Glueck studies showed that few boys, delinquent or otherwise, had parents who consistently mistreated them in the name of discipline. This finding does not mean that most parents of delinquents were kind and loving in discipline, although such discipline was found in the families of many nondelinquents. Relatively few parents of delinquents were kindly and consistent in discipline. Either erratic or lax discipline characterized most fathers and mothers of delinquents but was also found to some extent among parents of nondeviants.

The favorable home. The data cited so far help to outline the type of home conducive to the development of delinquency and one that favors nondelinquent behavior. The McCords conclude from their findings, only a few of which are cited here, that the home most likely to produce adult criminals is the quarrelsome home with neglecting parents and lax discipline. Conversely, the cohesive, love-oriented home is least likely to produce adult criminals. When one parent is loving and the other rejecting, the love of the one helps to offset the neglect or harshness of the other. The loving mother is of special significance in socializing her sons to conforming behavior. While these findings apply to adult criminality, the somewhat similar findings of the Gluecks suggest that they also apply to delinquency. In favorable homes, boys feel accepted and loved; they are drawn to their parents as models worthy to be followed.

Parental models. The loving relationship between parents and child is one side of the coin of identification. The other side is the

2 Glueck and Glueck, *op. cit.*, p. 129.

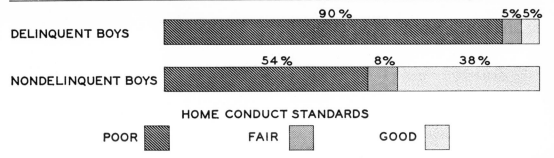

Figure 10. Home Conduct Standards for Five Hundred Delinquent and Five Hundred Nondelinquent Boys. (Data from Glueck and Glueck, *Unravelling Juvenile Delinquency,* Harvard University Press)

kind of model presented by parents to their children.

Criminal as well as noncriminal adults tend to uphold the mores of society in verbal statements. The parents of the adult criminals in the McCord study had, according to records from the youth of the men, condemned criminality in their sons. Nevertheless, for many boys the parental admonitions did not stop criminality, especially when the relation between parents and son was harsh or unloving. More significant is behavior of the parents. Both the Glueck and McCord studies show that many delinquents and criminals have had criminal or disorganized parents as models.

The Gluecks graded the homes of delinquents and nondelinquents as good, fair, or poor on the basis of the presence or absence of immorality, drunkenness, criminality, and unwholesome ideals. The great preponderance of poor standards in the homes of delinquents is shown in Figure 10. The fact that over half of nondelinquents came from homes with poor standards raises several points. Since both groups came from lower-class backgrounds, one would expect some deviations from what are essentially middle-class standards. But it is necessary to recall that the nondelinquents had an almost perfect record of behavior, lacking even the minor delinquencies tolerated by the public. Why was the conduct of these boys so excessively conforming, when over half came from homes with some immorality, drunkenness, criminality, or unwholesome ideals?

Several clues may point to an explanation. One is the higher proportion of nondelinquent than of delinquent boys who were neurotic (Chapter 5). Some of the nondelinquent boys may have reacted to the poor home situation through neurotic anxieties instead of through overt acts of delinquency. Another suggestion comes from Figure 11, which

shows the percentages of boys who felt their fathers were worthy of emulation. In contrast to the very high percentage of homes with poor parental standards (based, it is true, on both parents), few boys felt that their fathers were completely unworthy of emulation. Perhaps they were moved by loyalty to their fathers regardless of conduct. But it is also possible that the conditions that led the researchers to classify the homes as poor did not seem very much out of the ordinary from the lower-class point of view of the boys. A third clue comes from the McCords, who found that when the father and mother were both deviant, the association with adult criminality was very high.[1] When one parent was deviant and the other not, the association was less close. The love of one parent, especially of the mother, tended to offset the effect of deviation in the other parent.

The delinquent girl and family relationships. The dynamics of family relationships operating among delinquent girls may differ from those operating among delinquent boys. In view of the high percentage of girls who appear in court on charges of incorrigibility, ungovernability, and running away from home, the family situation seems to be a dominant factor in the delinquency of girls. Several Detroit studies show that, as compared with boys, a higher percentage of girl delinquents quarreled with their parents, felt "picked on" at home, disliked the father, and were hostile to the mother and especially to the stepmother if there was one.[2]

1 McCord and McCord, *op. cit.,* pp. 93–116.
2 William W. Wattenberg, "Differences between Girl and Boy 'Repeaters,'" *Journal of Educational Psychology,* 47 (1956), 137–146; Wattenberg, "Girl Re-

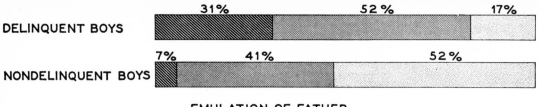

Figure 11. Emulation of Father among Five Hundred Delinquent and Five Hundred Nondelinquent Boys. (Data from Glueck and Glueck, *Unravelling Juvenile Delinquency*, Harvard University Press)

Since girls spend more of their time at home and are more closely supervised than boys, any latent tension is more likely to burst into open quarreling and hostility than is true for boys. The boy may escape into the community and find solace in his peer group in what is regarded as normal boy activity. The girl who attempts to escape from home is less likely to find a free-roving peer group. If she does, or if she runs away by herself, she is considered a delinquent. Thus the boy has an avenue of escape from home that is closed to the girl. Away from home, the boy may, however, affiliate with a delinquent group and eventually come to court attention, not for incorrigibility, but usually for some form of stealing.

Broken homes and their implications

Broken homes have been blamed for many years as the source of delinquent behavior. Older studies have little value, however, since the rates of broken homes among delinquents usually were not compared with corresponding rates among comparable groups of nondelinquents. Other studies grouped all types of broken homes together, whether from death, desertion, or divorce, disregarding the distinctive psychological reactions to each type of break. Others took no account of the social-class or ethnic attitudes toward broken homes and the possibility that in some groups, intermittently broken homes might be accepted as near-normal. More recent studies go beyond the rates to explore the implications of different types of

broken homes for the personality development and behavior of the child. As with many other topics, many studies of broken homes are confined to boys.[1]

Broken homes among delinquents and nondelinquents. When control groups of nondelinquents are used, the control groups show a persistent but moderate excess of unbroken homes. Table 17 shows the percentages of delinquent and nondelinquent children living with both own parents in different parts of the country for periods of time ranging from the twenties to the forties.

Contrary to popular assumptions, half or more of the delinquents live with their own parents. For this group, the broken home is not a distinctive factor in delinquency. The difference between delinquents and nondelinquents ranges from 6 to 24 per cent in the studies cited in Table 17. For these percentages of the cases, the broken home may be a determining factor in delinquency. However, the percentages are based on delinquent children brought to court attention. They often have brothers and sisters, living in the same broken homes, who are not delinquent. Healy and Bronner, in their study of 153 boy and girl delinquents, found that 65.5 per cent came from homes with both parents present, 34.5 from various types of broken homes.[2] These delinquents came from 133 different families that had produced a total of 194 de-

peaters," *National Probation and Parole Association Journal*, 3 (1957), 48–53; Wattenberg, "Recidivism among Girls," *Journal of Abnormal and Social Psychology*, 50 (1955), 405–406.

1 The first extensive study of broken homes among delinquent and nondelinquent children from comparable physical and social backgrounds was made by Clifford R. Shaw and Henry D. McKay, *Social Factors in Juvenile Delinquency, A Study* . . . for the National Commission on Law Observance and Enforcement, No. 13, volume 2, U. S. Government Printing Office, Washington, D. C., 1931, pp. 261–284. This study showed only a moderate excess of broken homes among delinquents; unfortunately broken homes were not classified into types. While the study made a tremendous impact on the thinking of the day, it is less useful today when interest centers in types of broken homes.
2 William Healy and Augusta F. Bronner, *New Light on Delinquency and Its Treatment*, Yale University Press, New Haven, Connecticut, 1936, p. 35.

Table 17

Percentage of Delinquents and Nondelinquents Living with Own Parents

Type of delinquent cases	Number of delinquent cases	Percentage living with own parents		
		Sex	Delinquents	Control Group
x Juvenile court cases, Chicago 1,675		Boys	57.5	63.9
† Juvenile court cases, California 300		Boys and girls	49.3	73.3
‡ Correctional school, Massachusetts 500		Boys	50.2	71.2

x Clifford R. Shaw and Henry D. McKay, *Social Factors in Juvenile Delinquency, A Study . . .* for the National Commission on Law Observance and Enforcement, No. 13, volume 2, U. S. Government Printing Office, Washington, D. C., 1931, p. 274.
† Maud A. Merrill, *Problems of Child Delinquency*, Houghton Mifflin Company, Boston, 1947, p. 66.
‡ Sheldon and Eleanor Glueck, *Unraveling Juvenile Delinquency*, Harvard University Press, Cambridge, Massachusetts, 1950, pp. 88–89.

linquent children among a total of 461 old enough to become delinquent. (Of the delinquent children, 153 had been selected for study.) Among all the children, 42 per cent were delinquent and 58 per cent nondelinquent. In other words, the broken home that produces one or several delinquents does not necessarily produce only delinquents. Conversely, according to Table 17 unbroken homes produce half the delinquents.

The mere fact of the absence of one or both parents is less significant than the relationships that exist in the family among whatever family members are present. The absence of one or both parents reduces the probability of adequate relationships but does not necessarily destroy all significant relationships. The preceding section of this chapter brought out the importance of a loving relationship, fair discipline, and adequate parental models and the fact that one loving nondeviant parent may offset the effect of a rejecting or deviant parent. Broken or unbroken, these relationships are significant. The type of break is important in terms of the different kinds of interference that it makes in good interpersonal relationships within the family.

Age of delinquents. Preteen-age boys come from broken homes in greater proportion than adolescent boys, according to the Chicago study by Shaw and McKay.[1] At age ten almost twice the proportion of delinquent boys as of school boys (control group) came from broken homes. At ages fifteen to seventeen, the proportions of delinquents and school boys from broken homes were almost equal. Comparisons for girls are not available. The conclusion might be drawn that at the earlier ages boys are still more in need of identifica-

tion with their parents and more dependent on them for affection and satisfaction of needs than are adolescents.

Sex and broken homes. Studies including both boys and girls show that fewer delinquent girls than boys live with both parents and that more come from broken homes. A third to a half of all delinquent girls live with both parents, compared with half to three-fourths of the delinquent boys.[2] A Philadelphia study (Table 18) of court cases from 1949 to 1954 showed that 72.4 per cent of all white boy first offenders lived with both parents, compared with only 48.4 per cent of the girls.[3] Among delinquent girls the broken home is more clearly linked with delinquency than among delinquent boys. However, since delinquent boys outnumber delinquent girls about four or more to one, the fact remains that more boys than girls come from broken homes. For example, in Philadelphia, the ratio of the total number of offenders brought to the juvenile court (first offenders and recidivists), was six white boys for every white girl. Of this number, 11,676 boys were living with their parents and 6,096 in some type of broken home; while 1,273 girls were living with their parents and 1,646 in some type of broken home. The broken home is not a factor in explaining the wide discrepancy between the numbers of boy and girl delinquents. It is a factor within girl delinquency.

Types of broken homes. The most common type of truncated family that remains after a break is the mother and children, according

1 Shaw and McKay, *op. cit.* p. 277.

2 For a summary of studies prior to 1953 see Ruth Shonle Cavan, *Criminology*, Thomas Y. Crowell Company, New York, 1953, p. 118.
3 Thomas P. Monahan, "Family Status and the Delinquent Child: A Reappraisal and Some New Findings," *Social Forces*, 35 (1957), 250–258.

Table 18

Family Status of Delinquent First Offenders Disposed of in Municipal (Juvenile) Court, Philadelphia, 1949–1954

Percentage distribution

A. With whom child lived	Whites		Negroes	
	Boys	Girls	Boys	Girls
Both of own parents..............	72.4	48.4	47.2	27.3
Mother only....................	15.5	26.1	35.2	46.7
Mother and stepfather...........	4.2	7.0	2.8	2.7
Father only....................	2.6	4.6	3.8	5.2
Father and stepmother..........	1.3	3.1	1.4	2.0
Adoptive parents...............	0.1	0.3	x	0.1
Other family home..............	3.9	10.5	9.6	16.0
† Institution....................	(0.4)	(0.9)	(0.1)	(0.1)
Total........................	100.0	100.0	100.0	100.0
Number of cases...............11,236		1,984	8,706	2,736

B. Marital status of parents				
Own parents living together.......	73.1	49.7	47.8	27.9
Parents unmarried..............	1.6	4.1	10.7	20.3
Mother dead...................	2.9	6.3	4.8	7.5
Father dead....................	7.7	11.0	9.8	10.4
Both parents dead..............	0.5	1.6	1.7	2.1
Father deserted mother..........	0.7	1.7	2.3	3.6
Mother deserted father..........	0.2	1.8	0.2	0.3
Both parents deserted...........	0.1	0.1	0.2	x
Parents living apart.............	7.9	14.0	20.1	25.4
Parents divorced................	5.3	10.7	2.4	2.5
Total........................	100.0	100.0	100.0	100.0
Number of cases...............11,244		1,906	8,643	2,717

Thomas P. Monahan, "Family Status and the Delinquent Child: A Reappraisal and Some New Findings," *Social Forces*, 35 (1957), 250–258.
x Less than 0.05 per cent.
† Not included in 100 per cent.

to a Philadelphia study (Table 18-A). The delinquent boy or girl, if not living with both parents, is most likely to live with the mother. The mother-child combination might be the result of separation, desertion, divorce, death, or failure to marry at all. Whatever may have gone before, at the time of delinquency the incomplete family nucleus is the mother and her children.

Broken homes are essentially ones in which the mother has not remarried (or never was married). Fathers and stepfathers very infrequently play a role. Stepmothers are also a rarity. The infrequent variant types of father only, stepfather (for whites), or stepmother include a higher percentage of girl than of boy delinquents.

Neither the broken home nor the mother-child home is found only among delinquents,

although every type of broken home is more characteristic of the delinquent than the nondelinquent group, according to the Glueck study of lower-class white boys (Table 19). Among the types of broken homes the mother-child combination far outranks other types among nondelinquents as among delinquents.

Difference between white and Negro delinquents. The diversification of types of broken homes for Negroes follows in general the pattern for whites, with one glaring exception. For both boys and girls the percentage of delinquents who live with both parents is only a little more than half the percentage of white delinquents who live with both parents. Table 18-A shows that only 47.2 per cent of the Negro boys as compared with 72.4 per cent of the white boys live with both

Table 19

Living Arrangements of Five Hundred Delinquent and Five Hundred Non-delinquent Boys

Percentage distribution

With whom boy lived:	Delinquent boys	Nondelinquent boys
Both his own parents	50.2	71.2
One own parent (the mother four times as often as the father among delinquents, three times as often among nondelinquents)	34.6	19.8
One own parent and one stepparent	8.0	4.4
Two stepparents, foster parents, other relatives, brothers and sisters	7.2	4.6
Total	100.0	100.0
Number of cases	500	500

Reprinted by permission of the publisher from Sheldon and Eleanor Glueck, *Unraveling Juvenile Delinquency*, Harvard University Press, Cambridge, Mass., Copyright 1950 by the Commonwealth Fund, pp. 88–89.

parents; the unusually low percentage of 27.3 of the Negro girls as compared with 48.4 per cent of the white girls live with both parents. Complementing this difference is the large proportion of Negro boys and girls who live with the mother only—roughly twice the proportion for whites. Negro children less often have stepfathers and more often live in other people's homes than do white children.

The chief key to this situation is the high percentage of unmarried mothers in the Negro group. Five or six times as many Negro delinquents as white have unmarried parents. Fathers more often desert mothers, and there are many more cases of separation of parents. (However, white delinquents' parents more often are divorced than Negro delinquents'.)

The greater proportion of unmarried, deserted, and separated parents among Negroes is not confined to delinquents. It is a general condition among lower-class Negroes, both in the South and in the North. For the total population, according to the 1950 census, 33 per cent of all Negro children under age eighteen lived in families headed by someone other than the married father and mother; the corresponding percentage for white children was only 7.[1] Even when a couple does head the household, the union may be unstable, as is shown by a study of 2,253 households in Atlanta, Georgia. In 12 per cent of the marital unions, both the man and the woman were temporarily living together; 38 per cent were common-law marriages without

legality but with more permanence than the temporary union; 50 per cent were licensed marriages. The lower the social-class level, the more often were the unions of the impermanent or nonlegal type.[2] A Chicago study also shows the prevalence of Negro families with female heads in the lower class —twice as high a proportion as in the Negro upper class.[3]

In many lower-class neighborhoods, the family headed by the mother or grandmother is the normal type. Negro men seem to have retained some of the role they had during slavery, when their masters rather than they were responsible for the support of their families. Negro mothers, accustomed to work during the slave period, continue the dual role of employed woman and mother. Many Negro lower-class households consist of a grandmother, mother, and dependent children. Continuity, stability, and authority are in female hands. Into these maternal households, men come, either as husbands or companions, but feel free to desert periodically or permanently. The term serial monogamy has been applied to this situation.[4]

1 T. P. Monahan, "Family Status and the Delinquent Child: A Reappraisal and Some New Findings," *Social Forces*, 35 (March, 1957), 250–258.

2 Mozell C. Hill, "Research on the Negro Family," *Marriage and Family Living*, 19 (February, 1957), 29.

3 E. Franklin Frazier, *The Negro Family in Chicago*, University of Chicago Press, Chicago, 1932.

4 St. Clair Drake and Horace R. Cayton, *Black Metropolis: A Study of Negro Life in a Northern City*, Harcourt, Brace and Company, New York, 1945, pp. 582–599; Walter B. Miller, "Implications of Urban Lower-Class Culture for Social Work," *Social Service Review*, 33 (September, 1959), 219–236. Miller's discussion is not limited to Negroes but is especially applicable to them.

Implications of the mother-child home. An important implication concerns the normal differences in roles played by the father and mother throughout American culture but especially in some lower-class subcultures. Usually the mother is the parent to whom the child first becomes attached, and, unless she rejects the child, she continues to exert an affectionate, understanding, and sometimes yielding influence on the child. The father usually is a more authoritarian figure with whom the child may come in conflict and who may react to the child more aggressively and punitively than the mother. Studies of nondelinquent, relatively well-adjusted children show these reactions, as well as the studies cited in the earlier portions of this chapter.[1]

Data already presented from the McCord and Glueck studies show that the mother is a warmer and more loving figure in the child's experience than the father and that this is true for both delinquents and nondelinquents. Absence of the father from the home therefore removes the parent who is most likely to be hostile and disliked. However, among delinquent children, the relationship with the mother often is not close, and she may not be able or willing to close the gap left by the father's absence. In other cases, although the mother is hostile, the father may be warm and compensate for her hostility. When he is absent, this possibility is removed. The suggestion may be made, without supporting data, that the mothers who have been deserted, separated, or divorced may generally have cold and unappealing personalities. The husband may have escaped; the child bears the brunt. The break in the family may be less important in the delinquency of the child than the personality of the mother which may have created the break in some cases.

Another handicap, especially for boys, is the absence from the home of a masculine model. The father usually passes on to his sons the self-concept and role of the adult man in his subculture and to his daughters the conception that they should have of men in the subculture. When the father is not present, any one of a number of outcomes is possible. The boy may continue to model himself after his mother, developing a somewhat feminine self-concept and seeking a

feminized masculine role, such as cook or some other service position. He may turn to some other adult male for a model, or he may find an adolescent version of the adult role through a delinquent gang.[2]

Two subtypes of mother-child families are distinguishable: the legally based family in which the parents married, with some anticipation of permanency, and the marriage then disintegrated through some form of separation with or without divorce; and the family in which a marriage never took place or disintegrated before a definite family pattern had developed, to be followed by a kind of serial monogamy, usually illegal but with more permanence than casual promiscuity. The effects of the two types on children are probably not identical.

1. Some form of separation removes the legally married father from the home two to three times as often as death (Table 19-B). Conflict between the parents often precedes a separation, and bitterness may follow it. The way in which the mother speaks of the father affects the attitude that children have for the father. Studies of nondelinquent children aged six to ten years, separated from their fathers by military service, throw light on the relation between the mother's spoken attitudes toward the father and the child's conceptions of the fathers.[3] When the mother always spoke of the absent father in derogatory terms, the child's fantasies pictured the father as fearful and aggressive. The opposite was true when the mother always spoke favorably of the father. It seems probable that in many cases of permanent separation of parents, the mother may deride her husband to her children. The child then is not only deprived of a daily father model but would not have in memory a favorable model.

In the much more rare case of a mother-child home resulting from the death of the father, there is less probability of bitterness and often a tendency for the remnants of the family to work together.

The addition of a stepparent, although infrequent (Table 19-A), often necessitates a difficult adjustment, whether or not the child is already delinquent, or it may contribute to the beginning of delinquency. Usually the

1 George R. Bach, "Father-Fantasies and Father-Typing in Father-Separated Children," *Child Development,* 17 (1946), 63–80.

2 Walter B. Miller, "Implications of Urban Lower-Class Culture," *Social Service Review,* 33 (1959), 219–236.

3 Bach, *op. cit.*

stepparent is a stepfather, an authoritarian figure, who may seek to exert authority over a stepchild without the compensating affection and need-satisfaction usually extended by the own father, whose authority is thus tempered. Stepfather and stepchild may mutually dislike and reject each other. On the other hand, if the stepfather develops affection for the child and if the child finds in him a trustworthy father model, the relationship may be helpful to the child and a preventive of delinquency.

The child may develop considerable hostility that he projects on weaker and less threatening figures than the stepfather. Or he may simply step out of the family and avoid home as much as possible. Typically, he steps into the street life of his neighborhood, which rarely offers an adequate substitute for a normal family relationship.

2. The second subtype of mother-child family is the one in which a legal or otherwise stable union was never effected between father and mother. This type of family has been termed a "female-based" family by a sociologist who has worked intensively with lower-class delinquent boys.[1] This family is especially commonplace among lower-class Negroes. Among Negroes and whites values, attitudes, and roles develop that are an outgrowth of this particular type of family and that affect the personality and behavior of children.[2] This family is not a breakdown of the more conventional American family, but a unique type, accepted in certain lower-class subcultures and perpetuated from one generation to the next. The mother assumes the responsibility of rearing her children and the expense of maintaining the home, often with help from relief agencies.

One result of the fluidity of relationships between men and women is the high rate of illegitimacy. Among whites, 2.1 per cent of all births are illegitimate; among nonwhites (primarily Negro), the percentage is 21.2.[3] Negro illegitimacy occurs much more often in lower-class than in middle- or upper-class levels, according to Chicago studies.[4] Deplored by the middle and upper classes,

illegitimacy has little stigma in the lower-class Negro family for either mother or child. The problems that arise are the result not of social stigma, but of inadequate care and the lack of a father to teach both sons and daughters responsible adult roles.

The illegitimate boy has a choice of roles. He may very well repeat the role of his father or later male associates of his mother—the ne'er-do-well, the drifter, the shirker of responsibility as viewed by more stable social classes. This role easily includes a variety of delinquencies for the boy and minor crimes for the adult.

When the boy does not blindly accept the role of irresponsibility, he may pattern himself after his mother in a modified feminine role, as suggested above.

A third possibility is the repudiation in adolescence of the feminine role and along with it of "goodness" as a feminine trait. The boy then attempts to be tough and "bad," modeling himself after tough men in the neighborhood and affiliating with a gang of boys who are equally in the pursuit of masculine toughness.[5] Delinquencies follow as part of the technique of learning a tough masculine role adapted to lower-class culture and lower-class manual occupations.

The illegitimate adolescent girl, following the pattern of her mother and other adult female relatives, may find herself accused of sexual promiscuity, or she may drift away from her family and enter prostitution, a following condemned by her own family and class as well as by the middle class. If she becomes a streetwalker, she is liable to arrest and perhaps commitment to a correctional school.

The disintegrated family. The small percentage of children who live outside the family group may be bereft of any intimate continuing relationship with an affectionate adult with whom to identify. Such deprived children differ from rejected children in that often they have literally had almost no opportunity for an emotional identification with any adult. Nondelinquent institutional children, paired with children in foster homes and studied at various ages between three and twelve years of age, were found to be generally impoverished mentally—they had poor memories, experienced difficulty in grasping general concepts, were unorganized in re-

1 Miller, *op. cit.*
2 Miller, *op. cit.*
3 *Statistical Abstract of the United States, 1960*, U. S. Government Printing Office, Washington, D. C., 1958, pp. 55–56.
4 Frazier, *The Negro Family in Chicago*, p. 189; Drake and Cayton, *op. cit.*, p. 604.
5 Miller, *op. cit.*

sponses to present situations, and were handicapped in planning ahead.[1] Although their
physical needs were well met and they were
not harshly treated, nevertheless emotional
needs were not satisfied. The children tended
to be placid and conforming. However, when
released from this situation and placed in
foster homes, they became hyperactive and
uncontrollable, and their behavior was characterized by tantrums, fights with other children, and running away. Their behavior was
impulsive, that is, not oriented toward a goal.
In early years in school they were unmanageable and impulsive, and, when blocked,
showed some hostility. In the foster home and
elsewhere they demanded a continuous display of affection, seemed never to be satiated,
but were unable to give affection in return.
The rejected child, on the other hand, has
usually spent some time with his parents and
has some identification with them, which
stimulates him to respond and to organize
his activities.

Redl and Wineman, in their discussion of
Children Who Hate, describe a boy of eight
who fits rather well the pattern of the deprived child.[2]

Larry was born in a charitable institution
where he remained for two years. His mother,
unmarried, visited him only occasionally. From
the time he was two years old, he was transferred from one foster home to another. When
he was six he went to live with his mother,
who had married. The mother was unable to
offer Larry a warm relationship. The stepfather
was an alcoholic, brutal and bullying. Larry
was severely mistreated physically by the stepfather, being beaten, kicked, thrown into a
drainage ditch, and locked into a shed for
hours at a time. Larry entered the residential
school for aggressive delinquent boys, of which
Redl was the director, shy, detached, and
afraid of adults. As he adjusted to the school
he became demanding, "commanding" someone
to bring him articles that were not available.
He was ridiculed by the other boys in the
school and often made the scapegoat of their
remarks and actions. He resented anything
that he regarded as a favor done by a counselor
to some other boy or as a slight to himself. His

reaction was to refuse to listen to explanations
and to scream his demands.

The other boys in the school (there were
five most of the time) seemed to fall somewhere between deprivation and rejection, or
to exhibit a combination. All were unable to
control their impulses, unresponsive to counselors, and at times uncontrollable in behavior. Their past records included stealing,
running away, and attempting to injure siblings.

Many such homeless children are shifted at
short intervals from one place to another. The
Gluecks found that 50.4 per cent of their 500
delinquent boys had had one or more changes
of family setting, compared with only 10
per cent of the nondelinquent group who had
not lived consistently in one household. Of
the delinquents, 19.6 per cent had made one
or two changes, 16.9 per cent three to five
changes, and 13.9 per cent six or more
changes.[3] Negro correctional school delinquents have an even higher proportion than
white delinquents from shattered homes.[4] In
a New York state correctional school, among
white boys the same proportion (50 per cent)
as in the Glueck study had lived continuously
in one family. The Negro boys had a very
different history of family stability. Only a
fifth had continuously lived in one family,
and 17 per cent had lived in four or more
different types of families. Under these conditions of constant change, many boys must
necessarily fail to establish a permanent satisfying relationship with any adult.

Poverty and employment of parents

Poverty, unemployed fathers, and employed mothers have often been held accountable for juvenile delinquency. Since the
Social Security Act was passed in 1935, the
sharp edge of dire poverty has been blunted
by such provisions as Aid to Dependent Children and Unemployment Insurance. Nevertheless much variation in economic status
remains, even within the lower class.

Poverty. In their study of 500 delinquents
and 500 nondelinquents, the Gluecks
matched the two groups on a number of
economic items. The usual occupation of the

1 William Goldfarb, "Psychological Privation in Infancy and Subsequent Adjustment," *American Journal of Orthopsychiatry,* 15 (1940), 247–255.
2 Abstracted from Fritz Redl and David Wineman,
Children Who Hate, Free Press, Glencoe, Illinois,
1951, pp. 55–56, 113, 121.

3 Glueck and Glueck, *op. cit.,* p. 121.
4 Sidney Axelrad, "Negro and White Male Institutionalized Delinquents," *American Journal of Sociology,*
57 (1952), 569–574.

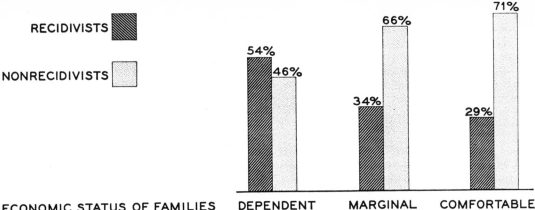

RECIDIVISTS

NONRECIDIVISTS

54%
46%

66%
34%

71%
29%

ECONOMIC STATUS OF FAMILIES   DEPENDENT   MARGINAL   COMFORTABLE

Figure 12. Economic Status of Families of Delinquents and of Recidivists, Cook County, Illinois. (Data from A. J. Reiss, Jr., "Delinquency as the Failure of Personal and Social Controls," *American Sociological Review,* 16 (1951), 200)

fathers was almost identical, with 68.4 per cent of the fathers of delinquents and 62.5 per cent of the fathers of nondelinquents doing unskilled and semiskilled work.[1] However, the usual economic status of the families of delinquents was far below that of nondelinquents. Almost none of either group were in comfortable economic circumstances and two-fifths of both groups were sporadically dependent. Here the resemblance stopped. Twice as many nondelinquents as delinquents were from families with marginal comfort: 41.0 per cent versus 20.0 per cent. In the lowest group, usually dependent, were 36.2 per cent of the delinquents but only 14.6 per cent of the nondelinquents.

Boys from the low-income group are also much more likely to repeat their delinquencies than are delinquent boys from comfortable or even marginal families. Figure 12 shows that among boys on probation in Cook County (Chicago), Illinois, the proportion who became recidivists increased as family economic status declined, with twice as high a proportion from the dependent level recidivating as from the comfortable level. Therefore, the conditions faced by the boy in the low-income family seem not only to permit or encourage delinquency but to lead to continued offenses.

The question immediately arises as to why low income is conducive to delinquency among boys. Most delinquency of boys is stealing, primarily for immediate use. This suggests that simple deprivation of food (especially luxury food), sports-type clothing favored by youth, and recreation equipment may be important. But other factors come

into play. Reiss, who compiled the data for Figure 12, suggests that economic deprivation may lead the boy to feel insecure and to doubt whether the economic system will provide for him in the future. Losing confidence in society, he loses his respect for the approval of society. He would therefore be able to justify his delinquencies and avert a sense of guilt.

Unemployment of the father. In addition, and perhaps as a more fundamental factor, are conditions within the family which underlie the low economic status. Of prime importance, according to Figures 13 and 14, is the inability of the father to support his family. Almost half of the delinquent boys in the Glueck study had fathers who were unwilling to assume responsibility for support, and 62 per cent had fathers (no doubt including most of the unwilling fathers) with poor or only fair work habits. Poor work habits were defined as loafing, laziness, dishonesty, waywardness, vagabondage, and instability; fair work habits were a combination of qualifications for work and periodic absences because of intoxication or vagabondage, or involved the choice of seasonal or other work with long unpaid periods of leisure.

These characteristics seem to link the unemployable fathers with fathers previously characterized as indifferent, hostile or rejective, as overly strict or erratic, or as absent from the home. It will be recalled that few

1 Glueck and Glueck, *op. cit.,* p. 106, 104.

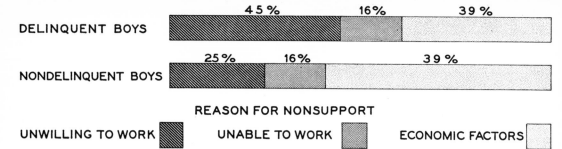

Figure 13. Major Reasons for Aid to Family from Relief Agencies and/or Relatives, among Five Hundred Delinquent and Five Hundred Nondelinquent Boys. (Data from Glueck and Glueck, *Unravelling Juvenile Delinquency*, Harvard University Press)

delinquent boys found their fathers the type of men whom they would unreservedly want to emulate. In addition, the mere fact of nonsupport lowers the status of a man, especially in families which are ordinarily self-supporting. With long-continued nonsupport and dependency on relief agencies, however, the family tends to adjust to its low status and to devise ways to exploit relief agencies or to supplement their contributions.[1] The man who manages to maneuver sources of money well, may have the respect of his family, while at the same time setting a model of work-avoidance and dupery for his children. However, in many lower-class dependent families, the father is personally disorganized and unable to provide support by work or otherwise.

In the light of this discussion, the suggestion arises that the association of the low economic condition of the family with excessive delinquency of boys is closely related to the character and personality of fathers who, even in a time of high employment, are unable to hold steady jobs.

Employment of the mother. Traditionally the employed mother is as much a deviant from social customs and good family policy as the unemployed father. The ideal was the mother who devoted herself fully to the task of homemaking and rearing children. The mother who sought work usually did so because the

family needed additional income for necessary expenses. She often was the mother without a husband in the home, or the wife of an unemployable or intermittently employed man. Economic need is still a motivation for employment of mothers; however, the percentage of mothers who are employed is increasing markedly and no longer represents dire economic need.[2] Employment often is a symbol of aspiration and of upward social mobility and as such may be an integrative and stabilizing influence.

The Glueck study shows only a moderate difference between the delinquents and nondelinquents, with both groups having more than half of the mothers at home (53.0 and 67.0 per cent respectively).[3] Approximately a fifth of the mothers of both groups had regular employment outside the home. More mothers of delinquents than of nondelinquents had occasional employment—26.6 per cent and 14.7 per cent. The part-time employment status of the mothers of delinquents and nondelinquents differed for only 12 per cent of the boys, with the delinquent boys in this group having an occasionally employed mother, the nondelinquents having the mother at home.

Within the delinquent group, mothers who worked tended somewhat more often than housewives to have husbands who were emotionally disturbed, had poor work habits, and were not supporting the family adequately.[4] Parents tended to be incompatible in the

1 Ruth Shonle Cavan, "Unemployment—Crisis of the Common Man," *Marriage and Family Living*, 21 (1959), 143–145.

2 The percentage of mothers with children under eighteen who were employed increased from about 20 to 30 per cent between 1948 and 1958; the percentage of all mothers of children under 6 who were employed increased from about 13 per cent to 20 per cent in the same decade. These percentages are still rising. *Children in a Changing World*, published and distributed by the White House Conference on Children and Youth, 1960, p. 10.

3 Glueck and Glueck, *op. cit.*, p. 112.

4 Sheldon and Eleanor Glueck, "Working Mothers and Delinquency," *Mental Hygiene*, 41 (July, 1957), 327–352.

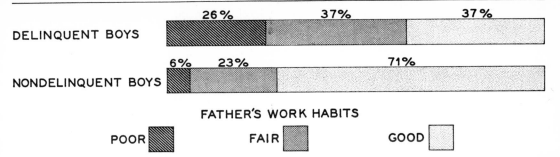

FATHER'S WORK HABITS

POOR   FAIR   GOOD

Figure 14. Usual Work Habits of Fathers of Five Hundred Delinquent and Five Hundred Nondelinquent Boys. (Data from Glueck and Glueck, *Unravelling Juvenile Delinquency*, Harvard University Press)

group with employed mothers, and the family lacked cohesion. Some of these situations were more acute in families in which the mother was occasionally employed than in those in which she worked regularly. Sons of employed mothers had less supervision and more freedom away from home than sons of housewives. However, many differences are not extreme and many of the sons of housewives also faced unfavorable situations in the home.

It seems difficult if not impossible to isolate the effect that employment of the mother has on delinquent behavior. Employment of the mother is part of a general family pattern involving an inadequate or disturbed father, low economic level, and lack of family cohesion, all of which are independently related to delinquent behavior. They are probably all closely interrelated. Together they create a disjointed family situation which fails to give the boy (and probably even more the girl) firm identification with loving and admired parents.

The delinquency-prone family

From the studies cited in this chapter and other less extensive studies much too numerous to be quoted, it is possible to draw some conclusions about the delinquency-prone family. In comparison with families of nondelinquent boys, delinquency-prone families as a group have a greater proportion of rejecting or harsh parents, parents who impress their sons as indifferent to their welfare, parents who are erratic or lax in discipline, or who offer little for the sons to admire or emulate. Delinquency-prone families are more likely than other families to be broken (for some delinquents there is no family at all), with the female-based family a common type in some groups. The delinquency-prone family frequently is financially dependent on outside assistance or public relief; when the

mother is employed it is usually at occasional jobs. There is evidence that an accumulation of unfavorable factors increases the likelihood that the boy will become delinquent and also that he will become a recidivist. However, some unfavorable factors can be balanced against favorable ones—for example, the effect of the harsh father may be neutralized by the loving mother. Thus families differ as to the number and combination of favorable and unfavorable factors.

It seems probable that with adequate analysis families could be placed in a continuity with reference to the likelihood that one or more children would become delinquent, ranging from families with a high degree of delinquency-proneness downward through intermediate stages to families with a very low degree of delinquency-proneness. The former type of family would tend to have many unfavorable factors associated with delinquent behavior, the latter type would have few unfavorable factors but many favorable ones associated with nondelinquent behavior. However, the delinquency-prone family usually would have some favorable elements, and the conformity-prone family some unfavorable elements.

Within a family proneness to delinquency differs from one child to another. Each child has his own personal relationship with his parents. One child in a family may be loved, another rejected; one child may be favored by the mother, another by the father. The ordinal position and the sex of a child may be factors. Moreover, children differ in physical and temperamental qualities. The strong boy may be treated differently than the handicapped boy, the bright child than the dull child, within the same family.

From this complicated web of family relationships each child acquires his first concept of himself, his first set of values, his first roles. If he is given a conception of himself as worthy, conforming, and good and acquires values that are aligned with those of the larger society and an opportunity to act out corresponding roles, he is not likely to become permanently delinquent, although he may as a child vacillate between good and bad behavior within the limits of tolerance for a child of his age and sex. The child who is rejected, who conceives himself as unworthy, who acquires a delinquent set of values or only a confusion of values, and who develops nonconforming or confusing roles to play is much more likely to become a delinquent.

Virtually all the material in this chapter is confined to the lower or possibly lower-middle class (McCord study), and it refers to children who have been sufficiently delinquent to become court cases, correctional school inmates, or adult criminals. Most of the data refer to boys. The moderately vacillating child, the middle-class delinquent, and the girl delinquent have not yet been adequately studied in their family setting. Additional research is urgently needed since it cannot be assumed that the discussion in this chapter applies to these groups in the same way or to the same degree as to the seriously delinquent lower-class boy.

Bibliography

Axelrad, Sidney, "Negro and White Male Institutionalized Delinquents," *American Journal of Sociology,* 57 (1952), 569–574.

Bach, George R., "Father-fantasies and Father-typing in Father-separated Children," *Child Development,* 17 (1946), 63–80.

Bettelheim, Bruno, *Truants from Life, The Rehabilitation of Emotionally Disturbed Children,* Free Press, Glencoe, Illinois, 1955.

Drake, St. Clair, and Horace R. Cayton, *Black Metropolis: A Study of Negro Life in a Northern City,* Harcourt, Brace and Company, New York, 1945.

Eissler, K. R., and Paul Federn, editors, *Searchlights on Delinquency, New Psychoanalytic Studies,* International Universities Press, Inc., New York, 1949.

Frazier, E. Franklin, *The Negro Family in Chicago,* University of Chicago Press, Chicago, 1932.

Gardner, George E., "Separation of the Parents and the Emotional Life of the Child," *Mental Hygiene,* 40 (1956), 53–64.

Glueck, Sheldon and Eleanor, *Unraveling Juvenile Delinquency,* Harvard University Press, Cambridge, Massachusetts, 1950, Chapters 8–11.

———, "Working Mothers and Delinquency," *Mental Hygiene,* 41 (1957), 327–352.

Goldfarb, William, "Psychological Privation in Infancy and Subsequent Adjustment," *American Journal of Orthopsychiatry,* 15 (1940), 247–255.

Healy, William and Augusta F. Bronner, *New Light on Delinquency and Its Treatment,* Yale University Press, New Haven, Connecticut, 1936.

Jenkins, Richard L., *Breaking the Patterns of Defeat,* J. B. Lippincott Company, Philadelphia, 1954.

McCord, William and Joan, *Origins of Crime, A New Evaluation of the Cambridge-Somerville Youth Study,* Columbia University Press, New York, 1959.

Merrill, Maud A., *Problems of Child Delinquency,* Houghton Mifflin Company, Boston, 1947, Chapter 3.

Monahan, Thomas P., "Broken Homes by Age of Delinquent Children," *Journal of Social Psychology,* 51 (1960), 387–397.

———, "Family Status and the Delinquent Child: A Reappraisal and Some New Findings," *Social Forces,* 35 (1957), 250–258.

———, "The Trend in Broken Homes among Delinquent Children," *Marriage and Family Living,* 19 (1957), 362–365.

Nye, F. Ivan, "Child Adjustment in Broken and in Unhappy Unbroken Homes," *Marriage and Family Living,* 19 (1957), 356–361.

———, "Employment Status of Mothers and Adjustment of Adolescent Children," *Marriage and Family Living,* 21 (1959), 240–244.

———, *Family Relationships and Delinquent Behavior,* John Wiley and Sons, Inc., New York, 1958.

Parsons, Talcott, "Certain Primary Sources and Patterns of Aggression in the Social Structure of the Western World," *Psychiatry,* 10 (1947), 167–181.

Redl, Fritz, and David Wineman, *Children Who Hate,* Free Press, Glencoe, Illinois, 1951.

Reiss, Albert J., Jr., "Delinquency as the Failure of Personal and Social Controls," *American Sociological Review,* 16 (1951), 196–208.

Roucek, Joseph S., editor, *Juvenile Delinquency,* Philosophical Library, New York, 1958, Chapters 4 and 9.

Shaw, Clifford R., and Henry D. McKay, *Social Factors in Juvenile Delinquency,* A Study . . . for the National Commission on Law Observance and Enforcement, Number 13, volume 2, U. S. Government Printing Office, Washington, D. C., 1931, Chapters 9 and 10.

Stoke, Stuart M., "An Inquiry into the Concept of Identification," *Journal of Genetic Psychology,* 76 (1950), 163–189.

Chapter **11**

Three delinquent boys

The purpose of the three case summaries given in this chapter is to illustrate the way in which various factors associated with delinquency operate together and the process by which minor delinquencies of early childhood develop into the serious delinquencies of later adolescence and (in two cases) into the criminal behavior of adults.

The cases show three different clusters of factors. One case is of a boy deprived of opportunity for identification with either a family or a peer group. He was set afloat in society without roots, preparation for employment, or a sense of social responsibility. Fortuitous circumstances had familiarized him with the use of firearms. Childhood attempts to solve certain problems by stealing found their adult counterpart in armed robbery. Another case depicts a boy with normal working-class family relationships, whose moral standards and habits were developed in close ties first with semidelinquent street-corner boys and later with adult criminals. As an adult he was a career criminal of moderate success. The third case concerns a typical gang boy, the influence of whose peer group far outweighed the influence of his family. Of more than average intelligence, he was eventually able to identify with adults who understood his problems and who were able to provide a way of life, status, and prestige that did not depend upon membership in a fighting gang.

All three cases are summarized from detailed first hand accounts, supplemented in one instance by careful study of agency rec-ords covering the entire life of the boy. All three cases are edited by journalists who specialize in reporting criminal events. The accounts are factual; they do not attempt an analysis.

The cases are not presented as typical of delinquency in general or of a certain type of delinquency. They were selected for very simple reasons. A limited number of detailed cases of delinquents is in print; unpublished cases are apt to be fragmentary, to be slanted toward one or another theory, or not to be available for publication because of their confidential nature. These three published cases were readily available in rather complete form. Moreover, in each case the history of the boy is carried on into adulthood, thus giving a complete longitudinal picture through the childhood years into a firmly fixed adult mode of life. In two cases, the youth of the boy occurred during the 1940's or 1950's and therefore is of sufficient recency to reflect current conditions.[1]

The delinquent deprived of family or peer group identification

The deprived child was described earlier in this book as one who has never had an opportunity to live intimately within a family group. Hence he fails to secure identification with parents. Learning of values and approved norms comes through the process of identification with the beloved parents or other adults. Their values and norms are accepted by the child as right; thus the basis of his conscience is formed. The deprived child does not go through this process. Sometimes an attachment to some other adult than the parent—a relative, minister, teacher, youth leader, or neighbor—acts as a partial substitute, but some children lack even this partial identification. The second source of identification usually is the peer group, which offers its version of values and norms. They may be congruent with or opposed to the

1 Some case studies prepared by professionals are in print. These were not used for a number of reasons. Some represent a past period; others do not carry the case beyond adolescence; still others are strongly slanted toward one or another theoretical interpretation. For the purposes of illustration, the unadorned accounts by journalists seemed most appropriate and provided opportunity for selection of a variety of factors associated with delinquency without strong emphasis on any one theory. The bibliography at the end of this chapter lists other published case studies.

adult values and norms. In either case, the child is incorporated into the peer group and has the security and control of his fellow members. When a child lacks both family and peer group, he picks up the pattern of his life in hit or miss fashion without much regard to the values and expectations of other people.

Identification with a close intimate group serves another function in addition to development of values and norms. It gives the child a sense of worth. The child without such close attachments often feels that he is no good and unwanted by anyone. Moreover, he has no opportunity to learn how to build up a close friendship or love relationship with anyone.

The deprived child is rootless. He drifts into and out of situations with little planning. He is concerned with his own impulses and needs; his behavior is unrestrained by consideration for others. He may be openly hostile or simply bewildered and ineffectual.

It does not follow that such a child necessarily becomes delinquent, but the usual restraints imposed by conscience and group controls are lacking. Fortuitous circumstances may cause the child to become delinquent. If his needs are met through his delinquency, he tends to continue in it. He does not feel moral or social qualms or responsibilities.

The case that follows traces the experiences of a deprived child from birth to his imprisonment at age twenty. His story illustrates the conditions of the deprived child who has never lived in one family long enough to build up close identifications with parent-substitutes. He usually lived in foster homes in some range of middle-class neighborhood where his position as a foster child set him apart from other children who lived with their own parents. He was taunted by other children and hence failed to build up associations with a peer group. Thus deprived of both adult and peer primary associations, he failed to develop a clear concept of his own personality or role. He also failed to absorb the moral values of society but lived in terms of immediate individual impulses and needs.

Robert Brown was born in 1928 in a hospital in New York City to a young woman who was not married to his father.[1] His

mother took him home with her and for two years seemingly supported him by working as a waitress. She left him alone or with neighbors while she was at work. When he was two years old she became ill and asked for help from the Federation of Protestant Welfare Agencies. They suggested a foster home or a day nursery while she recuperated, but his mother did not follow through on either suggestion. Six months later in December, 1930, the Society for the Prevention of Cruelty to Children investigated a complaint and found Robert and his mother in an unheated furnished room. The SPCC filed a complaint in Children's Court, charging Robert's mother with neglect of child. Robert was placed in the SPCC's child shelter, and the judge ordered an investigation. The Department of Welfare reported that Robert's mother was unable to support him, and the judge placed Robert in the care of the Department of Welfare for placement in a foster home. Robert did not see or hear from his mother again.

Robert's mother was born in England and at the age of twelve came to the United States with her father and four brothers and sisters. She attended high school for two years, was married at the age of seventeen, and had a son. Five years later she deserted her husband and son. Two years later, Robert was born, an illegitimate child.

Robert remained in the care of the Department of Welfare for about three weeks after the court took him from his mother, at which time he was accepted by the New York Foundling Hospital for care. This is a Catholic agency, chosen because Robert's mother was Catholic. Robert remained at the hospital for three weeks until he was placed in a foster home.

In the twelve years between the ages of four and sixteen, Robert lived in five foster homes and one orphanage. A general pattern developed in each foster home placement. At first he made a good impression, and the relationship with the foster mother tended to be friendly, even close. This period was followed by one of dissension or conflict with the foster

1 Summarized from Croswell Bowen, *They Went Wrong*, McGraw-Hill Book Company, New York, 1954, pp. 30–96. The account is based on study of agency records that began with the boy's birth, evidence brought out at the trial, and interviews with the boy and others. Comments in brackets are those of the author of this textbook; they emphasize factors that have been discussed in preceding chapters as significant in the development of delinquent behavior.

mother. The mother gradually became estranged from him and finally requested his removal. Each new foster home entailed a change of school; in addition, he was sometimes shifted from public to parochial school or vice versa. Usually, he adjusted well at first in school. Then he would begin to have trouble with teachers and pupils. Almost from the time he first entered school, he stole small sums at home and school. A brief summary of each placement shows the developing pattern.

1. The Foundling Hospital, which retained supervision throughout his childhood, first placed him in the Korowski home where there were three children of the parents and two other boarding children. The family lived in Jamaica, near New York. The parents became fond of Robert, and he sometimes returned to visit them after he left.

The initial good adjustment lasted until after he entered school at the age of six. There children were curious as to why his name was Brown rather than Korowski. He began to wonder about his parents. Also other children seemed to come from families with more money to spend than his foster parents had. He began to steal pennies from the teacher's desk that had been collected for milk. He bought candy to distribute to other children. He pinched other children and was mildly disorderly in the classroom. Both teacher and foster mother criticized him to the visitor from the Foundling Hospital with the boy present. The teacher asked other children to report his misdeeds before him.

He was transferred to a parochial school, but the stealing of pennies continued. He was again criticized before other children.

At this point, at the age of eight, he was given a psychiatric examination. His intelligence quotient was found to be 109, and he appeared to react normally.

2. The Foundling Hospital decided to try a different foster home. He was in the second home only a few weeks when he contracted diphtheria and spent several weeks in a hospital. While he was there, another child was placed in the foster home.

3. Upon release he entered his third foster home with the Dolsons, who lived on Long Island. Mr. Dolson was a municipal clerk in New York. At first Robert seemed to fit into the family, although he disliked Mr. Dolson

from the beginning. When he picked up a toy pistol belonging to the Dolson's son, Mr. Dolson laughed and said jokingly, "I see he's never going to be any good." Robert, already in some doubt about his status, blamed himself because he was no good; according to his later statements, he felt that this was because he didn't have a mother.

He asked Mrs. Dolson about his mother but she was unable to tell him anything; the visitor likewise could not help him. His concern about his parents was a dominant theme. He came to dislike Mrs. Dolson and was extremely jealous of her son, two years his senior. He was destructive of articles of which Mrs. Dolson was fond, and it seemed to her he did everything he could to hurt her feelings. Mrs. Dolson for her part denied him simple pleasures that neighborhood children enjoyed.

Robert attended a parochial school in the area, where again the children taunted him because his name differed from that of his foster parents. He shoved them around and stole pennies from them. He was transferred to a public school, where he adjusted well at first but in a few months seemed nervous and was not studying. Stealing at school continued; one time he stole from neighbors.

4. After four years at the Dolsons, Robert at the age of twelve was placed in his fourth foster home. He and Mrs. Dolson parted without any show of regret on either side. He remained only one year with the Snows. They accepted him as one of their own children, of whom they had two. Neighbors also accepted him, and he was invited to children's parties. He had an allowance; Mr. Snow found him a small job and then supplemented his earnings so that he could have a bicycle. Mr. Snow also took him to see a priest and he became an altar boy. He was adjusting well in school.

The end to this happy situation came four months after placement when a boy at school stood before a glass paneled door and said to Robert, "We don't allow orphans in here." He slammed the door, whereupon Robert crashed into the door, breaking the glass.

He began to steal again, at home and from a neighbor. He was persistent in questioning Mrs. Snow about his mother, but she was unable to tell him anything.

In January, 1941, Robert graduated from

elementary school and entered high school. He still lived with the Snows, who tried to help him. Twice Mrs. Snow took him to the city to see a psychiatrist, an experience that Robert enjoyed. His stealing had increased. He angered a grocer by stealing a pie and a little later was picked up by the police on a complaint that he had stolen money from a house. He admitted the theft, after having first accounted for the money to Mrs. Snow by saying he earned it caddying on the golf course. He used part of the money to treat children to rides on a merry-go-round.

5. The Foundling Hospital resumed care of Robert, and he was placed in his fifth foster home. Robert stayed with Mrs. Hubert, a widow, for about a year, when she decided to go to work in a factory.

6. Robert was now fourteen, an age when foster home placement is extremely difficult. The hospital therefore placed him in a Catholic orphanage about twenty-five miles from the city. He was not received by the other boys as well as had been expected he would be—since they, too, were orphans, he had expected immediate friendliness. Other boys were friendly to the nuns, but this repelled him. He ran away several times, refused to study, and as he approached the age of sixteen requested release to fend for himself. This request was granted, although he still remained under the nominal custody of the Department of Welfare.

At the orphanage he made one contact that seemed meaningful to him and that continued off and on until the time of his imprisonment. This was with Father Bernard Donachie, a young man preparing for the priesthood who, with other seminary students, took troublesome boys on picnics or to the movies. Father Donachie offered the boy friendship and understanding, which were accepted. He and the boy had long talks, and Robert later regarded him as his only real friend. Father Donachie was appalled at the lack of emotional depth or conception of moral values that Robert possessed.

[Comment by author. Robert's response to Father Donachie was normal for his age. In midteens if not earlier boys tend to emulate some man and to break their attachments to their mothers. Robert apparently had not had a close attachment to any foster father, with the possible exception of Mr.

Snow. His attachment to Father Donachie was thus especially significant, but a normal move for him to make. Robert had lacked a strong attachment to any woman. He seemed unable to accept the friendliness of any foster mother—and the mothers were drawn to him at first—because of his anxiety over his mother which seemed to stand in the way of the usual identification that a small boy would develop for an affectionate foster mother. At the orphanage he was beyond the age to find the nuns satisfactory mother-substitutes. In other words, he had completely missed the emotional development as well as the moral training that come from early identification of a boy with his mother, normally followed by identification with his father. Regardless of the material comforts in all the homes, Robert was a deprived child in the essentials for good personality development.]

With Robert's release from the orphanage, another phase of his life began, the most prominent feature of which was his rootlessness and his utter lack of ability to accept the responsibilities of work. For a time he changed rooms and jobs every few weeks, unable to earn more than a minimum wage as he lacked training and adequate education. He began to steal and for a time traveled around the East. Once he was arrested for vagrancy but released when it was learned he was still a charge of the Department of Welfare. He tried in vain to find his mother; he sought information about her from social agencies that had had contact with her but they either could not or would not tell him as much as he wished to know. He had a brief friendship with a girl from a respectable family, whose father, Mr. Harris, continued to aid him through various escapades.

Finally, by changing the date of his birth on his certificate of baptism, he enlisted in the marines. Soon he was associating with a marine who spent his time drinking and fighting. He deserted, after stealing a revolver, and returned to New York. With no job and no money, he began to steal, sometimes alone, sometimes with some other young man. At gun point, they held up people in taverns or on the street, in random fashion without preliminary planning. In one night Robert and a friend secured $225 and three wrist watches. He was arrested the same night and was sentenced to Elmira Reformatory, where he spent two years, including several periods of up to thirty-nine days in solitary confinement for misbehavior.

Released on parole, he was almost immediately involved in more armed holdups. He either could not stay with a job or could not find one. He lied to his parole officer and stopped seeing him. His lies were discovered, and a search was made to find him and return him to the reformatory. However, he was not found. He was now associating with other young criminals hanging around the Times Square area. He rented a small apartment and was generous with food and drink for various young people he met. He was especially fond of two waitresses who had rooms in the building. He paid his expenses by armed holdups, carried out alone, that netted him about $75 each.

He had no feeling of guilt about the holdups. His only remorse seemed to be that he had betrayed the friendship of Mr. Harris, who had tried to help him in his struggles. He resolved this feeling of guilt by sending Mr. Harris a false report that he had a job and would see him soon.

His final armed robbery was little different from preceding ones except that in the course of it he killed a man without provocation. He held up a small hotel at night, taking $175 and herding three employees into a rear office. He demanded that they open a cabinet that he thought was a safe containing more money. They were unable to do this, and Robert threatened to kill one. He maintained later that he did not intend to kill anyone, but his finger slipped, and one man was instantly killed. Robert fled and returned to his apartment in a state of agitation. He told one of his girl friends what had happened. She told a man friend with whom Robert had had a quarrel, although the girl did not know this. The man apparently tipped off the police, and Robert was arrested without resistance.

Robert was tried with three able attorneys appointed by the court to defend him. During the time when he was in jail awaiting trial he was visited by the Monsignor who was head of the Foundling Hospital and by Father Donachie who had befriended him when he lived in the orphanage. No one of his foster parents or friends came to see him.

Three psychiatrists examined Robert and brought in three different reports. Dr. Fred-

eric Wertham gave Robert a Rorschach test, the interpretation of which showed that Robert was disturbed mentally and was subject to periods of intellectual confusion. He functioned in an immature explosive manner, had deep fears, felt rejected, and was arrested in emotional development at a level before the normal one of puberty. Dr. Wertham felt that Robert was dominated by a fixation on the mother image, shown in his desire to travel as symbolizing his search for his mother and his daydreaming about her. With this preoccupation he had failed to develop emotional warmth or normal social relationships. Dr. Wertham also thought his violence stemmed from the comic books that he had read as a child.[1]

Dr. Wertham diagnosed Robert as having a schizoid psychopathic personality with obsessive and paranoid features; the stress was so acute that Robert was legally insane at the time of the killing, that is, he could not detect right from wrong.

Robert was also examined by Dr. Perry Lichtenstein, a psychiatrist attached to the staff of the district (prosecuting) attorney. His report was mainly a refutation of Dr. Wertham's report. He did not find that the murder was explosive, nor that Robert had a mother complex that affected his sense of right and wrong. He was not legally insane.

A third psychiatrist, Dr. Leo Orenstein, chief of the psychiatric clinic of the Court of General Sessions, also examined Robert. He characterized Robert as immature and poorly adjusted, with deep-seated feelings of insecurity, based on his childhood experiences. He had an attitude of indifference toward social and conventional demands and dramatized his aggressive behavior as an outcome of his difficulty in finding security. Because of his insecure childhood, he had failed to sublimate his infantile aggressive impulses and projected them on society. Robert was not psychotic or legally insane. He was classified as of average intelligence, with an aggressive personality.

Robert's own explanation was that he needed money; he could earn very little and he wanted some comforts and luxuries. He wanted to have a good time. He regarded

1 Dr. Wertham is noted for his belief that comic books are a major influence in the commission of violent crimes by youth. See his *Seduction of the Innocent*, Rinehart and Company, New York, 1953. Many psychiatrists do not share this view.

robbery as a way to "earn" money and prided himself on not robbing drunks or swindling people by selling fake jewelry. He resented the fact that the newspapers called him a "killer." He wanted to find his mother but did not believe that caused him to steal; he did not think comic books were a cause.

Robert confessed to second degree murder and was given a sentence of forty-five years to life in prison.

[Comments: As commented earlier, Robert's many moves during childhood from one foster home to another and the partial acceptance by each foster mother, followed by rejection, left him without identification with a mother (later with a father). He therefore did not receive the normal socialization in conventional morals that children in a stable family group usually receive. When he was finally without the supervision of the orphanage, he had no ties to an intimate group that would judge his behavior.

The taunting by schoolmates had interferred with the development of peer group associations. In the middle-class areas in which he lived, these associations would probably have been nondelinquent. He did not associate with delinquents as a child or young adolescent. He was socially isolated from any peer group contacts. His later contact with the Harris girl was shortlived; his contacts with the two waitresses were superficial. He seemed unable to make any deep friendships with people of his own age. His attempts to make friends as a child were through buying candy for other children. As a young adult he continued this method, buying food and whiskey and inviting acquaintances to his apartment.

His progress in stealing follows normal developmental stages: first, pennies at school, then larger sums from houses when he found an easy opportunity, then articles from stores. After he became familiar with firearms in the marines, he began to steal at gunpoint. He did not plan his crimes well in advance; he continued to operate on an opportunistic basis. He did not belong to a group of skilled criminals. He was an amateur throughout.

Robert represents one type of juvenile delinquent, who has never quite been assimilated into any primary group and who seeks through thefts a way to meet needs that more conventional people satisfy through social relationships and through earning money.]

From delinquent child to career criminal

This case illustrates the developmental character of delinquent and criminal behavior. It traces the progression from little-boy escapades for fun and food, to opportunistic or partially planned thefts of money as a sideline to normal family and school life, to a noncriminal occupation which collapsed under the weight of criminal acts, and finally to an adult career as a skilled thief.

Eugene was not the victim of tragic circumstances. He came from a working-class family; he was not neglected or mistreated. He did not live in an area with a high rate of delinquency. He was not a member of a thoroughly delinquent gang and did not as a young adolescent associate with adult criminals. But he and his pals found many opportunities to get money and other things they wanted without working for them. Apparently they were never effectively halted in their drift toward crime. Neither family nor school set future conventional goals for Eugene toward which he might work. They did not succeed in implanting in him stiff moral standards. As a youth he acted impulsively, looking for a quick money return for his efforts. Crime offered more opportunities to get what he wanted than the type of work he was prepared to do. Later, stealing became his occupation and guided his activities.

The case traces Eugene's life from childhood until he had reached the age of forty-five. At that time he had "retired" from his criminal career, not because of any inner reformation but because he feared one more arrest and conviction might send him to prison for the rest of his life.

Eugene's crimes were primarily in the field of theft; the list consisted of various types of thefts and other crimes related to theft. It included petty larceny, grand larceny, burglary and possession of burglar's tools, safe blowing, robbery, armed robbery, automobile theft, transporting stolen automobiles across a state line, bootlegging, receiving stolen property, arson, assault and assault with intent to kill, carrying concealed weapons, frequenting and operating a gambling place, vagrancy, bribery, perjury, subornation of perjury, jury tampering, conspiracy, and being a fugitive from justice. As a boy, this man of crime was a run-of-the-mill juvenile delinquent.

Eugene was born about 1905 to working-class parents who lived in a small Chicago suburb.[1] His father, a machinist, was regularly employed. Family relationships were satisfactory; other children in the family (two girls) turned out well. Even after he had become heavily involved in crime, Eugene maintained friendly intermittent contacts with his family. Since he rarely carried out a serious crime in the suburb, they were unaware of the extent of his activities.

Eugene's school relationships were superficial and not wholly satisfactory. He attended regularly but studied only enough to get by. When he entered high school, he became aware that some children came from wealthy families; others, like Eugene, were of working-class origin. Eugene was sensitive to the differences; the wealthy children had many more privileges and their own circle of friends. Their future was planned for them by their parents. Eugene felt unwelcome among them. He had no future plans and little motivation to remain in school. After one year of high school he ran away at the age of fifteen and succeeded in enlisting in the navy.

Eugene's childhood friends were five or six boys with backgrounds similar to his own, who found their recreation on the streets. They stole from fruit carts, partly for the fruit, but partly for the fun involved in being chased by the vendor. They made forays into nearby orchards for fruit to eat. They made friends with the driver of a bakery wagon and soon learned who the customers were. They then would order cake at the store and charge it to a customer. No one stopped them; they regarded these activities as normal and felt no sense of guilt.

With adolescence their activities expanded. They would wait on the station platform of the elevated railway until a train pulled in. Then just as it pulled out, they would reach through an open window and grab a purse that some woman had lying loosely in her lap. The train proceeded to the next station; the boys hastily left the platform. They spent the money at an amusement park. They carried off candy cases from elevated stations, locked and unattended at night, and ate the

candy. They were never caught in these escapades.

During Eugene's years in the navy, the pattern of his future life was set. He had already learned that many things can be achieved without work. Also, he was now thrown with young adults and soon found some who were exploiting their assignments for their own profit. Some officers were not adverse to making extra money. He paid an officer $50 to get him assigned to a job that would not involve drilling, which Eugene regarded as hard work. He became a night watchman with a key to the warehouse which he was expected to inspect for any fires. Soon he was spending a minimum of time on his job, bribing his way past the guard, and carrying bundles of goods from the warehouse to dispose of them through friends he had made at a nearby restaurant. Stolen blankets, pea coats, socks, sweaters, and other articles brought him a tidy income, much of which he lost in crap games. Eventually he was discovered; he lost his job in the warehouse and was sentenced to thirty days at hard labor.

Later he was assigned to a hospital ship on the West Coast. His shore leaves introduced him to the world of vice. His free time was spent with professional prostitutes, among whom he found a ready market for narcotic drugs stolen from the ship. He was caught participating in the burglary of a safe on shipboard and was sentenced to prison for two years and given a dishonorable discharge. In nine months he was released on parole. In prison he made contacts with older professional criminals and on release went to a hotel in San Francisco about which he had learned while in prison. This hotel was the hangout of experienced criminals, each with his own special type of crime. Eugene paid one of them $50 to introduce him to the crime of armed robbery. Eugene's share was several hundred dollars, soon spent on prostitutes. He began to travel about the country, riding freight trains, committing burglaries, getting arrested, bribing his way out of trouble when he could and spending short periods in jail when he could not. Eugene was now eighteen, just at the upper age of classification as a juvenile delinquent. He returned home, where he lived for a while. He worked but continued to burglarize and eventually was caught. His parents, thinking this was his first experience in stealing, secured a lawyer for

1 John Bartlow Martin, *My Life in Crime*, Harper and Brothers, New York, 1952. Martin is a responsible journalist who specializes in serious articles and books on crime. The present book is the life story of a criminal, whom Martin calls Eugene, as he told it to Martin.

him. He was placed on probation, which turned out to be very superficial and no impediment to continued stealing.

He transferred his activities to Chicago where he was affiliated with first one group of criminals and then another. He made no pretense of working. He never became integrated into organized crime but remained a burglar, working alone or with one or two associates. He moved from one part of the country to another, since a string of burglaries in one city might end in arrest. He never married, but lived from time to time with first one woman, than another, leaving each when he felt it expedient to move on. He never became involved in community affairs. He was always ready to move on at a moment's notice.

Several times he was convicted of stealing and spent several terms in state and federal prisons, including returns for violation of parole.

He stole and spent immediately some $18,-000 to $20,000 a year. In his total career as a criminal covering a span of about twenty-five years, including the time spent in prisons, he estimated that he had stolen money and goods worth a half million dollars, on which he had realized about $150,000, all spent as he got it. (The yearly average from this amount is less than his figure given above of $18,000 to $20,000 per year, which might have represented his best years.)

Long years in prison did not reform him. He never felt a sense of remorse or guilt. He did regret that he had not become a member of some organized criminal group, where he might have made more money and avoided arrests and convictions through a corrupt political fix. Imprisonment caused him to change his occupation from criminal to a legal job, since he feared that another conviction would send him to prison for life. He was never able to secure a job of any importance because he could not risk investigation of his past life. He dared seek only mediocre jobs, none of which paid more than a living wage.

[A comparison of Eugene's story with other published biographies or autobiographies of thieves indicates that it probably is rather typical of what happens to professional thieves. His childhood and adolescence seems fairly typical of the working class. Everyday activities include stealing of a minor nature that is common to the street life of lower-class urban areas, whether in the inner city or in industrial suburbs. The boys "pick up" the ways of stealing as they may also pick up the techniques of playing ball in a vacant lot. The stealing, as the ball playing, is all part of a boy's life, expected, tolerated.

Sometime during adolesence the boy's activities become predominantly either criminal or noncriminal. He does not necessarily make a decision to become a criminal. Usually he drops out of school, which seems to have no meaning for him. He associates with other dropouts. He may find a job but drop it because it too has no interest or meaning for him. Sometimes the job opens ways for stealing. Especially if he is not caught and the rewards are high, crime makes more and more appeal to him. He finds himself more at home in the hangouts of criminals than in the clubs of more conventional boys.

The final step is the acceptance of a criminal philosophy of life, with various rationalizations that protect the criminal from a sense of remorse or guilt. Common rationalizations of thieves are that thievery is a form of work, since it requires planning, specific skills, and personal risk. The thief may pride himself on stealing only from the rich, never from the poor. If he does not carry a gun, he takes pride in this fact and justifies his behavior by comparison with that of criminals who threaten people with guns or physical force.

The acceptance of a philosophy of crime apparently begins in childhood, partly because the rationalizations are part of the street culture and partly because no conventional agency has built up an opposing concept of what is good to insulate the boy against the impact of the philosophy of the delinquent and criminal world.]

A gang boy who redefines his concept and role

In certain disorganized areas of cities where conventional and law-enforcement agencies are inactive or weak, boys' gangs develop that not only prey on householders and business men but are in conflict with each other. Families are unable to compete with the pull of the gangs. Indigenous agencies and businesses, manned by residents of the area, often are tolerant of the delinquency of youth. To them, as to the boys, social agencies, school attendance officers, and the police often seem to interfere with their lives and to cause trouble. They tend not to seek help from these sources.

Not all gang boys grow up to be ne'er-do-wells or criminals. Many find places in conventional jobs. A few extricate themselves completely not only from their gang but also from the area that breeds gangs and crime.

The present case is of a Negro boy in a lower-class neighborhood in Brooklyn, a boy beyond the control of his parents, steeped in the delinquency of the streets, and leader of his gang. The description of his gang life can be duplicated many times in other published accounts. The case is important in that it shows the process by which the boy, separated from his gang, is led to change his self-conception and to seek a new, conventional role. The boy had an intelligence quotient of 160, which placed him far above the average in ability. His intelligence however did not save him from gang life nor did it cause him to reason logically that legal pursuits are any better than criminal ones. It did make it possible, however, for him to take a long leap from a lower-class area through college and graduate school into a respected professional middle-class occupation.

Frenchy, as the boy is called in the book about him, was the son of Jamaican Negroes who had migrated to New York.[1] His mother was from a middle-class family, whose proudest achievement was their co-operation in helping Frenchy's uncle secure a medical education. This uncle was constantly held up to Frenchy as the model after whom he should pattern his life. Only in late adolesence did this model come to have personal meaning for him.

Frenchy's father was a working man, lower in social status than the mother's family; her marriage to him had been disapproved but her contacts with her family remained close. The father worked steadily, except for periods of illness or unavoidable unemployment. The father followed the life of the lower-class man of the area, playing policy, gambling a little, and drinking a little but not to the extent that his job or family status was damaged. When Frenchy was a small child, it was a matter of pride that his mother did not

work outside the home. Later, such employment became necessary during a long period of illness on the part of the father, when the family sank to a poverty level. Later, the family was able to move to a somewhat better neighborhood than the typical slum where Frenchy began his life.

Frenchy's relationship with his mother was close; she was loving and sympatic, although she strongly disapproved of his delinquencies. His one regret seemed to be the pain that he gave her, yet the feeling was never strong enough to prevent his continued misbehavior. He and his father were antagonistic. The father was inclined to be authoritarian and to punish Frenchy for any trouble by severe beatings.

At school Frenchy found the work easy to do, so easy in fact that he was bored. He had the highest grades in his class. He misbehaved in school in ways annoying to the teacher: he drummed on his desk like a bongoman and sang calypso songs. Once he hit a teacher.

After his mother began to work, Frenchy spent all his free time with the neighborhood gang. After the family moved, he continued to return to the old neighborhood to be with them. At first he was simply a little boy hanging on the fringe, admiring the older boys. Later he was admitted to the activities and was head of a unit of the Bishops gang. By the time he was thirteen, his unit had broken away to form an independent gang, called the Deacons, of which he was the leader.

The activities of the gang were typical of street gangs—hanging around a meeting place, working a little at odd jobs, stealing a little, indulging in sex activities with girls who permitted it, experimenting with marihuana, and occasionally planning and executing brief but violent fights with a rival gang, sometimes with the use of guns.

By the time Frenchy was fourteen, he had been before the Children's Court thirteen times, all but the last time being released to his parents, who by the time he was out of elementary school had no control over him. On the thirteenth appearance in Court, Frenchy was committed to the Warwick State Training School for boys, at Warwick, with the approval of his parents.

He had expected his parents to plead for his release as they had done previously; their refusal was an admission of their defeat,

---

[1] Ira Henry Freeman, *Out of the Burning*, Crown Publishers, New York, 1960. Freeman is a journalist who has made Negro boys' gangs a field for special study. The history of Frenchy is the story, in fictional form, of one boy's experiences.

but to Frenchy it was evidence of their rejection of him.

Frenchy had been proud of his police record, which gave him status with the street gangs, but he had many misgivings about the training school. Terrible tales of mistreatment and beatings came back to the gangs from boys who had been there. To Frenchy's surprise there was no mistreatment as such, although the headmasters of the cottages on occasion might subdue a refractory boy by immediate physical force.

Frenchy at first had many difficulties in accepting the orderliness and restraints of institutional life. He had still more difficulty in realizing that the school might have anything of value for him. He faced one crisis when the Superintendent refused to grant him a home furlough because he felt sure Frenchy would immediately swing back into his old gang. He was assigned to a job as assistant to the librarian, a situation where his potential academic ability could find some expression.

In time, Frenchy adjusted sufficiently that he and another boy were enrolled at the public high school in the city of Warwick. They were the first training-school boys to have this privilege. Frenchy was able to rise to the trust placed in him. He worked hard, entered successfully into extra-curricular activities, and did not try to run away. He continued to live at the training school, commuting daily to the high school.

[This was probably the first time in his life that Frenchy had looked to a conventional institution and to law-abiding individuals for status and prestige. Several factors seem to be involved. His contacts with his gang had been effectively severed by distance and absence. To his surprise, he had found that he was not treated like a junior public enemy at the training school, an attitude he had come to accept as typical of school officials and police. He respected the authority of the officers who maintained order, apparently in much the same way that he had respected the authority of the leaders of his gang when he was an underling in membership. In his experience, leaders enforced their authority, by physical force if necessary. In addition, he appreciated the understanding extended to him, especially by the Superintendent, A. Alfred Cohen. He had also found his superior in the library to be friendly and encouraging. He was not treated as an outlaw; he was given an opportunity to gain prestige along new lines. At the public high school, he and the other training-school student apparently were something of a novelty. They were part of an experiment to determine whether delinquent boys could adjust in the community. Everyone wanted and expected them to succeed. He was no longer an outcast. Frenchy found it more difficult but as satisfying to meet these conventional expectations as he previously had found it to meet the expectations of his gang.]

Frenchy was finally released on parole at his own earnest request and somewhat against the best judgment of Mr. Cohen who was not sure his degree of rehabilitation had strengthened him enough to resist the pull back toward his gang once he had returned to the old situation. His release placed on him a personal obligation not to disappoint Mr. Cohen; he now took his model of behavior from a member of the conventional community and not from a gang leader.

Frenchy had many problems on parole. He did not re-enter the gang, in spite of their disgust over his refusal. His new goal was to complete high school. Because of his record, fourteen high schools refused to admit him before he found one that would accept him. He was able to weather this overt rejection by conventional society. Finding work was not easy, and he wavered between working for small wages and stealing. He settled into work. He graduated from high school a few months before he was seventeen with an average grade of B. By now, college seemed desirable and possible. He enrolled in evening courses, continuing to work during the day. Family approval was now a strong supporting factor. Even his father, who had previously "washed his hands" of him, was proud of him.

[Not every boy who is sent to training school achieves a success story, even on a lower academic level than was true for Frenchy. What happened to Frenchy, however, was essentially what must happen in the transition of a boy from complete identification with a delinquent gang to conventional life. The separation from his gang was a crucial factor; the boys were no longer at hand to admire him or to give him an outlet through delinquency. He might simply have found substitute friends of the same type at the training school. However, the association with the librarian followed by his enrollment in a school of well-behaved adolescents gave substitute intimate contacts unconnected with delinquency. Frenchy wanted prestige, success, and a role of leadership. He found them in legitimate ways.

Had Frenchy been allowed to remain in his own home and in contact with his gang, it seems probable that he would have become more deeply involved in stealing and gang violence, until it would have been im-possible for him to abandon such activities. In a few years he would have been beyond juvenile court age and a serious crime would have sent him to prison. Prison is an excellent place for a budding criminal to make contacts with more experienced criminals. Frenchy, who at the time his life story was published, had graduated from college and held a re-sponsible professional position, might simply have become one more added to the criminal population.]

Bibliography

Bowen, Croswell, *They Went Wrong*, McGraw-Hill Book Company, New York, 1954.

Freeman, Ira Henry, *Out of the Burning*, Crown Publishers, New York, 1960.

Freeman, Lucy, *"Before I Kill More—,"* Crown Publishers, New York, 1955. (The reference to Kennedy, Foster, *et al.* concerns the same case.)

"Girl Delinquent, Age Sixteen," *Harper's Magazine*, 164 (1932), 551–59.

Kennedy, Foster, Harry Hoffman, and William H. Haines, "Psychiatric Study of William Heirens," *Journal of Criminal Law and Criminology*, 38 (1947), 311–341.

Martin, John Bartlow, "End of a Boy's Life," *McCall's Magazine*, 75 (July, 1948), pp. 25 ff. Reproduced also in Barron, M. L., *The Juvenile in Delinquent Society*, Alfred A. Knopf, New York, 1954, pp. 3–10. (This account of the life of a boy aged twelve who killed a younger boy ends with his first trial and his commitment to prison for twenty-two years. His case was appealed to the state supreme court, and the decision was reversed on the ground that the boy was too immature to understand the significance of the guilty plea that he had made. In his second trial he was found not guilty on the ground that he was emotionally disturbed at the time of the mur-der and therefore unable to tell right from wrong. He was placed under the care of a guardian and sent to a private school for problem boys.)

Martin, John Bartlow, *My Life in Crime*, Harper and Brothers, New York, 1952.

Shaw, Clifford R., *The Jack-Roller*, University of Chicago Press, Chicago, 1930. (This and the following books by Shaw are famous among the life stories of juvenile delinquents. The autobiographical portions are in the boys' own words. Sociological, and in some instances psychological and psychiatric, analyses are included.)

Shaw, Clifford R., *et al.*, *Brothers in Crime*, University of Chicago Press, Chicago, 1938.

Shaw, Clifford R., in collaboration with M. E. Moore, *The Natural History of a Delinquent Career*, University of Chicago Press, Chicago, 1931.

Wertham, Fredric, *Dark Legend: A Study in Murder*, Duell, Sloan and Pearce, New York, 1941.

Part three

Patterns of delinquency

In spite of the tendency to speak of delinquency as though all delinquent acts were alike, the recognition has been growing for some time that a fruitful lead to an understanding of delinquency is the consideration of specific types as separate cultural complexes or systems of behavior existing within the total culture. Study of criminal systems has been applied to some types of adult crime, for example, professional theft, embezzlement, forgery, and white collar crime.[1] It is not to be expected that juveniles would integrate their entire lives as tightly about crime as a central interest as adult professional criminals do or that they would often confine themselves to one or a few related types of crime or have the types of crime completely systematized. Nevertheless, attempts to isolate types of delinquency and study each as a distinct behavior pattern have made some progress.

Such studies of one type of illegal behavior tend to divorce the behavior from the person who is involved and to draw upon the behavior of many persons to construct a detailed picture of the type. This procedure produces what is called an "ideal type," that is, the type of behavior as it would be found if fully developed and consistent throughout. In a sense the ideal type is an exaggeration of those traits common to any one person. It is useful in showing the extreme or ultimate development of a pattern of behavior, against which the specific cases may be measured. At times some cases will have only a vague resemblance to the ideal or perfect type so that they can no longer be considered as falling within the classification; other cases will parallel somewhat the ideal type; and finally some cases will approach perfection.

Not all types of delinquency have been studied as systems of behavior, and sometimes the types studied have been spectacular rather than the more common types. Chapter 3 has already shown that the most common delinquencies of boys brought before juvenile court are stealing, malicious mischief,

Chapter **12**

Offenses primarily injurious to others

and destruction of property. Truancy (discussed in Chapter 14) and traffic violations are also very common among boys. Rarely are juveniles brought to court because of assaults, murders, drunkenness, or drug addiction—although the last may be concealed behind crimes of theft. Girls' offenses—incorrigibility, running away from home, and sexual promiscuity—are discussed in Chapter 9.

This chapter discusses offenses which are injurious to the rights or the safety and life of other people. The following chapter is concerned with offenses that are primarily injurious to the health and the personality development of the offender himself. Throughout, the discussion is limited by the paucity of studies of specific types of delinquency.

General characteristics of juvenile offenses

Statistical reports often use broad classifications which obscure specific subtypes. For example, the reports of arrests issued by the Federal Bureau of Investigation show arrests for each offense at all ages, from the child under age fifteen to the elderly person: murder, robbery, sex offenses, gambling, and so on. What is not made clear is that the specific subtype of the offense, the conditions under which it occurs, and the motivations all change from one age period to another.

The offenses of children and adolescents fit into certain specifications, some of which are listed below:

1. The younger the child, the more likely is his offense to be limited to the possibilities of

---

1 Jerome Hall, *Theft, Law and Society,* Bobbs-Merrill, Indianapolis, 1952; E. H. Sutherland, editor, *The Professional Thief,* University of Chicago Press, Chicago, 1937; Donald R. Cressey, *Other People's Money: A Study in the Social Psychology of Embezzlement,* Free Press, Glencoe, Illinois, 1953; Edwin M. Lemert, "The Behavior of the Systematic Check Forger," *Social Problems,* 6 (1958), 141–149; E. H. Sutherland, *White Collar Crime,* Dryden Press, New York, 1949.

his home, immediate neighborhood, school, and a few local institutions. In other situations his mere presence while unattended arouses suspicion.

2. The younger the child, the more he depends upon stealth and secrecy.

3. Adolescents and youth tend to make use of brute physical force or to use weapons readily obtained or which can be made from materials at hand: the homemade gun, the garrison belt with heavy buckle, the sharpened cane, the knife ordered through a mail-order catalog. Adult criminals may have a whole arsenal of guns, but many adult criminals avoid weapons and depend upon manual skill, dexterity of movement, or the psychological manipulation of a victim who voluntarily succumbs to his wily schemes.

4. The younger the offender, the more likely he is to combine fun and play with his offenses; the adult criminal tends to be serious and calculating in his movements.

5. The younger the offender, the less he plans and the more likely he is to seize upon a good opportunity for theft, vandalism, or a fight. The older criminal plans ahead, and the more important the crime, the longer and more carefully he plans.

6. The needs satisfied by crime differ with age, following the general developmental trend of human beings, discussed in Chapter 4.

These characteristics will be brought out as specific types of behavior are discussed.

Stealing

By far the most common type of crime in the United States is some form of theft, classifiable under six headings: robbery, burglary, larceny, automobile theft, forgery and counterfeiting, and embezzlement and fraud. The value of thefts of various types totals over $500 million per year, with approximately half the value being recovered by the police.[1]

The types of stealing prevalent among the young are likely to require daring and physical agility or to rest on opportunism. Automobile theft, burglary, larceny, and robbery are distinctively crimes of youth. Table 20 shows that about one-fourth to two-thirds of all arrests for these crimes are of youth un-

der age eighteen. In fact, burglaries and larcenies are well-established activities of juveniles under fifteen years of age. By age twenty-five, two-thirds to nine-tenths of all arrests for these four offenses have been accounted for.

Arrests for several other types of stealing are rarely made of youth under eighteen. Only 2.4 per cent of arrests for embezzlement and fraud and only 7.6 per cent of arrests for forgery and counterfeiting are of persons under eighteen. Some of these offenses require skills of technique and of manipulation of other people not usually found among teenagers. Others, such as embezzlement, require that the offender be in a position of trust where he is in contact with large sums of money, for example, a bank official.

Among all offenses leading to arrests of persons under eighteen, larceny accounts for 20.2 per cent, followed by burglary (10.6 per cent), automobile theft (6.6 per cent), and robbery (1.2 per cent). Burglary and larceny outrank all other youthful arrests of whatever type.[2] Regardless of the high number of arrests of juveniles and youth for stealing, little research has been carried out to discover the situations in which stealing occurs, methods used by delinquents, or motivations involved. Therefore this discussion is necessarily fragmentary.

Larceny. In the classification used by the Federal Bureau of Investigation, larceny includes shoplifting, pocket-picking and thefts of money, bicycles, and automobile accessories as well as any other articles taken without the use of force, violence, or fraud. Theft of automobiles for use rather than for sale is not included under larceny. Larceny is a relatively safe type of stealing, since it does not involve injury to another person or breaking into a building, both of which carry heavier legal penalties than does larceny. The larcenist hopes to steal and escape without detection.

Especially among children, larceny may be opportunistic: the child sees an unguarded bicycle and rides away on it. He is attracted by some article in a store, thinks that he is unobserved, and slips it into his pocket. He takes money from his mother's or his teacher's purse. At school he makes off with articles belonging to the building or to some pu-

1 Federal Bureau of Investigation, United States Department of Justice, *Uniform Crime Reports, 1959*, U. S. Government Printing Office, Washington, D. C., 1960, p. 9.

2 *Uniform Crime Reports, 1959*, p. 100. The figures are based on 1,789 cities with population over 2,500.

Table 20

Persons Arrested for Various Types of Stealing by Age, Percentage Distribution

Offense*	Number	Age				Total
		Under 15	15–17	18–24	25 and over	
Automobile theft	33,409	15.8	47.8	24.3	12.1	100.0
Burglary	65,044	24.9	27.5	25.8	21.8	100.0
Larceny	132,441	25.3	23.6	20.2	30.9	100.0
Robbery	15,379	4.7	21.5	39.0	34.8	100.0
Forgery and counterfeiting	12,007	1.2	6.4	27.4	72.6	100.0
Embezzlement and fraud	21,009	0.5	1.9	17.1	80.5	100.0

Data: Arrest rates do not give a complete account of crimes committed. Crimes reported to the police far outnumber arrests made in connection with the crimes. The percentage of certain crimes "cleared" by arrest is as follows: murder, 92.7; negligent manslaughter, 88.5 per cent; forcible rape, 73.6 per cent; aggravated assault, 78.9 per cent; robbery, 42.5 per cent; burglary, 30.7 per cent; larceny, 20.9 per cent; and automobile theft, 26.2 per cent. Nor are all arrested persons convicted of crimes. However, it is only after an arrest has been made that the offender can be classified by age and sex; only then can he be identified as a juvenile delinquent or an adult offender. The juvenile court statistics published by the Children's Bureau are inadequate for a study of all offenses, since in some states serious crimes committed by persons over some stated age (often fourteen) can be and often are tried in the criminal rather than the juvenile court. On the other hand, minor offenses that often bring a child to police or court attention may not be included in the arrest figures. In the FBI reports police classify a young person as arrested when he has committed a crime under circumstances that would lead to an arrest if the individual were an adult. The arrest figures are therefore more complete for serious crimes or felonies than for minor offenses included in juvenile delinquency laws but not considered to be adult crimes. The percentages given above are from Federal Bureau of Investigation, United States Department of Justice, *Uniform Crime Reports, 1959*, Washington, D. C., 1960, p. 11; see also p. 98.

* The offenses are arranged in descending order according to the percentage of arrests of persons under eighteen years old.

pil. Especially among young children these episodes tend to be unplanned and the articles are for immediate use or consumption.

If the young child is caught and punished or his desire for certain articles is met, larceny disappears from his behavior. He is a larcenist because he has not yet accepted the fact that property belongs to specific people and cannot be acquired simply by taking it.

Older children, however, may plan larcenies, sometimes with co-operation between several children. Those who have contacts with criminals may learn the techniques of specific types of larceny from them.

Shoplifting is a type of larceny which ranges from amateurish thefts by children or housewives to the professional crimes of adults who carefully study a store, plan their approach, and have ready means of disposing of stolen goods. Since many shoplifters, especially amateurs, are not arrested when caught, no exact information is available on numbers, what is taken, or the characteristics of shoplifters, either for juveniles or adults. Children are active in shoplifting, however; the National Association of Food Chains in 1952 estimated that 20 per cent of all shoplifters were juveniles.[1] In a midwestern college town, during one year (1949–1950), 63 per cent of all shoplifters arrested were under

seventeen years old. The usual child shoplifter could be classified as a "sneak thief," who takes something for his own use and hopes not to be caught. Studies differ as to whether boys or girls are more active as shoplifters, but the general impression is that girls and women predominate, especially among amateurs. Boys and girls are likely to be amateurs, but men and some women shoplifters are professionals who strike for highly priced goods to be resold.

The amateurish, pilfering type of shoplifting typical of the juvenile can be illustrated by the activities of seven boys ranging in age from thirteen to fifteen. Among other things, they had stolen a crowbar, hair tonic, playing cards, gloves, magazines, ice cream, candies, comic books, wallets, staplers, cigarettes, padlocks, gum, flashlights, batteries, cigarette cases, peanuts, shirts, film, a wall soap dispenser, and four quarters from a hair dryer. These articles were taken from two drug stores, two department stores, a sporting goods shop, an office supply store, and a pet shop.[2]

Contrasting to the amateur are the professional shoplifters using planned, skilled methods. The location of the goods is studied in advance on some legitimate pretext. Exits and elevators are noted, mirrors are spotted through which a store detective might see the

1 Cited by Henry Angelino, "Shoplifting: A Critical Review," *Midwest Sociologist*, 15 (Spring, 1953), 17–22. This article summarizes a number of studies.

2 Newspaper item, city of 125,000.

In this scene, a boy is stealing a baseball glove from a sporting goods department and concealing it under his jacket. His companion is shielding his movements from view. This picture is posed. (Courtesy Director of Security, Carson, Pirie, Scott and Co., Chicago)

theft or through which the shoplifter or an accomplice can watch the detective, the working hours of salespeople are observed, and store detectives are identified. The procedure in stealing a fur coat often parallels the following:

A well-dressed young woman asked to look at mink coats and tried on several, finally selecting one but saying she would wait to make a final decision. Several days later she returned at noon to look at the coat again. Her saleslady was out for lunch (as anticipated), but another saleslady brought out the coat for her to try on again. When her accomplice in the background signaled that she seemed to be unobserved, she walked in leisurely manner to the elevator, wearing the coat. She had been observed, however, and the store detective trailed her to the elevator, with the accomplice in turn trailing the de-

tective. As a rule, an arrest for shoplifting cannot be made inside the store, since the shoplifter may claim that she is going to buy the article and may sue or threaten to sue the store for false arrest. As the detective followed the shoplifter to the door, she was tripped by the accomplice, who helped her to her feet and apologized profusely, thus giving the shoplifter time to escape still wearing the coat.[1]

Burglary. The Federal Bureau of Investigation defines burglary as any unlawful entry to commit a felony or a theft, even though no force was used to gain entrance. Breaking into or unlawfully entering a house, store, office, factory, or other building are examples; safecracking is also included. Shoplifting differs from burglary in that it is a theft committed during hours when the public is admitted to the building, and hence there is no unlawful entry.

Burglars are active at night and on week ends, when business houses are closed to the public. Houses are entered at night or when the householders are thought to be absent for a few hours or a longer period of time. Vacationists sometimes return to find their homes stripped of most valuables. The peak years of arrests for burglary are during the teens, particularly youths of age sixteen. Many burglaries are committed by children under age fifteen. The number of arrests declines after age sixteen and becomes negligible after age forty. It may be that the risk of being shot by a householder, a policeman, a night watchman or a guard offsets the desirability of burglary as a way to obtain money or goods. Or it may be that only the very daring and skilled remain, striking infrequently but obtaining large sums of money or valuable goods. These large undertakings require long periods of observation to determine the safest time to enter and entail elaborate plans of entry and exit. Such exploits are the work of professional criminals, not of children.

Children and teen-agers are usually small-scale burglars. Cases of juvenile delinquents are filled with episodes wherein two or three boys break a window or find an open transom in a small store or a gas station, enter, steal any available cash and small articles to be sold or used, and escape without detection. These boys are not professionals. Burglary is simply one of a number of illegal acts com-

1 Zeta Rothschild, "Why Shoplifters Get Caught," *Coronet*, 28 (August, 1950), 99–102.

mon to their way of life. Many live at home and use the money not for necessities but for luxuries and entertainment.

Automobile theft. Theft of an automobile is defined by the Federal Bureau of Investigation as stealing or driving away and then abandoning a motor vehicle; the joy-ride of the teen-ager is a common type. Taking an automobile for temporary use with the intention of returning to the owner, or the unauthorized use of a car by someone having lawful access to the car are not included in automobile theft. Stripping a car of accessories which are then sold is included under the heading of larceny. Many automobile thefts are committed by children not yet fifteen years old, and the incidence of thefts continues to be high until age seventeen, when it takes a sharp downturn; by the thirties automobile theft has become a rare occurrence. Thefts are primarily made by boys: for example, in Onondago County, New York, 98 per cent of all arrests for automobile thefts by juveniles were of boys.[1]

The theft by the teen-ager is not for the purpose of selling the car, but to use it for an evening or a few days, or occasionally for a cross-country trip. The car is usually abandoned, perhaps when the gas tank is empty. The car is stolen because the boy is too young to own a car, is not allowed to drive the family car, lives in a family without a car, or has no money with which to buy one of his own. Approximately 40 per cent of all persons arrested for automobile theft have not reached the age required by most states for a driver's license.[2]

Stealing of cars by adults usually is for resale, a transaction that involves changing the appearance of the car and finding a customer. The procedure must be carefully planned; it is the work of the professional automobile thief and differs radically from the quick "borrowing" and later abandonment of an automobile by the youth who wishes to have the temporary use of a car.

The urge of the teen-age boy for an automobile is not limited to the United States. As automobiles have come into more common use in Europe, automobile thefts for joy-riding have increased. These thefts are not regarded as a new type of delinquency but simply as the result of a new, desirable object for pleasure that replaces earlier objects. In the past the boy stole a horse and carriage, in the future he may steal a space ship.[3]

A United States study shows that a higher proportion of white than of Negro boys steal cars.[4] The explanation seems to be that parking lot attendants are more likely to question Negro boys than white boys found loitering in the lot and thus reduce their opportunities for stealing. Also, in some cities police almost routinely investigate credentials of Negro youth driving cars. Other findings of interest were that among the white boys, automobile thieves came from a slightly better socioeconomic background than did other delinquents. The thieves were also better adjusted socially to their peers than the common run of delinquents. The authors of the study suggest that automobile theft may be a kind of "white collar" crime more common to middle- than to lower-class boys. It would fall into the general pattern of delinquency as a social activity.

Robbery. Robbery is defined by the Federal Bureau of Investigation as stealing from a person by force, violence, or threats. Examples are strong-arm robbery, stickups, and armed robbery. Although arrests for robbery are rare among juveniles, several types can be identified. Two of the types, taking money from smaller boys by threats and "jackrolling" drunks are attacks on relatively defenseless persons. When persons of equal strength or adults are robbed, several boys often cooperate in the attack, which may include serious injuries to the victim and may, in fact, more truly be classified as assault than robbery.

Jackrolling refers to strong-arm robbery of a drunken person. Jackrolling is low on the status scale of criminal types; it requires little skill or finesse. Typically, two sturdy teenagers spot a drunken man in a skid-row area during the evening, follow him until he passes an alley or other dark area, drag him

1 Robert H. Hardt, *A Delinquency Profile of Syracuse and Onondaga County, New York, 1957–1958,* Youth Development Center, Syracuse University, New York, 1960, Table 12, p. 45.
2 Richard Wedekind, "Automobile Theft, the Thirteen Million Dollar Parasite," *Journal of Criminal Law, Criminology and Police Science,* 48 (1957), 443—446.
3 Discussion at the Second United Nations Conference on the Prevention of Crime and the Treatment of Offenders, London, August, 1960.
4 William W. Wattenberg and James Balistrieri, "Automobile Theft: A 'Favored Group' Delinquency," *American Journal of Sociology,* 57 (1952), 575–579.

to the ground, if necessary club him into submission with whatever weapon they carry, and search his clothes for money. Later in the evening they may enter some vacant building where skid-row bums sleep, many intoxicated, and systematically search each one. With reasonable care, the boys may evade arrest for long periods of time and make a small but regular income. For the boy who is headed toward professional criminality, jackrolling is simply an interim occupation until he is accepted by professional criminals for induction into more skilled ways of stealing.

Extortion of money from children is another type of juvenile robbery. Adult criminal gangs often extort money from merchants, construction companies, and other businessmen in return for "protection" from vandalism, delays in construction, or personal injury. If the businessmen do not comply, the "protection company" destroys their property or inflicts serious personal injuries on them. A replica of this type of extortion is sometimes found among children or teen-agers, who have found threats of a beating or other injury an easy way to extort money from children with spending money. Sometimes the money is collected regularly on a weekly basis. The victims often are afraid to report their tormentors to their parents or to the school principal—the extortion often takes place on school grounds. A popular article by members of the United States Senate Judiciary Subcommittee to Investigate Juvenile Delinquency gives an example of extortion in a Washington, D. C., junior high school.[1] A fourteen-year-old boy named Eddie, who had spent some time in a correctional school, found himself with little spending money in a school where other children received liberal allowances from their parents. With some friends, Eddie extorted money from thirty or forty other boys during a period of several months before one of the victims made a definite complaint. Eddie was arrested. A short time afterward the boy who complained and two of his friends were attacked by nine friends of Eddie and severely beaten. For some of the nine boys at least the attack was in the nature of an unprovoked assault. They had not shared in Eddie's extortion and in fact some of them did not know the boy whom they attacked.

Gang assault and robbery is another type of robbery carried out by a number of boys, with or without prior planning and selection of a victim in advance. In both New York and Chicago such crimes often occur in subway or elevated stations or on trains, where victims have little chance to escape, and police rarely are sufficiently numerous to guard stations and trains. An example is the holdup attack on a passenger in the Chicago subway by fourteen youths between the ages of fourteen and eighteen. The group had planned to attend a dance which they found on arrival had been cancelled. They took a subway to the center of the city and while walking through the subway tunnel to transfer to another line they decided to hold up someone on the train. Some of the boys blocked the exits from the train and others sat beside passengers to prevent them from coming to the victim's assistance. One boy then seized the man selected as a victim by the neck while another went through his pockets. When he resisted, a third youth hit him in the face; later he was also kicked in the face. The boys secured a wrist watch and $26.00. Their explanation was that it was "something to do" when they found the dance had been cancelled.[2]

Even though this assault and robbery was not planned in advance, the boys used techniques familiar to them and without doubt used on previous occasions.

Vandalism

Vandalism often is included under the general designation of malicious mischief or some other omnibus term when delinquent acts are classified. The exact amount of vandalism is therefore unknown, but limited studies and individual reports indicate that it is a specific and continuing type of delinquency. It consists of the deliberate damage or destruction of private or public property by persons (in this instance juveniles) who do not own the property.[3]

Types and cost of vandalism. The following

---

1 Richard Clendenen and Herbert W. Beaser, "The Shame of America," *Saturday Evening Post,* 227 (January 8, 1955), 78.

2 Reported in *Chicago Daily News,* September 23, 1960.

3 Based on definition used by Marshall B. Clinard and Andrew L. Wade, "Toward the Delineation of Vandalism as a Sub-Type in Juvenile Delinquency," *Journal of Criminal Law, Criminology and Police Science,* 48 (1958), 493–499.

excerpts from reports of individual acts of vandalism indicate some of the more costly and extensive types.

Over the Memorial Day week end, 1960, twenty-five Chicago schools received an estimated $50,000 worth of damage. Classrooms and offices were ransacked, a fire was set in a principal's office, windows were broken, and ink was splashed on walls and used to make crude drawings or write obscene phrases; in one school a radio, phonograph, and records were damaged. In some schools lunchroom ice boxes were broken into and food was thrown against walls and ceilings. Many schools not entered had windows broken from the outside.

In September, 1959, nine boys aged twelve and thirteen wrecked the inside of a Chicago elementary school, breaking windows, throwing ink and paint on desks and walls, pulling books off shelves, tipping over desks, pulling doors off metal lockers, and scattering school records. Damage was estimated at $7,000. The same boys together with several others wrecked another school a few days later, causing $5,000 damage.

Such reports are routine not only in Chicago but in all large cities. Vandalism is not limited to schools, although they provide a favorite target over week ends and holidays, especially when night watchmen are not employed.

In a city of 125,000 three boys, aged thirteen, fifteen, and sixteen, in the course of one evening damaged ten cars in a parking lot by breaking antennae, windshield wipers, and rear view mirrors. They also turned over a set of swings in a school playground, broke a window in the schoolhouse and one in a cleaning plant, broke a fence, and tore down a sign. They were caught before they did more damage. This was apparently unplanned vandalism, done "just for fun."

In New York, during the first year after a new school was opened, 598 windows were broken, costing $2,680 to replace.

New construction work offers many opportunities for youthful vandals. A survey of its members by the National Association of Home Builders described the following instances of vandalism: [1]

In Detroit a boy drove a bulldozer into a

1 Elizabeth W. Robinson, "Let's Build Them Better," *National Association of Secondary School Principals*, 40 (September, 1956), 119–124.

new house, with damage amounting to $650. A youthful vandal threw $600 worth of sewer crock into an excavation, breaking all. Two children in Baltimore shoved in the walls of two cottages while the mortar between the cement blocks was still wet. Workmen had to chip the mortar off each block and rebuild the walls. In Syracuse, the evening before six new houses were to be on display to the public, young vandals broke forty windows, flooded basements, plugged up drains, split the doors, and pounded nails into the plaster. In White Plains, New York, boys poured gasoline into the rooms of a house nearing completion. The damage was more than $35,000. (Incidentally, the builders noted that losses from adult theft were higher than the damage from youthful vandalism.)

Sex and age of vandals. All accounts indicate that, as in other outdoor types of delinquency of an active type, boys are primarily responsible. Pre-adolescent and adolescent boys are the chief culprits.

Cultural and social aspects. The United States culture is fairly tolerant of a certain amount of vandalism, provided the damage has little money value. Adults grumble but seem to expect to clean up after youthful disorderliness and to stand the minor expenses involved in slight damage. Halloween is celebrated by an institutionalized form of vandalism, which often threatens to get out of hand. Efforts are made to forestall such vandalism by offering instead parades, parties, and prizes for well-decorated store windows and substituting "treats" for "tricks."

Actual property damage is disparaged, but relatively little is done about the situation. Since most vandalism takes place after dark and around unguarded buildings or construction sites, the vandals are usually not caught. When they are, the children are unable and the parents either unable or unwilling to make restitution for large amounts of damage. Consequently, most companies and some householders carry insurance to cover such damage. Since the cost of repair and replacement is assured, the victims do not press for the discovery of the culprits.

Whether youthful vandals disproportionately represent any one social class or ethnic group is an unsettled question. The actual situation in which the boys find themselves, the dearth of outlets for energy or hostility, and the opportunities available in unguarded buildings with many windows may be determining factors.

Relation to other delinquencies. Studies disagree as to whether vandalism is closely related to other acts of delinquency—whether it is part of a generally delinquent way of life or whether it is a more or less casual and transient type of misconduct.[1] It may very well be both, since it seems to serve a number of different purposes so far as the vandals are concerned.

The widespread nature of vandalism among children and adolescents is evident from a survey of high school students. Of midwestern boys included in the survey, 60.7 per cent had at some time deliberately damaged property, with 17.5 per cent having damaged property more than once or twice. Among far-western boys the percentages were 44.8 and 8.2 per cent respectively.[2] In each instance only about a third as many girls admitted property destruction. The occasions for the vandalism are not given—whether on Halloween, in the excitement preceding or following a hotly contested football game, in a spirit of fun, or for revenge.

According to the same study, among inmates of a correctional school, the commission of vandalism was more widespread and more often repeated than among high school students. Since the correctional school was in the Far West, the percentage of inmates reporting property damage should be compared with the far-western high school students. The comparable percentages follow: correctional school boys, 84.3 per cent, high school boys 44.8; more than one offense, correctional school boys, 49.7, high school boys, 8.2. For girls, the percentages show the far greater frequency of property damage among correctional school than high school students: correctional school girls, 65.4, high school girls, 13.6; more than one offense, correctional school girls, 32.1, high school girls, 1.6. It should not be assumed that the correctional school inmates were convicted for acts of vandalism; this activity may well have been simply one of an array of delinquent acts. The data also do not show the relative values of the damage done by high school versus correctional school students, or by boys versus girls.

Variety of motives. A recreation element enters into some forms of vandalism; a number of boys may participate, to see who can break the first window or the most windows in a building. If the building is a school, an element of revenge may also be a motive. An abandoned house or vacant factory seems made to order for sport and adventure. Middle-class college students referring to childhood destructiveness reported excitement, adventure, and enjoyment of the activity as the obvious motives.[3] The members of the group stimulate each other and mild excesses lead to greater ones. The motivations seem very similar to competitive games in which children and youth attempt to outdo each other in skill or daring—shooting balls at a basket, playing darts, target practice, or shooting at a target in a sideshow.

Although one school of psychology assumes that a young child is naturally destructive, this view is not universally accepted. A. H. Maslow, a psychologist, asserts that children are as often generous, co-operative, and unselfish as destructive, aggressive, or hostile, and that destructiveness in children is never a direct primary response to a simple destructive drive.[4] Nevertheless, the child who is not accepted, who seems rejected, insecure, or hostile, may react in a vengeful fashion against the person or institution he holds responsible for his unhappy state.

Homicides and assaults

Physical assaults of all types, whether or not they result in death of the victim, account for a minor number of the total number of arrests. Without regard to age of the offender, arrests for physical assaults equal only 5.2 per cent of all arrests. Among juveniles under eighteen, they account for a still smaller percentage of arrests for all ages and offenses—0.5 per cent.[5] As measured by arrests, very

1 Clinard and Wade, *op. cit.*
2 James F. Short, Jr., and F. Ivan Nye, "Extent of Unrecorded Juvenile Delinquency: Tentative Conclusions," *Journal of Criminal Law, Criminology and Police Science*, 49 (1958), 297–298.
3 Walter Houston Clark, "Sex Differences and Motivation in the Urge to Destroy," *Journal of Social Psychology*, 36 (1952), 167–177. About half of the students, both boys and girls, reported destructiveness.
4 A. H. Maslow, "A Comparative Approach to the Problem of Destructiveness," *Psychiatry*, 5 (1942), 517–522.
5 Federal Bureau of Investigation, United States Department of Justice, *Uniform Crime Reports, 1959*, U. S. Government Printing Office, Washington, D. C., 1960, p. 100.

few physical assaults can be blamed on juveniles.

When specific types of assaults are considered, arrests of youth under eighteen cover only a small number of each type of assault. Of all murder and nonnegligent manslaughter cases, 6.6 per cent of all arrests were of persons under age eighteen; of all manslaughter cases by negligence, 5.7 per cent; of all aggravated assaults, 9.2 per cent; of all other assaults, 8.3 per cent; and of all forcible rape, 18.8 per cent. Arrests for physical assaults of all types are more typical of the twenties than of other age periods.

When total arrests of all persons under eighteen years old are taken as the base, arrests for assaults are only 3.67 per cent of all arrests.

Gang assaults and murders. A psychiatrist with wide experience among offenders states that most homicides by juveniles result from gang warfare and often are not premeditated.[1] However, when gangs do meet with intent to fight, they carry knives, guns, clubs, belts with heavy buckles, car antennas, sharpened canes and other weapons capable of inflicting death. Even with such an arsenal, neither armed gang intends to annihilate the enemy but hopes to surpass it in bravery and drive it back into its own territory. Actual murder may not be premeditated, but serious physical injury is often caused which may lead to death. A detailed discussion of gang fights is given in Chapter 14.

Assaults which may or may not cause death to the victim, may be directed by small gangs against someone unknown to the gang but who by chance is at hand when the gang is aroused or bent on adventure. The victim may be of another race or a person in authority who has unsuccessfully attempted to control the behavior of the gang. If a woman is the victim she may be raped before being injured or killed. These unplanned assaults and murders apparently are overt expressions of inner tensions or even momentary frustrations. The identity of the victim is incidental. In these cases the assault is not the first or only offense of the gang; it is part of a generally delinquent way of life.

An unprovoked attack is described below:

Five Negro youths were seized by police in a Chicago park after they had attacked two white married couples who were taking an evening stroll in the park, although not with each other. The two young women were raped three times and their husbands were stabbed and beaten with a baseball bat. Two men who tried to assist the victims were also beaten and stabbed. The youths were aged fifteen to eighteen.[2]

Rivalry between youths of two different gangs for the attention of a girl may also involve both gangs in fighting. In one instance, youths of sixteen and twenty arranged a meeting to settle their rivalry for the attention of a fifteen-year-old girl. Their friends accompanied them, and in the melee a seventeen-year-old boy was stabbed and killed by the older of the two contestants.[3]

Assaults by individuals. Sometimes individuals plan robberies that get out of hand and result in murder. An illustrative case is that of a seventeen-year-old youth who planned a robbery on an elevated train platform in Chicago in order to get money to support his sixteen-year-old mistress and her baby. The victim fought back, and the boy stabbed him. The boy said later that he did not mean to kill his victim but had to stab him to get away. He had a delinquency record going back to his eighth year and had been in a correctional school.[4]

Other individual assaults, often murderous, seem to be the explosion of deep emotions. They may be either planned or spontaneous. The victims may be parents, other family members, complete strangers with whom there is only a casual contact, or someone who has added to already existing tensions. The offender may have a previous record as an emotionally deprived or disturbed child—although not suspected of murderous impulses. He may previously have committed other kinds of delinquency. But sometimes he has seemed to be a normal— or even a model—youth.

Sometimes young children of ten or twelve commit such murders, but in general the offenders are in middle or later teens. Often the child or youth displays little comprehen-

1 Melitta Schnideberg, "Child Murderers." Abstract of a paper read at the Fifteenth Annual Meeting of the American Society of Criminology, 1958, *Journal of Criminal Law, Criminology and Police Science,* 49 (1959), 569–570.

2 Reported in *Chicago Daily News,* July 27, 1960.
3 Reported in *Chicago Daily News,* September 29, 1959.
4 Reported by UPI, Chicago.

sion of the enormity of his act and no guilt or repentance. Although these individual murders cover a wide variety of types and details, it is often assumed that the offenders are emotionally disturbed or even psychotic. Psychiatrists who have studied child murderers hesitate to pinpoint the problem. Although their reactions are abnormal, they cannot be lumped under such a catchall term as "sick," psychopathic, or schizophrenic.[1]

Motivation

The present discussion has been limited almost entirely to the pattern of behavior characteristic of each kind of offense. The attempt of some students of juvenile delinquency to attribute a specific motive to each specific type of crime has proved futile. Calling all thefts acts of aggression resulting from early failure to curb and channelize innate aggressive drives obscures the behavior instead of illuminating it. Equating physical aggression in all cases with immature or perverse sexual drives also does little to clarify the problem of either aggression or sexual perversion.

A more useful approach to an understanding of delinquency is first to discover the general pattern or behavior system of each type of offense. Once a behavior system has de-

1 Schnideberg, *op. cit.*

veloped, it becomes a part of culture to be passed from person to person, from older to younger, from professional to amateur. The means are chiefly first-hand contacts, and only secondarily through mass media.

Not all adolescents in a position to learn delinquent patterns of behavior do so, or having learned, put the system to use. It is at this point that motivation must be examined. The motivation for making use of a specific delinquent behavior system is not the same in all cases. The boy may steal because stealing is the accepted way in his gang to get money or goods; he therefore is not releasing destructive impulses. Stealing may be part of a group adventure—attempting to filch some object in a store without being caught. He may steal to show he is brave, to buy or get food because he is hungry, to avoid the steady monotony of work, or for other reasons.

Sometimes the performance of a delinquent does not fit the behavior pattern. He acts on the spur of the moment without knowing how to assure success or escape, or he may innovate a new system, yet for all his pains, he may still be caught. But in general, as the system is repeated, he tends to eliminate imperfections and to increase the chance of success. At this point, he begins to move into career-criminality.

Bibliography

Stealing

Angelino, Henry, "Shoplifting: A Critical Review," *Midwest Sociologist,* 15 (Spring, 1953), 17–22.

Shaw, Clifford R., and associates, *Brothers in Crime,* University of Chicago Press, 1938.

—— *The Jack-Roller,* University of Chicago Press, 1930.

Wattenberg, William W. and James Balistrieri, "Automobile Theft: A 'Favored Group' Delinquency," *American Journal of Sociology,* 57 (1952), 575–579.

Richard Wedekind, "Automobile Theft, The Thirteen Million Dollar Parasite," *Journal of Criminal Law, Criminology and Police Science,* 48 (1957), 443–446.

Vandalism

Clark, Walter Houston, "Sex Differences and Motivations in the Urge to Destroy," *Journal of Social Psychology,* 36 (1952), 167–177.

Clinard, Marshall B. and Andrew L. Wade, "Toward the Delineation of Vandalism as a

Sub-type in Juvenile Delinquency," *Journal of Criminal Law, Criminology and Police Science,* 48 (1958), 493–499.

Maslow, A. H., "A Comparative Approach to the Problem of Destructiveness," *Psychiatry,* 5 (1942), 517–522.

Michelson, Bettie E., "Vandalism in Our Schools," *Illinois Education,* 44 (1956), 294 f.

Robinson, Elizabeth W., "Let's Build Them Better," *National Association of Secondary School Principals,* 40 (1956), 119–124.

"Vandalism," *Federal Probation,* 18 (March, 1954), eight brief articles.

Murders and assaults

Kennedy, Foster, Harry R. Hoffman, and William H. Haines, "Study of William Heirens," *American Journal of Psychiatry,* 104 (August 1947) 113 ff.

Martin, John Bartlow, "End of a Boy's Life," *McCall's Magazine,* 75 (July 1948), 24 ff. This account ends with the first trial of a twelve-year-old boy who had killed a playmate. Subsequently, the State Supreme Court reversed the decision of the criminal court, and the boy was tried again. Arrangements were made for him to enter a private correctional school for problem boys where he could receive therapeutic treatment.

Reaching the Gang, New York City Youth Board, New York, 1960, Chapter 3.

Schnideberg, Melitta, "Child Murderers," Abstract of a paper read at the Fifteenth Annual Meeting of the American Society of Criminology, 1958, *Journal of Criminal Law, Criminology and Police Science,* 49 (1959), 569–570.

Van Waters, Miriam, "Why Hickman Hangs," *Survey,* 61 (October 1, 1928), 20–23.

Chapter **13**

Offenses primarily injurious to the delinquent

In the United States it is traditional to regard personal vices as legal offenses and to exact the same kind of penalties applied to crimes invading the rights of or injuring other people. When legal attempts to stamp out vices and injurious habits fail, strict legal regulations may curb such excesses. For example, when the prohibition amendment failed to eliminate the manufacture and drinking of alcoholic beverages, regulations were imposed to channel usage. Other practices generally condemned by the mores (although not by all subgroups) and hedged about by regulations are gambling, vagrancy, use of narcotic drugs, and certain irregular sex practices, especially perversions and prostitution. Experience has shown that without regulation, these practices expand into disorganizing habits and customs affecting both the individual and the society. Attempts to stamp them out entirely have not succeeded. The United States thus tends to take a middle ground between a wide-open policy and complete repression.[1]

1 Although opinions vary, it is possible to consider most of the practices listed above, except those in which other people are victimized, as moral rather than legal issues. In some European countries, normal sex relations outside marriage are not legally penalized as they may be in the United States. In England in 1957, a Committee on Homosexual Offences and Prostitution recommended that homosexual acts carried out in private between consenting adults should no longer be considered criminal; the committee also noted that in England prostitution itself was not an offense against criminal law. *Report of the Committee on Homosexual Offences and Prostitution,* Presented to Parliament . . . Septem-

Restriction of juvenile behavior

Juvenile delinquency laws generally hold youth responsible to all state or local laws. In addition, other regulations are often added restricting activities of children and adolescents beyond those placed on adults. Youth may be forbidden to buy alcoholic beverages until they reach a certain age; in some states they are "delinquent" if found in a place where liquor is sold. Pre- and extramarital sex relations are generally forbidden; the law, disregarded by many adolescents, requires postponement of sex relations until marriage, which in some states may not occur before the age of twenty-one. The "homeless man," the vagrant, or the hobo is not as a rule arrested unless he becomes a public nuisance or violates a definite law; but the runaway child or adolescent may be apprehended by the police even though his conduct is acceptable.

Many of the desires and impulses leading adults into misconduct are also present in youth. The restrictive laws applied to youth apparently hold that if the boy or girl can be restricted until the age of sixteen, eighteen, or twenty-one, he will no longer desire to break the law and will act in moderation. Actually, many youth feel the laws are unjustified impositions and challenges. Some break the laws in defiance, others to prove that they are adult. In some families and neighborhoods adults ignore the laws and impose little control over youth. Children and adolescents who observe the laws do so not so much out of respect for the law as such but primarily because they have a positive standard that excludes certain behavior, and they identify themselves as members of peer groups holding this standard.

Relation of juveniles to organized criminal syndicates

It is generally true that when there is a public demand for some service or article, an organized business will develop to supply the demand. The fact that the service or article is forbidden by law does not interfere with the mutual exchange. Organized criminal syndicates exist semisecretly or openly to enable people to gamble, find a house of prostitution, buy narcotic drugs, or buy alcohol illegally. Vagrancy, since it seems to be nonincome producing, is not sponsored by

ber, 1957, Her Majesty's Stationery Office, London, England, pp. 25, 79.

either legal or criminal business organizations.

Juveniles usually develop relationships with criminal syndicates indirectly. Nevertheless, certain vices could not be pursued unless a criminal syndicate existed; the adolescent drug addict may know only the "pusher" or street peddler—or become a pusher himself —but at the top of the hierarchy of drug distribution is a highly organized and efficient criminal organization smuggling drugs into the country and controling a system of distribution. The boy with cash may buy a numbers ticket in a policy game and meet only the underling selling the tickets, but this form of gambling is controlled by a well-organized criminal syndicate. Patronage at a house of prostitution is sometimes a mark of manhood to the boy. The promiscuous girl may look to the house of prostitution as a step upward professionally. Taverns that admit and serve teen-agers often are tied in with a criminal syndicate which protects the proprietor from arrest.

Juveniles do not begin their vices with any direct connection with organized criminal groups and in fact may never have a direct contact. But they are able to satisfy their desires because adult criminal groups exist to supply services and goods outside the restraints of the law, and with no regard for the effect that indulgence may have on young customers. The disregard for law is most likely to occur in disorganized neighborhoods when informal controls by public opinion or civic groups are weak, or in neighborhoods in which adults disregard the laws because they feel they are too restrictive or where they wish to have free indulgence themselves.

Eventually, a few teen-agers may step into jobs with organized criminal syndicates that operate in their neighborhoods. The system works very much as any large business organization works that is organized on a city-wide or larger basis and has many local outlets. The promising older boy or girl secures a job at the local level; he hopes to move upward, and his ideal of success is the powerful wealthy few at the top.

Not all indulgence depends upon organized criminal groups or illegal local organizations. Especially for the younger teen-agers, with little money, indulgence in vice is a homemade affair. The boy and the girl may have sex relations without recourse to profes-sionals or the passage of money. The entire gang may contribute small sums to make possible the purchase of a bottle of wine to be drunk in secret or in the hangout. Gambling goes on constantly among youth in the nature of betting, shooting craps, or card games, without the aid of a professional gambling establishment. Purchase of narcotic drugs necessarily has a connection with organized crime, but the juvenile addict's contact is with the petty peddler on the street. With more maturity, sophistication, and money, the transition to organized establishments is easy to make.

Incidence of vice

Arrest records published by the Federal Bureau of Investigation indicate that few persons under eighteen are arrested for most of the vices, compared with the many arrested for various forms of stealing.[1] It is probable that vice is far more widespread than the arrest figures indicate. Many activities are carried out in secret to avoid trouble; others are of a minor nature and are disregarded by police or momentarily ended by a police warning and order to disperse. Some vice will be concealed in the grab-bag classification of disorderly conduct, common among youth. The public disturbance may be the result of private drinking or a quarrel over the sexual favors of a girl.

The discussion that follows of individual offenses is limited by the irregularity of research focused on the different types. Studies of gambling are limited to adults, with the brief mention that youth do not have enough money to participate. The reference of course is to organized gambling and not to the back alley gambling of adolescents. Vagrancy is the eighth most common cause of arrest for youth under eighteen, who also account for 6 per cent of all vagrancy arrests. Nevertheless, only the adult vagrant seems to merit the attention of research.

Sex offenses, drinking, and drug addiction have received more detailed attention. These three offenses are therefore discussed in this chapter.

Sex offenses

Sex offense is a vague term which covers a

1 Federal Bureau of Investigation, United States Department of Justice, *Uniform Crime Reports*, 1959, U. S. Government Printing Office, Washington, D. C., 1960, p. 100.

variety of different acts. Normal heterosexual relations may be included when they occur outside of marriage, when the girl is below an arbitrary legal "age of consent," or when force is involved. Aberrant sex conduct is also included, such as homosexuality, exhibitionism, or unusual types of heterosexual relations regarded as degrading or unnatural. The combination of several types of sexual activity under one heading or the failure to separate male from female cases in court or arrest reports make it impossible to give a statistical report of frequencies. From other reports and limited studies, however, a fairly accurate description of sex offenses among juveniles can be given.[1]

Girls' offenses. The offense of girls is almost always normal heterosexual relations carried out under conditions that seem to threaten the girl's reputation or future personal development. She has become promiscuous and seems headed for a future as a professional prostitute. Or she has become pregnant without perhaps knowing who the father of the child is, or she has contracted a venereal disease which she will probably pass on to others. The delinquent girl's situation was further discussed in Chapter 9.

Also, only rarely is a girl really a victim of forcible rape, although marginal cases occur in which the girl has protested but not resisted sufficiently to justify a charge of forcible rape. Public revulsion to forcible rape is so widespread and so deep, especially if the girl is seriously injured or is very young, that boys and men who are engaged in criminal activities feel the same abhorrence to rape as the most upright person in the community. Occasionally, of course, vicious rape occurs with extreme newspaper publicity. These few, violent cases tend to obscure the true situation.

Statutory rape is also rare, in the sense that an older and experienced man takes advantage of a young unsophisticated girl. In the street life of the deteriorated city areas, knowledge of sex is part of the common culture into which children are inducted at an early age; in crowded tenements, children learn of sex relations without formal instruc-

tion. Although technically, men who have intercourse with girls below the age of consent may be charged with statutory rape, actually even young girls usually enter voluntarily into the relationship. Also, their partners usually are not adults but boys near their own age. The offense usually is one of boy-and-girl having normal heterosexual relations but under conditions where emphasis is on immediate physical pleasure without regard to the girl's reputation, possible parenthood, or venereal infection.

Normal heterosexual relations among boys. Normal heterosexual relations are more widespread among boys than girls, that is, almost all lower-class boys and a high proportion of middle-class boys have some experience with normal sex relations during adolescence. Many girls, especially middle-class, have none or little experience, but a few girls become involved in sex relations in a promiscuous manner.[2]

In the life of the streets, boys have very little status in their own age group until they have had sexual intercourse. Young teenagers strive for status by proving their sexual maturity, boldness, and nonchalance. In the middle class, status may be improved in some groups by heterosexual experience, but usually it is not demanded as the price of acceptance into a teen-age group, as is true in the lower-class street groups.

Boys rarely are arrested for involvement in normal sex relations, perhaps because they are a minor part of the boy's total round of activities in contrast to some girls for whom sex becomes a central activity. Also, it is rare that a couple is detected in the process of sex relations; thus a direct charge of illicit sex is difficult to make against the boy. The girl may become conspicuous in trying to pick up boys, or become pregnant with resulting investigation into her past by social workers, health officials, or police.

Abnormal sexual expression. Boys, more than girls, exhibit forms of sexual expression other than normal heterosexual relations. Sometimes these expressions indicate failure of an adolescent to develop normal heterosexual attitudes or to divert sexual impulses into ac-

1 An excellent discussion of the place of sex offenses in adolescent behavior is contained in Albert J. Reiss, "Sex Offenses: The Marginal Status of the Adolescent," *Law and Contemporary Problems,* 25 (Spring, 1960), 309–333.

2 Alfred C. Kinsey, *et al., Sexual Behavior in the Human Male,* W. B. Saunders Company, Philadelphia, 1949, 374–384; *Sexual Behavior in the Human Female,* W. B. Saunders Company, Philadelphia, 1955, 294–295, 331–333.

ceptable activities. Thus, some older adolescent boys exhibit their sex organs in public and perhaps especially before girls; some sexually attack a small girl or an old woman unable to resist them. These boys are few in number and now are usually regarded as in need of psychotherapy. Occasionally, also, a boy or a gang of boys forcibly attack some girl or young woman, often someone they have never seen before who may not live in their neighborhood. These attacks, which sometimes seriously injure the victim, may be part of a generally disorganized pattern of activity. When such person or gangs are accustomed to gain all advantages by force, sex is no exception. Friendships with girls or gaining a girl's consent seem unnecessary.[1]

Homosexuality is also more common among males than females. Most confirmed homosexuals are older men; to some extent they afford a threat to younger boys whom they seek as partners and who may thus be drawn into degrading situations. However, adolescent boys, already in delinquent gangs, may reverse these roles and exploit older men known to be homosexuals. They deliberately lure older men into compromising situations where they act as male prostitutes for a fee; or they arrange to be "discovered" by their companions who then steal what the man has knowing he dare not report the theft and have his homosexuality come to light. This type of exploitation may become an accepted way to get money in some delinquent gangs, and the technique is taught to younger boys by older, experienced ones. It is part of the system that the boy does not allow himself to become emotionally involved and consents only to certain types of aberrant sex relations. These boys are not homosexuals. They also practice normal sex relations with girls, and they are not homosexuals in adulthood as a result of the practice. The boys seem limited to members of certain thoroughly delinquent gangs, probably oriented toward adult criminality, who have found exploitation of adult homosexuals a relatively safe way to get money without working for it.[2]

Sporadic incidents of homosexuality between boys of the same age also occur, often as part of the rather wide range of sexual experimentation that many adolescents carry out before they have settled into approved adult types of sexual expression. Masturbation, either individually or among boys in a group, may be placed in the same category, although it is much more widespread.

Gang activities. The gang does not originate the interest of boys in sex, but it helps to shape its expression, both normal and abnormal. The approval of the gang urges the adolescent boy along into normal heterosexual activities. The gang itself sponsors exhibitionistic displays of sex, including group masturbation and intercourse in rotation with one girl.[3]

These activities, disapproved by the mores, are approved by the gangs themselves. No boy needs to feel guilty, since his own small social world gives approval. These activities do not dominate the gang life, but are only one of many ways in which the gang participates in building up an independent way of life separate from family and formal institutions.

Some gangs approve of exploitation of adult homosexuals by their members for money-making purposes. And a few gangs assault and rape. It should not be thought that all otherwise delinquent boys or delinquent gangs engage in abnormal, exploitative, or assaultive types of sex expression. These boys and gangs are the exception. In contrast, it is probably true to say that most lower-class boys, delinquent or otherwise, and many if not most middle-class boys regularly or sporadically engage in normal heterosexual activity and experiment with milder aberrant forms.

Offenses involving alcohol

Few youth of juvenile delinquency age are victims of alcoholism, which may be defined as "a chronic behavioral disorder manifested by repeated drinking of alcoholic beverages in excess of the dietary and social uses of the community and to an extent that interferes

---

1 Stanton Wheeler, "Sex Offenses: A Sociological Critique," *Law and Contemporary Problems,* 25 (Spring, 1960), 258–278.
2 Reiss, *op. cit.*

3 Harrison E. Salisbury writes as follows: "The 'circle jerk' or mass masturbation, is a common sex activity. Groups of as many as twenty Rovers join in such a ritual on a summer evening in a deserted public park. Sometimes, a boy and girl may give an exhibition in the center of the circle while group masturbation goes on." *The Shook-up Generation,* Fawcett Publications, Inc., Greenwich, Connecticut, 1958, p. 32.

with the drinker's health or his social or economic functioning." [1] The offenses for which youth are arrested are violation of state or local liquor laws, driving while intoxicated, and drunkenness. Taken together, these three offenses account for 6.5 per cent of all urban arrests of persons under eighteen made in 1959.[2] Four other offenses, chiefly thefts, far outrank these three offenses involving alcohol.

Youth under eighteen account for only a small percentage of the total arrests at all ages for drunkenness and drunken driving— 0.8 and 0.7 per cent respectively, according to the 1959 FBI reports. Arrests for both of these offenses increase rapidly after age twenty-one, when in many states the purchase of liquor becomes legal and therefore may be easily acquired, reaching a peak during the thirties, after which there is a slight decline. Violation of liquor laws, however, is an offense of the young, with most arrests at ages seventeen through twenty, the period during which young people, especially boys, wish to participate in adult activities but are often restricted in the purchase of liquor. The violations become an offense not because of any innate viciousness of the activity but because of the arbitrary limitations set by law on the age when liquor may be purchased. Unlike murder or larceny, forbidden to all people, purchase of liquor is permitted to adults but is made a legal offense for youth.

Among adults, violation of liquor laws does not involve illegal purchase alone but many offenses of proprietors of liquor stores, such as not observing closing hours and other regulations, including nonsale to minors.

Drinking is much more widespread among youth than the arrests indicate. Several surveys of high school boys and girls in the Middle West, Far West, and Kansas indicate that approximately 35 to 70 per cent of boys and 25 to 60 per cent of girls had drunk alcoholic beverages at least once and approximately 30 per cent of boys and 20 per cent of girls more often. The percentages vary with region and size of community. According to the Kansas study, few of the high school drinkers

were consistent or heavy drinkers; a survey in Racine County, Wisconsin, confirms this statement.[3] Drinking does not necessarily lead to drunkenness, nor drunkenness to arrest. Public disturbances or fighting as a result of drunkenness often lead to arrests but the youth may be charged with disorderliness instead of with drunkenness.

The concern about drinking among youth is not limited to the disorderly conduct which may follow but to a fear of future consequences in periodic drunkenness or eventually in alcoholism itself. Since the etiology of alcoholism has not been definitely established, it is difficult to make such assertions. Theories of the cause of alcoholism range from the presence of a biochemical defect to constitutional predisposition to personality problems rooted in childhood to environmental factors. Certainly among the many youth who drink, few will become alcoholics. More specific factors must be found than drinking in itself.

Age and sex differences. The FBI reports show few arrests under age fifteen for violation of liquor laws and few under age sixteen for drunkenness. Driving while intoxicated is rare until ages eighteen and nineteen. In the juvenile period, offenses involving liquor therefore are located in adolescence and especially later adolescence.

For both boys and girls, drinking tends to be a social activity, carried out in a group, often in connection with other social activities. However, the pattern of drinking varies between boys and girls. Only about three-fourths as many high school girls as boys drink outside their own homes; fewer girls have drunk more than once.[4] Fewer girls drink to the point of feeling "high" or becoming intoxicated. Both boys and girls most often had their first drink on special occasions, among family and friends, such as a marriage, or wedding or birthday anniversary. Boys more than girls drank before parties. They more often had their first drink of hard liquor (as distinct from beer) in automobiles. These facts indicate that boys

1 Mark Keller, "Alcoholism: Nature and Extent of the Problem," *Annals of the American Academy of Political and Social Science,* 315 (1958), 2.
2 Federal Bureau of Investigation, United States Department of Justice, *Uniform Crime Reports, 1959,* U. S. Government Printing Office, Washington, D. C., 1960, pp. 99–100.

3 James F. Short, Jr., and F. Ivan Nye, "Extent of Unrecorded Juvenile Delinquency: Tentative Conclusions," *Journal of Criminal Law, Criminology and Police Science,* 49 (1958), 297–298; E. Jackson Baur and Marston M. McCluggage, "Drinking Patterns of Kansas High School Students," *Social Problems,* 5 (Spring 1958), 317–326.
4 Short and Nye, *op. cit.;* Baur and McCluggage, *op. cit.*

drink with other boys as well as with girls. Girls rarely drink with their own sex only.

Cultural influences. In drinking, adolescents reflect the culture of their ethnic and social class groups. Ethnic groups who regard alcoholic beverages as food or as a condiment to meals, teach their children to drink wine or beer as a normal part of food consumption; in these groups drunkenness tends to be rare. Jewish, Italian, and Chinese ethnic groups are examples.[1] However, if the pattern whereby drinking is integrated into the daily life and controlled by family and community is broken by exposure to other customs, the controlled type of drinking tends to break down. Also, if in the process of social adjustment, stresses become intense, drinking may increase.

Social classes also tend to have distinctive attitudes toward drinking. The middle-class attitudes are most likely to be restrictive and critical of drinking among young people. If tolerated at all, parents and other adults expect it to be in moderation and preferably at home or in some controlled recreational setting. Use of alcohol, therefore, easily becomes a symbol of defiance and of independence. The triad of middle-class delinquency (automobile, alcohol, and sex) has already been discussed in Chapter 8. The upper-class is more lenient but tends to restrict the place of drinking by youth to homes, private clubs, and restaurants or bars whose patrons tend to be upper-class. As with other types of deviant behavior a protective wall is built around the drinking indiscretions of upper-class youth. Public tipsiness or drunken driving may also be kept from police records or public print by family influence.

Drinking in the lower class differs according to the ethnic background of the group. When drinking is integrated into ceremonial and eating patterns, it may remain at a low level even in public places. When drinking has not been so integrated and especially when hard liquor rather than wine or beer is the chief beverage drunk, a certain amount of male drunkenness may be accepted as part of the lower-class culture. The locale for

drinking is likely to be the public tavern (in the past the saloon), patronized primarily by men.

In lower-class communities where heavy drinking is tolerated by the mores, taverns do not hesitate to break laws and serve adolescents or sell bottled goods to them. Writing about Chicago in 1947, a long-time social worker for youth stated that illegal tavern conditions had become so entrenched and were so bound up with corrupt politics that interested groups of citizens could not force compliance with the laws.[2] Many of the taverns were also centers for gambling, prostitution, and obscene entertainment and were regarded as social recreational centers for the neighborhood. In small cities, also, taverns serve as social centers and illegally cater to youth who wish to drink.

In *Elmtown's Youth,* the function of drinking for the lower-class male adolescent is clearly stated for that city of 7,000.[3] As already described in Chapter 7 a claim to manhood may be made by the boy who can walk up to a bar, order a drink of whiskey, down it, and order another. Lower-class girls who drink in public, sit at tables in the taverns.

In these lower-class communities where drinking and drunkenness among adolescent males are accepted, adult males also drink heavily and thus set the pattern of drinking as a symbol of adulthood and masculinity.

Drinking and delinquency. Drinking seems less a cause of delinquent behavior than part of a pattern of behavior which has a variety of deviant facets. Drinking (and presumably drunkenness) is far more common in the past experiences of correctional school boys and girls than among high school students. The surveys in the Middle West and Far West already cited showed that 89.7 per cent of western correctional school boys compared with 57.2 per cent of western high school boys bought or drank alcoholic beverages; 79.4 per cent of correctional school boys but only 29.5 of high school boys had bought or used it more than once or twice.[4] Among girls twice as high a percentage of correctional school girls as of high school girls (90.2 ver-

1 Albert D. Ullman, "Socio-cultural Backgrounds of Alcoholism," *Annals of the American Academy of Political and Social Science,* 315 (1958), 48–54; Harrison M. Trice and David J. Pittman, "Social Organization and Alcoholism: A Review of Significant Research since 1940," *Social Problems,* 5 (Spring 1958), 294–307.

2 Jessie F. Binford, "Postwar Problems of Youth," *Federal Probation,* 11 (October–December, 1947), 7–11.
3 August B. Hollingshead, *Elmtown's Youth,* John Wiley and Sons, New York, 1949, Chapter 15.
4 Short and Nye, *op. cit.*

sus 44.5) had bought or used alcoholic beverages; among those who had used them more than once or twice the corresponding percentages were 80.5 and 17.6.

These same correctional school boys and girls had a high frequency of other offenses as compared with high school students, notably truanting from school, running away from home, expulsion from school, defiance of authority, reckless driving, stealing of various types, fighting, and illicit sex relations. The surveys do not indicate the relationships between these deviations from approved behavior, but individual cases from other sources show the intricate interrelations of motives and behavior which often make up delinquency.

Motivations for drinking by youth. It is probably impossible to assign all drinking to one motivation. For some youth it is an extension into public behavior of ethnic patterns of family drinking. For others, it is an attempt to prove manhood in the lower-class world of the tavern. For still others, it is part of recreational life such as a dance or other type of party where added daring or gaiety seems called for. Some find in it a means to defy adult restrictions. Within limits, many adults are tolerant of drinking by older adolescents, usually at home or at private parties where there is some adult control. When drinking exceeds these limits, it usually occurs in a small closed group of adolescents in an automobile or gang hangout. The illegality of most adolescent drinking outside the confines of the family calls for a certain amount of circumspection and secrecy, except, perhaps in the lower class, where the tavern, although a public place, actually serves as a private men's club.

Juvenile drug addicts

Drug addiction among adolescents creates great concern because of its debilitating effect and legal aspects. Since the sale of narcotic drugs is restricted by law, illegal possession or sale of drugs constitutes a crime; adolescents and adults alike who are discovered with drugs in their possession for illegal sale or use are subject to arrest and severe legal penalties. The law thus indirectly makes drug use or addiction a crime. Beyond this legal definition of crime, drug addiction has several other connections with delinquency and crime. An uneasy popular feeling that addicts become ma-

niacs when under the influence of drugs causes many people to fear the possible effects of widespread use of drugs by adolescents, especially those in gangs. For the most part, this fear is unfounded. A real relationship between drugs and crime exists, however, in the thefts and acts of prostitution carried out by boys and girls to buy the high-cost drugs on the illegal market in order to satisfy their craving.

Location of addicts. Narcotics use is not widespread in the United States, even among adults and still less among juveniles. It has aroused concern partly because of its concentration in certain areas and groups where it has become a real problem and partly because of the extreme difficulty of controlling or terminating usage once it has begun.

Drug addiction, regardless of age, centers in three states: New York, Illinois, and California. As of December 31, 1959, among 45,391 active addicts known to the Federal Bureau of Narcotics, 45.6 per cent were in New York State, chiefly in New York City, 14.2 per cent in California, and 13.6 per cent in Illinois. Only one other state had as many as 5 per cent of the total number of addicts. Even in the states with high percentages of addicts, only a minute proportion of the population is involved.[1]

Addicts are chiefly found in large cities, often port cities into which narcotic drugs are smuggled in excess of the amounts that are legally imported for medical, scientific, or industrial uses. It is virtually impossible for addicts to secure drugs by legal means through a doctor's prescription; therefore they buy surreptitiously from drug peddlers or storekeepers who secure drugs illegally, chiefly from organized criminal groups which have secured them by means of smuggling. The secrecy that must surround the entire operation is possible in a large city to an extent impossible in smaller communities. Within cities, adolescent addicts tend to live in a few areas, chiefly those in which certain deprived people live. In Chicago, youthful drug addicts are primarily Negroes living in slum areas.[2] In New York City, Negro and to

---

1 *Extract from Treasury—Post Office Departments Appropriations for 1961,* Hearings before the Subcommittee of the Committee on Appropriations, House of Representatives, Eighty-Sixth Congress, Second Session, U. S. Government Printing Office, Washington, D. C., 1960, p. 145.

2 Harold Finestone, "Cats, Kicks, and Color," *Social Problems,* 5 (1957), 3–13. Also unpublished report

some extent Puerto Rican youths are frequent among addicts.[1] In general, without regard to race, the areas of concentration are the deteriorated areas where social organization is weak and public tolerance of drug use high. Within these areas, drug use is highest in the most crowded and poverty-stricken neighborhoods, where education is low and family breakdown frequent.[2] These areas are essentially the same as those which have high rates of delinquency not related to drug use.

Age of addicts. Among the 45,391 active cases known to the Federal Bureau of Narcotics in December, 1958, only 12 per cent were below the age of twenty-one and very few of these were under eighteen. The offenders below twenty-one reported by local agencies to the Bureau vary from year to year; in 1959, youthful addicts constituted only 3.7 per cent of all cases. Slightly more than half of the cases were between ages twenty-one and thirty and the remainder were scattered through the older years.[3] Marihuana was not included.

Race of addicts. Among addicts of all ages known to the Federal Bureau of Narcotics, only 26 per cent are classified as white; 58 per cent are Negro, 8 per cent Puerto Rican, 6 per cent Mexican, and 2 per cent "other" races.[4] In the total population only about 10 per cent are Negroes.

When race is linked with what is known of the geographic location of addicts, addiction can be traced to Negroes, Puerto Ricans, and Mexicans in large industrial cities, chiefly in the North and Far West. Among northern cities, Negro addiction is a problem in Chicago, Detroit, New York City, Philadelphia, Newark, Pittsburgh, St. Louis, Baltimore, and Washington. Only one southern city, New Orleans, has a problem with Negro addicts. Puerto Rican addiction centers chiefly in New York City, where most Puerto Ricans on the mainland live. Mexican addiction centers in the Southwest and Los Angeles.[5]

Adolescent drug users and addicts. Addiction is defined as: "(1) an overpowering desire or need (compulsion) to continue taking the drug; (2) a tendency to increase the dose; (3) a psychological and sometimes a physical dependence on the effects of the drug." [6] When the user becomes dependent upon the drug, he finds it necessary constantly to increase the amount taken in order to achieve the same effect that resulted earlier from a smaller quantity. Thus he enters upon a spiral of increasing amounts, taken at shorter intervals of time, placing upon him a greater burden of acquiring money to buy the drug. For many, the central goal is to accumulate money, usually illegally, to buy drugs to satisfy the never-ending craving and avoid the pains of withdrawal.

Not all adolescent drug users become addicts. In areas of addiction, knowledge and folklore about narcotic drugs is widespread. Many boys begin the use as an experiment in new experiences or as sharing of a social activity with others. They may never become addicts, but may confine the use of drugs to the weekends, when social activities are most prevalent. For example, a study of 305 members of eighteen New York gangs, known for their active participation in intergang fights, showed that ninety-four used heroin more or less regularly. Only 43 per cent of the heroin users, however, took the drug daily and thereby qualified as addicts. The other 57 per cent of users were casual or "weekend" users. They did not become dependent on the drug nor find it necessary to increase the dosage. Their usage was a social activity. The drugs available to adolescents have often been diluted to such an extent that they are not completely habit forming. Casual users therefore have a chance to decrease or stop the practice without suffering excruciating physical pains.[7]

"Drug Addiction among Young Persons in Chicago," Illinois Institute for Juvenile Research and The Chicago Area Project, October 1953.

1 Donald L. Gerard and Conan Kornetsky, "Adolescent Opiate Addiction: A Study of Control and Addict Subjects," *Psychiatric Quarterly,* 29 (1955), 457–486.

2 Isador Chein, "Narcotics Use Among Juveniles," *Social Work,* 1 (April, 1956), 50–60.

3 *Extract from Treasury—Post Office Departments Appropriations for 1961, op. cit.,* pp. 135, 144.

4 *Extract from Treasury—Post Office Departments Appropriations for 1961, op. cit.,* p. 144.

5 *Extract from Treasury—Post Office Departments Appropriations for 1961, op. cit.,* p. 175.

6 This is the definition agreed upon by the World Health Organization's Expert Committee on Drugs Liable to Produce Addiction, Report on the Second Session (1950), cited in Roma K. McNickle, "Drug Addiction," *Editorial Research Reports,* 1 (March 28, 1951), p. 223.

7 Daniel M. Wilner, Eva Rosenfeld, Robert S. Lee, Donald L. Gerard, and Isidor Chein, "Heroin Use and Street Gangs," *Journal of Criminal Law, Criminology and Police Science,* 48 (1957), 399–409. The

Many adolescent users begin their experiment with drugs through smoking marihuana cigarettes (reefers), usually in company with a few friends. From this practice they may graduate to the use of heroin (horse), a drug that is a derivative of opium. Typically, the boy begins by sniffing the drug up his nose (snorting); he moves from this to injecting the drug subcutaneously (skin popping); and finally he injects it intravenously (shooting the main line). By this time he usually is an addict (hooked), or has "the habit."

A young woman witness before the Senate Crime Committee gave an account of her experiences with narcotic drugs.[1] An inmate of the federal hospital for addicts at Lexington, Kentucky, she was a voluntary witness. She began to use marihuana at the age of sixteen and a year later was injecting heroin subcutaneously. Finally for an added kick, she used "speed balls," or a combination of cocaine and heroin. The cost of the drugs ran from $30 to $70 per day. To secure this money she became a prostitute and also bought stolen checks for about half their face value, forged an endorsement, and cashed them for the full amount. She also exploited men, whom she lured to a place where they could drink, then put knockout drops in their drinks, robbed them and left.

Effect of narcotic drugs. Most juvenile offenders either smoke marihuana or use heroin. Marihuana may cause hallucinations. It is habit-forming but does not require an increase of dosage to give satisfaction, as do many other narcotic drugs. Also, when the habit is broken, the user does not suffer the severe pains and nausea that torment the heroin addict during the first few days after withdrawal of the drug. The use of marihuana is therefore not regarded as seriously as is the use of heroin. Often, however, it opens the pathway to the use of heroin with its more powerful effects and illusory pleasures.

Heroin has a sedative effect (unlike cocaine which tends to stimulate and excite). The effect of heroin is to reduce tensions, including those resulting from various insecurities and anxieties and from the sex drive.[2] Addicts develop a feeling of well-

being. For the harsh realities of their lives they substitute fantasies in which they play a grandiose role, featuring themselves as sophisticated, cultured, and well-dressed. They distinguish themselves as members of an exclusive addicted or "cat" culture which they view as superior to that of the ordinary person. As the drug wears off, they again become aware of reality and feel depressed until the next intake of the drug. They gradually become unfit for work and avoid a regular, routine job.

Addiction and boys' gangs. The majority of boys in typical delinquent and fighting gangs are not addicts, although some may be weekend users of small amounts of drug. In general, gangs exert pressure against the use of drugs by their members, and users do not try to induce their brother-members to use drugs nor try to sell drugs to them. Any proselytizing that they do is with nonmembers. However, drug usage is often begun in a little group of friends.[3]

Gang members feel that the addict is unreliable. He cannot be depended upon to carry out his role and if arrested may easily be induced to confess gang exploits by withholding of the drug. Since addicts often become involved in serious attempts to steal, they are more likely to be arrested than are other boys.

If the addict has previously had a place of leadership in the gang, he usually loses it as his addiction increases. Many users are not leaders, however. They may be fringe members, who may take drugs first in an effort to increase their prestige. The long-run effect is to lower it.

As addicts lose status in the gang and find their interests deviating from those of other members, they tend to form smaller cliques within the gang and eventually to withdraw, either because other members mature and branch out into adult pursuits or because they find themselves more comfortable among a group of addicts. In the clique they can share their beliefs and follow their practices without criticism or feelings of guilt.

Attitudes and life pattern of the youthful addict. Comparative studies between addicts and

article is one of a series from a study sponsored by the National Institute of Mental Health.
1 *Detroit Free Press,* Wednesday, June 27, 1951.
2 Harold Finestone, *op. cit.;* Paul Zimmering, James Toolan, Renate Safrin, and S. Bernard Wortis,

"Heroin Addiction in Adolescent Boys," *Journal of Nervous and Mental Disease,* 114 (1951), 19–34. The latter study, made by physicians, was based on twenty-two consecutive admissions of adolescent boys to the Boys' Ward of Bellevue Hospital.
3 Isidor Chein, *op. cit.;* Zimmering, *op. cit.*

nonaddicts show that youth do not fall into two distinct psychological types, addict and nonaddict.[1] Differences are relative.

Various studies bring out the characteristics of the youthful addict. It is not clear to what extent these characteristics preceded addiction and may have influenced the adolescent toward continued use of the drug, or to what extent they have resulted from addiction. Addicts seem unable to adjust well to other people. They tend to feel inferior and rejected and in turn reject others. Even when they form small cliques, each addict tends to maintain his individualism; they do not embark on projects requiring planning and close co-operation. They remain individuals without close group affiliations, although they may gather to listen to music records and drift off into their individual fantasies.[2]

For the addict, the objective of drug use is "the kick," defined as "any act tabooed by 'squares' that heightens and intensifies the present moment of experience and differentiates it as much as possible from the humdrum routine of daily life." [3] Addiction is not the only "kick" known in delinquency areas. Others are sex perversions and orgies and use of alcohol. But heroin is regarded among addicts as the ultimate "kick," as it is the most strongly disapproved. Thus addiction as a way to alleviate anxieties and escape from harsh realities comes to have a positive value. The drug transports the addict away from a world in which he cannot compete, into a fantasy world of his own making where he builds up a dream self-concept of himself as sophisticated and cultured. Music is important to the young addict, not only as something to soothe him but as a possible vocation in some illusive future.

Many young addicts suffer from a weak concept of their role as males. They have difficulty making normal contacts with girls, including sex relationships, an open symbol of masculinity in the areas in which they live. Some are homosexuals. The many families in areas of addiction headed by the mother may contribute to the failure in developing a masculine role and thus indirectly lay the foundation for some cases of addiction. However, most fatherless boys do not become addicts.

The addict leans toward criminal activity by his desperate need for money to buy the drug. Whatever his original potential for work may have been, he becomes unemployable both psychologically and physically as the addiction increases. Stealing provides some money. He tends to abhor physical force and hence tries to manipulate people by playing on their sympathies or finding some way to swindle them out of money. His ideal, however, is to have someone else supply him with money. He thus tends to reject the middle-class ideal that the adult male should work and seeks some way to have a woman who will work for him. He often becomes the pimp to a prostitute. This view among lower-class Negro addicts may be influenced by the prevalence of fatherless homes in which the mother supports the family.[4]

The outcome of addiction. It is generally agreed by those who work with addicts that physical withdrawal of the drug is not the whole answer. Among adolescent boys, those who use it casually seem to be able to control their demand without becoming addicts who are constantly impelled to increase the amount taken. They may voluntarily seek admission to a hospital for treatment. If their gang has few addicts, their friends may attempt to help them give up the habit.

The true addicts are in a more dangerous situation. Their physical addiction is often complicated by deep-seated psychological problems, held in abeyance by the drug but reappearing when the drug is not used. The

1 In one study, the research team found distinct differences between addicts and nonaddicts on the Rorschach test. But when an outside psychiatrist rated the Rorschach protocols, the differences, though present, were not great enough to be statistically significant. Gerard and Kornetsky, *op. cit.*

2 The discussion of attitudes and life patterns is based on Chein, *op. cit.;* Gerard and Kornetsky, *op. cit.;* Finestone, *op. cit.;* and Leo Gold, "Toward an Understanding of Adolescent Drug Addiction," *Federal Probation,* 22 (September, 1958), 42–48.

3 Finestone, *op. cit.,* p. 5. Finestone's conclusions are based chiefly on study of young Negro addicts in Chicago.

4 In *Call Girl,* the relation of the pimp to the call-girl (the elite of prostitutes) is discussed from the point of view of the girl. The successful call-girl who meets men only by appointment and favors well-to-do clients, has a comfortable if not large income but a dearth of companionable contacts. The pimp, a man whom the call-girl supports totally or in part, is the one to whom she turns for companionship or for sex relations more satisfying to her than those with her clients. The pimps usually have some connection with the underworld of crime and could arrange for police protection from exploitation. Often they were drug addicts, who liked to dress well. They are also described as passive and somewhat feminine. *Call Girl* describes a different social level than Finestone describes, but the relationship between the male drug addict and the prostitute seems to be the same. Harold Greenwald, *The Call Girl,* Ballantine Books, New York, 1958, Chapter 8.

supposedly cured addict soon relapses into his former habits. Because of the dependence on the drug and its availability, addicts can rarely be cured while they remain in their own neighborhoods. They must be removed and hospitalized where they cannot secure the drug and where psychiatric as well as physical treatment can be provided.

Addicts who are not voluntarily admitted to special hospitals—that is, who are committed by the courts—do not readily respond to the opportunity for therapy.[1] The drug has become a sure way to escape from frustrations and tensions; therapy seems uncertain and involves facing the problems they have been avoiding. Unless the therapist can secure the addict's cooperation, help him face and solve his problems, and achieve the maturity to face them alone after he leaves the hospital, he is not cured. The fact that he has had no drugs over a period of several months means nothing when he is released and returns to his old environment, friends, and problems. Among those who have had physical withdrawal alone, 90 per cent return to drug use.

The co-operative addict finds the hospital a place of refuge where his need for protection from stresses is met. He can gather strength within the hospital and learn to meet the low-level demands made there before he returns to independence and his old stresses. Even so, he may relapse and return several times before he can forego drugs.

The adolescent addict who is not cured faces a hapless future. He becomes more helpless in solving his problems and in holding a job. He turns to petty crime as an answer. He accepts intermittent jail sentences and the pains of quick drug withdrawal as an inevitable part of life. Sometimes repetition of these experiences forces him to admit his addiction and his low status in society in general. He may or may not seek a cure.

Other addicts are able to contain their addiction at a low level, integrated into a nonconventional pattern of life. A revealing study of the so-called "beat generation," presented by a sympathizer, analyzes the style of life of this group in Venice, California. Non-conventional in relation to the larger society, the group has conventionalized its ways into a little subculture which receives its valuation and confers status within its own little private world. Many of the characteristics described for youthful drug addicts in the studies cited are found in the beat community in subdued form permitting the members to live with little stress and tension and to avoid police attention even when their activities are illegal. The community described represents one type of adjustment in adulthood of youth who cannot adjust to the realistic and practical expectations of either conventional or criminal society.[2]

Wavering public opinion

Thefts, assaults, and murders are almost universally condemned in the United States. Public opinion wavers, however, about unusual or abnormal sex expressions, excessive drinking, and addictive use of narcotic drugs. One troublesome problem is definition—what is abnormal, excessive, addictive? The problem of definition is even more difficult when juvenile behavior is in question. The protective attitude toward juveniles easily leads to a repressive policy toward minor deviations which often are passing phases of development toward adulthood. The outcome in adults of certain types of sexual deviations, excessive drinking, and drug addiction tends to disintegration of personality and often danger to other people. An important need is to discover how to differentiate the transient experiments of youth from the beginnings of serious adult perversions and excesses.

Public opinion also wavers as to the way in which juveniles and adults should be treated when they become involved in sex offenses, drunkenness, and addiction. Are they vicious personalities, hardened criminals, to be severely punished? Or are they victims of maladjustment who should receive medical and psychiatric treatment? Research into development of the behavior and experimentation with different types of treatment may clarify some of these questions.

2 Lawrence Lipton, *The Holy Barbarians,* Julian Messner, Inc., New York, 1959.

1 Gold, *op. cit.*

Bibliography

Sex offenses

Gardner, George E., "The Community and the Aggressive Child, The Aggressive-Destructive Impulses in the Sex Offender," *Mental Hygiene,* 34 (1950), 44–63.

Kinsey, Alfred C., *et al., Sexual Behavior in the Human Female,* W. B. Saunders Co., Philadelphia, 1955.

————, *Sexual Behavior in the Human Male,* W. B. Saunders Co., Philadelphia, 1949.

Kirkendall, Lester A., "Circumstances Associated with Teenage Boys' Use of Prostitution," *Marriage and Family Living,* 22 (1960), 145–149.

Reiss, Albert J., "Sex Offenses: The Marginal Status of the Adolescent," *Law and Contemporary Problems,* 25 (Spring, 1960), 309–333.

"Sex Offenses," *Law and Contemporary Problems,* 25 (Spring, 1960), entire issue.

Whyte, William Foote, "A Slum Sex Code," *American Journal of Sociology,* 49 (1943), 24–31.

Use of alcohol

Baur, E. Jackson, and Marston M. McCluggage, "Drinking Patterns of Kansas High School Students," *Social Problems,* 5 (Spring, 1958), 317–326.

Trice, Harrison M., and David J. Pittman, "Social Organization and Alcoholism: A Review of Significant Research since 1940," *Social Problems,* 5 (Spring, 1958), 294–307.

Ullman, Albert D., "Sociocultural Backgrounds of Alcoholism," *Annals of the American Academy of Political and Social Science,* 315 (January, 1958), 48–54.

Wattenberg, William W., and John B. Moir, "A Study of Teen-Agers Arrested for Drunkenness," *Quarterly Journal of Studies on Alcohol,* 17 (1956), 426–436.

Juvenile drug addiction

Chein, Isidor, "Narcotics Use among Juveniles," *Social Work,* 1 (April, 1956), 50–60.

————, and Eva Rosenfeld, "Juvenile Heroin Users in New York City," *Law and Contemporary Problems,* 22 (Winter, 1957), 52–68.

Clausen, John A., "Social and Psychological Factors in Narcotics Addiction," *Law and Contemporary Problems,* 22 (Winter, 1957), 34–51.

"Drug Addiction among Young Persons in Chicago," A Report of a Study Conducted by the Illinois Institute for Juvenile Research and The Chicago Area Project, issued October, 1953.

Finestone, Harold, "Cats, Kicks, and Color," *Social Problems,* 5 (July, 1957), 3–13.

————, "Narcotics and Criminality," *Law and Contemporary Problems,* 22 (Winter, 1957), 69–85.

Gerard, Donald L., and Conan Kornetsky, "Adolescent Opiate Addiction: A Study of Control and Addict Subjects," *Psychiatric Quarterly,* 29 (1955), 457–486.

————, "Adolescent Opiate Addiction; A Case Study," *Psychiatric Quarterly,* 28 (1954), 367 ff.

————, "A Social and Psychiatric Study of Adolescent Opiate Addicts," *Psychiatric Quarterly,* 28 (1954), 113 ff.

Gold, Leo, "Toward an Understanding of Adolescent Drug Addiction," *Federal Probation,* 22 (September, 1958), 42–48.

Lipton, Lawrence, *The Holy Barbarians,* Julian Messner, Inc., New York, 1959.

McNickle, Roma K., "Drug Addiction," *Editorial Research Reports,* 1 (March 28, 1951), 221–237.

Prevention and Control of Narcotic Addiction, Bureau of Narcotics, U. S. Treasury Department, Washington, D. C., undated.

Rosenfeld, Eva, "Social Research and Social Action in Prevention of Juvenile Delinquency," *Social Problems,* 4 (1956), 138–148.

Wilner, Daniel M., Eva Rosenfeld, Robert S. Lee, Donald L. Gerard, and Isidor Chein, "Heroin Use and Street Gangs," *Journal of Criminal Law, Criminology and Police Science,* 48 (1957), 399–409.

Zimmering, Paul, James Toolan, Renate Safrin, and S. Bernard Wortis, "Heroin Addiction in Adolescent Boys," *Journal of Nervous and Mental Disease,* 114 (1951), 19–34.

Chapter **14**

Group and isolated delinquency and the nondelinquent

Delinquencies of children are much more often the actions of groups than of isolated individuals. In fact, James S. Plant, a psychiatrist, has said that "with the possible exception of marriage, no human arrangement is of a more social nature than delinquency." [1] Over the years various studies have shown that from 70 to 85 per cent of boy delinquencies are committed by two or more boys, only 15 to 30 per cent by one boy alone.[2] The small clique is the usual unit for delinquency. Among delinquencies carried out by more than one boy, 65 to 70 per cent were the work of two or three boys. The remaining groups rarely included more than four boys. Organized gangs were extremely rare in the commission of crimes, although some boys belonged to larger but loosely grouped crowds of delinquents, who did not however, participate as a unit in

1 James S. Plant, "Who is the Delinquent?" *Juvenile Delinquency and the Schools,* Forty-seventh Yearbook of the National Society for the Study of Education, Part I, edited by Nelson B. Henry, University of Chicago Press, Chicago, 1948, p. 24.
2 Clifford R. Shaw and Henry D. McKay, *Social Factors in Juvenile Delinquency,* A Study . . . for the National Commission on Law Observance and Enforcement, No. 13, volume 2, Government Printing Office, Washington, D. C., 1931, p. 195; William Healy and Augusta R. Bronner, *New Light on Denliquency and Its Treatment,* Yale University Press, New Haven, Connecticut, 1936, pp. 63–64; Sheldon and Eleanor Glueck, *One Thousand Juvenile Delinquents,* Harvard University Press, Cambridge, Massachusetts, 1934, pp. 94, 100; William C. Kvaraceus, *Juvenile Delinquency and the School,* World Book Company, Yonkers-on-Hudson, New York, 1945, p. 116.

delinquencies. After all, few delinquencies can be carried out successfully by large groups because of the increased likelihood of discovery with an increase in number of boys. Outright fights, riots, or mass vandalism are almost the only delinquencies that can be more successfully carried out by a large group than a small one. In spite of flaming newspaper headlines, such delinquencies rarely occur, the usual delinquency is to steal on a small scale. Drinking and sex parties are also sometimes carried out by an entire group or gang.

Table 21 shows for one disorganized Chicago neighborhood the division of delinquencies into those carried out by groups of delinquents and those committed by individuals or small cliques. Some forms of misbehavior are adaptable to both large and small groups and to the individual. But there is also a distinction among other delinquencies. Drinking and certain sex activities and fighting tend to be group activities. Both minor and major offenses involving property and annoyance or injury to other persons tend to be individual or clique offenses. The potentially most damaging of the large group or gang offenses is fighting.

The true function of membership by the delinquent in a large group is not for the successful perpetration of a delinquency but for social and status functions. Delinquent and nondelinquent peer groups serve many of the same functions for their members, although the activities by which these functions are achieved may differ. Delinquency is one —but only one—way by which the delinquent gang carries on its activities and meets personal needs of members.

Organization of delinquent gangs

Delinquent gangs may consist of loosely federated small cliques, of street clubs with informal natural leadership, or of organizations with an age hierarchy and specialized leadership.

Cliques. Some gangs begin, perhaps in preadolescent years, with a closely linked clique of four or five boys. If another small clique competes for dominance of a particular play space the two may combine without losing their identity. More members may be needed for some particular sport. In time other small cliques are added, not through formal action but because of something they can add to the

Table 21

Number of Group Members Involved in Classified Types of Antisocial Behavior during the Period from June 31, 1955 to December 31, 1955, Newly Disorganized Area, Chicago

	Group members engaging in antisocial behavior	
	Alone or with less than half of the group	With half or more of the group
Violations of city ordinances, including curfew laws, traffic laws, hopping streetcars, swimming in forbidden places, playing ball in streets, etc.	89	87
Minor offenses		
Against property, including truancy, trespassing, sneaking into movies, running away, petty stealing, minor defacing of property, etc.	62	—
Against persons, including abuse of younger children, marked annoyance of older persons outside of family or friendship circle, etc.	15	—
Drinking and sex within group.	—	75
Fight against another group.	—	41
Major offenses		
Against property including breaking and entering (burglary), larceny, major vandalism, etc.	15	—
Against persons, including strongarm or armed robbery, use of narcotics, knifing, forced sex relations, etc.	3	—
Total number of boys.	184	203

Rearranged from Charles H. Shireman, *The Hyde Park Youth Project, May 1955–May, 1958,* Welfare Council of Metropolitan Chicago, Chicago, undated, p. 129.

customary activities of the already established clique or cliques. Each clique tends to keep its leader but acknowledges a central leader when the entire group undertakes some enterprise.

When the group grows by individual accretions of members, the membership may tend to form small cliques of boys with special interests who nevertheless also wish to be part of a larger group. The cliques shift and angle for increased importance in the combined group, trying to place the clique leader in the top position and themselves in a favored status with reference to the other cliques.

The pair, triad, or small clique is the most frequent delinquency unit. This is true whether or not the boys are members of a larger gang. Several illustrations of minor and serious delinquencies involving the pair, triad, or small clique follow.

Two boys aged fourteen and fifteen left the city where they lived with their parents, in the car of one family and with a safe containing $1,300 belonging to the other family. They had crossed the country from north to south before police arrested them for erratic driving.

Three boys, aged thirteen, fourteen, and fifteen were separately attacked outside their school in Chicago by two older youths who had demanded a dime of each of the younger boys. Two of the boys were injured sufficiently to require hospital treatment.

A fifteen-year-old boy, Carl, killed Willis, aged fourteen after school as the climax to the following chain of events. Carl's brother Walter, aged fourteen had annoyed Willis' sister, Anita. This led Willis to beat Walter. Carl then warned Willis not to attack Walter again. Willis made a movement as though he were about to draw a weapon, whereupon Carl stabbed him with a ten inch butcher knife which he had with him. Willis was found to have a switchblade knife and a straight razor in his pocket.

Informal amorphous gangs. The fluid unstable quality of Chicago gangs was observed in the twenties by Thrasher.[1] He says that the "ganging process is a continuous flux and flow," with individual members joining and leaving and with more permanent breaks through conflict or arrest. The same quality was noted in Chapter 6 for Hyde Park gangs in Chicago. This type of gang has been referred to as a "near group," less formless than the temporary mob but without the more formal structure of a true group.[2]

According to the near-group theory, the gang builds up around a central core of five or six boys, who desperately need the gang as a group within which to work out personal problems that might vary from one boy to another. There is no consensus as to goals; each boy is trying to meet individual needs. Additional boys have a loose affiliation with the gang, participating or not as any particular activity meets each boy's temporary needs. A still more remote ring of boys do not identify themselves with the gang but on occasion may accompany a gang, for instance, on a fight, to enjoy the excitement as observer or participant. Thus there is no definite membership. In this loose affiliation, individual boys with many types of emotional needs may try to meet them without much responsibility for the group or its purposes.

Other writers who recognize the near-group as one form of gang or street club do not, however, emphasize the quality of emotional disturbance as a necessary quality for leadership or membership. In the work with street clubs in Hyde Park, Chicago, only about 10 per cent of members (not leaders alone) were found to be emotionally disturbed and were referred to a casework agency.[3]

Under adult leadership near-groups may move toward a firmer type of organization. The street workers assigned to work with the amorphous mass of boys in Hyde Park, Chicago, were able to separate out congenial groups who formed clubs, found purposes, and made plans. Progress was slow. Some boys remained on the fringe, some remained outside the clubs. It may be suggested that in a newly disorganized community both the boys who have grown up in the area and the newcomers, previously unknown to each other, may at first form amorphous groups of like race or subculture. Oldtimers and newcomers tend to feel the threat of the other and draw together for security. Only with a less uncertain relationship—either friendly or drawn conflict—do they seem able to organize into clubs.

Organized clubs or gangs. Some gangs have as one purpose—but not the only one—maintenance of their status and protection of their home territory from intruding gangs. Some of these gangs fulfill the qualifications of near-groups, but others are more fully organized, and groups of older boys often reach a high point in organization. Nevertheless, group processes are informal and methods of obtaining new leaders are so unformulated that the gang may disintegrate if the leader moves away, is arrested and committed to a correctional school, or fails to meet his obligations. However, usually other boys are ready and keen to step into the vacated position. Membership is handled by the simple method of testing out each new potential member.[4]

Some of the more definitely structured gangs have subsidiary gangs, arranged by age. Each subgang moves up step by step in status as the members grow older, with the oldest subgroup ready to replace the dominant gang as its members leave the gang for the armed forces, jobs, marriage—or sometimes prison. A typical organization is that of the "Outlaws," in which youth over nineteen hold the controlling position as Senior Outlaws. In lower levels are the Intermediates aged seventeen to nineteen, Junior Outlaws aged fifteen to seventeen, and Midget Outlaws aged thirteen to fifteen. Some organized boys' gangs have an auxiliary of girls, in this instance, Outlawettes aged fourteen to sixteen and Little Outlawettes aged twelve to fourteen. All these segments rarely meet together, but they maintain a sibling relationship with each other, with older segments overseeing and controlling the activities of the

1 Frederic M. Thrasher, *The Gang,* University of Chicago Press, Chicago, 1927, pp. 35–37.

2 Lewis Yablonsky, "The Delinquent Gang as a Near-Group," *Social Problems,* 7 (Fall, 1959), 108–117.

3 Charles H. Shireman, *The Hyde Park Youth Project, May 1955–May 1958,* Welfare Council of Metropolitan Chicago, Chicago, undated, p. 147.

4 Walter B. Miller, "The Impact of a Community Group Work Program on Delinquent Corner Groups," *Social Service Review,* 31 (December, 1957), 390–406; Miller, "Lower Class Culture as a Generating Milieu of Gang Delinquency," *Journal of Social Issues,* 14 (April, 1958), 5–19; *Reaching the Fighting Gang,* New York City Youth Board, New York, 1960, Chapters 2 and 3.

younger, gradually passing on to them the attitudes, codes, and approved behavior patterns of the older group. They set the traditions and reputation of the gang. The younger groups emulate the older ones. The total assemblage or aggregate using a given name and feeling part of the same organization might total as many as fifty to seventy members.

The age-group unit numbers fifteen to twenty boys and is itself broken into cliques of three or four boys, each with its own leader. When the larger group acts as a unit, different boys act as leaders for different functions, such as athletics, a dance, or an intergang fight. In addition to the vertical organization, some gangs have a horizontal organization and a brother relationship with one or more other gangs whereby they do not fight each other but will join together to attack or defend territory against an opposing gang. When members of such gangs move to other communities, they may organize a

This phalanx of youth, filling the street from curb to curb, typifies the gang that has become detached from ordinary community controls and lives according to its own code. In some cities, public or private agencies have initiated a program whereby group workers meet gangs of boys wherever they may be found, seek to gain their confidence, and gradually redirect their course of action. This gang is one that came under the care of the street-club worker program of the New York City Youth Board. (Courtesy New York City Youth Board)

new gang which then maintains a brother relationship with the original gang. A network of gangs may then project itself into several areas, not necessarily contiguous.

Conflict gangs

This term is applied to gangs, one of whose calculated activities is physical fighting with other gangs. The fights are not sporadic and spontaneous such as often occur between boys over some difference of opinion or small slight. Such individual fights may occur between members of the same gang as well as between boys who are not gang members. Conflict does not necessarily serve the same purpose in all gangs.[1]

Individual and gang status. Intergang skirmishes may take place at almost any time, but full-scale encounters are planned well in advance, either through clandestine messages to the gang to be attacked or with intergang arrangements of time, place, and weapons. Since fighting is always a potential activity, the fighting (or bopping) gangs tend to be well organized, with "war counsellors," and appointed members to store and, as needed, distribute weapons which may range from clubs to guns.

The fights serve no utilitarian purpose but are a way to maintain certain values important to the gang. One is the maintenance of a certain territory or "turf" which the gang holds for itself, free of interference from competing gangs. The intangible value is to demonstrate courage (heart) and a reputation for daring. Occasions for fights are sometimes contrived in order to redemonstrate possession of these values. The gang that defends its turf or successfully encroaches upon another's has higher status than the defeated gang and is regarded with fear and admiration by nearby gangs. Within its own territory it receives the admiration of young boys who either aspire to become members or who are in younger, auxiliary groups.

One hypothesis to explain the development of the cult of violence is that with all avenues to success closed, illegitimate or legal, the gang turns to violence as a way of gaining status which is under their control. Anyone may try to gain status by toughness and fighting; there is no need to wait for society to show them the way. Also, the bitterness and tension gang members have because of frustrations at home, in school, or in the community may be worked off through conflict.[2]

A high degree of disorganization and lack of adult or institutional control is also a necessary condition for the development of gangs that so thoroughly violate the orderliness of a community.

Conflict and prejudice. Fighting does not seem necessarily to follow ethnic or racial lines. The main necessity for membership in a conflict gang is residence within a limited area. However, it often happens that because of this basis of membership, one ethnic or racial group will be pitted against another. In this case, antagonism between the groups because of their differences may be an added factor in the continuance and bitterness of the conflict relationship.

The conflict that grows up between residentially separated groups harboring mutual prejudice differs from the intermittent conflict between gangs trying to protect their territory from all other gangs. The prejudice may be based on religion, general cultural differences, or race. It may be carried into the slum area from previous regions or countries of residence. Differences are evident through language, dress, customs, or skin color. When two such groups begin to compete for the same houses, park, or swimming pool, and to mingle in school and on the street, sparks of prejudice may easily be fanned into fights. Often a truce is reached, with each group remaining on its own side of a street, railway track, or park. If the groups are displaced by new ones, the tradition of separation and warfare along these same boundaries may continue.

Conflict gangs and riots. Some gangs fight when any opportunity is presented, whether the opponents are personally known or not. These fights seem most likely to occur when prejudice already exists between different classes of people, such as between races. Race riots are an example. Once started, a race riot tends to spread over a wide area and draws in gangs from areas outside the main territory of racial contact. For example, the Chicago race riot of 1919, arising basically out of a large influx of Negroes who overflowed the boundaries of the previous

---

1 The discussion of conflict gangs is drawn from a number of sources, chiefly the two Miller sources, *op. cit.; Reaching the Fighting Gang, op. cit.;* Ira Henry Freeman, *Out of the Burning, the Story of Frenchy, A Boy Gang Leader,* Crown Publishers, Inc., New York, 1960; Dan Wakefield, "Gang that Went Good," *Harper's Magazine,* 216 (June, 1948), 36–43.

2 Richard A. Cloward and Lloyd E. Ohlin, *Delinquency and Opportunity,* Free Press, Glencoe, Illinois, 1960.

Negro community, was prolonged and intensified by invasions into the Negro district of gangs from areas two or three miles away.[1] The rioting had been preceded by gang attacks on Negroes and in general the Negroes were the objects of hostility and attacks on the part of white gangs. These gangs were organized, had names, and had club rooms whose rent was often paid by local politicians in anticipation of future votes in their favor. The age range of the various gangs ran from fifteen to twenty-two. Negro youths, newcomers to the city, were less likely to be organized into gangs but entered into fights when attacked. The gangs along the border of the Negro area were especially active in harassing Negroes, and from time to time a gang from farther away made a foray into the Negro area for the purpose of "getting a nigger." Several murders resulted from these expeditions. During the riot itself, gangs of white youths played an important role. Members of a gang would wedge themselves into a truck, well armed with guns which were part of their normal equipment, and speed shouting through the streets to the Negro area. There they often formed the nucleus of a crowd which then attacked Negroes, destroyed their furniture, and burned their homes. Serious injuries and deaths often were the result. The riot, although not started by white gangs, provided the opportunity for a violent outlet of hostility toward a group whose territorial expansion was generally resented by Chicagoans of that period.

A comment on the origin of the white gangs throws some light on conflict gangs. Their members were residents of areas with a high proportion of foreign-born adults. They were the American-born children of immigrants, who had slipped out of the control of the parents' culture although they still lived in the foreign colonies. They were not fully acculturated to American values and modes of behavior and were not acceptable in American social groups. One group that accepted them consisted of politicians who manipulated voters in the foreign areas for their own benefit. Older foreign-born people

who had not been naturalized could not vote but in the younger American-born members of the community, many politicians sensed a future gold mine of political support. They therefore cultivated the allegiance of these youth, lent their names to the clubs, paid rent on a vacant store for a clubhouse, and arranged for police protection. For example, many of the gangs that attacked the Negroes, sometimes with guns, were not stopped by police who witnessed the attacks. Some gangs took a local policeman with them in their cars or trucks as protection against interference from policemen from outside their area. Thus a part of the background of the conflict gangs of the twenties was their own low status in the wider community. They seized any opportunity to displace resentment against those who rejected them by attacking groups of still lower status whom they dared to insult and injure.

Similar though less explosive and violent conflict situations have arisen in other cities than Chicago, between gangs or groups of unequal and low status. The flare up of trouble between Mexican-American youth and sailors and marines on leave in the port city of Los Angeles is a case in point. In 1941–1943 a series of fights broke out between groups of sailors or marines and groups of Mexican-American boys, referred to in newspaper headlines as zoot-suiters.[2] This term, of unknown origin, referred to the distinctive garb worn by many Mexican-American boys as a fad and mark of distinction among their own members. The trousers, full at the waist and tight at the ankle came from the garb worn by field workers in Pachuco, Mexico, to provide airiness and comfort and at the same time to prevent insects from crawling up the ankles. The remainder of the outfit consisted of a long coat, tight at the waist, from which hung a heavy key chain. Long hair, combed in duck-tail fashion, was topped by a broad brimmed flat hat. This garb led to the nickname among Mexican-Americans of Pachuco

1 Chicago Commission on Race Relations, *The Negro in Chicago, A Study of Race Relations and a Race Riot,* University of Chicago Press, Chicago, 1922, pp. 3, 7, 11–17, 54–57.

2 Emory S. Bogardus, "Gangs of Mexican-American Youth," *Sociology and Social Research,* 28 (1943), pp. 55–66. Sam Glane, "Juvenile Gangs in East Side Los Angeles," *Focus,* 29 (1950), pp. 136–141, reprinted in Clyde B. Vedder, editor, *The Juvenile Offender, Perspective and Readings,* Doubleday and Company, Garden City, N. Y., 1954, pp. 175–181. Harold L. Stallings with David Dressler, *Juvenile Officer,* Thomas Y. Crowell Company, New York, 1954, pp. 141–151

(Pachuca for girls who sometimes wore a modification of the coat), but was called a zoot-suit in newspapers.

Sailors and marines in their uniforms were equally well marked. They were strangers in the city, detached from family ties, and not always well regarded by middle-class groups.

The sailors and marines and the Pachucos came into conflict mainly in certain taverns over girls. In a sense the sailors and marines were invading the territory of the Pachucos, and this invasion was resented. Each group looked upon the other with suspicion, disdain, and perhaps envy. Some of the Mexican-American boys, who had delinquency records, had been rejected by the draft boards; out of school and without jobs, they felt inferior and were looked down upon by other groups. It has been suggested that they envied the men in uniform as well as resented their invasion of the civilians' pleasure spots.[1] The sailors and marines, for their part, may have mixed their scorn of the Pachucos with envy for their freedom and freedom from the restraints imposed by the service.

The foregoing discussion has identified and sketched three types of conflict gangs: (1) Gangs wedded to a particular territory whose fights are with rival gangs in adjacent territory. They fight to prevent invasion by the rival, to prove their bravery, and to retain monopoly of privileges. (2) Gangs that fight not only to preserve their territory but also because the rival is of a different, misunderstood, and often resented culture or race. In the twenties the opponents were primarily of different European nationalities; in the fifties and sixties they often are of different races. (3) Gangs that are deeply prejudiced against an entire ethnic, religious, or racial segment of society and rush out to enter any conflict even though it is in no sense a threat to their territory.

Tendency to overemphasize

The dramatic quality of gang fights leads to a tendency to overemphasize them. Some gangs have reached a high status and rarely have to fight to maintain it. Others are aggressive and provoke fights to establish status. Still others are defensive and try to settle disputes without fighting. Moreover, no gang makes fighting its chief activity; milling around, social events, vandalism, and stealing are also part of the gang activities.

Each fight is a separate and special event. Most gangs engage in only one or two major fights in the course of their existence. They may however have frequent weekend skirmishes. Ill feeling may build up on a Friday evening, after a week at school or on the job. Those with jobs have money to spend on girls or drink, quarrels easily erupt, and individuals fight. If the situation is taken as a serious threat by one side or the other, a later gang-versus-gang fight may follow.[2]

It must be cautioned, however, that gang members are not totally receptive to delinquent values. The gang, in spite of its delinquency, functions in a community which is generally law-abiding. Members more often than not have parents who lean toward legal conformity although the pressures of life and the lower-class culture may cause them to short-cut the corners of honesty and sobriety. Children have been subjected to conforming values by the school and through the agencies of mass communication. Therefore they are likely to have mixed attitudes toward both conformity and deviancy, toward honesty and dishonesty, toward avoidance of injury to others and assault. Even though seriously delinquent at times, they may accept the values of the larger society as basic, their delinquent values as secondary, and seek to rationalize or neutralize their delinquent behavior. They may do this in at least five ways: [3]

1. The delinquent may deny personal responsibility for his delinquent acts. Many delinquents are adept at picking up factors that have been found associated with delinquency and using them as excuses for their behavior —they place responsibility on a broken home, unloving parents, or bad companions. The delinquent persuades himself that these conditions caused him to be a delinquent and that he is not responsible.

2. The delinquent may define delinquency as only those actions that specifically harm some individual. He may define stealing a car for his own use as borrowing; vandalism as harmless, since the person whose property is damaged can probably afford the loss; truancy as harming no one.

1 Edward C. McDonagh, "Status Levels of Mexicans," *Sociology and Social Research*, 33 (1948–49), 449–459; Bogardus, *op. cit.*

2 *Reaching the Fighting Gang, op. cit.*, pp. 27, 94.
3 Gresham M. Sykes and David Matsa, "Techniques of Neutralization: A Theory of Delinquency," *American Sociological Review*, 22 (1957), 664–670.

3. The delinquent may deny that the person injured or wronged is really a victim. He has simply been rightfully punished for what he has done to the delinquent. The attack on a person or group of lower status is justified because this person has not "stayed in his place." School vandalism is "all right" because the principal or teacher was unfair.

4. The delinquent may "condemn the condemners," that is, accuse the persons (or segment of society) who criticize or condemn him as being delinquent themselves, of showing spite, or of being corrupt or brutal. He thus seeks to excuse or justify his own misbehavior.

5. The pull toward loyalty to the gang may override the awareness of the values of the larger society. The gang is a group bound by emotional ties. The immediate personal rewards of conforming to this intimate group's values are greater than the impersonal awards of conforming to law or abstract principles of ethics. For the gang boy, these abstract principles are not represented by personal friends but only indirectly or in formal relationships with teachers, ministers, social workers, and so on.

In these ways the delinquent boy tries to solve the dilemma of ambivalent attitudes toward legal conformity. The fact that he becomes delinquent does not necessarily mean that he completely rejects legal standards or ethical values of society. He knows these standards, and has accepted and internalized some of them. But under the conditions of gang life he does not always follow them and seeks to ease or avoid in advance feelings of guilt by strong rationalizations for his conduct.

However, a few delinquent individuals and gangs move so far away from normal values that they become unresponsive to conventional groups.

Special terms and symbols

Many delinquent groups use special terms and symbols which set them apart from conventional society. Such terms and symbols are characteristic of many groups, from Scouts to men's lodges. They seem to serve a common purpose: to identify the members as belonging to a particular group, to give a feeling of superiority to outsiders, and to create prestige among certain other groups. In general people look with amusement or admiration on the symbolic apparatus of groups in their own subculture, but are inclined to regard with fear, adhorrence, or disgust the symbols of groups of other subcultures. For example, Scout uniforms are worn with pride by middle-class boys and girls and regarded with approval by middle-class adults. Many lower-class boys and adults alike look on them with amusement and scorn. Likewise, the garb of many delinquent gangs is approved in lower-class culture but regarded as a symbol of crime by middle-class people.

The language and symbols of delinquent gangs throw light on gang values and activities.

Gang language. As is true of almost any group with the same background of interest and experience, gangs have developed a "little language" of their own which spreads generally throughout the delinquent contraculture. Similar specialized terminology is found in the professions, many occupations, the sports world, high schools, and the like.

Gangs do not refer to themselves as gangs, a word with unpleasant connotations to delinquent boys as to others. Their group is a club, a respectable word that implies that the gang does not regard itself as engaged in reprehensible activities.

Other special words reflect major interests. Some are given below with their meanings.

Names of gangs tend to have special significance. They may identify the territory that "belongs" to the gang; the name of a street, park, or area may be used. Other names attribute courage to the gang, for example, Warriors, Vikings, or Comanches; these also imply warlike qualities. Still others have a general connotation of danger: Cobras, Scorpions, Dragons, Tigers, or Daggers. Other names identify the gang with individuals or groups of high status, for example, Viceroys, Lords, Egyptian Kings, Dukes, and Gents. Ethnic names are sometimes used. Other names have no easily understood connotation but perhaps refer to special experiences of the gangs.[1]

The preoccupation of some conflict gangs with fighting and the fear of attack is shown

---

1 The terminology has been assembled from Harrison E. Salisbury, *The Shook-up Generation,* Fawcett Publications, Inc., Greenwich, Connecticut, 1958; *Reaching the Fighting Gang,* New York City Youth Board, New York, 1960, especially pp. 295–296. Exact terms may differ from one city to another, but serve the same purpose.

by the wide variety of terms having to do with fighting.

1. Bopping club—a street-fighting gang; to bop—to fight
2. Burn—use of guns in a fight
3. Cool (a noun)—agreement not to fight
4. Fair fight—stylized, arranged fight without deadly weapons
5. Go down—embark on a fight or rumble
6. Jap—an attack
7. Piece—a gun
8. Rumble—an intergang fight
9. Steel—a knife
10. Turf—territory claimed by a gang; to mind our turf—to protect our territory
11. War counsellor—the boy whose speciality is planning intergang fights
12. A win—victory
13. Zip gun—a homemade but dangerous gun

Sex is another abiding interest which has its own terminology, some of which follows:

1. Deb—a girl
2. Fish—close dancing without moving the feet, sexually exciting
3. Shack up—to have sexual intercourse

Status is extremely important and has its own vocabulary.

1. Chicken—a coward
2. Coolie—a boy who does not belong to a gang
3. Faggott—a boy who does not join a gang and is assumed to be a coward
4. Heart—bravery of a daring sort
5. Punk out—to show fear; opposite of heart
6. Rep—reputation for heart
7. Sounding—insulting someone, usually leads to a fight

Stealing is also a common activity, which, with fighting, may lead to arrests

1. Bust—an arrest
2. Con—to outwit someone
3. Hustle—a racket whereby money is extorted
4. Jackroll—robbing a drunken man

The lists could be greatly extended. Special forms of delinquency, such as illegal possession and sale of drugs and addiction have their own specialized vocabularies.

Symbolic dress. Gang unity is emphasized by some characteristic style of haircut or type of dress. Some gangs buy leather jackets and have their names inscribed on them. Girls who are friends or who form a kind of auxiliary may wear a similar jacket. In the southwest the pachuco or "zoot suit" has been popular with Mexican youth. A special kind of shirt or hat may characterize a gang. In like manner, many conventional groups have special uniforms, jackets, badges, or insignia.

Delinquency by individuals

Approximately 15 to 30 per cent of boys who come before the juvenile court have committed their delinquencies alone. The difference in percentages is probably due primarily to differences in definition of group and isolated delinquencies. At any rate, the isolated delinquency is of infrequent occurrence. Whether the isolated delinquency also indicates an isolated individual is another question. The fact has already been shown that most delinquencies are committed by two or three boys. These boys or the individual delinquent may be members of a gang. They may receive support for their delinquencies from the gang in the way of status for successful completion of a delinquency. They may, in fact, represent the gang and steal candy, cigarettes, alcoholic drinks, or equipment for the use of the gang.

Little has been done in studying the truly individual delinquent, who not only commits his delinquencies alone but who has no gang contacts. It is possible to do little more than speculate or offer isolated examples.

The isolated delinquency may be the act of a social isolate, who either is unable to make friends or who prefers to work or play alone. Throughout society there are people who do not make close affiliations with groups. If such a person is motivated by whatever reason toward delinquency, he would tend to carry out his delinquency alone, just as he prefers to study alone, read instead of play with others, or have a hobby that does not require co-operation. It is normal for him to act as an individual and not as a member of a clique or gang.

The isolate may be maladjusted in some way and express his difficulties overtly in secret crimes that somehow symbolize his dissatisfactions. These crimes may become continuous, repetitive in type, and sometimes progressively more serious. His satisfaction is completely covert and does not depend upon group applause. However, the crimes do not solve his problem but only temporarily relieve tensions; as tensions increase again, another crime is in order. If the maladjustment is deep and serious, the crimes may be serious and lie outside the usual run of juvenile delinquencies. A Chicago case will illustrate. A young boy of middle-class status became overly interested in sex and expressed this interest in symbolic ways, at one period through stealing and hiding women's underwear. In adolescence he found sexual satisfaction in breaking into apartments and finally was unable to resist the compulsion to murder any woman whom he found, although he did not molest her sexually. Three murders were committed before the boy, then just past sixteen years of age, was located and identified.

Other instances of isolated delinquency may not symbolize long-standing maladjustment but be an explosive outburst of long-smoldering emotions. Children and youth as well as adults sometimes commit murder when the tension of inner emotional turmoil reaches the point when it can no longer be contained. The murder may be planned or impulsive; it may be a single episode or one of a series of murders quickly performed. The offender may then run away in fear but meekly surrender when police find him, his emotional tensions having been discharged. Less serious assaults may follow angry quarrels. Destruction of property may be a displacement of anger toward some person. When these emotions are not shared by someone else and when they come to a head quickly and are immediately expressed in violence, the delinquency is likely to be the act of one individual. At other times and in other ways, the offender may be a member of a group and share in group activities.

In another Chicago case, a boy of twelve murdered a younger companion who had threatened to report a theft from his mother by the older of the two boys. The young murderer had a lifelong history of unstable family life, absence of his father, and rejection by his mother. He was so poorly adjusted in school that he had been referred repeatedly to a clinic. Therapeutic treatment was recommended but never carried through by his mother. The killing of his companion was the climax to twelve years of emotional turmoil. This boy lived in a lower-middle class neighborhood. He did not run with a gang and had few friends. He had been suspected in one or two minor thefts, committed alone, but was not regarded as a delinquent.

Individual acts of delinquency also occur when an individual wishes, through a hidden act of delinquency, to maintain or improve his position in some nondelinquent group. Thefts, juvenile or adult, often are motivated to obtain funds with which to improve an insecure position. The child may take money from his mother's purse or from a neighbor with which to buy candy or presents for other children, among whom he holds an insecure position. At the adult level, the person in a position of trust may embezzle money for much the same reason—to live on a social level otherwise beyond his means, to be accepted in a moneyed crowd, or even to impress his wife. Success in these social goals depends upon secrecy of the offense. If his theft is discovered, he loses all that he had hoped to gain, and more too. Since neither child or adult is essentially criminal in attitude, they find it necessary to rationalize their offenses and thus assuage a sense of guilt. The adult unrealistically plans to replace the money, the child insists he found the money or that someone gave it to him.

The isolated delinquent is limited in the kinds of delinquency he can carry out and in the satisfactions obtained. A delinquency that requires teamwork is beyond him. For example, a typical group pattern for breaking into stores is for one boy to act as look-out, one to wait at the wheel of a car, and one or two to enter the store. The delinquency requires co-ordinated work and trust among the boys. The individual thief must somehow combine the activities of the three or four boys; he must bear the full burden of responsibility and guilt. However, he does not need to share the stolen articles with anyone, and he avoids the possibility of an accomplice's being arrested and revealing the names of his companions.

The isolated delinquency also lacks the recreational aspects of many types of group delinquency. An individual boy may have sex relations with a girl, but the experience seems greatly enhanced when a group of boys engage in a "line-up" wherein one boy after another has relations with a girl who presumably is a willing participant. Stealing by a clique often has recreational aspects in the planning, risk, daring, and display of skill. Both the proceeds and the satisfaction of success are shared. Group vandalism also often takes on definite recreational features.

Group delinquency often affords some control of the behavior of each individual, since none wishes to be betrayed by the awkwardness or impulsiveness of a companion. Even in the violence of intergang fights, controls are exerted. When a limited planned fight between two gangs ends in a violent melee with serious injuries, the precipitating cause often is the impulsive act of one boy who lacked self-control. Avoidance of such control or censure for erratic types of delinquency may be one motivation toward individual delinquency.

Individual delinquency runs through all social classes. Its relation to class subcultures has not been studied.

The nondelinquent in the delinquency area

Even in areas of high delinquency rates, a minority of boys and many fewer girls than boys become seriously and persistently delinquent. Very little attention has been given to the reasons why some children do not become delinquent when many cultural and social pressures push children toward delinquency. Some light is gained from studies that compare delinquent and nondelinquent children.

Environmental factors. The comparison of delinquent children with an equal number of nondelinquent siblings, made by Healy and Bronner, emphasizes the importance of the different types of relationships that may exist between each child and his parents.[1] Even though outwardly the family appears to be the same for all the children, actually each child has his own special relationship with each parent. In general in Healy's study the family background was not completely favorable: in 54 per cent of families there was serious disharmony between the parents and in only 30 per cent was the relationship between the parents distinctly harmonious. Nevertheless, even in the disharmonious families, some children were nondelinquent. The authors point to the need to consider the constitutional characteristics of each child and the relationship of each child to each parent. They state, ". . . for any single case any of the supposed influences have to be evaluated as they may or may not have affected the child's conduct. If this were not so, how does it happen that such a considerable proportion of the children in these families

do not become delinquent?"[2] One strong positive relationship may offset other negative relationships.

The material presented in Chapter 10, "Family Setting of Delinquency," shows that nondelinquents more often than delinquents live in families that are unbroken, cohesive, warmly affectionate, and fair in discipline. The relationship with the mother is especially significant. Nevertheless, many delinquents come from homes with favorable family relationships and many nondelinquents come from homes with unfavorable ones. In the studies yielding these conclusions, it cannot be assumed that all children in the families represented by one delinquent member were delinquent, nor that all the siblings of the nondelinquent boys chosen for study were also nondelinquent. The favorable family conditions create a pressure toward nondelinquency; nevertheless, the specific family relationships for each child need to be taken into account, as Healy and Bronner pointed out.

The same reasoning applies to any given child's relationship with school or community. Individual clashes of personality and fortuitous experiences may be determining factors in the child's early turning toward delinquent or nondelinquent behavior. Even in those areas of a city where teachers find it most difficult to understand their students and where the traditional school program is least suited to the needs of students, some children find school a rewarding experience and continue until graduation. Friendly and understanding teachers, capable of teaching well, and curricula adapted to the needs of the children are positive forces against delinquency, but do not guarantee successful development of the child.

Self-concepts. Based on the unique combination that each child has in temperament, family, peer group, school, and community relationships, he develops a self-concept as either delinquent or nondelinquent. This self-concept is the real key to the fully developed delinquent as well as the nondelinquent child.

The self-concept is social in origin, growing out of the child's perception of what others think about him. What they think varies greatly and is not always closely related to the child's behavior. Toward some children there are biased stereotyped attitudes, for

1 Healy and Bronner, *op. cit.*

2 Healy and Bronner, *op. cit.*, p. 33.

example, the Negro is always shifty, the Jew is always grasping, the middle-class person places material success above human values, and so on. Simply by being born into a certain biological or social group, a child may find a prejudiced self-concept thrust upon him. His individual behavior is another factor that determines what others think of him and how they behave toward him.

In some communities that are highly unified in culture, the child may find a uniform set of attitudes toward him. He tends then to accept the self-concept offered to him, especially if it is a favorable one. Often, however, he finds that different people or different groups react differently to him. He has a choice of self-concepts and often wavers among them. This is the situation of the preadolescent school child who fluctuates between conformity and underconformity.

As the child finds certain self-concepts more rewarding to him, he tends to affiliate with the groups that approve of a given self-concept. It is often only in such a group that he is rewarded by approval and status. Other groups disapprove of him and project on him a different and unpleasant self-concept. This process goes on for both delinquent and non-delinquent children, until the preponderance of relationships of each is with groups that give him a self-satisfying self-concept. These groups whose opinions become especially important are called reference groups.

Roles. Self-concepts of all kinds are embodied in patterns of activity called roles. The delinquent gang has a variety of roles, one of which each incoming member must conform to if he is to become a functioning member of the group. Likewise, the nondelinquent finds roles waiting for him in various youth organizations and in school. The reactions of the group toward the member, his self-concept based on these reactions, and the roles he overtly carries out tend to fuse into one pattern that becomes highly satisfying to the member.

A person may have a number of self-concepts growing out of a number of different reference groups, each calling for different roles. For example, the good boy who conforms in school and who is active in church may also have a delinquent reference group. He does not have a consistent set of self-concepts. When the self-concepts merge into consistency, the person has a self-image that

tends to become the standard by which he measures much of his behavior. His groups also tend to become consistent, and he withdraws from groups that do not support the self-image. His roles are consistent with his self-image and with each other. With reference to delinquency, the extreme of this tendency is the underconforming contracultures.

The development of nondelinquent self-concepts. In high delinquency areas it cannot be assumed that the nondelinquent is what one should expect, with the delinquent being the one whose behavior alone must be explained. So deep and pervasive are the pressures toward delinquency that the need arises to account for nondelinquency.

What "insulates" some—in fact, the majority—of boys in high delinquency areas from becoming delinquent? Especially, what accounts for consistently obedient boys, well adjusted in school and community? Reckless and Dinitz studied sixth-grade boys in Columbus, Ohio, to find answers to these questions.[1] Teachers of sixth grade pupils in areas of highest delinquency rates were asked to classify the boys into three groups: those whom they felt would never have trouble with police or courts, those whom they felt sure would have, and ones about whom they were uncertain. Among these twelve-year-old boys, well below the peak delinquency age of sixteen, approximately half were classified as "good" and not headed for trouble, about 25 per cent as potential delinquents, and about 25 per cent as not showing clear tendencies in either direction.

The boys were given certain tests and questionnaires, and their mothers were also given tests and interviewed. Tests of delinquency tendencies and social responsibility confirmed the opinions of the teachers. Search of police and juvenile court records resulted in elimination of sixteen nondelinquent boys, since they had some type of record though never for a serious offense. The mothers or mother-substitutes of some boys could not be located. The final groups consisted of 125 "good" boys and 108 prospective delinquents, of whom 23 per cent al-

---

1 This study has been discussed in a number of articles listed in the bibliography under the names of Reckless, Dinitz, or Scarpitti. It is briefly summarized in Walter C. Reckless, *The Crime Problem*, Appleton-Century Crofts, Inc., New York, 1960, pp. 346–353.

ready had records with police or court, some for serious offenses.

The data assembled revealed that the socio-economic status of nondelinquent and delinquency-prone boys was approximately the same. Home conditions differed, giving the usual picture of greater stability and cohesion and better parent-child relationships in the nondelinquent than in the potentially delinquent group. The researchers did not stop with this finding but probed deeper, with the following results:

1. Nondelinquents more often than delinquency-prone boys felt that their parents were concerned about them and were fair to them; they felt that their families were equal or superior to any other family. They also felt that family relationships were harmonious.

2. Parents of nondelinquent boys more often than parents of delinquency-prone boys supervised their sons, were interested in them, and felt that they were good boys and would never be in serious trouble with the police. They felt that their sons had selected good friends.

3. The nondelinquent boys regarded themselves as "good," did not believe they would ever have trouble with the police, and in fact avoided trouble at all costs. Few of their close friends had ever had any trouble with the police, and the boys said they would drop a friend who was headed for trouble.

In general, the delinquency-prone boys and their parents held views that were the opposite of the above.

The conclusion drawn by Reckless and Dinitz is that the nondelinquent boys belonged to reference groups that defined them as good: family, school, peer groups. The boys not only played the role of good boy but had a self-image of themselves as good. Moreover, they were satisfied with their roles and their groups. They tended to avoid contacts and behavior that were not in accord with this self-image.

The next question that the researchers asked themselves was whether or not the self-image was well established at age twelve and would prevail during adolescence, when delinquency reached its height in the areas in which the boys lived. A follow-up study was made four years after the initial study when the average age of the boys was sixteen. Four

of the previously nondelinquent boys had had encounters with the police, respectively for violation of curfew and drunkenness, malicious mischief, school truancy, and auto theft; only the last delinquency was referred by police to the juvenile court. The attitudes of the boys toward family, friends, and bad conduct remained almost identical with those held at age twelve. The self-image of being a good boy already established at age twelve held at age sixteen for 96 per cent of the boys.[1] At the time (1960) that the follow-up study was published, a similar study of the delinquency-prone group was in process to determine whether their self-image as boys probably destined for trouble had also persisted.

A further word should be added about the delinquency-prone boys. Whereas family, school, and peer groups (probably also church, police, and community center, whose opinions were not investigated) held a good opinion of the nondelinquent boys, they held a poor and sometimes rejective opinion of the delinquency-prone boys. These groups which undoubtedly were significant reference groups helping to establish the satisfying self-image of the nondelinquents, thrust upon the delinquency-prone boys an unsatisfying self-image. It is under such circumstances that boys turn to the free peer groups and especially the delinquent peer groups as their significant reference groups, where they find approval and roles.

The psychologically disturbed delinquent. Reckless makes the point that the good or poor self-image derived from significant reference groups does not apply to compulsive acting-out neurotics who become repeatedly involved in fire-setting, ritualistic stealing, exhibitionism, or peeping-tom activities. Violent aggressive delinquents who feel no sense of guilt (psychopaths) also are immune to socially formed self-images. Other explanations must be sought for their often erratic behavior.

The comment should be added, however, that many of these difficulties have their origin in group contacts that have proved highly unsatisfactory or that have not socialized the child into a pattern of control, whether delinquent or nondelinquent.

1 The follow-up group consisted of 103 boys; twenty-two of the original group could not be located.

The critical point in juvenile delinquency

From the point of view of adult crime, the most serious phase of juvenile delinquency does not come during the tumultuous period of adolescence, regardless of how much nuisance value the depredations of delinquency have for teachers, community, and the police. Only a minute proportion of delinquencies cause the loss of any large amount of property or serious injury or death to someone. The critical point in juvenile delinquency comes toward the end of the delinquency period when adolescents face the pattern of adult life. Will they become conventional citizens in the terms of their subculture, small-time criminals, individual professional criminals, or possibly members of highly organized criminal rackets or syndicates? The seeds for their choice are germinated during childhood and adolescence; but their choice also depends upon the easy availability of adult crime and contacts that may lead to association with adult criminals. The choice may not be deliberately made; boys may drift into adult criminal activities just as they drift into conventional jobs. They must have attitudes, however, that condone or support their choice and they must have criminal "job opportunities."

From the point of view of society, the probability of the lower-class delinquent boy finding a "job opportunity" in crime is greater than the probability of the middle-class boy. The middle-class boy is more likely to be exposed to unethical or criminal practices after he becomes employed than when he is selecting an occupation, since many business men and corporations use questionable methods to avoid payment of taxes or to meet severe competition. The lower-class delinquent therefore is more of a nuisance or threat to society during adolescence and more likely to be drawn into crime as an adult.

The gang boy is likely to build up attitudes and behavior that make him susceptible to adult criminal activities. The gang affords fertile ground for the growth of a delinquent contraculture. As the gang becomes detached from conventional lower-class society it builds up its own delinquent codes and customs; its own systems of rewards and punishments; its own little social world. As gangs gain status and prestige in any particular area they attract other boys and quickly pass on to them the contraculture. Gangs that have an age-graded structure quite deliberately induct the younger boys into the codes, delinquent skills, and personal habits of the gang.

Boys identify themselves with the gang and do not respond to individual approaches from teachers or social workers. To leave the warmth and friendship of the gang would often mean both social and emotional isolation for the boy, and would require a self-confidence and self-sufficiency that most of the boys do not have. For this reason social workers sometimes make an appeal to the entire gang, seeking to convert it into a club of conventional athletic or social type.

The danger point to society from the gang as a whole comes at the point where the gang has cut itself off from acceptance of conventional ethical and moral values and has developed contravalues which not only differ from but are opposed to conventional values. Few gangs reach an extreme point in this process; those that do are almost immune to efforts to bring them back to acceptance of conventional values. In the delinquent contraculture, boys not only act in a delinquent manner but conceive of themselves as tough, hard, and superior to boys who endure the limitations of conformity, hard work, and the pursuit of future goals.

The emotionally disturbed adolescent may continue his delinquencies, falling as an adult into one of several types, the ne'er-do-well, the drunkard or drug addict, or the compulsive or violent criminal. What eventually becomes of him depends upon the tolerance of the community, the seriousness of his threat to society, and the availability of special facilities for treating him.

Bibliography

Bogardus, Emory S., "Gangs of Mexican-American Youth," *Sociology and Social Research*, 28 (1943), 55–66.

Chicago Commission on Race Relations, *The Negro in Chicago, A Study of Race Relations and a Race Riot*, University of Chicago Press, Chicago, 1922.

Cloward, Richard A., and Lloyd E. Ohlin, *Delinquency and Opportunity*, Free Press, Glencoe, Illinois, 1960.

Cohen Albert K., *Delinquent Boys, The Culture of the Gang,* Free Press, Glencoe, Illinois, 1955.

Dinitz, Simon, Walter C. Reckless, and Barbara Kay, "A Self Gradient among Potential Delinquents," *Journal of Criminal Law, Criminology and Police Science,* 49 (1958), 230–233.

Freeman, Ira Henry, *Out of the Burning, the Story of Frenchy, A Boy Gang Leader,* Crown Publishers, Inc., New York, 1960.

Glane, Sam, "Juvenile Gangs in East Side Los Angeles," *Focus,* 29 (1950), 136–141.

Healy, William, and Augusta F. Bronner, *New Light on Delinquency and Its Treatment,* Yale University Press, New Haven, Connecticut, 1936.

Miller, Walter B., "The Impact of a Community Group Work Program on Delinquent Corner Groups," *Social Service Review,* 31 (December, 1957), 390–406.

————, "Lower Class Culture as a Generating Milieu of Gang Delinquency," *Journal of Social Issues,* 14, No. 3 (1958), 5–19.

Reaching the Fighting Gang, New York City Youth Board, New York, 1960.

Reckless, Walter C., Simon Dinitz, and Barbara Kay, "The Self-Component in Potential Delinquency and Potential Non-delinquency," *American Sociological Review,* 22 (1957), 566–570.

————, and Ellen Murray, "Self Concept as an Insulator against Delinquency," *American Sociological Review,* 21 (1956), 744–746.

————, "The 'Good' Boy in a High Delinquency Area," *Journal of Criminal Law, Criminology and Police Science,* 48 (1959), 18–25.

Scarpitti, Frank R., Ellen Murray, Simon Dinitz, and Walter C. Reckless, "The 'Good' Boy in a High Delinquency Area: Four Years Later," *American Sociological Review,* 25 (1957), 555–558.

Shireman, Charles H., *The Hyde Park Youth Project, May 1955–May 1958,* Welfare Council of Metropolitan Chicago, Chicago, undated.

Sykes, Gresham M., and David Matsa, "Techniques of Neutralization: A Theory of Delinquency," *American Sociological Review,* 22 (1957), 664–670.

Thrasher, Frederic M., *The Gang,* University of Chicago Press, 1927.

Tuck, Ruth D., "Behind the Zoot Suit Riots," *Survey Graphic,* (August, 1943), 313–316, 335.

Wakefield, Dan, "Gang that Went Good," *Harper's Magazine,* 216 (June, 1948), 36–43.

Yablonsky, Lewis, "The Delinquent Gang as a Near-Group," *Social Problems,* 7 (Fall, 1959), 108–117.

Part four

Institutional controls and treatment

Juvenile delinquency is related to the public schools in three ways: serious misconduct in and around schools; truancy, both as a delinquency itself and as the open door to other kinds of delinquency; and the day-long idleness of boys and girls who drop out of school before graduation and find it difficult to become incorporated into conventional adult activities, such as steady employment. An examination of these three situations finds the schools in a paradoxical position of fighting a losing battle against misconduct and temporary or permanent absenteeism, and at the same time providing opportunities for prevention and control of delinquency.

Place of public schools in society

From approximately age six to sixteen, boys and girls are expected to be in regular school attendance during about nine months of each year. Outside the home, the school, then, is the most common organized milieu of the child and young adolescent. It is inevitable that the school both receives the brunt of misconduct generated by outside influences and creates dissatisfactions on the part of children who do not fit easily into the school program.

Reciprocal roles. Public schools, which the large majority of children attend, are institutions that, like all institutions, operate by a system of roles and rules. The principal has a role to play as the top authority within the individual school. The teacher plays a role, also authoritarian, consisting primarily of imparting knowledge and secondarily of helping the child in general adjustment to the school regime and to other children. The pupil also has his role, as an obedient and conforming learner. The school can function only when everyone accepts and is able to play his role reciprocally with the roles of others. For example, the teacher can handle her large number of children within the confines of a classroom only when children accept and play out the role of obedient child. She can impart knowledge only when pupils accept the role of learners. They in turn can learn only when the teacher acts out her role of helping them to learn.

The school operates by means of a system of stated purposes, codes of anticipated behavior, and rules of conduct. Principal, teachers, and pupils are all expected to work

Chapter **15**

Schools, delinquency, and employment

toward the goals and to follow the rules; disregard for goals and rules leads to pandemonium.

Public schools in both large and small cities tend to be highly institutionalized, with large classes and impersonal relationships between teacher and pupils. The admonition to teachers to know each child personally and to individualize her teaching is often an impossibility, in terms of what she is expected to accomplish, the number of hours that she is with the child (but rarely individually) each day, and the change in pupil-teacher combination each year.

Neither teacher nor pupil can legally escape from his relationship to the other unless one or the other transfers to another school or the child is promoted to another grade with a different teacher. The child cannot escape the school system legally until he reaches the age which marks the termination of compulsory school attendance, in most states age sixteen. The school system then becomes a kind of compulsory imprisonment of teacher (who, of course, may resign) and pupil who may not resign. Some children adjust and profit from the teaching offered; others do not adjust but resist and rebel or sit out the last years in resigned boredom and indifference.

Goals of education. Back of this situation lies the purpose for which public schools were organized, to create a responsible and literate citizenry, able to read both the Bible and the laws. At least some education for all children became the goal. This goal is supported by laws in all states that specify the age when a youth may legally withdraw from school. Most states had passed such laws by 1900, the last state in 1918. Since then, many states have lengthened the compulsory attendance period and tightened attendance laws.[1] The goal of public education for all children has been approached so far as elementary school education is concerned; high school education has been less well received, although the proportion of teen-agers graduating from high school has constantly risen.

Opposed to this goal is the fact that public schools actually have appealed to and set up curricula primarily for a limited portion of children headed for ever further training and education. These children come from middle-class families who anticipate higher education for their children. They come to school with enough cultural background and interest in learning to ease their adjustment to school and motivate them to fit into the learning pattern.

Contemporary types of pupils. In addition to middle-class children, favored by public schools, there are many lower-class pupils of all types of backgrounds. In large cities, some schools cater primarily to one social class or one ethnic or racial group, because of the voluntary tendency of people of like culture or skin color to live in little colonies within the city. Other school districts cut across ethnic or racial boundaries and bring together incompatible or antagonistic groups of pupils.

The problem also includes the marked difference between teachers and pupils in social class affiliation. One estimate is that 3 per cent of public school pupils are upper class, 38 per cent middle class, and 58 per cent lower class.[2] Teachers are predominantly middle class. Moreover, teachers are steeped in middle-class traditions of educational methods and values. Methods of evaluating the pupil's ability are based largely on intelligence tests standardized on middle-class children, tending to discriminate against lower-class children. The adequate child by these tests tends to be the middle-class child.

Public schools tend to emphasize middle-class standards and values, suited to the tested intelligence of the typical pupils of an earlier period. The values of the lower class and varied ethnic groups whose children now fill many schoolrooms, are largely unknown and when known depreciated.

The lack of harmony between school curricula and teachers' attitudes on the one hand and the values and customs of lower-class parents and their children on the other, often becomes apparent when the child first enters school. The lack of co-ordination is especially destructive when the child comes from a foreign-culture family and is unable to speak English easily or at all. Unless special classes are organized to teach such children English, they are hopelessly handicapped. When parents have little education in their own culture, the children find it all but impossible to maintain the level of work believed suitable for their age and year of school attendance. Many become academically retarded. Reading retardation is especially significant in their lack of progress, since success in most subjects depends upon reading speed and comprehension. Many children therefore suffer from occupying a low status in the eyes of the teacher and of more successful children. They may accept this evaluation and become passive and resigned; or they may rebel against their status.

Many lower-class parents and children come to regard school, especially high school, as unrelated to the values and life needs of the lower class. It is of value to the child to be able to fend for himself physically and to begin to earn money as soon as possible to help his parents and take care of his own expenses. Even those parents who desire better things for their children than they themselves have had, do not look beyond manual skills, such as those of a craftsman or a machine operator.[3] Most of the parents are themselves unskilled or semiskilled workers. They have only grade school education and their highest and often unfulfilled aspiration for their children is high school or trade school. Many, in fact, would be content to have their children leave school in the early teens if this were legally possible. The parents are not only unable to prepare their children for successful

1 W. H. Burton, "Education and Social Class in the United States," *Harvard Educational Review,* 23, No. 4 (Fall, 1953), 243–256. The author is on the faculty of the Graduate School of Education, Harvard University.

2 Burton, *op. cit.*

3 James S. Davie, "Social Class Factors and School Attendance," *Harvard Educational Review,* 23, NO. 3 (Summer, 1953), 175–185.

school adjustment, but often tacitly or openly encourage rebellion, truancy, or early withdrawal.

The above discussion should not blind the reader to two facts: some middle-class children do not adjust well to school; and approximately half of the lower-class children graduate from high school and a small number attend college. Nevertheless, the problem of poor school adjustment centers in lower-class children.[1]

Misconduct in and around the school

Gradually schools have assumed more and more responsibilities for the conduct and welfare of pupils within the school. To the basic purpose of intellectual training, many schools have added medical examinations, balanced lunches, counseling, vocational training, and supervision of conduct, even when misconduct threatens injury or harm to other pupils or the teacher, or leads to destruction of property, or disrupts the school regime to the point where teaching cannot be continued. Only in extreme cases does the school admit its difficulty in controlling misconduct and call for police aid.

Trends in school misbehavior. The variety and trends of school misbehavior can be estimated from a study made by the National Education Association in 1955–1956. A list of eighteen acts of misbehavior was submitted to a sample of 2,987 urban and 1,283 rural teachers in elementary schools and junior and senior high schools. The teachers were asked to check the items found among children and youth in the community at the time of the survey as compared with ten years earlier, not limiting themselves to actions in the classroom. Table 22 gives the list with the percentage of urban teachers who felt that misbehavior occurred more frequently, less frequently, about the same, or not at all, as compared to ten years before. It is important to note that the table simply shows stability or change in occurrence of each type of misbehavior and not relative frequency of occurrence of the type.

Considerable insight into school and community misbehavior can be drawn from Table 22. Several types of misbehavior, commonly regarded as among the most serious types of juvenile delinquency, did not occur at the time of the survey nor ten years earlier in more than 50 per cent of the school districts (column 5): carrying switchblade knives, guns, and other dangerous weapons, using narcotics, and physical violence against teachers. Some school districts had witnessed an increase in these three types of misbehavior, but the increase in both carrying dangerous weapons and physical violence against teachers was offset by decreased frequency or stability of occurrence in other districts. Only use of narcotics showed an over-all increase in frequency. From earlier discussion it is clear that juvenile drug addiction is a rare rather than common type of juvenile delinquency. Therefore increased use of narcotics does not indicate that a large percentage of all pupils have become addicts.

Other types of misbehavior have tended to remain stable, that is, a high percentage of teachers reported that they occurred with about the same frequency in 1955–1956 as ten years earlier (column 4). For example, 50 or more per cent of teachers reported stability of occurrence for cheating on tests and homework, lying, stealing small articles of little value, and unorganized fighting. Types of misbehavior reported as the same in 40 to 50 per cent of school districts were failing to do homework and other assignments, using profane or obscene language, truancy, and obscene scribbling in lavatories. By and large, these types of misbehavior are to be expected as children try to make adjustments to the pressures placed on them in the process of socialization. Such misbehavior in moderation is tolerated and not severely punished. Most of this misbehavior is handled by the school when it occurs on school grounds. Its control forms part of the normal school problem of training children. Only in cases of extreme persistence or when combined with other, more serious misbehavior, are these acts regarded as delinquency worthy of juvenile court attention.

Six types of misbehavior showed increased frequency in a third or more of school districts (column 2); impertinence and discourtesy to teachers, failing to do homework and other assignments, destruction of school property, drinking intoxicants, stealing of a serious na-

1 Davie, *op. cit.;* W. Lloyd Warner, Robert J. Havighurst, and Martin B. Loeb, *Who Shall Be Educated?* Harper and Brothers, New York, 1944, pp. 52–53.

Table 22

Trends of Misbehavior Over a Ten-year Period in School Districts With 2,500 or More Population

| 1 | All urban school districts—the act in 1955–1956, as compared with ten years before, is occurring— | | | |
| | 2 | 3 | 4 | 5 |
Acts of misbehavior	More frequently	Less frequently	About the same	No occurrence then or now
Impertinence and discourtesy to teachers...................54.9%	13.3%	27.4%	4.4%
Failing to do homework and other assignments.............46.0	7.2	44.2	2.6
Destruction of school property..........................43.1	22.3	30.5	4.1
Drinking intoxicants....................................38.6	4.3	17.8	39.3
Stealing of serious nature..............................38.5	15.1	31.0	15.4
Using profane or obscene language.....................33.6	14.9	42.1	9.4
Gang fighting..27.6	13.3	18.5	40.6
Truancy..27.0	27.2	40.2	5.6
Sex offenses...27.0	7.6	35.5	29.9
Carrying switch-blade knives, guns, etc...................24.6	8.7	14.2	52.5
Cheating on tests......................................23.0	11.4	62.1	3.5
Cheating on homework.................................22.3	8.2	64.1	5.4
Lying of serious type...................................21.5	15.1	55.7	7.7
Using narcotics..21.3	2.8	9.3	66.6
Stealing small articles of little value.....................21.2	19.3	57.0	2.5
Obscene scribbling in lavatories.........................17.2	31.7	43.4	7.7
Unorganized fighting...................................15.9	24.6	50.8	8.7
Physical violence against teachers.......................11.7	12.8	20.1	55.4

Teacher Opinion on Pupil Behavior, 1955–56, Research Bulletin, Vol. 34, No. 2, April, 1956, National Education Association of the United States, Washington, D. C., p. 93. Table 22 comprises columns 1, 10, 11, 12, 13 of Table 43 in the above source, entitled "Acts of Misbehavior now (1955–56) as Compared with Ten Years Ago, by Selected Sizes and Types of School Districts and Relative Frequency of Occurrence." Quoted with permission.

ture, and using profane or obscene language. Three of these clearly pertain to the school, and the other three may do so.

Certain offenses regarded as very serious among children were observed to increase in 20 to 30 per cent of school districts (column 2): gang fighting, sex offenses, carrying switchblade knives and other dangerous weapons, and using narcotics.

A part of the increase in some school districts is offset by decreased frequency in other districts, but in general the districts noting an increase exceed in number those with a decrease. The conclusion is that so far as we may judge from teachers' reports, serious misconduct as well as many types of school misbehavior is increasing in certain districts. At the same time the large percentage reporting nonoccurrence or stability cannot be overlooked.

The complete table in the published survey, of which Table 22 is a part, leads to certain other conclusions. Relatively few rural school districts or small city districts (2,500 to 5,000 population) showed increases in serious types of misbehavior, although a high percentage

reported increased frequency of impertinence and failing to do assignments. School districts of a million or more population have the worst record of increased frequency of misconduct, both for violations of school regulations and for serious delinquencies. For school misconduct, 70 per cent noted an increase in impertinence, 54.1 per cent in failure to do school assignments, and 42.5 per cent in use of profane and obscene language. For serious offenses, 57.8 per cent of school districts noted an increase in destruction of school property, 53.4 in gang fighting, 46.7 in carrying dangerous weapons, and 44.0 in serious stealing.

The teacher's first hand experience with violent misbehavior is shown in the following excerpt.

Roy came to class in an unresponsive mood. Soon he fell asleep at his table. Steve sitting next to him complained: "Roy smells like whiskey."

At 11:45 A.M. I awakened Roy for lunch. On the way to the clothes closet he heard Tony remark: "Roy's been drinking; he smells like booze." Roy punched Tony and a fight began.

Table 23

Percentage of Teachers Reporting Troublemaking and Physical Striking in Their Classrooms, According to Living Conditions of School Neighborhoods

Living conditions in school neighborhood	Per cent of teachers reporting that 10 per cent or more of their pupils were real troublemakers	Per cent of teachers reporting someone in their school had been struck by a pupil in the preceding twelve months
Very good	2.7	7.8
Above average	2.4	9.3
About average	4.4	**
Below average	9.1	20.3
Very bad (slum area)	32.9	48.0

Teacher Opinion on Pupil Behavior, 1955–56, Research Bulletin, Vol. 34, No. 2, April, 1956, National Education Association of the United States, Washington, D. C. Column 2 is unpublished data obtained in connection with Table 25, p. 78 of the Bulletin; column 3 is from p. 78. Used with permission.
** Percentage not given.

Roy pulled a kitchen knife from his trousers and drew back to stab Tony. Wilson grabbed a window stick and handed it to me. I whacked Roy across the buttocks and legs, then knocked the blade from his hand. Roy still raging grabbed a chair and hurled it at Tony, but missed him. This time I grabbed Roy from behind, pinning his arms behind him, and sent to the office for help.

Roy's mother, a former dope addict and a present alcoholic, brought charges against me for striking her son. On the stand I told the truth and was acquitted. Roy was transferred to another school. I don't know what has happened in the other school, but I do know that since our trouble Roy and his brother tried to kill their mother.[1]

Misconduct and social class. Obviously, such violent encounters occur only rarely. They and other serious types of misconduct are more likely to occur in slum (lower class) areas than in other areas. In the survey of teachers' opinions, school neighborhoods were classified by the teachers according to industrial or residential usage of land, living conditions, and income. When teachers' reports on classroom behavior were classified by living conditions, the results shown in Table 23 were discovered. Misconduct increased steadily as living conditions declined. Classroom misbehavior was reported twice as often in classrooms in essentially industrial neighborhoods as in totally residential neighborhoods. Income level was less closely related to classroom behavior; it seems probable that teachers were less able to estimate

the family income than to judge the living conditions or industrial-residential ratio. Specific types of misbehavior are not classified by type of school neighborhood. Other sources, however, show that the serious delinquencies and acts of violence are more frequent in schools in slum neighborhoods than in better residential neighborhoods (that is, in lower class than middle class). It is important to note, however, that even in slum neighborhoods, many children are not troublemakers. According to Table 23, only a third of teachers in slum areas regarded 10 per cent or more of their pupils as real troublemakers and slightly less than half reported physical violence in their schools (not simply classrooms) during a twelve month period.

Conditions responsible for misconduct. When teachers attempted to assess responsibility for misbehavior, they divided responsibility among family, school, and outside influences. They ranked conditions as follows: (1) family conditions; (2) lack of training or experience in moral values; (3) school conditions such as overcrowding and lack of special classes and curricula for special types of pupils; (4) certain external conditions, for example, lack of recreational facilities, undesirable TV programs, prevalence of comic books, and availability of automobiles; and (5) other internal matters of school policy, such as conflict of theories, lack of teacher authority, and failure of the principal to back up the teacher.[2]

Methods of dealing with misconduct. Whether the misbehavior originates in family, neigh-

---

1 *Teacher Opinion on Pupil Behavior, 1955–56,* Research Bulletin, Vol. 34, No. 2, April, 1956, National Education Association of the United States, Washington 5, D. C., p. 59.

2 *Teacher Opinion on Pupil Behavior, 1955–56, op. cit.,* pp. 99–103.

borhood, or school, the classroom teacher has the problem of dealing with the misbehaving pupil, often finding himself (or more likely herself in the elementary school) faced not only with violations of school rules but also of laws which he is nevertheless expected to handle without recourse to the police. The teacher is often in a helpless condition; the influx of unwilling pupils increases the disciplinary problem, especially as the teen years approach when pupils reach adult stature and dare open defiance. With problems increased, teachers have been shorn of their earlier stern, even harsh means of discipline.[1] In "the good old days," rules were strict and sternly enforced by corporal punishment before an audience of peers or by other forms of physical distress, such as solitary confinement in some dark corner or standing on one foot placed within a wooden shoe containing a sharp peg. A pupil might be forced to hold out a heavy object at arm's length or to stoop over touching a peg in the floor, with limbs held rigidly erect. Girls as a rule were less severely punished than boys— perhaps their misdemeanors were less serious. It should be noted that in the "good old days," pupils did not attend school for as many years as at present, and it seems probable that most of the corporal punishment was dealt out to children rather than to adolescents.

Today, some 86 per cent of elementary school teachers and 30 per cent of junior high school teachers may administer corporal punishment. However, theories of permissiveness, personality development, and motivation tend to preclude corporal or other types of painful or humiliating punishment. Teachers are aware of what they may not do to enforce discipline but feel that they have few positive measures to substitute for the older physical punishments. The admonition that they should make the classwork sufficiently interesting to hold the attention and motivate the best efforts of the pupils often is not realistic in terms of the school curriculum, overcrowding, and types of pupils. A Chicago case illustrates the teacher's dilemma.

The teacher, Mrs. T., after eight years of successful elementary school teaching, found herself faced with serious disciplinary problems. Her case was heard by the Board of Education, which voted, although not unanimously, to dismiss her from the school system. In defense of her inability to maintain discipline, she and other school personnel listed some of the things a teacher might not do either because of definite rules or because of objections of the principal. They could not assign home work as a penalty; keep children after school as they were then exposed to street hazards after the crossing guards had left their posts; keep a child out of a class he especially enjoyed; ask parents to come to the school for an interview, as experience had shown nothing was gained; grasp a pupil by the wrist or arm to escort him to his seat since the child might later exaggerate the amount of force used; or isolate him from other pupils, as this tended to stigmatize the child. Although principals were expected to give teachers suggestions and to come to their aid in severe disciplinary cases, not all principals gave positive and firm help.[2]

School boards and principals dislike to admit that they cannot maintain discipline and that occasional serious delinquencies or crimes occur in and around schools, sometimes of a type that would immediately command police attention if they occurred elsewhere. These would include serious thefts, major vandalism, physical attacks of various sorts; they might also include the retaliatory counter attacks of young men teachers or principals on impudent adolescent boys, especially in states that legally forbid corporal punishment.

Misbehavior in schools is not an isolated activity on the part of students. Many school troublemakers are also home and community troublemakers. These boys and girls are likely sooner or later to be arrested; they may have to be absent from school for a few hours to attend a court hearing or longer to carry out a period of detention in a state correctional school. They may return to school on probation after the hearing or on parole after release from the correctional school. If they have not reached the age for legal withdrawal from school they are expected to be in school attendance regardless of their out of school record or clash with police. Each such absence intensifies the school problem if for no other reason than that the pupil, often already retarded, falls still further behind the class. Moreover, he usually is degraded in the

1 John Manning, "Discipline in the Good Old Days," *Phi Delta Kappan*, 41 (December, 1959), 94–99.

2 *Chicago Daily News*, March 22 and 24, 1960.

eyes of the teacher, middle-class pupils, and upwardly mobile lower-class pupils. Among other poorly adjusted, semidelinquent or delinquent pupils his status may increase with his added experience with court and correctional schools. The school, which must receive him back, bears much of the burden of his readjustment.

Truancy

School absenteeism falls into a number of types: children lawfully absent because of illness; those unlawfully absent with the knowledge or connivance of the parents, for example, to care for younger children or to work even though legally under age for employment; and children unlawfully absent from school without the knowledge of their parents. The last type is truancy in the strict sense of the word. An occasional truancy is not regarded as serious, but continued truancy may bring both school and legal penalties.

The amount of truancy varies from city to city and within a city from one school to another. A New York City report states that every day about one child in ten is absent, but only about 18 per cent of the absentees are truants.[1] It is customary in most cities for schools to deal with truants through their own avenues of investigation and discipline. However, by definition habitual truancy is a legal delinquency in most states. The chronic truant, therefore, is the one most likely to be referred to the juvenile court, where he may be placed on probation or in extreme cases sent to a correctional school.

Characteristics of truants. Habitual truancy is primarily an adolescent phenomenon, occurring most frequently during the ages of fourteen to sixteen, the peak ages for delinquency. It begins, however, as early as the first grade; it decreases sharply after the terminal age for compulsory school attendance is reached. Approximately 60 per cent of truants are boys.[2]

Details about the truant closely resemble

details about the school troublemaker and in fact about juvenile delinquents in general. A study in San Francisco showed that the median I.Q. for truants was 95, with a range from 43 to 163, compared with a median of approximately 100 for all students.[3] Despite the small difference, the truants were academically poorly adjusted. Although 5 per cent of truants were accelerated and 25 per cent were in the appropriate grade, 70 per cent were retarded at least one semester. Retardation of two or more years was found for 15 per cent of truants but only 1 per cent of all students.

Many of the San Francisco truants tended to be school troublemakers, as judged from the fact that a third had grades of D or F in school citizenship; two-thirds, however, rated C or better. Thirty per cent of the truants had no other recorded symptom of poor adjustment than the truancy itself. Whatever motivated the habitual truancy was not readily evident to the agencies handling the truant. In 70 per cent of the cases, other difficulties were noted, such as illness, running away, stealing, nervousness, deviant sex acts, and fighting.

Types of truants. A loose classification of San Francisco truants, made from the records, resulted in the following distribution of types:

In 50 per cent of the cases, situational factors were prominent, such as a lack of clothing, the parents kept the child at home, the school was too difficult, or the child was not interested or accepted by other pupils.

In 30 per cent of the cases, the pupil was withdrawn, depressed, ill, daydreamy, and failed in school although he was capable.

In 20 per cent of the cases, the pupil was aggressive and apparently truanted to get even with the world; his record indicated defiance, fighting, cruelty, and stealing.

No single pattern of dissatisfaction is dominant in the cases. In an individual case of habitual truancy, only a study of that case would reveal whether the child was escaping from an intolerably frustrating or humiliating school situation, from rejection by other children, or from inner turmoil originating outside the school. Further, the truant might find those activities that he could carry out

---

1 *Children Absent from School,* Citizen's Committee on Children of New York City, 1949; Alfred J. Kahn, "Who are our Truants?" *Federal Probation,* 15 (March, 1951), 35–40. Professor Kahn, with the New York School of Social Work, is also consultant for the Citizen's Committee on Children of New York City.

2 *Children Absent from School, op. cit.;* John L. Roberts, "Factors Associated with Truancy," *Personnel and Guidance Journal,* 34 (1956), 431–36.

3 Roberts, *op. cit.,* The truants comprised a sample of 175 from the Bureau of Attendance, 66 from the Child Guidance Service, and 97 from the Juvenile Court, all from the San Francisco Unified School District.

away from school more desirable to him than those in the school.

Social class and truancy. The San Francisco study found that half of the truants came from families on public assistance, which suggests lower-class placement at least economically.

Truancy and delinquency. Habitual truancy itself may bring a child before the juvenile court. It also has other repercussions. The retardation typical of many truants is increased by the pupil's absence; therefore, his poor adjustment and dissatisfaction with school increase, and truancy may seem all the more attractive. The pupil is caught in a vicious circle. When truanting, the pupil usually must remain more or less in hiding. The store where he typically hangs out after school may not welcome him during school hours; community centers and recreation areas are not organized to operate during school hours for school pupils and again, the presence of a pupil would bring inquiries and perhaps lead to a report to the school. Most would hesitate to go home. The truants— several together perhaps—are forced to hide in a "club house," along the railroad tracks or in an empty building. Whether they plan delinquency to be carried out then or later would depend very much upon the type of children. It seems probable that their activities would be related to other customary activities and not be isolated events. It does not seem that truancy per se would lead into delinquency, but that the high percentage of truants found among delinquents would indicate a more general tendency of the boy or girl not to fit into an orderly way of life.

Early withdrawal from school

Most states have laws requiring school attendance until age sixteen. Some pupils virtually leave at a younger age through habitual, long-continued periods of truancy. If the truant teen-ager leaves home, as sometimes happens, or if parents are unco-operative, the attendance officer may not locate the truant for weeks or months. If a pupil has been especially troublesome in school and seems impervious to all attempts to help him, he may be allowed to drop out with tacit approval of teacher and principal. Most dropouts, however, are at, or past, the legal age limit but have not completed high school.

Unlike habitual truants, they are not delinquent by definition. They do not need to hide. They are old enough to go to work.

Early dropping out at a time when a greater percentage of young people are graduating from high school and entering college creates concern on the part of educators, many of whom believe that the schools are failing a segment of the population. The specialist in delinquency problems has a different interest. Early dropouts find it difficult to get and hold jobs, especially jobs that will provide them with money to buy the clothing and afford them the amusement they want. They readily congregate at favorite hangouts and become typical street-corner boys. Many drift into stealing to supply the money they are unable to earn.

Frequency and social class. The number of pupils who drop out before graduation from high school shows the extent of the problem. Approximately half of the pupils who are in fifth grade (prior to the age for legally leaving school) do not complete high school.[1] States vary greatly in dropout rates. In 1954, Wisconsin had the best record with a loss of only 200 per 1,000 pupils between fifth grade and graduation; Georgia, with the worst rate, lost 770.

Within an individual city, the percentage of dropouts is not evenly distributed among all schools or all communities. The percentage increases sharply as social-class level or socio-economic status declines. For example, a study of 3,736 youths in New Haven showed that in the upper-upper-class areas 98.2 per cent of adolescents aged sixteen and seventeen were in school.[2] The percentage dropped to 57.4 per cent of attendance by youths in the lower-lower-class areas.

Studies using other measures of social class or socio-economic level show the same trend. Various studies show that 72 to 84 per cent of dropouts are from lower-income families.[3] When occupation is used as the measure, professional, managerial, clerical, and sales groups contribute many less than their share of dropouts; farmers, skilled laborers, and homemakers have an average proportion of dropouts; unskilled laborers and especially unemployed, retired, or unclassified groups

1 R. A. and L. M. Tesseneer, "Review of the Literature on School Dropouts," *Secondary School Principals Bulletin*, 42 (1958), 141–153.
2 Davie, *op. cit.*
3 Tesseneer, *op. cit.*

contribute two to three times their share.[1] Dropouts are also likely to have poorly educated parents.

Characteristics of dropouts. A study of 10,000 dropouts prior to graduation in cities of 30,000 to 350,000 population in seven different areas of the country, made by the United States Department of Labor, helps to pinpoint the type of student who drops out.[2] In all cities, the legal age for leaving school was sixteen years; nevertheless, 10 per cent of dropouts were under this age, having left because of ill health, marriage (of girls), and the like. Thirty-four per cent of the dropouts left school at the legal age of sixteen, 27 per cent remained an additional year, 17 per cent dropped out at age seventeen, and 12 per cent at age nineteen or older.

Age is not a clear indication of the amount of schooling received: 31 per cent had only eighth grade education or less; 30 per cent ninth grade; and 39 per cent tenth or eleventh grade. Slightly over half were two or more years behind the proper placement for their age, and another third one year or more retarded. Only 15 per cent were in their proper grade. Many had attended school enough years to have graduated but because of retardation were far behind the boys and girls with whom they first started school. Part of the answer is in mental ability as shown by the Otis Mental Ability Group Test: 46 per cent of dropouts as compared with 21 per cent of graduates rated below 90 (below normal) I.Q.; 48 per cent compared with 63 per cent had scores between 90 and 109 (normal); and 6 per cent as compared with 16 per cent had I.Q. scores of 110 or higher (superior). However, many dropouts have the ability to graduate.

Assigning reasons for leaving school is a difficult task. School records state the reason as seen by the administration; pupils themselves give very similar reasons. Some reasons have to do with the school situation: the pupil either is unable to do the work or he sees no relationship between school work and his major needs or what he foresees as his occupational future; the pupil is unable to achieve satisfactory interpersonal relationships with the teacher or with other pupils— he is not popular or he feels left out of things. But there are also pulls from the outside: the pupil wants or needs money or his family expects him to begin to earn; military service catches up with some of the older boys; girls want to marry. Thus the pupil balances his dissatisfactions with school against his anticipated satisfactions if he drops out of school.[3] If school has meaning for him personally or in terms of future occupation or further education, he tends to remain in school, even though his mental ability is rather low; if school has less meaning than the things he can find or hopes to find outside, he tends to leave school, often when he has the mental ability to graduate.

Although the dropout rate is high both for boys and girls, boys are slightly more inclined than girls to leave school before graduation.[4] Among those who drop out, girls fare better than do boys.[5] About a fourth of the girls soon marry, thus accomplishing one of the major life goals of most girls. Those who go to work find jobs as clerical workers, saleswomen, and waitresses. If they have taken business courses, their opportunities for good job placement are improved. Almost two-fifths of the boys find unskilled jobs, as they have no definite vocational training. High school graduates tend to find better-paying jobs and to remain in them longer than the dropouts, who tend to have an irregular work record at least during their first period after leaving school. Many occupations now require high school graduation and the dropout finds himself in a low-wage, deadend job. The boy's dream of a large income, new, smart clothing, a car, a girl to entertain, and eventually marriage have to be reduced to fit reality. When the boy is unable to make this adjustment and especially if he becomes unemployed he often is a candidate for an idle street-corner group, a delinquent gang, or for personal debilitation.

1 Joseph C. Bledsoe, "An Investigation of Six Correlates of Student Withdrawal from High School," *Journal of Educational Research,* 53 (September, 1959) 3–6.

2 Seymour L. Wolfbein, "Transition from School to Work: A Study of the School Leaver," *Personnel and Guidance Journal,* 38 (1959), 98–105.

3 Wolfbein, *op. cit.: Retention in High Schools in Large Cities,* Bulletin No. 15, 1957, U. S. Department of Health, Education, and Welfare, U. S. Office of Education, 1957; Joel B. Montague, "Social Status and Adjustment in School," *Clearing House,* 27 (September, 1952), 19–24; J. S. Caravello, "The Drop-out Problem," *High School Journal,* 41 (1959), 335–340.

4 Bledsoe, *op. cit.; Retention in High Schools in Large Large Cities,* Bulletin No. 15, 1957, *op. cit.*

5 Wolfbein, *op. cit.;* Caravello, *op. cit.*

Before the pupil drops out of school he often has been one of the troublesome pupils in school and/or a habitual truant. Dropping out for many students is simply the last step of a process that began soon after they entered, growing out of poor school adjustment academically and often socially and out of failure of family and community to give support to continuance in school. Actual ability of the student may be less important than the family and community factors.

The school's responsibility

To what extent is the school directly or indirectly responsible for delinquency? To what extent can the school reduce troublesomeness, habitual truancy, and early withdrawal?

Indirect responsibility. No general statement can be made that schools are directly responsible for delinquent behavior. Occasionally inept methods of teaching or the resentment of a teacher may contribute directly to individual cases of delinquency. Primarily, principals and teachers—those in direct relationships with children—are handicapped by deficiencies which they cannot control. Some of these are as follows:

1. Laws that require attendance of virtually all children except the most seriously handicapped between fixed ages, usually six to sixteen.

2. Failure of many school boards and of city or county governmental units to provide special education for misfits, whether mental, physical, or social.

3. Overcrowding of schools, with large numbers of pupils per teacher, or with half-day sessions and no provision by any governmental agency for filling the released time of pupils.

4. Poorly prepared teachers, especially during the fifties and sixties when the demand for teachers has exceeded the supply of well-trained applicants.

5. Over the years, gradual assumption by schools of more and more responsibility for various functions and the corresponding public attitude that most of the child's development—physical, personality, and academic—rests with the schools. The public tends to expect schools to handle all types of children, whether or not they have special facilities for dealing with those not able to benefit by the existing kind of education.

6. The widely accepted attitude by principals, teachers, and public that the schools should push children up the socio-economic ladder, whether or not the children wish or are able to make the ascent.

Serious questions have arisen as to whether the schools have overreached reasonable boundaries of responsibility. Should other agencies provide special programs for the misfits, leaving to the schools the function of education in the narrower sense of academic and vocational training for childern prepared to benefit by it? In larger cities, especially, school systems have made numerous approaches to the problem of nonacademic needs of students.

Special programs of schools

Special programs for schools usually are not couched in terms of delinquency prevention but in positive terms of better academic and personal development. Nevertheless, they often prevent delinquency. They help children adjust or relieve the classroom physically of troublesome children.

School counselors or social workers. School counseling services have been added to a number of schools. Teachers may refer individual children to the service, whose staff members analyze the child's difficulties, interpret his problems to the teacher, and often visit the child's home. The counselor assigned to the case may continue some relationship with the child in school, but as a rule, refers a family in need of expert help to an appropriate community agency. If the child has serious personality problems, an attempt is made to have the family arrange for psychiatric treatment outside the school. The counselor then interprets, helps to adjust school problems, and acts as a liaison among school, family, and community agencies. Since only individual pupils with special problems are referred to the counseling service, one specialist may provide adequate service for a large number of pupils. Los Angeles County estimates that the following specialists are needed for elementary schools:

Director of pupil-personnel services—one for each district

Psychologist or psychometrist—one for each 2,000 pupils

School social workers—one for each 2,000 pupils

Counselor—one for each 1,200 pupils

Physician—one for each 5,000 pupils

Nurse—one for each 1,000 pupils

Child welfare and attendance worker—one for each 2,500 pupils

Special teachers—determined by survey of pupil needs.[1]

A program of special services is not established solely for the benefit of delinquent children. Its aim is to bring all children to the point where they can learn to their fullest capacity. In this process delinquency-prone children may be identified in early stages of difficulty and straightened out.

Special classes and schools. Some cities have established special ungraded classes in some schools, or entire special schools for children who do not adapt to the usual school program.[2] The pupils in special classes and schools often represent a potpourri of problems: withdrawn children, emotionally unstable children, aggressively active children, habitual truants, and others. Usually attention can be given to children as individuals, especially if classes are small and the services of various specialists are provided. One rule of the effective special class or school is an individual approach to catch the attention and interest of the pupil and then build on that interest to meet some of the specific needs of the child. The ideal end objective is to adjust the child and return him to his regular school in condition to fit into the classroom. In some situations, however, the special class simply becomes a catch-all for misbehaving children; its function then is to remove the child from a classroom and permit other pupils to do their work although the special program may not be of much benefit to the troublemaker himself.

Chicago has long had a system of special schools. The Montefiori school (established in 1929 as part of the public school system) and the Moseley school receive boys in a day-school program which operates throughout the year. One branch of each of these schools is for girls. The Chicago Home for Girls, a branch of Montefiori, operates ten months of the year for girls who need to be removed from their own or foster homes, and the Chicago Parental Home is a year-round residential school for boys. Other units of the public school system are operated throughout the year in the detention home, the House of Correction, and the Cook County jail. The public school system also maintains twelve adjustment rooms in elementary schools for boys under twelve years of age.[3]

Pupils enter these special schools on transfer from their regular schools, without recourse to the juvenile court, and may be transferred back in the same way when they seem ready to readjust to the usual program and routines. At the special school, after individual study, each pupil is given a program suited to his abilities and needs. Many are in need of remedial work in basic skills. The academic program is paralleled by crafts and vocational courses. In Montefiori school, the boys find courses in woodwork, electric shop, general metalwork, shoe repairing, print shop, mechanical drawing, general mechanics, and crafts. Girls are offered homemaking, hairdressing, personal grooming, sewing, cooking, and typing. Counseling and guidance are provided as needed.

Many of the students transferred to Montefiori are in the dull-normal group, many are retarded in school, and many have personality difficulties. Almost 90 per cent of the pupils are already known to one or more social agencies before referral, the average referral per pupil being to 3.5 agencies. Over 50 per cent of the pupils or their families are known to the Family Court, which includes the juvenile court.

Adjustment of boys after they leave Montefiori varies. About half leave school permanently at age sixteen to find employment; the school's responsibility then ends. About 60 per cent of these dropouts do not get into difficulty. Of those who return to regular schools, about 70 per cent make good records in school.

New York City opened special classes in some elementary schools in 1940 for potential delinquents. In 1947, special schools known as "600 schools" were established, consisting of ten institutional schools, two remand (detention) centers, ten day schools, and six annexes to institutional organizations.

---

1 William C. Kvaraceus, William E. Ulrich, and collaborators, *Delinquent Behavior, Principles and Practices,* National Education Association of the United States, Washington, D. C., 1959, p. 136. Pages 134–173 constitute a chapter on "Providing Help Through Integrated Special Services," containing statements from many school systems.

2 Kvaraceus and Ulrich, *op. cit.,* chapter 6, "Providing Help through Special Classes," describes both special classes and special schools.

3 Kvaraceus and Ulrich, *op. cit.,* pp. 215–219; Edward H. Stullken, "Chicago's Special School for Social Adjustment," *Federal Probation,* 20 (March, 1956), 31–36.

Approximately 3,500 pupils are in these schools.[1] Only one of the schools is for girls. The pupils include children who are trouble-makers, delinquent, emotionally disturbed, and psychotic. Most pupils have had some court experience. One function of the schools is to remove the children from regular class-rooms where their behavior prevents learn-ing by themselves and others, and to re-habilitate them when possible for return to the regular schools.

Other large cities have similar special classes and schools. Most of them remain more or less experimental, still discovering what services are needed and what results can be expected.

Special programs for retention of students. Many students who lose interest in school and become chronic truants or early dropouts are not emotionally maladjusted. From working-class backgrounds, they anticipate entering some form of manual or skilled employment. If they have not been able to secure voca-tional training of a practical nature, school may easily seem unnecessary and superflu-ous. If such boys drop out of school and do not find jobs they often tend to drift into delinquent behavior. The lower-class Elm-town boys, already described in Chapter 7, are illustrative. An expansion of practical and vocational types of education to fit these boys specifically for the jobs they may rea-sonably hope to fill would undoubtedly re-duce early dropping out and also place them in a position to work at jobs with better re-muneration than they often secure.

Another special type of training suggested for lower-class pupils has been to prepare them in general for law-abiding lower-class life.[2] This point of view recognizes, first, the differences in values and objectives of the middle and the lower class, and, second, the fact that many lower-class youth probably will not be upwardly mobile and, therefore, should be prepared for lower-class life as a worthwhile level of society. Respect for lower-class values would ease the adjustment of the youth who wishes to rise but cannot for any one of a number of reasons, and who often finds delinquency an outlet for his feel-ings. This point of view seems to run counter

to the usual school emphasis on middle-class values as superior to lower-class values and to the pressure on students to move if possi-ble toward middle-class status. An adoption of this approach should be made with cau-tion, in order not to create a permanent lower "caste," and to keep the way of upward mo-bility open for students desiring and able to move upward in accordance with the tradi-tional American ideal.

Employment as delinquency preventive

Since many lower-class youth become chronic truants and early school dropouts, the suggestion has been made that the age for compulsory education and for a work permit should be lowered. The boy or girl would then be able to leave school early in the teens and go to work. Heated arguments between the advocates of continued schooling and of early employment have found their way into print.

Early employment. A juvenile court judge has assailed the school and child labor laws as the chief cause for adolescent idleness, es-pecially by youth not interested in attending school.[3] Other statements emphasize the fact that in our culture work gives prestige and carries the adolescent on into adult status.[4]

Various facts cast doubt on the wisdom of lowering the age for leaving school and seek-ing work. Early dropouts find it more difficult to find and hold well-paying jobs than the high school graduates.[5] Unemployment is much more common among the dropouts.

In addition, the trend of business and in-dustry is away from unskilled labor and toward greater use of machines, whose opera-tion requires maturity and specialized train-ing. In discussing job placement, one guidance counselor has called attention to the fact that in seventy-one occupations with labor shortages, the minimum educational require-ment is four years of education at the high school level.[6] Undisciplined delinquents and

1 Kvaraceus and Ulrich, *op. cit.*, pp. 182–183.
2 William C. Kvaraceus and associates, *Delinquent Be-havior, Culture and the Individual*, National Educa-tion Association of the United States, Washington, D. C., 1959, pp. 62–75.
3 William C. Long, "Let's Put Our Idle Teen-agers to Work," *American Magazine*, October, 1955. For views on both sides see "An Open Letter to Judge Long," *American Child*, 38 (March, 1956), 1–2; "Two Views on Child Labor Laws," *American Child*, 37 (May, 1955), 4; "Are the Child Labor Laws to Blame," *American Child*, 40 (May, 1958), entire is-sue.
4 "Federation Employment and Guidance Service," *Special Youth Board Project Report*, New York, mimeographed, April 21, 1958, p. 2.
5 Wolfbein, *op. cit.*
6 Caravello, *op. cit.*

early dropouts are not eligible for good jobs. They may find their way into unskilled, deadend jobs or drift from one job to another. Whether the kind of work they can enter is delinquency-preventive is open to question, especially for the boy who has unrealistically dreamed of a glamorous job.

The statement that work gives prestige seems less true of lower-class than of middle-class types of work. In a study of the attitudes men hold toward their jobs, a number of men were asked what they would do if they inherited sufficient money to stop work. The skilled and unskilled workers showed a much greater willingness to stop work than men in prestige jobs.[1] When asked whether they would continue in their same jobs if they inherited money but wished to continue to work, 61 per cent of middle-class but only 34 per cent of the total working-class group said they would continue in the same job; only 16 per cent of unskilled workers would want to continue in their category.

Early school dropouts come primarily from the unskilled class or from families in which the father is unemployed or retired. Unprepared to do more than their dissatisfied fathers do, it is questionable to what extent work would build up their feeling of worth and status, or provide money to fulfill their ambitions.

Integration of school and employment. A halfway program has been suggested whereby students work and attend school, with the job integrated into the school program.

In various communities some organization has taken the initiative in screening youth in or out of schools and finding jobs for them. The organization may act as a liaison between an employer who is solicited for job openings for youth, the school counselor who recommends students, and the recommended student who wishes to work. The work may be part time during the school year or for a portion of the summer. The response of the employed youth is reported from various cities as very good: they like to work, spend their money wisely, and so on.[2] It is not clear in these efforts to place youth in jobs whether seriously delinquent youths are likely to be selected for placement. Also, the effect of the attention received all along the line would tend to heighten the youth's sense of value regardless of the effect of working and earning money. Follow-up studies are needed as to the adjustment when these special attentions are withdrawn and the youth is on his own.

Various individuals and organized groups advocate a system of publicly supported work-study programs adapted to youth, especially to adolescents who are not well adjusted in the usual school program: the retarded, the truants, the troublemakers.[3] The programs should be co-ordinated with the public school program, beginning with boys aged thirteen or fourteen. Its objectives would be to teach such elementary work disciplines as "punctuality, ability to take orders from a boss, ability to work cooperatively with others in a team, responsibility on the job." It should lead into stable adult jobs. The work should be of a useful variety, such as conservation of natural resources or some form of public service. The aid of business leaders would be needed at the point where boys transferred from the work program into regular jobs. For well-rounded development the boys would need to continue certain studies and also have a well-developed social life supplied by community organizations. Work alone would not be sufficient to check the tendency of dissatisfied youth to look to delinquency for a solution to their problems.

To the extent that such a program incorporated youth into a project that enlisted their interests and efforts it should check some of the drift toward delinquency as a way to find satisfactions not now supplied by schools. The advocates of the program suggested in the preceding paragraph believe that it might be expected to reduce delinquency as much as 50 per cent, but not more, since many delinquents do not fall into the group that is failing in school and rebellious over their situation. The school alone cannot be expected to prevent delinquency. It has a responsibility, however, to co-operate with other agencies in a more skillfully designed youth-training program than presently exists.

1 Nancy C. Morse and Robert S. Weiss, "The Function and Meaning of Work," *American Sociological Review*, 20 (1955), 191–198.
2 *Youth and Work*, National Child Labor Committee, New York 16, New York, 5 (October, 1958).
3 Robert J. Havighurst and Lindley J. Stiles, "National Policy for Alienated Youth," *Phi Delta Kappan*, 43 (1961), 283–291. This article was prepared with the approval of the Phi Delta Kappa Commission on Prevention of Juvenile Delinquency and therefore is not limited to the opinion of the two authors.

Bibliography

Caravello, S. J., "The Drop-out Problem," *High School Journal,* 41 (1959), 335–340.

Cohen, Eli E., and Lila Rosenbaum, "Will Relaxing Child Labor Laws Help Prevent Delinquency?" *Federal Probation,* 23 (March, 1959), 44–47.

Franklin, Adele, "The All-day Neighborhood Schools," *Annals of the American Academy of Political and Social Science,* 322 (1959), 62–66.

"From School to Work," U. S. Department of Labor, Bureau of Labor Statistics, Washington, D. C., 1960.

Havighurst, Robert J., and Lindley J. Stiles, "National Policy for Alienated Youth," *Phi Delta Kappan,* 42 (1961), 283–291.

Hill, Arthur S., Leonard M. Miller, and Hazel F. Gabbard, "Schools Face the Delinquency Problem," *The Bulletin* of the National Association of Secondary-School Principals, 37 (December, 1953), 118–221.

Henry, Nelson B., editor, *Juvenile Delinquency and the Schools,* National Society for the Study of Education, Yearbook No. 47, Part 1, University of Chicago Press, Chicago, 1948.

Kvaraceus, William C., Walter B. Miller, and collaborators, *Delinquent Behavior, Culture and the Individual,* National Education Association, Washington, D. C., 1959.

———, William E. Ulrich, and collaborators, *Delinquent Behavior, Principles and Practices,* National Education Association, Washington, D. C., 1959.

"Reading and Delinquency," *National Probation and Parole Association Journal,* 1 (1955), 1–30, seven articles.

Retention in High Schools in Large Cities, Bulletin 1957, No. 15, U. S. Department of Health, Education, and Welfare, U. S. Office of Education, Washington, D. C., 1957.

Roberts, John L., "Factors Associated with Truancy," *Personnel and Guidance Journal,* 34 (1956), 431–436.

Samuels, Gertrude, "Visit to a '600 School'," *New York Times Magazine,* (March, 1958), 12, 57–58.

"School and Delinquency," *Crime and Delinquency,* 7 (July, 1961), entire issue.

Smith, P. M., "The School as a Factor," Chapter 7 in Joseph S. Roucek, editor, *Juvenile Delinquency,* Philosophical Library, New York, 1958.

"Social Class Structure and American Education," *Harvard Educational Review,* 23 (Summer 1953) and 23 (Fall, 1953), entire issues.

Spence, Ralph B., *Reducing Juvenile Delinquency,* New York State Youth Commission, Albany, New York, revised 1955.

Stullken, Edward H., "Chicago's Special School for Social Adjustment," *Federal Probation,* 20 (March, 1956), 31–36.

———, "The Schools and the Delinquency Problem," *Journal of Criminal Law, Criminology and Police Science,* 43 (1953), 563–577.

Taber, Robert C., "The Potential Role of the School Counselor in Delinquency Prevention and Treatment," *Federal Probation,* 13 (September, 1949), 52–56.

"Teacher Opinion on Pupil Behavior, 1955–1956," *Research Bulletin of the National Education Association,* 34 (April, 1956), 51–107.

Tesseneer, R. A. and L. M., "Review of the Literature on School Dropouts," *The Bulletin* of the National Association of Secondary School Principals, 42 (May, 1958), 141–153.

Warner, W. Lloyd, Robert J. Havighurst, and Martin B. Loeb, *Who Shall Be Educated?* Harper and Brothers, New York, 1944.

Wolfbein, Seymour L., "Transition from School to Work: A Study of the School Leaver," *Personnel and Guidance Journal,* 38 (1959), 98–105.

Over the years in addition to special school programs, numerous efforts have been made to prevent delinquency or to rebuild the attitudes and redirect the behavior of delinquent children. From decade to decade the spotlight of hope fastens on first one then another program or agency. In general, new approaches reflect the dominant interest of the society at a given time or are the application to delinquency of some newly developed educational or therapeutic philosophy or method. Regardless of these efforts, delinquency continues.

Since no effort to date has succeeded, communities are reluctant to abandon old methods, but at the same time are often willing to try new ones. Earlier programs may be kept alive by small devoted groups. New programs are begun by equally devoted groups. The result is a conglomeration of projects to blot out or control delinquency, always growing by the accretion of new projects. The projects are not co-ordinated and, in fact, may be in conflict with each other in their basic philosophy or practical programs. A small urban neighborhood with a high delinquency rate may have a number of unrelated agencies seriously trying to influence the same boys and girls as though each were the only agency in the community.

Each agency may have a measure of success, sometimes by appearing to calm the community as a whole, sometimes through the spectacular rehabilitation of one or two notoriously delinquent youths. Since, as has been shown, delinquency is not a homogeneous type of behavior and does not develop from one given type of temperament or personality, the efforts that appeal to and are effective with some delinquent boys and girls may have no effect whatever on others.

In general, agencies may be placed in two categories: those open to all children in a community whether delinquent or not and those focused especially on children already engaged in delinquent behavior. Agencies of the first type, discussed in this chapter, are usually preventive; the second, discussed in the following chapter, are remedial and perhaps preventive of continued or more serious delinquency. The first are exemplified by churches, schools, community centers, and youth organizations; mass media also fall into this category, although whether they are preventive or productive of delinquency is a con-

Chapter **16**

Community preventive efforts

troversial issue. The second includes case work and group work with children or youth already becoming delinquent.

From the point of view of the child, his contact with an agency may be voluntary on his part, or it may come as a decree of the juvenile court. In general, this chapter and the following are concerned with the voluntary relationships. The special agencies and measures used by juvenile courts are discussed in connection with courts and other legally constituted programs and institutions, such as probation, correctional schools, and parole.

Meaning of prevention and rehabilitation

Prevention in its strictest sense would somehow bar the child from all serious acts of misbehavior that might be construed as delinquency. Since there are many such acts and no means of knowing in advance what acts a child might engage in, if any, purely preventive programs are difficult to initiate. They have no definite objective toward which to work. An organization sponsoring a preventive program tends either to pin its faith on one form of activity, recreation, for instance, or to try to enlist children in a number of varied activities in an effort to absorb most of their free time, as some community centers do.

Positive quality of preventive programs. Preventive programs are better thought of in positive terms rather than negative, as a movement toward some stated goals rather than prevention of vague possible misbehavior which cannot be pinpointed but which, if it should appear, would be undesirable. Commonly accepted positive goals are acceptance by the child of the high values of his society, integration of personality around these values, maximum use of abilities, and organization of associates and activities to give socially approved kinds of satisfaction to basic needs and interests. These objectives usually are stated in terms of concrete goals to be striven for, such as honesty, fairness, industriousness, maximum use of mental ability and any special talents, good companions, and a well-rounded circle of activities.

A child who is positively guided toward such goals by supervising adults no doubt is less likely to become delinquent than the child who is exposed to pressures that push him toward unapproved objectives and toward companions engaged in delinquency. The child who finds himself in a delinquency cul-de-sac may feel that his way of life is satisfactory and may defend it and cling to it regardless of well-meaning efforts to persuade him to abandon it. He does not foresee that he is quite likely to be increasingly rejected by conventional social groups and made to feel unwanted and inferior, and that he is likely to be arrested and imprisoned from time to time during a large part of his youth and adult life.

Whether he moves toward delinquency or toward conformity, the process is very much the same: inclusion in and identification with small groups, acceptance of their values and goals, learning of roles co-ordinated with the roles of others, and learning of techniques for carrying out the activities attached to the roles. The nondelinquent boy may be a member of a normal family, a member of Scouts or some similar organization; identified with his father, some teacher, or the scoutmaster; have status as and adopt the role of a student, an athlete, an "all-round" boy; learn to study, engage in team sports, hold a Saturday job, and the like. The delinquent boy may be a member of a poorly organized family and of a street-corner or delinquent group; become identified with older delinquent boys or successful criminals; have status in his group as war counselor, a clever thief, a courageous fighter; learn to evade or trick the police, break into a store, fight other boys, and the like.

The processes that lead the child toward conformity differ in two ways from those that turn the child toward delinquency: usually they are planned and supervised by adults who represent the dominant social values; and the child is publicly rewarded for conformity by approval, titles, badges, good grades, and tangible prizes.

The process toward delinquency is informal. Children imitate slightly older youth who often are without any clear future goals; they learn from them by observation, association, and at times through direct teaching of the techniques of delinquency. The rewards are bestowed by these older youth in the way of praise and eventual inclusion in their organization. At any time, however, the representatives of the larger society may express their disapproval and impose penalties for nonconformity.

Reversing the delinquency process. When the child has already become delinquent, the process of rehabilitation is more complicated than the process of inducting a child directly into conformity. The delinquent child has already developed attitudes favorable toward delinquency and found roles among delinquent companions. If the child is simply on the fringe of delinquency and still finds many satisfactions in nondelinquent groups, he may more easily be brought back to conformity than the child or adolescent whose most vital activities are encompassed by delinquency. Stated in the terminology of Chapter 2, the further he has been incorporated into a contraculture of delinquency, opposed to the dominant culture or even the class subculture, the more difficult the task of rehabilitation becomes. The process of rehabilitation has two stages. First, the delinquent attitudes, roles, and associations must be destroyed; second, attitudes, roles, and associates favorable to conformity must be made important and vital to the child. He must pass from a contraculture group into a subcultural or dominant cultural group. The two processes should go on simultaneously. If the child's identification with and acceptance by the delinquent group is destroyed and no conforming person or group has already gained some hold upon him, he is a "lost" person. It is not enough therefore to break up the delinquent gang by sending key members to different jails or correctional schools, to close the hangout, and to institute severe police measures. The remnants of the gang will cling together and recruit new members; in correctional schools new cliques will form. The necessity for the second part of the process often is not clearly understood.

Measuring success. The success of either preventive or rehabilitative efforts is very difficult to measure. If the community center, the church, or the public playground were not operating in the delinquency area, how many more children would be delinquent? How can the effects of any program be separated from the effects of family life, ethnic culture, the prevalence or nonexistence of neighborhood gangs? In all except perhaps certain small areas of a city, most children do not become confirmed delinquents or adult criminals. Many do not enter into preventive programs; even if preventive programs did not exist in the community they would not become delinquent.

Rehabilitative programs directed toward the individual child or gang have slightly less difficulty in evaluating their efforts. The child or gang has already shown evidences of delinquency. He (or the gang members) do or do not continue in delinquency. If they do, where has rehabilitation failed? If they become conforming, is it necessarily due solely or principally to the rehabilitative efforts?

Probably most preventive and much rehabilitative work goes forward on faith. In terms of our cultural values, certain experiences are thought to be good for children. If children accept the values and fit into the approved pattern, the program tends to take the credit. If the child fails, the tendency is to search outside the program for the cause of failure—the slum area, the lack of playgrounds, the broken home, and any one of a number of other situations that either are or are thought to be related to delinquency.

From time to time, new insight is gained into the development of delinquency and new programs are instituted.

Changing the child's environment

One type of effort to prevent or reduce delinquency is in changing the immediate situation in which the child lives. This may be accomplished in two ways: actually changing community conditions or removing the child to a different type of community, usually without his family.

Housing. The deteriorated housing in high delinquency areas led to the mistaken idea that decent housing and general cleaning up of slums would automatically reduce delinquency. Favorable public opinion was sought to acquire public subsidies for housing by asserting that delinquency would thus be eliminated. Early surveys made before and after slum clearance often did show a reduction in the rate of delinquency in the blocks where condemned buildings or other deteriorated houses had been razed and modern public housing erected. However, the reduction was found to be illusory. The families forced out of the old housing usually did not move into the new housing. In the interval of time involved in building the new structures, the families had found other housing in other slum areas. Also, although many of the new projects were on a low rent basis, the rent was still often higher than the former families could pay. A slightly different type of family moved in, often apparently oriented toward nondelinquency.[1]

In other instances, delinquency has flourished in the projects and occasionally delinquent gangs have made a project area their turf to be protected and fought for. The situation in certain housing projects in New York City has been described and presumably might be duplicated in other large cities. Physically, the projects are an improvement on the old slums; but often the human problems of the residents have been overlooked.

Many New York projects are large—the largest houses 3,400 families, running to perhaps 17,000 persons. This is a small city in itself. These families have come together from diverse backgrounds in a short space of time, much too rapidly for people to come to know each other, form community organizations, develop community sentiment or public opinion, or exert control over conduct of the residents. Added to these disorganizing factors is the new arrival of many of the residents (Puerto Ricans and southern Negro migrants) to the industrial city and its ways. Thus the housing project often is a city of strangers.

Some housing projects include club or recreation rooms within the project. Without some help, however, the residents often do not know how to organize their little commu-

---

1 Although the early claims of public housing as delinquency preventive were not substantiated, the housing can be defended on many other grounds: sanitation, health, less overcrowding, more privacy, more play space, and less family tension.

nity or build up public opinion and control through use of a common gathering place. They are not only strangers to each other, but several languages may be spoken in the project, and the residents may not have had experience in organizing themselves into effective groups. In time the strangers are welded into a true community which can act for itself.

Another lack in newly built areas is the dearth of community organizations, such as churches and community or youth centers. Some such agencies may have lost their buildings in the slum clearance that preceded building of the housing project; others have lost some of their clientele when families moved from their areas to make way for the project. The new residents may be of another race or religion—the Jewish synagogue may be surrounded by Catholic Puerto Ricans; the center staffed with whites may have a clientele of Negroes.

A practice in some housing projects in New York City has been especially vicious—the immediate eviction of any family when a boy is found to belong to a gang or when someone is arrested. The family is forced back into the situation from which it was trying to extricate itself, and the delinquent finds himself not only in trouble with the police but blamed by his family for its problems. Other projects close their recreation rooms to all youth because they are thought to be destructive, or to all but the members of one gang to prevent intergang conflicts. The projects thus tend to be rejective, exiling those having trouble, instead of instituting positive programs of adjustment.[1]

The replacement of slums by adequate housing certainly can be justified on many grounds, but it does not automatically change behavior. Parents and children alike bring problems with them and, in addition, need help in establishing friendly relationships and developing a consensus of opinion as a basis for control of behavior within the project.

Removing the child from an unfavorable environment. Usually this step involves removing the child from an unfavorable family en-

vironment and placing him in an institution for children or in a foster home. Institutionalizing a child in a correctional school is omitted from the present discussion, since this is by order of a court and usually has overtones of punishment. When a child is placed in a children's home or a foster home, it is usually with the consent of the parents and is carried out by a social agency or by the juvenile court acting as a social agency. The motive is to remove the child from an inimicable situation and place him in a group that in some way will function as a family. The children as a rule are not seriously delinquent. Sometimes they are merely dependent and in other cases neglected to the point where they are rapidly moving toward delinquency. It is the hope of social workers, judge, and parents (if they agree to the placement) that the child will find in the new home warm relationships with adults who will serve as satisfactory parent-substitutes and provide an adult model with whom the child can identify. Young children usually are placed in foster homes if any are available; older children usually are placed in various institutional homes.

Institutional homes. Institutions for delinquency-prone children usually take the form of residential schools. They are variously operated by religious groups or private boards. Most of them are for boys. In the older type of school, only the first step in the process from delinquency to conformity was attempted—to break the boy's affiliation with delinquent associates and destroy his delinquent pattern of behavior by removing him from the environment where he lived. Often the family was included among the undesirable associates. The schools rarely attempted to implant substitute attitudes, attachments, and self-motivated behavior patterns—often because this part of the process was not understood. An attempt was made to change overt behavior by authoritarian exhortation, repression, regimentation, hard work, drill, and punishment.

The newer and more modern type of school attempts both steps. Some of the staff are trained to guide the program and to counsel the boy. Others—especially house parents —are selected because they are warmhearted (though firm on occasion) and not too far removed in background from the boy's own so-

1 For a rather impassioned indictment of New York City's housing projects see Harrison E. Salisbury, *The Shook-up Generation,* Fawcett Publications, Greenwich, Connecticut, Chapter 5, "The New Ghettos."

cial-class level but adhering to approved so-cial values. It is hoped that they may become not merely supervisors but substitute parents in the best sense of the word.

Many problems are met in instituting such a program. The physical plant itself is soon outdated, as ideas change on the best kind of environment. Homes built to accommo-date several hundred children under one roof now are considered a hindrance to the child's best development, and "cottages" for thirty to fifty children are advocated—or fewer if there is money for an adequate number of independent buildings.

Staffing is difficult, both in terms of profes-sionally and technically trained staff and the special types of personality needed among those in close contact with the children.

Money is always a problem and often lies at the foundation of inadequacies of build-ings and staff.

When children come in, they are often frightened, apprehensive, resentful, or an-tagonistic. They are abruptly torn away from friends and family who before had given meaning to their lives. More orderliness, obe-dience, and co-operation are expected than has been demanded of them before. The shock of such a sharp change creates resist-ance. A long period may be necessary before any constructive work can be done with the child to instill conforming attitudes and readi-ness for retraining.

Not the least of the problems is the return of the child to the community, for few children remain in these schools indefinitely. The re-turn to the community is the test of the ade-quacy of the institutional experience. Boys who leave the schools with the best of inten-tions to avoid trouble find themselves unable to resist their old companions (after all, they have no other friends in the home commu-nity) and soon the temporary effect of the school experience has disappeared.

These discouraging remarks are not meant to disparage the schools. They often make a sufficient break with the past so that the boy can adjust on a new basis at home, especially if some work has been done with his family, or some community agency is ready to give him some help. Also, the period in the school may tide some boys over a few crucial years until they are old enough to go to work and move on into adulthood.

Foster homes. Foster homes are private homes in which children are placed instead of in an institution or school of some kind. The husband and wife ideally are people who have older children of their own and who re-tain a warm and natural interest in children. Arrangements for foster-home placement are made with the consent of the parents by a so-cial agency which then pays the expense of the child in the foster home or by the juve-nile court through its social workers or a com-munity social agency, with the city or county paying the expense. The original concept of the foster home, however, was that the family accepted the child because of their interest in children and not as a money-making project.

Foster homes are used primarily for de-pendent children who are well below adoles-cence. However, delinquent children are sometimes placed in foster homes when the supervising agency thinks that normal home life may check delinquent tendencies.

Good foster-home placement calls for skill in matching child and foster parents, giving foster parents some insight into the child's problems and how they may be handled, and helping the child accept the foster parents as parents. When the child is taken directly from his own home to a foster home, an added problem is adjustment of the parents to having their child become attached to the foster parents. The child is often reluctant to leave his parents and home even though the parents may have neglected or mistreated him. If a crowded, ill-kept home and deterio-rated community are all that the child has known, a clean and orderly foster home and neighborhood may seem so strange that the child cannot adjust, and his delinquency may increase.

Foster parents are under no obligation to keep the child for any specified length of time. If the child misbehaves at the new home, quarrels with children in the family, is a problem at school, or is delinquent in the neighborhood, the foster parents may notify the agency that placed the child with them and request that the child be removed. Chil-dren who have difficulty in adjusting may have a record of three or four different fos-ter homes in the course of a year to two. Un-less an especially fortunate placement is finally made, the child may progressively deteriorate in personality and behavior, since each removal from a home constitutes rejection in the eyes of the child as well as posing one more new situation to which he must try to adjust.

Rehabilitative efforts within the existing environment

Changing communities physically from slums to well-equipped neighborhoods is a slow process; special institutions and foster homes provide for a small number of delinquent children. Most attempts to prevent delinquency are carried out in the environment in which children and their families live, through such organizations as churches (synagogues, temples, other religious organizations), settlement houses and community centers, youth organizations, and supervised recreational programs, such as public parks and playgrounds with supervisors. Objectives of these various organizations vary. They may be limited to a specific goal or may cover a number of approaches. Leaders may be professionally trained in community organization, group work, or recreation, or they may be untrained. The membership may be limited to one age or sex or may cover all residents of the community who wish to participate.

When these agencies first developed, the customary procedure was for a group or organization (as a church) from a favored, perhaps upper-middle-class area to penetrate the lower-class area, secure or erect a building, and institute and finance a program, depending upon the program to catch and hold the interest of the residents of the lower-class neighborhood. More recently, some projects have been organized with at least some indigenous leadership, requiring a minimum of control and financial support from outside the area served.

Organizations sponsored primarily from outside the area. Many of these organizations are locally sponsored, and hence each one has its own special characteristics. They may be federated into a national body and conform to a general pattern but nevertheless have local autonomy. Only general patterns and trends are attempted in the discussion.

1. Religious organizations. The effectiveness of churches and similar religious organizations (for brevity, referred to here collectively as churches) in prevention of delinquency is not clear. A principal purpose of churches is to instill the beliefs and values of a specific religion. Although these may differ from one major religion to another and from one denomination to another, the basic values are very similar among the many religious groups in the United States (over 200). Since most of them derive from the Judeo-Christian tradition, such similarity is to be expected. However, the theological creeds may differ and also the customs through which creeds and values are expected to be expressed in daily life. Consequently, one important relation of religion to delinquency prevention is whether the church in a specific neighborhood corresponds to the religion traditionally followed by the residents. The social class, ethnic, and racial clustering of people into rather compact colonies seems at first glance to provide natural congregations for their traditional religions. However, some time may elapse before a church is established on a firm footing, unless it is sponsored by a strong church organization which is able to come into the neighborhood, finance a church, and supply outside leadership. Ethnic Catholic communities in large cities often are served by a Catholic church in which the ethnic language is used and by parochial schools in which the teaching is in the ethnic language. Social service and recreational programs may also be established with Catholic leadership. For the ethnic community as a whole these programs provide stability in the early years of the settlement. The use of the foreign language, however, may in time serve as a barrier to adjustment to the city as a whole.

The relationship between church and community often is not a stable one. Urban mobility is high, especially in the lower-class areas where one ethnic or racial group succeeds another. The newcomers may be of another religion than the preceding residents. The formerly Protestant or Jewish community may be taken over by Catholic migrants (for example, Mexicans or Puerto Ricans); or the former Catholic or Jewish areas by Protestants (for example, southern Negroes). If the already established church remains, it must either continue to draw back its older adherents or attempt to draw in people of a different religious affiliation. Even when the religion remains the same, the language of the group may differ; Catholic churches that

formerly served Italians may now be surrounded by Spanish speaking migrants.

Many families that come into the areas have either had no affiliation or only a nominal one with a church or they lose the affiliation in the confusion of becoming integrated into the American city. Children are likely to escape from a church's influence or, if they attend religious services, fail to integrate religious values into their personal values and attitudes. Certainly attendance at religious services is no guaranty of nondelinquent behavior, as several studies show. In Passaic, New Jersey, among delinquent boys and girls referred to the Children's Bureau, 54 per cent attended church regularly, 25 per cent seldom or never, and the remainder irregularly.[1] Some 2,000 boys interviewed by Detroit police after complaints of their behavior had been received had a similar record of church attendance: 44 per cent attended regularly,

Centers sponsored by a specific religious group gain in effectiveness when they work among people of the same religion. In this picture volunteers aid children in Our Lady's Youth Center, El Paso. The Center caters to a lower-class Mexican Catholic community. The priest assigned to this community had studied Spanish but found it necessary to improve his speech in order to come to friendly terms with many of the people in his parish. As in many community centers, work is not limited to adolescent clubs and gangs, but includes recreation for younger children, in the general effort to build constructive attitudes and interests. (Courtesy Our Lady's Youth Center, El Paso)

25 per cent occasionally, 16 per cent seldom, 14 per cent never, and 1 per cent gave no information. Recidivists had a slightly—but only slightly—poorer record than the one-time offenders.[2] The comparison of 500 correctional school with 500 nondelinquent

1 William Kvaraceus, "Delinquent Behavior and Church Attendance," *Sociology and Social Research*, 28 (1944), 284–289.

2 W. W. Wattenberg, "Church Attendance and Juvenile Delinquency," *Sociology and Social Research*, 34 (1950), 195–202.

boys, made by the Gluecks, showed that 39 per cent of delinquents attended church regularly, 54 per cent occasionally, and 7 per cent never; among nondelinquent boys the corresponding percentages were 67, 29, and 4.[1]

Even among children who attend regularly, the impact of religious training may be superficial. It has long been known that knowledge about the Bible or about moral precepts is rarely sufficient to control behavior.[2] Many churches are beginning to recognize the necessity of understanding children's interests and problems and relating their teaching to the daily lives of the children. Some theological seminaries have instituted special programs to bring ministerial students into direct association with delinquents.[3] Penetration of religious teaching into community and legal programs for delinquents is also urged by those who wish to see a more aggressive approach of churches to delinquency prevention and rehabilitation. Clergymen are urged to serve as chaplains in detention homes and correctional schools, to stimulate lay church members to become volunteers to work with delinquents, to equip themselves or enlist the services of trained persons for counseling, to initiate social action to clean up conditions breeding delinquency, and to organize community programs within church buildings.[4]

Protestant churches or denominations often maintain missions of various sorts in deteriorated areas. Some have proselytizing as their objective to draw people without church connections or sometimes with some other kind of religious affiliation into a Protestant church. Others are "rescue" missions, aimed at converting the debilitated inhabitants of skidrow areas to Christianity. Special religious organizations, such as the Salvation Army, have assumed this task as well as programs for children in deprived areas.

Churches also sometimes operate neighborhood houses that closely approximate secular community centers; emphasis is placed less on a specific religious affiliation than on supervised group activities and recreation, especially for children and youth.

2. Settlement houses and community centers. Settlement houses originally were the physical embodiment of the belief that people of education and culture should share their lives and learning with people of little education who had few opportunities for learning or appreciation of art, literature, philosophy, and other cultural studies. From this association, the educated would learn at first hand of the deprivations and problems of the poor and deprived and perhaps be able to alleviate the problems; the uneducated would enrich their lives and improve their chances for good citizenship. The original settlement house was Toynbee Hall in the East End in London, opened through the initiative of Canon Samuel Barnett. Through his vigorous influence, young men from the universities came to reside for a season or for a few years in Toynbee Hall. Jane Addams, who in 1889 founded one of the first settlement houses in America—Hull House in Chicago—caught her inspiration from Toynbee Hall. Hull House was preceded by the Neighborhood Guild in New York City by two years.

Like churches, settlement houses are not primarily devoted to delinquency prevention. Their function has always been to spearhead movements to improve conditions in slum areas through legal and voluntary reform and to give personal service and opportunities for growth and education to people living in the immediate neighborhood of the settlement house. Nevertheless, they have often been noted for their contribution in the way that any constructive program is so credited.

When settlement houses were first established in American industrial cities, these cities were struggling with the adjustment and assimilation of immense masses of European immigrants, huddled in compact colonies, whose language not only differed from English but also from that spoken by the adjacent immigrant colony a few blocks distant. They were not only poverty-stricken but were prey to every type of economic and political exploitation. Laws to protect them and public welfare services did not exist. The areas

1 Sheldon and Eleanor Glueck, *Unraveling Juvenile Delinquency,* Harvard University Press, Cambridge, Massachusetts, 1950, p. 166.
2 Hugh Hartshorne and Mark A. May, *Studies in Deceit,* Macmillan Company, New York, 1928–1930.
3 Richard V. McCann, "The Self-Image and Delinquency: Some Implications for Religion," *Federal Probation,* 20 (September, 1956), 14–23.
4 Robert and Muriel Webb, "How Churches Can Help in the Prevention and Treatment of Juvenile Delinquency," *Federal Probation,* 21 (December, 1957), pp. 22–25; Robert and Muriel Webb, *The Churches and Juvenile Delinquency,* Association Press, New York, 1957; Guy L. Roberts, *How the Church Can Help Where Delinquency Begins,* John Knox Press, Richmond, Virginia, 1958.

Community centers may supply equipment for all types of play, in this case hula hoops, a popular fad of the late 1950's. (Courtesy Our Lady's Youth Center, El Paso)

where immigrant families lived were also the areas of highest crime and delinquency rates. Since the immigrants themselves were not criminal in background the assumption seems sound that the delinquency of their children was bred in the American slums. In a sense, then, whatever the settlement-house staffs and residents did to aid the immigrants was indirectly preventive of delinquency.

Many changes have occurred since then. Some settlement houses have seen their original neighborhoods swept away for business expansion, spacious highways, or public housing. Others are still surrounded by slums but the ethnic character of their residents has changed. Still others are serving the children and grandchildren of the original immigrants, now American in culture with only traces of the ethnic culture. In the last situation, residents have often been admitted to more and more participation in the direction and leadership of the settlement houses, functions that they could not perform when the houses were first established.

The original residents of settlement houses were volunteers who paid their own expenses but gave volunteer services to the house and the neighborhood. The spirit of service and co-operation ran high. As professional social work developed, trained salaried workers were added to the staff, and at present they form the backbone of settlement work although volunteers still perform many services. The program has tended to develop into group and recreational work. Individual case work is less often a part of the services provided.

Settlement houses are sometimes criticized because they have not swept delinquency from their areas. Such criticism overlooks the changing character of some neighborhoods, where one alien group has

This dance, at a lower West Side community house in Manhattan, took gang members off the street and gave them something new in their world of fun. They like the simple dances like this "Bunny Hop," a version of follow the leader. (Courtesy New York City Youth Board)

followed another, to repeat the process of adjustment to industrial urban life. It also overlooks the very real service of settlement houses in helping people of another culture (whether foreign, regional, rural, or social class) to become integrated effectively into the urban culture. In Chapter 7 the problem of upward mobility for youth in deprived areas was discussed. Settlement houses offer many avenues for the upwardly mobile young person. Children who are not delinquency prone, although they live in areas with high rates of delinquency, find companionship in settlement houses and similar institutions. They often find the middle-class models they need in the volunteers and pro-

fessional staff. Since these leaders are dedicated to the task of helping youth and often define help as movement into middle-class culture, they give youth the support they need to break away from the pull into lower-class culture or into delinquent groups. Schools may offer the upwardly aspiring youth the formal education they need; the settlement house offers out-of-school activities which fit them for middle-class participation; and the leaders provide friendly personal models.

Upwardly aspiring youth are not the only ones who come to settlement houses. Some studies show that some delinquent boys, especially overly active ones, join clubs, teams, and recreational groups in many kinds of organized agencies, including settlement houses. However, they are not always loyal or cooperative members.[1] They seemingly make

1 William Healy and Augusta F. Bronner, *New Light on Delinquency and Its Treatment,* Yale University Press, New Haven, Connecticut, 1936, pp. 71–72. Sheldon and Eleanor Glueck, *op. cit.,* p. 64.

use of facilities but do not identify with adult leaders. The middle-class leaders, helpful to upwardly mobile children, may lack understanding of delinquent children. Other delinquent children give settlement houses and other organized agencies a wide berth, scorning to participate in their programs. After a certain stage in delinquency-development has been reached, the programs of the agency lose their appeal and seem tame in contrast to the more exciting activities of stealing, joyriding, and fighting.

The discussion has been given from the point of view of the settlement house, one of the earliest types of community organization in deprived areas. Many similar institutions are called community centers. Community centers tend to differ from settlement houses in that they may be found in any type of area and may be completely operated and financed by the residents of the area. They are found in upper-middle-class suburbs as well as lower-class inner-city neighborhoods, where they usually receive outside support. The neighborhood houses sponsored by some churches, already discussed, have many of the same problems as settlement houses, which usually operate on a nonsectarian basis.

3. Youth organizations. Organizations whose programs are tailored to appeal only to youth take many forms. The boys' club may be locally autonomous with a building and staff of its own, although it may belong to a national federation. Such clubs usually are located in or near high-delinquency areas and regard their program of clubs and sports as generally delinquency preventive. Other youth organizations, such as the Boy and Girl Scouts, have narrowly defined programs; they are usually sponsored by a local group or organization which provides a meeting place. At one time many of these organizations termed themselves "character-building agencies," thus suggesting that they prevented delinquency; they have tended to redefine themselves in wider terms as group-work agencies, emphasizing that they work with groups for a wide variety of constructive objectives.

4. Supervised recreational projects. Recreation, defined as enjoyable pursuits carried out for their own sake, falls into several categories: commercial, where the participant or observer pays the operator for the privilege of attending; unsupervised, in which the person provides his own recreation; and supervised, in which adult leaders plan or help plan and oversee the recreation. With reference to delinquency, the tendency is to condemn the first two types and to laud the third. Closer examination, however, is needed, as any of the three may be constructive and any one may open the way for, or actively encourage, delinquency.

When commercial recreation is condemned in connection with delinquency, it is easy to overlook that the finest plays, motion pictures, and concerts are commercial recreation as well as the strip-tease exhibition, gangster film, and public dance hall, which serves as the prelude to prostitution.

Unsupervised play is not necessarily destructive; in fact, for most children it probably is constructive in that it gives scope for imaginative play and free experimentation not always found in supervised recreation. It is true, of course, that unsupervised play more than supervised play may lead to vandalism, minor stealing, and fighting. It is doubtful whether the motivation for delinquency arises from the lack of supervision so much as from unsatisfied needs and restlessness of the children.

Many supervised recreational projects have been established, taxes levied, money contributed, and tremendous effort expended by professional leaders and volunteers in the name of prevention of delinquency. It has been difficult to prove, however, that supervised recreation actually prevents delinquency in any widespread way. Recreation of course can be justified on other grounds—health, pleasurable use of leisure, development of leadership and of co-operation among children and between children and adults, and other such benefits none of which are necessarily preventive of delinquency.

Not many objective studies have been made to arrive at valid conclusions about supervised recreation as a preventive, nor do they always agree with each other. Mass recreation (in parks and playgrounds) and small groups or clubs are often combined in one study. Some of the results follow:

A Chicago study that combined parks, playgrounds, settlement houses, and church programs covered four slum and one middle-class areas. Children and youth aged ten to seventeen were divided into delinquents (both official and unofficial, that is, no police or court record) and nondelinquents. In each area a much higher percentage of nondelinquents than of delinquents used the recreational facilities. In slum areas, a higher proportion of delinquents participated than in the middle-class area. Nevertheless, the proportion of nondelinquents exceeded them. In the different areas, a third to two-thirds of the delinquents did not use the recreational facilities. Either the supervised recreation offered did not appeal to them, or they were already so incorporated into other activities that they felt no need for the supervised recreation.[1]

The delinquent boys who did attend spent more time in the facilities than did the nondelinquent boys. This suggests (although no evidence on this point is given) that the delinquent boys may have found little of interest in extracurricular activities at school or in recreational opportunities in their own homes. The study shows that they preferred types of recreation which were not closely supervised, such as game rooms where they could check out games to be used among themselves without an adult leader, or competitive sports. They were not attracted by clubs in which members and adult leader worked closely together. In other words, they fitted the recreational opportunities into their way of life but did not expose themselves unnecessarily to close relationships with supervising adults.

In all the Chicago areas studied, for all children, younger children participated in greater proportions than adolescents. This finding is supported by a Cincinnati study which showed that as boys approached adolescence they tended to drop out of organized groups. Boys brought before the juvenile court tended not to be affiliated with organized youth groups, although younger children from the same areas were affiliated.[2] Contrary evidence comes from a study of one specific boys' club in a deprived area in New York City. This club appealed more to adolescent boys than to younger ones and to delinquents than to nondelinquents. Delinquency continued during the time that the boys were actively engaged in club activities.[3]

These contradictory findings are no doubt related to the different programs in the agencies studied and to competing possibilities for activity in the neighborhoods.

Recreational programs absorb only a limited portion of the free time of children. The Chicago study revealed that the total number of hours per year spent in supervised recreation was only 43 to 87.5, or less than two hours per week. Almost twice as much time was spent seeing motion pictures. Nevertheless, delinquent acts occurred slightly less often among participants than among nonparticipants. It is not possible to determine whether the difference was the result of the supervised recreation or rested on initial choice of children in joining or shunning supervised recreation.

From general knowledge of how children's behavior is affected, it seems probable that the preventive and remedial results are greater for children in small groups or clubs than in mass recreation. The leader of a club of fifteen to twenty boys or girls has a closer relationship than does the supervisor of fifty or more boys and girls. Opportunity for identification of children with the leader is possible and the leader may know individually the needs of each child. Also, membership in the club with a name, symbol, and specific planning of programs increases the probability of continued attendance. However, if the child does not like or cannot identify with the leader, he or his entire club may more quickly fade away than in the mass program where contact with the leader is less close. If the child is a member of a street club, this group may exploit the opportunities for recreation in the mass program without yielding any of its integration as a group or giving up delinquent activities. Some community or youth organizations have experimented with drawing in an entire street club or gang and working with them as a group. Great patience and skill of leadership are required for successful conversion of the street club into a more conventional form.

5. Pros and cons of mass media. Included under mass media are motion pictures, radio and television broadcasts, and crime comics, all of which in turn have been condemned as delinquency producing. Most of the criticism has failed to note that many programs are

---

1 Ethel Shanas and Catherine E. Dunning, *Recreation and Delinquency,* Chicago Recreation Commission, Chicago, 1942.

2 Ellery F. Reed, "How Effective Are Group-Work Agencies in Preventing Delinquency?" *Focus,* 28 (November, 1949), 170–176.

3 Frederic M. Thrasher, "The Boys' Club and Juvenile Delinquency," *American Journal of Sociology,* 42 (1936), 66–80.

educational and cultural in nature; criticism should be directed toward programs that glamorize criminal or other undesirable behavior, or that show in detail the techniques of committing crimes.

A great deal of constructive learning goes on through the use of reading, pictures, motion pictures, and radio and television programs. When these means are used under controlled conditions in the classroom, they are dignified by the term audio-visual aids, and their effective use has become almost a science. Usually, students are prepared beforehand for the audio-visual material to be presented and afterward participate in a discussion based on it. The material thus is integrated into a general learning situation.

The commercially presented materials may or may not fall on fertile ground. The simple viewing of a crime motion picture or television show, or the reading of crime comics is not likely to create a juvenile delinquent. In the United States, adults and children alike have an intense interest in crime as drama and eagerly read, view, and listen

Many community and youth centers in deprived neighborhoods work with already formed street clubs and gangs as the natural unit. They offer sports, the center's insignia, and adult leadership as substitutes for street fights, gang insignia, and adolescent leadership often in conflict with conventional standards. This is one approach made by Our Lady's Youth Center, working with lower-class youth of Mexican descent in south El Paso. Begun by a parish priest, the Center expanded into a fully supported community project. Its first approach was to conforming children and youth; from this focus the work expanded to include and to specialize with delinquent gangs. In time it was necessary to try to meet the needs of a clientele consisting of about 35 to 40 per cent "good kids" without gang affiliations, 50 per cent "borderline kids" loosely affiliated with gangs, and 10 or 15 per cent troublesome hoodlums. For a penetrating analysis of the processes involved in working with this clientele, see Harold J. Rahm, S. J., and J. Robert Weber, *Office in the Alley, Report on a Project with Gang Youngsters,* Hogg Foundation for Mental Health, Austin, Texas, 1958. (Courtesy Our Lady's Youth Center, El Paso)

to criminal events as well as crime fiction. Nevertheless, most adults and children behave in a reasonably conforming manner. Certain conditions are necessary to create receptivity of the contents of crime stories and programs.

The degree to which the child is already oriented toward delinquency is important. An early study of crime motion pictures in which delinquents and nondelinquents were compared, showed that the viewing of crime motion pictures was widespread, but more frequently indulged in by delinquents than by nondelinquents. This study of motion pictures—the most complete study of the effect of crime audio-visual presentations made to date—did not indicate that motion pictures motivated the beginning of delinquent behavior. Among delinquents studied, only 10 per cent of males and 25 per cent of females seem to have been clearly affected in their delinquency by motion pictures.[1] The pictures that contributed to their delinquency covered a panorama of subjects, and, of course, were seen by thousands of others who did not become delinquent. The significant factor is not the motion picture (telecast, radio broadcast, crime comic) but the relation between the program content and the already developing interests and activities of the person. Previous interest in crime or delinquency makes the person receptive to stories of crime. Criminal attitudes are reinforced and specific techniques may be learned. The nondelinquent, however, has no occasion to use such techniques. With regard to a related area, illicit sexual relations, the motion picture study showed that boys often took girls to a sexually exciting motion picture as a preliminary to intercourse. However, inexperienced girls or ones not desiring to have intercourse were not receptive and resisted the boys' efforts.

Nondelinquent boys and girls who viewed crime motion pictures often interpreted them very differently than did the delinquents. They saw the successful criminals as objects of horror, not as successful men.

"Harmful" comic books and those of "questionable" content are more often read by delinquents than nondelinquents, according to a study comparing delinquents and nondelinquents matched for age, sex, school level, and socio-economic status.[2] Both groups read about the same number of "harmless" comic books. Actual relation to delinquent behavior was not probed by the study. Other studies have failed to find a relationship between comic book reading and delinquency or poor personal adjustment.[3]

Many of the stories presented through audio-visual means, however, may have a general effect on children's attitudes and beliefs through the repetitive impact of the same themes: police are brutal; physical strength is the means to gain an objective; wealth is a supreme goal; sex experience is a plaything to be seized at any time. However, these attitudes may be offset by other attitudes learned at home, or in school, church, or youth organization. Attitudes learned in these agencies through personal contact are likely to be more powerful than those learned through the impersonal means of motion picture, television, or comic book. However, if the child is associating with a delinquent gang, then the impersonal means of learning may reinforce the attitudes acquired through personal contacts.

Opposing the criticism and fear of crime programs and comics are those who regard them as ways to release dammed-up frustrations through vicarious aggressive behavior. Children often engage in imitative play based on telecasts or motion pictures or comic book stories, which may be a way to release emotions. This imitative play is not restricted to crime stories but may include romance, space travel, or any other theme that at the time meets the child's need. Harmless release depends upon the child's ability to distinguish between play and reality. The occasional incidents reported in the press of several children harming another child in imitation of a telecast usually relate to young children who are not fully aware of this dis-

1 Herbert Blumer and Philip M. Hauser, *Movies, Delinquency and Crime,* Macmillan Company, New York, 1933.

2 Thomas Ford Hoult, "Comic Books and Juvenile Delinquency," *Sociology and Social Research,* 33 (March, 1949), 279–284. The classification was made by Hoult.
3 Paul Witty, "Comics, Television, and Our Children," *Today's Health,* 33 (February, 1955), 18–21; Florence Heisler, "A Comparison between Those Elementary School Children Who Attend Moving Pictures, Read Comic Books and Listen to Serial Radio Programs to an Excess, with Those Who Indulge in These Activities Seldom or Not at All," *Journal of Educational Research,* 42 (September, 1948–May, 1949), 182–190; "Comic Books and Character," *School and Society,* 66 (1947), 439.

tinction. Adolescents who act in a similar manner almost invariably are already delinquent and would continue to be so even if they did not see or read crime stories.

Research to date has been too fragmentary and scattered to settle the heated controversy over the degree of harmfulness of crime stories, whether read, heard on radio, or seen in motion picture or on the television. The controversy is largely one of opinion. Nevertheless, it has led to attempts to control each type of presentation. Legal censorship prohibits certain types of stories. Groups of citizens, churches, and parents' and children's magazines often constitute screening agencies, recommending some programs and condemning others. The motion picture industry and the comic book industry have each established a system of self-censorship.

Each of the mass media may be and often is used constructively for delinquency prevention, for example, through documentary productions of the progress of drug addiction in youth, methods of social work with delinquent gangs, methods of rehabilitation used in correctional schools, and similar subjects. In some cities, the police department puts on television programs regarding their work with youth. Organized youth and recreational agencies present their work. Whether or not such programs influence youth depends upon their receptivity to them. No doubt the nondelinquent youth are more receptive to these constructive programs than are delinquent youth, just as the reverse is true for crime programs.

Indigenous community approaches

The programs described so far have all been brought into—in some cases imposed on—a neighborhood by outside groups or agencies. The organized agencies seek to pass on to a deprived area the values and ways of life of a better educated group from a higher socio-economic level. When they were initiated, many of the receiving neighborhoods were peopled with newly arrived immigrants who were helpless in solving their problems or even in securing their legal rights for opportunities and protection. In time, the nature of many of these communities changed and indigenous organizations grew whereby residents could handle many of their own problems. Some of the organizations were illegal in method—criminal rackets and syndicates—but brought financial gain to the operators and channeled potentially antisocial activity into a system. This organizing ability has now been directed by outside leaders against crime and delinquency.

Chicago Area Project. Widely known is the Chicago Area Project initiated by Clifford R. Shaw and his associates at the Institute for Juvenile Research, a state-supported child-guidance clinic. The first area project was begun in 1932. By 1959 projects had been established in twelve Chicago neighborhoods under a central civic board called the Chicago Area Project and in a number of other Illinois cities under the state Illinois Youth Commission.[1]

The philosophy of the Project reflects the sociological theory that a child's personality and satisfactions come from his personal or reference groups—the people among whom he lives most intimately and for whose good opinion he cares. If the companions with whom he associates are delinquent and find status and satisfaction in their roles, and if the adults are indifferent or themselves engaged in illegal activities, the child will accept delinquent behavior as the natural way to live. The basic idea of the Project is to mobilize the adults of a neighborhood to promote nondelinquent behavior and thus change the public opinion of the area from indifferent or prodelinquent to antidelinquent. When adults do not condone but disapprove delinquency, then, it is assumed, children and youth will respond to these new expectations and themselves disapprove of delinquency.

In order to implement these ideas, an employed staff member enters an area with high rates of delinquency; perhaps he has been reared or has had previous experience in a similar area. By slow, patient work he seeks out the conforming leaders of the area, and persuades them of the need for a strong local movement against delinquency. A local committee or council is then organized and helped to establish a program and to raise funds, supplemented as needed by the state or an outside source.

The facilities and programs seem to parallel

1 Solomon Kobrin, "The Chicago Area Project—A 25-Year Assessment," *Annals of the American Academy of Political and Social Science,* 322 (March, 1959), 19–29; Anthony Sorrentino, "The Chicago Area Project After Twenty-five Years," *Federal Probation,* 23 (June, 1959), 40–45.

those of settlement or neighborhood houses, with a club and recreational building and program, camping site, and money raising projects. They differ in significant ways. The controlling committee and most of the leaders working directly with youth are drawn from the community and represent run-of-the-mine residents, often working men or small business operators. The responsibility for the center and its activities thus is with the parents and relatives of the children involved. As a consequence of this policy, there are few professionally trained workers, guidance being provided by consultants or program directors provided by the Illinois Youth Commission. Ideally, in time, local leaders will secure needed training.

Special attention is given to delinquents and to boys and men released from correctional schools or penal institutions. Instead of rejecting them as outcasts, the local group accepts them and helps them to readjust on a new level. The staff begins where the children and youth are and does not impose standards which they cannot reach. There is not the gap between local staff and children that is often found in agencies with professionally trained workers from a more favored socio-economic background.

The Project and the local committees have faced many problems. This radical departure from the ever-increasing professionalization of social work has brought criticism and opposition from organized agencies dedicated to a professional approach. The area itself has often presented problems. Different political, nationality, and racial groups may characterize an area and be unable to work together collectively, or they compete for control of the local project. Mobility and the physical destruction of old organized neighborhoods by highways or slum clearance have also tended to destroy a unity that had been carefully fostered. Nevertheless, the work continues.

Few claims for widespread delinquency reduction have been made, although in some of the areas rates have declined. The Project staff and sponsors recognize, however, that rates may change for many reasons, as other agencies also change their approach or as population changes in character.

Individual delinquents have been rehabilitated and sometimes have become staunch supporters of the project. Unity of neighbor-

hoods has been accomplished and indigenous controls have been established. Co-operation among agencies working with children, delinquent or otherwise, has resulted. Children know better what is expected of them and find satisfactory ways to organize their lives.

Co-ordination of efforts

The various organizations discussed operate independently of one another. Each has its own controlling board or agency, sets its own budget, formulates its own policies, and establishes its own program. Different values may be found and certainly different techniques. Sometimes agencies in one area compete for children or funds or oppose each other.

Various ways have been developed to achieve some degree of co-ordination and to avoid duplication of effort. The principal methods of co-ordination are as follows:

1. Community Chest or Community Fund, a joint money-raising organization for a number of welfare agencies. The agencies voluntarily agree not to raise money independently without approval of the Fund. They submit their budgets to the Community Fund, which sets up a committee of laymen to review all budgets and modify them if it seems wise. The agencies then share in the money raised in proportion to their budgets. Through the budget review and possibility of modification the Fund maintains a certain degree of balance among the agencies.

2. Council of Social Agencies or Community Welfare Council, composed of representatives of all social agencies working with problems of health, family and child welfare, and recreation and meeting standards set by the Council. This is an organization of organizations, whose representatives seek to understand each other's problems, avoid duplication of effort, co-ordinate their work, develop public understanding, and act jointly on community problems.

3. Co-ordinating Council of citizens and representatives of social agencies represents a wider spread of interests than the Council of Social Agencies and usually focuses on some specific problem, often delinquency. It attempts to bring all appropriate agencies in the city to bear on this problem. It may develop new services.

4. Social Service Exchange, lists the names of all clients of agencies and records which

agencies have served each person. Duplication of similar services by agencies dealing with one case may be avoided and co-operation of dissimilar agencies working with a multiproblem family may be achieved through the Exchange.

Through these and similar types of coordination, agencies may come to understand each other's philosophy and methods and the probability of co-operation may be increased. The combined efforts of a number of citizens or agencies may result in the establishment of a new agency (for instance, a mental health clinic) in a city or in needed expansion of services into some newly settled area in need of specific help.

Bibliography

General

Kvaraceus, William C., *The Community and the Delinquent,* World Book Company, Yonkers-on-Hudson, New York, 1954.

Witmer, Helen L., editor, "Prevention of Juvenile Delinquency," *Annals of the American Academy of Political and Social Science,* 322 (1959), entire issue.

—— and Edith Tufts, *The Effectiveness of Delinquency Prevention Programs,* Children's Bureau Publication No. 350, U. S. Government Printing Office, Washington, D. C., 1954.

"Housing and Community Development," *Marriage and Family Living,* 17 (1955), entire issue; see especially articles by Catherine Bauer, H. Warren Dunham and Nathan D. Grundstein, Astrid Monson, and Daniel J. Ransohoff.

Salisbury, Harrison E., *The Shook-up Generation,* Fawcett Publications, Inc., Greenwich, Connecticut, 1959, Chapter 5, "The New Ghettos."

Institutional and foster homes

Palmieri, Henry J., "Private Institutions," *National Probation and Parole Association Journal,* 4 (1958), 51–56.

Kellar, Gladys I., "Court Foster Home Program," *National Probation and Parole Association Journal,* 4 (1958), 57–65.

Stroup, Herbert H., *Social Work, an Introduction to the Field,* American Book Company, New York, 1960, Chapter 4, "Children in Institutions," and Chapter 5, "Children in Foster Homes."

Religious organizations

Dominic, S. M., "Religion and the Juvenile Delinquent," *American Catholic Sociological Review,* 15 (1954), 256–264.

Kincheloe, Samuel C., *The American City and Its Church,* Friendship Press, New York, 1938.

Lee, Robert, "The Church and the Problem of Delinquency," *Religious Education,* 52 (1957), 125–129.

McCann, Richard V., "Juvenile Delinquency and the Church's Opportunity," *Religious Education,* 50 (1955), 88–92.

——, "The Self-Image and Delinquency: Some Implications for Religion," *Federal Probation,* 20 (September, 1956), 14–23.

Moore, Paul, Jr., "Religion's Role in Preventing and Treating Crime and Delinquency," *Crime and Delinquency,* 6 (1960), 376–379.

Rahm, Harold J., S.J., and Weber, J. Robert, *Office in the Alley, Report on a Project with Gang Youngsters,* Hogg Foundation for Mental Health, Austin, Texas, 1958.

Robert, Guy L., *How the Church Can Help Where Delinquency Begins,* John Knox Press, Richmond, Virginia, 1958.

Webb, Robert and Muriel, *The Churches and Juvenile Delinquency,* Association Press, New York, 1957.

——, "How the Churches Can Help in the Prevention and Treatment of Juvenile Delinquency," *Federal Probation,* 21 (December, 1957), 22–25.

Settlement houses

Addams, Jane, *Spirit of Youth and the City Streets,* Macmillan Company, New York, 1909.

——, *Twenty Years at Hull House,* Macmillan Company, New York, 1910.

Recreation

Brown, Roscoe C., Jr., and Dan W. Dodson, "The Effectiveness of a Boys' Club in Reducing Delinquency," *Annals of the American Academy of Political and Social Science,* 322 (1949), 47–52.

Reed, Ellery F., "How Effective Are Group-Work Agencies in Preventing Delinquency?" *Focus,* 28 (1949), 170–176.

Shanas, Ethel, and Catherine E. Dunning, *Recreation and Delinquency,* Chicago Recreation Commission, Chicago, Illinois, 1942.

Thrasher, Frederic M., "The Boys' Club and Juvenile Delinquency," *American Journal of Sociology,* 42 (1936), 66–80.

Audio-visual sources of recreation

Blumer, Herbert, and Philip M. Hauser, *Movies,*

Delinquency, and Crime, Macmillan Company, New York, 1933.

Cavanaugh, John R., "The Comics War," *Journal of Criminal Law and Criminology,* 40 (May, 1949), 28–35.

Committee on the Judiciary, U. S. Senate, 83rd Congress, Subcommittee to Investigate Juvenile Delinquency, *Juvenile Delinquency (Comic Books),* U. S. Government Printing Office, Washington, D. C., 1954.

Murphy, Charles F., "A Seal of Approval for Comic Books," *Federal Probation,* 19 (June, 1955), 19–20.

Roucek, Joseph S., editor, *Juvenile Delinquency, Philosophical Library,* New York, 1958, Chapter 10, "Mass Media and Juvenile Delinquency."

Wertham, Fredric, *Seduction of the Innocent,* Rinehart and Company, New York, 1953.

Witty, Paul, "Comics, Television, and Our Children," *Today's Health,* 33 (February, 1955), 18–21.

Chicago area project

Bright Shadows in Bronzetown, South Side Community Committee, available through the Chicago Area Project, 160 N. LaSalle Street, Chicago.

Burgess, E. W., J. D. Lohman, and C. R. Shaw, "The Chicago Area Project," *Coping with Crime,* National Probation Association Yearbook, 1937, pp. 8–28.

Hopper, Edward P., "Putting Neighborhoods on Probation," *Federal Probation,* 19 (September, 1955), 38–43.

Kobrin, Solomon, "The Chicago Area Project— A 25-Year Assessment," *Annals of the American Academy of Political and Social Science,* 322 (1959), 19–29.

Sorrentino, Anthony, "The Chicago Area Project after Twenty-five Years," *Federal Probation,* 23 (June, 1959), 40–45.

Community organization and co-ordination

Friedlander, Walter A., *Introduction to Social Welfare,* Prentice-Hall, Inc., New York, 1955.

Hillman, Arthur, *Community Organization and Planning,* Macmillan Company, New York, 1950.

Stroup, Herbert H., *Community Welfare Organization,* Harper & Brothers, New York, 1952.

Churches, settlement houses, community centers, recreational units, and other socializing institutions have diverse and unspecialized programs, aimed at attracting and benefiting all classes of children and youth. Another category of agencies is therapeutic in nature, that is, remedial or curative. These agencies work directly with individuals whose behavior is in some way disturbing or who are delinquent. The philosophy that underlies the therapeutic treatment is that the basic cause of misbehavior lies within the personality of the individual. Delinquency and other nonnormal behavior is regarded as a symptom of the underlying maladjustment. If the maladjustment can be eliminated, the individual will feel no further need to express himself in delinquency, which then will fade away. This type of diagnosis and treatment is in the hands of psychiatrists, clinical psychologists, and psychiatric social workers.

Other agencies, stemming from group work and recreational units, make a direct approach to delinquent groups, seeking to change the attitudes and redirect the activities of the group as a social unit.

Both the individual or casework approach and the group approach to delinquency-prone children and youth are discussed in this chapter.

Discovery of delinquency-prone children

Any treatment directed at specific delinquency-prone children depends upon discovery of the children who, although not yet known to be delinquent, may become so in the future. At present, selection of such children usually rests on observed continuous misconduct of a minor nature or on recommendations of teachers, parents, and others in a position of responsibility for the children's conduct. The need to select at an early stage of development has generated interest in the possibility of constructing prediction devices which will pinpoint specific children who are not yet in serious misbehavior but who probably will become so by the time adolescence is reached. If they could be located, remedial treatment might forestall the development of delinquency. Predicting or forecasting is carried out successfully in many areas, especially biological or physical. Forecasting human behavior is extremely difficult since many factors are involved, physical, so-

Chapter **17**

Treatment of delinquency-prone individuals and groups

cial, and cultural. Nevertheless, attempts are constantly being made to predict at a young age whether or not children will later become delinquent.

Construction of a delinquency-prediction scale. In general, prediction rests on the assumption that a combination of factors that has been found associated with a certain outcome in the past will, in the future, have the same association. In the case of delinquency, work begins with a known group of delinquents and a group of nondelinquents, usually matched by age and sex. The two groups are compared on items that the researcher has reason to believe might differentiate the two groups. These items are selected from prior research, clinical experience, social work records, and the like. Firsthand investigation by interviews or by paper and pencil inventories is then made of the two groups to determine the percentage of each group that is characterized by each item. Any item that is found among approximately the same percentage of delinquents and nondelinquents is discarded, since it does not differentiate between the two groups. When the difference in frequency of any item is found to be sufficiently great (by statistical techniques) to represent a real difference and not a chance one, that item is retained. The differentiating items are formed into an inventory, check list, or scale. Each item is given a score, related to the greater frequency with which the item is found among delinquents as opposed to nondelinquents. The partial scores are added to give a total score for each child. These scores may then be ranked from low to high and arranged into a table to show what percentage of children in each range of scores has been delinquent and what percentage nondelinquent. This table based on known cases of delinquent and nondelinquent children must be validated by using the inventory, check list, or scale on another group of children to discover whether the same results are obtained. This step precludes the possibility that some chance factor might have caused the association of items with delinquency in the original group.

Delinquency prediction devices are worked out on known delinquents and nondelinquents, usually in adolescence when delinquent behavior is well established. For predictive purposes, however, the device must be given at a much younger age, before delinquent behavior has developed. For final validation of the device, therefore, it must be administered to young nondelinquent children and a score assigned to each child. Some scores will be those made by older delinquents, some those made by older nondelinquents, thus seeming to predict future delinquency or future nondelinquency. It is necessary, however, to wait until the children reach later adolescence to determine whether the device really did predict delinquent behavior accurately. If the prediction is validated, a probability table can be constructed based on the percentage of children with each range of scores who have become delinquent. The score of any nondelinquent child can then be compared with the table to determine the chances out of a hundred that he will later become delinquent.

A probability table of this type cannot be used to predict an absolute outcome for any individual child except perhaps for extremely high and low scores. In an unselected group of children (for instance, a grade school class), most children will have scores in the middle of the range from low to high. These scores are least predictive; for example, the original research may have shown that of children with these moderate scores 40 per cent were delinquent and 60 per cent nondelinquent. With a newly tested group of young children there is no way to determine whether a specific child with a moderate score will in the future be delinquent or nondelinquent. It is possible only to say that the child has forty chances out of a hundred to become delinquent and sixty chances to remain nondelinquent.

In addition to the practical problems of time and expense involved in setting up and validating a prediction device for delinquency, there are a number of theoretical problems. Delinquency is not a homogenous activity. Can one prediction scale be valid for predicting such diverse delinquencies as murder, larceny, chronic truancy, or sexual misconduct? The word delinquency is used to mean anything from casual, intermittent acts to the central organizing factor in the delinquent's way of life: can one prediction device be valid for the entire range? How many of the numerous items known to be associated with delinquency must be included in the device to make it a dependable instrument? Within the range of scores in which children may be predicted as either future delinquents or nondelinquents in almost equal proportions, how can the truly delinquency-prone be selected?

Prediction among young children. Experience of child-guidance clinics working with individual children has shown that the probability of success in remedial work is much greater among children whose maladjustment is in the beginning stage than among those with deeply imbedded problems. Often this means beginning to treat young children rather than adolescents who have been building up maladjustment over ten or more years of time. But prediction of delinquency at a young age for purposes of treatment poses its own special problems.

Prediction for very young children is based on the theory that personality is set in the family in preschool years and that delinquency grows out of poor personality adjustment. Later social experiences are assumed to be of minor importance, since they do not make themselves felt during early childhood. Therefore, a device that attempts to predict on the basis of family alone omits the influences of peer groups, institutions, and community culture which many studies have shown to be significant in the development of delinquent behavior.

Practical problems also beset the attempt to predict at a young age. All children in a given area or of a given age would have to be included in the prediction. This inclusive approach would necessitate house to house canvassing for preschool children or waiting until children enter school. During the first few years of school, it would be difficult for children to report objectively on their families or to fill out answers on the paper and pencil check lists and scales which may be used among older children. For young children, long hours of observation, play techniques, or interviews with parents would be needed. Gaining rapport with child or parents usually would require several meetings. Parents who are suspicious or who do not understand the importance of the study might resist the investigation. Skilled investigators would be needed. The more laborious and expensive an investigation becomes the less likely it is to be used in any widespread manner.

With older children, information may be gathered directly from the children. However, the number of items to be covered increases as the child's experience outside the home widens. The increase in the task of scoring because of added items may be offset by the increased validity given by the added factors upon which prediction is based. Also, with each advance in age, some loss occurs in a preventive program, since some children will already have become delinquent.

Reports often appear in print of limited investigations that show the association between personal or social items and delinquency and suggest the possibility of a prediction instrument. Few go beyond this stage in order to validate the instrument. Three research projects are discussed that have been in process, independently of each other, for a number of years. All are still in the process of validation; none has been put to practical use as of 1960.

The Glueck Prediction Tables. From the great number of comparisons in *Unraveling Juvenile Delinquency* the Gluecks selected three sets of related items that seemed feasible for the basis of three scales to predict future delinquency among currently nondelinquent children. Only one of the scales has been subjected to continued research.

1. Glueck Social Prediction Table. This table is composed of five family relationships, each of which was found to differentiate markedly between the correctional school and the nondelinquent control group of boys whom they studied. The accumulation of several or of all five unfavorable relationships in the experience of some boys was very highly

Table 24

Glueck Social Prediction Table

Social Factors	Weighted score
1. Discipline of boy by father	
Overstrict or erratic	72.5
Lax	59.8
Firm but kindly	9.3
2. Supervision of boy by mother	
Unsuitable	83.2
Fair	57.5
Suitable	9.9
3. Affection of father for son	
Indifferent or hostile	75.9
Warm (including over-protective)	33.8
4. Affection of mother for boy	
Indifferent or hostile	86.2
Warm (including over-protective)	43.1
5. Cohesiveness of family	
Unintegrated	96.9
Some elements of cohesion	61.3
Cohesive	20.6

Sheldon and Eleanor T. Glueck, "Early Detection of Future Delinquents," *Journal of Criminal Law, Criminology and Police Science,* Northwestern University School of Law, 47 (1956), 175. The weighted score is the percentage of the total of delinquent and nondelinquent boys in each subcategory who were delinquent.

associated with delinquency while the accumulation of favorable aspects was very highly associated with nondelinquency. Each item was assigned scores in proportion to the frequency with which it was found in the delinquent group. Table 24 gives the five relationships, the types, and the weights. Theoretically the scores could run from a low (nondelinquent) score of 116.7 to a high (delinquent) score of 414.7. Table 25 shows the actual distribution of scores for the original delinquent and nondelinquent groups upon whom the table was established. Both delinquents and nondelinquents run the limit from high to low, but with decided bulking of the two groups at opposite ends of the range of scores. The middle scores (200 to 299) are the least predictive, but include approximately a third of each group. If the scale were given to young children, with the idea of selecting potential delinquents for special preventive treatment, children with scores in this middle range could not be placed with any confidence in either the potentially delinquent or the potentially nondelinquent classification. As was pointed out earlier, this difficulty is not a characteristic only of the Glueck scale, but is typical of prediction scales in general.

Table 25

Percentage of Delinquents and Nondelinquents in Each of Seven Weighted Score Classes Based on Five Factors of Social Background (Glueck Scale)

Weighted score class	Delinquents No.	per cent	Nondelinquents No.	per cent	Total
Under 150......	5	2.9	167	97.1	172
150–199........	19	15.7	102	84.3	121
200–249........	40	37.0	68	63.0	108
250–299........	122	63.5	70	36.5	192
300–349........	141	86.0	23	14.0	164
350–399........	73	90.1	8	9.9	81
400 and over...	51	98.1	1	1.9	52
Total cases......	451		439		890

Sheldon and Eleanor Glueck, "Early Detection of Future Delinquents," *Journal of Criminal Law, Criminology and Police Science,* Northwestern University School of Law, 47 (1956), p. 178.

The Gluecks have proposed the use of this scale when children first enter school at age six. If children could be identified at this early age as potential delinquents, they might receive special treatment and thus become adjusted and delinquency averted. One of the difficulties has just been pointed out—the nonpredictability of the scores except at the extremes. Another question is whether the scale, based upon adolescent boys, is applicable to six-year-old children. Still another is whether so much reliance can be placed on family background—important though it is— with complete disregard for peer group and criminal influences in the community.

A test of the scale is underway which should answer some of these questions. In 1952–1953 pertinent information was gathered from the parents of all boys in the first grades of two public schools in a deprived area of New York City, and scores were computed for each boy. From time to time, investigation is made of the behavior records of the boys. The study is being carried out by the New York City Youth Board, with the guidance of the Gluecks. Interpretation of results to date are a matter of extreme controversy between the Youth Board and the Gluecks on the one hand and a number of critics on the other. It is agreed by all that the final interpretation will not come until about 1962 to 1964 when the boys are sixteen to eighteen years old and nearing the end of the juvenile delinquency period.[1]

1 *Delinquency Prediction, A Progress Report, 1952– 1956, An Experiment in Validation of the Gluecks' Prediction Scale,* New York City Youth Board, New

2. Other Glueck scales to predict delinquency. The Gluecks have also taken the initial steps toward construction of a predictive scale based on five traits of character structure derived from the Rorschach Test, and of still another scale based on five traits of temperament drawn from the psychiatric interviews.[2] The use of two or three of these scales increased the differentiation between the delinquent and nondelinquent boys in the original groups, but not to the point where the Gluecks felt that the Social Prediction Scale alone was not adequate to identify potential delinquents. The Rorschach test and psychiatric interviews would create tremendous practical problems in locating adequately trained specialists who would have time for extensive testing and interviewing and in financing such a program once the tests moved out of the experimental stage into the area of practical use. The Social Prediction Scale itself presents certain problems since the data for classifying the children must be collected through home interviews by trained social investigators.

The Kvaraceus Delinquency Scale. Called the KD Delinquency Proneness Scale and Check List, this device consists of seventy-five multiple choice items for children to check and a list of seventy items to be checked by someone other than the child, usually a teacher. The items cover personal, environmental (home and family) and school factors.[3]

Examples of the multiple choice items in the Proneness Scale follow:

Parents usually understand their children: very well; quite well; not very well; not at all.

Failure in school is usually due to: bad company; lack of ability; lack of hard work; unfriendly teachers.

All items included in the Scale differentiate between known delinquents and nondelinquents. Each answer has been given a score

York City, 1957; Sheldon and Eleanor Glueck, *Predicting Delinquency and Crime,* Harvard University Press, Cambridge, Massachusetts, 1959, pp. 133–136. For references to the controversy, see the following authors in the bibliography for this chapter: Burgess, Herzog, Keniston, Reiss, and Rubin.

2 Glueck, *op. cit.,* pp. 236–240; Sheldon and Eleanor Glueck, "Early Detection of Future Delinquents," *Journal of Criminal Law, Criminology and Police Science,* 47 (1956), 174–182.

3 W. C. Kvaraceus, *The Community and the Delinquent,* World Book Company, Yonkers-on-Hudson, New York, 1954, pp. 139–154; W. C. Kvaraceus, "Forecasting Juvenile Delinquency," *Journal of Education,* 138 (April, 1956), 1–43.

and the addition of the scores provides a total score for each child filling out the Scale.

The Scale has made a rather wide appeal to researchers and a number of studies have been carried out independently comparing various categories of delinquents (official, unofficial, misbehaving) and of nondelinquents (typical school children, "high morale" children, different age groups, and so on). The Check List has not been submitted to the same type of research.

The many test items of the Scale indicate that it differentiates delinquents from nondelinquents to some extent, that is, the mean (average) scores for the groups differ significantly. However, there is a great amount of overlap in scores among the different groups; if the Scale were given to children whose record of delinquency or nondelinquency was not already known, it would not be possible to identify the present or future delinquents with any degree of assurance. Children with extremely high (delinquent) or extremely low (nondelinquent) scores might be selected with some certainty as to their future behavior, but the behavior of children with middle scores would not be predictable; they might or might not turn out to be delinquents.

The final test of the validity or predictability of the Scale has not yet been made— the application of the scale to children below the age of delinquency followed by a record of their experience in delinquency by the time they reach age eighteen. The author of the scale, Kvaraceus, questions whether complete predictability can be obtained by prediction tests but believes that groups of children can be identified who need some type of help.

Minnesota Multiphasic Personality Inventory (MMPI). This inventory of 550 statements covers neurotic and psychotic factors as observed in maladjusted adults and also indicators of psychopathic and paranoid behavior. It was standardized on adults and only later was tried in experimental fashion with junior and senior high school students. It is not usable with young children since the person filling out the inventory must be able to read and understand the many statements. Also, it was not originally intended as an indicator of delinquency or crime, but as an indicator of personality disorders. Its relation to delinquency, therefore, comes about through the relation of delinquency to personality dis-

orders. This relation is not of a type to link juvenile delinquents to any specific pattern of adult mental illness.[1]

After it was determined that delinquent and nondelinquent boys differed with reference to certain traits, a test of predictive value was made. An unselected sample of ninth grade boys with a modal age of fifteen was tested with the inventory. Boys who had records as delinquents in the police department, juvenile courts, or private agencies were excluded. Two years and four years later, the nondelinquent boys were again checked for delinquent behavior, when the modal age of the group was seventeen and nineteen years. The delinquent boys were then compared with the nondelinquent on their original inventory traits, to determine the degree to which the original findings would have predicted later delinquency.

On four traits, the nondelinquents and delinquents were almost identical in the number of boys in each group who had one of the traits as the highest point of their personality profile, and it is therefore assumed that these characteristics are not related to delinquency:

Hypochondriasis, or abnormal concern about bodily functions.

Hysteria, or solving of problems by physical symptoms or immaturity.

Paranoia, or suspiciousness, oversensitivity in social situations, rigidity of personality.

Psychasthenia, or fears, inferiority feelings, compulsive behavior, indecisiveness.

Three traits were found to be inhibitory, that is, a lower percentage of delinquents than of nondelinquents exhibited these traits. Their presence in the personality tends to lower the delinquency rate. These traits are:

Social introversion, or social withdrawal.

Depression and unhappiness.

Tendency toward feminine interests on the part of males.

Three traits were excitatory, that is, a higher percentage of delinquent than of nondelinquent boys had these traits, which follow:

Psychopathic deviation, or absence of deep emotional response, inability to profit from

---

1 Starke R. Hathaway and Elio Monachesi, *Analyzing and Predicting Juvenile Delinquency with the MMPI*, University of Minnesota Press, Minneapolis, Minnesota, 1953; Hathaway and Monachesi, "The Personalities of Predelinquent Boys," *Journal of Criminal Law, Criminology and Police Science*, 48 (1957), 148–163.

social training, disregard of social mores.

Schizophrenia, or bizarre thoughts or behavior, failure to be or feel in good social contact.

Hypomania, or overproductivity in thought, overactivity, transient enthusiasms, expansive.

It was further discovered that boys who were unable to fill out the inventory had 36 per cent who were delinquent, most of them seriously so. The failure to fill out the inventory might have been due to inability to read the inventory, carelessness in answering, or emotional disturbance.

The differences in percentages between delinquents and nondelinquents is moderate, even for the characteristics that are most differentiating. At best they indicate a tendency or proneness toward delinquency which perhaps comes to actual overt delinquency only under certain social conditions. The Inventory indicated that other boys had deviant traits that did not find expression in delinquency but which indicated that they needed some help in making better adjustments.

The authors have selected thirty-three items from the 550 in the complete Inventory that are the most highly differentiating between delinquents and nondelinquents. They are not, however, formed into a scale for practical use.

Work continues with the MMPI in the attempt to select individual items that might predict delinquency.[1]

Comment on prediction attempts. The three prediction instruments described take very different approaches. The Gluecks depend entirely upon family relationships as predictive factors; Kvaraceus brings in a wider range of influences—personal factors, family, and school; Hathaway and Monachesi deal with personality traits, resembling major types of maladjustment. The original tables set up in the three studies in which delinquent children are compared with nondelinquent, are arranged to isolate items that distinguish delinquents from nondelinquents as groups. The items can be formed into a scale and the scale scored. In each type of scale, however, there is a wide overlap of scores between delinquents and nondelinquents, which reduces

the practical usefulness of the scales. The final validity of the scales in prediction comes only when a scale is given to children at a fairly young age who do not have a record of delinquency. These children must then be examined for subsequent delinquency at the end of the adolescent period. When the early scale scores of the delinquents and nondelinquents are compared, are they sufficiently different to have made it possible to separate the children into potential delinquents and potential nondelinquents at the time of the early testing? Such experiments are in process and the final outcome is not known. It seems probable however from reports so far published, that prediction will be reliable only for children with scores at the extremes of a given scale and that most children will fall into intermediate score groups for whom positive prediction cannot be made.

In the meantime, in an effort to identify children in need of help, many children who show early and sometimes serious tendencies toward misconduct are singled out on a common sense basis for specific treatment and re-education.

Treatment of individual delinquents

Treatment of individual children with conduct disturbances is carried on by psychiatrists, clinical psychologists, and psychiatric social workers. These specialists may have a private practice and charge a fee to the client. Since fees tend to be high, only families with ample incomes can afford to have their children treated by a specialist in private practice. Treatment is also offered through child-guidance clinics, agencies organized on a service basis with a controlling board of directors and an employed staff of specialists. Such clinics are usually publicly supported through taxation or subsidized by the local community fund or other philanthropic funds. When fees are charged, they are small and adjusted to the ability of the client to pay.

The first child-guidance clinic in the United States was opened in Chicago in 1909, the funds being provided by a local philanthropist. First called the Juvenile Psychopathic Institute, in 1917 it became the state-supported Institute for Juvenile Research. Its director, William I. Healy, spearheaded the movement for case studies of individual delinquent children.

In the fifties there were approximately 650

1 Clara Kanun and Elio D. Monachesi, "Delinquency and the Validating Scales of the Minnesota Multiphasic Personality Inventory," *Journal of Criminal Law, Criminology and Police Science,* 50 (1960), 525–534.

psychiatric clinics in the United States, providing child guidance, with about 400 operating on a full-time basis. Most of the clinics are in the larger cities; many small cities and rural areas are without access to such clinics.

Underlying philosophy. Psychiatrists do not agree as to the basic causes of misbehavior or other nonnormal behavior in children. Some tend to attribute it to inborn causes, others to failure of the parents to instill a sense of security in the child at an early age, and others to failure of family and other social groups to help the child inhibit or find approved expressions for the inborn savage impulses which are assumed to motivate a child's behavior.

Regardless of the specific philosophy, child-guidance clinics to not limit themselves to the treatment of delinquents. They are interested in helping children with any kind of emotional or behavioral disturbance. Whatever the outward show of disturbance—withdrawal, compulsions, aggressiveness, defiance of authority—it is assumed to be only a symptom of underlying maladjustment of the child. The specialists seek to diagnose the basic difficulty and relieve it. If the basic readjustment can be made, the child's outward behavior will lose its peculiarities and the child will be better able to accept the demands of society and to find approved ways of meeting his inner needs. With this philosophy, clinics do not seek a group or community approach to preventing delinquency, but an individual-by-individual approach.

Since many psychiatrists and clinical psychologists view the mother as the most influential person in the child's early satisfaction of needs, they are gradually moving away from treating only the child to treating the child and his mother. But even this has been found to be too narrow, since the most significant person in the family may not be the mother, but the father, an uncle, or a grandmother. Often the entire family is involved in strained relationships, the root cause of an especially disturbed child. The close relationship of family to delinquent behavior is shown in the statement that 75 per cent of the delinquents in New York City come from 1 per cent of the families.[1] It might be added that these families are concentrated in certain areas where delinquency rates are very high, with social disorganization, adult criminal activities, and demoralizing behavior very common. Gradually the child-guidance specialists are gaining an awareness that the community as well as the family in which the child lives is responsible for the specific attitudes and activities that the child develops. The child can define what his needs are and work out his satisfactions only in the social world in which he finds himself. This theory differs from a commonly held sociological theory that in some areas delinquency is learned as games or sports are, because it is part of the common culture. The psychiatrist places the origin within the child but grants that inner tensions may find an expression in types of delinquency that are part of a community pattern. If each individual is readjusted, it is assumed that each will be able to cope with his environment.

Selection of clients. Clinics usually use an element of selectivity in accepting children for treatment. Some clinics have learned by experience that they can give little help to children with certain extreme personality maladjustments. One such type is the extremely egocentric maladjusted child who is not responsive to the opinions or overtures of other people. Children with less severe maladjustments, neuroses, and even near psychoses have been helped.[2] Many clinics further limit their clients to children whose parents are able to concede a relationship between the family and the child's delinquency and, therefore, are willing to accept therapy for themselves. Clinicians who feel that the basic difficulty lies in the parent-child relationship think that little can be done to help the child without help to the parents also.

Group therapy with delinquents

Group therapy is not, as its name might imply, an attempt to prevent or control delinquency through working with naturally formed delinquent groups. It is a type of individual therapy in which clients of a psychiatric clinic are artificially grouped together in a balanced combination of types under a leader familiar with the theories of psychiatry

1 *New Directions in Delinquency Prevention, 1947–1957,* New York City Youth Board, New York, undated, p. 10.

2 Helen L. Witmer and Edith Tufts, *The Effectiveness of Delinquency Prevention Programs,* Children's Bureau Publication No. 350–1954, U. S. Government Printing Office, 1954, pp. 39–40, referring to studies made in the 1940's at the Judge Baker Guidance Center, Boston.

and skilled in the techniques of group therapy. Group therapy had its origin much later than therapy with single individuals. Its use with children was developed by S. R. Slavson during the thirties and was eagerly seized upon by many agencies as a hopeful new approach to curbing delinquent behavior. The procedure has been used in a variety of situations, with both adults and children: in clinics, mental hospitals, veteran's hospitals, prisons, correctional schools, and with probationers and clinic cases. When children are members of a therapy group, their mothers may be gathered into a separate therapy group.

Formation of groups. Group therapy is often used as a last resort in treatment of delinquency-prone children, after individual therapy has been carried on for a year or more without beneficial results. Typically, a child-guidance clinic will sort out such children and form them into small groups of eight or ten children each. Except among very young children, boys and girls are separated. Children's case histories are carefully reviewed by a staff committee before the therapy group is formed. Children having different problems are included in one group, but not in hit-or-miss fashion. If a number of the children are shy, a moderately (but not extremely) aggressive member or two may be added; or in a group of aggressive children will be placed some who are conforming in behavior. Group therapy has been found not suitable for the severely neurotic child nor for extremely aggressive psychopathic children or psychotics, who would become violent in behavior in the permissive atmosphere that characterizes group therapy. The children meet at a regular time and place usually once a week, with a specially trained leader.

Objective and method. The objective is not to weld the children into a permanent group nor to encourage them to meet outside the appointed time and place. The leader is fully as concerned with the therapy of each individual boy as was the psychiatrist or social worker whose treatment often precedes the entrance of the child into group therapy. The group situation has advantages over individual casework for certain children. In successful casework, the child must achieve a personal relationship with the caseworker, marked by trust, confidence, and respect. Some children cannot do this because of the nature of their problem; for example, the

basic problem may be distrust and fear of an authoritative parent, and the child associates all adults in a position of leadership, such as the teacher or case worker, with that parent. Or the child may be so aggressive that he cannot conform to the expectations of an office interview. In the therapy group, the child may ignore the leader for many meetings. In a group, his reticence is less noticeable and he feels less conspicuous than when confined in an interview with the case worker.

Among children his own age, with problems similar to or different from his own, the child begins to realize that he is not the only child with problems. The atmosphere of the group is permissive since there is no set program to be carried out (as in normal organized groups or clubs). He is thus relieved from a feeling of pressure to accomplish something at a time when he is inhibited by his emotional problems. He also can express his feelings freely, short of injury to himself or others. Therapy usually must continue for many months. Gradually, the child loses some of his fear of the leader, his timidity with other children, or conversely, his aggressiveness toward equipment, children, and leader. Often individual therapy is carried on simultaneously with both the child and his mother.

With young children, the room provided for the meeting usually is equipped with sturdy toys, games, and simple tools. With older children and adolescents, therapy goes on primarily through free discussion in which the leader plays a minimum role and offers no reprimand regardless of what is said. The members slowly begin to express verbally their resentments, to compare experiences, and to develop an interactive therapy in criticizing each other and in offering suggestions as to how one individual may handle a specific problem. Gradually, the leader is admitted to the discussion and may judiciously guide or help the youths to round out their discussions of their own problems.

The leader usually has training as a psychiatric social worker. He must be aware of each child's difficulties and note carefully the changes which occur. These are recorded in notes after the meeting. His attitude during the sessions is passive and neutral. He does not permit himself to be used by the children. The child who has found he had to comply explicitly at home in order to get along with his parents soon finds that he is always treated in friendly fashion by the leader, whether or not he is docile and obedient. The child who feels he must do favors for adults is not encouraged along this line, but is told he may do some special thing if he wishes. Thus the leader is warm and friendly but does not cater to the children's needs or to his own through the children.

Benefits of group therapy. The benefits of group therapy (not confined to therapy with delinquents) as reported in 300 articles yields the following list of nine most often reported mechanisms that take place: [1]

1. Acceptance by the group: the member acquires a warm comfortable feeling toward other members.

2. Altruism: in time the members wish to do something for others.

3. Universalization: the member realizes that he is not alone in his problems.

4. Intellectualization: he gains insight through acquiring knowledge in the group.

5. Reality testing: the group situation is permissive and nonthreatening; the member may try out expression of attitudes or behavior without fear of reprisals.

6. Transference: the member achieves a strong emotional attachment to the leader, to separate members of the group, or to the group as a whole. Eventually, in the course of therapy he will free himself of this dependence.

7. Interaction of whatever type seems to be beneficial.

8. Spectator therapy: each member gains in some way from listening to and observing himself and others.

9. Ventilation: the member releases pent-up feelings or expression of ideas usually not expressed in other situations.

In addition to these nine specific categories, twenty-six other mechanisms were mentioned in the articles one or two times, but do not fall into any general pattern.

In successful group therapy, the child eventually recognizes that he no longer needs the contact with the group. A typical pattern seems to be an initial distrust of the group with irregular attendance, then dependence on the group and regular attendance, followed by ability to adjust in his family and in the normal community and gradual withdrawal from the group.

Treatment in special residential centers

Emotionally disturbed and delinquent children sometimes become so disorganized and unable to control their behavior that family and community can no longer tolerate them and the children in turn can no longer tolerate the family and community. They withdraw mentally, repeatedly run away, or make violent attacks on people and property, or threaten or attempt suicide. Such children make little progress toward adjustment unless removed from the family and sometimes from the community. Foster home placement rarely suffices as the foster family expects some degree of orderliness and co-operation. Even when the child's behavior is delinquent in nature, the correctional school is unsuitable as it usually imposes greater restrictions and is more impersonal in nature than the situations against which the child is struggling.

Here and there special residential schools and camps exist for the full-time care and treatment of these children. These institutions are not limited to delinquent children. Children are admitted on the basis of their emotional problems, delinquency being considered one of many overt symptoms of the inner disturbance.

The schools and camps are difficult to staff and expensive to operate. Although the children sleep, study, play, and eat together in small groups, their inability to form attachments makes it difficult to handle them as a group. Each child must be treated on an individual basis by carefully trained counselors and teachers and, in addition, requires the services of a psychologist and psychiatrist. Rehabilitation is slow and a period of several years' residence may be necessary with follow-up contacts after the child is able to leave the school.

A residential school. An example is the Sonia Shankman Orthogenic School in Chicago, equipped to give residence to and treat some forty children who are so deeply disturbed that their rehabilitation is impossible while they remain in their own homes, foster homes, or institutional homes. The basic problem faced by most of them is great insecurity because of faulty relationships with their parents. They fear their needs will not be met;

1 Raymond J. Corsini and Bina Rosenberg, "Mechanisms of Group Psychotherapy: Process and Dynamics," *Journal of Abnormal and Social Psychology,* 51 (November, 1955), 406–411.

they lack self-confidence; and they are unable to postpone fulfillment of desires and drives.

The policy of the School is to remove repressions and not to curb the child's outbursts until the child himself is able to adjust to orderliness and restrictions. Every effort is made to help the child build up a close relationship with his counselor which will bring him the love and security he did not receive from his parents. Once he has identified with his counselor and comes to love and trust her, many of his symptoms subside and he gradually adjusts to the life of the school and accepts the guidance of his counselor. Three or four years are usually needed for the child to respond to this treatment, and in some cases success is only partial. Regardless of how violent or dangerous to himself or others a child's behavior is, he is never punished for it; safeguards, of course, are used. Treatment is directed toward uncovering and correcting the underlying emotional conditions. When this has been accomplished, the child's violent behavior—his delinquency—lessens and disappears.[1]

Residential camp. Another example of a residential treatment center for disturbed children is the Salesmanship Club Boys Camp in Texas, maintained by the Salesmanship Club, a civic organization of Dallas. The boys in the camp had failed to respond to efforts to adjust them in their normal environment. Their behavior ranged from withdrawal and inability to talk to violent attacks and stealing. In the camp they live in small groups of ten boys with two counselors, each unit separated by woods from other units. Although the boys and their counselors live in tents under primitive conditions, the camp is a year-round one in which some boys have lived for three or four years. Removed from the pressures and strains of their families (or lack of family), the school, and the community to which they could not adjust, they are slowly helped to build up a close relationship with adults and to solve their inner problems

with a consequent change in outer behavior.[2]

A problem faced by residential schools and camps that place disturbed children in a simplified environment, isolated from the normal community, is the return to that community after personal adjustment has been achieved and the child has learned to adjust to the simplified environment. In all probability he returns to the same environment from which he came. If the treatment has not strengthened him beyond the pressures of the school or camp, he may relapse into his previous behavior. The staff of the treatment center follows the boy or girl through the period of readjustment to the outside world.

Guidance of street clubs

All the types of preventive efforts so far described have necessitated the approach of the child or his parents to the agency. The philosophy of treatment has included the idea that successful treatment rests on the voluntary co-operation of the client with the social worker or psychiatrist, symbolized by the client's request for help. This philosophy has greatly limited the clientele not only in numbers but in type of client, since a certain amount of knowledge is needed before youth or parents realize the need and know about the facilities for treatment. The tendency, therefore, has been for voluntary clients to be drawn from middle-class families. Children from lower-class families, often new to the city and unfamiliar with its agencies, tended to come to the attention of treatment agencies only when their behavior had become intolerable to schools or they had been referred to the juvenile court. The method of referral often made it difficult, if not impossible, for the agency to carry out effective treatment, since the children tended to associate it with their previous clash with school, police, or court. It became apparent to public officials and agencies concerned specifically with delinquency that a more direct approach to delinquents and delinquency-prone children and youth was needed.

A new philosophy and approach slowly developed, referred to as aggressive social work or by the catchy phrase "reaching the unreached." The essence of the approach is that the social worker seeks out the client instead

1 Bruno Bettleheim has amply described and discussed the Sonia Shankman Orthogenic School: "The Special School for Emotionally Disturbed Children," Chapter 7 in Nelson B. Henry, editor, *Juvenile Delinquency and the Schools,* Part 1 of the Forty-seventh Yearbook of the National Society for the Study of Education, University of Chicago Press, Chicago, 1948; *Love Is Not Enough,* Free Press, Glencoe, Illinois, 1950; *Truants from Life,* Free Press, Glencoe, Illinois, 1955.

2 Bert Kruger Smith and Campbell Loughmiller, *The Worth of a Boy,* Hogg Foundation for Mental Health, Austin, Texas, 1958.

of the traditional reverse relationship. The
approach is based on the conviction that
many people who do not come to seek help
can nevertheless be made aware of their
needs and brought into rapport with the
proper specialists provided a trained social
worker makes the first approach and persists
in breaking through the reserve of the prospective client.

Street-club work. The aggressive approach
has been applied to street-corner groups or
clubs whose behavior is already delinquent
or moving toward delinquency. It is applied
specifically to groups whose members refuse
to affiliate themselves with community or
other organized centers and conform to their
regulations. These groups constitute the unreached or the hard-to-reach groups, clubs,
or gangs. The procedure is for some agency
to assign a well-trained group or recreation
worker to make rapport with a club, known
or suspected to operate in a specific neighborhood. Usually the worker is young, and often
he has originated in an area similar to the one

White, Negro, and Puerto Rican boys join in an
animated discussion on the littered sidewalk outside club rooms provided by the New York City
Youth Board. The street-club worker seems to be
accepted as one of the group. The boys are from
a mixed racial and ethnic area, but seem to be
well-integrated in their group. Such discussions can
become informal group therapy sessions for airing
misunderstandings, exchanging opinions, and
building up more mature attitudes. (Courtesy New
York City Youth Board)

where he works. If race is a problem, the
worker selected is of the appropriate race.[1]

The worker, called a street-club worker, inconspicuous in dress and manner, begins to
spend many hours in the neighborhood, loafing, observing, talking with storekeepers and
others in the area. Soon he finds the hang-out
of the group and learns its routine of behavior. He loafs in the confectionary, lunch
room, or drug store, or on the corner favored

1 See Bibliography: Guidance of Street Clubs.

Older youth in the areas where street clubs and gangs flourish are often woefully lacking in knowledge of job opportunities or of how to go about applying for jobs. One function of street-club workers is to help boys in applying for jobs and to give them pointers on how to become dependable workers. (Courtesy New York City Youth Board)

by the group; he eats the favored food and plays the favored records.

At first, the boys look on the street-club worker with suspicion and resentment; he may be a member of the police force or a "do-gooder," either of whom might interfere with their activities or get them into trouble. Gradually the boys become accustomed to him and test him out in various ways as to his motives and trustworthiness. Eventually an understanding is reached; he is a social worker but not intent on forcing them into a fixed mold. He can get things for them they want most—a basement or storeroom for a club room and means to clean it up; a place to hold a dance, often refused by neighborhood agencies because of bitter past experiences with gang fights. He can help them learn about jobs; he can widen their experience in the city. But he cannot enter into illegal activities with them nor condone such activities; in fact, in extreme cases, he may be compelled to report them to the police. Progress is very slow and there are many relapses, some of which may lead to arrests and end in boys being sent to correctional schools.

Objective of street-club work. The objective of the work, unlike that of group therapy, is to deal with the group as a naturally formed association. If individuals appear to need special help, they are induced if possible to accept it from the appropriate agency. The naturally formed groups have many assets: they constitute a more or less congenial group, with some structure, and with natural leadership. Members are loyal to each other; they usually live in a limited area so that there are no problems of transportation. Beginning with these assets, the street-club worker tries to supply what they do not have. Superficially, he supplies practical satisfactions; more fundamentally, he probes into background situations. Usually, the background is characterized by the family and community disorganization already discussed in earlier chapters.

The street-club worker tries to get himself accepted as an informal adviser, whose purpose is not to impose rules on the club but to induce the club to arrive at new objectives and accept new methods of handling internal conflicts and of dealing with other antagonistic street clubs. For example, instead of struggling for the position as dictator leader, the boys are made familiar with democratic procedures of voting. Instead of gang fights, it is suggested that sports competitions may suffice to demonstrate ability and courage. If a fight is unavoidable, then the adviser tries to arrange a pre-fight meeting of leaders to arrange terms for the fight, without deadly weapons, or accept a fight between representatives rather than the entire gangs. Sometimes these methods are accepted and carried out, sometimes the arrangements break down completely.

Time works for the street-club worker. As the boys pass from mid-adolescence to later adolescence, their need increases for jobs, social activities with girls suitable for wives, and wider contacts in the city. The club with a worker has a genuine advantage over the one without.

Limitations of street-club work. Experience has shown that the street club already dedicated to delinquency or crime as a central activity or affiliated with an older criminal gang is virtually "unreachable." Work therefore tends to concentrate on younger groups of boys, whose activities may be reorganized along nondelinquent lines before the pattern of the club has been firmly set. In the long run, if this diversion can be accomplished, the boys will not organize their club activities around delinquency as they grow older, and they will not readily affiliate with older criminal groups. In fact, in theory at least, in time there should be no older delinquent gangs with which younger groups could affiliate.

The number of clubs that any one worker can handle is limited, not only because of the amount of time consumed in the continuous contact with one club, but because of jealousy that sometimes arises between clubs when they share a worker. He may become the object of competition for his time and attention and the interclub relationship may move toward, instead of away from, conflict.

Street-club work is confined almost entirely to boys since they, more than girls, tend to form into semiorganized street clubs and hence afford a nucleus for work. Also, their depredations are more conspicuous and more damaging to property and life than are the delinquent activities of girls. Workers are aware, however, of the auxiliary relationship of girls to the boys' clubs and indirectly must take them into account in working with the boys.

The street-club worker faces various problems aside from the basic one of gaining rapport with the club. In some cities it has been found that if he works out of a local community center, the boys associate him with the agency. Since their selection as a group has been in part because they refused to affiliate with the local center, association of the street-club worker with the center makes it extremely difficult for him to gain acceptance by the club. Whatever repelled them from the center is associated with the worker, and he is regarded with suspicion. Hence in some areas it has been found advisable for the worker to be on the staff of some central city agency with which the boys have not had direct contact. This arrangement, however, increases the difficulty for the worker. He has no immediate headquarters and no ready association or companionship with other professionals. He may become too detached, too involved emotionally with the boys, perhaps even identified with them. His work depends upon a sympathetic understanding of the boys but not emotional identification with them, as this obscures his objectivity about them and their activities.

The worker also has to adjust to irregular hours. He cannot keep office hours or confine his contacts to stated times and places. He must be where the club is, whatever the time or place.

Evaluation. Street-club work began about 1950 and is still in an experimental stage in various cities. Results are not quickly evident. The worker must continue his contacts with the club through the period of adolescence; check-up and evaluation would come later. However, methods of approach and influence are being evolved. Workers are being accepted by clubs and have made headway in inducing the clubs to find constructive purposes for themselves and to work toward them in acceptable ways.

A comprehensive community approach to prevention and treatment

Many communities have devised some degree of co-ordination of preventive work, usually through co-operation of autonomous agencies. The comprehensive community effort described here goes beyond this and is an attempt on the part of one city-wide agency to penetrate into all the high delinquency areas and to supply or stimulate other organizations to give needed facilities and services. This tremendous task has been in operation in New York City since 1947; reports have been numerous but evaluation is difficult.

In 1945 the state of New York established the New York State Youth Commission. One of its obligations was to aid cities struggling with youth problems, by providing half of the cost of approved projects for the prevention

and control of juvenile delinquency, up to a total cost depending on the youth population of the city. New York City established the New York City Youth Board in 1947, composed of eighteen representative laymen and ten heads of the following city agencies: schools, parks, welfare, health, police, housing, correction, and several of the courts. The Board began its work with a survey of delinquency, which enabled it to select eleven areas most in need of preventive work. The greatest concentration of effort remains in these areas.

The multifaceted approach includes planning at the city-wide level, co-operation with agencies already in existence, supplementation of their work, and operation of local projects. Laymen in the communities in which concentrated effort is being directed, are also worked into the projects. The organization is as follows:

1. Citywide Planning and Co-ordinating Unit, which works through committees of laymen and professionals to appraise current resources for delinquency prevention and to make recommendations.

2. Department of Borough Planning and Community Co-ordination, which stimulates local interest and action and acts as an intermediary between the Citywide Unit and the needs of the Borough. The effort to involve residents of the high delinquency areas in prevention resembles in purpose the Chicago Area Project.[1]

3. The Research Department which maintains up-to-date records of the incidence and location of delinquency, as well as a central register of offending youth and evaluates the various methods used by the Youth Board, which are still in an experimental stage. Typical research projects include:

a. Street-club study, which covers not only study of gang boys but evaluation of the efforts of street-club workers.

b. Evaluation of project whereby child guidance clinics were established in three schools. This project was begun by the Youth Board and later assigned to the Community Mental Health Board.

c. Study of 150 multiproblem families

1 The Chicago Area Project is credited in various Youth Board reports with offering a method of approach to reach adults and children in delinquency-prone neighborhoods.

in the caseload of Service to Families and Children. The study is both quantitative and qualitative in nature.

d. Index of multiproblem families in recognition of the fact that these families contribute more than their share of children to the ranks of delinquency.

e. Prediction of juvenile delinquency, a long-term project in which the Glueck Social Prediction Scale was applied to first graders, whose behavior is being followed until they reach later adolescence, in order to test the validity of the Scale.

4. Referral Unit. Operated by the Board of Education, a unit is stationed in each of the areas of high delinquency. The unit actively seeks to learn of poorly adjusted children, both the withdrawn type and the overtly delinquent type. Once discovered, the children and their families are referred to appropriate agencies.

5. Service to Families and Children is the Board's special casework project, whose chief function is to make an active approach to families that are so deprived, deteriorated, and depressed that they have been given up by other agencies as beyond help. Certainly, the families do not take the initiative in seeking help. This Service is regarded as the key service since almost two-thirds of the children in such families become delinquent. It is estimated that there are some 20,000 "hard-core" families in New York City (less than 1 per cent of all families) who contribute 75 per cent of the city's delinquency.

In addition to operating its own Service to Families and Children, the Board enters into contract with existing welfare agencies to increase their staffs and reduce their long waiting list of clients.

6. The Department of Group Work and Recreation works actively with existing agencies, specifically with the Board of Education's School Community Centers, the Police Athletic League Centers and Playstreets, and Housing Project Community Centers operated by the Board of Education.

7. Council of Social and Athletic Clubs, commonly known as the Street-Club Project. In 1959, work was carried on with one hundred antisocial conflict groups. This type of work has already been discussed. The Council is assisted by a Technical Advisory Committee of outstanding citizens who offer sug-

gestions to the Council and help interpret the work of the Council to the local areas. The future goal of the Council is to have a street-club worker for every conflict youth group in the city.

8. In-service Training Department which orients new workers to the purposes and the "reaching out" philosophy of the Youth Board and provides continued contacts with established workers.

9. Community Relations Department, whose chief purpose is to disseminate information about delinquency and the work of the Board.[1]

At the end of its first ten years of activity, the Youth Board did not make any extravagant claims to have stamped out delinquency. A published chart covering the years 1951–52 to 1955–56 on annual trend in delinquency shows that during 1951–52 delinquency dropped in the areas served by the Youth Board but increased in other areas. After this year the trend of Youth Board and non-Youth Board areas followed the same path of ups and downs, but the increases were less and the decreases greater in the Youth Board than in the non-Youth Board areas. Delinquency is far from disappearing but some set of influences—perhaps predominantly provided or stimulated by the Youth Board—has had a favorable effect on the high delinquency areas.

The outstanding features of the New York City Youth Board are that it is a joint function of state and city; it is supported by public funds; it attempts to penetrate into every area where delinquency rates are high; it drives toward modification of many types of situations known to be associated with high delinquency rates; it co-operates in providing expanded constructive services; it focuses directly on delinquents and their families; and it takes the initiative in seeking out and helping delinquents, other poorly adjusted youths, and their families. Many other cities are also co-ordinating and expanding their work with delinquency-prone children and inadequate families, but none perhaps on the scale or with the vigor of the New York City Youth Board.

1 *New Directions in Delinquency Prevention, 1947–1957,* New York City Youth Board, New York, undated; *Reaching the Fighting Gang,* New York City Youth Board, New York, 1960.

Bibliography

Glueck social prediction table

Burgess, Ernest W., "Can Potential Delinquents Be Identified Scientifically?" *Twenty-fourth Annual Governor's Conference on Youth and Community Service,* Illinois Youth Commission, Springfield, Illinois, 1955, pp. 33–39.

Delinquency Prediction, A Progress Report, 1952–1956, An Experiment in the Validation of the Glueck Prediction Scale, New York City Youth Board, New York City, 1957.

Glueck, Eleanor T., "Status of Glueck Prediction Studies," *Journal of Criminal Law, Criminology and Police Science,* 47 (1956), 18–32.

———, "Spotting Potential Delinquents: Can It Be Done?" *Federal Probation,* 20 (1956), 7–13.

Glueck, Sheldon, "Ten Years of *Unraveling Juvenile Delinquency,*" *Journal of Criminal Law, Criminology and Police Science,* 51 (1960), 283–308.

Glueck, Sheldon and Eleanor, "Early Detection of Future Delinquents," *Journal of Criminal Law, Criminology and Police Science,* 47 (1956), 174–182.

———, *Predicting Delinquency and Crime,* Harvard University Press, Cambridge, Massachusetts, 1959, Chapters 9–11 and pages 233–255.

———, *Unraveling Juvenile Delinquency,* Harvard University Press, Cambridge, Massachusetts, 1950, Chapter 20.

Herzog, Elizabeth, *Identifying Potential Delinquents,* Children's Bureau Report No. 5, U. S. Government Printing Office, Washington, D. C., 1960.

Keniston, Kenneth, "Entangling Juvenile Delinquency," *Commentary,* 29 (1960), 486–491, and comment, *ibid.,* 30 (1960), 165.

Reiss, Albert J., Jr., "*Unraveling Juvenile Delinquency,* An Appraisal of the Research Methods," *American Journal of Sociology,* 57 (1951), 115–120.

Rubin, Sol., "*Unraveling Juvenile Delinquency,* Illusions in a Research Project Using Matched Pairs," *American Journal of Sociology,* 57 (1951), 107–114.

"Symposium on *Unraveling Juvenile Delinquency,*" *Harvard Law Review,* 64 (1951), article on "Prediction" by Edwin Bidwell Wilson, pp. 1039–1041.

Thompson, Richard E., "A Validation of the Glueck Social Prediction Scale for Proneness to Delinquency," *Journal of Criminal Law, Criminology and Police Science,* 43 (1952), 453–470.

———, "Further Validation of the Glueck Social Prediction Table for Identifying Potential Delinquents," *Journal of Criminal Law, Crim-*
inology and Police Science, 48 (1957), 175–184.

Kvaraceus delinquency proneness scale

Kvaraceus, W. C., "*The Community and the Delinquent,*" World Book Company, Yonkers-on-Hudson, New York, 1954, pp. 139–154.

———, "Forecasting Juvenile Delinquency," *Journal of Education,* 138 (April, 1956), 1–43.

Balogh, Joseph K., and Charles J. Rumage, *Juvenile Delinquency Proneness, A Study of the Kvaraceus Scale,* Annals of American Sociology, Public Affairs Press, Washington, D. C., 1956.

Minnesota multiphasic personality inventory

Kanun, Clara, and Elio D. Monachesi, "Delinquency and the Validating Scales of the Minnesota Multiphasic Personality Inventory," *Journal of Criminal Law, Criminology and Police Science,* 50 (1960), 525–534.

Hathaway, Starke R., and Elio D. Monachesi, *Analyzing and Predicting Juvenile Delinquency with the MMPI,* University of Minnesota Press, Minneapolis, Minnesota, 1953.

———, "The Personalities of Predelinquent Boys," *Journal of Criminal Law, Criminology and Police Science,* 48 (1957), 148–163.

Treatment of delinquents individually

Friedlander, Walter A., *Introduction to Social Welfare,* Prentice-Hall, Inc., New York, 1955, Chapter 13, "Mental Hygiene and Psychiatric Social Work."

Peck, Harris B., and Virginia Bellsmith, *Treatment of the Delinquent Adolescent,* Family Service Association of America, New York, 1954.

Witmer, Helen L., *Psychiatric Clinics for Children,* The Commonwealth Fund, New York, 1940.

———, and Edith Tufts, *The Effectiveness of Prevention Programs,* Children's Bureau Publication No. 350, U. S. Government Printing Office, Washington, D. C., 1954.

Group therapy

Corsini, Raymond J., and Bina Rosenberg, "Mechanisms of Group Psychotherapy: Process and Dynamics," *Journal of Abnormal and Social Psychology,* 51 (1955), 406–411.

Grunwald, Hanna, "Group Counseling in Combating Delinquency," *Federal Probation,* 22 (December, 1958), 32–36.

Konopka, Gisela, *Therapeutic Group Work with Children,* University of Minnesota Press, Minneapolis, Minnesota, 1949.

Rosenthal, Leslie, "Group Therapy with Problem Children and Their Parents," *Federal Probation,* 17 (December, 1953), 27–34.

Slavson, S. R., *An Introduction to Group Therapy,* International Universities Press, New York, 1943.

Stranahan, Marion, and Cecile Schwartzman, "An Experiment in Reaching Asocial Adolescents through Group Therapy," *Annals of the American Academy of Political and Social Science,* 322 (1959), 117–125.

Residential treatment centers

Bettleheim, Bruno, *Love Is Not Enough,* Free Press, Glencoe, Illinois, 1950.

Bettleheim, Bruno, "The Special School for Emotionally Disturbed Children," Chapter 7 in Nelson B. Henry, editor, *Juvenile Delinquency and the Schools,* Part 1 of the Forty-seventh Yearbook of the National Society for the Study of Education, University of Chicago Press, Chicago, 1948.

————, *Truants from Life,* Free Press, Glencoe, Illinois, 1955.

Redl, Fritz, and David Wineman, *Children Who Hate,* Free Press, Glencoe, Illinois, 1951.

————, *Controls from Within,* Free Press, Glencoe, Illinois, 1952.

Smith, Bert Kruger, and Campbell Loughmiller, *The Worth of a Boy,* Hogg Foundation for Mental Health, Austin, Texas, 1958.

Guidance of street clubs

Bernstein, Walter, "The Cherubs Are Rumbling,"
New Yorker (September 21, 1957), 120–147.

Dealing with the Conflict Gang in New York City, Interim Report No. 14, Juvenile Delinquency Evaluation Project of the City of New York, The City College, New York, 1961.

Furman, Sylvan S., editor, *Reaching the Unreached,* New York City Youth Board, New York, 1952.

Gandy, John M., "Preventive Work with Street-Corner Groups: Hyde Park Youth Project, Chicago," *Annals of the American Academy of Political and Social Science,* 322 (1959), 107–116.

Jones, Stacy V., "The Cougars, Life with a Brooklyn Gang," *Harper's Magazine,* 209 (November, 1954), 35–43.

Miller, Walter B., "Preventive Work with Street-Corner Groups: Boston Delinquency Project," *Annals of the American Academy of Political and Social Science,* 322 (1959), 97–106.

————, "The Impact of a Community Group Work Program on Delinquent Corner Groups," *Social Service Review,* 31 (1957), 390–406.

Milner, John G., "Working with Juvenile Gang Members," *California Youth Authority Quarterly,* 12 (Spring, 1959), 3–7.

New Directions in Delinquency Prevention, 1947–1957, New York City Youth Board, New York (undated).

Reaching the Fighting Gang, New York City Youth Board, New York, 1960. Comprehensive community approach—New York City Youth Board.

Whelan, Ralph W., "New York City's Approach to the Delinquency Problem," *Federal Probation,* 17 (December, 1953), 19–25.

A misbehaving child may be neglected or handled informally by police and various institutions such as the school without being designated as a juvenile delinquent. If his behavior passes the toleration point of the community or he commits a serious offense and the police take him into custody, his misconduct becomes a matter of record. At this point he officially acquires a record as a juvenile delinquent (although it may be confidential) and enters upon a sequence of events prescribed by law or developed by practice. Not all children follow through the entire sequence. Depending upon the seriousness of the misconduct, the provisions for supervision, and the child's own response, the child may be permitted to leave the sequence at various points.

Chapter **18**

Background of present legal handling of juvenile delinquents

Sequence of practices

The complete sequence or process, if followed through from beginning to end, begins when the police arrest a child and ends with his discharge from parole after he has been confined in a correctional school. The steps are given below in outline form.

1. Police intercept a child in misconduct, respond to a complaint about a child, or on investigation find evidence that a child has been involved in certain misconduct. The child is taken to the police station. Depending upon the organization of police services and the policy of the police and of the juvenile court, the child is either reprimanded and released, or turned over to the police juvenile bureau (if there is one), or referred to a social agency or to the juvenile court.

2. If the child is referred to a fully developed juvenile court, his case is reviewed by an intake department. Certain children are released; others are referred to social agencies for treatment, and some are held for a hearing before the juvenile court judge. A minority of children reach court attention through direct referral by parents, school officials, or others without reference to the police. The court hearing and subsequent procedures are the same as when the police refer a child.

3. If an interval of time must elapse before the hearing, the child may be released to his parents or held in detention in jail or a special juvenile detention center.

4. When the judge hears the case, he has information available not only on the offense but also on the child and his family, assembled by social workers or probation officers attached to the court. If intervals of time elapse during the course of the hearing, the child may continue to live at home or be held in the place of detention.

5. The child may be dismissed with a warning to him and his parents.

6. The child may be placed on probation, under supervision of the probation officer or of some agency in the community. He usually continues to live at home, attend school, and follow a normal round of activities.

7. If his home is unsuitable for him, he may be placed in a foster home (if a young child) or in a private institution for borderline delinquents (if an older child).

8. If he has committed a serious offense or is a recidivist, he may be committed to a state correctional school for a period of time.

9. When he is released from the school, he is usually placed under the supervision of a parole officer.

10. Eventually he is discharged from probation or parole.

11. In some states, if his offense is a serious adult-type crime, he may be tried in the adult criminal court. Somewhat the same procedure is followed but in a more formal manner; if he is found guilty he may be sentenced to an adult prison, perhaps for a sentence that will keep him imprisoned for many years. In extreme cases, an older adolescent may be given a death sentence, although this rarely happens.

Ideally, except in the case of criminal court procedures, the child is shielded from exposure to adult criminals and is spared a formal criminal trial. Emphasis is placed on discovering why the child has become delinquent and on mapping a plan of action that will prevent future delinquencies. In practice, of course, the ideal is not always reached.

Development of the juvenile court

The juvenile delinquency concept. Until 1899, except in a minor way, all children except the very young, were subject to the same laws and procedures as adults. In general, the United States followed the English tradition in legal matters. In English common law, children under age seven were not held accountable for criminal acts. From age eight to fourteen, children could be held responsible if it could be shown that they were sufficiently intelligent to understand the nature and consequences of their misdeeds and if they could distinguish between right and wrong. Such children could be subjected to the same type of trial and punishment as adult criminals, even to infliction of the death penalty in extreme cases. Blackstone, writing in 1795, refers to several earlier cases in which children of ten to thirteen years of age were subjected to execution for murder or other wanton crimes. Occasional similar cases of capital punishment are found in the history of the United States; for example, in New Jersey in 1828 a thirteen-year-old boy was hanged for an offense committed when he was twelve.[1]

The English common law dealt in a protective manner with other classes of children, in contrast to its treatment of delinquent children. As *parens patriae* (father of his country), the King was responsible for the care of children; this care he delegated to the Court of Chancery, whose objective was the common welfare. This court was founded on the idea of equity; it was able to act in a more flexible manner than was possible under the rigid legal rules of the common law. The original purpose of chancery wardship of children was directed primarily toward protection of the property interest of wealthy children.

Two precedents then existed for the mod-

ern concept of juvenile delinquency: first, that children under a certain age were not responsible for criminal acts; second, that some children were in need of protection by the courts. The concept of juvenile delinquency merged these two approaches. The age of non- or limited responsibility was raised from seven to sixteen or eighteen; and the delinquent was placed in the same position of care by a court of chancery as were dependent and neglected children. This move eliminated most criminal trials for children and led to the development of the juvenile court and a series of auxiliary institutions and practices to implement the purpose of protection and care, chief among them being detention centers, children's clinics, probation services, and special correctional or training schools.

Juvenile courts in the United States. The first juvenile court in the world was established in 1899 in Cook County (Chicago), Illinois. The court had control over three categories of children—dependent, neglected, and delinquent. The delinquent child had ceased to be a criminal and had the status of a child in need of care, protection, and discipline directed toward rehabilitation. As with the other two categories of children, he became a ward of the state.

Although the juvenile court as a formal institution did not appear until 1899, various concessions previously had been made toward removing children from criminal courts, while in the criminal courts, the trend was to soften the harshness of the laws. Massachusetts enacted a statute in 1869 providing that an agent of the state board of charity should attend trials of juveniles, investigate their cases, protect their interests, and make suitable recommendations to the judge. Special trials for children's cases were provided in laws of 1870, 1872, and 1877. New York, Indiana, and Rhode Island followed the lead of Massachusetts. The juvenile court is the culmination of a long-term trend.

Laws providing for juvenile courts were not immediately enacted in all states. The last state to enact the necessary legislation was Wyoming, in 1945. Juvenile courts are of various types in the different states and, within a given state, range from the simple situation in a rural county where the judge of some adult court sits as juvenile court judge as needed, to the highly complex system of related institutions constituting the juvenile

---

1 Cited by Frederick B. Sussman, *Juvenile Delinquency,* Oceana Publications, New York, revised, 1959, p. 12.

court and its allied services in a populous urban county.

Juvenile courts in other countries. Other countries, especially England and European countries, have also shown marked concern about the treatment of juvenile delinquents. England established juvenile courts through the Children Act of 1908, and Belgium and France through legislation of 1912. The Scandinavian countries have developed child welfare boards to handle delinquent as well as neglected and dependent children. Norway established such boards by the Child Welfare Act of 1896; Sweden and Denmark shortly thereafter provided for similar boards. These countries continue the use of child welfare boards and feel no need for special juvenile courts. The Near Eastern countries have moved more slowly into the juvenile court movement, with the exception of Eygpt which set up its first juvenile court in 1905 and, as of 1953, had courts in Cairo and Alexandria. As of that date, Syria had laws to provide for juvenile courts but actually had not yet established any. Lebanon had opened one court in Beirut. Turkey, Iraq, Iran, Saudi Arabia, and Yemen dealt with juvenile cases in the regular criminal courts. In the Far East, countries formerly under the influence of, or attached to, Great Britain or the United States, tend to have juvenile courts following the pattern of the dominant country. Pakistan has one juvenile court, which has functioned in Karachi since 1938. In India, various Children Acts were passed in different areas during the 1920's, giving rise to a limited number of juvenile courts. Japan's family courts, which handle all juvenile cases, date from the post-World War II period and are modeled after those of the United States.[1]

Juvenile courts are gaining acceptance throughout the world. Except in some cases of very serious crimes, they protect children from a criminal court trial and relieve them of full responsibility for minor and some serious offenses. As will appear later, however, many court problems remain to be solved.

Development of probation

Probation, now widely used, had its origin before the establishment of juvenile courts. Massachusetts established the first probation system without age restrictions in 1880, soon to be followed by Illinois, New York, and Indiana.[2]

Development of juvenile training schools

The development of special correctional or training schools for juveniles long preceded the coming of the juvenile court. This movement was part of the general trend that eventually brought the juvenile court into existence—a trend recognizing the immaturity of children and youth, and the right of delinquents to special training. In both England and the United States, training schools were a development of the nineteenth century.

Early institutions. In Europe, a few now famous schools were established much earlier. An early school was the Hospital (home) of Saint Michael in Rome, founded in 1704 by Pope Clement XI. Here orphan as well as delinquent boys and infirm old people were housed. Hard work, silence, and solitude were the methods of corrective discipline by which delinquents were to be converted into upright youth.

Another development in England and Europe was the house of correction or workhouse beginning as early as the latter part of the sixteenth century in England and on the continent. These institutions received a motley lot of unfortunates, vagrants, beggars, vendors unable to secure licenses, and petty criminals of all ages. Although the first ones were established in England and Amsterdam, the most famous was in Ghent, Flanders (now Belgium). In 1773 Hippolyte Vilain, burgomaster of Ghent, founded the workhouse as a response to the hordes of vagrants who wandered over Europe. Unlike most institutions of its day, the Ghent workhouse segregated prisoners according to seriousness of their misbehavior, sex, and age. One part of the institution was reserved for children. Hard work, complete obedience, and the learning of a trade were emphasized.

Schools of the nineteenth century. In the early nineteenth century, institutions specifically for delinquent children, separate from those for adults, were developed in England, Europe, and the United States. The first concern was for the homeless, uncared-for children wandering the city streets, sleeping in gutters and alleys, and living by their wits. Some were orphans, some deserted by their parents,

---

1 Various sources, including United Nations' reports.

2 Sussman, *op. cit.,* p. 13.

some runaways from other cities. By our present classification they were neglected, dependent, and delinquent. The first institutions for their care were founded by wealthy philanthropic individuals or organizations dedicated to the care of children. In England, voluntary groups established correctional schools to which courts could send young criminals. They would be granted a pardon upon condition of placing themselves under the care of a charitable institution until they were "reformed." Following this step, they would be sent to the Colonies. The Reformatory Schools Act of 1854 enabled courts to commit offenders under sixteen to a reformatory, after serving a period of not less than fourteen days in prison. Gradually the government assumed more and more responsibility for support and management of correctional institutions. In Acts of 1857 and 1866, industrial schools were established for children under fourteen needing care and protection, and for legal offenders under twelve.[1] Nevertheless, many children under sixteen and some as young as ten were in prison. European countries were also beginning to separate children from adults.

In the United States the first break with the older policy of imprisoning children and youths with adult offenders came in 1825 when the Society for the Reformation of Juvenile Delinquents succeeded with state assistance in opening the New York City House of Refuge. A vacated barracks for soldiers was first used. The purpose of this institution was to care for and educate children apprehended by the police as minor offenders or vagrants, children often picked up on the streets and typically sentenced to six months in the penitentiary.

The House of Refuge received much the same public acclaim that the juvenile court received seventy-five years later. Clearly it marked a forward step in that children were segregated from adult offenders and provided with a special program of training. The state gave some support and later assumed entire responsibility for the House. Its location was moved several times and, more than a hundred years after its founding, it ceased to exist as a separate entity and was merged with

the New York State Vocational Institution at West Coxsackie, a state training school for boys.

In 1826 a similar institution was founded in Boston, and in 1828 another in Philadelphia, both as the result of efforts by private organizations. By 1850 the trend for state-supported training schools was well established, and state after state established such schools. State-supported schools now far outnumber private schools.

These schools which preceded the creation of the juvenile court, represented a growing concern for delinquent (often also destitute) children, that they should not mingle with adult criminals in prisons and that some effort should be made to train them. Children were still tried in adult courts and were subject to the same kind of sentences given to adults. Many, especially serious offenders, were still confined in prison.

The early institutions were prison-like in structure. However, in England and Europe experiments were being carried out with separation of delinquent children into small units within the institution, to create groups somewhat modeled after families. The first cottage type training schools in the United States were the girls' institution at Lancaster, Massachusetts, opened in 1854 and the boys' institution at Lancaster, Ohio, in 1858. The cottage system is now the customary type of training school.

Lack of central administration

In the United States the various legal agencies dealing with a delinquent suffer from a high degree of decentralization and lack of co-ordination. Each stage of the process from arrest to eventual freedom is under the control of a different administrative set-up. Consensus of policy may not exist at all; co-ordination of activities usually comes about only on a voluntary basis and may degenerate into conflict.

The city child is dealt with by municipal police operating under some municipal officer or body. Outside the city, the county sheriff or county police have charge of law enforcement, and are accountable to the county government. At times the state police arrest a delinquent. Lines between the jurisdiction of these police bodies are not always clear; moreover, the delinquent may have passed

---

1 Fox, Lionel W., *The English Prison and Borstal Systems,* Routledge and Kegan Paul, Ltd., London, England, 1952, pp. 327–328.

from one jurisdiction to another. If a serious crime has been committed by a juvenile, the city, county, and state police may each have some connection with the case and compete for the "honor" of handling it.

The juvenile court is usually on a city or county basis, but is not related administratively to the city or county police. The judge is usually elected and operates more or less independently under the state law or he may be part of a federation or council of judges. The probation officer is usually a subordinate of the judge.

The correctional school to which the judge may commit a delinquent may be administered by a private board of directors or by a state group, such as a welfare or correctional department. When the child is released and placed on parole, the parole officer usually is attached to a state department.

Although all these agencies and institutions operate within state laws, the laws have been passed from time to time without complete integration into one system. Moreover, each level of government lower than the state—county and municipal—makes its own regulations which are legal so long as they fall within the general state laws. County and city need not co-ordinate their regulations, and in fact within either county or city, confusion may reign between different agencies.

Whoever is in charge of each correctional agency supervising the child—the police chief, the judge, the chief probation or parole officer, the director of a correctional school—makes policies and sets practices for the operation of his specific agency. Co-ordination may be worked out on this level for smooth operation of the cumbersome, disjointed machinery. Agreements may be made between police and juvenile court judge as to which types of cases police will handle independently and those to be referred to the juvenile court. The judge may have understandings with the various agencies to which he may commit the care of delinquents as to the kind of delinquent each agency can best handle. Nevertheless there are many misunderstandings and actual conflicts. The individual child may be passed smoothly and with a minimum of delay from one agency to another, or he may be shuttled back and forth between agencies which seem less concerned with the child than with their own autonomy.

Lack of a standard pattern. When municipal, county, and state agencies dealing with delinquency are considered *in toto,* literally thousands of different laws, policies, and practices are revealed. Some are very good; some are deplorable. Not only are there fifty states (and Puerto Rico, The Virgin Islands, the District of Columbia, and the federal government) each with individual sets of laws and systems of agencies, but in addition, there are the regulations and ordinances of more than 3,000 counties, and 16,000 municipalities. Even within one state there is no uniformity of excellence among counties or cities. Moreover, it is virtually impossible to achieve uniformity of laws, regulations, ordinances, and agency systems by legal means.

For a number of years attempts have been made, with constant pressure and a measure of success, to induce cities, counties, and states individually to accept and enact into law or put into practice standard laws or practices devised by national or federal bodies. Significantly active have been the Children's Bureau of the federal government and the National Council on Crime and Delinquency (formerly the National Probation and Parole Association) which, independently or in co-operation, have published many reports and standard practices. The United Nations through its two world Congresses for Prevention of Crime and Treatment of Delinquents (1955 and 1960) and attendant conferences and publications is taking world leadership in establishing standard policies and practices toward which individual nations may work. The reports and recommendations of these and other agencies are referred to frequently in the succeeding chapters.

Special terminology

In the effort to differentiate legal procedures for juveniles from those for adults, a special terminology has developed. The intent was to remove from the child the stigma attached to criminal terminology; unfortunately, the new terms now have become stigmatized. Since this terminology will be used in the chapters to follow, the words and phrases are given for future reference in the list which follows on page 238, including full definitions and their equivalence in terms used in adult legal procedures:

Juvenile term	Adult term
Adjudication: decision by the judge that the child has committed delinquent acts.	Conviction of guilt
After-care: supervision given to a child for a limited period of time after he is released from the training school but still under the control of the school or of the juvenile court.	Parole
Commitment: decision by the judge that the child should be sent to a training school.	Sentence to imprisonment
Detention: holding a child, usually prior to trial, in close physical custody in jail or whenever possible in a special juvenile detention center.	Holding in jail
Hearing: the presentation of evidence to the juvenile court judge, his consideration of it, and his decision on disposition of the case.	Trial
Petition: document stating the alleged delinquent acts of the child, filed with the juvenile court.	Accusation or indictment
Probation: supervision of a delinquent child after the court hearing but without commitment to a training school.	Probation, with the same meaning
Take into custody: act of the police in securing the physical custody of a child engaged in delinquency; avoids the stigma of the word arrest.	Arrest

Bibliography

Abbott, Grace, *The Child and the State,* University of Chicago Press, 1938.

Fox, Lionel W., *The English Prison and Borstal Systems,* Routledge and Kegan Paul, Limited, London, England, 1952, Ch. 9 & App. B.

Nyquist, Ola, "How Sweden Handles Its Juvenile and Youth Offenders," *Federal Probation,* 20 (March, 1956), 36–42.

Sellin, Thorsten, "Sweden's Substitute for the Juvenile Court," *Annals of the American Academy of Political and Social Science,* 261 (1949), 137–149.

Wines, Enoch C., *State of Prisons,* Cambridge University Press, Cambridge, England, 1880.

The juvenile court is always hailed as the most significant of the agencies that deal with delinquents, and it undoubtedly is in setting policies and making decisions on the disposition of children responsible for serious delinquencies. The police, however, have contacts with many more misbehaving and outright delinquent children than does the juvenile court. Of all children picked up or arrested by the police, only one-fourth are referred to the juvenile court. Three-fourths are handled independently by the police; moreover, the police decide which three-fourths they will handle and how. In addition to dealing with delinquents, police have many informal encounters with children on the streets and in places where children loiter. Here they exercise general supervision as part of their function of maintaining order and protecting younger children from harm. The police exercise an extraordinary degree of authority quite independently of the juvenile court. Especially among young and minor delinquents, the police department is the one official agency that the child sees. It is extremely important, therefore, that police understand and exercise well this vast power that they have.

As long as misbehaving children were regarded simply as small-sized criminals, the police function toward them was very much the same as toward adult criminals, to repress misbehavior and crime when they saw it occurring and to bring offending children and adults alike to the police station with whatever force was necessary. The conception of children as immature and still developing personalities and of juvenile delinquents as not fully responsible for their acts has gradually led to new conceptions of police functions where children and youth of juvenile delinquency age are concerned. These new conceptions and functions are not limited to the United States but are found in many other countries, especially in highly industrialized cities.

Law enforcement

A basic function of all police is to enforce laws. This function may involve interfering with a crime that is in process, stepping in to prevent a crime that seems to be brewing, or making routine inspections of places, such as taverns or dance halls, operating under special regulations. Foot patrolmen, motorcycle

Chapter **19**

Police contacts

police, and squad car units carry on these activities day and night without regard to the age of persons who may be involved. The constant surveillance is one of the chief ways in which order is maintained and delinquency and crime reduced in amount and seriousness.

Regulatory activities are protective as well as preventive. Many cases heard in court are for offenses of adults against children. Police action to prevent sale of liquor to minors, sale of narcotics to children, loitering of girls in questionable restaurants or taverns, or sexual approaches of men to young girls or boys is protective, in that it reduces the dangers to children. It is preventive also inasmuch as children who participate often are violating juvenile delinquency laws. If police supervision reduces or eliminates the illegal acts of adults, delinquency in these areas of behavior is also reduced or eliminated.

When juveniles are involved in delinquent or criminal acts, the police are empowered to interfere. The drunken youth, the girl loitering on the streets late at night, boys found trying the locks on doors or windows, rowdyness, and fighting all call for police action. Complaints received by the police department of delinquent activity also require police action.

What the policeman does with the child or youth of juvenile delinquency age is partly a matter of decision on his part. In most instances he warns the child on the spot, or he may take the child to the police station, call in the parents immediately, and warn both

An outbreak of gang fighting often leads to general roundups of youth and adults whose actions seem questionable if not outright delinquent. These five boys were among ninety picked up by New York police in Times Square, July 31, 1954, and brought to a police station where they stand in front of the booking officer. (Wide World Photos)

parents and child. Usually no record is made of these on-the-spot adjustments. They far outnumber the instances in which a record is made.

These encounters may seem trivial; however, they are important for the future behavior of the child and his relationship with the police. If the policeman on the beat has warned a child and the child repeats his misbehavior, the time will come when the policeman will take more positive action. If the policeman is kindly (but firm) in his attitude toward the child, a warning or two may hold the child's behavior in line. If the policeman is hostile and threatens to or actually does use physical force unnecessarily, the child is very likely to respond with defiance, ridicule

of the officer, and baiting of the officer to make him angry. In any case, the policeman is a figure of authority. How he displays the authority is extremely important.

With repeated or serious offenses the child receives more direct action. He is taken into custody by the police. In theory it would seem that the child would be referred immediately to the juvenile court. However, preliminary screening is often carried out by the police. The police thus make the first decision as to what will be done with the child, even when his offense is serious enough to warrant the police in taking him into custody.

Screening and referrals by police

Opinions differ as to the amount of investigation police should make of a case before determining disposition.

Investigation. Agreement is general that the police should investigate the facts of the offense thoroughly; otherwise children may be falsely accused of delinquent or criminal behavior.[1] Sufficient social information about

1 *Police Service for Juveniles,* Children's Bureau Publication No. 344, U. S. Government Printing Office,

the child and his background is also needed by police in order to determine whether to return the child to his family, refer him to a health, welfare, educational or recreational agency, or refer him to the juvenile court, which assumes responsibility for whatever further investigation is needed. The Children's Bureau suggests that a total investigation by the police, might include the following:

1. Facts of the offense, including all details necessary to sustain a petition in court.
2. Record of any previous police action.
3. Record of any previous court or social agency action.
4. Attitudes of the child, his parents, and the complainant in the offense, toward the act.
5. Adjustment of the child in home, school, and community.[1]

While making this investigation, police may release the child to his parents or hold him at the police station. Opinion is divided as to how long the police are justified in holding a child while they investigate. The opinion of the committee that set up the Standard Juvenile Court Act was that it should not be more than two or three hours.[2] However, police may not be able to complete their investigation in this time.

To protect the child, the Standard Juvenile Court Act recommends that a child should not be held longer than twenty-four hours, excluding Sundays and holidays, unless a petition alleging delinquent behavior has been filed with the juvenile court. When a special juvenile detention center is available, the child should be held there instead of in the jail.

Release of child and voluntary supervision. First minor offenses, contrite attitude on the part of the child, adequate parents, and good social adjustment tend to facilitate release of the child to his parents without court hearing and legal disposition. Police sometimes exercise an unauthorized "voluntary" supervision

over the child. Although the police maintain that the parents voluntarily accept this supervision, critics of the practice point out that the police represent authority and parents are afraid not to agree to the plan. Police also sometimes collect money from the child or his parents in order to make restitution for damage done by the child.

The conference of chiefs of police and representatives of related services held in 1953 revealed three points of view on these practices. One group felt that these informal methods of supervision and adjustment by police are justified by the effect they may have on the child's behavior. A second group thought the police should expand their regular police functions into the supervisory field only if the community was lacking in other facilities for this work. Other justifications for police supervision were that some parents will not seek casework with community agencies, children eventually realize that the police are not punitive but are continuously aware of their conduct, and that some police are trained to offer treatment.

A third group was opposed to all types of voluntary supervision by police. Arguments against such supervision were that the police were overstepping their authority and acting as prosecutor and judge as well as investigator, that the supervision was not voluntarily accepted by child and parents, that few police are trained to do casework, that police supervision duplicates services provided by other agencies, and that personnel must be increased with increased cost to the taxpayer.[3]

Under the circumstances, each police department, with or without consultation with the juvenile court, devises its own policy.

Referral of child by police to social agencies. When the child is referred to a social agency, he is also released to his parents. The referral is on a voluntary basis, that is, the police do not have legal authority to demand a referral. They can, however, bring considerable pressure to bear on the parents, especially if the alternative seems to be referral to the juvenile court. Children so referred usually have exhibited somewhat serious misconduct but are not "hard core" delinquents with a long-established pattern of delinquency. Sometimes the trouble seems to lie within the family itself, and referral

---

Washington, D. C., 1954, pp. 7–10. The report incorporates the deliberations, range of opinion, and consensus of a conference of about fifty leading police officials and representatives of related fields, held in East Lansing, Michigan, August 3–4, 1953, under the sponsorship of the Children's Bureau and the International Association of Chiefs of Police.

1 *Ibid.*, p. 10.
2 *Standard Juvenile Court Act*, sixth edition, National Probation and Parole Association, New York, 1959, pp. 37–43.

3 *Ibid.*, pp. 24–27.

may lead to readjustment of the entire family relationship.

Referrals depend upon the availability of appropriate social agencies in the community and their readiness to accept the cases. They also depend upon the ability of the parents to comprehend what a social agency may be able to do to help them and their child. Especially among newcomers to the city, services offered by social agencies may not be understood. Parents may be afraid or suspicious of them.

Referrals to juvenile court. Usually, referral to the juvenile court is reserved for the one-fourth of delinquents having the most serious and persistent offenses. The conference of chiefs of police (East Lansing, 1953) agreed on the following reasons as justifying referral:

1. The particular offense committed by the child is of a serious nature.
2. The child is known or has in the past been known to the juvenile court.
3. The child has a record of repeated delinquency extending over a period of time.
4. The child or his parents have shown themselves unable or unwilling to co-operate with agencies of a nonauthoritative (social agency) character.
5. Casework with the child by a nonauthoritative agency has failed in the past.
6. Treatment services needed by the child can be obtained only through the court and its probation department.
7. The child denies the offense and the officer believes judicial determination is called for, and there is sufficient evidence to warrant referral or the officer believes that the child and his family are in need of aid.[1]
8. There is apparent need for treatment.[1]

Agreement is general among police, court officials, and social workers that screening must take place before cases come to the attention of the juvenile court. Otherwise, in most cities the court would be so crowded with minor cases that a long delay would follow referral of the child. The alternative would be an expensive duplication of courts. Also, many children are really candidates for social work procedures and, if they can be distinguished, may be spared the court appearance. It must be recalled also that the juvenile court judge is not a social worker but a lawyer by training; his services are best reserved for cases in which authoritative legal action is needed.

There is controversy, but not over the need for screening and diversified referring of cases. The controversy concerns the agency best fitted to screen. In some cities a preliminary screening is made by the police, with another screening made by a social worker or a probation department attached to the juvenile court and at its best staffed by trained social workers. The more elaborate organizations are in large cities. In small cities, cases are handled either by police or the juvenile court judge with little formal screening procedure.

Organization of police work with juvenile delinquents

Police work with delinquents is usually organized in three ways.

1. Especially in small cities, the regular force is the only one available for all types of police work.

2. In some cities in addition to the regular force there are special youth police or youth squads, attached to the investigative branch of the police department. These youth police supplement the regular police, taking over as much of the work of apprehension of delinquents and investigation of delinquency as is possible. However, the regular policeman on the beat would still interfere in an act of delinquency or crime if he were present and the youth police were not.

3. Juvenile control unit. Most of the large cities in the United States have their youth police organized into an independent department or juvenile control unit called by some such name as crime prevention bureau, juvenile bureau, youth aid division, or juvenile division. Duties of the juvenile control units vary from city to city, but are likely to include some of the following: making use of information gained in investigations by other police units to arrange the disposition of the case; patrolling known juvenile hangouts where conditions are harmful to the welfare of children; maintaining records of juvenile cases; and planning and coordinating a delinquency prevention program.[2] Some units routinely investigate certain types of situations inimical to children, such as family neglect or abuse, employment of minors, immoral vocations, admission of minors to im-

1 *Ibid.,* p. 20.

2 *Ibid.,* p. 39.

proper places, possession or sale of obscene literature to children, bicycle thefts, offenses committed on school property, sex offenses involving juveniles except forcible rape, and gang fighting among juveniles.

Some juvenile control units have experimented with case studies and treatment, notably the Juvenile Aid Bureau of the New York City police department, during the early part of its experience. This function has now been stopped. It was the opinion of the conference of chiefs of police in East Lansing in 1953 and also of a special committee of the International Chiefs of Police in 1958 that police should not undertake social casework or individual rehabilitation.[1] For these services trained case workers are needed. The latter group defined the duties of police as patrol, investigation, and public education. The police should carry investigation to the point where the child is released as not in need of further aid or where he is referred to a social agency or the juvenile court.

Special youth police in other countries

The trend toward special police for youth is not confined to the United States. Since 1926, with increasing emphasis, the need for police specially selected and trained to work with children and youth has been discussed in the General Assemblies and included in reports of the International Criminal Police Organization—Interpol. The First United Nations Congress on the Prevention of Crime and the Treatment of Delinquents, held in Geneva in 1955, strongly urged the creation of special police services for juveniles on the part of nations not already providing such services.[2]

Industrialized nations more often have specialized police than do nations still essentially in an agrarian and handicraft stage of development. In the latter, special police may be found in one or two industrialized cities. In general, until large industrialized cities develop, delinquency tends to be infrequent and to be controlled through strong family organization. As in the United States,

family organization tends to weaken or collapse in large cities, and delinquency becomes a public problem.

Surveys made by the Department of Social Affairs of the United Nations showed that in 1953 the following statement could be made for the Middle and Near Eastern countries of Egypt, Iran, Iraq, Jordan, Lebanon, Saudi Arabia, Syria, Turkey, and Yemen: "In this region there exist no special legal provisions concerning the apprehension of juvenile offenders, which is usually carried out by the ordinary police under the same rules of procedure followed in respect of adult criminals."[3] In Asia and the Far East in 1953, no special provision for the arrest of juvenile delinquents was found in the laws of Burma, Ceylon, the Philippines, Pakistan, Thailand, and the various states of India. However, in cities like Manila, Rangoon, and Bombay, special juvenile control units in the police force worked with juvenile delinquents. In 1953 Bangkok joined this list. Japan had special provisions.[4] European countries, in general, either have specially trained police to work with delinquents, or the regular police officers are aware of special problems and often work closely with various child welfare committees. The impression given by the various surveys is of an awakening awareness of juvenile delinquency as a public problem and a slow approach to special police services. In some countries services are well developed. As in the United States, large cities are more likely to have special services than small cities or rural areas.

Probably because much of it is new, police work with children does not fall into a standardized pattern. A few illustrations of police work with juveniles show the variety of approaches:[5]

In Federal Germany the chief police group that is active in delinquency prevention and control is the women's criminal investigation department (W. P. K., Weibliche Kriminalpolizei), first established in 1930 and now

1 *Ibid.,* p. 8; Alexander Aldrich, "The Police Role in Social Investigation," *The Legal Aid Review,* 57 (Fall, 1959), 14–19.
2 *Special Police Departments for the Prevention of Juvenile Delinquency,* submitted by the International Criminal Police Organization—Interpol, General Secretariat, Paris, to the Second United Nations Congress for the Prevention of Crime and the Treatment of Delinquents, London, August, 1960.
3 *Comparative Survey on Juvenile Delinquency, Part V, Middle East,* ST/SOA/SD/1/Add. 4, United Nations, Department of Social Affairs, Division of Social Welfare, New York, 1953, p. 8.
4 *Comparative Survey on Juvenile Delinquency, Part IV, Asia and the Far East,* ST/SOA/SD/1/Add. 3, United Nations, Department of Social Affairs, Division of Social Welfare, New York, 1953, pp. 18–20.
5 *Special Police Departments for the Prevention of Juvenile Delinquency, loc. cit.*

operating in all the states of the federation. In addition, all states except the Saar have young people's advisers (jugendsachbearbiter) attached to the police forces; given special training, these advisers deal with offenses committed by adolescents aged fourteen to eighteen. Some large cities have other special provisions. The W. P. K. is regarded as the section of the police force that is most concerned with control of juvenile delinquency.

Since 1947, Vienna, Austria, has had a special department to deal with juveniles (Jugendpolizei) at the federal police headquarters. A specially trained officer, wherever possible a woman, attached to each of the local federal police departments deals with cases involving juveniles. The Vienna federal police established a youth hostel (Jugendheim) in 1950 so that children in immediate physical or moral danger and suspects could be held until a decision was made to send them either to welfare centers or to the juvenile court detention center. About 600 children per year spend some time in this hostel.

Rangoon, Burma, has had a Special Juvenile Squad since 1958 that handles all cases of juvenile delinquency. Police officers serve on the committees of three children's hostels.

In India, the cities of Bombay, Calcutta, and Hyderabad each have a juvenile aid police unit composed of both men and women. Work is chiefly preventive and the units co-operate with welfare agencies and schools. In Hyderabad a specially trained police officer maintains relations with the press, with good results.

In Japan, the National Police Agency in Tokyo has organized a Juvenile Sub-Section in the Crime Prevention Section. Each of seven regional police bureaus has a Juvenile Safety Section. All the police stations in the country have special juvenile branches, first established in 1949. Police co-operate with special public movements against delinquency, such as the month-long yearly campaigns organized by the Central and Prefectural Juvenile Deliberation Councils, and the work of the various guidance centers. These centers are credited with aiding the police in detecting both delinquents and predelinquents.

England has no special juvenile officers or unit; however, policewomen, who are a normal part of the police departments all over the country, make a special point of trying to spot predelinquents. All children are a special concern of all police, who decide individually whether merely to caution a misbehaving child or to take formal action. Liverpool, a city of 800,000, has innovated a plan to control delinquency which has been hailed as a great success. The Crime Prevention Branch of the police appointed a police juvenile liaison officer for each section of the city. The fifteen liaison officers work primarily with first offenders and are responsible for working with all criminal, social, or moral cases involving children under eighteen. They work with parents and co-ordinate the work done by various community and social agencies. In 1957 a special unit of policewomen was formed to work with girls up to the age of seventeen who seemed likely to become prostitutes.

Selection, training, and special practices of police for juveniles

Selection. Various conferences in the United States and abroad as well as individual professionals in the field emphasize the importance of assigning to juvenile work only those officers with a special interest in and ability to gain rapport with juveniles. Routine assignment of police officers to juvenile work is regarded as a quick way to failure. Much juvenile work is preventive in nature. Children and youth are warned when they seemed headed for delinquency or are engaged in minor delinquencies. If the warning is not effective, delinquencies may increase in seriousness and frequency until a court referral becomes necessary. Warnings backed by threats or force are less effective than those supported by explanations and a genuine interest on the part of the policeman. Another attribute of the police for youth is firmness; a buddy-buddy attitude is avoided. The police officer must hold himself apart from the child as one who firmly believes in orderliness and obedience to the law. He thus sets a barrier between the child and delinquency but not between himself and the child.

Women are often recruited to work with children. Policewomen are usually given special responsibility in dealing with all preadolescent children, both boys and girls, and with adolescent girls. For the preadolescents much of their work is protective; they visit places where children may be exploited or permitted to break laws, and they are especially on the lookout for sexual approaches to young children. Much of their work with older girls also revolves around sexual exploitation or a drift toward prostitution. Men police officers usually work with adolescent boys, who often commit serious delinquencies or crimes necessitating arrest rather than warnings and preventive supervision.

There is no general agreement as to whether the officers working with juveniles should be selected from the already-operating police force of a city or should be especially selected for youth work. Since they are police officers, a compromise position is that they should be specially recruited for youth work but should be assigned for six months to regular police work before being assigned to youth work. In this way they would be familiar with police problems and also trained sufficiently for reassignment to other than youth units if necessary.[1]

Three qualifications emphasized by the International Criminal Police Organization—Interpol for youth police—are that they should be "volunteers," that is, eager for this type of work; they should be young and in good physical condition; and they should be mentally and morally well-balanced. Otherwise, their effect on youth may be deleterious rather than beneficial.[2]

Training. Since the regular police, even in cities with special youth officers, have many contacts with children and youth, all police should have some training both in laws concerning children and in how to approach and handle misbehaving or criminal children and youth. Without such training, the tendency is for police to follow a "get tough" policy, with many arrests of children for trivial misconduct and excessive physical roughness with adolescent boys. Far from reforming children and youth, such treatment only arouses hostility and resentment and reduces the possibility that police will be effective in preventing or reducing delinquency.

Special youth officers require additional, intensive training. This training may be on an in-service basis, although only the largest police departments as a rule have such programs. For smaller cities, regional training

programs are a possibility, drawing upon professionals outside the department for teachers, such as judges, trained probation officers, social workers, lawyers, professors in local colleges or universities, and others with training that qualifies them to participate in such a training program. The Children's Bureau makes the following suggestions for subjects to be covered:

1. Philosophy of police work with juveniles.
2. Laws pertaining to juveniles.
3. Conditioning factors in juvenile delinquency.
4. Duties of a juvenile control unit.
5. Intra-departmental relationship between the juvenile control unit and other police units and personnel.
6. Interviewing.
7. Screening process.
8. Dispositions.
9. Knowledge and use of community resources.
10. Records.
11. Developing good relationships with related agencies and the public.
12. Preventing delinquency through community organization.[3]

A number of colleges and universities sponsor institutes on juvenile law enforcement running from two days to ten weeks, and leading either to a certificate or to college credit.[4] A few universities have special degree programs in criminology or police administration which sometimes include individual courses applicable to youth police work. The social-work program is also applicable to some phases, as are courses in sociology and psychology. Standards for training are still in flux, but agreement is general that special training is needed.

Special practices. In line with a rehabilitative philosophy and the avoidance of stigmatizing a child or youth as delinquent, certain special practices have developed. Usually members of the special youth police unit do not wear uniforms. It is regarded as especially important that they should not when calling at a child's home or school to interview him, his parents, or his teachers. He would of course identify himself as a member of the police force, but his civilian clothing would shield the family from curious neighbors. Also some

1 *Police Services for Juveniles, loc. cit.,* pp. 40–41.
2 *Special Police Departments for the Prevention of Juvenile Delinquency, loc. cit.,* p. 45

3 *Police Services for Juveniles, loc. cit.,* pp. 42–43.
4 A list of universities, program titles, and length of institutes is given in the Appendix.

children or families might regard the uniform as a symbol of force and be reluctant to co-operate from fear. The automobile in which the youth police officer rides should not carry an identifying symbol for the same reasons.

Police are agreed that complete records should be kept when a complaint has been received, an investigation made, or a child taken into custody. This record should be confidential and should be opened only to persons with a legitimate concern about a case. Otherwise children may be harmed by widespread knowledge of some minor offense or, as a law-abiding adult, be prevented from securing work because of a "police record." There is less general agreement about keeping records of children with whom the police have had informal contacts only. On one side, some argue that such records reveal harmful community conditions or provide light in case of later more serious delinquency. Others call attention to the only occasional value of such records, the amount of time involved in making them, and the later harmful effect they may have if they become public.[1]

Strong arguments for and against photographing and fingerprinting juveniles prevent any clear statement of policy or practice. In some states laws forbid these methods of identification; in states where they are permitted, individual police departments may have a policy opposing them. Such methods are contrary to general juvenile court principles, since they may later become part of general files which are checked by prospective employers at a time when the former misbehaving juvenile has become an upright adult. However, those who favor photographing and fingerprinting point to their usefulness as means of identification.

A middle course is suggested by the Children's Bureau: to fingerprint only on authorization of the juvenile court; to limit fingerprinting to children suspected of committing such acts (felonies in adults) as robbery, rape, homicide, manslaughter, or major acts of burglary, to children with a long history of delinquency, and to runaways who refuse to reveal their identity. If a child is found not guilty of the act of which he was accused, the prints should be returned to the court for destruction. If fingerprints are filed

in local, state, or federal bureaus they should be filed as civil identifications only.[2]

These and similar special practices are all designed to protect the child from stigmatization in his own eyes or among friends and neighbors. If he can be treated as an erring child or youth, subject to regaining or achieving conformity, the chances of rehabilitation are much greater than if he is officially or publicly designated a delinquent.

Expansion of police functions to preventive programs

Much inspection and patrol work that police do is preventive in that it clears up doubtful situations harmful to children or checks the activities of children before they reach the point of actual lawbreaking. In some cities police have gone further and established clubs and recreational programs designed to prevent delinquency. In such situations police officers are assigned to operate these projects, to serve as youth leaders, or to raise money by solicitation; civilians may also be employed.

Police Athletic League, New York City. The most widely publicized of police recreational programs in the United States is the Police Athletic League, or PAL. With its roots in a Junior Police program begun in 1914, the organization developed full status in 1932. Although it is independently incorporated, it has always remained a unit of the police Juvenile Aid Bureau (JAB), (reorganized and made a part of the Police Department's Youth Division in 1959). At first, PAL offered recreational services only in high delinquency areas, where recreational facilities were inadequate. Later it expanded into all areas. It was staffed by the Education and Recreation Department of the federal Work Projects Administration during the existence of this agency, which was closed in 1943. Thereafter, PAL raised money to meet all expenses through one dollar fees of associate members, private contributions, and the proceeds of annual benefit performances. During the latter fifties the organization declined. The parent organization, Juvenile Aid Bureau, was under heavy criticism, contributions were inadequate, facilities were in disrepair, and salaries were too low to retain the staff. In 1959, new impetus was given to the

---

1 *Police Services for Juveniles, op. cit.,* pp. 27–29.

2 *Police Services for Juveniles, op. cit.,* pp. 29–31.

program under new and vigorous leadership.

The PAL program reaches some 150,000 boys and girls each year and is reported to be the largest privately financed recreation agency in New York City. In 1959, eight full-time and forty part-time centers were in use and seventy-eight precinct programs were operated. The activities duplicate those of any typical community center, with athletics, dancing, clubs, games, arts, and crafts. Special programs are put on by children at Hallowe'en, Thanksgiving, Christmas, and other occasions. In the summer, playgrounds and blocked-off streets as well as a summer camp provide outdoor recreation. Certain scholarships are available for excellence in athletics and the arts.[1]

Other recreational programs. The sponsorship of some type of recreation for youth by police departments is widespread. Among 611 police departments responding to a questionnaire in 1952, half reported that they had juvenile specialists on the force, and about the same number reported that they conducted recreational programs for children.[2]

The type of recreation sponsored by police departments covers a wide range, from the extensive program of PAL to sponsorship of Boy and Girl Scout units. Some departments with a police band have a junior band.

Police clubs abroad. Sponsorship of recreation and clubs is not limited to the United States. The police of many other countries have also expanded their preventive work into the recreational area. Clubs are reported in Australia, Belgium, Burma, Canada, Denmark, India, and Sweden. Usually the clubs are found only in major cities. Mannheim, Germany, initiated police-sponsored dance halls, an activity that has spread to other German cities. In these halls young people from sixteen to twenty-five may come to dance. Only nonalcoholic drinks are served. In England, especially in London, the police operate youth clubs. In addition, thirty-seven cities in England and Wales operate "attendance centres" under the 1948 Criminal Justice Act. They are run by volunteer police officers in their spare time. The courts may send offenders aged twelve to twenty-one to these centers for a maximum of three hours a day. They receive physical training, courses in handicrafts, and lectures on good citizenship. For some of the boys, the activities in the centers prepare them for entrance into various youth organizations.[3]

Evaluation of recreational programs. It is difficult to evaluate the programs sponsored or operated by police departments. As preventives to delinquency, they are subject to the general criticism of recreational programs discussed in Chapter 16. On the other hand, there is general concensus that well-planned, supervised recreation is a constructive experience for all children and youth. There is some doubt as to how appealing the programs are to already-delinquent adolescents.

Younger children and active adolescents often find them attractive. The extent to which they may prevent delinquency is almost impossible to measure.

Special criticisms have been directed toward many of the programs operated by police. The charge is made that police are not trained for recreational or club leadership that needed programs should be operated by professional recreational organizations. Another charge is that assigning police to recreational projects weakens the department as a whole and that these police would be more effective if engaged in their regular role. Police counter with the charge that recreational facilities are inadequate in many areas and they are simply filling a need not met by recreational agencies and that the contacts with youth generally improve the relationship between police and youth and make police work more effective.

On the basis of recommendations and comments from the National Sheriffs' Association, the International Association of Chiefs of Police, and the National Conference on Prevention and Control of Juvenile Delinquency (1946), the Children's Bureau makes four points for consideration by a police department interested in the recreational aspect of police work:

1. The police have the responsibility to keep the community informed about recreational needs, particularly in underprivileged areas.

1 *Annual Report, 1959* and other pamphlets from the Police Athletic League, New York.

2 *Police Services for Juveniles, loc. cit.,* pp. 53–57. The questionnaire was distributed by the Special Juvenile Delinquency Project of the Children's Bureau and the International Association of Chiefs of Police. Replies came primarily from the larger cities.

3 *Special Police Departments for the Prevention of Juvenile Delinquency, loc. cit.*

2. All communities should provide recreation based on community needs and developed through broad community planning.
3. Police participation in providing recreational service should be determined through this joint community planning.
4. Recreation supervisors should be trained in the field of recreation, and recreation programs should meet recognized standards.[1]

Other preventive activities. Police both in the United States and abroad engage in a variety of other activities not strictly in line with traditional police functions designed to prevent delinquency. These include lectures to school classes or assemblies and to parent-teacher groups; radio and television programs focused on delinquency prevention and the work of the police; teaching traffic safety to youth; and encouraging youth to visit police stations and to come for advice.

The efforts of police at delinquency prevention follow the pattern found in the community as a whole. Not being sure how to prevent delinquency, they try numerous approaches, many of which are undoubtedly constructive in nature although unproven as to their effectiveness in actually decreasing delinquency. They testify to the great interest in delinquency prevention that has become part of the concern of police departments across the country and to their readiness to accept the juvenile court philosophy of prevention and rehabilitation as a substitute for the outmoded philosophy of force and punishment.

Co-ordination of police and other agencies

Many agencies in a community have a stake in delinquency prevention and control: the police, the juvenile court, the schools, and social agencies in general. As the first agency to have official contact with misbehaving children, the police are in an especially vulnerable position with reference to the functions of other agencies. Agencies tend to believe that their own approach is better than that of many other agencies and to be zealous in carrying out their functions. Many possibilities, therefore, exist for misunderstanding and conflict.

Relationship with the juvenile court. The degree of authority undertaken by the police in dismissing children or in referring them to

1 *Police Services for Juveniles, loc. cit.,* p. 55.

other agencies may be a point of conflict. Some screening and diverting of children from the court is needed. The question is, which agency is best qualified to do it? In some cities most preadolescent children and minor adolescent offenders are handled by the police delinquency control unit. At the other extreme, all children taken into custody by the police are immediately taken to the juvenile detention center where the probation officers attached to the juvenile court assume responsibility for the screening. One point to be considered is the division of labor between police and the probation branch of the court. Which children can be adequately screened by police, with or without special training for juvenile work? Which children require the more specialized services of a probation officer before decision is made as to release, referral to a casework agency for treatment, or referral to the juvenile court? Another question concerns the adequacy of training of the probation officers. Questions of screening are related to the training of police and court staff and especially to a policy agreed upon by police and court. Too much assumption of authority by the police may mean that many children in need of special services slip out into the community again. Or, children without basic delinquency trends are needlessly referred to the court, where they are screened out without a court hearing.

Police sometimes do not understand the philosophy and practices of the juvenile court. In the suburb of an eastern city, police felt that when they had taken a child into custody and escorted him to the juvenile court in the core city, the child should be institutionalized and therefore removed from the suburb. The judge placed a large number of children on probation; the sentiment of the police was that the child was back in the suburb before they had had time to return. They therefore instituted an illegal form of probation, instructing the child to report to them at regular intervals and requiring their parents to see that this was done. The parents did not know that this action by the police was illegal.

Relationship between police and private social agencies. Whereas the court and its staff must accept the children referred by the police and make some decision about the case, the private social agency is not under this compulsion. A given agency may provide only a special type of service which may be limited to children of some specific race, religion, or nationality. It may have an overload of cases and simply place the name of a child on the waiting list, in order not to jeopardize the work already in process. The staff may have an interview with a child, look into the background situation, and dismiss the child as one the agency cannot hope to help. Police must work within these limitations in referring children. It is necessary for them to know the limitations and policies of each agency and to establish workable relationships with each one.

When police attempt to do casework, even through specialized units, they often are severely criticized by social agencies, whose trained staff assert that the police are first police, and second, social workers. The police social workers are actually, or in the minds of clients, backed by the authority of the police department. Most social workers react negatively to the idea of such authority and feel that case work can be done successfully only when the client comes voluntarily. This point of view has been attacked recently through the philosophy of "aggressive case work," in which social workers make the initial approach to a family or child in need of treatment of some sort.[1]

Co-operation with schools. Since schools serve as quasi-legal agencies of delinquency control, a division of labor needs to be established between the police department and the school administration. Truancy is a case in point. Schools typically expect to handle truants themselves up to a certain point, but truancy is one of the specified acts of delinquency in many state laws on delinquency, and beyond a certain point, schools rely on juvenile courts to enforce the school attendance law. Where

1 See Chapter 17.

this point lies, however, is open to question. Police and schools also need to define the outdoor boundary around a school building that separates police supervision from school supervision of children, both for their protection and for delinquency control. Residents in the neighborhood also need to understand the kind of misbehavior by children on the way to and from school which should be reported to the school or to the police. Other decisions need to be made jointly on the use of school records by police in the course of an investigation, as to when the police may approach a suspected delinquent in school and for what large gatherings police should be on hand for regulation and control of traffic and behavior. None of these overlapping areas needs to involve conflict; all need clarification.

Relationships with co-ordinating bodies. The police department, and especially the delinquency control unit or specialized youth police, need affiliation with any community planning or co-ordinating bodies. They may be the source of useful information on the local problem of delinquency, and their work should be geared with the work of other social agencies which are members of the co-ordinating body.

Some cities have special city-wide councils concerned only with delinquency. For example, Washington D. C., has a body known as the Commissioners' Youth Council, established in 1953 by the Board of Commissioners governing the District of Columbia. The Council has units in each of a number of areas, whose task is to co-ordinate the efforts of all agencies (represented in the Council) concerned with delinquency prevention and control. The police are one such agency.[2]

2 John E. Winters, "The Role of the Police in the Prevention and Control of Delinquency," *Federal Probation*, 21 (June, 1957), 3–8.

Bibliography

Police

Annual Report, Police Athletic League, New York, 1959.

Greenblatt, Bernard, *Staff and Training for Juvenile Law Enforcement in Urban Police Departments*, Children's Bureau Publication No. 13, U. S. Government Printing Office, Washington, D. C., 1960.

Kahn, Alfred J., "The Functions of Police and Children's Courts," *The Community and the Correctional Process*, 1951 Yearbook, National Probation and Parole Association

(now National Council on Crime and Delinquency), New York, 1951, pp. 60–74.

Kenney, John P., and Dan G. Pursuit, *Police Work with Juveniles*, Charles C. Thomas, Publisher, Springfield, Illinois, 1954.

Millikin, Rhoda J., "The Police and Children in Trouble," *Federal Probation*, 19 (March, 1955), 24–27.

Police Services for Juveniles, Children's Bureau Publication No. 344, U. S. Government Printing Office, Washington, D. C., 1954.

Russell, Bernard, *Current Training Needs in the*

Field of Juvenile Delinquency, Children's Bureau Publication No. 8, U. S. Government Printing Office, Washington, D. C., 1960.

Selvidge, Jean, "The Police Juvenile Bureau's Job," *National Probation and Parole Association Journal,* 3 (1957), 39–47.

Special Police Departments for the Prevention of Juvenile Delinquency, submitted by the International Criminal Police Organization—Interpol, General Secretariat, Paris, to the Second United Nations Congress for the Prevention of Crime and the Treatment of Delinquents, London, August, 1960.

Winters, John E., "The Role of the Police in the Prevention and Control of Delinquency," *Federal Probation,* 21 (June, 1957), 3–8.

Delinquency control in New York City. The delinquency control unit, known for many years as the Juvenile Aid Bureau, was included in a Youth Division in 1959. It has been under severe criticism and in process of reorganization. The following references deal with this unit but also provide much general information about police preventive and control efforts.

Aldrich, Alexander, "The Police Role in Social Investigation," *Legal Aid Review,* 57 (Fall, 1959), 14–19.

Chwast, Jacob, "Police Methods for Handling Delinquent Youth," *Journal of Criminal Law, Criminology and Police Science,* 46 (1955), 255–258.

Kahn, Alfred J., *Crisis in the New York City Police Program for Youth,* Citizens' Committee for Children of New York City, Inc., New York, 1959.

———, *For Children in Trouble,* Citizens' Committee for Children of New York City, Inc., New York, 1957.

———, *Police and Children,* Citizens' Committee on Children of New York City, Inc., New York, 1951.

The Police Department, Juvenile Delinquency Evaluation Project of the City of New York, City College, New York, 1956.

The Police Department: One Year Later, Juvenile Delinquency Evaluation Project of the City of New York, City College, New York, 1957.

Smith, Bruce, *The New York City Police Survey,* Institute of Public Administration, New York, 1952.

Detention of delinquents refers to keeping them in restrictive custody twenty-four hours a day when necessary during the process of investigating an offense, during any waiting period prior to the court hearing, and after the hearing but prior to admittance to a correctional school if they are committed to one. Detention is not punishment. A child is not "sentenced" to detention as he may be to a correctional school. Detention is a form of holding a child prior to a court hearing or between a hearing and transfer to a correctional school.

Limited need for detention

Not all children are or need to be detained in custody. Approximately two-thirds of children referred to the juvenile court are released to the custody of their parents or to a responsible adult. The other third are detained, at least over night and some for much longer periods prior to their court hearing.[1] When children are released, their parents are responsible for bringing them to the court hearing, which may not be held until some days or weeks after the child is first taken into custody by the police or referred to the court without police action by parents, teachers, or others.

Some children, however, cannot safely be placed in the hands of their parents and permitted the freedom of the community. If the child has been dangerously aggressive with threats or actions, he may be detained for the safety of others. If the parents or others are hostile toward the child because of his misdeeds, the child may be detained for his own safety. The delinquent who is known as a runaway or who has made suicide threats is also likely to be detained. The emotionally disturbed child may be detained for close psychiatric study. Runaways from other places who are picked up by the police often must be kept in safe custody until they can be returned to their homes or to police or to a welfare agency in their communities. As will be explained later, only about 10 per cent of all delinquents who come to police attention need detention.

The decision whether or not to place in detention a child referred to the court rests

---

1 I. Richard Perlman, "Delinquency Prevention: The Size of the Problem," *Annals of the American Academy of Political and Social Science*, 322 (1959), 6.

Chapter **20**

Detention of delinquent children and youth

with an intake officer, usually a probation officer, who functions under policies set up by the juvenile court judge. The decision is part of the total intake process of the juvenile court, which is described in Chapter 22.

Except in four states where a state system of courts and detention prevails, juvenile delinquency is handled on a county basis. The number of children in need of detention is closely related to the number of delinquent children in a county and, therefore, indirectly to the population of the county. Rural counties may have only one or two children per year who must be placed in detention; counties with small cities may detain several hundred while large cities detain thousands. For example, Philadelphia holds approximately 12,500 children per year. The children detained in no instance include all delinquent children referred to the juvenile court. The period of detention is short—from a few days to a few weeks. Therefore, at any one time during the year, only a few children are detained. Philadelphia has a daily average of only 170 children in detention. A midwestern county of 210,000 population detained 816 children in 1959 but at any one time had only an average of ten in detention.

The small number of children who need detention at any one time, combined with the custom of providing detention on a county basis, poses one of the major problems of suitable detention for children.

It is now widely accepted that children should be separated from adult offenders while in detention. When the number of children makes it feasible, boys are separated from girls and younger children from older thus facilitating specialized programs and control. These stipulations for good detention demand special quarters, even though they may not be fully used at any given time. Best detention practices also call for something more than physical safekeeping of the child. Especially for children who must remain in detention for several weeks while investigation or special studies are being made, a normal round of activities is needed as well as counseling in order to avoid demoralization of the child and to begin or lay the groundwork for rehabilitation that may be carried on after release in the community or in a training school, if the child is committed to one. These provisions necessitate suitable space beyond that occupied by sleeping quarters, such as indoor and outdoor recreational areas, dining area to avoid eating meals in the sleeping rooms, school room, and interviewing room. A specialized staff is required to operate the program, in addition to the maintenance staff that takes care of the physical plant. These standards can be met only in special detention centers limited to children, constructed (or remodeled from some other structure) for the purpose.

Few counties need or can afford special detention centers. Approximately 85 per cent of all counties—about 2,550—have populations of less than 50,000 and hence, few delinquents in need of detention.[1] One per cent—about 30 counties—have populations running from 50,000 to 100,000 with only a small number of delinquents at any one time in need of detention. Slightly more than 400 counties have a population in excess of 100,-000; only these could reasonably be expected to support special detention quarters for delinquent children, and the financial strain would be grave for many of the less populous counties in this group. Many of these counties make no special provision, and others use makeshift arrangements. In general, only the larger counties have specially constructed juvenile detention quarters.

From this situation two main questions arise: What means of detention do the counties with small population use? To what extent do the populous counties provide adequate detention quarters and program?

1 Sherwood Norman, *Detention Practice,* National Probation and Parole Association, New York, 1960, p. 165.

Detention without special juvenile detention centers

A variety of places for detention is used by counties without special centers. Within the facilities available, many attempt to provide comfortable quarters. If an adjacent county has a juvenile detention center, arrangements may be made to pay this county for detention of the few children in need of it. A nearby state correctional school may accept children for detention. A dwelling house may have detention screens or bars placed over the windows of certain rooms and locks provided for room doors, perhaps in the home of a couple willing to assume supervision. A few rooms in some institution, as an old people's county home, may be screened or barred and used. Sometimes a few rooms in the court house or some other public building are similarly reinforced. These methods provide for the physical custody of children, but too often in barren jail-like rooms and without any provision for exercise or schooling, much less counseling.

Detention in jails

More often than any of the above, the county jail is used when there is no special juvenile detention center, even though the effect of jail detention is almost certainly harmful to the child.

The traditional place of detention for children and adults alike is the city or county jail. The practice dates from the period prior to juvenile court legislation when delinquents and criminals of all ages were thrust into a common jail to await trial, to serve a sentence as punishment, or to await transfer to a prison or, in earlier days, infliction of some form of physical punishment. With the establishment of juvenile courts, it became evident that the protective care and rehabilitation with which the juvenile courts were charged was vitiated by imprisonment in jails. Gradually makeshift centers were used and in time specially designed juvenile detention centers were constructed.

Nevertheless, it is estimated that each year from 75,000 to 100,000 children of juvenile court age are housed for some period of time in county jails, almost invariably without special accommodations for children. Others may be detained in city jails for short periods.

Condition of jails. Jails are operated by a

municipal government under the administration of the city police department or by the county government under the direction of the county sheriff. As a class, jails are the most backward and neglected of all detention, correctional, and penal institutions. They have been called a public nuisance, a human garbage can, and the Black Hole of Calcutta, American style. A typical jail is a series of small-barred cells, resembling cages in a zoo, at best equipped with a narrow cot, with or without mattress, a flush toilet, and a wash bowl with running water; although the wash bowl is often lacking, and one toilet may serve a number of cells. Meals are served in the cells. Exercise space is usually lacking, as

Many juvenile delinquents are housed in jails to await a court hearing, especially in counties with too few delinquents to justify a special detention home or in cities when the detention home is filled. This Utah jail cell is barren of any means of activity. It is, however, clean, and the beds are well supplied with blankets. In some communities juveniles find themselves in dirty cells with only a bare wooden bench or metal cot without bedding. (Courtesy Bureau of Services for Children, Department of Public Welfare, Utah)

are activities of any kind. Prisoners, even before their guilt is proven, often simply sit or stand in the cell day after day. Some jails have a day room in which prisoners may mill around, with the stronger ones sometimes abusing the weaker and smaller ones. The jail may be kept well painted and clean, or not, depending upon the local situation. Many jails are so old that even an attempt at cleanliness and sanitation is only partly successful.

Only estimates exist as to the number of county and city jails in the United States. Estimates run from 3,000 to 4,000.[1] Most jails are very small. Fully 54 per cent (1,723) of jails have a capacity for less than twenty-five persons. At the other extreme are ten city jails with a capacity for a thousand or more people.[2] Children are more likely to be detained in the small jails than the large urban jails, since most large cities have special detention centers for children.

From time to time some state surveys its jails, and annually the Federal Bureau of Prisons surveys some five to eight hundred jails in order to designate those suitable for the detention of federal prisoners awaiting trial. The following rating scale has proved useful:

	Points
Custody and security	5
Food	5
Administration	4
Inmate control and discipline	4
Housekeeping, sanitation, and personal hygiene	4
Building and equipment	3
Medical and health service	3
Inmate employment	2
Inmate activities (religious program and educational and recreational opportunities)	1

Each jail is given a percentage rating for each factor; each percentage is then multiplied by the factor's weight and the sum of the products is divided by thirty-one—the total value of the weight. A rating of 90–100 is excellent, 75–89 is good, 60–74 is fair, 50–59 is poor, and under 50 is bad.[3]

Each year the Bureau drops from the list

jails that rated poor the year before and adds some additional jails. Year after year, almost no jails are rated excellent, about half rate as good, about a third as fair and 6 or 7 per cent as poor. For the 474 jails inspected in 1953, none were excellent, 11 were good, 287 fair, 143 poor, and 33 bad. These ratings are made in terms of suitability for adults, not children. In spite of this dismal picture, the federal inspectors note some improvement over the years, chiefly in food and medical care when needed by the inmates. Idleness remains the chief jail problem. Adults are rarely provided with any employment (even when serving sentences which may run to a year or more), and provisions for recreation, education for youths, and religious program almost never exist aside from a weekly religious service.

In addition to these drawbacks, personnel in charge of the jail are almost universally untrained and often elected or appointed on a political basis rather than for their aptitude or preparation for jail administration.

Unsuitability for children. Especially from the point of view of children detained, little or no provision is made for segregating children from older offenders, ranging from the chronic alcoholic to the skilled thief or occasional murderer among males, and from shoplifters to prostitutes among females. When some attempt is made to separate children from adults, the result may be virtually complete isolation for the one or two children who may be in the small jail at any one time. Also, lack of supervision makes it possible for older children to torment or abuse younger ones. Certainly most jails, small or large, offer little or no opportunity for exercise, recreation, or schooling for children, and make no provision for counseling.

Attempts to improve. The Federal Bureau of Prisons has no authority over jails, not even the ones in which federal prisoners are housed. It does, however, offer several types of training to jail personnel: a correspondence course for jail employees; short training courses given by the Bureau's jail inspectors; and conferences, often in co-operation with other agencies. The training is aimed at the improvement of jails in general and not in converting them into children's institutions. So far as children are concerned, the slow trend is to move them from jails into special detention centers adapted to their needs and

1 For general information on jails, see Louis N. Robinson, *Jails,* John C. Winston Company, Philadelphia, Pennsylvania, 1944; Roy Casy, "Catchall Jails," *Annals of the American Academy of Political and Social Science,* 293 (1954), 28–34.

2 Myrl E. Alexander, "Let's Look at Our Jails," *Federal Probation,* 16 (September, 1952), p. 15.

3 *Federal Prisons, 1953,* United States Department of Justice, Bureau of Prisons, 1954, pp. 44–48.

equipped to lay the foundation for rehabilitation.

Juvenile detention centers

Special juvenile detention centers are advocated by specialists in child delinquency
and by two standard-setting agencies, the
federal Children's Bureau and the National
Council on Crime and Delinquency.[1]

Regional detention homes. Juvenile detention
homes to serve a number of sparsely populated counties are recommended as the best
substitution for jail detention and other inadequate types of detention in sparsely populated counties. In several states, counties
have been authorized to co-operate on building a detention home, but with one exception, nowhere have counties taken advantage
of this permissive legislation. Either no one

1 Edgar W. Brewer, *Detention Planning*, Publication,
  No. 381, Children's Bureau, Washington, D. C., 1960,
  pp. 9–10; Sherwood Norman, *Detention Practice, loc.
  cit.*, Chapter 13. Most of the discussion on detention
  homes is based on these two publications.

This secure, family-type detention home is planned
to accommodate five boys and three girls and a
resident couple to provide care and supervision.
This type of home is suitable for counties with
few children in need of detention. A regional home
would offer many advantages in the way of added
facilities and specialized staff. (Courtesy National
Council on Crime and Delinquency; model by
Sanzenbacher, Miller and Brigham and Charles D.
Scott, Architects)

takes the leadership, or administrative tangles
cannot be straightened out. In lieu of such
permissive arrangements, state initiative is
advocated, with the state establishing and
operating regional detention homes to serve
a number of counties. State and counties
could combine in the financing. The plan
seems especially feasible in states that have
regional juvenile courts. However, state
sponsored detention homes are still a prospect
for the future rather than a present reality.

In 1960, Massachusetts, Delaware, Maryland, and Connecticut operated regional juvenile detention homes, with Connecticut also operating a statewide juvenile court system. Each of its three district courts has its own regional detention center.

County juvenile detention centers. Most detention centers or homes are found in populous counties with large cities. In 1960, 174 such centers served as many counties, although not all met present standards for construction and staffing. Many counties are at the stage where they are discarding remodeled or outmoded detention homes and embarking on new buildings.

To aid in planning, the National Probation and Parole Association has published plans for different types of juvenile detention homes. In general, they group the centers into three types.[1]

1. The family-type home. Planned for a maximum of eight boys and girls, separate in sleeping quarters but with common areas for activities, the building also provides living quarters for a resident couple and sleeping rooms for people needed to relieve them. The photograph on page 255 shows the model for such a home. Security features consist of the fenced or walled recreation area and stainless steel detention screens inside the glass panes at the windows prevent runaways or the breaking of the glass.

Such homes are most suitable for young and co-operative delinquent children. The small number of children virtually precludes a specialized staff, such as a recreation leader, teachers, or counselors. Dependence must be placed on the services of other agencies or on temporary appointments depending upon the needs of whatever children are in the home at any given time.

Family-type homes rarely provide the degree of security or the specialized supervision and services needed for overly aggressive or disturbed adolescents, who often are confined to the county jail in lieu of any other place of high security. The family home therefore only partially solves the problem of suitable detention.

The county that constructs a family deten-

tion home is the one with few delinquents. In the long run, it would provide better detention services by working with other counties for a regional home that could provide a greater variety of facilities for different types of children and a specialized staff.

2. The single-unit detention home. This type of center is designed for fifteen to twenty boys and girls, with separate sleeping quarters but common living areas. The usual design has a central section with a reception area in front and a service area in the rear. On either side extends a wing for sleeping rooms (one wing for boys, the other for girls.) Toward the center of the building are dining, living, recreational, and school areas.

3. The multi-unit home. This home duplicates many of the features of the single unit home, with a number of units for fifteen (or possibly twenty) children each. Separate units can be used for different age groups, and often one unit is reserved for disturbed children. Units may be semidetached buildings of one story (popular in California) or built with several stories (more suitable for large cities.)

4. Decentralized units. When a city finds it necessary to have more than a hundred children in detention at one time, it is advisable to have several district detention homes located close to probation offices serving the same district. Certain professional members of the staff such as doctors and psychiatrists could serve several district centers.

Recommended plans emphasize attractiveness and comfort of the building and provision for a normal round of activities. At the same time, the building is intended for custody and hence should be escape proof, with stainless steel detention screens over all windows, tamperproof protection of light and ventilator panels as well as of all ducts, and locked outer doors. This makes it possible for staff and children to concentrate on program activities without anxiety. Supervision is necessary at all times; to this end, corridors should not have turns that cut off the view of a supervisor. The sleeping rooms and other rooms should have heavy tempered glass panels in the doors. Activities rooms should have safety glass panels built into the walls. Many other provisions are necessary in construction to prevent attempts at escape, to prevent the securing of some object which a youth

---

1 Sherwood Norman, *op. cit.*, Chapter 2; *Standards and Guides for the Detention of Children and Youth*, National Probation and Parole Association, New York, N. Y., 1958, Part 4.

may use as a weapon, and to forestall suicide. A temporary isolation room (or possibly in large centers more than one) is needed, into which a boy or girl may be placed if he is drunk or fighting when first brought in or later becomes so unruly that he cannot remain with others.

Detention in practice

A general discussion of detention may be made more graphic by a description of how the counties of one state met problems of detention when no special center existed or when the center was overcrowded or not appropriate for certain delinquents. The survey upon which the discussion is based also suggests specific problems based on age and sex distribution of children detained. The survey, of Pennsylvania, highlights some of the realities of juvenile detention.[1]

Variations in number of children detained. Pennsylvania is a state with both rural and urban areas, including the large cities of Philadelphia and Pittsburgh and many intermediate sized cities. The number of children detained in a year varied from none at all in eleven counties to 12,486 in Philadelphia County. With 2,972 children detained in Allegheny County (Pittsburgh), the two largest cities account for three-fourths of all children detained. Both counties have detention homes, although Philadelphia County places only two-thirds of children in the detention home, and one-third in other facilities. Seventeen other counties with detention homes held a total of 2,443 children, an average of 144 per county. Fifty-one counties without detention homes detained 2,518 children during the year, an average of forty-nine children per county. All counties except two that detained as many as seventy-five children during 1959 had special detention centers.

Facilities other than detention homes. A question growing out of the above paragraph is how counties without special detention centers managed the problem of detention. The county jail most frequently provided the an-

1 *Children Held in Juvenile Detention—1959,* prepared by the Office of Program Research and Statistics, Commonwealth of Pennsylvania, Harrisburg, May 13, 1960, mimeographed. Clarification of certain points was secured by correspondence. The report covers sixty-four counties; three counties did not respond to the query sent out.

swer: 1,899 children were detained in county jails, or 9.3 per cent of all children detained in the state. Less than 1 per cent of the children detained were held in detention homes of other counties, in the quarters of the jail warden, training schools, court house annex, foster or boarding homes, child-care institutions, or police lock-ups, accounting in all for 3 per cent of all children detained in the state. Thus, second to special detention centers stands the county jail as the place of detention.

Detention in jail in counties with detention homes. In Pennsylvania the existence of a detention home is not a guaranty that all children will be kept out of the jails. The Juvenile Court Act of Pennsylvania includes the provision that youths aged sixteen or seventeen may be detained either in the county jail or a detention center. Practice differs from county to county: some counties never confine a juvenile to jail; others use the jail extensively; others may use the jail only when the detention home is overcrowded.

In practice, 8.3 per cent of children detained in counties with detention homes were nevertheless placed in jail. Some of the counties using both facilities placed only one or two per cent of children in jail; five counties placed a third or more of children in jail—one placed two-thirds in jail. The survey does not indicate to what extent the use of the jail was due to overcrowding of the detention home or to a policy of placing older delinquents in jail and reserving the detention home for younger delinquents.

Problems related to age and sex of detained children. Some idea of the practical problems can also be gained from the Pennsylvania survey. Only 4.7 per cent of the children detained were under twelve years of age; hence small-child care was not a necessity of the detention program. Half of the detainees were aged twelve through fifteen, still of school age and in the active period of early adolescence. The remainder, 45 per cent were aged sixteen and seventeen, adolescents on the verge of adulthood, with the seventeen-year-olds being past the compulsory school attendance age and hence eligible for employment.[2] The age distribution suggests

2 In Pennsylvania jurisdiction of the juvenile court ends at age eighteen; compulsory school attendance ends at age seventeen.

that some part of the facilities would have to be adapted to man-sized and man-strong boys and that the help given during detention should take into account problems of job training and job placement.

The sex ratio was 4.4 boys to one girl. The ratio differed, however, with age. For the under-twelve group, there were eight boys to one girl; for the twelve through fifteen group, there were only 2.7 boys to one girl; among the older adolescents, aged sixteen and seventeen, there were four boys to one girl. Facilities and program need to take account of these differences and of the relatively large number of young adolescent girls.

Length of detention period

Counties vary greatly as to the average length of time that children remain in detention centers. A survey of twenty-three detention centers, made by the National Probation and Parole Association, shows that the average number of days of detention varied from five to thirty.[1] The period of detention should be controlled by the length of time required to prepare the case for the court hearing. Ten days to two weeks is the length of detention recommended by the National Probation and Parole Association. Only in exceptional cases should the social investigation preceding the court hearing require more than this length of time. Children detained for two or three days usually might well have been released when first apprehended, since this period is scarcely adequate for a social investigation and is simply a disturbing experience to the child. Children who are detained longer than two weeks usually suffer a lowering of morale because of the separation from their family and friends, anxiety as to how the juvenile court judge will decide their case, and general dislike of confinement. Occasionally children must be detained longer than two weeks to permit a more thorough investigation or study, perhaps by a psychiatric clinic.

Children are sometimes detained longer than necessary for a variety of reasons. The juvenile court judge or the detention personnel may feel that in detention the child is "safe" from further trouble and also will be on hand for the court hearing. Detention may also arise from the unvoiced feeling that the child deserves some punishment, which he

may not get after the court hearing. Both of the above practices are in violation of the purpose of detention, which is simply to detain a child until the hearing when he cannot safely be released to his parents or some other responsible adult.

Detention sometimes drags on simply because no terminal date has been set. A judge participating in the formulation of a standard juvenile court act recommended that the juvenile court judge should order detention for a limited period, the exact number of days to depend upon his estimate of the time needed to prepare each case for a hearing.[2] For example, an order of detention not exceeding one or ten days, as the case might be, should replace an order of detention until further order of the court. Such an order would signify that the probation officer was to make the social investigation promptly. If it became apparent that the child did not require detention, he could be released before the end of the specified period; the detention could not be extended, however, without another order from the judge.

Detention is also sometimes prolonged because the training school to which a child has been committed is so overcrowded that it refuses to accept another child until some child in the school has been released. Thus, although the policy of the juvenile court is to transfer the child to the training school as soon as commitment is made, the child may have to be retained in the detention home. Since the detention home is under county supervision and the training school under state supervision, a co-ordinated policy may be difficult to establish. The mingling of committed children with those who are still awaiting hearings and who may be released on probation is not good for the morale of either group. Moreover, for the committed child to receive the greatest possible benefit from the training school program, he should be inducted into it as soon after commitment as possible.

Staff and services

The staff of a detention center is usually large and is related to the program. A basic staff is required for operation of the center, regardless of the number of children in resi-

1 Norman, *op. cit.*, pp. 220–221.

2 *Standard Juvenile Court Act*, sixth edition, National Probation and Parole Association, New York, 1959, p. 42.

dence. In addition, trained people are needed for specialized functions and counseling, each with a limited number of children. The National Probation and Parole Association lists eight services as necessary for any detention center.[1]

1. Administrative, including secretarial, bookkeeping, and telephone services, community relationships, and staff development and supervision.

2. Health services providing for medical and dental examinations and care.

3. Casework services with the children, with reports to the probation office and court on each child's needs and potentialities.

4. Clinical services including psychological testing, psychiatric diagnoses as needed, and assistance to the staff in handling children.

5. Group work services, such as recreational and creative activities and daily living activities.

6. School, since many children are of school attendance age, and also to help structure the child's day. The Board of Education typically supplies teachers, who must adjust their teaching to each child's customary placement in school so that they may return to school when released.

7. Religious activities.

8. Institutional services, such as housekeeping, laundry, food services, and maintenance of buildings and grounds.

This array is perhaps the ideal. In small centers, one person may be assigned several of these functions. Volunteers and community service groups may also contribute to the program, for example, religious services and recreation. In large centers, each service may represent a separate department. In any case, the services must be co-ordinated. The highly professional services are the most difficult to supply, especially in small communities. Part-time services of professionals in the community (medical, dental) may be used as needed.

The problem of staff is heightened by the necessity to duplicate certain services to provide three eight-hour shifts to cover the around-the-clock care and supervision that the children must have. Five staff members are required to staff one post around the clock when provision is made for sick leave, holidays, and vacations.

1 *Standards and Guides for the Detention of Children and Youth, op. cit.,* pp. 34–35.

Illustrations of detention facilities and programs

How detention homes operate can best be shown by descriptions of specific homes. The first is of a home with a capacity of fourteen children, the second of a large institution for 650 children. With essentially the same objectives, different methods of reaching these objectives are used. The small home depends upon supplementing staff with part-time services from professional people in the community and excellent use of volunteers. The small number of children in the home at any one time automatically provides small-group contacts and contacts between adults and children. In the large detention center, highly specialized full-time staff is possible; small-group contacts and personal relationships between adults and children are attained by living and activity units of twenty children each.

A small detention home. Parkview Home, South Bend, Indiana, serves a county of 232,-000 population.[2] Built in 1953, it replaced the county jail as the place of detention. It has accommodations for fourteen children, primarily in single rooms, but including one dormitory for three boys. Boys and girls occupy separate wings but share a large living-dining area, a gymnasium, and activity rooms. The superintendent has a four-room apartment. Usually about nine children are in residence for an average of six days each. In 1960, some 400 children were cared for, 74 of them being detained at two or more times. Four out of five boys and girls are adolescents between the ages of fourteen and seventeen inclusive.

Upon admission, each child is examined by a staff member for external evidence of injury or disease, and his temperature is taken. Within twelve hours, a physician makes a general examination. The physician supervises medical care of sick children in the Home; seriously ill children are transferred to a hospital. Parents pay for this care if they are able; otherwise, payment comes from the county.

Boys and girls share in many activities, always under supervision, such as group discussions that are held daily and various types of recreation. Other activities are carried out

2 Based on Norman, *op. cit.,* pp. 49–50, 59, 71–72, 126, and 186, and information supplied by Superintendent Ralph D. Rogers of the Home. The Home was constructed following a survey by the National Probation and Parole Association.

A modern small detention home is shown in this view of Parkview Home, South Bend, Indiana. The boys' wing is in the right background, the girls' wing at the extreme left, and the probation officer's wing in the center foreground.

separately, as is customary in ordinary school programs. Boys and girls have separate gym periods and usually separate outdoor recreation. The staff feels that the joint activities reduce exaggerated interest in the other sex and avoid the infatuations that sometimes arise when boys and girls share the same detention home but have few contacts.

Religious counseling is provided by a minister from the community when the child's parents have not arranged for their own pastor to visit the child. The minister also confers with the superintendent regarding his impressions of the child. A one-hour interdenominational program is conducted each Sunday morning; Catholic children may attend mass at the local church, under the care of a Catholic layman. In addition, two Protestant church groups hold their services in the Home on alternate Sunday afternoons, with the children in the Home participating.

In addition to a staff of eight people (full time or the equivalent in part-time services), the Home has a well-developed service of volunteers to supplement and enrich the program without staggering costs for additional staff. Volunteers also provide children with a contact with the world outside the Home and remind children that many people are interested in their welfare. Depending upon their interests and talents, volunteers do such things as run movie shows, join the boys in the gym, give art lessons, teach simple crafts, lead in singing, and help girls with cooking, sewing, and personal grooming. Students from the Physical Education Department of Notre Dame University contribute to the program by volunteering their learning and talents to the recreational program. The following schedule gives the volunteer services for one week:

Monday, 2:00–4:30   Art class conducted by an artist for all children.

Tuesday, 7:00–9:00 P.M. Recreational program with assistance of a sociology major from Indiana University Extension Center.

Wednesday, 2:00–4:00 On alternate Wednesdays representatives from the Red Cross direct the children in helping with various Red Cross projects; for example, the children help assemble a Red Cross news letter or arrange small boxes with various items for distribution overseas.

Thursday, 3:00–4:30 A sewing class for girls is conducted by a woman volunteer. The Home furnishes the materials, and girls make blouses, skirts, and pajamas for their use while in the Home.

7:00–8:00 P.M. The men from St. Anthony's Church show movies for the children at the Home.

Friday, 3:00–4:30 Sewing class as outlined above.

8:00–9:00 P.M. A retired scoutmaster conducts a handicraft class for boys.

Saturday, 1:00–3:00 Outside recreational

All detention homes face the problem of providing for the boys and girls throughout the day and of giving their programs more significance than merely the filling of time. Parkview Home has a Red Cross project to aid in the overseas relief program. Boys and girls assemble sandals under the supervision of a member of the staff.

activities with the volunteer help of Notre Dame physical education majors.

3:00–4:00 On alternate Saturdays a youth group from the Gospel Center Church hold their services at the Home, with children participating.

Sunday, 9:30–10:30 A minister, supplied by the Council of Churches of St. Joseph County, comes to the Home to hold Sunday School for the children.

4:00–5:00 A youth group from the Calvary Temple hold their services at the Home with children participating. This group comes on alternate Sundays.

Los Angeles County Juvenile Hall requires many buildings for its 650 boys and girls. Shown is one of the girls' dormitories, containing two living units, each with sixteen individual sleeping rooms, a four-bed dormitory, dayroom, and so on. The roof of the chapel is visible in the background. The three food carts on the walk are part of a fleet of electrically heated carts used to transport food from the main kitchen to the dining rooms situated in different buildings. Nine or more carts are hitched to a small truck, which delivers one cart to each dining room. In the foreground of the picture is part of the large grass playing field for the girls.

Parkview Home has one lack, provision for a certified teacher to conduct classes. For most children the period of detention is short and does not entail much loss of school attendance. The children spend an hour each morning and each afternoon in classes conducted by the superintendent, his assistant,

and volunteers. These periods consist of informal classroom activities, stressing reading, writing, and arithmetic, since a large proportion of the children lack ability in the three R's.

Each child's day from 7:30 A.M. to 9 P.M. is completely filled with scheduled activities, except from 3:00 to 4:30 when the children have a rest period in their rooms, during which they may read, write to their parents, or do school work. They help prepare the meals, keep the building clean on an assigned schedule, have indoor and outdoor recreation, carry out the two hours of classroom work already described, and have time for personal grooming. In the evenings the children may have visitors, view TV in separate groups for boys and girls, or have organized play in the gym.

Included in the detention home is a room for court hearings which are held once a week or oftener if necessary.

A large detention home. The Los Angeles

County Juvenile Hall serves an area of some 6 million people.[1] Established first in 1906 and since expanded several times, it now occupies eighteen buildings spread over twenty acres. The institution has wide lawns and recreation areas and is enclosed by a high wall. The Hall is equipped to care for 650 boys and girls, the majority of whom are between the ages of fourteen and seventeen inclusive. During recent years Juvenile Hall has been greatly overcrowded with the population rising far beyond the maximum capacity. One reason is that the rapid growth of population in Los Angeles County has overcrowded all institutions dealing with delinquent children—the detention home, courts, and training schools. Children must first wait in the Hall until their cases can be investigated and heard in the court; then another wait often follows until there are vacancies in the training school. Therefore the Hall is not only overcrowded, but the average length of stay is thirty days.

Juvenile Hall is administered by the Los Angeles County Probation Department. The staff is organized into four divisions, Medical-Psychiatric, Boys' Care and Training, Girls' Care and Training, and General Services. A large staff of 517 full-time (or equivalent) persons, including thirty teachers assigned by the public schools is required to operate this large detention home.

Children are housed in groups of twenty. In the newer buildings each living unit has sixteen individual sleeping rooms and a four-bed dormitory. (Older buildings have larger dormitories.) Girls and boys are housed in separate areas, and the program is not co-educational.[2]

---

1 Norman, *op. cit.*, pp. 67–68, 99–100, 106, 123–124, 136–137, 154–155, and 217–218, and correspondence with Superintendent David Bogen.
2 In regard to a specific question regarding coeducational activities, the Superintendent stated that the staff felt that "the hazard of undesirable relationships resulting from having boys and girls from various parts of our large metropolitan community become acquainted during the time when they are under the emotional stress of being detained for delinquent behavior, would outweigh the benefits they might derive from coeducational activities in the detention home. It appears that coeducational activities have been used to advantage in the detention homes of smaller communities without any serious adverse sequals." He refers to the discontinuance of coeducational activities in two other urban detention homes after boys and girls who had met in the homes were found living together after their release.

The group of twenty stays together all day, in school, at meals, during recreation, and in attendance on Sunday at religious services, always under the supervision of counselors. The large number of children makes it possible to group children according to age, physical development, and special types of problems. Thus in spite of the large size of the institution, children have the advantages of small group association and attention of adults.

Children remain longer than is usually customary in detention centers—an average of thirty days. The number of children and the long stay make possible various special services and necessitate a more elaborate program than many detention centers require where children are held an average of a week or two.

Medical care is in the hands of three full-time physicians, two half-time dentists, and thirty-eight registered nurses. The medical unit includes an infirmary for boys and one for girls, each adequate for nineteen patients, examining rooms, two dental offices, physicians' offices, and a dispensary. The medical staff also provides psychiatric and medical examinations for children under care of the juvenile court who are not resident in Juvenile Hall.

Separate schools with numerous classrooms and an auditorium–gymnasium in each are provided for boys and girls. Each school has its own outdoor playgrounds. The county superintendent of schools operates these schools as "special" schools. The program consists of academic subjects and a variety of other subjects suited to the interests of boys or girls. Emphasis is placed on developing favorable attitudes and interest in learning. An effort is made to help boys and girls who are detained for long periods to keep up with their school work. The school is in session throughout the year, except for vacation periods at Christmas, Easter, and the beginning and end of the summer term.

A library with approximately 2,000 volumes and numerous magazines is maintained. Use of the library is co-ordinated with the school. Boys and girls may also take out books and magazines to read in their living units.

Recreational activities are fitted around the school program, with all-day recreation

At Juvenile Hall, County of Los Angeles, girls have classes in sewing, cooking, arts and crafts, personal grooming, and physical education, as well as in academic subjects. Classes for boys are adjusted to their special interests.

planned for week ends and during school vacations. Active recreation is carried on both outdoors and in the gymnasium. Quiet recreation centers in the living units which are equipped (through gifts) with radios and television sets. Table games, handicrafts, and reading are among the types of recreation. As with other activities, the living unit of twenty boys or girls shares recreation. Occasionally two or more units are brought together for games or other recreational activities.

A chapel provides the setting for separate religious services for boys and girls for each major religious group. Classes in religion are held in the living units on Sunday, and religious counseling is available during the week for children who wish it. The clergymen who have charge of these services come from outside religious groups and are not on the regular staff of the Hall.

A psychiatric clinic has operated in the detention home since 1928. The staff includes fifteen (part time) psychiatrists, six psychologists, and five psychiatric social workers. The staff studies about 180 children per month (approximately 15 per cent of the total number of new cases appearing before the juvenile court). Other services include consultation with Juvenile Hall staff provided by a psychiatrist who visits the various living units during the week to see children who present exceptional problems; consultation with probation officers in regard to individual cases; and in-service training for staff. The clinic also provides training for psychiatric residents.

A step toward rehabilitation. These descriptions amply demonstrate the ways in which the process of rehabilitation can begin in the detention home. The provision for the everyday needs of the boys and girls; the continuation of normal educational, recreational, and religious activities; and the special counseling are a start toward rehabilitation. Important also is the necessity for each individual to adapt to a group, accept regulations, and adjust to adult supervision. These relationships may seem to some delinquent boys and girls to be repressive, even inhuman. To others they may be the first steps toward bringing orderliness and dependable personal relationships into a precarious and insecure way of life.

Detention of juvenile serious offenders

A special problem of detention is posed by youth of juvenile court age who commit certain serious offenses. In all states except three some provision is made in the law whereby the criminal court may take jurisdiction over certain children in lieu of the juvenile court. The provisions are not uniform from state to state but in general pertain under specific conditions to children accused of crimes for which a sentence of death or life imprisonment may be imposed, or in some states all crimes for which a penitentiary sentence may be given. Sometimes a minimum age, usually between thirteen and sixteen, is imposed below which the criminal court cannot take jurisdiction. Sometimes the juvenile court initiates transfer to the criminal court, and sometimes the criminal court has the power to select cases it wishes to try. Whatever the provisions, a small trickle of boys and girls within the ages ordinarily assigned to juvenile court jurisdiction find their way to the adult criminal courts.

Once it has been decided that a child will be tried in the criminal court, he is no longer eligible for the detention home but is transferred to the county jail, where he is held for a criminal trial, on an adult basis. Since the philosophy of speedy disposal of cases, common in the juvenile court, does not apply to jail, the youthful suspect may remain in jail for many months.

In 1960, a fourteen-year-old Chicago boy accused of killing a five-year-old girl (which he denied) remained in jail four and a half months before trial. He was found guilty and sentenced to fourteen years in prison. His attorney moved for a new trial, a request which if granted could lead to many more months in a jail cell waiting for the time of the second trial.

In the later forties, a twelve-year-old Chicago boy spent a period of eighteen months in the Cook County jail waiting for a murder trial and retrial. He was in no way mistreated, but, in order to segregate him from adults waiting trial, he was kept in virtual isolation, having contacts with only a few prison officials.

Most children held in the Cook County jail are older than these two, have committed some type of theft, and remain in jail for only a short period of time. According to a study of 319 boys and girls held in the Cook County jail at some time during the years 1938–1942, two-thirds were aged sixteen, and only seventeen were as young as fourteen years.[1] Almost half were detained for less than a month, 42 per cent from one month up to six months, and 12 per cent from six months to more than a year.

The continued use of jail detention and trial in the criminal court indicates either a distrust of the juvenile court or a failure to provide the juvenile court with facilities to deal with older serious offenders. The situation is better, however, than in 1898, the year before the juvenile court law was passed; in that year 575 children were held in the Cook County jail, compared to an average of 106 per year for 1938–1942. The rate of detention was much higher in 1898, inasmuch as the population of Cook County was much smaller then than in 1940.

The situation in Cook County is not an isolated instance. Across the country many other children whose cases will be tried in criminal court are detained in jails for varying periods of time. After trial, some serve their sentences in the same jails in which they were detained; typically a jail sentence does not exceed one year.

1 Fred Gross, *Detention and Prosecution of Children,* Central Howard Association, Chicago, Illinois, 1946, pp. 33, 72.

Bibliography

Allaman, Richard, "Human Relations at the Detention Home," *Federal Probation,* 16 (December, 1952), 38–41.

———, "Managing Misbehavior at the Detention Home," *Federal Probation,* 17 (March, 1953), 27–32.

Brewer, Edgar W., *Detention Planning,* Publication No. 381, Children's Bureau, Washington, D. C., 1960.

Kneisel, Stephan H., "Detention Home Programing," *Reappraising Crime Treatment,* 1953 Yearbook, National Probation and Parole Association, New York, 1954, pp. 141–149.

Norman, Sherwood, "Detention Intake," *Crime Prevention through Treatment,* 1952 Yearbook, National Probation and Parole Association, New York, 1952, pp. 140–155.

————, *Detention Practice,* National Probation and Parole Association, New York, 1960.

————, "Juvenile Detention," *National Probation and Parole Association Journal,* 3 (1957), 392–403.

————, "New Goals for Juvenile Detention," *Federal Probation,* 13 (Dec., 1949), 29–35.

————, and John B. Costello, "Juvenile Detention and Training Institutions," Chapter 22 in Paul W. Tappan, editor, *Contemporary Correction,* McGraw-Hill Book Company, Inc., New York, 1951.

Shulman, Harry Manuel, "The Detention of Youth Awaiting Court Action," *National Probation and Parole Association Journal,* 2 (1956), 116–122.

Standards and Guides for the Detention of Children and Youth, National Probation and Parole Association, New York, N. Y., 1958.

The juvenile court is the special court devised to remove children from the jurisdiction of criminal courts, which are dominated by a philosophy of punitive justice. In the criminal court an accused person is given a formal trial to prove his guilt or innocence of a specific criminal act; traditionally he has been held responsible for this act, and conviction has been followed by punishment prescribed by law for the specific crime. In removing children from the jurisdiction of the criminal court, the law swept away both the punitive philosophy and the method of trial and punishment so far as children were concerned. A new philosophy was stated—the child was regarded as immature and hence not wholly responsible for his acts; he was entitled to protection and retraining or rehabilitation. The court was to act as a wise parent who would plan for the total welfare of the child rather than punish for one specific act. Such a drastic shift in philosophy called for new personnel, new procedures in the court room, and different methods of treating the offender. Much confusion and many conflicts resulted in the transition from the old to the new, and not all of these have been resolved.

Only gradually have standards evolved to guide legislators in improving laws concerning juvenile courts and to guide juvenile court judges in their work. Such standards have been formulated and are constantly being revised by three national agencies that work in co-operation, The National Probation and Parole Association (now the National Council on Crime and Delinquency), the National Council of Juvenile Court Judges, and the United States Children's Bureau.[1] These standards, differing in some details, nevertheless, all support the same philosophy and general practices. In discus-

1 *Guides for Juvenile Court Judges,* prepared by the Advisory Council of Judges of the National Probation and Parole Association in Co-operation with the National Council of Juvenile Court Judges, National Probation and Parole Association, New York, 1957; *Standard Juvenile Court Act,* prepared by the Committee on the Standard Juvenile Court Act of the National Probation and Parole Association in co-operation with the National Council of Juvenile Court Judges and the U. S. Children's Bureau, National Probation and Parole Association, New York, 1959; *Standards for Specialized Courts Dealing with Children,* prepared by the U. S. Children's Bureau, in cooperation with the National Probation and Parole Association and the National Council of Juvenile Court Judges, U. S. Government Printing Office, Washington, D. C., 1954.

Chapter **21**

The juvenile court: jurisdiction and organization

sing the unsolved problems of the juvenile court, these standards will be referred to collectively as the national standards.

Socio-legal aspects of the juvenile court

The juvenile court is balanced precariously on a tightrope that marks the dividing line between legal procedures and safeguards to the individual on one side and the educational and social work procedures needed in rehabilitation on the other. Legalistic-minded people urge greater adherence to legal procedures similar to those used in criminal courts; social-work-minded people urge abandonment of these procedures and the freer use of education and social work.

Jurisdiction over types of delinquents. The legal jurisdiction of the juvenile court is fixed by state law. It can assume control only over children who are within the legal definition of juvenile delinquency. As was pointed out in Chapter 2, all state laws define delinquency as violation of federal, state, and local laws and municipal ordinances. Except for complications with criminal court jurisdiction, to be discussed later, this area of jurisdiction is clear. In addition, juvenile courts have jurisdiction over children who commit any number of minor acts thought to be injurious to the development of the child. Some of the state laws specify these acts; in others the court may take jurisdiction over any child whose behavior is injurious to its own welfare or the welfare of others or who is beyond the control of parents or guardian.

These loosely worded phrases give tremendous scope to the jurisdiction of the juvenile court and expose the court to a wide range of interpretation and sometimes misintepretation. No exact measurements of delinquency can be automatically applied. The judge must decide when a child's behavior has passed the area of toleration by a community and is considered injurious. How far may a child deviate from local standards before his behavior is injurious to himself? What constitutes incorrigibility and what degree of resistance to parents constitutes delinquency? The judge cannot depend on legal definitions for his decision. He must depend in part upon his own good sense and knowledge of child psychology but also upon the temper and standards of the community. At this point the judge passes from a strictly legal interpretation of his area of jurisdiction into a psychological and sociological interpretation.

One solution suggested has been to limit the concept of juvenile delinquency—and hence the jurisdiction of the court—to clear cases of violation of stated laws. For example, the delegates from eighty-four countries attending the Second United Nations Congress on the Prevention of Crime and the Treatment of Offenders in 1960 recommended:

(a) That the meaning of the term *juvenile delinquency* should be restricted as far as possible to violations of the criminal law, and (b) that even for protection, specific offenses which would penalize small irregularities or maladjusted behavior of minors, but for which adults would not be prosecuted, should not be created.[1]

The United Nations delegates would turn over to schools and social agencies the prevention and solution of such behavior problems

as truancy and incorrigibility since they are not comparable to crime as traditionally understood.

In the United States, however, the tendency is to expand the jurisdiction of the juvenile court. The national standards advocate bringing into the jurisdiction of the juvenile court not only children who have violated specific laws but also children who are beyond the control of their parents or guardians or whose behavior threatens or is damaging their own or the community's welfare.

Thus the world standards would draw back to a strictly legal conception of juvenile delinquency, whereas, the United States seems to be moving toward an ever broader and less precise definition, which tends to place one part of the work of the juvenile court in the area of general social work for poorly adjusted children.

The imprecision of juvenile court jurisdiction is enhanced by the general practice in the United States of bringing under the same court children who are neglected or dependent. A neglected child is one whose parents or guardians do not provide it with the care, training, and education expected by community standards. A dependent child is one whose parents or guardian do not provide it with physical care, such as adequate food, clothing, and shelter. The three concepts— delinquency, neglect, and dependency—may overlap, in that many incipient cases of delinquency have their roots in lack of supervision or failure to provide for physical needs. The judge must often make his own decision as to which classification is appropriate. The decision is important since ways of handling the children in the three categories differ. For example, the delinquent child might be committed to a correctional school, the neglected child removed from his parents and placed in a foster home, and the parents of the dependent child provided with financial relief through some agency other than the court. Since the origin of many delinquencies lies in the family, a given child may be delinquent, neglected, and in need of more adequate support.

The national standards recommend removing from the jurisdiction of the juvenile court all children whose problem is dependency uncomplicated by either neglect or delinquent behavior. Such children, the discussion by national agencies states, do not require legal

1 The United Nations Congress on the Prevention of Crime and the Treatment of Offenders is the world organ for setting standards. Countries participating in the Congress are not obligated to accept the standards, which, however, represent the consensus of opinion of the nations of the world. The first Congress was held in 1955, replacing the earlier and less pretentious voluntary organization of the International Penal and Penitentiary Commission. For brief discussions of the work of the two Congresses see Ruth Shonle Cavan and Jordan T. Cavan, "World Trends in Criminology," *Federal Probation*, 19 (December, 1955), 42–47; William P. Rogers, "The Geneva Conference on Crime: Its Significance for American Penology," *Federal Probation*, 19 (December, 1955), 39–42; Charles V. Morris, "Worldwide Concern with Crime," *Federal Probation*, 24 (December, 1960), 21–30.

action, and the child and his parents would be more appropriately handled by various public or private relief agencies, established to provide financial help to families and individuals who are unable to support themselves. Such agencies are represented by public general relief agencies, Aid to Dependent Children, and various private agencies providing shelter, vocational training to make employment possible, or temporary financial aid during illness of the wage earner.

Due process of law. As a legal institution, the juvenile court has wide powers of authority over a delinquent child. The child becomes the ward of the court, often until age twenty-one. The court may place a delinquent child on probation, arrange for his placement in a foster home, or commit him to a correctional school. The child and his parents have no choice about the disposition chosen by the judge, even though it may break up the family and cause personal distress. The assumption is that the judge is acting for the best interests of the child and the community. However, the typical judge is untrained in child psychology or the sociology of the family. He may or may not have recommendations from a child guidance clinic or a social worker. He may be unconsciously motivated by various prejudices. Even the most well-meaning of judges may violate the rights of child and parents.

In order to safeguard all individuals, the federal Constitution and state constitutions and laws place certain legal safeguards around individuals in court, whether they are being tried in a criminal or a civil court. Many people are concerned about the seeming disregard of the juvenile court for these safeguards. Those who view the juvenile court as a kind of social agency dedicated to the welfare of children feel that strict observance of many of the safeguards would prevent the effective operation of the court and that dependence can be placed in the judge and other court personnel to deal fairly with the child in terms of his welfare.

The legal safeguards alleged to be neglected in some courts are included in the phrase, due process of law.[1] The juvenile

1 A staunch defender of due process of law in juvenile courts is Paul W. Tappan whose professional interests are both sociological and legal. See his *Juvenile Delinquency*, McGraw-Hill Book Company, New York, 1949, pp. 204–212; also "Treatment without Trial," *Social Forces*, 24 (1946), 306–311.

court has been accused of hiding behind its designation as a civil court to avoid safeguards used in the criminal court; but civil courts also have safeguards. The juvenile court is accused of being negligent in the following ways:

1. Some juvenile courts are inclined to assume jurisdiction over a child without specific proof of legal violation. Often, especially in the twilight zone of incorrigibility or injurious behavior, legal violation may be hard to prove. Nevertheless, well-meaning judges may proceed as though they had jurisdiction.

The national standards make clear in their recommendations that the court has no jurisdiction unless the child has committed some act that legally brings him within the jurisdiction of the court; this fact should be established at a preliminary hearing, with as little delay as possible after a child is taken into custody. If the child does not come within the legal jurisdiction, he should be released or referred on a voluntary basis to some appropriate agency. Only if the child comes under legal jurisdiction is the court entitled to take any authoritative action, whether informal without a petition being filed, or formally after a petition has been filed. In the former case, also, what the court does should be limited to referral to another agency or to voluntary conferences with parents to reach agreements. No compulsion should be placed upon the parents. Children who are dealt with informally, without a petition, should not be placed in a detention home.

2. The juvenile court is also sometimes accused of ignoring safeguards in bringing a child before the court. In a large city, most of the work of screening and determining which children come under court jurisdiction and whether a petition should be filed is done by an intake worker, typically a probation officer who should be, but often is not, trained in social work theory and techniques. The work is carried on under the direction of the juvenile court judge. By way of contrast in a criminal court the accused person would reach the court through action of a court with limited jurisdiction (magistrate's court, justice of the peace, municipal court, and so on), a grand jury indictment, and the decision of the prosecuting attorney. This procedure is dispensed with in the juvenile court, and a more general investigation is made into the child's whole round of behavior. So-

cial workers rather than legally trained personnel make the decisions.

3. Another safeguard is that a person suspected or accused of an offense cannot be required to testify against himself. Children are queried by the probation officer and the judge about their alleged offenses, and often admit to their delinquencies.

4. Other rights observed generally in other courts, but which are dispensed with in many juvenile courts are the right of the accused person to hear the evidence against him, to be released on bail, to be represented by an attorney, to be tried in public for a specific act, to have a trial by jury, and to have the right of appealing to a higher court. The safeguards are needed in a criminal court, where a trial resembles a verbal jostling match between a prosecuting attorney trying to convict an accused person of a specific crime and a defense attorney trying to prove him innocent. The juvenile court procedure has been a deliberate attempt to escape from the contest between prosecuting and defense attorneys with its many formal rituals. The hearing tends to resemble a conference of the judge with persons not only aware of the child's misdeeds but interested in his welfare.

The national standards provide for observance of legal rights of the child, although recommending an informal procedure. Before the hearing, parents should be informed that they have a right to be represented by counsel, that is, employ an attorney to be present at the hearings and to guard their rights. It must be shown that the case comes within the court's jurisdiction, with reference to such things as age, residence of the child, and the delinquent act itself. It must also be shown that all people needed at the hearing have been notified. The second step is presentation of evidence to prove that the child actually performed the delinquent acts of which he is accused; this step is called the adjudication, corresponding to conviction in the case of an adult criminal. Only after such proof, is the court in a position to make some plan for the child. If the parents or guardian of the child are dissatisfied with the adjudication, they have a right to appeal the decision to a higher court, and it is part of the duty of the court to inform the parents of this right.

Not all courts observe these recommendations; hence there are occasional instances in which rights of parents or of children are overridden, although often with good intentions, or in which the court oversteps the bounds of its jurisdiction in its zeal to help children. The national standards carefully separate these legal safeguards from the informality of the court, providing for both legality and informality.

The socialized aspects of the juvenile court. Within the legal limitations of the juvenile court, a socialized program is carried out. At its best, the plan devised for the child is not punishment but treatment. This does not mean that the child will necessarily like everything about the plan—in fact, he may regard it as severe punishment. In some unfortunate instances the treatment phase is lost in repressive and punitive measures either during probation or in correctional institutions. But even a plan designed to help the child meet his problems and to retrain him to conformity may not be to the child's liking. Nevertheless, the objective is to help the child.

Probation officers or other court social workers are active at this stage of proceedings. They make a social investigation of each case and present their findings to the judge, together with recommendations. If the child is placed on probation, the probation officers supervise the child.

The work of the juvenile court in its full development is team work between judge and social workers, between law and social work practices. The laws provide legal authority and safeguards; social work practices provide for individualizing the plans for each child and for rehabilitative treatment.

Organization of juvenile and related courts

The fully developed juvenile court is essentially an urban institution. Just as juvenile detention homes are impossible for sparsely populated counties, so are fully staffed juvenile courts beyond the financial resources of such areas. Only in counties with large cities are all or most of the provisions for a fully operating juvenile court achieved.

County and regional courts. Most juvenile courts are organized on a county basis, as are other courts, detention homes, and many welfare agencies. However, in specific instances the area served is the city, a judicial district larger than the county, or a special region within the state. Connecticut, Rhode Island, and Utah have organized their juvenile courts on a state basis, administered and financed by the state. Connecticut has three districts, each with a full-time judge; Rhode Island has two full-time judges who handle all juvenile delinquency cases for the state; and Utah has a juvenile court judge in each of six districts, three of whom are on a full-time basis. When a judge handles a district, he usually travels from one county to another on a regular schedule, holding court in each county. The state-administered court with a limited number of judges is especially advantageous to sparsely populated states or areas within states, since it permits judges to devote themselves exclusively to children's cases and encourages them to develop specialized experience in children's needs and treatment possibilities.

Relation to other courts. Juvenile courts may be independent of other types of courts. Such independent courts are especially suitable to large cities where the number of cases necessitates the full services of a judge. Another arrangement, especially found in sparsely settled counties, is for the court to be a part or function of another court of general jurisdiction such as the county, circuit, district, or probate court, all of which hear civil cases; at certain times the judge of this court hears juvenile cases and at such times his court becomes for the time being the juvenile court. In other systems, the juvenile court is one unit within a court of general jurisdiction, to which a judge may be assigned permanently or on a rotating basis. The latter arrangement involves periodic change and tends to prevent development of professional interest in juvenile court work on the part of the judge. Still another system merges the juvenile court work with that of other courts concerning children and families to create an integrated or family court.

Family court. Some juvenile courts cover types of cases other than the customary three of delinquency, neglect, and dependency. For example, in some states cases of adults who have committed offenses against children may be tried in juvenile court. A family court goes beyond this; it has jurisdiction over all types of cases involving children or other family members where laws have been violated, necessitating legal action. The focus is on intrafamily relationships, especially those that affect children. The Standard Family Court Act recommends the inclusion of the following situations and offenses in the family court act: [1]

1. For children, exclusive original jurisdiction should extend over children who have violated federal, state, or local laws or municipal ordinances; whose environment is injurious to their welfare; whose behavior is injurious to their own or others' welfare; who are beyond the control of parents or custodians; or who are neglected or abandoned by their parents or custodians. The family court should also have the authority to determine the custody of any child or appoint a guardian; arrange for adoption; terminate the legal parent-child relationship; give judicial consent to the marriage, employment, or enlistment of a child when such consent is required by law; and arrange treatment or commitment of a mentally defective or mentally ill minor.

2. For adults, exclusive original jurisdiction to try a parent, guardian, or custodian for any offense against a child; to try an adult charged with deserting, abandoning, or failing to support any person in violation of law, or charged with committing an offense, other than a felony, against a member of his family; to handle proceedings for support, alimony, divorce, separation, annulment, and paternity of a child born out of wedlock; and for commitment of an adult alleged to be mentally defective or mentally ill.

In offenses for which an adult is entitled to a trial by jury and demands it, the juvenile court judge may certify him for criminal proceedings in the appropriate court.

Although all these provisions may not be included in any one court, family courts are now found in eight counties in Ohio and six in North Carolina, as well as in the cities of Portland, Oregon, Des Moines, Omaha, and St. Louis. The first court was established in 1914 in Cincinnati as a division of the Hamilton County Court of Common Pleas. Eighteen family courts in the entire United States does not constitute a major inroad into the traditional court system.[2]

1 *Standard Family Court Act,* prepared by the Committee on the Standard Family Court Act of the National Probation and Parole Association in cooperation with the National Council of Juvenile Court Judges and the U. S. Children's Bureau, National Probation and Parole Association, New York, 1959.

2 *Standard Family Court Act, op. cit.,* p. 3.

A number of arguments can be advanced in favor of family courts:

1. The philosophy of the family court is similar to that of the juvenile court, to regard the family as a group or unit and deal with it as such, just as the juvenile court treats "the whole child." At present when a family is in difficulty, one court may hear divorce proceedings, another may deal with failure of the husband to support his family, another with abuse by one member of the family, and another with delinquency or neglect of children. Policies in the different courts may differ radically. The family is fragmented, each member being treated as an individual who has committed some offense. The family court would enable the judge to see the family as a whole and consider what was for the benefit of the family and its individual members.

2. The social, probation, and clinic services now used by the juvenile court could be brought into service for all family problems. When social services are now used in different courts dealing with family problems, they represent a duplication and added expense. Many courts having jurisdiction over some aspects of family matters do not have social services.

3. The same approach would be used as in the juvenile court, with legal safeguards but a socialized approach.

Objections center around the vested interests of different courts and lawyers, whose function is usually minimized in a socialized court; possible increase in cost to provide adequate social services; and possible inadequacy of a socialized approach to handle problems that arise.

It seems probable that in the course of time, greater provision will be made for family courts, and a unified, socialized handling of family problems, within a framework of legal safeguards.

Youth courts. A youth court implies the extension of the juvenile court philosophy and methods to the next age group above the juvenile court age, that is, up to age twenty-one. Few such courts exist, and those that do are part of the criminal court system. But justification for them can be found, especially in states where juvenile court jurisdiction ends with age sixteen or seventeen. The commission of serious delinquencies and felonies increases in later adolescence and often con-

stitutes a serious threat to the community. Nevertheless, many boys and girls between sixteen or eighteen and twenty-one are not yet settled into an adult pattern—they are not yet securely anchored into conventional life by jobs and marriage. Some, of course, will always resist such conformity, but for many others the possibilities of rehabilitation would be greater with a socialized than with a punitive approach. In a sense, the youth court is a "last chance" court before the criminal court is allowed to take its course and the deviant youth is classified as a criminal.

Some of the special youth courts in operation are limited in their jurisdiction to misdemeanors—that is, minor offenses, the penalty for which would be a fine or less than a year's imprisonment. The criminal courts still receive later adolescents who have committed serious crimes or felonies.

An example of a youth court is the Boys Court of Chicago, established in 1914 and operating as one of the complex of specialized courts that comprise the Municipal Court of Chicago.[1] The court has jurisdiction over boys between the ages of seventeen and twenty-one. It operates under the criminal code that governs adults. The case of a boy is tried under conventional legal procedures with the purpose of determining whether the boy is guilty. If he is not, his case is dismissed; the boy may be given suggestions for securing help if he seems to need counseling or other help. When a boy has been found guilty, the judge has a choice of dispositions. The boy may be committed to an adult penal institution, usually the municipal House of Correction or the county jail; placed on probation under the probation department; placed under the supervision of a private family casework agency, usually for six months with possible renewal; or recommended for psychiatric treatment. When the case is referred to an agency, it is continued for the requisite period of time and then at the end of the period comes back to the court for a renewal of continuance or a final disposition. If the boy has made adequate progress, he is dismissed; if not, one of the other possible dispositions may be used. The continuance gives an opportunity for social

1 Paul Reizen, "Family Casework with Boys under Court Jurisdiction," *Social Casework*, 36 (1955), 208–214.

work but does not free the boy from the control of the court. Most of the offenses for which boys come to Boys' Court are minor in nature; through the court, many of the boys are given an opportunity for rehabilitation without imprisonment.

Girls over juvenile court age do not have a special court in Chicago. If they are guilty of minor offenses, they may be tried in the Women's Court, which handles all law violations of women over eighteen except felonies and traffic violations. Many of the problems have to do with irregular sex relations, prostitution, or minor thefts. The Social Service Department of the Municipal Court aids in investigation of these young women, many of whom are referred to co-operating private social agencies.

Philadelphia also has youth courts within the Municipal Court to handle youth of both sexes aged eighteen to twenty. Cases are limited to misdemeanors.

New York City has several different types of youth courts which do not cover all types of cases nor all portions of the city. Unlike the youth courts of Chicago and Philadelphia, which operate under the criminal law, the youth courts of New York are organized under special Wayward Minor statutes, first passed in 1923 and later amended from time to time. The statutes give to both criminal courts and Children's (juvenile) Courts jurisdiction over youth between the ages of sixteen and twenty-one who are habitually addicted to the use of liquor or drugs, who habitually associate with undesirable persons or prostitutes, who are wilfully disobedient to the reasonable and lawful commands of parents or guardian, or who are morally depraved or in danger of becoming depraved.[1] Serious offenses and felonies are not covered by the statute.

Under this Act, an adolescents' court was established in Brooklyn in 1935 for boys; it is part of the City Magistrates' Court. In the Borough of Queens, an adolescent court was established in 1936 as part of the Felony Court. With jurisdiction over the whole of New York City, the Wayward Minors' Court for girls, known as "Girls' Term," operates as part of the Women's Court.

In 1943 the Youthful Offender Act provided for a Youth Part to the criminal courts of New York, applicable to youth between the ages of sixteen and nineteen who have committed crimes not punishable by death or life imprisonment.[2]

The various youth courts, although they fall into the classification of adult courts, tend to use techniques similar to those of the juvenile court, with social investigations, a liberal use of probation, and emphasis on rehabilitation. In some cases it is also possible for a charge of a serious crime to be reduced to a misdemeanor for youth who seem adaptable to rehabilitation. The youth courts may be considered as an extension of the juvenile court point of view and methods into youth or young adulthood.

It is not mandatory that all youth should be tried in the youth courts in the various cities. Therefore some youth, even though their offenses are minor, are tried in the criminal courts.

The juvenile court and the criminal court

Children who have violated federal, state, or local laws formerly were tried in criminal courts. Their removal to juvenile court jurisdiction has caused uneasiness among legislators and lawyers who fear that criminal law is being flaunted and that juvenile courts are too easy or "soft" for "young criminals." Criminal court judges often do not like to give up their vested interests in trying criminal cases, and many prosecuting attorneys see the successful conviction of a youthful criminal as a spectacular chance to make a name for themselves. For these and other reasons in many states, the line between criminal and juvenile jurisdiction is not clearly drawn, or the two jurisdictions overlap for the adolescent years. The controversy applies only to serious offenses that would be felonies if committed by adults. The minor offenses included in juvenile court laws that are not illegal if done by adults are firmly lodged in the juvenile courts; the criminal court has no interest in these offenses. As a result minor offenders receive the rehabilitative treatment provided by the juvenile court, but seriously criminal youth are deprived of it.

1 John Otto Reinemann, "The Expansion of the Juvenile Court Idea," *Federal Probation*, 13 (September, 1949), 34–40, reprinted in Clyde B. Vedder, *The Juvenile Offender, Perspective and Readings*, Doubleday and Company, Garden City, New York, 1954, pp. 280–288.

2 Frederick J. Ludwig, *Youth and the Law, Handbook on Laws Affecting Youth*, Foundation Press, Brooklyn, New York, 1955, Chapters 8 and 9.

Juvenile courts with exclusive jurisdiction.[1] In only three states, Oklahoma, Virginia, and New Hampshire, does the juvenile court have original exclusive jurisdiction for all offenses of all children within the juvenile delinquency age limits. The national standards for juvenile courts recommend this jurisdiction for all juvenile courts.

Juvenile courts with overlapping or concurrent jurisdiction. In thirty-eight states, juvenile and criminal courts have overlapping or concurrent jurisdiction, sometimes for children of all ages, sometimes only for older adolescents. In some of these states, the juvenile court may waive its jurisdiction and transfer the child to the criminal court; in others officers of the criminal court may make the decision and take a case away from the juvenile court.

The national standards recommend that the juvenile court judge should have the authority to transfer a case to the criminal court, provided that the child is sixteen years of age or older and that the offense would be a felony if committed by an adult. This recommendation is to provide for older adolescents who could not be adequately confined in the typical training school or who are thought not to be amenable to the treatment provisions and facilities of the juvenile court. The National Council of Juvenile Court Judges would prefer age fourteen as the dividing line between exclusive juvenile court jurisdiction and authority to transfer to the criminal court in order to include the rare cases of a child of fourteen or fifteen who might be already well steeped in criminal attitudes and behavior.[2] Whether the age limit is fourteen or sixteen, the cases requiring transfer to the criminal court are few in number and a very small proportion of all juvenile court cases.

Exclusive jurisdiction to criminal court. In twenty-three states the criminal courts have exclusive jurisdiction over some offenses, that is, they must be tried in the criminal courts regardless of the opinion or wish of the juve-

nile court. Almost without exception the offenses are ones punishable by long prison terms or execution when committed by adults. When the criminal court assumes jurisdiction, the child becomes subject to the penalties provided by law for adults. The children are no longer juvenile delinquents but juvenile criminals.

In fifteen of the twenty-three states giving exclusive jurisdiction over some offenses to the criminal courts, the criminal courts also have concurrent or overlapping jurisdiction with the juvenile courts in regard to less serious offenses. In these states the criminal courts may easily be more dominant in the handling of juvenile delinquents than the juvenile courts.

Age of criminal court jurisdiction. As a rule, criminal courts may assume jurisdiction, even for the most serious offenses, only over children who have reached a certain age, whereas the juvenile court has jurisdiction over children usually beginning with the age of seven (or shortly thereafter). In two states the youngest age at which a child may be tried in the criminal court is ten; in two states, twelve; in four states, fourteen; in two states, fifteen; in nine states, sixteen; and in one state, seventeen. It should be recalled that in a few states, sixteen is the upper age for all juvenile court cases, after which all offenders are tried in the criminal court.

In actual practice, some young adolescents or even preadolescents are tried in criminal courts, found guilty, and sentenced to the adult penitentiaries of the states. On the other hand, criminal judges are not insensitive to the possibility of injustice, especially to young adolescents who are not generally delinquent but may have committed one serious crime. Certain practices are permitted by law or have developed administratively to ameliorate the harshness that otherwise might result.[3] When there is concurrent jurisdiction, the criminal court may waive its right and agree that the child should be tried in the juvenile court. In other instances in which a youth comes under the jurisdiction of the criminal court, he may be placed on probation, given a suspended sentence during good behavior, or have his case continued. The charge may be held in abeyance without a trial; or the charge may be reduced from a

---

1 Paul W. Tappan, "Children and Youth in the Criminal Court," *Annals of the American Academy of Political and Social Science,* 261 (1949), 128–136. The information on jurisdiction is based on a questionnaire survey and correspondence with the offices of attorney generals and state crime commissions, supplemented by examination of statutes. A similar classification, differing in some details, is given in Ludwig, *op. cit.,* pp. 30–36.

2 *Standard Juvenile Court Act, op. cit.,* p. 33.

3 Tappan, "Children and Youth in the Criminal Court." *op. cit.,* 133–134.

felony to a misdemeanor, for example from assault to disorderly conduct, with a different pattern of trial and punishment.

The Criminal Court of Cook County. Not all children tried in the criminal courts are found guilty, as a study of children tried in the Criminal Court of Cook County (Chicago), Illinois shows. In Illinois, the criminal and the juvenile court have concurrent jurisdiction over all cases of children aged ten and over, and the criminal court has exclusive jurisdiction for all crimes of violence. In the years 1938 to 1942, 270 children, three of whom were repeaters, and fifteen of whom had convictions on more than one offense, were held for trial in the criminal court.[1] Fifteen or 5.5 per cent were discharged without a trial; eight or 2.8 per cent were found not guilty, or a total of 8.3 per cent.

The remaining 250 children had a total of 265 different sentences, many with heavy penalties. Of the sentences, 105 or 39.6 per cent consisted of probation, although fifteen of the children were given another sentence on a second charge. The most frequent sentence was to the state penitentiary, given to 107 boys. Another fifty-three boys were sentenced to municipal or county jails. Only five boys were committed to the state training school for boys—all others were committed to adult penal institutions.

Sentences to the municipal house of correction or the county jail were relatively short, running from thirty days to a year. Most of those sentenced to the state penitentiary had sentences with a minimum stay of one year, but with possible maximums of ten years to life. Parole is possible for a large part of this time. Smaller numbers, however, were given fixed sentences of fourteen to ninety-nine years, with the possibility that parole would reduce the time spent in prison.[2]

Children in state and federal prisons. Each year in many states a number of boys and girls of juvenile court age are admitted to state and federal prisons after conviction in criminal courts. In 1950, the last date for which reports on commitments by age were published, fifteen boys and one girl, aged fourteen or under, were sent to prison; 1,828 boys and fifty-three girls aged fifteen through

seventeen; and 8,411 boys and 297 girls aged eighteen to twenty-one.[3] Those aged fourteen and under constituted less than 0.1 per cent of the total number of prisoners committed to prison in 1950. Boys aged fifteen through seventeen equalled 3.3 per cent of all males and girls of the same age, 2.2 per cent of all females. Boys aged eighteen through twenty made up 15.2 per cent of the male total, and girls in this age group, 12.6 per cent of the female total. Not quite all these prisoners were of juvenile court age in the state from which they came, although most of those under eighteen years old were.

Children committed to prison are not only a very small proportion of all prisoners but also a very small proportion of children whose cases are brought to a juvenile court. In 1950 it was estimated that about 325,000 children came to the attention of the juvenile court, about half of whom were handled as informal cases, half with a petition of delinquency and a hearing before the judge. The juveniles under eighteen who entered prisons that year (1,897) after criminal court conviction constituted much less than 1 per cent of the number who were handled by the juvenile court. The method of handling children and adolescents in criminal courts and prisons, therefore, deplorable though it may be, touches only a minute fraction of delinquents, but for them it may be a major disaster.

Crimes are given in the national report for males only. Most of the crimes are of the same order as the delinquencies of boys—forms of stealing—but of a more serious nature. Assaults are more frequent. Of the fifteen boys aged fourteen or under, seven had been convicted of burglary, two each of robbery and larceny, and one each of murder, manslaughter, forgery, and carrying and possessing weapons. Boys totaling 7,085 aged fifteen through nineteen had the following offenses: burglary, larceny, and other types of property offenses, 81.9 per cent; murder, assaults, rape, 9.3 per cent; various forms of vice (sex, drug, liquor violations), 3.2 per cent; military court martial, 2.5 per cent; and other, 3.1 per cent.

Executions of youth. The ultimate penalty—loss of life—is also exacted of a few youths

1 Fred Gross, *Detention and Prosecution of Children*, Central Howard Association, Chicago, Illinois, 1946, p. 134.
2 Gross, *op. cit.*, pp. 132–133.

3 *National Prisoner Statistics, Prisoners in State and Federal Institutions, 1950*, U. S. Department of Justice, Bureau of Prisons, Washington, D. C., 1954, p. 51.

still in their teens. For the years 1948 through 1952, twenty-four youths aged nineteen and under were executed. Four were whites and twenty Negroes. Sixteen of the executions took place in southern states and four in northern and western states. Seven of the executions were for rape, one for robbery, and sixteen for murder.

Judge of the juvenile court

The central figure in the juvenile court team and in many rural areas is the juvenile court judge. He is almost invariably a lawyer by training, prepared to handle cases where a point of law is at stake, but with no training in child psychology or family sociology. For making decisions regarding a child's treatment and rehabilitation, he is no better prepared than the engineer, the architect, the dentist, or the doctor, or any other intelligent educated person. He is professionally prepared only to establish that a case legally comes within the jurisdiction of the juvenile court, to apply legal safeguards, to interpret the law, and to protect the child from illegal disposition of his case. It is important that the judge should have sound legal training, but more than this is needed. The original conception of the juvenile court judge was that he should be a wise and kindly father. More recent attempts to state desirable personal qualifications depict a paragon of perfection that has rarely existed. One formulation of qualities follows:

1. The experiences of an attorney who has been successful in practice and who is conversant with the rules of law and the ways of the courtroom.
2. Intellectual flexibility and the capacity to absorb the elements of new disciplines, particularly in the behavioral sciences, and to utilize the guidance and skill of professionally trained people in these various disciplines.
3. An emotional capacity for understanding, sympathy, and dedication to his task of helping people, coupled with a strong sense of fairness.
4. The will to work hard and the physical stamina to put in long hours.
5. The ability to see community needs and the capacity to act as a leader in helping the community develop or create services and facilities for the welfare of children and families.
6. The willingness and capacity to work with all interested people and agencies who want to help children and families.
7. Humility toward his responsibilities—humility that is derived from a critical self-awareness of his intellectual and emotional weaknesses and biases.[1]

One difficulty in securing the best person possible for juvenile court judge is that in the main judges are elected by popular vote. No statutory qualifications exist by which a panel of adequate persons could be selected from among whom a judge might be elected. No provision is made whereby an impartial body of professional people—lawyers or other judges, welfare officials, educators, and responsible citizens—might draw up a list of candidates qualified not only in legal training but in personal characteristics and knowledge of human nature.

Another difficulty is that only in large cities does the juvenile court judge devote all his time to the juvenile court. In smaller cities he may be primarily a judge in a court handling civil affairs or minor criminal cases and only on occasion act as a juvenile court judge. His mind-set and probably greatest interest are in his other court duties. Only occasionally is such a judge able to play his dual role with advantage for the children who come to the juvenile court.

Difficulties exist also in some cities where the juvenile court is one of a number of specialized courts in the court system. The judges are usually organized under the headship of one judge, who assigns the judges to the respective courts. Some of the courts are heartily disliked by the judges, either because of the type of cases brought before them or because they do not serve as a steppingstone to higher status in the judicial system or open the way to political office. To relieve this situation, judges are often rotated through the specialized courts, serving perhaps a year in each one. In some cities the juvenile court is the least liked of the courts. It does not give status, it does not permit a display of acumen in handling a difficult legal case. The judges accept their term as a necessary but disliked part of their duties. The result is that none of the judges become expert in handling children's cases, nor are they motivated to acquire the knowledge of human nature needed by the juvenile court judge.

The usual tenure in office of a judge is a few years; then the judge must seek re-elec-

1 *Guides for Juvenile Court Judges, op. cit.,* p. 127. Printed with permission of the publisher, the National Council on Crime and Delinquency, formerly the National Probation and Parole Association.

tion. The settlement of difficult and widely publicized cases or conviction of criminal cases catches the public eye and increases the probability of re-election. The juvenile court judge may have handled difficult cases and may have set numbers of children on the road to rehabilitation. But the cases are not made public. Notorious cases of young delinquents more often than not are tried in criminal courts and add to the public's knowledge of the criminal court judge. The full-time juvenile court judge must be the anonymous official who works because of genuine interest in children and not because he regards his court record alone as the best means to re-election or to advancement into higher judicial positions or political life.

Some of the difficulties are overcome for smaller communities when a number of counties are grouped together to make possible a full-time juvenile court judge.

Regional juvenile court judges are more likely to be appointed by state officials than elected; they are therefore not handicapped by the specter of losing an election if they do not make a public showing of trying spectacular cases. If, however, appointments are made on the basis of political affiliation, other problems may arise. In Utah, juvenile court judges are appointed by the Public Welfare Commission, for four-year terms. Usually those selected are affiliated with the political party in power. Although good judges may be selected in this way (and apparently have been in Utah), more assurance of high qualifications in all appointments would be given if judges were appointed from lists established by merit system evaluations, with reappointment when the judge's work had been satisfactory.[1]

Services to supplement the work of the judge

Since the responsibilities of the judge are many and varied, supplementary services in large cities are part of the equipment of the juvenile court.

Referee. In many states the judge may appoint a referee to assist him. The referee usually hears cases and makes recommendations to the judge about the disposition of the case. The court is not compelled to accept the recommendation; he may change or reject it. However, since the referee often handles uncomplicated cases, his recommendations are likely to be accepted by the judge. The referee needs either legal training or a sound knowledge of law. In some courts the referee is a woman who handles girls' cases.

Probation staff. The probation staff, at its best, is composed of professional social workers. However, this standard is not always reached. The appointment of probation officers usually rests with the judge. The staff at its worst consists of people who have helped the judge secure enough votes to be elected; they may have neither training nor personal qualifications for the work. If the judge loses an election, the probation staff appointed by him is expected to resign so that the incoming judge may make his own appointments. Under these conditions, the best trained social workers regard probationary work as professionally undesirable. Only when qualifications are established and appointments taken from the judge and placed under some form of civil service with permanent tenure can a well-qualified staff be secured. Sometimes an intermediate stage is reached in which a committee of leading citizens, including members interested in education and welfare, is appointed by the court to recommend or screen candidates for probation work; from the list presented, the judge makes his appointments. With a change of judge, the incoming judge would still be entitled to make new appointments.

Most probation officers have a bachelor's degree, according to a survey of 2,000 probation officers in 405 courts.[2] The distribution by education was as follows: no college degree, 14 per cent; bachelor's degree, not in social work, 62 per cent; bachelor's degree in social work, 4 per cent; graduate degree, not in social work, 10 per cent; graduate degree in social work, 9 per cent; not reported, 1 per cent. The larger the city, the greater the percentage with college degrees of some type: in cities of less than 50,000 population, 55 per cent of probation officers had college degrees; in cities of 500,000 and over, 92 per cent fell into the college-trained group. Supervisors had only slightly better educational qualifications than the rank and file. Although the college training is rarely in social work, it may be in such allied fields as psychology, sociology, or education—this in-

1 *Concerning the Administration of Juvenile Courts,* Biennial Report of the Director of Bureau of Services for Children, State Department of Public Welfare, Salt Lake City, Utah, 1953–1956, p. 8.

2 Gladys M. Krueger, *Survey of Probation Officers, 1959.* Children's Bureau Report No. 15, U. S. Government Printing Office, Washington, D. C., 1960.

formation was not secured. College education should also simplify the acquisition of some social work training through inservice training, workshops, or short courses. Fully trained social workers seem to be at a premium in probation work.

The survey also indicated that about two-thirds of probation officers are men, probably a result of the predominance of boys over girls among delinquents.

Psychiatric and psychological services. Even though all children coming to court are not mentally or emotionally disturbed, some give indications of disturbance either in their past history or through the delinquency itself.

Rarely, however, do juvenile courts have the services of specialized psychological and psychiatric services. Only a few courts in large cities have their own clinics, and medium-sized or small cities may not have access to any services at all.

When a child's mental ability is in question or when his intelligence test scores and academic grade do not agree, it is important to have testing and interpretation of the results by a psychologist experienced in working with delinquent children. Interpretation of the results and of the child's response to the testing situation often reveal far more than the test score itself.

Bibliography

Beemsterboer, Matthew J., "The Juvenile Court—Benevolence in the Star Chamber," *Journal of Criminal Law, Criminology and Police Science,* 50 (1960), 464–475.

"A Chronology of Corrections, The Last Half Century in the United States," *National Probation and Parole Association Journal,* 3 (1957), 413–468.

Caldwell, R. G., "The Juvenile Court: Its Development and Some Major Problems," *Journal of Criminal Law, Criminology and Police Science,* 51 (1961), 493–511.

Goldberg, Harriet L., and William H. Sheridan, *Family Courts—An Urgent Need,* Children's Bureau Report No. 6, U. S. Government Printing Office, Washington, D. C., 1960.

Gross, Fred, *Detention and Prosecution of Children,* Central Howard Association, Chicago, 1946.

Guides for Juvenile Court Judges, National Probation and Parole Association, New York, 1957.

Herman, Stephen M., "Scope and Purposes of Juvenile Court Jurisdiction," *Journal of Criminal Law, Criminology and Police Science,* 48 (1958), 590–606.

Kohler, Mary Conway, "The Courts for Handling Youth," *National Probation and Parole Association Journal,* 2 (1956), 123–141.

Krueger, Gladys M., *Survey of Probation Officers, 1959,* Children Bureau's Report No. 15, U. S. Government Printing Office, Washington, D. C., 1960.

Lou, Herbert H., *Juvenile Courts in the United States,* University of North Carolina Press, Chapel Hill, North Carolina, 1927.

Ludwig, Frederick J., *Youth and the Law,* Foundation Press, Brooklyn, New York, 1955.

Morris, Charles V., "Worldwide Concern with Crime," *Federal Probation,* 24 (December, 1960), 21–30.

Nunberg, Henry, "Problems in the Structure of the Juvenile Court," *Journal of Criminal Law, Criminology and Police Science,* 48 (1958), 500–516.

Pound, Roscoe, "The Place of the Family Court in the Judicial System," *National Probation and Parole Association Journal,* 5 (1959), 161–171.

Reinemann, John Otto, "The Expansion of the Juvenile Court Idea," *Federal Probation,* 13 (September, 1949), 34–40.

Reizen, Paul, "Family Casework with Boys under Court Jurisdiction," *Social Casework,* 36 (1955) 208–214.

Roucek, Joseph S., editor, *Juvenile Delinquency,* Philosophical Library, New York, 1958, Chapter 11.

Standard Family Court Act, National Probation and Parole Association, New York, 1959; also printed in *National Probation and Parole Association Journal,* 5 (1959), 99–160.

Standard Juvenile Court Act, sixth edition, National Probation and Parole Association, New York, 1959.

Standards for Specialized Courts Dealing with Children, U. S. Government Printing Office, Washington, D. C., 1954.

Tappan, Paul W., "The Adolescent in Court," *Journal of Criminal Law,* 37 (1946), 216–230.

———, "Children and Youth in the Criminal Court," *Annals of the American Academy of Political and Social Science,* 261 (1949), 128–136.

———, *Delinquent Girls in Court,* Columbia University Press, New York, 1947.

———, "Treatment without Trial," *Social Forces,* 24 (1946), 306–311.

Young, Pauline V., *Social Treatment in Probation and Delinquency,* McGraw-Hill Book Company, Inc., New York, 1952.

The function of the juvenile court is to investigate all cases referred to it that come within its jurisdiction and decide upon the best plan for the delinquent's immediate future, in terms of community welfare and the delinquent's own rehabilitation. Rehabilitation may be carried out under the immediate supervision of the court, through probation, or may be delegated to some other agency.

Intake and classification of cases

Children are referred to the juvenile court by other agencies or by individuals. The court itself does not send representatives into the community to discover which children are delinquent. The court's work begins when a child is brought to the detention facility or when a complaint is made against the child.

Sources of referral. Most children come to the attention of the juvenile court by way of the police, either because the police have encountered children in the acts of delinquency or because a complaint has been made to the police and their investigation has implicated children. As stated previously, the police make minor adjustments without referral to the court.

About 70 per cent of all referrals of children to the juvenile court are made by police.[1] The remaining 30 per cent are referred by parents, teachers, social workers, and others. Parents and teachers are likely to refer children because they are incorrigible or beyond their control. Schools may refer destructive or disorderly students or persistent truants, although most schools handle truancy as an institutional problem without referral to the juvenile court. Police refer children for community delinquencies, such as disorderliness in public places, vandalism, theft, and fighting.

Intake. Intake refers to the preliminary steps taken to determine whether the child comes under the jurisdiction of the court and requires a court hearing. The term is commonly used in social work for the initial interview that a prospective client has when he comes to the social agency to ask for help. In this interview, the social worker in charge of intake determines whether the person's

1 I. Richard Perlman, "Delinquency Prevention: The Size of the Problem," *Annals of the American Academy of Political and Social Science*, 322 (1959), 6.

Chapter **22**

Functions of the juvenile court and probation office

problems are ones that the agency can handle, and makes an appointment when the person may talk with one of the case workers who will then handle the case.

In the juvenile court the purpose is the same but the procedure may be more formal. The intake procedure usually is handled by a probation officer and constitutes one of the specific functions of probation officers. In a large court, a special intake department or intake officer may specialize in this phase of the court procedure. In smaller courts, one probation officer may handle intake along with other duties. If there is no probation officer, the judge makes the decision.

Screening of cases. In juvenile courts with a sufficient number of cases to have a well-developed staff, probation officers supplement the complaint made by police or others when they refer a child to court. They make a preliminary investigation to determine whether the child's case comes within the jurisdiction of the court and whether a petition should be filed against the child.

Usually some children who are referred have problems that do not come under the legal jurisdiction of the court. The officer in charge of intake does not simply turn these cases aside, but refers them to some community or social work agency that offers the help needed. This procedure is a voluntary gesture of help and is not backed up by the authority of the court.

Cases that come under court jurisdiction fall into two types: unofficial and official. In the first type, if a petition does not seem necessary and the complainant does not insist upon one, the probation officer works out an informal and voluntary plan with the parents and the child. The judge may review these cases in whatever degree he thinks necessary, but typically this stage of the proceedings lies in the hands of probation officers or other social workers provided for the juvenile court.

The term unofficial case is loosely defined to include several types. In some instances it refers to cases where delinquency has been alleged but not proven or adjudicated; the judge makes some type of adjustment informally, perhaps by talking with parents and child or referring the parents to some social agency. The term is also applied to cases in which the probation officer feels that the child needs social casework but that legal action is not needed. Also the term may be used for cases that have formally come before the court but in which the delinquency is too trivial to demand court action.[1] In general, in unofficial cases a formal complaint or petition is not filed and the case is not entered on the juvenile court calendar for a formal hearing, but some action is taken by judge, referee, or probation officer to adjust the case. Presumably all would come within the official jurisdiction of the court. Legally, there is no compulsion on the child or his parents to conform to the recommendations made to them. However, if the child's behavior does not improve and he is again referred to the court, the next step normally would be an official hearing.

The third or official group of cases consists of those under the jurisdiction of the court that seem to need further investigation and a firm treatment plan. These are the official cases which receive a court hearing. These are also the cases from which children held in detention are most often selected.

Complaints and petitions. A written complaint on a standard form is made by the police or by the agency or individual that refers the child to the court. Only for the third group is a petition filed. The petition does not allege that a delinquent act has been committed, but usually opens with such a phrase as "In the interest of ——, a child under —— years of age." The specific behavior that

brings the child under the jurisdiction of the court is given, as well as the names and addresses of the parents or guardian. This petition is then filed, and the case is scheduled for a court hearing.

Procedures vary somewhat at this point. A preliminary investigation by the probation officer may be necessary in addition to the police investigation to determine whether the child actually does come within the jurisdiction of the court. In some courts the probation officer makes the determination at this point; in others, the judge holds a preliminary hearing. Again, the final decision may come at the beginning of the official hearing. Whatever the exact procedure, a social investigation is made by the probation officer before the official hearing, and as soon as possible the time for a court hearing is set. Parents are then advised by a written summons to appear with the child before the court at a certain time and place.

Social investigation

The second task of the probation officer is the social investigation. This investigation is more thorough and extensive than the police investigation which has been limited to establishing the facts of the delinquency. The social investigation secures background data on the child to help the judge understand the case and decide what should be done about it.

In assembling data for the report, the probation officer may use a number of sources. If the county has a social service exchange, listing the names of all people who have sought aid from all types of agencies and the names of the agencies, the probation officer may start with this agency. If the child or his family have had contacts with other agencies, they are asked to contribute helpful information. Other sources of information are schools, the church that the family attends, community or recreational centers where the child has said he goes, employers of the older child or possibly his parents, and others acquainted with the child. Police records are also consulted. The investigation expands beyond the child's delinquencies to include the total round of his life and that of his parents. Much of the investigation is carried on by telephone.

The above may be said to be the ideal situation. Often the probation officer is so rushed with duties and cases that the investi-

---

1 Pauline V. Young, *Social Treatment in Probation and Delinquency,* McGraw-Hill Book Company, Inc., New York, 1952, p. 244.

gation is superficial. Also, probation officers untrained in the techniques of social case investigation, are less likely to uncover the more subtle aspects than those who are trained. With the untrained investigator the report may be simply a statement of agency contacts, school performance, and neighborhood gossip.

When the report is drawn up for the judge's use, it usually contains suggestions or recommendations by the probation officer for the rehabilitation of the child. For adequate recommendations, the probation officer needs to be thoroughly familiar with the facilities of the community as well as with legal provisions and restrictions. Community facilities include mental health clinics, residential institutions for predelinquent or mildly delinquent children, community and youth centers, recreational facilities, churches, and various types of schools and school programs. Formal knowledge of the facilities and programs is not sufficient. The probation officer should also know the attitudes of these agencies toward working with delinquent children—some agencies do not want them, regarding the delinquent child as the bad apple who may contaminate otherwise good apples.

During the social investigation, the services of a court clinic or community mental health and medical clinics may be sought for diagnosis and recommendations.

The court hearing

The court hearing is the equivalent of the trial in a civil or criminal court. Unlike a trial, it may assume the nature of a conference under chairmanship of the judge. It is not simply a conference, however, for the final decision is not made by majority vote but by the judge, with the authority of his position behind him.

Attendance at the hearing. Unlike other trials, a juvenile court hearing is not an open or public meeting that anyone may attend. The minimum attendance at the hearing includes, beside the judge (or referee), the probation officer, the parents or guardian of the child, and the child. In some courts, a court reporter is present to make an exact record of everything that is said; if the case is appealed, this record is transcribed, but not otherwise. Since few cases are appealed, many judges do not regard a court reporter as necessary. The parents or guardian are enti-

tled to employ an attorney to protect their rights, but rarely do so. In some courts, the prosecuting attorney may have a representative present; again this is not customary.

Other persons who may be present are individuals interested in the child's welfare, especially if they are in a position to help the child, such as a minister, school social worker or principal, or representative of a social agency. Their presence is regarded as desirable, especially if they give the child a feeling of friendliness and can actually aid in the child's rehabilitation. They may also add to the reassurance of parents, who may feel wholly at the mercy of a judge whom they perhaps have never seen before and whose powers they do not understand.

Publicity. From time to time the question of publicity for juvenile court hearings becomes an issue. Secrecy of court proceedings has always been opposed in the United States, since it may open the way for exploitation of or injustice to the accused person, perhaps in the interest of other persons who would stand to lose or gain in prestige, power, or finances, according to the outcome of a trial.[1] The question with reference to juvenile court hearings does not revolve around absolute secrecy so much as around who should be eligible to attend hearings and how much of the case should be made public. Specifically, should newspaper reporters be admitted? Although there have been some recent changes, the conditions found by a survey made in 1939 still give an essentially true view of the laws and policies regarding publicity on juvenile court hearings or cases. At that time, the public was legally excluded from juvenile courts in seven jurisdictions and might be excluded in an additional twenty-four.[2] Eight states had statutes that prohibited the publication of names of juveniles without the consent of the juvenile court judge. In addition, judges have wide discretion about the ad-

1 Secrecy has bred brutality and resulted in false confessions when police have illegally held adult suspects in secret places or have secretly used brutal methods to exhort a confession. The brutality that comes to light from time to time in correctional schools or prisons is largely the result of the secrecy that surrounds what goes on within these institutions.

2 Referred to in Gilbert Geis, "Publicity and Juvenile Court Proceedings," *Rocky Mountain Law Review*, 30 (February, 1958), 1–26; reprinted in *National Probation and Parole Association Journal*, 4 (1958), 333–355. This well-documented article traces changes in laws and public opinion regarding publicity for juvenile court cases.

A conference-like atmosphere is maintained in this juvenile court hearing before Judge Paul W. Alexander of the Court of Common Pleas, Division of Domestic Relations, Toledo. Judge Alexander is noted for his understanding of delinquency as a personal and family crisis. Those present at the hearing are limited to the probation officer, the boy, and his parents. Some judges believe that a stenographer should be present to make a record in case an appeal is made. A few judges cling to the high judge's bench and robes as symbolic of the authority of the court. Judge Alexander prefers an informal but dignified office setting. On the wall back of the Judge is a favorite legend, "Who doth not answer to the rudder shall answer to the rock." (Courtesy National Council on Crime and Delinquency)

mission of newspaper representatives and vary to some extent in their policy as to which if any hearing they may attend. In general, when news is given out, judges and newspapers have followed the policy of not publishing the names of delinquents or other identifying data.

An outburst of a few lurid crimes committed by juveniles in the mid-fifties led to pressure by newspaper publishers to be allowed to print more specific data. Many readers demanded more details. Several state legislatures yielded to the pressures and lowered the bar to newspapers. Some arguments offered for greater publicity are given below, with answering arguments.

It is argued that the public is entitled to receive all the news through all means of information—newspapers, radio, television, and motion pictures. Less than full coverage gives an incomplete and unrealistic view of the world. The newspapers or other media are the only ones capable of deciding which news should be printed, and they may be trusted to judge wisely and to set their own standards collectively or individually. Such news will arouse public interest and lead to eradication of delinquency and its causes.

Opposed to this argument is the doubtful

beneficial result of the publication of stories on individual cases. Public demands for dramatic stories of individual delinquents or criminals often indicate a morbid interest, a need for vicarious participation in crime, or a hidden desire for punishment. Constructive movements do not grow out of these interests. Newspapers and other news media have done a valuable service in excellent feature or documentary stories which give a well-rounded conception of factors causing delinquency or of treatment methods. Such stories do not endanger the rights or the welfare of any particular child.

Another argument that favors publicity is that the juvenile court needs a watchdog to protect public and individual interests and that the best watchdog is the press.

It is true that some newspapers by persistent campaigns carried on over long periods of time have shocked the public into realization of disastrous situations in slums, prisons, and correctional schools. These are situations whose remedy requires legislation and public money. If the juvenile court needs a watchdog to protect family and child, this service could be better rendered by a committee of responsible citizens who would not necessarily feel that individual cases should be made public, but who could judge of unmet needs and bring them either to the public or to the proper authorities, as would seem wise.

Another argument for publicity is plainly punitive in origin: "punks," "hoodlums," young "gangsters" should have their names held up to scorn and should receive public condemnation. It is asserted that the knowledge that their names would be printed would act as a deterrent.

Opposed is the fact that no studies have been made of the effect of publicity on the individual delinquency-prone youth. But in general, making a public spectacle of a criminal has not stopped crime and has had some very ill effects in public sentiment. When executions, whipping, and other physical punishments were held in public they became the occasion for great hilarity and ribaldry; public sentiment if anything became calloused. Crime continued without a ripple of deterrent effect; pickpockets found the crowds gathered at public whippings or executions a good place to ply their trade; the fact that a fellow pickpocket was being punished or executed did not deter them. Kidnapping was not

stopped by publicity—although it is conceded that it lost much of its popularity in this country through the persistence with which the Federal Bureau of Investigation discovered the criminals and brought them to justice. It is notable that the FBI usually prohibits any publicity during the time that they are working on a case.

Among juveniles, publicity has sometimes boomeranged and far from humiliating the delinquent has given him a sense of importance as a public figure and has raised his status among other juveniles.

In any case, rehabilitation—never easy to accomplish—becomes more difficult. The less publicity an individual case has, the better is the chance to bring the delinquent back into conformity and to protect him in the future from either delayed hero worship or a stigma that he cannot cast off. Rehabilitation does not go on in the glare of publicity but through personal relationships of the delinquent with adult nondelinquents and when needed through specialized case work or clinic services.

Another unfortunate aspect of full publicity is that it spreads the mantle of guilt over the delinquent's entire family, perhaps over his neighborhood. Parents, younger brothers and sisters, and other members of the family are held up to scorn, and for years to come their name may be associated with a particular crime. In one well-publicized case of a notorious juvenile crime, the family legally changed its name and moved to another city to try to escape from the stigma and to protect younger children in the family.

Adjudication. In order that the judge may act legally, it must be determined that the child did actually commit a delinquent act. Unless there has been a preliminary hearing, the first item of the official hearing is the presentation of evidence in the presence of the child and his parents. The policeman who made the first investigation may present his facts. A complainant may state his reasons for filing a complaint or petition against the child. The probation officer may review facts as he found them. The child will be asked whether he behaved as these people have said. In most cases, children admit their delinquencies. When they do not or protest that they are innocent, they or their parents have the legal right to present opposing evidence. If it becomes clear that the child did not com-

Table 26
Official and Unofficial Cases in Juvenile Courts of Counties Containing the Principal Cities of Ohio, 1959

County	Principal city	Total number of cases	Percentage handled Officially	Unofficially
Butler	Hamilton	1,131	20	80
Clark	Springfield	580	22	78
Cuyahoga	Cleveland	3,864	62	38
Franklin	Columbia	694	40	60
Hamilton	Cincinnati	3,809	19	81
Loraine	Loraine	550	26	74
Lucas	Toledo	2,302	26	74
Mahoning	Youngstown	1,016	13	87
Montgomery	Dayton	2,203	28	72
Stark	Canton	94	100	0
Summit	Akron	2,413	4	96
Trumbull	Warren	508	35	65

From *Juvenile Court Statistics, 1959,* Children's Bureau Statistical Series No. 61, Children's Bureau, Washington, D. C., 1960, based on page 17.

mit the delinquent act, he is dismissed. Otherwise, he is adjudicated to be delinquent and a decree of this finding is placed on the child's record.

Review of the social investigation. At this point, persons who have been called to the hearing simply to give evidence on the child's behavior may be asked to withdraw, except of course the probation officer. Now that it has been established that the child comes under the jurisdiction of the court, the hearing shifts emphasis from proof of misbehavior to review of the child's social situation and disposition of the case. At its best it may resemble a case conference of a social agency; at its worst an authoritarian and punitive judge berates the child and imposes penalties and punishment upon him.

The judge may have read the report of the social investigation made by the probation officer prior to the hearing, or he may see it for the first time at the hearing. The first, of course, is preferable. In any case, the competent judge usually reviews pertinent points with the parents and child, trying to give them some understanding of, and insight into, the background of the child's delinquency.

Disposition of the case

The judge has a number of choices as to the disposition of cases that come under the jurisdiction of the court.

Official or unofficial handling. The first, made by the judge or by the probation officer assigned to intake, is whether to handle the case officially or unofficially. Taking the country as a whole, unofficial handling is widely used; in 1957, 52 per cent of all cases in fifteen states were handled unofficially. Individual courts, however, differ widely, even within one state, as Table 26 shows for the state of Ohio. Variation over the United States runs from no cases handled unofficially to almost all cases so handled, according to Table 27. Differences are related to the philosophy and policy of the individual judge and, no doubt, to the facilities available for different kinds of disposition under the two methods of handling cases. Certainly the differences are not an indication of the proportion of serious cases in each county represented. These tables represent clearly the great authority vested in the judge. In a given county almost all the children may receive the stigma of being officially declared to be delinquent; in a similar county, almost all are protected from the stigma.

Choice of disposition. The judge may choose among a number of possible ways in which to dispose of each case, as Table 28 shows. More than half of the unofficial cases are dismissed, adjusted informally through discussion or referral, or held open without further hearing. A variety of other dispositions are used in other unofficial cases.

The official cases more often lead to probation than any other method of disposition, with 38 per cent receiving this disposition. The percentage of unofficial cases placed on probation is low, a result of the large per-

Table 27

Official and Unofficial Cases in Juvenile Courts Handling more than 3,000 Cases per Year, 1959

State and county	Principal city	Total number of cases	Percentage handled Officially	Unofficially
Arizona, Maricopa County	Phoenix	8,066	87	13
California				
Alameda County	Oakland	4,699	37	63
Los Angeles County	Los Angeles	10,232	88	12
Orange County	Santa Ana	3,136	41	59
San Diego County	San Diego	4,640	38	62
San Francisco County	San Francisco	3,727	32	68
Florida, Dade County	Miami	3,237	68	32
Louisiana, Orleans County	New Orleans	7,804	13	87
Maryland	Baltimore	3,768	88	12
Michigan, Wayne County	Detroit	3,322	75	25
Missouri	St. Louis	3,526	13	87
Ohio				
Cuyahoga County	Cleveland	3,864	62	38
Hamilton County	Cincinnati	3,809	19	81
Pennsylvania				
Alleghany County	Pittsburgh	5,694	84	16
Philadelphia County	Philadelphia	9,301	100	0
Texas, Dallas County	Dallas	4,130	14	86
Wisconsin, Milwaukee County	Milwaukee	6,070	28	72

From *Juvenile Court Statistics, 1959,* Children's Bureau Statistical Series, No. 61, Children's Bureau, Washington, D. C., 1960, pp. 15–18. Several counties have been omitted because of incomplete data.

centage released without definite action being taken. These low percentages receiving probation are in contrast with the judgment of Austin H. MacCormick, an outstanding authority in corrections. He has stated that with a good juvenile court and adequate social resources in the community, as many as 90 per cent of juvenile delinquents can be placed on probation after the first court appearance, and as high as 50 to 75 per cent of children appearing in court for the second or third time. From 75 to 80 per cent of these probationers will adjust successfully.[1] Such extensive use of probation would reduce the number of children released without definite action and also the number (28 per cent) committed or referred to institutions, agencies, or individuals.

Reasons for different types of disposition. Each judge makes his own decision as to disposition. The probation officer or a clinic may make recommendations, but the judge is under no compulsion to follow them if he thinks something else may work better. Parents may make appeals, and the child may make requests, but these too are subject to the judge's authority. The personal element is a very profound factor.

1 Austin H. MacCormick, "The Community and the Correctional Process," *Focus,* 27 (May, 1948), 88.

In general young children, first offenders, and minor offenders are likely to be placed on probation. The child with a stable and intact family, or who is accompanied to court by an interested and responsible minister, recreation leader, or other adult willing to help, may be granted probation.

The recidivist who has perhaps failed to

Table 28

Disposition of Delinquency Cases (Excluding Traffic Offenses) by Juvenile Courts in Fifteen States, 1957, Percentage Distribution

Type of disposition	Total	Official	Unofficial
Total...................	100	100	100
Dismissed, adjusted, or held open without further hearing....................	45	23	54
Probation officer to supervise.	27	38	15
Committed or referred to:			
Public institution for delinquents...............	7	14	1
Other institution, agency, or individual..........	9	14	11
Other disposition..........	12	11	19

From *Juvenile Court Statistics, 1957,* Children's Bureau Statistical Series No. 52, Children's Bureau, Washington, D. C., 1959, p. 7. The fifteen states included were California, Connecticut, Florida, Iowa, Michigan, Mississippi, Missouri, New Mexico, North Carolina, Ohio, Oregon, Utah, Vermont, Washington, and Wisconsin. The table covers almost half the delinquency cases in the country.

amend his conduct under previous probation, the serious offender, and the older offender are more likely to be committed to a training school. The child from a broken and perhaps completely disintegrated home is often sent to the training school, especially if no one comes forward to befriend him and give him care. The young child in this situation may be thought of as neglected more than delinquent, even though his behavior is troublesome, and may be placed in a foster home or an institutional home for such children, but not as a rule the training school. (A few unfortunate children of this type are committed to correctional schools.)

Some judges find it difficult to project their thinking to understand the motives, aspirations, and frustrations of a child from another social class. Most judges are middle-class; most juvenile delinquents who come before the court are lower-class children. The differences in values of the two classes have already been discussed at length. Behavior that seems normal and advantageous to the lower-class child—or his parents—may seem delinquent to the judge. Even when the lower-class child commits a delinquency that his own class condemns, the middle-class judge may find it impossible to understand how the lower-class situation nevertheless led the child into the delinquent act. Commitment is likely to follow.

Judges are sometimes accused of prejudice and bias in making commitments. Critics point out the disproportionate number of Negro children in some correctional schools. It is true that the judge may suffer from race prejudice. But it is also true that in the Negro slum areas many families lack a father and many have completely fallen apart, with the children being shuffled from one relative to another. A judge who places faith in the value of a stable family is very likely to feel that the correctional school may be a safer haven for such a child than the streets and alleys of a typical city slum.

Some judges are punitive in their attitude toward delinquency. They may hold a personal philosophy of vengeance or retribution, or, if they serve part of the time as criminal judges, they may be unable to shake off the punitive philosophy of the criminal court and assume the rehabilitative attitudes appropriate for the juvenile court judge. The urge to punish may be especially strong when the judge faces a child of another race or social class, who is to him an ununderstandable alien. Such judges tend to commit children to correctional schools.

Most judges, however, accept the general philosophy in the United States that children should not be sent to training schools except as a last resort. The small percentage of delinquents committed to training schools confirms this statement. Harsh treatment and brutality in a few schools tend to overshadow the rehabilitative treatment of other schools. Also, unless the family has already disintegrated, commitment separates the child from his parents, which approaches violation of the right of parents to have their children with them. In addition, the fear always exists that the mildly delinquent child will become more delinquent from association with more thoroughly delinquent children in the school. He may come to think of himself as a delinquent—an outcast—and carry this attitude back to his home, public school, and community when he is released. But in his own peer group he may achieve status and importance because he has "done time" in a training school, associated with older "big shots," and learned new ways to "get by." Because of these hazards, many juvenile court judges hesitate to commit a child.

In his effort to find the best solution, the judge may linger too long on the margin between probation and commitment. If the child's family cannot give him stability and guidance even with help from the probation officer or other concerned people and, if the training school has a rehabilitative program, commitment may bring the child up short before he has deviated so far in attitudes and behavior that he cannot be brought back to conformity.

The judge has no set rules to guide him, as has the judge in a criminal court whose decision, if not already made for him by the jury, must fall within rather narrow legal limits that set the range of punishment for each crime. In theory at least, the juvenile court judge's concern is not punishment per se but the welfare and future development of the child and the safety of the community. Each case is an individual one, and each disposition should be made in terms of the needs of the individual child and the welfare of the community. The responsibility of the judge is considerable, and it is for this reason that he needs the personal qualities listed in the preceding chapter as well as a knowledge of law. He also needs the assistance of well-trained probation officers and a well-staffed clinic.

Probation

The child placed on probation remains in the community, usually in his own home, and carries on the normal activities of a child of his age and sex. Although there may be a slight stigma to being on probation, it does not condemn a child as a delinquent, as commitment to a correctional school does. The purpose of probation is variously stated. The Children's Bureau defines it as a "process of helping the individual accept and live with the limitations required by society by developing his potentials." [1] A much more limited definition is that the purpose of probation (or function of the probation officer) is "to help the offender comply with the order of the court." [2]

A more explicit, comprehensive statement, given in terms of the objectives of probation includes the following, drawn from a California study:

1. In accordance with the scope of the Welfare and Institutions Code of the state of California, to make plans for and to readjust delinquent, dependent, and neglected children by:
   (a) Helping the child recognize and understand his needs and problems and develop personal resources to meet them;
   (b) Assisting parents to understand their children and give them guidance;
   (c) Co-ordinating appropriate community services for the benefit of the family.
2. To protect children from harmful community influences, including unfit parents and other adults, and to help them develop resistance to the impact of these influences.
3. To protect the welfare of the community through reduction or elimination of delinquent behavior. [3]

The probation plan. Whatever the local conception is of the purpose of probation for the child, it begins with a plan agreed upon by the judge and the probation officer. This plan takes into account the social investigation, the child himself, his parents, and community facilities.

The judge may place certain obligations upon the child and his parents. In general the conditions include obedience of the child to his parents, regular attendance at school, being at home at an early hour in the evening, and avoiding disreputable companions and places. In addition, the judge may make special stipulations. Depending upon the acumen of the judge, such stipulations may or may not be helpful. If they are beyond the powers of the child or his parents to accomplish, they hinder adjustment. Such was the requirement that one judge laid on a child of mediocre intelligence that he must make grades of B. Another judge forbade earnest but helpless parents to whip a teen-age daughter but gave no help on how they should help her control her behavior. Other stipulations may lead toward rehabilitation, for example, that a moody or explosive child should be taken to a guidance clinic or that a restless child should explore the possibilities of a community center.

Judges differ greatly in their attitudes toward financial obligations. The Advisory Council of Judges of the National Probation and Parole Association states that fines and financial restitution for damages should be imposed only when they can be made part of the plan of treatment for the delinquent. [4] In either case, the amount should be small enough for the child to be able to earn most of it himself, without imposing an overwhelming burden on his parents. In cases of major vandalism or serious personal injury it is virtually beyond the capacity of children to earn any appreciable proportion of the cost. Even small amounts pose difficulties for children still in school. Money payment as fine or restitution may cause the child to feel that such a payment cancels his poor behavior. It may actually interfere with his rehabilitation and development of a feeling of personal responsibility. However, if the amounts are small and help to impress on the child the wrong he has done to some other person, the payments may become a part of rehabilitation.

1 *Standards for Specialized Courts Dealing with Children,* Children's Bureau Publication No. 346, Children's Bureau, Washington, D. C., 1954, p. 70.
2 Dale G. Hardman, "The Function of the Probation Officer," *Federal Probation,* 24 (September, 1960), 4.
3 Gertrude M. Hengerer, "Organizing Probation Services," *Reappraising Crime Treatment,* 1953 Yearbook, National Probation and Parole Association, New York, 1954, pp. 45–59.

4 *Guides for Juvenile Court Judges,* National Probation and Parole Association, New York, 1957, pp. 80–82; Joseph L. Thimm, "The Juvenile Court and Restitution," *Crime and Delinquency,* 6 (1960), 279–286.

Table 29

Distribution of Professional Probation Staff Time into Major Activities, Field Units, Los Angeles County

	Per cent
Interviewing.............................	33
Family...........................12	
Juvenile and family............... 9	
Juvenile........................ 7	
Collateral...................... 5	
Desk work.............................	33
Office routine....................17	
Dictation........................ 8	
Case planning.................... 4	
Reports......................... 4	
Travel................................	17
Court.................................	7
Hearings........................ 4	
Waiting......................... 3	
Telephone.............................	4
Other................................	6
Staff development................ 3	
Public relations.................. 1	
Miscellaneous.................... 2	
Total.................................	100

Based on diagram in Gertrude M. Henerger, "Organizing Probation Services," *Reappraising Crime Treatment*, 1953 Yearbook, National Probation and Parole Association, New York, 1954, 51.

The question of who is to pay for damage to property or for hospital and medical bills in case of personal injury is a serious one, since the injured person may not be in a position to pay the expense. Corporations and many individuals carry insurance to cover the cost of various losses and injuries caused by children. A mother who was employed and whose children had but scant supervision carried insurance to cover any damage caused in the neighborhood by her children. The children knew of this insurance and sometimes were impervious to cautions from neighbors because they felt that their mother could pay for any damage they did. Laws differ in various states as to whether fines can be used in juvenile court and the degree to which parents can be held responsible for damage caused by minor children.

Implementation of probation plans. The task of interpreting the conditions of probation to the parents and the child, and of helping them implement the tasks assigned to them, falls to the probation officer. If the parents have been instructed to secure certain community services, the probation officer acts as the go-between. The officer also explains that from time to time he will wish to see the child and perhaps the parents, at home, at his office, or in some other convenient meeting place.

The induction of the child and parents into probation is made most smoothly when the probation officer who made the social investigation will also supervise the probation. He is already familiar with the child's situation and at least some of his problems and has made initial contacts with the family.

Any program of redirection or rehabilitation requires time. Theoretically, in many states the wardship of the state, through the juvenile court, may extend until the child's twenty-first birthday. In practice, the judge sets a probation term of six to twelve months. On recommendation of the probation officer and following a review of the case by the judge, this term may be shortened and the case closed. On the other hand it may be extended, or it may be terminated and the child committed to a correctional school. Thus the probation period has considerable fluidity, depending upon the improvement or deterioration of the child's attitudes and behavior.

Many probation officers, especially if they have had training in social casework, view their function in wide terms, extending far beyond simply helping the child abide by court orders. Their goal is not only to bring the child's overt behavior into line but also to rebuild the child's personality.

To carry on casework the probation officer needs not only professional training but also a limited caseload. Fifty children as a caseload is recommended by the Children's Bureau, with a reduction in number if the officer also makes social investigations. It seems doubtful whether many probation officers are able to keep their caseloads to this number. In 1953 in California, usually ranked high in correctional matters, caseloads averaged 84 per officer in Los Angeles and 125 in Riverside.[1] These numbers are probably moderate compared with the numbers handled by many probation officers.

Time schedule of probation officers. The California study included a detailed analysis of the time schedule of probation work in Los Angeles County, given in Table 29. Interviewing, the key to casework, absorbed a third of the time. It was not distributed evenly over all individuals in the caseload.

1 Hengerer, *op. cit.*

New cases, and especially those involving a serious delinquency, required as much as ten or fifteen hours for the social investigation. Cases of recidivists were also time consuming. On the other hand, minor offenses required little time for investigation.

Supervision of children already on probation was minimal for at least half the cases. Supervision interviews often lasted only ten or fifteen minutes, time for a few questions and a warning. Other children did not require service, for example, those established in satisfactory foster homes or children awaiting return to another city. However, some children needed more service than they received; recommendations for special medical or clinical care sometimes were not carried out by parents; or the children were known to be continuing in delinquency. These children needed the time that the probation officer did not have to devote to them. It often seemed that routine office matters could not wait, but services to children could be delayed.

The large amount of time spent in travel was for investigations and home interviews; transporting children to court, to clinics, to a new foster home, to a correctional institution; or for returning a runaway child to his home or bringing back a runaway to the local community. In a city where the geographic area served by a given probation officer may be small, travel time may be limited, but in rural areas it may consume many hours. In the California study, probation officers in compact areas in the city of Los Angeles averaged 200 miles a month, but in rural areas mileage might run to 1,500 or even 2,000 miles per month.

The California study raises the question of the importance and necessity of some of the travel and some of the desk work when both cause a reduction in interviewing time and, hence, in case work services.

Other cities face many of the same problems as Los Angeles, as a study of probation in New York City makes clear.[1] There was the same crowding out of time for adequate interviewing by other obligations, some of which was time consuming but of little positive contribution to the treatment of a child. Travel time was increased by a policy of as-

signing children to probation officers of the same religion; the officer, therefore, often had a widely scattered distribution of cases, with several officers of different religious backgrounds covering the same area. The probation officer had to be in the courtroom when one of his cases was called; while he knew the day upon which the case would come up, he might not know the hour since some preceding cases required little time and some a long period. In one New York City court, facilities for calling the probation officer from his office to the courtroom were inadequate with the result that the officer had to wait in the courtroom or adjacent corridor for his case to be called. Sixty to ninety minutes was regarded as routine, with some waits of two or three hours.

According to the New York study, contacts with children were difficult to handle, partly because of lack of time and partly because arranging meetings with the children was extremely difficult. One officer had arranged to interview his boys in a library where he had a comfortable room for the purpose. He planned to see them twice a month. Thirty boys would be notified when to come; about twenty would appear. In three hours these boys were interviewed, an average of nine minutes each. For the city the average interview was ten to twelve minutes. Some boys had longer interviews, compensated for by very brief contacts with others. The interviews tended to become a matter of routine inquiry, about school, recreation, home, and church. Interviews held in the regular office of the probation officer were often far from satisfactory, with many interruptions and lack of privacy.

Visits to the boys' homes were also scheduled, but, since they were required to be unannounced, the officer found no one home in approximately half the cases. Officers who were especially interested in their work sometimes made calls after the working day had ended in order to catch employed parents at home. No extra compensation was allowed the officer, although evening hours at his office were paid for.

Even well-trained and dedicated probation officers find themselves seriously handicapped by the multiplicity of duties and the drain on their time through travel, waiting for cases to be called, and fruitless house calls.

Authoritarian aspects of probation. A widely

1 Alfred J. Kahn, *A Court for Children, A Study of the New York City's Children's Court,* Columbia University Press, New York, 1953, Chapter 7.

held tenet of casework is that the client must come voluntarily to the agency and be able to reach good rapport with the caseworker. The caseworker must be permissive and non-authoritarian. Casework agencies sometimes do not like to accept children referred by juvenile courts because the child may feel he is compelled to come. Many trained caseworkers do not like to accept positions as probation officers because they must work within the confines of legal and court conditions of probation.

The real danger in this authoritarian situation is not that there are legal boundaries—there always are—but that the probation officer may use his position and relation to the court to threaten the child with another court hearing or commitment to an institution. In order to help the child and his parents in more than a superficial manner, the probation officer must gain their trust and confidence. It is not necessary, possible, or desirable for him to set aside the responsibilities of his position. He is charged not only with helping the child but with preserving the safety and welfare of the community. At times the latter function takes precedence over the former. The child and his parents should never be permitted to look upon the probation officer as their ally in evading their responsibilities. They need to trust him as a representative of orderliness and legality who stands ready to help them in the areas where they have failed to restrain their behavior to fit into the community's expectations and demands.

The child and his parents should understand from the beginning both the position of the probation officer and the legal consequences that will surely follow if they do not or cannot conform. This knowledge is not a threat but a facing of reality. The probation officer should stand ready to help them learn how to conform, but not to protect and condone if they fail. He may have to report the child to the court or recommend institutionalization, psychiatric treatment, or transfer to a special school. The child and his parents should know from the beginning that there are possibilities from which the probation officer cannot shield the child, but that he will do all he can to help the child marshal his moral strength to live in a normal way in the community. If more specialized treatment or institutional confinement becomes necessary, it is part of the function of the probation officer to try to give some understanding of why such a step is necessary and the benefit that may result. He does not abandon the child or family if events turn out for the worst rather than the best.

Working with probationers in groups

The interest in group therapy has led to its use with small groups of probationers. Los Angeles County has been especially active in several types of group probation, despite the crowded time schedules already discussed.

Groups of boys.[1] The purpose of gathering probationers into groups is to give them an opportunity to define, understand, and redefine their problems and how they may meet them. This is done through interaction among the boys, with some guidance by the probation officer, who is the adult leader. As the plan operates, eight boys are chosen from a narrow age range, with similar intelligence, and able to communicate with each other. They are invited to attend the meetings; no penalty follows if they do not come. The sole activity is discussion, free and open. The leader makes clear at the beginning that he has some responsibilities to the community in his position as probation officer. This fact seems not to interfere; in fact, the boys seem to desire some control and direction and feel insecure if no guidance is given to the discussions. The leader is not authoritarian or oppressive, however, but warm, accepting, and friendly. The boys learn to express themselves freely and to see their own problems in the light of those of the other boys in the group. They gain some insight into the problems of their parents and recognize that various ways exist in which problems may be met.

Many of the problems of the boys are related to rebellion against authority, usually that of parents or school officials. In the leader they discover a figure with authority who nevertheless is friendly, accepting, and helpful to them. They learn that authority can give them strength and protection as well as thwart and oppress them.

The leader also serves as an acceptable adult male figure for some of the boys whose fathers are absent, weak, or alcoholic. In the leader the boys find an adult whom they can

1 Glenn J. Walker, "Group Counseling in Juvenile Probation," *Federal Probation,* 23 (December, 1959), 31–38.

admire and like and who likes them but at the same time stands for certain principles of conduct.

Not all boys come to the group regularly or seem to benefit from it. Boys already deeply set in attitudes and patterns of delinquency seem unable to detach themselves from dependence on their peer group or gang. They are therefore unable to think their way through their problems independently. Deeply disturbed boys also are unable to benefit; their entanglement with their emotions prevents rational thinking or insight into their problems. The groups are most successful, therefore, with boys not yet set in crime nor emotionally maladjusted, but perhaps not very happy in their role as delinquents. With insight and temporary dependence on the probation officer, they tend to learn how to manage their life situations less disastrously than through delinquency.

Although the boys meet as a group and the therapy goes on through group interaction, the leader does not attempt to form a permanent club, with officers and a variety of activities. The membership is expected to be fluid; as one boy is discharged from probation or drops out, another takes his place. The boys are not encouraged to associate together outside the meeting, since they might reinforce their delinquent attitudes; nor should the boys be allowed to attach themselves too firmly to the probation officer. For any one boy the meetings continue only for the length of probation and are designed to give the boy added strength to meet his problems by himself.

Group therapy with probationers and their parents. Another use of group therapy in Los Angeles County has a dual purpose—boys meet in one group, and, at the same time, their parents meet with other leaders in another group.[1] Each group has two leaders, a probation officer and a professional consultant, all of whom confer together after each meeting. The groups are formed at the time a boy is placed on probation (groups of girls have not been organized), with about nine boys in a group. Ideally both parents should attend, but in practice only the father usually attends. The scheme depends upon regular attendance not only of the boy but of at least one parent.

As with the groups of boys described in the preceding section, highly aggressive, schizophrenic, or regressed boys and those with other severe emotional disturbances are banned since they impede rather than enhance the therapy for other members and gain little for themselves. The boys tend to be run-of-the-mine active delinquents, able to express themselves within the normal range of personality deviation.

The boys are encouraged to express themselves freely but within the context of their behavior problems. The leaders guide and limit the discussion when necessary, in order to make it as constructive as possible and to prevent verbal brawls. Gradually the boys think through their problems and become aware of different interpretations given to their acts by adults, especially adults in a position of authority.

Meanwhile, the parents are helped to examine their own problems and their relationship to their children and to the community. They are helped to distinguish their marital problems from problems that originate with their children. If they can understand and directly approach their own problems, they are less likely to "take out" their feelings or project blame on their children. They may thus come to see that they are in part responsible for their children's delinquency and need to solve their own problems in order indirectly to help their children. Another value to the family is that they gain a more realistic and less fearful view of probation, as a helping rather than a punitive procedure.

Other juvenile courts and probation officers are also experimenting with group probation. In Washington County, Hagerstown, Maryland, more formally organized classes are available for both probationers and parents, meeting separately and with different programs. In the parents' groups, short talks followed by discussion and motion pictures are used. The subjects tend to be practical in nature.[2]

Camps for probationers. Counties in California have been authorized by law to establish camps under the control of the county probation department for boys who otherwise would be sent to correctional schools.[3] The

---

1 Robert H. Geertsma, "Group Therapy with Juvenile Probationers and Their Parents," *Federal Probation,* 24 (March, 1960), 46–52.

2 Evan Crossley, "Group Training for Predelinquents, Delinquents, and Their Parents," *Federal Probation,* 22 (June, 1958), 25–30.

3 Bernard Kogon, "Probation Camps," *Federal Probation,* 22 (September, 1958), 34–40.

boys then remain in the status of probationers unless they cannot adjust in camp, when they are returned to the court for further action. The boy's probation officer, who has previously made the social investigation, retains a contact with the boy while he is in camp, and supervises him for some months after his release from camp.

Los Angeles County maintains two reception camps, one for boys aged thirteen to fifteen and the other for boys aged sixteen to eighteen. After a period of time in the reception center where the boy's capacities are evaluated and he is prepared for the camp, the boys are transferred to their permanent quarters. The County operates four junior probation camps for the younger boys, all oriented toward school. In addition to the conventional subjects, the flexible program includes such activities as woodshop, ceramics, painting, and photography. In some way the boy is given an opportunity to feel a sense of accomplishment. In addition, each boy works for two hours per day.

Older boys are placed in three forestry camps, with the program oriented toward work, with counseling, recreation, and school in the evening.

Through the camp program and a feeling of success in it, and in more subtle ways, as well as in the direct observation of the removal from camp of boys who do not adjust, the boys slowly grasp the idea that good behavior "pays off." The term in camp is indeterminate, but usually lasts from six to nine months. The true test of the program comes, of course, after the boy has returned to his family and customary community environment. Have the changes been deep enough to carry him through readjustment to the community on a nondelinquent level? Information on this point is not given, although the need for research is recognized.

As with the other group-therapy programs discussed, boys who have a long record of delinquent behavior perhaps with previous commitment to a correctional school or who are emotionally maladjusted do not adjust to the camp nor benefit from it. Physically weak or handicapped boys cannot stand up to the physical stresses of camp life. The boys must be of average intelligence or better. Since the camps are unwalled the boys must have enough of a tendency toward rehabilitation and conformity not to walk away.

How successful is probation

Most attempts to measure the success of probation are limited to the percentage of children who misbehaved so thoroughly during the probation period that they were considered to have violated probation or whose behavior was increasingly delinquent and necessitated commitment to a correctional school. Two studies in Minnesota and Detroit concluded that about 20 per cent of the delinquents placed on probation had failed.[1] A report from the Catholic Charities Probation Bureau of New York stated that 85 per cent of cases were considered permanently adjusted by the end of the probation period —15 per cent were failures. A Chicago study of boy probationers showed that 32.7 per cent violated their probation.[2] In general then, about 15 to 30 per cent are unable to meet the obligations of probation and are returned to court.

Whether violation of the conditions of probation or even the commission of a new delinquent act is necessarily an indication of complete failure of the child to conform is debatable. Some conditions of probation may be impossible for the child to achieve. He may continue to run away or to defy his parents because of intolerable conditions in the home. He may run with his gang and get into difficulty because to do otherwise would subject him to jibes and ridicule and necessitate his becoming a social isolate. In some cases violation of probation may be a healthy sign; certainly it may be an indication that the probation officer needs to probe more deeply or that the judge needs to review the case and make new plans not as punishment for violation but as an improvement on the original plan for probation.

Another attempt to measure the success of probation comes with follow-up studies made some years after the end of probation. Even though the child appears to adjust during probation, does he keep out of trouble later? Many do not. For example, in 1940 in Allegheny County, Pennsylvania, of 280 delin-

1 Luther W. Youngdahl, "Give the Youth Correction Program a Chance," *Federal Probation*, 20 (March, 1956), 3–8; Paul Schreiber, *How Effective are Services for the Treatment of Delinquents?* Children's Bureau Report No. 9, Children's Bureau, Washington, D. C., 1960, 5–6, citing the Detroit and Catholic Charities reports.
2 Albert J. Reiss, Jr., "Delinquency as the Failure of Personal and Social Controls," *American Sociological Review*, 16 (1951), 200.

quents placed on probation, 16 per cent were convicted of other offenses within ten years, (about 10 per cent for misdemeanors and 5 per cent for felonies).[1] A more extensive study of Essex County, New Jersey, covered 131 juvenile delinquents placed on probation in 1937. Eleven years later, 42 per cent had committed major offenses and approximately 25 per cent minor offenses.[2] Other studies tend to show percentages of failure between these two figures.[3]

Many other factors than the experience as probationers contribute to the delinquent's future status as criminal or noncriminal. The type of probation supervision itself is one factor. Others are the family and community pressures for or against conformity, the type of marriage the delinquent makes in adulthood, his work experience, and his associates. Probation usually lasts not longer than one year. By the time the follow-up studies are made, the person has lived some twelve to fifteen years prior to probation and ten years after, for a total of twenty-three to twenty-six years. Probation cannot be held accountable for all that the person has done, whether laudable or discreditable.

Some studies have attempted to go beyond arrests or convictions to study the social adjustment in general of the former probationers. But here again, changes cannot be attributed only to probation.

Much more subtle methods are needed to evaluate probation, beginning perhaps with a realistic conception of what probation as now practiced can be expected to do. For children whose habits of delinquency are deeply ingrained, probation may have little effect; if the family or community situation is especially corruptive, again probation may be almost hopeless. For the milder delinquent, probation may stabilize the delinquent, give him support to work out his problems, and tide him over until such time as his situation changes with increasing age. The disorderly school boy and truant eventually reaches the age when he may leave school; the rejected girl who seeks security and money through casual sex relations eventually reaches the age when marriage may stabilize her behavior and meet her needs. Probation is only one of many factors influencing behavior.

Regardless of the difficulty in evaluating the effectiveness of probation, the concensus of opinion of those deeply interested in helping delinquents is that probation is the best method so far devised for helping the great majority of delinquents and especially those whose families are not able to incorporate the delinquent into a stable family group. The problems relate to the way in which probation is carried out rather than to the value of probation itself. Probation officers need more training in case work techniques and more time in which to do casework. Also a better rapprochement is needed with community casework and mental health agencies, which may assume responsibility for long-term treatment when needed, with the probation officer acting as representative of the court and as co-ordinator of services for the child.

1 Lewis Diana, "Is Casework in Probation Necessary?" *Focus,* 34 (January, 1955), 1.
2 Jay Rumney and Joseph P. Murphy, *Probation and Social Adjustment,* Rutgers University Press, New Brunswick, New Jersey, 1952, pp. 162–163.
3 Paul Schreiber, *op. cit.,* pp. 6–9.

Bibliography

Boswell, Charles H., "The Role of a Citizens Advisory Council in a Juvenile Court Program," *Advances in Understanding the Offender,* 1950 Yearbook, National Probation and Parole Association, New York, 1951, pp. 40–49.

Brucker, Herbert, "The Right to Know about Juvenile Delinquency," *Federal Probation,* 23 (December, 1959), 20–22.

Chudd, William V., and Agnes A. Donnelly, "Characteristics of the Investigative Process in a Children's Court," *Social Casework,* 40 (1959), 262–268.

Crossley, Evan, "Group Training for Predelinquents, Delinquents, and Their Parents," *Federal Probation,* 22 (June, 1958), 25–30.

Diana, Lewis, "Is Casework in Probation Necessary?" *Focus,* 34 (1955), pp. 1–8.

Gardner, George E., "Publicity and the Juvenile Delinquent," *Federal Probation,* 23 (December, 1959), 23–25.

Geertsma, Robert H., "Group Therapy with Juvenile Probationers and Their Parents," *Federal Probation,* 24 (March, 1960), 45–52.

Geis, Gilbert, "Publicity and Juvenile Court Proceedings," *Rocky Mountain Law Review,* 30 (February, 1958), 1–26; reprinted in *National Probation and Parole Association Journal,* 4 (1958), 333–355.

Guides for Juvenile Court Judges, National Probation and Parole Association, New York, 1957.

Hardman, Dale G., "The Function of the Probation Officer," *Federal Probation,* 24 (September, 1960), 3–10.

Hengerer, Gertrude M., "Organizing Probation Service," *Reappraising Crime Treatment,* 1953 Yearbook, National Probation and Parole Association, New York, 1954, pp. 45–59.

Hoover, J. Edgar, Editorial in the FBI Law Enforcement Bulletin, 26 (February, 1957), reprinted under the title "The 'Mollycoddling' Charge," *National Probation and Parole Association News,* 36 (May, 1957), 1–3, 8.

Kahn, Alfred J., *A Court for Children, A Study of the New York City Children's Court,* Columbia University Press, New York, 1953.

Kogon, Bernard, "Probation Camps," *Federal Probation,* 22 (September, 1958), 34–40.

"More than Meets the Eye: The Shaping of Public Opinion," *National Probation and Parole Association Journal,* 36 (1957), 5–6.

Reinemann, John Otto, "Probation and the Juvenile Delinquent," *Annals of the American Academy of Political and Social Science,* 261 (1949), 109–119.

Rumney, Jay, and Joseph P. Murphy, *Probation and Social Adjustment,* Rutgers University Press, New Brunswick, New Jersey, 1952.

Standards for Specialized Courts Dealing with Children, Children's Bureau Publication No. 346, Children's Bureau, Washington, D. C., 1954.

Tappan, Paul W., editor, *Contemporary Correction,* McGraw-Hill Book Company Inc., 1951, Chapters 3 and 24.

Thimm, Joseph L., "The Juvenile Court and Restitution," *Crime and Delinquency,* 6 (1960), 279–286.

Walker, Glenn J., "Group Counseling in Juvenile Probation," *Federal Probation,* 23 (December, 1959), 31–38.

Weber, George H., "Explorations in the Similarities, Differences, and Conflicts between Probation, Parole, and Institutions," *Journal of Criminal Law, Criminology and Police Science,* 48 (1958), 580–589.

Young, Pauline V., *Social Treatment in Probation and Delinquency,* McGraw-Hill Book Company, Inc., 1952.

A training school is a custodial residential school for children, usually operated by the state. It receives delinquent children committed to it by the courts, primarily juvenile courts. Occasionally it is used also for other children in need of care, such as children awaiting trial, or feebleminded, neglected, or dependent children. In general, however, it is limited to delinquent children. In distinction from detention homes, the training school is designed for long-term care, that is, the period of time children remain is not measured in days or weeks, as in the detention home, but in months and years.

In addition to the minimum function of maintaining custody over the children and thus segregating them from the community, the training school has the full-time care of the children and must provide housing, food, education, recreation, religious training, adult supervision, and medical and dental care for them. The responsibilities of parents are superseded by those of the school and state. In addition, the school has the function of trying to change the delinquent attitudes and habits of the children so that when they leave they at least will not get into further trouble with police or courts and at best will have better balanced personalities and constructive attitudes. The formulation of training school functions and the methods used to achieve them differ from school to school and have changed several times since training schools were first established.

Changing methods

The various institutions for children have typically had as a main objective reforming children and giving them a better chance to become self-supporting and law-abiding than they had on the streets or in adult prisons. The means advocated and practiced reflected period by period the general philosophy of child training of the times.

Suffering. An early means of reform, which still tends to persist, was that the child should suffer for his misdeeds before the attempt at reformation began or concurrently with reformation through strict discipline and severe punishments for any lapse, however slight. For example, a unique training school near Mettray, France, that was built on the cottage system, received delinquents only after they had served a part of their sentences in prison. For insubordination while in the

Chapter **23**

Organization of training schools for treatment

reformatory, the inmate could be returned to prison. Discipline was strict and punishments included isolation, reduced diet, whipping, and other types of severe physical pain. Various of these punishments are still in use in some training schools, now usually carried out in secret and often illegally.

Hard work. Along with severe discipline went hard and tiring work. Many of the children and youth admitted to the early reformatories were vagrants and thieves. Hard work was thought of partly as punishment and partly as training in staying at a job. From the present-day point of view, the training was inadequate and indeed often brutal in its effect on the children; it was, however, in harmony with the general philosophy of child-training of its period. Belief in hard work as a preventive and curative device for misconduct permeated the training of all children, nondelinquent as well as delinquent; prior to the introduction of the public school system, learning of a trade at an early age was regarded as the proper education for the children of the common man. In the children's institutions, the training took the form of contract labor, whereby a contractor paid a set price for the labor of a given number of children, provided materials, and supervised the work, with discipline vested in the hands of the institutional management. Long hours of work, heavy pressure on speed of production, and severe discipline were usually concomitants of the contract system. In many institutions for children, contract labor was not abolished until near the end of the nineteenth century and then only to be replaced by other forms of labor.

Military-type training. Training in habits of obedience, cleanliness, good manners, and extreme orderliness at all times became important as the general condition of children improved and as they entered the reformatories with some grounding in education and some familiarity with group living acquired from home and school. Often former military officers were appointed as superintendents, in accord with the philosophy of strict discipline. Many evidences of this training are still apparent. Children may stand stiffly when an official or guest enters a room; they may be forbidden to talk at mealtime; they may march in a long column of two's, perhaps with an attendant, from one building to another. All clothing, books, and other personal articles must instantly be put in place as soon as discarded or not in use. In addition to orderliness and obedience, training covered a wide spread of activities, physical education, supervised recreation, academic education, vocational training, religious training, all according to a rather set pattern uniform for all, with the exception of academic education which was adjusted to the child's capacity to learn.

Names of institutions. As these changes occurred, names for institutions for delinquent children also changed: from refuge to reformatory, to industrial school, to training school.

Present methods of treatment. Since about 1930 a new trend is discernible in the United States and abroad. With the development of clinical psychology and psychiatry, training schools (the term is still used) began to consider the delinquent child as an individual, many of whose needs could be met in a uniform program, but with other needs calling for individualized programs or special treatment. The place of attitudes and of emotional sets in behavior has also been recognized. In the school, the child may still adjust to a rigid regime in order to avoid punishment and secure an early release, but he is unlikely to carry his habit training into the community when released unless his attitudes are changed and his emotional problems solved. Also, the strong influence of a child's peer group and of his adult identifications is conceded, with more attention to his peer asso-

ciates in the school and to the kinds of adults placed in supervisory positions.

The new concept of the training school is that it is a treatment center, whose functions may be described in the words of a publication prepared by the Children's Bureau in cooperation with the National Association of Training Schools and Juvenile Agencies:

The word "treatment," as used in training schools today, means help given to the child— the total effort made by the school to rehabilitate the child and the aftercare services in his home community. It denotes helping a child by providing a new and more satisfying experience in community living together with any special services that he may need. It includes a proper diagnosis of the child's problems and a plan of care based on that diagnosis. It implies providing an environment in which all activities are directed to getting the child ready for a successful return to community living. It covers every aspect of the child's institutional life and involves the total staff, as well as the neighboring community. Every staff member, including the cottage supervisor, teacher, clerk, maintenance man, cook, and nurse, has a definite and important contribution to make to treatment.[1]

Rehabilitation is to be accomplished not alone by special psychological or psychiatric services but through the entirety of the child's experiences in the school. Most important agents of change for the child are the adults —all the adults—with whom he has contact in the school. These adults need to "establish warm, friendly and sensitive ties based upon a respect for the personality of each individual child and . . . [to] elicit mutual respect and understanding in return."[2] The relationship must be developed and maintained within the restrictions of the school. As much permissiveness may be granted as children (or an individual child) can accept without abusing it. As the child grows in self-control, permissiveness may be increased. In the rather relaxed atmosphere, the child has an opportunity to learn how to adjust to other people co-operatively and to accept the necessity for supervision and authority. In time, he experiences satisfactions in adopting socially approved behavior. Most children respond to this atmosphere; a few however are emo-

1 *Institutions Serving Delinquent Children, Guides and Goals,* Children's Bureau Publication No. 360, U. S. Government Printing Office. Washintgon, D. C., 1957, p. 5.
2 *Ibid.,* p. 6.

tionally disturbed at the time of entrance or become so later to the point that they need individual therapy.

The program of activities may seem no different from those in the typical training school. However, less insistence is placed upon regimentation, although limitations are set upon the child's freedom of activities. A genuine attempt is made to adapt the program to the child, rather than as in the past to force all children into one set of activities. Living groups can become smaller to permit a better social relationship with adults. Children are studied upon entry and placed in units according to their needs. Populous states have begun to establish a series of schools, each adapted to children with special needs.

In a country like the United States, a change from training to treatment does not come all at once. Some states have made marked progress toward the treatment ideal; others give lip service only; and still others regard a strict regime as the main ingredient of rehabilitation. No new generic name has emerged to supplant that of "training school." The tendency is to use individual names which conceal the purpose of the school as training or treatment. Thus in California one school is named the Fricot Ranch School for Boys, another the Pine Grove Forestry Youth Camp; the District of Columbia has the Children's Center; Kentucky has Kentucky Village and Maryland, Boys' Village of Maryland; Oregon has the MacLaren School for boys and the Hillcrest School for girls; and Washington has the Maple Lane Village for girls. Most schools, however, contain in the name the words training school or industrial school.

State organization—youth authority

The first privately sponsored houses of refuge and reformatories were controlled by a board of directors. This pattern was followed when states first began to establish and finance reformatories and training schools. Each training school had its own board, which guided the policies and practices of the training school, under the laws of the state. Gradually, training schools were brought under the control of state commissions or departments, which were usually charged with the operation of other types of institutions. In time, the state department of public welfare became popular as the body to control juvenile train-

Table 30

Central Administrative Body in Control of State Training Schools and Forestry Camps for Juvenile Delinquents, 1956

Central body	Number of states
State department of public welfare	13
State department of correction	3
State department of institutions	9
State department of health	1
State board of education	2
Other state board (control, charities and reform, etc.)	8
Special boards for training schools:	
Separate board for each institution	5
One board for all training schools	5
Youth authority type of agency	6
Total	52

Statistics on Public Institutions for Delinquent Children, 1956, Children's Bureau Statistical Series, No. 48, Children's Bureau, Washington, D. C., 1958, p. 15. In addition to states the Children's Bureau tables usually include Hawaii, Puerto Rico, Virgin Islands, and the District of Columbia. Alaska has no training schools.

ing schools, along with control of other institutions dealing with children, such as schools for the feebleminded, as well as with mental hospitals and women's reformatories. The tendency here was to avoid grouping the training schools with adult prisons. A still later tendency has been to establish separate departments or subdepartments controlling juvenile training schools only. All these methods of control continue as Table 30 shows.

The state department of public welfare is used in more states than any other administrative body. It tends to support the philosophy that delinquent children are children in need of help—that they are but one of many types of children for whom special provisions are needed. A slightly different approach is made by the boards known generically as youth authorities, but often carrying such titles as Youth Commission or Youth Board. These boards attempt to bring all state agencies dealing with delinquent children into one co-ordinated system, that is, one including a center to study the child after adjudication as a delinquent, specialized types of training schools and treatment centers, and parole supervision. Probation tends to remain a function of the juvenile court, although fuller development of the youth authority idea would place probation in the state system also.

Origin and provisions of the Youth Authority Model Act. The model for youth authorities was devised by the American Law Institute

DIVISION OF CHILDREN AND YOUTH SERVICES
JUVENILE REHABILITATION FACILITIES
1959 – 1961 BIENNIUM

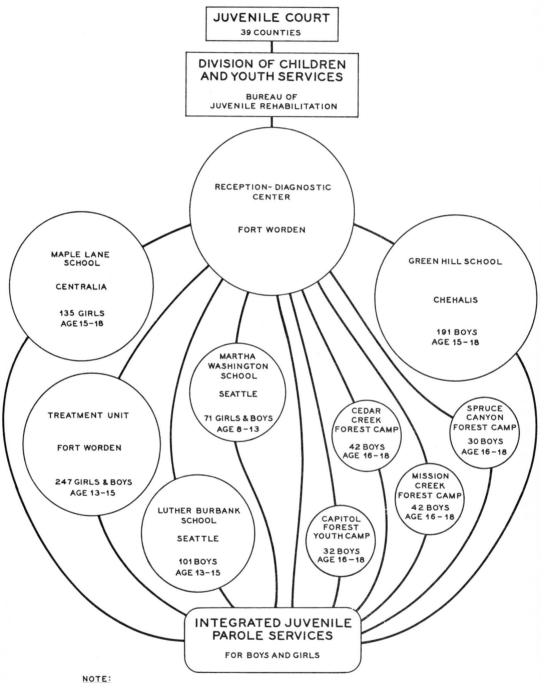

NOTE:
THE AREA OF EACH CIRCLE IS PROPORTIONAL TO THE CAPACITY OF THE FACILITY.
BOYS AND GIRLS MAY BE TRANSFERRED BETWEEN THEIR RESPECTIVE FACILITIES.

in 1940 after study and consideration for several years by a committee of advisers composed of some of the most outstanding judges, criminologists, professors of law, and welfare specialists in the country. Their concern was for the treatment of youthful offenders, the age group above the juvenile court jurisdiction, who typically are tried in criminal courts and committed to adult reformatories and prisons. The model act which was published with the hope that the various states would adopt it had the following provisions:

1. Name: Youth Correction Authority
2. Administrative organization: board of three persons with staggered nine-year terms, appointed by the governor; the board to select its chairman.
3. Age of jurisdiction: sixteen to twenty-one, from criminal or juvenile court.
4. Type of commitment: mandatory commitment to the Youth Authority by the court for all persons under twenty-one at the time of apprehension, convicted of a crime punishable by imprisonment for less than life; children aged sixteen and over might be committed by the juvenile court. The Authority, not the judge, would make the decision whether to grant probation or commit to an institution.
5. Type of commitment: the commitment to the Authority would be for an indeterminate period; the Authority would make the decision when to terminate commitment, release on parole, and so on; however, persons might not be held after age twenty-five and those under eighteen committed by the juvenile courts not after age twenty-one. If release would be dangerous, the court might approve of continued control.

Figure 15. This chart shows the state organization for Washington, where all facilities for committed delinquent children are parts of a unified system. Children committed by all juvenile courts in the state enter the Reception-Diagnostic Center for study and classification. They are then assigned to the institution whose program seems best suited to their needs. Upon release, all are under the supervision of a state-wide parole service. These varied facilities and services are operated by the Division of Children and Youth Services of the Department of Institutions, which also includes the Divisions of Mental Health, Adult Correction, and Veterans' Homes. (Courtesy, Department of Institutions, State of Washington)

6. Administration of facilities for diagnosis and retraining: the function of the Authority was to be mainly diagnostic, but it was also permitted to administer training schools and similar facilities.[1]

The above are the provisions of the model act. To date, no state has passed laws that put the model act in its entirety into operation. Many modifications have been made, and, in fact, states have been slow to swing behind the movement.

Youth authority in operation. California was the first state to establish a Youth Authority, using this shortened form of the original title. Other states have created their own titles: Youth Conservation Commission in Minnesota, Youth Commission in Illinois, Youth Council in Texas, and similar titles. Each youth authority (to use a general term) has modified the original model act, and, in addition, no two are alike. Certain general provisions can be found, however.

The governor usually appoints the board, with or without the assistance of an advisory committee of citizens; state officials may also serve on the board ex-officio. Staggered terms are customary. The membership of the board is extremely important. If the governor is able to fill the board with political appointees rather than with persons qualified to operate a program on sound rehabilitative principles, little is gained.

More emphasis than in the model act has been placed on juvenile delinquents and in some states, the act limits control by the youth authority to juvenile delinquents.

The judge retains the power of probation, that is to place the delinquent on probation after adjudication; only those whom he believes should be committed to an institution come under the control of the youth authority. The authority, however, may then release some of these children or youth on probation.

The youth authority tends to assume management of the various training schools of the state. This makes possible co-ordination of the schools and, where several exist, designation of each school for a special type of delinquent or of treatment. Authorities have tended to press legislatures for additional funds to establish special schools, camps, or reception and diagnostic centers to fill out the needs for rehabilitation. Establishment of a

1 Sol Rubin, "Changing Youth Correction Authority Concepts," *Focus*, 29 (1950), 77–82.

reception and diagnostic center has become a goal of most youth authorities, where children and youth may be subjected to careful study before the decision is made as to where they should be placed or whether they should be released on probation immediately.

The commitment is indeterminate but control may be retained until age twenty-one to twenty-five, in different states. The maximum age for commitment is the upper age limit for juvenile court jurisdiction or, in the case of youth, twenty-one years. Thus the authority may retain control, if it seems necessary, for several years after the maximum age for commitment. Provisions are made for extension of commitment for dangerous persons.

The authority has the power to release the delinquent at any time. Ideally, release is to be determined by progress toward rehabilitation. Actually, in many overcrowded training schools, children are released after a few months to relieve the pressure of inadequate capacity.

It has been pointed out that all the provisions contained in the various youth authority acts already existed in various states and that they might be put into operation under most existing forms of state organization without the passage of new laws and the creation of another board.[1] However, the youth authority movement has seemed to advance the cause of rehabilitation in several ways.

Especially in the forties, a great amount of publicity was given to the model act, which served to call attention to the shortcomings of training schools and of provisions for youthful offenders. Many states were induced to look closely at their provisions. The time was propitious for change. Several surveys of training schools had called attention to their deficiencies.[2] Attention diverted to the war effort had begun to swing back to civilian needs, including the needs of delinquent children. The model act, backed by the prestige of the American Law Institute provided a plan with which each state might compare its own provisions, whether or not it adopted the

youth authority type of organization. It was possible for individual provisions of the act to be adopted without a change in previous organization.

In addition to stimulating rethinking and revising of treatment, the youth authority when adopted, provided for a tightening of the organization of services specifically for delinquents. It is often regarded simply as a reorganization of services, with a sharp focus on the delinquent. However, it is not limited to services. Its focus has been on rehabilitation, the study of each delinquent child with a thoroughness not possible in many local communities, and an expansion of training facilities. It has tended to bring under one board the services previously carried out by several boards, often without much co-ordination; for example, control of training schools and of parole were sometimes vested in two separate state boards or departments.

Creating a youth authority does not guarantee perfection. Any betterment is limited by the type of persons appointed to the board. In one state with political appointees making up the board, scandals have broken out over the connection of one chairman with a gambling syndicate and over gross brutality in one training school. Only persons of the highest integrity and with specialized training in various phases of rehabilitation can convert outworn methods to a program based on respect for human beings.

The work of the youth authorities is limited also by the appropriations made by state legislatures. Some training schools, built many decades ago, resemble prisons or mass institutions, and are almost beyond conversion to modern treatment needs. New facilities are needed, especially a reception and diagnostic center and a system of training units graded from open camps or similar institutions through the secure training school to the close-custody institution; specialized treatment centers for deeply disturbed delinquents are also needed. Even when the legislature is generous, this array of institutions is within the financial capacity of only the more wealthy and populous states. Regional youth authorities would give a workable base for a modern plan of treatment.

Many youth authorities experience an initial period of difficulty. If the staff of a training school has been following older disciplinary methods, they may be unable to change

1 Rubin, *op. cit.*
2 Alida C. Bowler and Ruth S. Bloodgood, *Institutional Treatment of Delinquent Boys,* Part I, Children's Bureau Publication No. 228, U. S. Department of Labor, Washington, D. C., 1935; *Handbook of American Institutions for Delinquent Juveniles,* Vols. I–IV, Osborne Association, 1938–1943; a slightly later, popular book is Albert Deutsch, *Our Rejected Children,* Little, Brown and Company, Boston, 1950.

their attitude and habits toward rehabilitation. New staff may be added in positions that reduce the authority of the old staff. The children in residence respond to the tensions in staff and change in policy; disciplinary problems and runaways may increase temporarily. Often the values of change become visible only after months have passed. It is important that new staff or replacement should be selected by the youth authority on the basis of qualifications for the work and not on the basis of political affiliation or of success in getting out votes for the political party in power.

If the youth authority's province is limited to delinquents, it will have to work out new lines of co-ordination with other state agencies in charge of other groups of children, such as the feebleminded, dependent, and near-psychotic, so that lines can be drawn to exclude them from the training schools and provide for them elsewhere.

The youth authority also has an important relationship to maintain with the juvenile court judge and other judges who may commit children to the authority. The law requires commitment to the authority instead of to specific institutions. However, since the

The entrance to the Youth Authority's Paso Robles School for Boys shows the simple style of architecture characteristic of the present period in contrast to elaborate, ornate styles of the past. This school houses around 450 boys with an average age of sixteen. The boys receive academic education (usually of a remedial nature), vocational training, and work experience. They have an athletic program, and two chaplains conduct religious services and instruct the boys in religion. Two cottages, one of which is a detention unit, house boys unable to adjust in the regular program. Group counseling is emphasized. The cottages are also used to give in-service training to the school personnel in understanding and treating troublesome youth. (Courtesy California Youth Authority)

youth authority as well as the judge may place a child on probation, a possible conflict of authority is present. If the youth authority places a child on probation who has been committed to it (presumably for treatment in the training school), the judge may regard this step as a criticism of his judgment. However, in doubtful cases some judges may welcome the chance to pass the decision as to probation on to the youth authority. If the judge does not have access to clinics and so-

cial workers he may genuinely appreciate
the services of a state diagnostic center. Or he
may not wish to take the responsibility of
placing doubtful cases on probation and of
receiving the sharp local criticism if the child
again commits delinquencies. A clear understanding of policy is necessary between the
judge and the authority as a basis for the
best service to youth.

In some states the youth authority has
added functions. Usually the supervision of
delinquents on parole from the training
school is under the control of the authority.
In some states an attempt is made to work
with the child's family before his release. If
the family has disintegrated or refuses to accept responsibility for the child, the authority
must make other provisions for the child.
In this way the work of the authority flows
into the local community, and its services follow the child after release.

In some states the authority is also charged
with delinquency prevention, especially with
establishing recreation and community centers in local communities. Usually this move
involves participation from the local community and is not imposed upon them.

Types of institutions and services

In 1958 in the United States, the residential care of committed delinquent children
was lodged in 132 state institutions, fifty-two
local county training centers, and twenty-nine
forestry camps.[1] Reception and diagnostic
centers are not included. A minority of states
maintain such centers; an inspection of annual reports for different years indicates that
more such centers are being built. In addition,
diagnostic facilities for wider use are often
available in an individual institution. In addition to these publicly supported institutions,
there are a number of privately supported
homes and treatment centers. The statistics
that follow pertain only to the state and
county institutions and public forestry camps.
They are estimates for all institutions based
on actual reports from 162 institutions.

Groups served. Training schools and camps
for boys far exceed those for girls in both
number and capacity; this is in line with the
greater number of boys than of girls brought

to juvenile courts. Institutions for boys number 129, for girls 65. Only nineteen institutions have ventured into coeducation. These
institutions actually are two separate institutions with housing for boys and girls well
separated.

In the south, separate institutions for white
and Negro children are customary; in other
parts of the country, institutions are shared by
all races. Of the total number, twenty-eight
are for white children only, twenty-six for
Negro, and 159 for both. The Children's
Bureau survey does not state to what extent
whites and nonwhites may live in separate
houses within the same institution. Outside
the South, children of all races become accustomed to mingling in school and in public
places, but not to living together. It is possible
that mixed houses would increase tensions
and lead to exploitation or abuse of one race
by another. The practice in this respect is not
given.

The capacity of the institution is important
in terms of creating the close adult-child relationships now thought fundamental to rehabilitation. One-hundred-fifty children is regarded as the maximum number that can be
handled in one institution without a loss of the
therapeutic value of the various interrelationships. Slightly over half (54 per cent) of institutions are under 150; the other half range
upward, a few having a capacity of 600–700.
Many institutions are now overcrowded, due
to a combination of increasing child population, increased rate of delinquency, and failure of state legislatures to appropriate money
for additional buildings and staff.

Training schools attempt to break up the
mass of children by using cottages. However,
a cottage often holds forty to eighty children,
often jammed into space originally intended
for many fewer children. Individual rooms intended for one girl may house two or three;
boys' dormitory rooms may have double-
decked bunks placed so close together that
there is scarcely space to climb into them.
Slightly more than a third of training schools
are housing more than the number of children for which they were constructed. Some
have half again as many children as their official capacity. On the other hand, states with
building programs may erect small cottages
for twelve to fifteen children, in which some
semblance of family life may be developed
about a married couple as houseparents.

Staff. Although physical plant may facilitate

1 *Statistics on Public Institutions for Delinquent Children, 1958,* Children's Bureau Statistical Series, No.
59, Children's Bureau, Washington, D. C., 1960.
Further statistics are drawn from this report unless
otherwise stated. Comments are based on a variety
of sources including reports from states and schools.

or restrict a program of retraining, the heart of rehabilitation is the staff. The ratio of staff to children is high—one full-time staff member for every 2.6 children. When staff in state and local public training schools and forestry camps is broken down by function into three classes, the treatment and educational group accounts for 60.6 per cent, operational and maintenance 28.3 per cent, and administrative 11.1 per cent.

The treatment and educational group includes cottage supervisors and night attendants, (a group that accounts for about 40 per cent of this classification). The treatment and educational group also includes a widely diversified list of specialists: academic and vocational teachers, social workers, recreational workers, psychologists, occupational supervisors, physicians, psychiatrists, dentists, nurses, medical aides, and chaplains. Aside from the cottage personnel, the next most numerous groups are the academic teachers and the occupational supervisors, each comprising about 14 per cent of the treatment and educational personnel.

For staff in general, training and salaries are lower than in other fields where the same kinds of positions exist; the turnover is very high, with a median length of employment for full-time staff of 3.3 years. Personnel come into positions with virtually no previous experience in other institutions. Annual reports of many training schools report vacancies of key staff positions of a year or more.

Inadequate as these facts are to give a complete picture of the staffing of training schools, they are sufficient to indicate some of the difficulties in implementing a program of rehabilitation.

The trend toward treatment is set. The objective of training schools has scarcely changed since the early nineteenth century; at all times the goal has been to change delinquent and criminal children into upright citizens. The philosophy of method, however, has changed drastically, from severe punishment and grueling work to re-education and personal rehabilitation. Traces of past methods remain in many places—in the structure of old buildings, the inadequately trained staff, the furtive use of severe punishments, and repressive training. The idea of personal rehabilitation through change of attitudes, personal values, and goals is still new and threatening to many people. A few states forge ahead, many move part way, and some cling to the old ways. But the movement toward personal rehabilitation slowly gains ground.

Bibliography

Bowler, Alida and Ruth S. Bloodgood, *Institutional Treatment of Delinquent Boys,* Part I, Children's Bureau Publication No. 228, U. S. Department of Labor, Washington, D. C., 1935.

Deutsch, Albert, *Our Rejected Children,* Little, Brown and Company, Boston, 1950.

Handbook of American Institutions for Delinquent Juveniles, Vols. I–IV, Osborne Association, New York, 1938–1943.

Hardman, Dale G. and Margaret P., "Three Postulates in Institutional Care," *National Probation and Parole Association Journal,* 4 (1956), 22–27.

Institutions Serving Delinquent Children, Guides and Goals, Children's Bureau Publication No. 360, U. S. Government Printing Office, Washington, D. C., 1957.

Jeter, Helen, *State Agencies and Juvenile Delinquency,* Children's Bureau Report No. 12, U. S. Government Printing Office, 1960.

Some Facts about Public State Training Schools for Juvenile Delinquents, Children's Bureau Statistical Series, No. 33, U. S. Government Printing Office, Washington, D. C., 1956.

Statistics on Public Institutions for Delinquent Children, 1958, Children's Bureau Statistical Series, No. 59, Children's Bureau, Washington, D. C., 1960.

Studt, Elliot, and Bernard Russell, *Staff Training for Personnel in Institutions for Juvenile Delinquents,* Children's Bureau Publication No. 364. U. S. Government Printing Office, 1958.

Training Personnel for Work with Juvenile Delinquents, Children's Bureau Publication No. 348, U. S. Government Printing Office, Washington, D. C., 1954.

Zald, Mayer N., "The Correctional Institution for Juvenile Offenders: An Analysis of Organizational 'Character'," *Social Problems,* 8 (1960), 57–67.

Youth authority

California Youth Authority, Program and Progress, 1943–1948, California Youth Authority, State of California, Sacramento, California, 1949.

Beck, Bertram M., *Five States: A Study of the Youth Authority Program as Promulgated by the American Law Institute,* American Law Institute, Philadelphia, 1951.

Rubin, Sol, "Changing Youth Correction Authority Concepts," *Focus,* 29 (1950), 77–82.

Chapter **24**

The delinquent and the training-school program

Each year an estimated 14 per cent of all children whose cases are officially heard in juvenile court are committed to public training schools; only 1 per cent of unofficial cases reach the training schools.[1] The estimated number committed in one year amounts to about 40,000 children. Approximately three boys are committed to every one girl. The boys stay on an average of nine months, the girls one year; a few, however, remain two or more years. They are then released with or without supervision, usually to return to their old communities.

The children committed

The committed child has been rejected by the community and temporarily exiled. Sometimes the parents, in despair, urge the judge to commit their child, thus explicitly rejecting him. The child tends to look upon commitment as a form of imprisonment and enters the institution in a hostile and sometimes fearful frame of mind. A few children, however, welcome entrance; these are ones from unhappy or deprived backgrounds who have previously been in the institution and have found that it offers comfort, food, and many activities, and protects them from many of the deprivations and hazards of life. Most children learn to accept institutional life and to adjust to it. A few do not; they continue to rebel or they run away. Children committed

to training schools then are not all of one type. They are individual personalities who react in many different ways to the institution and its regime.

Offenses. The offenses of committed children do not differ from those which bring children to the attention of the court, but the concentration of offenses in certain categories does differ. Only estimates and rough comparisons can be made but the general picture seems sufficiently accurate to indicate violations that have led to commitment. In this comparison the offenses of court cases are those given by the Children's Bureau for fifteen states.[2] The offenses of committed children are based on annual reports from nine states for boys and six states for girls.[3]

Among juvenile court cases, 48 per cent of the boys had indulged in some form of theft, automobile theft, burglary, and robbery being the most common. Among training school boys, approximately 65 per cent had thefts as their principal delinquencies. Sex offenses and injuries to others are slightly more numerous among the training school than the court delinquents, but are low in both instances. The more trivial offenses among the court cases— truancy, running away, ungovernability, and acts of carelessness or mischief are almost nil in the institutional cases. A miscellaneous category, called "other" appears among both court and training school boys, in some schools including a general classification of "general delinquency."

Among girls, the wide range of delinquencies found among court cases tends to shrink

1 *Juvenile Court Statistics,* 1957, Children's Bureau Statistical Series No. 52, Children's Bureau, 1959, p. 7.

2 *Juvenile Court Statistics, 1957, op. cit.,* p. 7. The fifteen states are California, Connecticut, Florida, Iowa, Michigan, Mississippi, Missouri, New Mexico, North Carolina, Ohio, Oregon, Utah, Vermont, Washington, and Wisconsin; these states were not chosen as a representative sample but apparently because they published juvenile court statistics on a statewide basis. See also Chapter 3 for a distribution of offenses.

3 The information was assembled from the reports of training schools in California, Colorado, Delaware, Illinois, Iowa, Nebraska, Oregon, Texas, and Washington for boys, and California, Illinois, Nebraska, Oregon, Washington, and Texas for girls. A nationwide request was made for reports and these were among the states that responded and whose reports contained the desired information. Not all reports were for the same year, but all represent the latter part of the fifties. Crude though this type of data is, it has some substance; approximately 6,000 boys and 1,000 girls are represented, or more than a sixth of all training school children. Comparison of the distribution of offenses for the individual states showed a decided similarity, obscured at some points it is true by differences in classifying some offenses.

to three principal offenses for training school girls: incorrigibility, sex offenses, and running away—including truancy. Stealing accounts for a very low percentage, and injury to others and destruction of property are rarely listed.

The experienced delinquent. A number of the training school reports remind the reader that usually the offense listed is simply the one that led to commitment—the straw that broke the camel's back—and that most of the boys and girls had a long list of other delinquencies in their past experience as well as failures on probation; some had had previous commitments, and failures on parole.

Among the children in training schools at any one time, about 57 per cent only are directly from the juvenile court; 12 per cent have previously been released but have violated the terms of their aftercare; and 30 per cent have been transferred from some other institution, usually from a reception and diagnostic center where they have spent a few weeks immediately after commitment.[1]

A more detailed report (Table 31) comes from the state of Washington. Comparable reports from other states were not found; hence the Washington report cannot necessarily be considered typical. However, general information indicates that, as the Washington report states, committed children are "a sophisticated group in regard to juvenile delinquency." All but 6 per cent of the boys and 12 per cent of the girls were known to have had at least a brush with the police prior to the events leading to the present commitment.

Intelligence test scores and school retardation. A number of state reports on training schools give some information on mental ability. Among those that reported on mental tests, the percentage of normal (I.Q. 90 to 110) children ranged from 27 to 57 per cent. In an unselected population of children, about 60 per cent would fall into this classification. Many of the schools have almost as many mentally normal children as the public schools from which they came. Training school children, however, included few with I.Q.'s above normal, that is, few who were superior in mentality according to the mental test scores. Three to eight per cent was typical, compared to an anticipated 20 per cent among public school children. Children with I.Q.'s below normal—the dull and borderline feebleminded—were numerous in the training schools, running from 36 to 70 per cent in the schools that reported scores. Ordinarily, about 20 per cent of children would fall into this group.

The intelligence test scores are closely related to retardation in school of children admitted to training schools, but whether as cause or effect or both one cannot say. The median age of boys when admitted to training schools was about fifteen years and of girls fourteen years. The median number of years of school attendance prior to entrance was about seven, indicating a school retardation of about two years. Various reports stated that the children were retarded an average of three years; some were retarded as much as six years. A western state reported that 60.8 per cent of boys were retarded a half year or more in reading and 64.9 per cent a similar amount in arithmetic.

Without speculating on the relation of mental ability and school retardation to delinquency, we, nevertheless, see here the framework within which the training school must adapt its program if it is to be of help to the children in their future adjustment after they leave the institution.

Table 31

Prior Police, Probation, and Training-School Experience of Boys and Girls Committed to the Division of Children and Youth Services, Washington, 1957, Percentage Distribution

Experience prior to commitment	Boys	Girls
Previous training school experience	13	36
Juvenile court probation, without any training school experience	60	35
Referral to police or court but without probation or commitment	21	17
None of the above	4	11
No information	2	1
Total	100	100
Number of cases	336	167

Juvenile Correctional Program, an Annual Statistical Report, Department of Institutions, Division of Children and Youth Services, Olympia, Washington, 1958, p. 14, based on Table 5.

Age

The legal ages for commitment to training schools cover a wide range. The upper limit

---

1 *Statistics on Public Institutions for Delinquent Children, 1958*, Children's Bureau Statistical Series, No. 59, Children's Bureau, Washington, D. C., 1960. Unless otherwise stated, further statistics in this chapter are drawn from this source.

Play suited to their age is an important part of therapy at the Fricot Ranch School for Boys, where the median age is thirteen years and some boys are as young as eight years. In this training school, each counselor has no more than ten boys. Each boy may select a counselor as his "Fricot Dad," with whom he may develop a close personal relationship. This school is one of eleven training schools and camps operated by the California Youth Authority, each devised for a certain age and sex group. (Courtesy California Youth Authority)

for commitment is the upper age of juvenile court jurisdiction. In many states, however, youth may be retained in the school until age twenty-one, provided they have been committed for a delinquent act that occurred before the upper age of juvenile court jurisdiction. The legal lower-age limit varies greatly, as Table 32 shows. In fifteen states (30.6 per cent) there is no minimum age for boys and in thirteen (27.1 per cent) none for girls; the minimum age for juvenile court jurisdiction would automatically set a minimum age. In a few states with no minimum age for this jurisdiction, very young children theoretically might be committed to the training school. Only a few states will allow a child of six or seven to be committed, and, in general, age eight is the minimum age permitted for commitment. The most frequent minimum age is twelve for girls and ten to twelve for boys.

In practice, few public state and local training schools have children under age thirteen as column 4 of Table 32 shows. Ninety per cent are between the ages of thirteen and eighteen. Training schools are thus adolescent schools. In some states separate schools receive young adolescents and older adolescents, with modification in the program, especially as regards the relative emphasis placed on education and work.

Health. In many training schools each child is given a thorough physical examination upon entrance, and an effort is made not only to treat obvious illnesses but to upgrade the child's general standard of health and to give care. Testing and treatment for venereal disease and tuberculous conditions are routine, not only for the health of the child but to prevent infection of others in the school. Some schools immunize all students against polio, diphtheria, whooping cough, and tetanus and vaccinate all against small pox.

Table 32

Legal Minimum Age for Admission to State Training Schools and Actual Age Distribution of Children in Residence, Percentage Distribution

Age	Legal minimum age * Boys	Girls	Actual age of children in 109 schools, 1953 **
No minimum	30.6	27.1	}
Six	—	2.1	less than 0.1
Seven	2.0	4.2	
Eight	18.4	14.5	
Nine	2.0	2.1	0.7
Ten	22.5	20.8	
Eleven	2.0	—	4.8
Twelve	22.5	29.2	
Thirteen-fourteen			20.9
Fifteen-sixteen			48.1
Seventeen-eighteen			23.3
Over eighteen			2.2
Total	100.0	100.0	100.0
Number of states	49	48	
Number of children			17,032
Median age			16.0

* *Directory Public Training Schools for Delinquent Children, 1955*, U. S. Government Printing Office, Washington, D. C., 1955. Hawaii is included; Alaska has no training schools; Arizona has none for girls.
** *Some Facts about Public State Training Schools for Juvenile Delinquents,* Children's Bureau Statistical Series, No. 33, U. S. Government Printing Office, Washington, D. C., 1956, p. 16. Later reports do not include an age distribution.

Glasses are supplied when needed. One school which admits approximately 160 students each year and has a total residence group of 350 students, gives a complete dental examination upon entrance, supplies whatever dental work is needed, and meets dental needs as they arise later. In a period of two years, 1,200 fillings were put in, fifteen dentures were supplied, and other dental work was done for the students.

Mental health is also a problem among a small minority of boys and girls. Various reports comment on the lack of any special institution or hospital in their states for the treatment of seriously disturbed children. Although all children committed have a similar background of delinquent behavior, and probably experienced severe social deprivations and handicaps, the great majority are not neurotic to the point of being unable to adjust, nor are they psychotic. The few who are emotionally disturbed not only are unable to benefit from a program keyed to the average delinquent but are a disruptive element in school. Nevertheless, many schools apparently have to cope with a minority of such children.

Family background. In general, reports from training schools give little specific information about the families of boys and girls committed to them. Available information indicates that more training school children come from broken homes than is true for delinquents in general or for nondelinquent children. Even in the smaller training schools with a limited number of children, the variety of broken and incomplete homes is very great, each suggesting different problems in the child's background. In one training school with 129 boys, parents were living together in 40 per cent of the cases, while the remaining 60 per cent were unevenly distributed into the following twelve types: parents separated, parents divorced, mother deserted, father deserted, mother insane, stepfather in the home, stepmother in the home, father dead, mother dead, father in prison, foster parents, child illegitimate (not stated where he lived). Other lists include children with adoptive parents or a background of residence in institutional homes.

When economic or occupational background of parents is given, the number receiving public assistance or who are unemployed or working at unskilled labor is large. Information on parental deficiencies indicates a high percentage of alcoholic parents or ones who are criminally inclined. All these factors have already been shown in earlier chapters to be more highly associated with delinquent than with nondelinquent children. Training school children are more likely than other delinquent children to have parents who have been unable to meet the stresses of life.

What the training school has to cope with. Training school boys and girls are not the savages nor the mental defectives that they are sometimes popularly thought to be; nor are they a cross section of public school children. They form a unique population withdrawn from normal community life for a few months or years and placed under a special regime. They are children less well equipped than the average child, who have failed to conform to community expectations. To be effective, the training school must adapt its program to the youth committed to it.

A description of a typical training school boy, based on the annual reports, is of a youth of fifteen, committed for a serious theft. The chances are two out of three that he has

Typical of the reception centers that are becoming part of the normal training school program is the one at Lyndon, Kentucky, opened in 1953. Although the capacity of the center is eighty children, almost 800 pass through the center each year, staying for limited periods of time. While there they are tested, interviewed, and observed to make possible a diagnosis of each one's difficulties. A few children may be referred back to the court that committed them—chiefly feeble-minded children for whom the training school has no facilities, but also a few older adolescents who have previously been in the training school and whose current delinquencies indicate that they should be considered as adults rather than juveniles. Most of the children, however, are either returned to their home communities under supervision, placed in wage homes, or sent to the training school or camp. (Courtesy Department of Welfare, Kentucky)

been on probation prior to his commitment, and either failed to adjust or committed a

new offense. Intelligence test scores show him to be normal or dull, and retarded about two years in school. Physically his health has been neglected so far as protective measures against disease are concerned, but he is not afflicted with malnutrition or serious physical handicaps. His personality is normal. He comes from a low economic background, and his parents have not been able to handle their personal problems adequately.

The training school girl has many of the same characteristics. She is, however, a year younger, and her offenses are a related complex of incorrigibility, sex offenses, and running away from home. She is much more likely than the boy to have had a prior commitment to a training school, less likely to have been on probation.

Program of training and treatment

The impact of training and treatment is to some extent related to the period of time spent in the institution. Training schools vary greatly as to the length of time that they retain children before release. In a few schools the median length of stay is less than six months; in a few others eighteen or more months. The median for all schools, however, is 9.3 months for boys and 12.0 for girls. Each school has its own formal program; these programs are similar in many ways but vary according to the degree to which methods have shifted from punitive toward rehabilitative.

Reception-orientation. A state with a number of training schools operating under one state agency may have a special reception and diagnostic center, usually of recent origin. Boys and girls are received at this center directly from the court and remain a matter of weeks. A psychologist gives tests, to determine intelligence, proper school placement, degree of maturity, social attitudes, aptitudes, and other facts valuable in planning a program for the child. A complete physical examination is given not only to rule out infectious diseases but to reveal strengths and weaknesses and any handicaps that may be remedied. A psychiatrist may interview all children or only those apparently in need of special therapeutic treatment. A report from the court may come with the child, covering his social background; otherwise, a social worker investigates this area. The chaplain usually talks with the child. The child's behavior is also observed during the period in the reception center, and he is given some help in orienting himself to institutional life and its restrictions and possibilities. A complete report is drawn up. A case conference on each child results in a summary of his needs and abilities, and a program is outlined for him.

In many more states, the reception-orientation process is carried out in the school itself, where one building or a suite of rooms may be set aside in which each child can be studied, usually on a less extensive basis than outlined above, and a plan made for him before he is assigned to his cottage, classes, work, and so on. In small institutions, the procedure may be very limited and informal. The superintendent, chaplain, school principal, and perhaps a few other members of the personnel talk with the child, advise him on acceptable behavior, and assign him to his cottage and activities. Often there is very little choice of living quarters or activities. Many small institutions have little or

none of the psychological or social work services found in larger institutions.

Education. The activities in a typical training school fall into several well-defined areas, all together designed to fill the student's time as well as to retrain or rehabilitate him. Younger children, especially, spend a large part of their time in school. As a rule, training schools do not attempt an exact duplication of the public school program, although they provide for academic training. By testing or experience, students are placed in groups where they can do the work or are allowed to work along an individual plan under the supervision of the teacher. In many training schools, an effort is made to give the student an experience of success at whatever level he can manage. At the same time, academic education cannot be overlooked, since within a year most boys and girls will return to their homes and must re-enter public school.

Students who seem totally unsuited to an academic program, are given training in simple skills, not necessarily with vocational intent. A group of girls unable to benefit from additional academic work may sit happily in a schoolroom whose walls are lined with woven, knitted, or embroidered articles they have made. They continue with such work in a relaxed atmosphere. While the girls may use or send home some of the articles they make, many are sold to the public at an annual fair. The money is used in various ways, usually for the benefit of the entire school. Boys of limited capacities are relieved of most or all academic work and assigned to various types of work on the grounds. Most training schools operate farms—a carryover from the agricultural dominance of the period when they were established. Boys spend considerable time doing farm work under supervision. Since they are usually city boys this work cannot be thought of as vocational in purpose; it does, however, give the experience of steady occupation under supervision and often opens the way for a friendly relationship between boys and farm supervisors.

Training schools also have some specific vocational training that is orientated toward the time of release. For the boys such things as woodworking, machine shop, shoe repairing, painting, printing, auto mechanics, and electrical work are popular. The objective is not to turn out skilled craftsmen but to give some orientation to an occupation. Girls are

A standard part of the procedure in reception centers is testing to reveal clues to intelligence and personality traits. Such testing is only part of the thorough study of delinquents received from the courts at the Northern Reception Center and Clinic, maintained by the California Youth Authority. (Courtesy California Youth Authority)

usually given experience in houskeeping through the operation of their cottage. Sewing classes are popular, and work is stimulated by the motivation of making attractive clothes to wear and to take along when they leave the institution. In some training schools, girls may learn the entire routine of the beauty parlor and, if they are successful, secure a state license to practice as a beautician, with no indication on the license as to where the training was received.

Some schools expand training by arranging for employment in some nearby community, under careful supervision.

Recreation and social life. Another round of activities comes under the heading of recreation. For both boys and girls much of this is of the active type, carried on outdoors in warm weather. Boys may have a highly developed system of athletics, sometimes playing against community teams. Marching bands are popular in some schools. Such activities calling for observation of regulations and for close co-ordination of activities among boys may offset some of the lack of orderly habits with which many boys enter the school. They also demonstrate advantages to be gained from working in a group for a shared objective. Girls may also play team games but are less likely to enter into any serious or outside competition.

Informal activities cover a wide range, including reading and hobbies which may be carried on alone, club activities, motion pictures shown in the school, group singing, and many other recreational activities normal to the age and sex of the students.

Some schools produce fairly complicated performances or skits to which parents may be invited. All-school events develop around the holidays, often with picnics in the summer.

Other schools make an effort to involve

students in community activities off the grounds; their success depends in part upon the willingness of the community to participate and the degree to which the boys and girls are able to adjust to community expectations of good behavior.

Some schools permit visits home during the stay in the school, perhaps for a long weekend, with a longer visit at Christmas or in the summer. The student travels by himself, or his parents are encouraged to call for him and return him. He must, of course, have a home or other assigned place to visit. These visits have a number of therapeutic advantages: they maintain the inclusion of the child in his family and neighborhood; they provide an opportunity for meetings with interested adults such as a school principal, minister, or social worker; and they test the student's ability to avoid getting into trouble back in the old environment and to assume personal responsibility for his own return. On the whole, these visits work out well, with only a few failing to return or causing trouble during the visit.[1]

A full activity program is offered at the pool each summer at Los Guilucos School for Girls, California. About 200 girls, aged eight to sixteen, are assigned to this school. Another school receives girls aged fifteen to twenty-one. At Los Guilucos School, most of the girls are in accredited junior and senior high school classes, with emphasis on homemaking and commercial subjects. Recreation is carried on in outdoor play areas, gymnasium, and auditorium. (Courtesy California Youth Authority)

Coeducational activities. The few training schools with both boys and girls in the same institutions, though usually in well-separated cottages, may plan a limited number of joint activities. Some school classes may be shared as well as a limited number of parties, dances, and programs of various sorts, all closely supervised. Free time is not spent together, nor is dating allowed.

A few training schools for girls attempt to arrange an occasional party to which boys or

1 The superintendent of one training school for boys, with emphasis on rehabilitation, told the author that the impact of their training was sufficient to carry the boy over a short period of a few days or a

week, but often the changes accomplished during a few months in the training school were not ingrained deeply enough to offset the pull back to old companions and old delinquent activities when the boy was permanently released from the institution.

young men from some club or church group in a nearby town are invited. Since the young men must be appealed to from a philanthropic motive, the gatherings lack spontaneity. Natural pair interests are discouraged from developing since there is no opportunity for dating.

Several motives underlie the efforts to have some mixed activities. The customary interest of youth in the other sex is given some satisfaction, and an opportunity is given to teach some of the values of social intercourse to boys and girls (especially) who have been all too accustomed to promiscuous sex relations.

Religious instruction. All schools provide some religious instruction, ranging from a service on Sunday, when a local minister comes to the training school, to the work of a full-time chaplain. Large schools near urban centers with a mixture of boys or girls of different religious backgrounds engage on a part- or full-time basis the services of ministers of the major religions—the Protestant minister, the Catholic priest, the Jewish rabbi. Schools provide chapels which either are reserved primarily for religious services or are multi-purpose rooms with the religious paintings or altar concealed by a curtain when the room is used for motion pictures, entertainments, or even athletics. Each religion provides its own equipment for worship.

Living arrangements

The hours not spent in organized programs of education, work, and recreation are spent in the living quarters. In most training schools, every effort is made to provide comfortable quarters with as much similarity to normal family living as is possible under the conditions of large numbers of children, of overcrowded buildings, and of enforcement of strict rules to prevent mass disorderliness and running away.

Training schools for girls. Training schools for girls usually provide several residential houses if the number of girls makes this economical. Thirty to sixty girls may be in one house or cottage, as it is usually called. Each girl may have her own room, or small dormitory rooms may be used. The rooms are simply but comfortably furnished, usually with a cot, chest of drawers, chair, and small table. Girls are encouraged to make their rooms attractive by embroidering pillow cov-

ers or scarves for the chest. They may have photographs of close relatives.

Many schools pride themselves on providing individual styles of clothing for the girls, although these fall within a narrow range of choice in style and material. When uniforms are used, an effort often is made to introduce variety and color. In a southern school, each color indicates a different group of girls or different type of occupation. Blue uniforms are worn to work and after school. Raspberry colored uniforms are worn by the girls who are serving in the dining room, with a change to kelly green for Sundays and special occasions. Chartreuse uniforms are worn by the girls chosen by an instructor to take care of her room and clothing—a position of honor signifying that the girl is trustworthy. White is worn on Sunday morning, with a change to skirt and sweater (color of the girl's choice) for church services. Girls in the isolation cottage wear green for work and yellow for leisure-time activities. A variety of colors are worn by the girls when in school—aqua, rose, moss green, gold, tomato red, pink, mint green, and wine. The uniforms are made at the school. Although a group of girls wear the same color of uniform, each girl has her own individual garments. The color aids supervisors in placing a girl in her proper classification. The use of uniforms instead of personal clothing reduces differences in status which would exist if each girl were allowed to wear the clothing that her parents could provide.

The training school cottage typically has a living room, dining room, and kitchen, and sometimes a simple recreation room in the basement. Girls are assigned to different tasks in the course of their stay, working at all the routines and skills of homemaking. In a typical dining room, the girls eat at small tables for four or six girls, with supervisory staff at another table in the same room. An effort is made to teach the girls good manners in dining and quiet comportment at the table. The living room is fully furnished in simple style; sometimes framed pictures painted by the girls are hung on the walls. A radio and television set are typical equipment. The recreation room in the basement may have simple sports equipment or may simply be a room to work off energy. In one training school, girls could roller skate in the basement.

All activities are carried out on a time schedule under supervision. Girls are not allowed to come and go at will. Each girl or small group of girls must be in a certain part of the house at a given time. They all arise at the same time, have a stated number of minutes in which to dress, a certain time when all put their rooms in order, a time to eat, and so on. All retire to their rooms at the same early hour of the evening, and at a given moment lights are turned off from an outside control box. A typical time schedule follows:

6:30 Rising bell
7:00 Early morning crews begin work. Girls clean rooms and dress for breakfast
7:45 Breakfast
8:15 Girls clean house and dress for school
8:55 Girls report to school or work assignment
11:45 School and work assignments dismissed
12:00 Lunch
1:00 School and work assignments resumed
3:30 Swimming, skating, basketball, or other physical education classes for girls in school
(Girls on work assignments have a period during work time for instructional swimming class)
4:15 School and work assignments dismissed
5:00 Supper
5:40–7:00 Cottages take turns participating in swimming, basketball, and skating
7:00–8:30 Indoor activities: dancing, television, arts and crafts classes, classes in various activities directed by local clubs or individuals
8:30 Cottage devotions and preparation for bed
9:00 Lights out (Friday and Saturday nights later)

Attendants are assigned to supervise specific areas. An attendant is in charge at night, not only to prevent misconduct or escape attempts but for security of the girls in case of fire or illness.

Security is increased by screened or barred windows. Doors to remote or unused portions of a building are kept locked, as are outside doors. Doors to sleeping rooms are often locked during the day, thus keeping girls in the common rooms. At night, girls are locked in their rooms.

In appearance the newer structures closely resemble a well-kept small college campus, landscaped and set with attractive buildings distinguishable as living quarters, classrooms, gymnasium, and often a chapel. The interiors of the cottages also suggest college dormitories. It is only when security features are examined that marked differences appear.

Planning activities for thirty to sixty girls to account for all the hours spent in the cottage calls for ingenuity and skill. Simply locking girls in their sleeping rooms is condemned. Activities should be fitted into the general plan for rehabilitation. At the same time, good conduct and security are necessary for the operation of the program.

Training schools for boys. Quarters for boys tend to be more institutionalized than those of girls, although often not more so than college quarters and certainly less in many ways than military quarters.

Boys usually sleep in large dormitory rooms, usually with cots or double deck bunks set close together. The rooms tend to look very bare, in contrast to the colorful and livable effects achieved in many of the rooms of girls. Usually an attendant is in charge all night, to prevent any disorderliness or attempt of boys to wander around.

Living and dining rooms and sometimes a recreation room are provided, usually simply but adequately furnished. When the school has a number of cottages, each one usually has only a small serving kitchen; the food is cooked in a central kitchen and brought to the cottages to be served. Boys may have the task of serving, washing dishes, and mopping or sweeping the floors—perhaps after each meal. Boys may eat at small tables but sometimes are forbidden to talk during the meal, to reduce the time needed for the meal as well as the likelihood of horsing around.

As in the girls' quarters, every minute must be accounted for. Free time is filled in with radio or television program, reading, crafts, or discussion groups. The boys are closely supervised at all times.

Weekends and holidays. A special problem is presented by weekends and holidays. Usu-

Preston School of Industry, with a capacity of 740 boys, is the largest training school in the California system. With boys ranging in age from fifteen to twenty, the emphasis is on vocational training and experience. The offerings include industrial work, trades, and farm work. Preston is also the site of a new psychiatric treatment unit opened in 1958, the forerunner to a number of similar units to be opened in other training schools. (Courtesy California Youth Authority)

ally, parents may visit the training school for some limited period during the weekend. In some schools, students may visit their parents over the major holidays. However, for various reasons, some boys and girls receive no visitors or are not permitted to leave the institution. A program must always be provided for them.

The precision and detail of planning for a holiday is shown by the following schedule in a girls' training school for Thanksgiving Day:

(No Laundry)

8:00–10:00   Breakfast in cottages . . . buffet style in kitchen . . . fix your own . . . wash your own dishes.

After breakfast, clean your own rooms and the day room.

11:00–12:00   Fix nails and hair, press dresses, etc. Some girls will help with dinner.

12:00 Noon   Thanksgiving religious Service

1:00–1:30   Dinner

Special Note:

On Thursday and Friday afternoons girls may make choice of activities in school building, or T.V., cards, games, or even study on floor. Miss A. and Mrs. B. will have charge of the school activities.

2:30–3:10   Dancing in music room and
1st group   volleyball in the gym, or T.V. in cottages, etc. (same as above). Girls may then leave school building for cottages . . . or cottage to school for activity at 3:10 P.M. Girls may remain in

	school from 2:30 until 4:00 P.M. if they so desire.
3:10–4:00	Dancing in music room . . .
2nd group	Volleyball in gym and T.V. on floors.
5:30–6:00	Dinner
7:00–9:00	Movie
9:15–9:30	Snack time
9:30	In rooms
10:00	To bed

Cottage personnel. The time spent in the cottage is usually regarded as especially significant in rehabilitation. In spite of scheduling and supervision, the boy or girl has more freedom than in school or at work and is thrown into close association with other students. A different set of personal qualities is revealed, and a new and less formal relationship with adults (the house parents and other cottage personnel) is possible than in the formal program.

Cottage personnel and especially the cottage parents are extremely important. They are not simply custodians but should be considered part of the treatment staff. In fact, two persons closely associated with services to delinquent children in Utah have stated: "From the treatment standpoint, the most significant person in the institution is the cottage parent." [1]

The emphasis on the treatment aspect of cottage relationships does not imply that house parents should have professional training as social workers or psychologists. They do need certain personal qualities and education to give understanding of human behavior. In a discussion of the qualities that the house parent ideally should have, the Children's Bureau includes the following items: attitudes of genuine interest toward the child; sympathy, understanding, and respect; capacity to relate to the child; flexibility; toleration of deviant behavior without condoning it or repressing it punitively; emotional maturity and stability; ability to take hostility; alertness and sensitivity to group situations; moral integrity; acceptable physical appearance; imagination; understanding of the treatment philosophy; ability to make decisions, accept criticism,

work under pressure, and follow directions.[2] He must be an organizer, preferably skilled in group leadership; he should know when and how to use authority, finding a balance between over-permissiveness and domination. Graduation from college with a sequence in social science or its equivalent in education and experience are desirable.

Salaries offered only infrequently approach the going market values of such persons. As a result, few cottage personnel reach these qualifications. Of the important large group of cottage day personnel, 26 per cent have less than high school education, 30 per cent are high school graduates, 20 per cent have had some college work, 19 per cent have been graduated, and 5 per cent have had some graduate education. Salaries of day personnel are among the lowest paid, with the night attendants falling lower; but the salary of the cottage supervisors ranks with that of the better-paid professional workers in other areas.

Infractions of regulations

As in any grouping of children where rules are imposed, some of the boys and girls break the rules. Such behavior is common in public schools, community centers, churches, and other normal community institutions. It may occur more often in the training school, for these are boys and girls who have been unable to conform to the laws and regulations of their communities and its institutions. Moreover, the training school imposes more rules than most of the children have met before because greater orderliness is expected.

In addition to the cottage regulations already discussed, there are other regulations extending throughout the day. Some institutions pride themselves on not having children march from one building to another with an attendant or two; but inquiry often reveals that when a child or children leave one building, the attendant there telephones to their destination to state that they have left the one building and should be at the other in a certain number of minutes. If they do not arrive, a search is begun. They are checked at numerous times during the day, unobtrusively, but nevertheless checked.

1 Dale G. Hardman and Margaret P. Hardman, "Three Postulates in Institutional Care," *National Probation and Parole Association Journal*, 4 (1958), 22–27. The authors are respectively Placement Supervisor, Utah State Industrial School, and caseworker, Children's Service Society of Utah.

2 *Institutions Serving Delinquent Children, Guides and Goals,* Children's Bureau Publication, No. 360, U. S. Government Printing Office, Washington, D. C., 1957, pp. 44–45.

The constant surveillance creates serious tensions for some boys and girls. They rather deliberately break rules, start fights, run away, or occasionally attack a staff member.

Penalties. Violations of regulations are met in various ways. In a thoroughly rehabilitative school, an effort may be made to discover why a student rebels, to help him accept regulations, or to make some modifications in his program. When the institution has a reception center and diagnostic clinic, the professional staff has a good chance to identify aggressive or explosive boys and girls at the time of their entrance to the institution and may be able to suggest ways to meet their special problems. When the regular staff must cope with these students alone, they often resort to punishment in a kind of helpless desperation.

For breaking of minor regulations, privileges are often denied for a limited period as a penalty. Good behavior is rewarded by special privileges, awards, transfer to an honor cottage, temporary paroles, and eventually early release.

Disrespect or insubordination to staff is regarded as extremely serious. An impudent or refractory boy or girl usually is promptly removed from the group before disorderliness becomes general. In one boys' school a special officer (equivalent to a police officer in the community) made the rounds and could be called in case of any disturbance. The house parents and professional staff, therefore, did not have to attempt to subdue or control a refractory student. This method placed control in the hands of a burly man who could quickly remove a boy, and it also reduced the probability that the boy would become hostile to the house parent or staff member.

Institutions typically have some isolation rooms where a recalcitrant boy or girl may be placed. In modern institutions, these rooms may differ little from the usual residence room, except that they are sparsely furnished. In older institutions or those built under the domination of a punitive philosophy, the rooms may be little more than dungeons. In some old institutions they are located in the basement of a building, have little or no light, no furniture, and a heavy solid door with a small observation window through which an attendant may peer. Food may be reduced in quantity and may be very unsavory. Some institutions place a child in isolation only until he quiets down, acknowledges his unruliness, and promises not to repeat his offense; others leave the child confined as punishment for many days or weeks. During this confinement he may be visited by the chaplain, social worker, or psychologist, and some effort may be made to get at the root of his problems. Where such services are provided, the place and conditions are usually less uncomfortable than when the confinement is thought of as punishment.

A modern isolation unit observed by the writer in a boys' training school had well-lighted rooms, with an ample outside window and a small window in the door, all unbreakable by the inmate. An attendant was in the building at all times; the chaplain visited every day. The professional staff worked with the boy. The rooms were unfurnished. At night a mattress was placed in each room, but these were removed during the day as some boys relieved their tensions, anxieties, and boredom by tearing at the mattress. The boys were allowed, one at a time, to have frequent shower baths to reduce tensions. Some of the inside walls of this unit were painted pink.

Physical punishment is generally condemned and often is forbidden by state statutes. However, it continues in many forms and in many institutions, if not as a regular method of discipline then as a way of meeting crises or of dealing with especially obstreperous students. In a boys' training school with many rehabilitative aspects, the superintendent denied the use of physical punishment, but added that if a boy turned on a staff member, "we let him have it." Physical punishment is more likely to occur in boys' institutions than girls because of the generally excessive aggressiveness of boys and the differences in types of offenses that bring boys or girls to training schools.

The problem of unruliness in training schools should not be minimized. Among most boys and girls orderliness may be maintained by rewards for orderly living and denial of privileges for failure to observe regulations. But the schools often receive very aggressive boys or girls, who do not respond to these methods. Rather than have these few wreck the entire program, schools lock them up or severely punish them either in despair or in retaliation. Sometimes provision is made for their removal from the institution. Many states provide that unmanageable older boys or girls may be transferred to adult reformatories or prisons where close custody is part of the regular regime. A few states provide institutions for psychiatric treatment of definitely psychopathic children. But all too often the training school must cope with all the children committed to it.

Running away. Not all problems arise from rowdiness, fighting, and insubordination. In general, incidence of running away during a year's time equals about 13 per cent of the number of children in the institution. The percentage of children involved might be less, since each incidence of running away is counted. The rate varies of course from one institution to another. It is highest in local institutions, perhaps because they are less secure. State institutions have a runaway rate of about 11 cases per 100 children, and forestry camps (usually in remote areas) a rate of 8.4.

In the absence of adequate studies, one can only surmise from case studies what some of the reasons are for running away. Children may rebel against a harsh program and try to escape. They may be homesick, not necessarily for their parents but for their clique or gang. Older boys or girls may become fearful of losing the interest of girl friend or boy friend, respectively.[1] They may feel that other children have received privileges that they also deserved—perhaps a visit home. The program may be unstimulating and fail to hold the interest of the child. The student may be on the way to rehabilitation but unable as yet to accept responsibility for remaining in the school.

Running away is usually treated as a disciplinary problem, and many training schools have a standard penalty for it, regardless of the reason. Those with individually oriented rehabilitative programs may refer the runaway to the counseling service to ferret out the underlying reason and find a solution to it instead of dealing with the running away directly. The boy or girl might still be subject to some disciplinary action, since one of the lessons to be learned is that conforming to rules and seeking help for problems are wiser ways to get along than insubordination or running away.

The pregnant girl

Since one of the common problems of delinquent girls is their failure to control their sexual activities, it is inevitable that from time to time a girl who is pregnant is committed to

the training school, or a girl already in residence becomes pregnant while on a visit home or in some community contact. Training schools make various provisions for the girl. An earlier practice of arranging for confinements in the infirmary at the school is giving place to taking the girl to a community hospital at the time of confinement or to arranging for her transfer to a home for unmarried mothers. The training school makes arrangements ahead of time for the confinement and also for care of the baby.

It is no longer thought advisable for the baby to remain with the mother in the training school, even though it would be housed in a nursery. If relatives of the girl are not willing or suitable to take charge of the baby, a welfare agency steps into the picture. The baby may be cared for temporarily until the mother is released. In other cases, arrangements may be made for its adoption if the mother so desires or if she seems incapable of caring for the child. In all arrangements, the rights as well as the wishes of the mother must be observed, as some girls wish to keep the custody of their babies and to assume some responsibility for them after their release. Others look upon adoption as the best way out for them and the babies; and of course some girls have poor prospects of becoming dependable mothers able to support and care for their children.

Specialized treatment services

The total institutional program constitutes a generalized treatment service. In addition, many training schools now have on their staff specialists in human behavior, such as a psychiatrist (perhaps not full time), clinical psychologist, case worker, and group worker. These are in addition to or in lieu of the staff of a reception center. In addition to working with students individually or in groups, these specialists provide leadership in building the entire program into a treatment environment and in giving other staff personnel better insight into the motivations for behavior and some knowledge of skills useful in dealing with boys and girls. In order to do their best work, the specialists must be integrated into the total staff and institutional program and not be regarded merely as a group apart to whom the other members of the staff may turn when a crisis arises.

Psychiatrist. Few training schools have the full-time services of a psychiatrist, some none

1 *Statistics on Public Institutions for Delinquent Children, 1958, loc. cit.*, pp. 6–7.

at all. Ideally, there should be a ratio of one psychiatrist for every 150 children; preferably he should have a specialty in child psychiatry.[1] Since psychiatrists command high salaries and are in great demand among institutions and for private practice, few training schools are in a position to meet these ideal standards. Schools that are located near large cities or near some other institution with psychiatric services are in a better position to secure part-time services than are small rurally located training schools.

Psychiatrists serve several functions. When they are regularly attached to the school, they head the entire staff of psychologists and social workers, directing the work and acting as chairmen of case conferences. They may interview all children as they first enter the school; diagnose any child whose behavior suggests some special psychological problem; and carry on individual therapy when necessary. Psychiatrists who serve in a consulting capacity only usually are called upon only when individual children exhibit especially unusual emotional or behavior problems. Except in the few cases requiring individual therapy, the psychiatrist's function often is to develop a plan for the child's informal treatment by the regular staff and to help them in understanding the problem.

Clinical psychologist. The clinical psychologist may perform several functions. He is responsible for administering and interpreting the various tests given to children upon entrance. He usually counsels individual students and confers with other staff members. When there are no psychiatric services, he often extends his work into psychological therapy. The ideal ratio of psychologists to children is one psychologist to 150 children, a ratio reached by few training schools.[2] In terms of training, the psychologist whose main function is testing should have a Master's degree and a year of supervised experience; the psychologist who carries on therapy should have a degree of Doctor of Philosophy and two years' experience. Actually, these standards are rarely met. A survey of 162 training schools (out of a total of 213 for the United States) revealed only seventy-two psychologists of all types.[3] Eleven per cent had an undergraduate college degree only, 18 per cent had had some graduate work, and 70 per cent had a graduate degree—the level is not stated.

Caseworker. Social workers—chiefly caseworkers—are more often found on training school staffs than are psychiatrists or psychologists. They perform numerous duties, in the institution and in the child's home community. If a sufficiently detailed report from the juvenile court does not accompany the child to the training school, the institution's caseworker assembles such material to be used in the case conference when the child's program is laid out. The caseworker participates in this conference. The caseworker maintains an individual relationship with students during their stay in the institution, recording their progress, talking with them individually, and conferring with other staff members. He also often establishes a relationship with the parents of the child. The exact order of duties and the distribution of time among caseworkers depends upon the institution.

The ideal ratio of caseworkers to children is one caseworker to thirty children; sometimes one caseworker per cottage is used as the standard.[4] A Master's degree in social work is advised. In practice, these standards are infrequently met. The 1958 survey of 162 training schools with approximately 32,000 students reported 519 social workers of all types (but primarily caseworkers) or one social worker for sixty children.[5] Educationally, as a group they fell far below the ideal standard. Only 22 per cent had advanced (usually Master's) degrees in social work; 7 per cent had such degrees in other fields. Twenty-nine per cent had had some graduate work; 34 per cent had an undergraduate degree. However, as many as 8 per cent had not completed college; in fact a small percentage had had no college work.

Group worker. Many opportunities exist in a training school where a group worker may be effective. One of the most important is in

1 *Training Schools for Delinquent Children,* American Psychiatric Association, Washington, D. C., 1952, p. 20; *Institutions Serving Delinquent Children, Guides and Goals, loc. cit.,* p. 58.
2 *Training Schools for Delinquent Children, op. cit.,* p. 20; *Institutions Serving Delinquent Children, Guides and Goals, op. cit.,* p. 57.

3 *Statistics on Public Institutions for Delinquent Children, 1958, op. cit.,* p. 21.
4 *Training Schools for Delinquent Children, op. cit.,* p. 20; *Institutions Serving Delinquent Children, Guides and Goals, op. cit.,* pp. 52–53.
5 *Statistics on Public Institutions for Delinquent Children, 1958, op. cit.,* p. 21.

the residential cottage, where perhaps thirty or more boys or girls must learn to get along together without conflict and preferably with friendship and helpfulness, among themselves and with the houseparents. Students are brought together in classes, recreational groups, and work groups with little regard to compatibility. In addition to groups that grow out of living arrangements and activities, other groups are formed as clubs of one sort or another which the group worker may head. He operates in much the same way as the group worker in a community center, trying to develop leadership, acceptance of leadership, democracy, co-operation, and acceptable goals. His difficulties may be greater, since membership may be compulsory or at least under pressure, and many of the boys and girls have characteristics that impede the development of good group relationships. The students are not without group experience, since many have been members of cliques and gangs. However, they often lack adjustment to adult leadership and to a democratic process in group activities.

Group therapy. Group therapy is now used in some training schools to help small, specially selected groups of students discuss their problems, talk over the problems of others, and gain insight into and some degree of control over their behavior. The method usually is discussion, guided to some extent by a skilled adult leader, who allows great freedom of expression but does not permit the discussion to become diffused or desultory. An example of such discussion about a common problem is given below, telling how the Utah State Industrial School handled a problem of persistent running away on the part of a small number of boys.[1] As it happened, none of the three leaders was experienced in either group work or group therapy, but their work with the boys was effective nevertheless.

The boys were formed into three groups of five, each with an adult leader. The groups met one evening a week for several months. Each leader developed his own approach. One leader, the assistant superintendent, structured the discussions around specific topics, such as running away, more privileges, use of the lockup (usual penalty for running away), and home visits; the director of group living

used a looser structure with discussion directed to running away but with a flexible range. The psychologist used an unstructured method, permitting the boys to find their own subjects. In addition to the discussions, the three groups carried on a round-robin basketball tournament with the loser treating the other groups. The boys developed friendships within their group and achieved a feeling of group identification. A few of the boys ran away during the initial stage of discussion, but they were accepted back into the groups, and with one exception, running away ceased.

The three group leaders analyzed the processes that went on to reduce and eventually almost eliminate running away. The group meetings seemed to achieve three things:

1. The boys had been an outgroup who achieved status through unacceptable behavior; they became an ingroup by achieving status through special activities.

2. The boys were able to form a socially acceptable group, with its own values, status, and goals.

3. The boys were given a new and to them acceptable environment for treatment.

Psychologically, the following effects occurred:

1. The boys had an opportunity to express individual hostilities; when they found these hostilities shared by other boys, their feelings of guilt about them were reduced.

2. The leaders accepted aggressive actions against themselves without retaliation, thus breaking through the cycle of anxiety-aggression-guilt-punishment-atonement-anxiety felt by the boys.

3. The membership in a special activity group bolstered the boys' self-concepts, which often were not high.

4. The group and leader gave boys who felt rejected and isolated a feeling of belonging to a group and of being wanted by someone.

5. The weekly sessions served as a series of short-term goals to steady the boys between meetings.

6. The leaders were accepted by the boys as an authority to whom they could have a meaningful relationship.

The authors stated that although deep personality changes were not attempted nor achieved, the discussions eliminated the running away, replaced previous punishment by locking up the boys, and shortened the period until the boys could be released. They do not

1 John D. Cambareri, Paul S. Sagers, and Donald F. Tatton, "The AWOL from a Juvenile Institution," *Crime and Delinquency*, 6 (1960), 275–278.

know whether there was any carry-over to adjustment after release.

Difficulties encountered in implementing special treatment services. Two widespread difficulties have already been mentioned: shortage of personnel and inadequate professional training. Other difficulties inhere in the institutional setting.

Training schools are still in a period of transition from punitive to rehabilitative treatment. The staff of some schools cling to a "get tough" philosophy even though professional treatment staff have been added to the personnel of the school. The board or state department under which the school operates and the legislature which makes appropriations may be divided in opinion, so that the professional staff does not have complete support for their work. The treatment staff therefore often works against barriers of ignorance and under-financing.

Overemphasis on custody continues, often preventing the therapeutic use of a certain degree of liberty and choice on the part of students—who very soon will be returned to the community with full liberty. Experience has borne out that students rarely take advantage of a moderate amount of freedom. Schools which regularly take groups of students on field trips or for participation in community activities, under minimum supervision, find that students act in a responsible way; they do not run away, riot, steal, or attack. Only rarely are there violations of acceptable behavior.

The pressure of time on all staff members is a great hindrance. A psychiatrist has described the situation in a boys' training school with nearly 500 boys and a yearly turnover of about 75 per cent.[1] The staff plan called for five psychiatrists, but actually only one full-time and one part-time psychiatrist were on the staff. Much time was consumed in reading the case history of each new boy, conducting a short interview, and writing down opinions and recommendations. There was no time for follow-up of individual cases or for psychotherapy, although the institution supposedly provided such treatment. Crisis situations involving individual boys were referred by the staff to the psychiatrist. These also had to be handled quickly on a surface

basis to restore order and permit the program to continue to function. The pressure of time on the entire staff made it difficult for staff members to attend conferences or participate in discussion sessions.

Training school students often resist treatment, even when it can be offered. They associate the professional treatment group not only with other staff members who may still be punitively oriented but also with stern figures of authority in the community. Their general feeling toward all adults in authoritative positions often is suspicious and rebellious. This shell of resistance can be penetrated, but again time and a relaxed situation are needed to accomplish it even by well-trained psychiatrists, psychologists, and social workers.

The authoritarian atmosphere also is often regarded by professional staff as a hindrance. Lack of agreement on this point is evident in the writings and discussions of social workers in general and in the correctional field. Correctional social workers feel that the authoritarian framework of the training school need not be a hindrance—in fact, it can be a help—provided it is not used by staff members autocratically and oppressively. One of the difficulties that has brought boys and girls to training schools has been their inability to adjust their lives to the necessary controls of community life. The tendency in training schools has been to increase authoritarian pressures and to use them to hold students in a rigid strait jacket. But authority need be made no more strict than necessary to secure effective operation of the school; students can be given an understanding of the necessities and advantages of regulations, leadership, and conformity. Thus authority can become part of the rehabilitative process to fit students to accept community authority and control upon release.

A time for transition

The nineteen-sixties form a propitious period for increasing the rate of change from punitive to rehabilitative programs. The number of delinquent children has increased because of both the present large child population and the increased rate of delinquency. The pressure of commitments on training schools is gaining intensity. Pressure of officials and of interested welfare and citizens' groups on state legislatures is increasing in efforts to stimulate additional legislation and

---

1 F. Gordon Pleune, "Effects of State Training School Programs on Juvenile Delinquents," *Federal Probation,* 21 (March, 1957), 24–32.

appropriations to enlarge training school facilities. In some states this situation has been the occasion for remodeling or adding new buildings embodying new concepts—small cottages, well-equipped classrooms, modern equipment. In other states, entirely new institutions have been built, with resulting specialization among the schools, perhaps on an age basis or in terms of type of treatment needed. The additional number of delinquents to be cared for has also aroused doubt about the old methods of excessive custody and repressive punishment. Some states have shown themselves willing to apply to delinquents

what is known about rehabilitation in general. The reception center for the study of incoming delinquents is one result. Professionals in human behavior on the regular staff are another.

Two additional steps need to be taken. One is constant research on the effectiveness of new methods. The other is a flexible attitude so that the current new methods do not harden into a fixed pattern which would prevent the introduction and experimentation of yet newer methods which undoubtedly will develop in the years to come.

Bibliography

Barker, Gordon H., and W. Thomas Adams, "The Social Structure of a Correctional Institution," *Journal of Criminal Law, Criminology and Police Science,* 49 (1959), 417–422.

Bowers, Swithun, "The Application of Social Work in the Correctional Field," *National Probation and Parole Association Journal,* 5 (1959), 16–20.

Cedarleaf, J. L., "The Chaplain's Role with Delinquent Boys in an Institution," *Federal Probation,* 18 (March, 1954), 40–45.

Costello, John B., "Institutions for Juvenile Delinquents," *Annals of the American Academy of Political and Social Science,* 261 (1949), 166–178.

Davidson, Harold E., "The Chaplaincy in the Juvenile Institution," *National Probation and Parole Association Journal,* 6 (1960), 69–74.

Freeman, Ira Henry, *Out of the Burning, the Story of Frenchy, a Boy Gang Leader,* Crown Publishers, Inc., New York, 1960.

Gardner, George E., "The Institution as Therapist," *The Child* (January, 1952), 70–72.

Institutions Serving Delinquent Children, Guides and Goals, Children's Bureau Publication, No. 360, U. S. Government Printing Office, Washington, D. C., 1957.

Keith-Lucas, Alan, "The Role of the Houseparent in the Training School," *National Probation and Parole Association Journal,* 4 (1958), pp. 156–160.

Konopka, Gisela, *Therapeutic Group Work with Children,* U. of Minnesota Press, 1949.

Lippman, Hyman S., "Difficulties Encountered in the Psychiatric Treatment of Chronic Juvenile Delinquents," in K. R. Eissler and Paul Federn, editors, *Searchlights on Delinquency,* International Universities Press, 1949, pp. 156–164.

McCorkle, Lloyd, "Group Therapy," in Paul W. Tappan, editor, *Contemporary Correction,* McGraw-Hill Book Company, 1951, Chapter 14.

Papanek, Ernest, "The Training School: Its Program and Leadership," *Federal Probation,* 17 (June, 1953), 16–22.

Pleune, F. Gordon, "Effects of State Training School Programs on Juvenile Delinquents," *Federal Probation,* 21 (March, 1957), 24–32.

Schepses, Erwin, "The Academic School Experience of the Training School Student," *Federal Probation,* 19 (June, 1955), 47–51.

Slavson, S. R., "Social Reeducation in an Institutional Setting," *1950 Yearbook, National Probation and Parole Association,* New York, 1950, 50–64.

"Some Aspects of Authority," *Crime and Delinquency,* 6 (July, 1960), entire issue.

Training Schools for Delinquent Children, American Psychiatric Association, Washington, D. C., 1952.

Weber, George H., "The Boy Scout Program as a Group Approach in Institutional Delinquency Treatment," *Federal Probation,* 19 (September, 1955), 47–54.

Chapter **25**

Trends toward treatment

The gradual supplanting of punishment by treatment has led to the development of new types of rehabilitation to supplement the standard training school. Three are discussed in this chapter: forestry camps, psychiatric treatment centers, and guided group interaction. These and other specialized programs call for a high degree of integration within a state; an example of such integration is described as found in the California Youth Authority.

Work camps

Work camps, often called forestry camps, are not a general substitute for training schools, but are a special means of rehabilitation for certain types of boys. The movement toward establishment of work camps is gaining approval by state agencies, camp supervisors, and observers.

Background of work camps. In the background of work camps for delinquent youth lies the experience of the thirties with work camps for unemployed nondelinquent youth through the Civilian Conservation Corps. Established during the depression to stabilize unemployed youth who had a tendency to wander back and forth across the country living by their wits or who restlessly milled about their home neighborhoods, the Civilian Conservation Corps was a federal program of work on public projects, usually outdoor conservation or improvement projects. Barracks-like camp buildings were constructed across the country in areas where useful work programs could be developed. The center of the

camp organization was work. A full complement of other services was provided, such as education, recreation, medical care, and religious services. The camps had a semimilitary aspect, since many of the directors were reserve army officers. The boys were paid for their work, a portion going to their parental families on relief and a portion being saved for them for the day of their release.

The youth who entered these camps were not adjudicated delinquents and were not committed by the courts. The program was administered as a relief and welfare program. The program seemed to work well; boys responded to the opportunity to work in the outdoors, enter other activities, and earn money. They gained physical strength and learned to apply themselves to work, to live co-operatively, and to accept supervision.

With the entrance of the United States into World War II, the camps were no longer needed, as many of the youth were of draft age and others found employment in war production. The persistent question has remained, however: If work camps were accepted by unemployed youth and were beneficial to them, would they not also be of benefit to delinquent youth?

Origin and development of camp movement for delinquents. California made the first definite step toward work camps for delinquents, beginning with a short-lived county probation camp and moving on to a camp for transient boys, full development of county camps, and finally state camps.[1] The first camp was established in 1927 in Riverside County, as a project of the probation office. Although it was regarded as successful it was terminated in 1932 because of lack of funds. The next venture was a forestry camp, opened in Los Angeles County in 1932 for the retention of transient boys who, without employment or the controls of family and home community, soon became delinquent.

1 The discussion of California camps is based primarily on the following sources: O. H. Close, "California Camps for Delinquents," *1945 Yearbook, National Probation Association,* New York, 1945, pp. 136–147; Allen F. Breed, "California Youth Authority Forestry Camp Program," *Federal Probation,* 17 (June, 1953), 37–43; Karl Holton, *California Youth Authority, Report of Program and Progress, 1943–1948,* California Youth Authority, Sacramento, California, 1949, pp. 92–99; articles in the *California Youth Authority Quarterly;* and *Biennial Reports* of the California Youth Authority.

This camp later became one of twenty-eight county camps for youth on probation. The state legislature recognized the county camps officially in 1935. The Youth Authority Act of 1941, as amended in 1943, granted permission for the Authority to establish state camps as part of the total program of state training facilities for delinquents. The county camps continue and through the Youth Authority are provided with state funds; they are operated under the direction of the chief county probation officer.

The first state camp operated by the Youth Authority was opened in 1943 at Calaveras Big Trees Park with fifty boys transferred from county jails. These boys built a camp for 100 boys, using portable buildings transported from the Benecia State Guard Camp. The next step came in 1944, when the Youth Authority entered into an agreement with the U. S. Army for introduction of delinquent boys into production of war materials. Two camps of 150 boys each were opened at

Kentucky Boys' Camp is equipped for thirty-two boys, all minor delinquents. Kentucky Village, the state training school, has about 350 delinquent boys and girls. In the camp the boys have a varied program, outdoor life, and individual attention. They work half of the day and spend the other half in school and recreation. The camp is used for boys requiring only a short period (three months) of training. (Courtesy Department of Welfare, Kentucky)

Benecia Arsenal and Stockton Ordnance Depot, to which boys were transferred from county jails. After the war ended, these camps were disbanded and the Youth Authority entered upon its present plan of forestry camps, operated co-operatively with the state Division of Forestry. In 1961, California operated four forestry camps and three subsidiary or spike camps.

In 1944, the Federal Bureau of Prisons opened the Natural Bridge Camp in buildings originally used by the Civilian Conserva-

Work in a forestry camp of the California Youth Authority is suited to the older adolescent who responds to the conditions of outdoor life and the relative freedom of the camp situation. (Courtesy California Youth Authority)

tion Corps, near Natural Bridge, Virginia, to which boys are transferred from the National Training School in Washington, D. C. This camp is well established as part of the federal training program for delinquent boys and is regarded as a successful venture.

Soon various states had established one or more camps: Illinois, Kentucky, Massachusetts, Minnesota, Ohio, Washington, and so on. Admittedly, the movement is in its infancy. *The Directory of State and Federal Correctional Institutions,* published in 1960, lists twenty-two state camps in nine states.[1] Three were opened prior to 1950, five between 1950 and 1954, and twelve between

1955 and 1959. Two were opened in the first few months of 1960.

The number of boys so far resident in forestry camps at any given time is a small proportion of boy delinquents in state institutions—only 5.7 per cent.[2] However, interest is sufficient so that the Children's Bureau has issued a special guide for the planning and operation of work camps.[3]

Organization of work camps. The usual pattern of organization at the state level is cooperation between the state administrative agency in charge of training schools and the state agency in charge of forestry, conservation, or state parks. The camps seem to thrive in forested states, to the extent that most camps are referred to as forestry camps rather than work camps. However, in some states other types of public work are done by the boys. Since the boys carry out useful work (not "made" or contrived jobs), the forestry or conservation department pays an agreed-upon sum to the training school agency. The

1 *Directory of State and Federal Correctional Institutions of the United States, Canada, England, and Scotland,* American Correctional Association, New York, June, 1960. The number of work (forestry) camps is given as twenty-nine in *Statistics on Public Institutions for Delinquent Children, 1958,* Children's Bureau Statistical Series No. 59, Children's Bureau, Washington, D. C., 1960, p. iv.

2 *Statistics on Public Institutions for Delinquent Children, 1958, loc. cit.,* p. 33.

3 George H. Weber, *Camps for Delinquent Boys, A Guide to Planning,* Children's Bureau Publication, No. 385, U. S. Government Printing Office, Washington, D. C., 1960. This pamphlet outlines acceptable standards and procedures.

boys usually are paid a small sum for wages, channeled through the training school agency. Usually the boy may spend part of this money with the remainder being saved for him until he is released. The training school state agency operates the camps.

On the level of the individual camp, the work done by the boys is taught to them and supervised by employees of the forestry department. The training school agency provides the camp administrator, his assistants, cooks, supervisors for the boys, and other staff. Although the center of the program is work, under the forestry or other appropriate department, the camp is part of the training school facilities of the state.

The camps tend to develop in states with an integrated state agency in charge of a number of phases of training. In some situations, boys are assigned to the camps directly from the reception and diagnostic centers, when study of the boy and his record indicates that his chances of adjustment and rehabilitation will be better in a camp than in a training school. Such boys include ones who will probably be unable to secure technical training for a job and hence will fall into the ranks of laborers, those without the ability to profit from the training school academic program, or those who will respond better to the freer atmosphere of the camp than to the greater regimentation of the training school. Other boys are transferred to the camps from training schools to which they were originally committed. These boys either have been unable to adjust well to the training school, or they are nearing the time for release and need a gradual transition from the controls of the school to the freedom of the community. Conversely, boys who abuse the freedom of the camp may be returned to the training school. At their entrance to training, boys pass through the same reception center as all other delinquents; at the termination of their stay in camp, they share the same parole or aftercare services.

Characteristics of camps. The camps are developed around the concept of rehabilitation more closely than are the training schools and are still in an experimental stage. The characteristics of the camps do not derive from traditional methods nor are they handicapped by outmoded buildings. The camps have been constructed or remodeled and organized with definite aims in mind

calculated to aid the delinquent in adjustment to conventional roles.

1. Camps are small. The capacity of camps is purposely kept small in order to maintain an informal atmosphere. Of the twenty-two camps, eleven have a capacity of less than forty, nine between forty and sixty-nine, and only four seventy or more. In general, the camps are not overcrowded but are held at or under capacity.

2. Camps are simple in structure. Especially when first established, many camps resembled barracks. Some began in old camps of the Civilian Conservation Corps or other work or military camps. Although adequate, soundly constructed, and clean, they lacked many of the niceties of schools or cottages and hence required less in the way of regulations and restrictions in the way the boys lived.

3. The camps are work-centered. The work is constructive, needed work in public service, calculated to give the boy a sense of worth and usefulness. Most of the skills needed are quickly learned and immediately applied. There is no long delay between learning and use. For the most part the boys work in the open, up to eight hours a day, five days a week. Other parts of the program are scheduled for evening or weekends. The types of work bear a marked similarity from camp to camp, but with some variations. The forestry camps provide such work as operating a nursery for forest trees, replanting, clearing out underbrush, building fire lanes, constructing roads, and building camp sites for public use. In states without heavy forestation, the work may center in the development and care of state parks.

The criticism has been made that the boys in the camps are usually from cities and that the skills learned do not prepare them for any kind of city work. Camp administrations make no pretense of teaching the boys urban skills. They are intent upon teaching the boys to work steadily, to become accustomed to manual labor and co-operation, and to accept supervision. The experience of working steadily (holding a job) rather than specific skills is the objective.

4. A well-rounded program supplements the work. Since most of the youth in camps are aged sixteen or over and, therefore, are past the age of compulsory school attendance, school usually is made secondary. In all

Approximately a third of the boys at Natural Bridge Camp for Boys work in the forests each day. Under supervision of a counselor, the boys carry out work planned by the local forest ranger, such as clearing trails, building picnic and camping areas, repairing roads, preventing soil erosion (see photograph), and thinning and pruning trees. The camp population is trained in fighting forest fires and is called upon in such emergencies. The purpose of the work is not vocational training but is part of a total program for developing wholesome and constructive interests, encouraging a sense of fair play and group loyalties, and building healthy bodies. (Courtesy Federal Bureau of Prisons)

probability boys interested in continued academic training would remain in the training

schools. Often remedial training in one subject, such as reading or arithmetic, is provided.

In all camps the boys are encouraged to participate (voluntarily) in hobby clubs, photographic classes, nature study clubs, and other informal means of expanding their horizons and learning indirectly. Active sports and quiet games are available. Arrangements are made for boys to attend church in the community, or a part-time chaplain comes to the camp. Medical service is secured from a community physician with return of the boy to the training school when serious illness or accident occurs.

Natural Bridge Camp requires attendance at a primary class in academic subjects for boys who have not completed fifth grade.[1] Classes for voluntary attendance are provided in shop mathematics, drafting, auto mechanics, woodworking, electric housewiring, first aid, and social development. All

Boys are placed in teams of eight at Natural Bridge Camp for Boys. Each team lives, works, and plays together and has its own counselor with whom the team meets at least once weekly for discussion of personal and institutional problems. Boys may also confer with the counselor individually. The close relationship of boys and counselor is regarded as one of the strongest factors for rehabilitation. (Courtesy Federal Bureau of Prisons)

classes are held in the evening, since the daytime is devoted to work.

5. Counseling. From the point of view of rehabilitation, the heart of the program is a close relationship between each youth and his immediate supervisor, often called a counselor to emphasize the type of relationship.[2] Each counselor works with a limited number

1 *Natural Bridge Camp for Boys,* Bureau of Prisons, Department of Justice, Washington, D. C., 1959.

2 *Cedar Creek Youth Forest Camp,* Division of Children and Youth, Department of Institutions, State of Washington, Olympia, Washington, 1957; Allen F. Breed, "California Youth Authority Forestry Camp Program," *Federal Probation,* 17 (June, 1953), 37–43.

Boys are learning to make cinder blocks for construction at Natural Bridge Camp for Boys. Although forestry work is the most popular type of work at the camp, some boys prefer more specialized work such as carpentry, electrical work, construction, sign-making, baking, cooking, or auto mechanics. Work is an integral part of treatment, through which the boy may achieve an interest and desire to excel in a certain field and develop a sense of responsibility. (Courtesy Federal Bureau of Prisons)

of boys. In Washington, a camp of thirty-two boys has five counselors; in California, each Youth Authority staff member has five boys, upon each of whom he makes a weekly written report; at the federal camp at Natural Bridge, boys are placed in teams of eight, each with its own counselor.

The relation of the counselor to his group of boys is not left to chance, but is structured. Each camp has its own method of assuring frequent contacts.

At Natural Bridge Camp, each boy is a member of a team of eight which forms a living unit. These boys live together in the dormitory, work together, and compete as a unit in sports. Each team elects its own boy leader and is assigned an adult counselor who is in contact with the boys throughout their stay. Team meetings with the counselor are held at least once a week for discussion of personal and institutional problems. The counselor is also available for individual counseling, which may occur at the boy's request or informally when opportunity arises. The boy team leaders form a camp council with whom the staff consults on activities that the boys would like, planning of special programs, selection of movies, and so forth. The staff and boys also discuss such problems as how to receive boys, get boys up in the morning, prevent waste, stimulate boys not to neglect their duties, and a variety of other problems for which boys have some responsibility.

In addition to the planned and informal meetings of boys and counselors at Natural Bridge Camp, formal group counseling sessions are held under the leadership of a man trained and experienced in this field. One-hour meetings with eight or ten boys are held weekly.

The counseling carried on in work camps makes no pretense of handling deep-seated problems. It is not individual therapy for severely maladjusted boys. The counseling deals with current personal and camp problems, attempts to give a boy insight, and provides some support to the boy as he changes his attitudes and conduct. Boys with serious emotional disturbance would be out of place in the usual work camp; they can be helped only in special situations with professionally trained therapists.

Selection of boys for camp. The broad classifications of boys served by the camps has already been stated.

Individually, boys are selected to meet certain qualifications found by experience to be necessary for successful adjustment to camp life. Usually, only older boys are selected, capable of performing a day's work at manual labor. At Natural Bridge Camp the boys tend to be between fifteen and eighteen years old; in Illinois and California, sixteen to twenty-one. In some states, even though the maximum age for commitment to training schools by the juvenile court is sixteen or eighteen, boys once in, may be detained until age twenty-one if they seem to need prolonged training. In other states, older boys may be routed to training schools or camps from adult courts. When boys under sixteen are assigned to camps, they are usually separated from the older boys and have programs oriented toward education rather than work.

Kentucky, for example, has only one camp for thirty-two mildly delinquent boys between the ages of six and seventeen; the actual age of boys in residence is not stated.[1] Academic instruction is offered the year round for all boys. The boys also work three hours daily, under supervision of the Division of Forestry. Much of this work is in the tree nursery.

Another criterion for selection is that the boy will probably respond to the full day of physical labor. First, this requires health and physical endurance; second, disinterest in

academic advancement; and third, acceptance of manual labor as a worthwhile occupation. The boy must also be able to adjust to the conditions of camp life, which lack some of the comforts of a training school. The bathhouse may be separated from the dormitory without a covered passageway. Work may take the boy into the open in severely cold or wet weather.

The boys tend to be "average" rather than exceptional boys. The dull normal boy may be adjustable, but not the mentally defective boy who may nevertheless be committed to a training school rather than an institution for defectives. The bright boy is acceptable but the brilliant boy would more likely be placed in the training school, because of its greater opportunities for academic education. The definitely maladjusted boy or the overly aggressive boy would probably be unable to adjust to the need for co-operation and supervision. The rebel would find it difficult to fit into the work camp pattern expected by the forestry or other work supervisory service. Likewise, the excessively dependent or truly immature boy would find the demand for self-sufficiency beyond him. The boys assigned tend to be "normal" late adolescent boys, capable of conforming and of responding to the responsibility of a job. However, they are not expected to adjust without help, which is given by work and camp supervisors, counselors, and other staff members.

The camps achieve some of their success because of the careful selection and also because they function in the shadow of the training school, to which boys may be transferred if they do not adjust in camp. The training school has no choice but to take them, and because it must accept all types, it has stricter regulations and closer custody than the camp uses.

Reduction of isolation. The isolation of camp life is often offset by planned contacts with the nearby community, which usually consists not of mammoth cities but of villages or small cities. Under supervision, boys may be taken to see a motion picture (in addition to the showing of motion pictures in camp) or to attend some special function. Arrangements are sometimes made for boys to attend church in nearby communities, perhaps as guests of townspeople (although camps have their own religious services). Camp teams may play nearby high school teams, either at

---

1 *Directory of State and Federal Correctional Institutions, op. cit.,* p. 15; Annual Report, Department of Welfare, 1959–60, Frankfort, Kentucky, 1960, pp. 73–75.

In State Boys' Camp, Kentucky, boys work in the tree nursery of the Division of Forestry as part of a retraining program that includes recreation, education, religious activities, and the services of a social worker. (Courtesy Department of Welfare, Kentucky)

the camp or at the high school. In some camps, boys may visit their parents at intervals, and parents are encouraged to visit the boys in camp or are permitted to take them from the camp for a stated number of hours. Each type of contact has certain advantages for the boys, not only in giving variety but in teaching boys how one behaves in an orderly community, or how to compete with or accept defeat from an opposing team. Contacts with parents are designed to strengthen the family relationships.

Regulation and discipline. Informality does not imply chaos. A pattern of work, recreation, classes, and household arrangements is established. However, there is less compulsion than in a training school for boys to participate in set activities. They are encouraged to have a well-rounded set of activities, but voluntary participation is sought as part of the training and treatment. Compulsion often means that upon release the boy will immediately avoid activities into which he was forced in the training school; voluntary participation gives an opportunity for the boy to build up a genuine interest which will carry over into his life after release. The choice of occupation is possible because supervision can be informal with a small number of boys in a limited number of buildings. Although supervision is inconspicuous, it is maintained.

Discipline is maintained through counseling, close contact with adults, and, when necessary, denial of privileges. Usually, the camp has no isolation rooms, and in extreme cases, when disruption of the program is threatened by a boy, he is returned to the training school. In emergencies, it is occasionally necessary to lodge a boy temporarily in the county jail. Occasionally, a boy runs away. However, the runaway rate is lower than in training schools, a fact that may be attributed to the selection of boys, the closer tie to adults, and the greater interest of the program.

Time in camp. The length of time spent in camp is variable and depends upon the progress toward rehabilitation made by the boy. The average length of stay for all forestry camps is 6.8 months as compared to 9.8 months in state training schools.[1] Several factors account for this: boys selected rarely include seriously maladjusted boys; boys may already have spent some time in a training school before transfer; they may have been sent to the camp for only a few months before release on parole as a halfway measure to freedom.

Evaluation. Careful follow-up studies have not been published showing the adjustment of camp inmates to the community after release. Boys are assisted in this adjustment by aftercare officers. One would anticipate a high degree of good adjustment. First, the boys sent to camp are usually those amenable to rehabilitation. Second, the informality, reduction of frustrating rules and regulations, and counseling should reduce tensions. Counseling should help the youth to understand his problems and the necessity for many social regulations and demands in the free community. The work experience should ready him for employment.

On a practical level, the camps are credited with being more economical than training schools, since construction is less costly. However, the ratio of staff to inmates is higher in the camps. According to the report of the Children's Bureau, the annual per capita operating expenditure is $2,149 for state training schools and $2,232 for forestry camps. In this statement, it is not clear how payment for the boys' work is handled.

Handicaps are that the boy often does not acquire any skills that he can use in an urban environment. He may so thoroughly adjust to the simplicity of camp life that adjustment to the complexities of urban life may be more rather than less difficult.

Another criticism or at least need for caution concerns the possibility of exploitation of boys in the desire to further the work of the state forestry or conservation department with low cost labor. However, the final con-

trol of the activities rests with the state agency for training schools, and treatment-oriented staff should effectively check any tendency toward exploitation.

Whatever the final conclusion as to the value of work camps, at present they seem to meet many requirements for rehabilitation, and their establishment is a growing movement in the United States.

Psychiatric treatment centers

Another movement in institutional treatment is the establishment of special institutions for seriously maladjusted delinquents. This movement may be placed in contrast to the forestry camp movement. Forestry camps remove from the training school minor, readily adjustable delinquents, able to live in a relatively free environment; psychiatric treatment centers remove seriously maladjusted delinquents who cannot fit into the regime of the training school, with the combination of restrictions and freedoms that characterize most training schools.

Need for psychiatric treatment centers. When punishment was accepted as the means for reformation of delinquents, the child who did not fit into the pattern—who was emotionally disturbed, aggressive, defiant, unstable—was pressured or punished into submission or was placed in a dark isolation room sometimes for months at a time. With newer ideas of reformation and rehabilitation, the easing of repressions and the use of more normal activities, delinquents who could not conform to the pattern acceptable to most inmates became conspicuous. They interfered with the carrying out of activities, induced other inmates to follow them into defiant acts, and seemed unable to improve their own conduct. In contrast, most inmates were able to conform either to save themselves trouble or because they were genuinely responsive to the staff and interested in the program.

These disturbers are neither completely psychotic nor feebleminded. Usually, the former can be placed in a mental hospital and the latter in a special school for mental defectives. The trouble-makers and the nonconformers lie somewhere between the seriously afflicted children and the normally misbehaving inmates who are, however, capable of responding to the customary regime of the school.

The California Youth Authority, which

---

1 *Statistics on Public Institutions for Deliqunet Children, 1958, op. cit.,* p. 7.

opened treatment centers in 1957–1958, refers to the type as "special problem delinquents." [1] How many of these difficult cases there are would depend upon the exact definition. In California it is estimated that 17 per cent of boys and girls admitted to the Youth Authority are "special problem delinquents."

The New York special treatment facility, opened in 1947 and called Annex of Boys' Training Schools, cites the following types as suitable transfers to it from the regular training schools: ". . . the aggressive, impulsive youngster who is constantly challenging authority and by his example disrupting the group, requiring constant individual attention, and encouraging repressive counteraction . . . the withdrawn, weak, or seductive youngster whose presence in a group creates anxiety for other boys and whose protective needs entail great burdens on supervisors . . . the neurotic, anxiety-ridden boy unable to withstand frustration of any kind, always ready to plot, or run, or steal, and in need of psychotherapy for an extended period." [2] A new center, opened in 1962 is capable of housing 100 boys which is equivalent to about 7 per cent of the total population of the training schools which make transfers to it. However, since the boys in the treatment center remain on the average longer than those in the training schools, the percentage of boys who can be accommodated at one time is somewhat smaller.

A special psychiatric treatment center that opened in Ohio in 1960 defines children suitable for referral as, "those suffering from any of the serious emotional disturbances who are considered to be more amenable to help by psychiatric treatment in this Unit than in the programs of the industrial schools or some other placement. These types, then, include a wide range of the neurotic and sociopathic overly-aggressive and behavior disorders, exempting only the overtly psychotic." [3] The

100 beds in the Unit are equal to about 9 per cent of inmates in the training schools. However, since the period of treatment is longer than the period typically spent in the training schools, a lesser percentage than this can be treated during a given year. The personnel of the Unit do not regard the Unit as large enough to accept all the children in need of such treatment.

These three examples indicate that about a sixth or less of training school students are regarded as in need of therapeutic treatment in a specialized type of institution.

Publicly supported psychiatric treatment centers. In addition to the three states already mentioned—California, Ohio, and New York—a few other states also have opened special treatment centers, for example, Massachusetts (1955) and Washington (1958). These special treatment centers are in addition to reception and classification centers where boys and girls are examined at entrance to training schools and sometimes at intervals thereafter. They also do not replace psychological and psychiatric services available at individual training schools for delinquents resident in these schools. The special treatment centers are residential centers for "special problem" delinquents. They may be adjacent to a classification center (Ohio), a completely independent institution (New York), or attached to a training school (California). These three centers will be described to the extent that information is available.

Annex of State Training Schools for Boys, New York. [4] The Annex at first was thought

1 Mark Lewis Gerstle, "The California Youth Authority Psychiatric Treatment Program, Its Historical Significance and Philosophy," *California Medicine,* 92 (April, 1960), 277–279.

2 *Transfers to the Annex of the Boys' Training Schools,* Annex of State Training Schools for Boys (New York State Department of Social Welfare), New Hampton, New York, undated but in use 1961.

3 *Psychiatric Treatment Unit of the Juvenile Diagnostic Center,* Department of Mental Hygiene and Correction, Columbus, Ohio, undated, received July, 1961, 4 pages.

4 The discussion is a compilation of material from mimeographed papers secured through the New York State Department of Social Welfare or from the Annex: Benjamin J. Hill, *Security Need Not Be Punishment,* paper delivered at National Conference of Social Work, May, 1952, Chicago, mimeographed, 8 pages; Willard F. Johnson, *Institutional Care and Treatment of Juvenile Delinquents in New York State,* paper given at a general session of the St. Lawrence University Institute on Delinquency and Crime, Canton, New York, July 19, 1950, mimeographed, 7 pages; Ernest H. Tilford, *Some Administrative Aspects of Individual and Group Treatment in an Institution for Delinquent Juveniles,* presented at National Institute on Crime and Delinquency, June 2, 1959, 6 pages; *Annex of State Training Schools for Boys, New Hampton, New York,* July 1, 1959, 3 pages; *Regulations Governing the Transfer of Boys from Warwick, Industry, Otisville, New Hampton, and Highland to the Annex of the Boys' Training Schools,* New Hampton, May 26, 1961; 3 pages; *Transfers to the Annex of the Boys' Training Schools,* undated 3 pages.

After operating since 1947 in former reformatory buildings, the Annex of State Training Schools for Boys, New York, acquired its own building in 1962. The institution retrains and treats boys who have been unable to adjust in the regular training schools.

of in terms of close custody for trouble-makers and runaways from the training schools. The idea was furthered by the fact that the center opened in buildings leased from the New York City Reformatory, built in typical prison style with individual cell-like rooms opening into long corridors and bar gates inside the main entrance and at the entrance to each wing, and surrounded by an eight-foot woven wire fence, topped with three strands of barbed wire. However, soon the bar gates and some of the fence were removed. Custody remained closer than in the training schools but the central emphasis was soon shifted from custody to psychiatric and social treatment. The Annex, housing about 65 boys, continued in these quarters until 1962, when it moved into a specially constructed center of minimum security status; the training schools are open institutions.

Boys under the age of sixteen (except in rare occasions) are received from the boys' training schools, after they have failed to adjust there, on written order of the Commissioner of Social Welfare. The boy comes to the Annex in custody of a staff member from the referring unit, clad in street dress; he may bring with him a few personal belongings. His record has preceded him. The referring school notifies the judge who has committed the boy and the boy's parents or guardian, conveying to them the constructive aspects

of the transfer. Since any move from one living situation to another typically produces anxiety in a child and this transfer may be especially threatening, the referring school tries to give the boy some understanding of why he is being transferred. An attempt is made, in understanding fashion, to get him to face the conduct that led to the transfer; he is told that he must expect to stay at the Annex "a long time," but that the length of time depends upon the progress that he makes in overcoming his problems. When the boy understands his own conduct, he is prepared to accept the transfer and to enter into the treatment.

The referring school continues to be responsible for contacts with the boy's family and makes the plans for the boy's parole. His aftercare rests with the regular aftercare agency.

When the director of the Annex after consultation with the staff considers that the boy is ready for release from special treatment, the boy is either returned to the referring school or released on parole. The average length of stay at the Annex is eighteen months.

The following remarks apply to the last year in the old Annex. The staff for sixty-five boys included forty-nine full-time and eight part-time staff members, consisting of three psychiatrists, a psychologist, a physician, and three chaplains.

The staff regards the best treatment for the boys as the experience of a warm and consistent relationship with adults who care for them. The staff is well educated but also must have "patient and sympathetic understanding" of the boys and of each other. Cottage staff, social workers, and clinic staff work together, since all services must be integrated in order to create a therapeutic atmosphere. The peak point of treatment is in the individualized clinical services. Group therapy is used as a diagnostic tool and in the future will probably be extended to treatment. A sociological approach is developing with recognition of the influence of the boy's group contacts prior to and in the institution in determining his values. When group affiliation is strong, the boy may resist the individualized clinic approach that induces him to look at himself objectively and hence seems to isolate him from his peer group. Thus a combined individual and group approach is foreseen for the future.[1]

According to one theory of rehabilitation of disturbed delinquents, they should be given complete freedom in which to express their emotions, both verbally and in action. At the Annex, such a high degree of permissiveness is not found. Limits are defined, and controls are maintained. However, the boys are given all possible opportunities for a variety of forms of self-expression: academic and vocational education, recreation, religion, and clinic help. Groups of boys are taken on off-campus trips under the supervision of a staff member; 3,000 "boy trips" are made in a year. Community groups often bring various activities to the Annex.

No long range follow-up study to evaluate

the program has been made. It is known that about half of the boys are making satisfactory adjustments two years after release, at the time parole ends. This is comparable to the record for all boys placed on parole in New York City and the southern counties. For the year April 1, 1960 to March 31, 1961, 716 boys from all institutions were released from parole; of these, 45 per cent had made a good adjustment, 37 per cent were recidivists, 7.5 per cent were unresponsive to supervision, 7.5 per cent could not be located, 2 per cent had been committed to mental hygiene services, and 1 per cent had left the state.[2] The Annex staff regards the degree of success as satisfactory and freely admits inability to reach some of the more confirmed and disturbed delinquents with methods so far devised.

Psychiatric treatment program, California. California has approached the problem of treatment of recalcitrant delinquents by authorizing the establishment of a special treatment unit within each training school, the first two of which were opened in 1957–1958. The legislature passed an amendment to the Welfare and Institutions Code which provided that the Youth Authority should accept certain delinquent youth who formerly had been shunted from one type of institution to another without fitting into any. The amendment stated that the Authority should accept "a person committed to it . . . if he is a borderline psychotic or borderline mentally deficient case, if he is a sex deviate unless he is of a type whose presence in the community under parole supervision would present a menace to the public welfare, or if he suffers from a primary behavior disorder."[3] The legislature authorized the establishment of a Psychiatric Treatment Unit in each training school, on a staggered basis, with the first two being opened at the Preston School of Industry for boys and the Los Guilucos School for girls. In these two units, various methods of treatment are being developed. Each unit is headed by a full-time psychiatrist and staffed by psychologists and social workers. Emphasis is on individual and group therapy. In the first year of operation, the treatment center at Preston School had eighty disturbed boys

1 A study of the informal group relationships in an unnamed New York training school for boys (not the Annex) was made in 1943 by F. E. Robin as a doctoral dissertation at Columbia University. It is reported in detail in Sophia M. Robison, *Juvenile Delinquency, Its Nature and Control,* Henry Holt and Company, New York, 1960, Chapter 23; see also Lloyd E. Ohlin and William C. Lawrence, "Social Interaction among Clients as a Treatment Problem," *Social Work,* 4 (April, 1959), 3–13.

2 *Fifth Annual Report, April 1, 1960 to March 31, 1961,* Boys' Training Schools Home Service Bureau, New York (undated), p. 25.
3 Gerstle, *op. cit.*

under treatment and the center at Los Guilucos School a hundred disturbed girls.

In a statement published in 1960, Dr. Gerstle, Chief Psychiatrist to the Youth Authority, outlined several principles of psychotherapy as carried out by the Youth Authority.[1] The patient (that is, disturbed delinquent) is permitted to say anything that comes into his mind which he thinks will express his feelings. Verbal expression helps to control or prevent overt expression of tensions, aggressions, or anxiety. The permissiveness between patient and therapist is regarded as a safety valve. Such permissiveness does not remove the need for discipline and self-control. In the process of psychotherapy the patient is helped to achieve greater control and to reduce compulsive urges and obsessions to act out his problems. The end result sought is that the delinquent shall respect other people, gain self-esteem, and lose the conviction that he is an outlaw rejected by society.

Psychiatric Treatment Unit, Ohio. When a new Juvenile Diagnostic Center was built in Columbus to house a service begun about 1915, a hundred-bed separate Treatment Unit was also constructed and opened in 1960. The Diagnostic Center studies delinquents either already committed by the juvenile court or referred by juvenile court judges who wish aid in coming to a decision on the disposition of a case.

The Treatment Unit is independent of the Diagnostic Center except that it receives children on recommendation of the Center immediately after study of the child or after a period spent in a training school during which he exhibited symptoms of disturbance.[2] These children are between the ages of ten and eighteen and formally are in the custody of the state Juvenile Division of the Department of Mental Hygiene and Correction. The time they remain in the Treatment Unit varies between six and twenty-four months; legally, they might be retained until age twenty-one if necessary. However, this would probably rarely occur.

1 Gerstle, *op. cit.*, p. 278.
2 Paul Kirch, *The Juvenile Diagnostic Center,* paper prepared for field staff, 5 pages; *Psychiatric Treatment Unit of the Juvenile Diagnostic Center,* 4 pages. These are mimeographed statements received in 1961 from the Psychiatric Treatment Unit, Department of Mental Hygiene and Correction, Division of Juvenile Research, Classification and Training, Columbus, Ohio.

The staff consists of psychiatrists, psychiatric residents, psychiatric social workers, psychologists, educators, recreational and occupational therapists, psychiatric nurses, psychiatric aides, and attendants, all functioning under the supervision of a psychiatric director. This list of professions indicates both the emphasis on psychotherapy and the range of activities open to the boys and girls. All activities are part of the treatment program. In addition to those carried out in the Unit, tours are arranged to such educational centers as museums, art galleries, television studios, and so forth.

Boys and girls live in completely separate units, in wards or cottages housing eight to twelve inmates. Each such living unit is self-contained with its own day room, dining and craft areas, and serving kitchens to handle food prepared in a central department and to serve snacks. The arrangement makes it possible to use the small group itself as a means of therapy.

Most of the patients receive individual therapy. Group therapy is used when it seems advisable. Recreational and occupational therapy are part of the treatment. All staff personnel are aware of the treatment goals for each child they work with, to the end that a unified, interdisciplinary approach may be made. Staff conferences on each child are held.

The program has been established too recently for any evaluation to be possible.

Private psychiatric treatment centers. Treatment centers in public correctional systems are relatively new. Somewhat more experience and experimentation have been achieved in privately supported institutions.

Exploratory and experimental treatment often comes more readily through private institutions than public. Less red tape and inertia are met in persuading an individual philanthropist, organization, or foundation that a new type of treatment is needed than in persuading a state legislature. A privately supported residential school for disturbed children (some of whom have been delinquent) is described in Chapter 17 of this book—the Sonia Shankman Orthogenic School in Chicago. In this and other private schools the child is accepted as a patient not because he is delinquent but because he is emotionally disturbed. Delinquency is regarded as symptomatic of his basic maladjustment. Some children may be referred after an appearance before juvenile court. The private residential school, however, is not compelled to accept the child; on the basis of its own examination it determines whether the child can probably be helped by its psychiatric services.

A private school that has received nationwide attention partly because it is featured in the motion picture, *The Quiet One,* is Wiltwyck School for boys in the state of New York.[1] This school can accommodate 100 boys. They are referred by the courts in New York City as delinquents whom psychiatrists have found to be in need of special treatment. Boys between the ages of eight and twelve are accepted; they stay from one to four years, with an average of eighteen months.

The school was originally opened in 1935 as a residential camp for Protestant Negro boys. Later it became interracial and interdenominational; the majority of the boys— about 60 per cent—are Negro. Support comes from several foundations, individual contributions, and New York City and state. It is not a public training school.

The philosophy and program of the school were developed under the leadership of Ernest Papanek, executive director until 1958.[2] Children in training schools "have experienced frustration, insecurity, anxiety, and tension, exploding into aggressive, antisocial behavior." When unguided feelings of guilt result from their aggressive behavior, they feel still greater insecurity, anxiety, and tension, which explodes into vengeful behavior in retaliation for their hopelessness and frustration. A vicious cycle thus is set into motion. Punishment intensifies the build-up of emotions. Understanding and readiness of society to co-operate with the delinquent reduces the tensions and in time teaches him to understand and to co-operate. At the same time the child needs to learn to face the consequences of his acts. The consequences do not include

punishment, isolation, or arbitrary denial of privileges, but a realistic recognition of what normally follows misbehavior. For example, when a newly arrived and aggressive boy broke thirty-two windows in the school dining room, he was told that each week some money would be deducted from his allowance to pay for replacement. Three weeks later, the boy was told that the staff were his friends and wanted to help him; no further deductions would be made. The boy was thus helped to understand that destruction had impractical consequences, but that other people were willing to help him find a way out of his difficulties.

The child is allowed more freedom of action than in the usual training school. However, he is required to attend school (provided by the state) and attends religious services. No walls or locks hold him in the institution, and boys often run away only to be returned by police or staff.

The children live in units of twelve or fifteen boys, under the guidance of professional counselors. They do not function as substitutes for the boys' families, to which the boys must soon return. Often a boy arrives at the school in a very belligerent state of mind (as was true of the boy who broke the windows) then becomes overly attached to some member of the staff in the attempt to find a parent usually of a type he has not experienced at home. The staff member, however, maintains that he is a friend, and in time the boy accepts him as such.

The school has the customary activities of any training school, but the heart of the program is in the constant guidance of the boys by adult leaders. "Socializing the antisocial or asocial child is simply showing him, interpreting for him, making him understand, accept, and respect the role and function of others and his own role in society," according to Papanek. Children participate in the administration of the community by helping to plan functions which are clear to them, such as serving on a food or sports committee.

The school is staffed with a psychiatrist, a psychiatrically trained resident director, an assistant director who is a social worker, four psychiatric social workers, ten counselors, six teachers, an art therapist, and a music therapist.

When a boy is released from the school he comes under the supervision of the schools'

---

1 William and Joan McCord, "Two Approaches to the Cure of Delinquents," *Journal of Criminal Law, Criminology, and Police Science,* 44 (1953), 442–467; Ernest Papanek, "The Training School: Its Program and Leadership," *Federal Probation,* 17 (June, 1953), 16–22; Edward Linn, "Wiltwyck: Home of the Wild Ones," *Reader's Digest,* 72 (February, 1958), 192–196.

2 Papanek, *op. cit.,* p. 18. Papanek's basic philosophy is related to that of August Aichhorn, with whom he had worked in Vienna. See Aichhorn, *Wayward Youth,* New York, Viking Press, 1935.

aftercare program in New York City. A social worker helps the boy and his family to readjust on a better basis than the one existing before his entrance to the school. If this proves to be impossible, the boy may be placed in a foster home or private school.

A follow-up of a sample of sixty-five boys five years after they left the school showed that 43.2 per cent had not had any court appearance; 27.6 per cent had had court appearances for one of three reasons, request to return to Wiltwyck, boy ran away from home, or boy truanted irregularly; 20.2 per cent were failures, having appeared in court on serious charges of assault, burglary, robbery, or sex offenses. Thus 70.8 per cent had made a good or reasonably good adjustment after release from the school.[1] As compared with the average run of training schools, this percentage is high.

A carefully controlled study of Wiltwyck and of a traditional type of New England training school whose program was based on strict discipline and formal education, showed that Wiltwyck exceeded the training school in the following ways: Wiltwyck boys more often than the training school boys liked a staff member best of everyone in the school; regarded an understanding and companionable person as a good counselor or cottage master (in contrast to a disciplinarian); showed decreased anxiety during their stay in school, decreased dependence on authoritarian procedures, and decreased prejudice. Aggressiveness did not show significant decrease at either institution, according to a paper and pencil test. Wiltwyck boys tended to regard the world as good and did not feel that one had to fight to get ahead. More often than the training schools boys, they regarded themselves as good and were satisfied with themselves. They also more often thought a good parent was one who "treats you well or respects you"; the training school boys more often thought the good parent was of the disciplinarian type.[2]

The researchers in this study concluded that the better attitudes of the Wiltwyck boys as compared with the New England training school boys as well as the low percentage of recidivists are the result of the therapeutic way of life at Wiltwyck.

1 Study by Lois Wiley, cited in McCord and McCord, *op. cit.*
2 McCord and McCord, *op. cit.*

Wiltwyck was not able, however, to guide all boys into acceptable attitudes and roles. These failures apparently have not been studied to determine why they resumed seriously delinquent behavior or what further might be done at the school or in the community to which they returned to reduce the number of failures.

In comparing the methods and results at Wiltwyck with those of public treatment centers, it should be noted that the Wiltwyck boys are younger—none over twelve when admitted, whereas most of the boys in public treatment centers are well into adolescence. The Wiltwyck boys represent an age group who are not yet considered appropriate for a training school for delinquents. They have had less experience in delinquency and less time in which to build up the "hard-core" attitudes that present an almost impregnable front to therapy among many older boys.

Significance of treatment centers. Whether publicly or privately supported, special treatment centers are a significant innovation in handling delinquency. They are a movement away from an earlier point of view that indiscriminately labeled all delinquents as psychopathic as well as away from a philosophy of punishment. They recognize that the majority of delinquents need resocialization in a controlled environment which can be achieved in the usual training school that uses modern psychological and sociological methods to break down old attitudes and build in new ones. The special treatment centers are designed for the small minority who need also to achieve fundamental personality changes before they can be resocialized.

Most of the centers are psychiatrically oriented, that is, they place individual therapy as the central method and tend to overlook the powerful effect of a child's identification with a delinquent peer group and of the feeling of rejection felt by both individual and group. As more is learned through sociological studies of delinquent groups, sociological methods will undoubtedly develop in co-ordination with the individual methods. The New York Annex is in the process of developing along this line.

Intensive short-term treatment—the Highfields experiment

A unique experiment in intensive short-term group therapy was begun in 1950 in

New Jersey at the Residential Group Treatment Center at Highfields.[1] The Center is limited to twenty boys aged sixteen and seventeen, sent by juvenile court judges as an alternative to commitment to the boys' reformatory or to immediate placement on probation. Boys with former commitments to correctional schools are not accepted. The program is not suitable for deeply disturbed nor mentally deficient youth.

The Highfields Center was established on the premise that with intensive methods rehabilitation could be accomplished in three or four months. The key part of the program is the group session, called Guided Group Interaction, a name chosen because it avoids the controversy over what is meant by group therapy and also avoids any implication that delinquent boys are mentally abnormal. The philosophy and techniques were developed by Lloyd W. McCorkle, who had had experience in group therapy with army prisoners. Each discussion group consists of ten boys and the director, meeting together five evenings each week. In the free discussion, the boys not only bring out their problems and gain an understanding of the motivations for their misbehavior, but are welded into a primary group. Boys learn that others have the same problems which they have; they feel the impact of the group's approval or disapproval. Success is not measured however by the response of the boy to the discussion group. Eventually he will leave the Center and return to his own family and community. Successful adjustment there depends upon his increased understanding of his motivations and his ability to control his behavior when surrounded perhaps by members of an earlier delinquent group of which he was a member.

Although the discussion sessions provide the most intensive therapy, the entire way of living is thought of as therapeutic in nature. During the day the boys all work at the New Jersey Neuro-Psychiatric Institute; Saturday morning they clean up their residence; Saturday afternoon is free. Sunday they may attend church and receive visitors. Rules are very few, and the boys have great freedom in choice of leisure activities and movement around the grounds. However, they are forbidden to leave the grounds without permission. With permission they may go to nearby villages—sometimes with an adult—, go with their parents when the parents visit them, and leave and return unattended for scheduled furloughs home. The regime is easy and relaxed, but most of the time is scheduled and the boys are in constant association with adult staff members.

Not all boys are able to adjust to the Center. Some run away; others are too aggressive and rebellious to fit into the program; a few commit new delinquencies of a serious nature. These boys are returned to the court that committed them to be handled in some other way. Also, not all boys keep out of trouble after they are released.

In order to test the success of the program, a comparable group of boys committed to the New Jersey State Reformatory for Males at Annandale was selected. Both the Highfields and the Annandale boys were tested and otherwise studied at the time of commitment and also after they had been released and spent some time in the community. A lower percentage of Highfields than of Annandale boys recidivated. However, the results are a matter of debate, since the Annandale boys tended to be a little older, more experienced in delinquency, and from poorer social backgrounds than the Highfields boys. When it is recalled that Highfields returned its nonconformers to court, a step that the Reformatory is unable to take, the differences in recidivism seem less clearly to point to superior effectiveness of the Highfields method.

It seems clear, however, that the Highfields method was at least as successful as the Reformatory in rehabilitation, in a much shorter period of time, and at much less expense. It may also be that more subtle changes were not revealed by the methods of testing. Highfields has shown sufficient promise to continue and is regarded as pointing the way toward new methods of rehabilitation for youthful offenders.[2]

---

1 Lloyd W. McCorkle, Albert Elias, and F. Lovell Bixby, *The Highfields Story: A Unique Experiment in the Treatment of Juvenile Delinquency,* Henry Holt and Company, 1957; H. Ashley Weeks, *Youthful Offenders at Highfields,* University of Michigan Press, Ann Arbor, Michigan, 1958.

2 In October, 1960, the Ford Foundation announced a grant to the New Jersey Department of Institutions and Agencies to be used in an experiment with guided group interaction while the boys continue to live at home, reporting daily to a center in their neighborhoods. The object is to prevent a complete break between the boy and his family and friends. Another grant from the same source was assigned to the Jef-

Necessity for integrated state program

When training centers range from the open forestry camp through several types of training schools graded by age, sex, and program, to centers for psychotherapy, all within one state, the necessity of co-ordinating the numerous facilities is paramount. The separate units cannot operate in independence but must function as parts of a co-ordinated system. A number of states have achieved such co-ordination. California, one of the first to develop an integrated system, is used here as an illustration.

Development of youth authority program

Under its Youth Authority, California has developed a state-wide integrated program for the care and treatment of delinquents from the time the court commits the child to the Authority until he is released from supervision. The judge retains the authority to place the child on probation without commitment. The original Youth Authority Correction Act was passed by the state legislature in 1941 and amended in 1943 to broaden its powers, including assumption of operation of training schools. At that time California had three state training schools with a total capacity of approximately 1,050 boys and girls. The schools and program of treatment were of the traditional type. In 1957–1958, the Authority operated two reception clinics, five institutions for delinquent boys, two for girls, and three (later increased to four) forestry camps, housing a total of approximately 4,000 delinquent children and youth. It also supervised more than 8,000 children on parole. Each institution is designed for a specific age group or type of delinquent. In addition, the Authority provides assistance and leadership to communities in delinquency prevention. Emphasis of program has changed from custody and punishment to supervision, education, and treatment.[1]

The changes were not all accomplished at once. Year by year new schools have been

constructed and old ones enlarged and modernized. The program also has changed slowly, from an emphasis on basic education, vocational training, and work (especially war work during World War II) to classification and individualized assignments to institutions and program. Special classification centers were not opened until 1954, although the work was carried on earlier in certain training schools. It was not until 1957–58 that the first Psychiatric Treatment Units were opened. A Division of Research was also organized in 1958.

The Youth Authority therefore has three important qualities: it penetrates into a wide variety of problems related to delinquency; it establishes practical programs and co-ordinates them; and it remains flexible both with reference to changes in facilities and programs and in the addition of new services.

Organization. The agency responsible for juvenile delinquents after commitment by the courts is the six-member Youth Authority Board. Composed of five men and one woman, the board is appointed by the governor, subject to confirmation by the senate. The chairman of the Board is also director in charge of administration of the reception centers, the various training schools, and camps. The other members of the Board are responsible for the wards, as the committed delinquents are officially called. They study the record of each boy and girl after the case has been analyzed at the reception center, decide upon the school to which he should be sent, review the case—on the average—three times a year, and decide when the ward should be released on parole. Board members are assisted by careful records maintained on the progress of each ward.

In addition to the administrative staff, the work of the Board is carried out through four divisions. The Division of Diagnosis and Treatment is responsible for medical, psychiatric, psychological, and educational services. It administers the program of custody and treatment in the two reception centers and all training schools and camps. Each ward spends about six weeks in one of two reception centers. He receives a complete physical examination upon entrance, and an effort is made to correct deficiencies. He also is given various psychological tests and interviews. On the basis of this study the Board makes its first decision as to where the ward shall

---

ferson County, Kentucky, Juvenile Court to establish a new residential center near Louisville, with a program modeled after that at Highfields. After a period of time, the effectiveness of the program will be compared with that of the conventional program at Kentucky Village.

1 The development of the California Youth Authority up to 1948 is given in Karl Holton, *op. cit., California Youth Authority Quarterly*, which began publication in 1947, and the *Biennial Reports* of the Authority.

begin training; occasionally, a ward is immediately paroled and returned to the community under parole supervision.

The Division of Field Services consists of two bureaus, the Bureau of Probation and Delinquency Prevention and the Bureau of Paroles.

The Bureau of Probation and Delinquency Prevention has a staff of consultants who are ready to assist cities and counties in preventive work and supervision of delinquents not committed to the Authority but remaining in the community on probation (a county function). They function at the request of the local community.

The Bureau of Paroles supervises all wards in the state after their release from the training centers and arranges supervision with other states when the wards are placed out of the state. The parole agents operate out of a number of offices distributed over the state. Each office supervises all parolees in its area, regardless of the school from which they were released. Thus the parole agent may become familiar with his area and is accessible to parolees and their parents.

The Division of Administrative Services does not work directly with the wards. It unifies all business and financial matters, plans and controls a joint budget, has charge of construction programs and maintenance, and either operates or supervises the financial operations of individual schools. The Division also plans the food programs, makes the annual food budget, and controls expenditures. Personnel supervision also falls into this Division.

The Division of Research has a records and statistics unit and a research unit.[1] One of the chief functions of the research unit is to make studies to provide a basis for evaluation of the program and for future planning.

Specialization in individual schools and camps. One advantage of an integrated system into which wards enter by way of diagnosis and classification is that different schools may be organized for groups with different needs. The five institutions for boys are designed respectively for boys aged eight to fifteen, twelve to sixteen, fourteen to seventeen, fifteen to twenty-one, and seventeen to twenty-two. The program of each includes both education and work but emphasizes one or the other depending upon the age of the boys. The overlap in ages makes further selection possible in terms of special emphases of the school and special needs of the individual boy.

In addition, four small conservation (forestry) camps are provided for older boys, capable of hard work and often nearing the time for parole.

Girls are assigned to two schools, one for girls aged eight to sixteen, the other for girls aged fifteen to twenty-one. The programs reflect the needs of the two age groups.

All institutions have provision for recreation suited to the age and sex of the wards, religious services, and counseling. Most of the schools (not the camps) have special cottages for the minority of wards who are psychologically disturbed to the point that they cannot adjust to the program or live at peace with the staff and other wards. Psychologists attached to the schools counsel these wards, institute group counseling, and train staff members to work with them.

Students may be transferred from one school to another or to the conservation camps to increase rehabilitation.

Values of the integrated system. A number of values can be found for the integrated system. From the point of view of the state, a number of individual boards and projects are brought under one board; duplication of staff and therefore expense is reduced. The concentration of operations under one board justifies the employment of specialists leading to more efficient administration and operation. For the staff there is opportunity for promotion within the system. For the ward there is initial study and classification, assignment to the school thought best suited to him, transfer to another school if this later seems advisable, repeated studies, and finally release on parole. Staff is of a high caliber. The effort is toward rehabilitation; in a fully developed system this includes readjustment of seriously disturbed wards. Although it cannot be said that all steps in the process of handling delinquents is centered in one agency, the statement is true from the time the court commits the delinquent to the Youth Authority. As he passes from reception center to school to parole and in and out of various services and programs his treatment is part of one plan operated in accordance with one set

1 Keith S. Griffiths, "New Youth Authority Research Program Readied," *California Youth Authority Quarterly,* 11 (Spring, 1958), 1–5.

of principles. He is not punished at one point, coddled at another, and thrown into educational programs which he cannot handle at a

third. The same state policies operate throughout.

Bibliography

Breed, Allen F., "California Youth Authority Forestry Camp Program," *Federal Probation,* 17 (June, 1953), 37–43.

California Youth Authority Quarterly, published quarterly, Room 401, State Office Building No. 1, Sacramento, California.

Gerstle, Mark Lewis, "The California Youth Authority Psychiatric Treatment Program, Its Historical Significance and Philosophy," *California Medicine,* 92 (April, 1960), 277–279.

Holton, Karl, "California Youth Authority, Eight Years of Action," *Journal of Criminal Law and Criminology,* 41 (1950), 1–23.

Linn, Edward, "Wiltwyck: Home of the Wild Ones," *Reader's Digest,* 72 (February, 1958), 192–196.

McCord, William and Joan, "Two Approaches to the Cure of Delinquency," *Journal of Criminal Law, Criminology, and Police Science,* 44 (1953), 442–467.

McCorkle, Lloyd W., Albert Elias, and F. Lovell Bixby, *The Highfields Story: A Unique Experiment in the Treatment of Juvenile Delinquency,* Henry Holt and Company, New York, 1957.

Natural Bridge Camp for Boys, Bureau of Prisons, Department of Justice, Washington, D. C., 1959.

Ohlin, Lloyd E., and William C. Lawrence, "Social Interaction among Clients as a Treatment Problem," *Social Work,* 4 (April, 1959), 3–13.

Papanek, Ernest, "The Training School: Its Program and Leadership," *Federal Probation,* 17 (June, 1953), 16–22.

Robison, Sophia M., *Juvenile Delinquency, Its Nature and Control,* Henry Holt and Company, New York, 1960, Chapter 23.

Weber, George H., *Camps for Delinquent Boys, A Guide to Planning,* Children's Bureau Publication, No. 385, U. S. Government Printing Office, Washington, D. C., 1960.

Weeks, H. Ashley, *Youthful Offenders at Highfields,* University of Michigan Press, Ann Arbor, Michigan, 1958.

Chapter **26**

Release, aftercare, and the delinquent's future

The time that a delinquent boy or girl spends in a training school is a period of retraining and rehabilitation to enable him to make a better adjustment than previously to the community, usually the same one from which he came. In all probability the community and the family that receive him back are little changed. The child or young adolescent returns to the same school from which he was perhaps a chronic truant. The older adolescent finds his old gang waiting for him, with some other boys perhaps also returning from training schools. He finds the merchants, community center, church, parks unchanged. This is the community in which he became a delinquent. In the relatively few months spent in training school, has he gained a new perspective on his future and a new strength of character adequate to help him withstand the same pressures and pulls toward delinquency that he experienced before commitment?

Release

When to release. In some training schools, the boy or girl is required to remain in the school for a specified period of time, but in most schools the length of commitment is conditional upon the progress toward rehabilitation made by the student. Progress is sometimes measured in part by the acquisition of a certain number of merit points. In most schools the student's adjustment to the school is used as a measure of successful rehabilitation. None of these methods necessarily in-dicates the changes in attitude and goals which signify real, that is, inner rehabilitation.

Schools with satisfactory treatment services are in the best position to determine when a child is ready for release. When professional treatment personnel are on active duty at a training school, the original diagnosis may be followed by periodic checkups and eventually by a conference of the staff to determine whether the boy or girl is ready to re-enter the community.

The period of time for residence in the training school should not be set in advance. Some students are ready to return to the community within a few months, some not for a much longer period of time. It has previously been stated that the average time in training schools is nine months for boys and a year for girls. In individual schools, however, the average stay may be as low as six months or as high as two or more years. A short average does not necessarily mean that the school is especially successful in rehabilitation; it may simply indicate overcrowding and the premature eviction of students in order to make room for others awaiting entrance after court commitment. In one training school, criticized for ill treatment of boys and for the high rate of recidivism, an official stated that the school was so overcrowded that it was like running the boys through on a conveyor belt. On the other hand, long terms do not always lead to rehabilitation; they may indicate failure to restore the boy or girl to the point where release seems justified, with final release as the youth reaches the age beyond which the school cannot hold him, or a judge may have specified a long term because the boy or girl has committed a serious offense. An example concerns a sixteen-year-old youth found guilty of manslaughter in a criminal court and sentenced to five to ten years. Placed in a training school instead of prison, he served almost five years and then at age twenty-one was released on parole for approximately three years.

Temporary release. Since many boys and girls are unable to adjust well after release, some schools have devised methods of trial release, either through granting a long furlough home or using some form of pre-release; if the young person misbehaves he can be returned to the training school with very little formality and later given another chance at outside adjustment.

Many schools have devised various ways in which to give the student continuing contacts while in the school with their homes and with community life in general. These include periodic visits home, work under supervision in the community in which the school is located, or a final period for boys in a forestry camp where formal supervision is relaxed. Recreational contacts with the community are sometimes developed. These methods have several advantages: they prevent the youth from becoming so immured in the institution that he tends to forget what community living is like; they keep him aware of what the community expects in the way of good behavior; and they give him actual practice in work and in self-discipline under conditions where running away has few obstructions.

Obstacles to adjustment on release

One of the major problems to good community adjustment after release is that little if anything has been done to modify family and neighborhood conditions. Rehabilitation of families when needed and preparation of the family for the return of the young person is theoretically regarded as a necessary part of the successful adjustment of the young person, but it is rarely carried out either because of lack of personnel for the intensive work which would be necessary or the failure of families to co-operate. Nevertheless, most children return to their families. Only a few are placed in foster homes or some residential type of institution.

For boys and girls still in school, readjustment to school is a major problem. Chronic truancy has often been one of the facets of the delinquent behavior that led to commitment to the training school. Especially if the training school program has attempted to find the student's true level of ability and has adjusted his educational program to this, he may find it extremely difficult to step back into the traditional school pattern. Sometimes attempts are made to help him in this transition. The aftercare or parole officer may visit the school and talk with the principal and teacher or arrange a transfer to a different school where the student may make a fresh start. Many training schools release students toward the end of a school term or during the latter part of summer vacation so that they may re-enter school at the beginning of a term. Nevertheless, the boys and girls who entered the training school with a history of school maladjustment often slip back into their old habits of coming late to school, cutting classes, displaying aggressive behavior in school, or truanting.[1]

The older boy or girl who does not wish to return to school faces the problem of finding employment. Aftercare officers usually try to help them secure employment, perhaps finding willing employers ahead of time and accompanying the youth for his first interview with the prospective employer. Many business concerns do not wish to employ someone who has been in the training school. Many young people are not able to accept the degree of industriousness, honesty, and co-operation required to hold a job. Case histories often show that a boy comes from training school filled with good intentions, accepts a job in good faith, but soon yields to some opportunity to pilfer or begins to come late to work or to find obviously false excuses not to come for a day or two at a time. Soon the boy is dismissed.

At all times, the pull of old companions and habits is very strong, even for the boy or girl who has determined while still in the training school to start a new life. Nondelinquent young people and their parents often refuse to associate with the training school youth; church and community center groups may admit them with reluctance. The one group that will accept them is the old clique or gang. Here they may occupy a position of importance and are eagerly questioned about the training school.

Aftercare supervision

Almost all released boys and girls are placed under aftercare supervision, which may be provided by the training school itself, by the state body administering all training schools, the probation office of the court that committed the child, by various social agencies, or by volunteers.[2] Each system has its supporters and each is adjusted to specific

---

1 Erwin Schepses, "The Academic School Experience of the Training School Student," *Federal Probation,* 19 (June, 1955), 47–51.

2 Frank L. Manella, "Aftercare Programs," *National Probation and Parole Association Journal,* 4 (1958), 74–80. This article presents the great variety of administrative arrangements for aftercare.

344   FIVE *Legal Methods of Dealing with Delinquency*

The responsibility of the Youth Authority extends to supervision of paroled delinquents. The parole officer assists the youth to secure work (in the photograph in a lumber yard) and keeps in touch with him during his period of parole. (Courtesy California Youth Authority)

situations. The juvenile court without a probation officer is unable to accept the supervision of released boys and girls. When several training schools in one state individually supervise aftercare for their students, a diversity of care and quality may exist within one state. When a state agency supervises, one officer may be assigned a wide territory and find it difficult to keep in close touch with his case load. No one however seems to question the necessity of working closely with each child in his readjustment to the community.

Supervision of released boys and girls is a form of social work. Hence the officer should be a trained social worker; however, as with probation officers and social workers in training schools, many of them are not. They experience many of the same problems as probation officers—too many children to supervise, scattered over wide areas thus consuming much time in travel, and the association in the student's mind of aftercare with authority, the training school, police, and revocation of parole.

Failure on release

Not all boys and girls released from training schools make good adjustments in the community. Table 31 has already shown that many young people enter the training school with a background of experience on probation or in training schools. These are youth who previously have failed to adjust on probation or parole, and have committed new delinquencies. In addition, among students released to aftercare, some will fail to adjust and will be returned as parole violators. An inspection of the annual reports of training schools shows as typical the following number of students placed on parole in a given year and the number returned to the training school for violation of parole: School A, 204 boys placed on parole, 42 returned for parole violation; School B, 1,646 boys and girls released on parole, 488 returned from parole and 19 recommitted; School C, 263 boys and girls released on parole, 93 returned for violation; School D, 330 boys and girls paroled, 90 returned as violators; and School E, 138 girls paroled, 28 returned for violation. The ratio of students released to those returned for violation runs from about 3:1 to 5:1. This is the record for one year only; in succeeding years, additional boys and girls resume delinquency. Some annual reports note that individual sudents have been released twice during the year on parole and returned twice for violation.

Whether or not failure on parole should be regarded as a condemnation of the training school is open to serious question, although it it is sometimes interpreted in this way. Perhaps one should give more weight to the majority who are not returned instead of to the minority who are. Perhaps the training schools should not be expected to erase in a short period of time the effects of twelve to fifteen years of development of delinquent attitudes and habits, nor to be able to offset completely the continued family neglect nor the strong pull back to delinquency in the community.

The above point of view does not condone the continuation of inadequate and untrained staff, political rather than professional control of training schools, and punitive instead of rehabilitative methods. It is difficult to evaluate all the effects of the newer rehabilitative methods. It is not possible simply to compare parole violation rates before and after changes in administration and staffing, since often the total system of handling delinquents is changed, institutional programs are revised, new training schools are opened, and new methods of parole instituted. Also, a number of years should elapse in order to permit tracing the subsequent careers of released delinquents at least into adulthood. Some states have had rehabilitative programs for a sufficient period to merit such a study.

The future of juvenile delinquents

One reason for the great concern about failure during aftercare and recidivism is the fear—and popular belief—that teen-age delinquents become adult criminals. The progression from delinquency to criminality is true in many cases but by no means all.

Limitations of research. Research has not progressed very far in tracing the future development of unselected samples of delinquents, perhaps because a long drawn-out program of study must be set up, designed to follow the teen-agers through some ten to twenty years; or an adequate set of records made in the past must be located, with follow-up in the present.

In the studies that exist, delinquency is sometimes treated as a unitary type of behavior; more valuable are studies which recognize delinquency as a collective term for different kinds of behavior. Each type of delinquency may have its own form of future development. The future of a young thief may be expected to be different from the future of a youthful drug addict. The problem is complicated by the fact that many delinquents carry out a variety of delinquent acts; therefore it is almost impossible to classify them as fitting into a single category of delinquency. As delinquents mature, they often tend to specialize in one type of offense.

Studies tend to be based on delinquents who have appeared before a juvenile court or who have been studied in a child guidance clinic. These children usually are the more serious or persistent offenders. The future of children who are dealt with by the police directly or through a police juvenile bureau is not included in the more comprehensive studies.

Temporary delinquency

Ample evidence has been given in Chapter 3 to show that most children and youth break laws defining juvenile delinquency or adult crime, but that only a few are arrested. Likewise, many children after their first arrest or court appearance do not again have their names appear on police or court records. Preadolescent children, especially, commit delinquencies sporadically without continuing or intensifying their delinquency. In Detroit, for instance, a series of complaints to the Youth Bureau of the police department included 207 boys ten years old; in the following two years only 43 boys (20.8 per cent) had additional police contacts. Among eleven- and twelve-year-olds, only 20 per cent had more than one police contact. For the 80 per cent who had only one arrest, the author of the study concludes that their early offenses were chance episodes and not prognostic of future delinquency or criminality. These boys were contrite about their conduct and worried about their predicament. They did not rebel, lie, or blame others as did the persistent delinquents.[1]

Children who are temporarily delinquent do not develop attitudes to justify their behavior. They do not think of themselves as delinquents, nor do they consistently follow delinquent roles. They are in no particular danger of organizing their lives around delinquency or crime as the central core of their personalities or of their way of living.

One thousand delinquent boys fifteen years later

An intensive follow-up study of a thousand seriously delinquent boys during three five-year periods showed a marked decline in number of arrests and seriousness of offenses, but not the elimination of all crime. The Gluecks, who made the study, selected as their group boys who had been referred to the Judge Baker Foundation (A child-guidance clinic now called the Judge Baker Guidance Center) by the Boston Juvenile Court during the years 1917–1922. Each child was

studied and recommendations were made to the court, but the Center did not enter into the treatment of the children. Eighty per cent of the children were seen only once by the Center; only 2.3 per cent were seen as many as three or more times. The recommendations concerned such things as where the boys should live, improvement of physical condition, type of supervision, education, industrial adjustments, disciplinary control, recreation, and need for further examination. Many of the recommendations were not carried out by the court.[2] These facts indicate that the cases were a run-of-the-mine series and not a selected group of boys who had received psychiatric therapy.

The description of the boys prior to referral to the Center coincides with descriptions of other delinquents brought to police and court attention: low family income, low educational attainment of parents, large families in overcrowded living quarters, family disorganization, lack of affiliation by the boy with organized youth agencies, but affiliation with other delinquents in commission of offenses. Of the thousand boys, two-thirds had been arrested prior to the "crucial arrest" that brought referral to the Center (and incidentally inclusion in the Glueck study). Most of the boys had had only one other arrest, but some had been arrested as many as five times. Two-thirds of the arrests were for forms of stealing; a fifth were for petty statutory offenses against public peace, morals or order; an eighth for such distinctly juvenile offenses as waywardness, truancy, and malicious mischief; about 2 per cent were for assaults and less than 1 per cent for sex offenses.

Since the Gluecks were interested in the degree to which the recommendations of the Center were carried out and the effect of these recommendations on future behavior, the first follow-up period was placed five years after the end of treatment as prescribed by the court. For boys whose treatment did not follow any of the recommendations, this time span was five years after court appearance; for the remainder it was about six years after court appearance, since the treatment period in the great majority of cases

---

1 William W. Wattenberg, "Ten-Year-Old Boys in Trouble," *Child Development*, 28 (1957), 43–46; Wattenberg, "Normal Rebellion—or Real Delinquency," *Child Study*, 34 (Fall, 1957), 15–20.

2 The study is reported in two volumes: Sheldon and Eleanor Glueck, *One Thousand Juvenile Delinquents*, Harvard University Press, Cambridge, Massachusetts, 1934; *Juvenile Delinquents Grown Up*, The Commonwealth Fund, New York, 1940.

Table 33

Trends in Commission of Offenses, Percentage Distribution

	Prior to crucial arrest	At time of crucial arrest	End of first follow-up	End of second follow-up	End of third follow-up
Average age	Under 13.5	13.5	19.0	24.0	29.0
Approximate number *	1,000	1,000	941	877	846
Not arrested during period	37.4	0	20.2	33.9	42.1
Average number of arrests for those arrested	2.3	—	3.4	3.7	3.7
Crimes leading to arrest					
Against property	62.9	73.6	48.7	24.6	18.2
Against public welfare	21.7	5.6	22.2	30.3	22.5
Against person	2.5	1.6	4.4	7.3	6.8
Against chastity	0.3	0.9	1.6	2.4	2.6
Against family and children	0	0	0.5	1.6	3.3
Drunkenness	0	0	9.3	29.0	43.0
Drug selling	0	0	0.1	0.3	0.6
Other †	12.6	18.3	13.2	4.5	3.0
Number of arrests	1,333	1,000	2,719	2,547	2,195

Based on material in Sheldon and Eleanor Glueck, *One Thousand Juvenile Delinquents,* Harvard University Press, Cambridge, Massachusetts, p. 100; and *Juvenile Delinquents Grown Up,* The Commonwealth Fund, New York, 1940, pp. 23, 43, 59, 309, 311, 316, 310, 317.
* The total number of cases decreased with each period due to deaths, failure to locate, or inability to secure information. The totals may also vary slightly from table to table, due to the last reason or because items are not equally applicable to all subjects.
† "Other," especially at the lower age periods, refers to such distinctly juvenile offenses as stubbornness, waywardness, disobedience, truancy, and malicious mischief.

lasted less than a year. The later follow-up was made some ten years after the first, but was organized in such a way that data could be assembled for two five-year periods. Thus the entire study covers four periods: prior to the crucial arrest; the first five years after treatment ended; the second five years, and the third five years.

The average age of the boys was 13.5 years at the time of the crucial arrest, 19 years at the end of the first follow-up period, 24 years at the end of the second, and 29 years at the end of the final period. What are the trends of behavior during this period stretching from early childhood to young adulthood?

1. Trend toward nondelinquency. Table 33 summarizes some of the trends. Prior to the arrest that led to the referral, at which point all were delinquent, 37.4 per cent had not been arrested. The first five years after treatment ended saw a fifth of the boys again in the nonarrest group. In each follow-up period, the number without arrests increased, reaching 42.1 per cent in the nonarrest group approximately fifteen years after the crucial arrest. This group reached its peak of delinquency as measured by arrest at age 13.5 and steadily rejected delinquent behavior with consequent arrest after that time.

2. Decline of unofficial delinquency. The Gluecks delved further into misconduct other than that shown by arrests and found a high percentage of "unofficial" delinquent and criminal acts, by which they mean acts for which the person might have been arrested but was not. The percentage of these incidents was very high (36.7 per cent) in the childhood period prior to the crucial arrest and no doubt signified acts regarded as trivial or as the normal misdeeds of childhood. In the follow-up periods, unofficial acts accounted for only 6 or 7 per cent of instances of misconduct.

3. Decrease of serious crimes. The pattern of offenses moved radically from serious to nonserious or noncriminal from the teen period to the adult period as judged by arrests. Offenses against property declined markedly; these comprised breaking and entering, larceny, pickpocketing, receiving stolen goods, forgery, and the like. A decrease also appeared in the offenses subsumed under "other," a classification that referred to typical juvenile misbehavior in the earlier years, such as stubbornness, running away, truancy, malicious mischief, and the like, and in the older years to default in carrying out court orders.

Crimes against public welfare remained at

Table 34

Changes in Behavior of Minor and Serious Delinquents During Fifteen Years

Number of boys	Trend from first to third period of study	Percentage
109	Nondelinquent throughout	13.3
88	Minor offenders throughout	10.8
226	Serious offenders throughout	27.6
162	From serious to minor	19.8
130	From serious to nondelinquent	15.9
63	From minor to nondelinquent	7.7
40	Erratic shifting about	4.9
818		100.0

Summarized from Sheldon and Eleanor Glueck, *Juvenile Delinquents Grown Up*, The Commonwealth Fund, New York, 1940, pp. 87–88. For the remainder of the boys, data were insufficient to trace a trend. Although "unofficial" offenses (no arrest) are included, 93 per cent of the evaluations of behavior are based on arrests.

about the same proportion of offenses in all four periods of time; these included disturbing the peace, gaming or being present—as juveniles—at gaming, peddling without a license, trespassing, vagrancy, loitering, begging, and similar offenses, all usually treated as misdemeanors rather than felonies. Crimes against the person (assaults) increased but at all periods were a small proportion of the total. Crimes against chastity (lewdness, unnatural sexual acts) also increased, but again were a small proportion of the total. Three crimes, against family and children (such as neglect or nonsupport), drunkenness, and drug selling, not found among juveniles, appeared in early adulthood and increased. Drunkenness became a major reason for arrest by the last period studied, when the average age was twenty-nine years. Considered as a whole, arrests for the serious offense of stealing declined as did also those for the minor juvenile-type offenses under "other." The arrests that increased were dominated by drunkenness. When the Gluecks grouped offenses as serious or minor they found a general trend of decline for serious offenses and of increase for minor offenses.[1]

Some of the changes in offenses are linked with age. Many juvenile offenses are not regarded as serious among adults. Neglect of wife and children does not occur until after marriage, drunkenness becomes widespread only after the age for legal purchase of liquor, and drug selling affects only a few juveniles. Within each category it is also probable that

specific types of offenses rise or fall with advance into adulthood. From other evidence presented in earlier chapters we know that types of stealing change with age and that some types of sex offenses regarded as a serious threat to the young are not so regarded for adults.

The discussion above has dealt with arrests —with types of offenses—and not with the classification of the boys themselves, other than to show that the percentage arrested greatly decreased. For the boys themselves certain trends of conduct are clear. According to Table 34, 27.6 per cent of the original group may be thought of as "hard core" delinquents, who have been guilty of serious offenses throughout the fifteen years of study, from an average age of 13.5 years to an average of twenty-nine years. In addition, 10.8 per cent were minor offenders throughout. These high percentages support the contention that juvenile delinquents are the future criminals and trouble-makers. However, for all other boys the record was much more optimistic: 13.3 per cent had no further record of delinquency after the crucial arrest, and 15.9 per cent of early serious offenders and 7.7 per cent of early minor offenders were nondelinquent by the third period of study. In addition 19.8 per cent shifted from serious to minor offenses during the fifteen years.

Juvenile delinquents thirty years later

Another important study on the outcome of delinquency is a thirty-year follow-up study of a consecutive series of children referred to the St. Louis Municipal Psychiatric Clinic between 1924 and 1929. The 524 children, whose median age at first contact was thirteen years, came to the clinic because of a wide variety of problems; 37 per cent had had juvenile court referrals at the time they first came to the Clinic. Certain criteria were set up for inclusion in the study group: age under eighteen at first clinic contact; Caucasian race; I.Q. (Stanford Binet) not less than 80; referral because of problem behavior (not as part of school survey, for vocational advice, or the like).[2]

Since not all children interviewed at the

1 *Juvenile Delinquents Grown Up*, *op. cit.*, p. 317. Definitions of offenses are given on pp. 16 and 77.

2 Lee N. Robins and Patricia O'Neal, "Mortality, Mobility, and Crime: Problem Children Thirty Years Later," *American Sociological Review*, 23 (1958), 162–171.

Table 35

Police and Court Contacts of Clinic Clients and Control Group, St. Louis, Percentage Distribution

	Total clinic group	Group 1 Juvenile court			Group 2 Antisocial behavior			Group 3 No antisocial behavior			Group 4 Control group		
		M	F	T	M	F	T	M	F	T	M	F	T
Juvenile court before clinic	37	100	100	100	—	—	—	—	—	—			
Juvenile court only after clinic	6	—	—	—	17	8	14	2	2	2	1	—	1*
Juvenile police brushes only †	13	—	—	—	31	17	26	14	5	11	7	—	5
No juvenile police trouble	44	—	—	—	52	75	60	84	93	87	92	100	94
Total per cent	100	100	100	100	100	100	100	100	100	100	100	100	100
Number of clinic cases	525	156	38	194	141	65	206	84	40	124	70	30	100

Lee N. Robins and Patricia O'Neal, "Mortality, Mobility, and Crime: Problem Children Thirty Years Later," *American Sociological Review*, 23 (1958), 165, headings modified.

* Juvenile court at any time, since control subjects did not attend Clinic.

† Arrests without court proceedings.

Clinic were court cases, it was possible to compare the adult adjustment of the court cases with that of children referred for other reasons. In addition, a control group was selected that in childhood matched the clinic group with respect to sex, race, and year of birth. The individuals were chosen from the same neighborhoods in which the Clinic patients lived. Children with I.Q. of less than 80 were excluded, as were children with behavior problems. The control group was randomly selected from public school records. A careful current checkup by records and interviews of Clinic cases and controls forms the basis for a series of reports.

The Clinic cases were classified according to the contacts they had had with court and police, as shown in Table 35. Group 1 with 37 per cent of Clinic cases is composed solely of children who had had an appearance before juvenile court prior to or at the time of the referral to the Clinic. They were typical delinquents for whom it was thought the Clinic would be helpful. Group 2, with 39 per cent of Clinic cases, consisted of children whose behavior brought them into court after the Clinic referral or brought a brush with police, that is, arrest and dismissal without a court hearing. Their conduct is considered in conflict with the mores but not sufficiently serious to be definitely delinquent. The children in Group 3, 24 per cent of the total, were referred to the Clinic because of behavior or neurotic problems not related to delinquency. Group 4, the control group, is

virtually without behavior or emotional problems that the child and his family could not handle. The four groups may be thought of roughly as a continuum, with behavior ranging from seriously delinquent, through delinquent-type misbehavior, through other kinds of behavior problems, to nondelinquent and well adjusted.

Thirty years after the time to which the above classification refers, the four groups were classified according to adult arrests and imprisonment. Table 36 shows the marked difference both in total percentage of arrested persons as well as in frequency of arrests in the four groups, with 60 per cent of group 1 (juvenile delinquents), 43 per cent of group 2, 20 per cent of group 3, and only 11 per cent of group 4 (nondelinquents) having had one or more nontraffic arrests as adults. Percentage of persons imprisoned followed the same trend.

Comparison between Glueck and St. Louis studies

A direct comparison between the two studies is not possible, because of different conditions of the studies, different approaches, and different time spans. Both studies show a marked carryover into adulthood of offenses on the part of juvenile delinquents. During the third five-year period of the Glueck study, 58 per cent of offenders were arrested; during the entire thirty years of the St. Louis study, 60 per cent of juvenile court cases were arrested. Since some of

Table 36

Relation of Childhood Behavior to Adult Arrests and Imprisonment, St. Louis, Percentage Distribution

Childhood behavior

Adult arrests	Group 1 Juvenile court		Group 2 Antisocial behavior		Group 3 No antisocial behavior		Group 4 Control group	
Any nontraffic arrests	60		43		20		11	
Three or more		38		20		9		3
One or two		22		23		11		8
Prison		28		13		6		1
No prison		32		30		14		10
Traffic only	2		4		3		5	
No arrests	38		53		77		84	
Total per cent	100		100		100		100	
Number	176		191		119		97	

Lee N. Robins and Patricia O'Neal, "Mortality, Mobility, and Crime: Problem Children Thirty Years Later," *American Sociological Review*, 23 (1958), 168. Numbers exclude those known to have died, been institutionalized (not in prison), or permanently out of St. Louis before age twenty-five. Title of Table modified.

the Glueck cases were arrested at earlier periods but not in the third period, the total percentage arrested at some time would be greater than for the St. Louis cases; at the same time, the span covered by the Glueck study was less. It seems therefore that the delinquents in the Glueck study had a higher percentage arrested as adults than was true for the St. Louis delinquents. However, the difference might be due to different types of delinquents or to differences in police practices. Moreover, the St. Louis delinquents were about one-fourth girls, who had a lower proportion of adult arrests than did the boys. It does not seem possible to rule out these factors for a direct comparison.

The Glueck study shows a minority hardcore group of serious or minor offenders who persisted throughout the fifteen years of study; a slightly larger group, however, showed a gradual improvement in behavior with the passage of time. The St. Louis study shows that the more serious the childhood misconduct was, the more likely is the person to be arrested and arrested often in adulthood.

An important fact is that both the Glueck and the St. Louis studies show a minority of delinquents (13.3 per cent and 38 per cent) with no arrests at any time after the time of Center or Clinic referral. Again differences in the studies make an exact comparison impossible.

General conclusions based on the two studies indicate that juvenile delinquency serious enough to bring arrests or court hearings leads to three outcomes in adulthood: a large minority of offenders continue into adulthood either at a serious or minor level of offense; another minority group conforms to the laws after early adolescence; and a larger group than either of these continues offenses but with decreasing seriousness and frequency.

Future outcomes other than crime

The seriousness of juvenile delinquency cannot be dismissed with the finding that many delinquents do not become adult criminals. Problems of adjustment other than crime beset many delinquents when they become adults.

The St. Louis study shows that almost half of the juvenile court cases among clinic clients became alcoholics and a fourth heavy drinkers. Among children who violated the mores but did not appear in court, a fourth became alcoholics and more than a third heavy drinkers. Among clinic clients with no antisocial behavior, only 15 per cent became alcoholics and about a fourth heavy drinkers. The control group of public school children had the startling record of no alcoholics, 2 per cent of probable alcoholics, and only 18 per cent heavy drinkers. Nondrinkers increased for the four groups from 28 per cent to 37 to 58 to 80. Thus high percentages of the court cases and the misbehaving noncourt cases used alcohol excessively as adults. Many of these men and women of course are included among those arrested in adulthood, but the arrests would not all have been for drunkenness. Over and above criminal behavior, many delinquent children as adults faced the problems of excessive use of alcohol.[1]

Another portion of the St. Louis study relates the childhood status with adult psychiatric status. Adults diagnosed as having no psychiatric diseases increased from 14 per cent among the former juvenile court cases to 60 per cent in the control group. The chief adult problem of the court cases was socio-pathic personality (37 per cent); an additional 14 per cent showed neurotic reactions. Socio-pathic personality is characterized by rebellion, belligerency, stealing, excessive use of alcohol, vagrancy, and irresponsibility—in other words, varied conduct that threatens the welfare of society. The outcome for the group in conflict with the mores was chiefly neurotic reactions (30 per cent) and psychotic reactions (30 per cent). The children who came to the clinic for nondelinquency problems, chiefly neurotic, and diagnosed later when adults, had neurotic reactions in 37 per cent of the cases and psychotic reactions in 15 per cent. The controls diagnosed had neurotic reactions in 23 per cent of the cases.[2]

It is important to note that the lowest percentage of adults who exhibited neurotic reactions were the former court cases. Few of these definitely delinquent youth later developed psychotic reactions (6 per cent). Their chief difficulty, socio-pathic personality, seemed to be a continuation of their early delinquencies—chiefly thefts and destruction of property. Children who had been referred to the clinic for truancy, incorrigibility, running away, and fighting were most likely to show psychotic reactions as adults. Sexual misbehavior, learning problems, and tantrums were associated with neurosis in adulthood. The associations between childhood misbehavior and adult maladjustment were not complete; however, the highest rates of well-adjusted adults came from among children whose troubles arose from fighting, common childish neurotic traits, tantrums, and

sexual misbehavior. Thus, only in a general way was it possible to forecast the adult maladjustment from the childhood behavior.

The St. Louis study further shows that the clinic clients who were court cases were much more likely to become divorced as adults than were any of the other groups. Fifty-seven per cent of court cases were divorced, 37 per cent of those guilty of violating the mores, 22 per cent of the nondelinquent problem group, and 12 per cent of the control cases.[3]

Direct lines of development from youth to adulthood are difficult to trace. Children and adolescents usually do not confine their misconduct to one type but range over a number of types. This is especially true of delinquencies carried out by groups of youth. A related cluster of delinquencies is the rule rather than one form only. Although adult offenders may limit their behavior to a narrow pattern, they also may be guilty of several, often related types. A given kind of juvenile delinquency may herefore be associated with more than one kind of adult behavior.

The childhood delinquency alone cannot be said to be responsible for adult crime or other types of abnormal conduct. The family background always appears as a factor whose influence follows the child into his adult years. The way in which the child is handled—whether he appears in court or is referred to a clinic, whether or not he is sent to a training school—is also a factor.

Nevertheless the evidence from the St. Louis study shows strong trends from certain types of childhood behavior—delinquent, neurotic, normal—to certain general patterns of adult behavior. The juvenile delinquents most frequently have serious criminal, socio-pathic, alcoholic, and marital problems when they become adults.

The linkage of juvenile delinquency and adult crime

A study of the entire trend of delinquency and crime shows that juvenile court appearances reach a peak at ages fourteen to sixteen and that arrests as reported by the Federal Bureau of Investigation reach a peak at ages sixteen to eighteen. Many of these young

1 Lee N. Robins, William M. Bates, and Patricia O'Neal, "Adult Drinking Patterns of Former Problem Children," dittoed, Department of Psychiatry and Neurology, Washington University School of Medicine, St. Louis, Missouri.

2 Patricia O'Neal and Lee N. Robins, *American Journal of Psychiatry*, 114 (1958), 961–969. The diagnoses indicate personality set and do not imply commitment to a mental hospital.

3 Lee N. Robins and Patricia O'Neal, "The Marital History of Former Problem Children," *Social Problems*, 5 (1958), 347–358.

people have only one arrest, court appearance, or short term of imprisonment. They do not, thereafter, continue in crime. Others more slowly adapt to conventional life. Some continue at whatever level of minor or serious criminal behavior they have achieved as juveniles.

Several reasons may account for the one official offense. The act may have been one that really was contrary to the personality set—the attitudes and moral standards—of the person and would perhaps not have been repeated even if arrest or court appearance had not followed. For some offenders, the arrest and court hearing may have given sufficient shock to turn the person back to conformity. Friends and family may have strongly disapproved of the misconduct but accepted the delinquent back and helped him to reaffiliate himself with conventional society. Various studies indicate that offenders who persist in misconduct or move toward continued criminal behavior more frequently come from disorganized areas and families than those whose foray into crime is short-lived. We may surmise that only certain types of delinquents coming from certain types of backgrounds are likely to become adult criminals.

For complete understanding, another factor is important. What effect does a year or more spent in a training school or a few years in a prison have on the offender? Opportunities for re-education and personal rehabilitation differ radically from one institution to another. The months spent in some institutions may draw the offender into closer relationship with other offenders and build up permanent attitudes favorable to crime; in other institutions, lasting re-education and rehabilitation may be accomplished for some of the offenders.

Bibliography

Release and violations

Betz, Elizabeth A., "Release from Training School," *1950 Yearbook, National Probation and Parole Association,* New York, 1950, pp. 75–88.

Institutions Serving Delinquent Children, Guides and Goals, Children's Bureau Publication, No. 360, U. S. Government Printing Office, Washington, D. C., 1957, pp. 111–117.

Manella, Frank L. "Aftercare Programs," *National Probation and Parole Association Journal,* 4 (1958), 74–80.

Rappaport, Mazie F., "The Possibility of Help for the Child Returning from a State Training School," in Sheldon Glueck, editor, *The Problem of Delinquency,* Houghton Mifflin Company, Boston, 1959, pp. 947–955.

Schepses, Erwin, "The Academic School Experience of the Training School Student," *Federal Probation,* 19 (June, 1955), 47–51.

Schreiber, Paul, *How Effective Are Services for the Treatment of Delinquents?"* Children's Bureau Report No. 9, U. S. Government Printing Office, Washington, D. C., 1960.

"Training for Probation and Parole Work," *National Probation and Parole Association Journal,* 2 (July, 1956), entire issue.

Wogahn, Lester E., Edith Sommer, and Lawrence Lawsen, "An Experiment in Group Placement of Juvenile Parolees," *National Probation and Parole Association Journal,* 4 (1958), 66–73.

The future of delinquents

Bates, William, Lee N. Robins, and Patricia O'Neal, "Prisons and the Problem Child," address given at the Midwest Sociological Society, 1960.*

Berlin, Louis, "Adolescent Recidivism," *National Probation and Parole Association Journal,* 4 (1958), 275–277.

Frum, Harold S., "Adult Criminal Offense Trends Following Juvenile Delinquency," *Journal of Criminal Law, Criminology and Police Science,* 49 (1958), 29–49.

Glueck, Sheldon and Eleanor, *One Thousand Juvenile Delinquents,* Harvard University Press, Cambridge, Massachusetts, 1934.

———, *Juvenile Delinquents Grown Up,* The Commonwealth Fund, New York, 1940.

Michael, Carmen Miller, "Follow-up Studies of Introverted Children, III, Relative Incidence of Criminal Behavior," *Journal of Criminal Law, Criminology and Police Science,* 47 (1956), 414–422.

O'Neal, Patricia, and Lee N. Robins, "Childhood Patterns Predictive of Adult Schizophrenia: A Thirty-year Follow-up Study," *American Journal of Psychiatry,* 115 (1959), 385–391.

———, "The Relation of Childhood Behavior Problems to Adult Psychiatric Status," *American Journal of Psychiatry,* 114 (1958), 961–969.

———, Jeanette Schaefer, John Bergmann, and Lee N. Robins, "A Psychiatric Evaluation of Adults Who had Sexual Problems as Children: A Thirty-year Follow-up Study," *Human Organization,* 19 (Spring, 1960), 32–39.

Robins, Lee N., "Mental Illness and the Runaway: A Thirty-year Follow-up Study," *Hu-*

man Organization, 16, No. 4 (undated reprint), 11–15.

Robins, Lee N., William M. Bates, and Patricia O'Neal, "Adult Drinking Patterns of Former Problem Children." *

————, and Patricia O'Neal, "The Adult Prognosis for Runaway Children," *American Journal of Orthopsychiatry,* 29 (1959), 752–761.

————, "The Marital History of Former Problem Children," *Social Problems,* 5 (1948), 347–358.

* Dittoed, Department of Psychiatry and Neurology, Washington University School of Medicine, St. Louis, Missouri.

Wattenberg, William W., "Factors Associated with Repeating among Preadolescent 'Delinquents,'" *Journal of Genetic Psychology,* 84 (1954), 189, 196.

————, "Juvenile Repeaters from Two Viewpoints," *American Sociological Review,* 18 (1953), 631–635.

————, "Normal Rebellion—or Real Delinquency," *Child Study,* 34 (Fall, 1957), 15–20.

————, "Ten-year-old Boys in Trouble," *Child Development,* 28 (1957), 43–46.

————, and Frank Quiroz, "Follow-up Study of Ten-year-old Boys with Police Records," *Journal of Consulting Psychology,* 17 (1953), 309–313.

Appendix

Institutes on Juvenile Law Enforcement Granting Certificates and/or College Credits
1959

	Institution and location	Program title	Length
1	Arizona State College, Tempe, Arizona	Delinquency Control Institute	10 weeks
2	Fresno State College, Fresno, California	Workshop on Children and Youth	6 weeks
3	University of Southern Calif., Los Angeles	Delinquency Control Institute	12 weeks
4	Florida State University, Tallahassee, Florida	Delinquency Control Institute	12 weeks
5	University of Illinois, Champaign, Illinois	Police Work with Juveniles	2–3 days
6	University of Indiana, Bloomington, Indiana	Juvenile Officers' Training Conference	2 weeks
7	University of Louisville, Louisville, Kentucky	Delinquent Youth and Society	2 weeks
8	Louisiana State University, Baton Rouge, La.	Law Enforcement with Juveniles	2 days
9	University of Maryland College Park, Maryland	Delinquency Control Institute	10 days
10	Michigan State University, East Lansing, Michigan	Juvenile Police Training Course	5 days
		Police-Community Relations (Juv.)	5 days
11	University of Minnesota, Minneapolis, Minn.	Juvenile Officers' Institute	10 weeks
		Institute on Problems	2 days
		Institute for Law Enforcement Officers Dealing with Juvenile Offenders	3 days
12	Rutgers University, New Brunswick, N. J.	Police Officers' School in Juvenile Problems	—
13	St. Lawrence University, Canton, N. Y.	Institute on Delinquency and Crime	1 week
14	Syracuse University, Syracuse, N. Y.	Summer Workshop on Juvenile Delinquency	3 weeks
15	University of Oklahoma, Norman, Oklahoma	Conference on Handling Juveniles	3 days
16	University of Texas, Austin, Texas	Texas Institute on Children and Youth	1 week
17	University of Wisconsin, Madison, Wisconsin	Juvenile Law Enforcement Institute	3 days

From Bernard Greenblatt, *Staff and Training for Juvenile Law Enforcement in Urban Police Departments*, Children's Bureau Publication No. 13, 1960, U. S. Government Printing Office, Washington, D. C., 1960.

Books

Primarily books that have marked changes in thinking about delinquency or are so comprehensive that they apply to a number of different phases of delinquency.

Cohen, Albert K., *Delinquent Boys, The Culture of the Gang,* Free Press, Glencoe, Illinois, 1955.

Cloward, Richard A., and Lloyd E. Ohlin, *Delinquency and Opportunity, A Theory of Delinquent Gangs,* Free Press, Glencoe, Illinois, 1960.

Eissler, K. R., and Paul Federn, editors, *Searchlights on Delinquency; New Psychoanalytic Studies,* International Universities Press, Inc., New York, 1949.

Glueck, Sheldon, editor, *The Problem of Delinquency,* Houghton Mifflin Company, Boston, Massachusetts, 1959.

Glueck, Sheldon and Eleanor, *One Thousand Juvenile Delinquents,* Harvard University Press, Cambridge, Massachusetts, 1934.

————, *Juvenile Delinquents Grown Up,* Commonwealth Fund, New York, 1940 (a sequel to the last named book).

————, *Unraveling Juvenile Delinquency,* Harvard University Press, Cambridge, Massachusetts, 1950.

————, *Predicting Delinquency and Crime,* Harvard University Press, Cambridge, Massachusetts, 1959.

Healy, William, *The Individual Delinquent,* Little, Brown and Company, Boston, Massachusetts, 1915.

————, and Augusta F. Bronner, *New Light on Delinquency and Its Treatment,* Yale University Press, New Haven, 1936.

Hollingshead, August B., *Elmtown's Youth,* John Wiley and Sons, New York, 1949.

Jenkins, Richard L., *Breaking the Patterns of Defeat,* J. B. Lippincott Company, Philadelphia, 1954.

McCord, William and Joan, *Origins of Crime, A New Evaluation of the Cambridge-Somerville Study,* Columbia University Press, New York, 1959.

Reaching the Fighting Gang, New York City Youth Board, New York, 1960.

Roucek, Joseph S., editor, *Juvenile Delinquency,* Philosophical Library, New York, 1958.

Sellin, Thorsten, *Culture Conflict and Crime,* Social Science Research Council, New York, 1938.

Shaw, Clifford R., and Associates, *Brothers in Crime,* University of Chicago Press, Chicago, 1938.

————, *The Jack-Roller,* University of Chicago Press, Chicago, 1930.

General Bibliography

————, and M. E. Moore, *Natural History of a Delinquent Career,* University of Chicago Press, Chicago, 1931.

(The above three books relate the "boy's own story," supplemented with discussions of background and analysis of factors playing upon the boy.)

————, *Delinquency Areas,* University of Chicago Press, Chicago, 1929.

————, and Henry D. McKay, *Juvenile Delinquency and Urban Areas,* University of Chicago Press, Chicago, 1942.

(The above two books present evidence on the unequal distribution of delinquency in small areas within a city, with the highest rates in slum areas.)

————, and Henry D. McKay, *Social Factors in Juvenile Delinquency,* No. 13, Vol. II, National Commission on Law Observance and Enforcement, U. S. Government Printing Office, Washington 25, D. C., 1931.

Annals, Journals, and Yearbooks

Featuring numerous articles on delinquency.

American Journal of Orthopsychiatry, 1790 Broadway, New York 19.

American Journal of Sociology, University of Chicago Press, Chicago 37.

American Sociological Review, American Sociological Association, New York University, Washington Square, New York 3.

Annals of the American Academy of Political and Social Science, 3937 Chestnut Street, Philadelphia 4.

(Two entire issues have been devoted to delinquency: "Juvenile Delinquency," 261, January, 1949; and "Prevention of Juvenile Delinquency," 333, March, 1959.)

British Journal of Criminology (formerly *British Journal of Delinquency*), handled in the United States by Quadrangle Books, Inc., Chicago.

Crime and Delinquency, National Council on Crime and Delinquency, 1790 Broadway, New York 19. (Begins with volume 7, formerly National Probation and Parole Association Journal.)

Federal Probation Quarterly, United States Probation System, Supreme Court Building, Washington 25, D. C.

Journal of Criminal Law, Criminology and Police Science, published for Northwestern University by Williams and Wilkins Company, Baltimore 2.

Journal of Negro Education, Howard University Press, Howard University, Washington 1, D. C. (See especially Yearbook No. 28, volume 28, summer 1959, entire issue devoted to "Juvenile Delinquency among Negroes in the United States.")

Journal of Social Issues, Society for the Psychological Study of Social Issues, Dorothy S. Jochem, Institute for Social Research, University of Michigan, Ann Arbor, Michigan. (See especially "New Light on Delinquency," volume 14, No. 3, 1958, entire issue.)

Mental Hygiene, National Association for Mental Hygiene, Inc., 1790 Broadway, New York 19.

National Probation and Parole Association Journal, see *Crime and Delinquency.*

Social Casework, Family Service Association of America, 192 Lexington Avenue, New York 16.

Social Problems, Society for the Study of Social Problems, Indiana University, Bloomington, Indiana.

Social Service Review, University of Chicago Press, Chicago 37.

Sources of Reports and Surveys

Children's Bureau, U. S. Department of Health, Education, and Welfare, Washington, D. C. Publishes Statistical Series on juvenile court statistics, reports on training schools, bibliographies, pamphlets on many phases of delinquency.

National Council on Crime and Delinquency, 1790 Broadway, New York 19, formerly National Probation and Parole Association. Publishes standards for juvenile and family courts, probation and parole, detention, and many other reports dealing with current problems of delinquency.

Uniform Crime Reports, Federal Bureau of Investigation, U. S. Department of Justice, Washington, D. C. Includes but is not limited to juvenile delinquency.

United Nations publications, handled by International Documents Service, Sales Section, United Nations, New York. Numerous reports for a variety of countries.

Index of Names

Offenses, 25 (*See also* names of individual offenses)
as behavior systems, 141–142
of boys, 28, 29, 101–102
in correctional school, 34–36
of girls, 28, 101–102
in high school, 34–36
in public schools, 183–187
Opportunities for criminal careers, 82–85, 89
Oriental groups, 108

Parents (*See also* Family, Father, Mother)
identification with, 111–116
punishment of, 10
Parole, 233 (*See also* Aftercare)
Pathology, 63–64, 176
Peer groups, 45–46, 49, 71–74, 81, 84–85, 92–94,
133–134 (*See also* Corner boys, Gangs)
of girls, 108–109
Personality, 53, 61–64
Petition, defined, 238
Police, 21, 31, 233, 239–249
abroad, 243–244
functions of, 239
investigation by, 240–241
juvenile control unit, 242–244
and other agencies, 248–249
and prevention, 246–248
referrals by, 241–242, 279
selection of, 244–245
training of, 245
Police Athletic League (PAL), 246–247
Poverty, 122–125
Prediction of delinquency, 213–218
Prevention
by community efforts, 195–211
and employment, 192–193
by police, 246–248
Probation, 233, 235, 284, 287–293
defined, 238
success of, 292–293
Probation officers, 277–278
investigation by, 270, 279, 280–281
supervision by, 288–291
time schedule of, 288–289
Prisons, children in, 275
Psychiatric services
in camps, 222
in clinics, 218–219
by group therapy, 219–221
for juvenile court, 278
in residential schools, 221–222, 335–337
in training schools, 317–318, 320
in treatment centers, 331–335
Psychiatric Treatment Unit, Ohio, 335
Psychiatric Treatment Units, California, 334–335
Psychological services
for juvenile court, 278
in training schools, 318
Publicity for court cases, 281–283
Puerto Ricans, 7, 69–71, 72, 107
and drug addiction, 159
Punishment, 9

Race, 7 (*See also* Negro)
Rates of delinquency
European, 12

Rates of delinquency—*Continued*
rural, 27
United States, 5–6, 25–31, 103
Reception centers, 309
Recidivists, 27, 34–36, 292–293, 346–352
Recreation, 11, 205–207
sponsored by police, 246–247
in training schools, 310–311, 313–315
Referee, 277
Rehabilitation, 137–138, 195–197 (*See also* Case-
work, Group therapy, Psychiatric services)
Release from training school, 342–343
Religion, 200–202
Retreatist delinquency, 90 (*See also* Drug addic-
tion)
Riots, 168–170
Robbery, 145–146
Roles, age-sex, 42, 49
Rural rates, 27

Schools, public, 181–193 (*See also* Training
schools)
and delinquency, 183–187
and drop-outs, 188–190
after the training school, 343
and treatment, 190–192, 221–222
and truancy, 187–188
Self-concept, 21, 41, 175–176, 177
Settlement houses, 202–206
Sex delinquencies, 95–96, 153–155
of girls, 104–107, 154
Shoplifting, 36, 143–144
Slum clearance, 11
Social class (*See* Lower, middle, upper)
and alcohol, 157
and delinquency, 99, 186, 188
and schools, 182
Staff
cottage personnel, 315
of detention home, 258–259
probation, 277–278
of training schools, 303, 317–319, 320
Statistics, 23–38
Stealing, 142–146
Street-club workers, 72–73, 166, 222–226 (*See also*
Group work)
Symbols of gangs, 171–172

Theories, 53–65 (*See also* Hypotheses)
Tolerance, 18–20, 35–38, 45, 51
and vice, 162
Traffic violations, 28–30
Training schools, 136–138, 233, 295–321
children committed to, 304–308
development of, 235–236
discipline in, 315–317
living arrangements in, 312–315
methods, 295–297
release from, 342–343
staff of, 303
state organization of, 297–302
treatment in, 308–312, 317–320
Treatment, 9
preventive, 213–227
in psychiatric centers, 331–337
short-term, at Highfields, 337–338
in training schools, 296–297, 308–312, 317–320
in work camps, 322–331